STAGES OF EMERGENCY

STAGES OF EMERGENCY

COLD WAR NUCLEAR CIVIL DEFENSE

TRACY C. DAVIS

DUKE UNIVERSITY PRESS   DURHAM AND LONDON   2007

TO MAX

all the white space on these pages is my thanks

for this, and so much else

CONTENTS

ACKNOWLEDGMENTS

The intellectual and gustatory debts that accrue in researching an international study such as this are daunting. I start with my late colleague Dwight Conquergood, who listened, was intrigued, and encouraged this work from its inception; Beverly Wright, who asked zinger questions at crucial moments; and exceptional colleagues — Peter Glazer, Baz Kershaw, and Tom Postlewait — who took a great deal time from their own work in order to substantially improve mine. Richard Schechner and Paul Boyer are also singled out for particular thanks. Special thanks also to Stefka Mihaylova, Sheila Moeschen, and Natalie Hanemann who helped prepare the final manuscript. Many Northwestern colleagues, students, and connections put information in my hands or smoothed the road in myriad ways, including Kamran Afary, Henry Binford, Steve Caruso, Beth E. Clausen, Paul Edwards, Gary Fine, Cindy Gold, Marva Golden, Virgil Johnson, Jacob Juntunen, Liz Luby, Bill McHugh, Russell Maylone, Sara Monoson, Barbara O'Keefe, Patrick Quinn, Celeste Pietrusza, Sally Roberts, Jim Schwoch, Daniel Smith Jr., Claire Stewart, Harvey Young, and Dan Zellner. Colleagues near and far have contributed instrumentally, including Aaron Anderson, Scott Bennett, Carol Burbank, Gay Gibson Cima, Mary Croarken, Jim Davis, Lesley Delmenico, Jody Enders, John Emigh, Penny Farfan, Dennis Kennedy, David Krasner, Ric Knowles, David Krugler, Michael McKinnie, Rosemary Mariner, Lisa Merrill, Kurt Piehler, Lionel Pilkington, Della Pollock, Joseph Roach, Laurence Senelick, Rose Whyman, and Jutta Wildes. I am also grateful to some of their students who assisted, including Amy Benner of the University of Tennessee, Carolyn Bain of the University of Maryland, and Melissa Hurt of Virginia Commonwealth University as well as her father Donald Hurt, an exemplary interviewee. Laurel Borisenko pointed me to important sources on international refugee protocols. Miriam Stanford and Charlene Senn taught me that not everyone in our neighborhood grew up dreading the sound of droning engines overhead, but Vera Klement reassured me I was not the only one who listened warily.

Mary and Neville Davis arranged my first visit to the Diefenbunker and hosted me for all my returns, never verbalizing doubts about this wacky preoccupation. Thanks to them and all the clan in Ottawa, and my parents, Thora and Ernie Davis, for being there too and for all the intangibles. Special acknowledgment is due to Dave Peters for guiding me through the Diefenbunker that first day and many other occasions; and to the Diefenbunker's archivist Doug Beaton, who gave me the run of the place, insightfully assembled countless incomparable treasures, and patiently answered all queries; along with Barrie Bruce, Bob Borden, Bob Biggs, Ken Farrell, Louise Fox, Hugh Gamble, Connie Murray, and Andy Renault, all vital informants.

The White House Historical Association and Dwight D. Eisenhower Presidential Library funded research trips, along with Northwestern University's faculty research grants program and the Ethel E. Barber bequest. A Benjamin Meaker Professorship from the Institute for Advanced Studies at Bristol University helped in the later stages of work, and I am indebted to the whole Theatre and Film Department at Bristol for their warm welcome. I am grateful to archivists and librarians at the National Library of Canada, National Archives and Records Administration in College Park (especially Tab Lewis), Library of Congress (Humanities and Social Sciences; Manuscripts; and Motion Picture, Broadcasting and Recorded Sound Division), Federal Emergency Training Center Learning Resources Center in Emmitsburg, Md. (especially Julie Beacon), Swarthmore Peace Collection, John F. Kennedy Presidential Library (especially Stephen Plotkin and Sharon Kelly), Dwight D. Eisenhower Presidential Library (especially David Haight), National Library of Medicine in Bethesda, Md., Historical Society of Washington, D.C., Stanford University Libraries Department of Special Collections, and Harold Washington Library of the Chicago Public Libraries (Municipal Reference Collection).

Robert Jurquet and Anne-Marie Smith of the NATO Archives in Brussels are singled out for special appreciation. Thanks also to the Public Record Office (London), British Library, Imperial War Museum Department of Film and Video (especially Matthew Lee), Corporation of London Record Office, Scout Association in London (especially Pat Styles), British Red Cross, Bristol Record Office, Bristol Central Library, National Archives of Ireland, East Sussex Record Office, Boosey and Hawkes, and David Scott of the Central Emergency Planning Unit of the Office of the First Minister and Deputy First Minister of Northern Ireland. Thanks also to Nelson Block who assisted by correspondence.

Portions of this book appeared in other forms in *Modern Drama, TDR: The Drama Review, The Handbook of Performance Studies*, and *Asaph*.

Finally, thanks to my editors at Duke, Ken Wissoker and Courtney Berger, for their faith in the project and unwavering good counsel.

ABBREVIATIONS

ABC	American Broadcasting Company (U.S.)
A-bomb	Atomic bomb, measured in KT
ACTICE	Agency for Coordination of Inland Transportation in Central Europe (NATO)
AFB	Air Force Base (U.S.)
BBC	British Broadcasting Corporation
BCL	Bristol City Libraries (U.K.)
BMEWS	Ballistic Missile Early Warning System
CBC	Canadian Broadcasting Corporation
CBS	Columbia Broadcasting System (U.S.)
CEGHQ	Central Emergency Government Headquarters, also known as the Diefenbunker (Carp, Ontario)
CENTO	Central Treaty Organization (Turkey, Pakistan, Iran, U.K., and originally Iraq)
CFB	Canadian Forces Base
CIA	Central Intelligence Agency (U.S.)
CND	Campaign for Nuclear Disarmament (U.K.)
CONELRAD	Control of Electromagnetic Radiation, a system for utilizing AM radio frequencies 640 and 1240 during a nuclear emergency (U.S.)
CRP	Crisis Relocation Plans, or Planning (U.S.)
CRU	Central Relocation Unit (Canada)
CTV	Canadian Television network
D- or D+	The number of days before or after an attack commences, e.g. D-3 (three days before attack) or D+2 (two days after attack); see also H+ and H-

DA	Diefenbunker Archives at Canada's Cold War Museum (Carp, Ontario)
DCPA	Defense Civil Preparedness Agency (U.S. 1971–79)
DDEPL	Dwight D. Eisenhower Presidential Library (Abilene, Kans.)
DEFCON	Defense Condition, readiness alert status of U.S. military
DEW Line	Distant Early Warning Line, the most northerly radar sites dotted across the Arctic
DHS	Department of Homeland Security (U.S. 2002–present)
DND	Department of National Defence (Canada)
DOD	Department of Defense (U.S.)
EMO	Emergency Measures Organization (Canada 1957–80)
EMP	Electromagnetic pulse
EPC	Emergency Planning Canada (1980–present)
FBI	Federal Bureau of Investigation (U.S.)
FCDA	Federal Civil Defense Administration (U.S. 1950–58)
FEMA	Federal Emergency Management Agency (U.S. 1979–present)
FMAU	Forward Medical Aid Unit (U.K.)
FRG	Federal Republic of Germany (West Germany)
GNP	Gross national product
GZ	Ground zero, the coordinates of a bomb's detonation and epicenter of destruction
H- or H+	The number of hours before or after the commencement of attack, e.g. H-1 (one hour before attack) or H+2 (two hours after attack); see also D+ and D-
H-bomb	Hydrogen bomb, also known as thermonuclear bomb, measured in MT
HEW	Department of Health, Education and Welfare (U.S.)
HMSO	Her (or His) Majesty's Stationery Office (U.K.)
HO	Home Office (U.K., the ministry responsible for civil defense)
HQ	Headquarters
HWLC	Harold Washington Library (Chicago, Ill.)
JFKL	John F. Kennedy Library (Boston, Mass.)
ICBM	Intercontinental ballistic missile
IRBM	Intermediate range ballistic missile
ITV	Independent Television (U.K.)
KT	Kiloton, equivalent to the explosive force of a thousand tons of TNT
MAF or MAFF	Ministry of Agriculture and Food [and Fisheries] (U.K.)

MEGHQ	Municipal Emergency Government Headquarters (Canada)
MOD	Ministry of Defence (U.K.)
MRBM	Medium range ballistic missile
MT	Megaton, equivalent to the explosive force of a million tons of TNT
NAC	National Archives of Canada (Ottawa)
NARA	National Archives Records Administration (College Park, Md.)
NASA	National Aeronautics and Space Administration (U.S.)
NATO	North Atlantic Treaty Organization
NBC	National Broadcasting Corporation (U.S.)
NLM	National Library of Medicine (Bethesda, Md.)
NORAD	North American Aerospace Defense Command
NUDET	Nuclear Detonation, a reported incident of A-bomb or H-bomb explosion
OAS	Organization of American States
OCD	Office of Civil Defense (U.S. 1961–68)
OCDM	Office of Civil Defense Mobilization (U.S. 1958–61)
OEP	Office of Emergency Planning (U.S. 1961–64)
OPAL	Operation Alert, a series of U.S. exercises from 1954–61, e.g. OPAL 55, the 1955 installment
PF	Protective Factor, a scale rating structures' internal shielding from radiation
PRO	Public Record Office (London)
psi	Pounds per square inch, indicating the strength of blast forces
PTA	Parent-Teacher Association
PTSD	Post-Traumatic Stress Disorder
r	Roentgen, a unit of ionizing radiation
RACES	Radio Amateur Civil Emergency Services, an affiliation of ham radio operators (U.S.)
RADEF	Radiological Defense, usually in reference to bomber or missile tracking networks
RAF	Royal Air Force (U.K.)
RAND	Think tank founded in 1946, a contraction of "research and development"
RCMP	Royal Canadian Mounted Police
REGHQ	Regional Emergency Government Headquarters (Canada)
RSG	Regional Seat of Government (U.K.)
SHAPE	Supreme Headquarters Allied Powers Europe (NATO)

SITCEN	Emergency Government Situation Centre (Canada), the area of the CEGHQ where radiological monitoring was plotted and predicted
SPC WRL	Swarthmore Peace Collection, War Resisters' League (Swarthmore, Pa.)
TWX	Teletypewriter Exchange, a telegraphic technology that allows a single operator to type in data that automatically prints at other stations
UN	United Nations
U.K.	United Kingdom (England, Scotland, Wales, and Northern Ireland)
U.S.	United States of America
USAF	United States Air Force
USDA	United States Department of Agriculture
USGPO	United States Government Printing Office
USSR	Union of Soviet Socialist Republics, also known as the Soviet Union
WVS	Women's Voluntary Service, a British voluntary civil defense organization (1938–present); in 1966 it became the Women's Royal Voluntary Service
ZEGHQ	Zonal Emergency Government Headquarters (Canada)
Z-zone	One of three concentric areas of damage and radioactive danger (U.K.). The X-zone is the area closest to GZ, where no rescue would be attempted; the Y-zone is an area of extensive fire damage and high radiation where immediate rescue was unlikely; and the Z-zone is the area where rescue efforts could be concentrated and survivors either ushered into fallout protection or evacuated to safer areas

INTRODUCTION

Acting is an emergency, and in an emergency you do whatever works. What you do in a fire drill may bear no resemblance to what you do in an actual fire, but your odds of survival are greatly improved by a past enactment of the drills.

—Deb Margolin

In mass media coverage of the domestic War on Terror, some things "look staged." No wonder, for throughout modern history civil defense has been deeply implicated with performance, pretense, and scripted pretexts. During the Cold War, citizens' perception that the effects of nuclear bombing could be mitigated led to judicious preparation and coordinated campaigns of rehearsal. We now execute our part in the new protocols of civil defense —presenting laptop computers for scanning at airport security checkpoints, passing through metal detectors in federal buildings, and scrutinizing our neighbors' behavior in response to the latest warnings of terrorism—and thus provide continuity with Cold War practices.[1] No longer merely an arcane by-product of the Cold War characterized by kitsch artifacts and memories of ducking under school desks or dispensing ID tags to children, civil defense is resurrected as homeland security.[2] Our small gestures— globalized through compliance at foreign airports and corporate offices, on public transport, and in gatherings of all kinds—occur on a massive scale and are habituated into routines. They are precautions whose status as quotidian or fateful may be revealed only when the next moment transpires and either the status quo is breached or peaceable normalcy is maintained. The mantra of "what if" keeps the gestures fresh. When the public and governments cease to ask "what if"—assuming that this comes to pass—security behaviors will once again become comprehensible as vestigial legacies of arcane beliefs, bygone fears, and vigilance without a clear reference point. Until then, it is prudent to understand the antecedents of our routines.

When the sociologist Guy Oakes called the United States' Operation Alert ("OPAL") series of nationwide civil defense drills that transpired from 1954 through 1961 "full-scale annual rehearsals for World War III based on this managerial conception of nuclear crisis," he echoed a wide selection of the documentation of this Cold War phenomenon. "These yearly rituals," he went on, "enacted simulations of nuclear attack in an elaborate national socio-drama that combined elements of disaster relief, the church social, summer camp, and the county fair."[3] Oakes invoked performative language—rehearsal, ritual, socio-drama, play, drama, and theater—as organizing metaphors for the preparations that constituted applied policy on civil defense in the event of nuclear war. But like many casual invocations of performance in academic or popular writing, the deeper implications of these ascriptions were left unexplored. *Stages of Emergency* insists on going beyond the superficial resemblance between civil defense and theater and reveals that civil defense draws directly upon the traditions and techniques of the stage: Cold War nuclear civil defense is not *like* something that is theatrical but is an embodied mimetic methodology that is *inherently* and *crucially* theatrical. Documentation of civil defense exercises repeatedly invokes rehearsal, acting, and theater as operating terminology; this book explains why it is important to take this seriously.

What are the implications of "playing" at biological, cultural, and economic survival on the scale necessary for surviving nuclear war? "Acting" involves pretense, but it has a different burden of continuity and completeness in rehearsal than performance. If events such as OPAL exercises were "rehearsals," how did people take part, who was on the sidelines, and how did they anticipate an eventual—though perhaps perpetually deferred—performance? What forms did civil defense rehearsals take, for what purposes, under whose auspices, and with what results? Just as acting accounts for the narrative "what if" pretense adopted by participants, rehearsal accounts for continuities between otherwise disparate kinds of exercises, uniting empirical experiments, rote behaviors, and systems analysis under a common methodology of embodied practice.

This is a multinational comparativist study. Since members of the NATO alliance recognized the same threat and shared an interlocking military defense, how do the civil defense practices of three close allies—the United States, Canada, and the United Kingdom—compare in their implementation of rehearsal techniques? How did these nations—whose history intertwined for centuries as they articulated their distinct ethos, acquired complications from immigration and their multicultural ethnos, and coped differently with post-1945 economic challenges and opportunities—seek to involve the populace in their own defense and plan for the preservation of governance against the overwhelming odds of surviving massive nuclear attack? Studying the United States, Canada, and the United Kingdom in concert produces certain efficiencies: each nation created and preserved different kinds of evidence about similar exercises, and conducted some exercises in common, so one nation's archives can yield information that assists the interpretation of another's practices. The reluctance of each nation to declassify certain kinds of documents can significantly cloud understanding of civil defense preparedness, but fortunately the three do not agree about what should be kept out of the public domain, and so the openness of one nation's records can significantly illuminate areas that remain classified elsewhere. Just as important, however, the differences between the three nations' strategies can be revealed by contrasts between their tactics. These allies were resolute in even spelling civil defense differently: to Canadians and Britons it is "defence" (n.) and "defense" (v.). This matters, for in essence civil defense policies were nouns in theory but verbs in practice; only in the United States was the concept of the subject (defence) and its execution (defense) elided into a single word. If adopting the American spelling convention (defense) sacrifices this denotative subtlety, the comparativist approach opens up insights that are both subtle and salient.

Since 11 September 2001, increased surveillance and the public's vigilant acts are predicated on risk abatement. Cold War civil defense took many forms, but it comes down to one thing: risk management. In the Cold War, nuclear attack was assumed to be a nationwide or multinational catastrophe, literally not symbolically, tangibly and factually, jeopardizing not just liberty and the pursuit of happiness but life itself for millions or even billions of people simultaneously, as well as all who might come after them. Scenarios envisioned various risks, depending on population distribution, geography, resource allocation, or assumptions about the enemy's targets, and endless variations were possible. Civil defense exercises focused on making this plethora imaginable, manageable, and most of all, capable of being acted upon, at least in part. Chapter 1 sketches in the historical background for this planning and some of the basic techniques of testing contingencies. Unlike earlier analyses, this study is not about the rhetoric of civil defense so much as the actions invested in it, and not as politics but as policy testing. Chapter 1 draws upon the rich literature in social history, sociology, and political science about American civil defense and adds to it a distinct disciplinary orientation and the compound perspective that results from comparing three allied nations, the exercises in two of which are entirely new contributions to the historiography. While the United States gave scientific and military leadership, each nation often meant something different when civil defense was organized, corporeally demonstrated, physically enacted, and environmentally embodied.

Stages of Emergency is not a history of civil defense but a historical treatment of how problems were investigated through theatrical techniques and rehearsal methodologies. A vast range of primary documents and commissioned research reports are consulted beyond civil defense historians' usual purview of the popular press and the undeniably important Project East River and Gaither Commission reports.[4] The argument is not that everything was "performance" but a more sophisticated (and limited) claim that theater (and not merely spectacle) had a utility in twentieth-century governance, education, and social life, central not only to how anxiety was expressed but more importantly to how people envisioned ways to identify and resolve anxious problems. For reasons explained in detail in chapter 2, it is not "performance" that matters here but the preparation for it: namely, rehearsal and what was accomplished through it.

Rehearsal is invoked neither as a metaphoric motif nor an aestheticized product, but rather a technique and mode of doing: not an omnipresent saturation resulting from modernity but something called up selectively, strategically, and purposefully. This was not the art and entertainment known as "the theater" yet it was staged; this was not "performance" yet it was performative, both in the sense of display and something that was done subject to evaluation. It could be spectacular, or not; well coordinated, or not; involve extensive predetermined activity, or not; depend upon fakery, deceit, and illusion, or not. Rehearsal was a methodology for exploration, inculcation, and discovery, referential of real-world problems, like games; dependent upon real-world skills, like work; and addressing real-world fears, like ritual. Chapters 3–7 examine the implications of this for rehearsals involving private citizens. Chapters 8–12 detail what was done in the name of the public by civil servants but behind closed—and sometimes bolted, obscured, and buried—doors.

While military personnel are accustomed to thinking of their profession's dependence upon staged games, it may be more surprising for civilians to discover the pervasiveness of such practices executed on their behalf. War, after all, is serious and its prosecution is of utmost consequence. Nuclear bombs gave rise to a new profession dedicated to planning for the aftermath of their use. These profes-sionals, and the public at large, acknowledged the hazards of living in the nuclear world by anticipating and rehearsing their responses. Nuclear bombs shifted the theater of war to the home front; the rehearsals that anticipated their detonation may have faded in the collective memory but they were pageants of angst and its antidotes, exhibitions of knowledge and laboratories for further discovery, and potent demonstrations of Cold War realities in the midst of uncertainty. Recover-ing the fullest possible range of these exercises reveals their dependence upon theater. Indeed, it shows the instrumental centrality of theater to this critical en-gagement with unprecedented peril. The identified perils have changed since the end of the Cold War, and there are more technologically sophisticated tools for monitoring them, but has our recourse for practicing risk management or abate-ment fundamentally altered?

Part I

DIRECTING APOCALYPSE

Chapter 1 **CIVIL DEFENSE CONCEPTS AND PLANNING**

To rationally plan for mass nuclear war is an attempt to claim that after the routines of everyday life are gone they can still be had. The very existence of such planning constitutes a claim that adequate thought and hard work can allow adequate control over highly uncertain, unpredictable events. More broadly, it is a rhetorical claim that a meaningful knowledge base can be constructed: that the information can be gathered, that it will be valid and reliable, that it can be drawn upon.

—Lee Clarke

Civil defense planning in Canada, the United Kingdom, and the United States hinges on a few key developments in science and politics that had direct consequences for policy and hence the exercises that rehearsed and tested policy. The use of A-bombs on Japan in 1945 and the unexpectedly early Soviet demonstration of nuclear weapons technology in 1949 are the first of these developments. In response, American schoolchildren were indoctrinated to answer the perspicacious Bert the turtle's interrogative "What are you supposed to do when you see the flash?" with a choral declamation "DUCK and COVER!"[1] This hung in the collective imaginary long after the A-bomb's destructive power was dwarfed by the H-bomb which could destroy, not just harm, entire cities. Deployed en masse, the H-bomb could probably wipe out civilizations. As President Eisenhower put it: "In the old dispensation, the slogan was 'duck and cover.' Now it is 'beat it.'"[2]

The H-bomb awed even RAND scientists forecasting the "super" bomb's effects in 1951–52, for "nobody had ever killed 35 million people on a sheet of paper before."[3] The director of the United States' Federal Civil Defense Administration (FCDA) told Canadian civil defense officials about seeing a film documenting the first H-bomb test and being immediately convinced "that 'Duck and Cover' was dead. You don't duck from the explosion of a nuclear weapon, you die, that's all."[4]

Nuclear Weapons and Civil Defense

American and Soviet testing of H-bombs in 1952 and 1953 resulted in NATO's "New Assumptions" doctrine of November 1954, which stipulated that henceforth any direct attack by the Soviets would receive a massive thermonuclear response.[5] It took a few years for this military posture to transform civil defense policies, but this phase marks the period of greatest tension and most intense activity. Bomber delivery was superseded by missiles capable of greater and greater distance and accuracy in the 1960s. Rhetoric cooled after the Cuban Missile Crisis of October 1962, and by 1970—due to the economic strains of the Vietnam War and public hostility toward civil defense—policy shifted to "dual-use" rationales explicitly folding preparations for wartime scenarios into agencies simultaneously geared toward any kind of civil disaster or natural calamity.[6] As the number of nuclear warheads in the United States' arsenal peaked, civil defense spending tanked.

Although the majority of this book is devoted to the earlier phases of civil defense planning (the 1950s and 60s), it is relevant to round out the story with aspects of latter-day civil defense policy that could not be folded into dual-use planning. This is typified by the United States' new concept for mass evacuation in the 1970s (Crisis Relocation Planning, or CRP) and the Thatcher government's imperative that local authorities write nuclear war disaster plans in the 1980s. As NATO's forward nuclear base, Britain was extremely vulnerable to attack, especially following the decision to deploy medium range ballistic missiles (MRBMs) to Europe in 1979. For a while, Canada allowed the United States to deploy Bomarc-B nuclear missiles on its soil, but renounced a nuclear role in 1971. Though Canada was technically a non-nuclear power, its geographic position— literally between the Soviet Union and the United States—kept it keenly interested in the geopolitics of proliferation, the technology of delivery systems, and the prognostication of disaster. This did not, however, result in public rehearsals for civil defense after the late-1950s. The United Kingdom also abandoned public rehearsals in 1968. While the United Kingdom's density of population made civil defense measures seem hopeless and the United States' economic hubris made civil defense seem worth trying, Canada trusted that with so few people spread over so much land mass some would survive, but no crystal ball could predict where they might be.

It can be misleading to bundle together this forty-odd-year history. The exercises that tested and refined policies were in response to an evolving set of circumstances. As the weaponry changed, the scale of its consequences also changed. As new weaponry was tested, factors were newly discovered or more explicitly understood, effecting exactly what civil defense would need to take into account in order to preserve life and restore nations to recognizable form. The civil servants who wrote these policies responded to the data trickled down to them by the U.S. Atomic Energy Commission and related agencies investigating atomic and thermonuclear weapons, conscious of the need to project plans into a scenario of the near future but rarely able to do it. To many artists, however, thinking ahead was irresistable, envisioning not war as it had been or even war that could happen at any given moment, but the war of the future, attending to the ambitions of science in order to envision the strategies needed five or ten years into the future.

"Pilot Lights of the Apocalypse" (1946) is a particularly prophetic example of speculative fiction, written by the American physicist Louis N. Ridenour. Adapted as *Open Secret*, a one-act play produced by Stage for Action in 1947, it depicts the United States launching atomic bombs into permanent satellite orbit. The American scientists and generals are more than a little surprised and dismayed when the cameras sent up with the missiles discover that their 2,700 bombs joined 2,641 others of unknown origin already circling the earth. Proliferation on this scale is shocking, yet the scientists and military barely have time to absorb the fact that a balance of power is achieved when a technician's console lights up indicating that San Francisco has been hit. Who did this? Fascist Spain, with which the United States has trade disputes over uranium and oil? The console lights up again, recording the American retaliation on Madrid. Apparently, the Spanish assume they were hit by the Norwegians and so fire at Oslo. The Norwegians think France bombed them so retaliate on Paris. Someone fires on London. The British think they were hit by the Americans, and strikes are registered on New York, Boston, New Orleans, Los Angeles, St. Louis, Detroit, and Atlanta, as well as Moscow, Shanghai, Prague, Vienna, and Budapest. In a matter of seconds, the situation escalates into global war. It no longer matters who fired at whom: the world is engulfed in computer-activated trigger-finger warfare before anyone can even try to communicate. And when it is discovered that San Francisco was not hit by an atomic bomb but stricken by a massive earthquake, the whole chain of destruction becomes the epitome of human and technological folly. Secrecy, technical superiority, and belligerent posturing—once the ethics and strategies of supremacy—become the downfall of the North American and European defense alliance and, ultimately, the world. Ridenour, who received the Presidential Medal of Merit for wartime work on radar, depicts an orbiting nuclear shield protecting Fortress America and mutually assured destruction resulting in nuclear Armageddon.[7] Imagining such radically new scenarios did not require an artistic career, and this combination of scientific knowledge and creative insight was frequently the hallmark of civil and military foresight and effective planning. Civil defense is what would happen in response to a scenario like this.

Though planners needed to be futuristic in thinking about weaponry, planning what to actually do for civil defense always involved examining historical precedents.[8] Britain, the United States, and Canada were combatants in World War II but did not experience a ground war at home. They studied data on aerial bombing of Germany and Japan, reflected on Britons' ability to cope during the Blitz, and forecast new tactics.[9] In the era of atomic weaponry, instead of bombers blanketing a city they could target an entire nation, each bomb multiplying the destructive factor, creating new challenges to military and civilian defense. Weapons were so much more destructive that the defense of civilian populations took on new urgency. Successive twentieth-century wars took successively heavier tolls on civilians, and yet nuclear war could cause as many deaths in a few moments as all the twentieth century's wars added together. As junior partners in the Manhattan Project, Canada and the United Kingdom joined with the United States in tackling a wide range of problems that the project's success had wrought.

Even in the brief A-bomb era, it was H-bombs that were the urgent (unmet) priority. In 1950, William L. Laurence, the *New York Times* journalist who had been "embedded" in wartime Los Alamos, where scientists toiled in secret on the bombs destined for Hiroshima and Nagasaki, revealed that something called the hydrogen bomb had been in the minds of Manhattan Project scientists all along and would soon be a reality for both the United States and Soviets. Such a weapon, he predicted, could revolutionize warfare by causing severe flash burns over a 1,250 square-mile territory and total destruction in an area over 300 square miles: "Had we possessed it at the Battle of the Bulge, just one could have wiped out the entire Bulge." Downplaying radioactivity, he warned that the explosive force of H-bombs could kill 50 million Americans in just a few minutes. Russia's comparative lack of urbanization gave it an immediate strategic advantage.[10] This prospect, along with tension in Berlin and Korea, spurred Britain, Canada, and the United States to plan for civil defense. They never funded it extensively, but

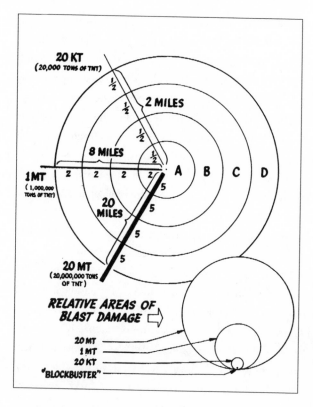

1. Damage from blast. Reprinted from *The National Plan*, 1958.

civil defense was in principle part of a layered defense that included conventional and nuclear weaponry.

Even before the first Soviet nuclear test—and long before it was thought possible—Britain, Canada, and the United States shared the scientific information that became the basis of their civil defense plans. In 1948, the Americans permitted British physicians to observe tests in the Pacific, contributing a report on medical aspects of the trials. Even though Britain pursued its own weapons research program, while waiting for this to materialize it made sense to share what data existed on the biological consequences of radiation and collaborate on the development of protective respirators and clothing. The British sought permission to let Canada's Department of National Defence (DND), with which they hoped to collaborate, into the information loop.[11] Months before it was published, the British received draft and advance copies of the U.S. Atomic Energy Commission's *Effects of Atomic Weapons* in order to offer comments and ensure its conformity with their own draft manual.[12] This indicates significant scientific and tactical exchange on topics including the principles of fission bombs; consequences of air, ground, and water bursts (shock, thermal radiation, and residual radiation); decontamination; and effects on personnel.[13] In 1951, Canada and the United States established eleven joint working groups on civil defense; most of these remained active into the mid-1960s (some into the 1970s), holding joint conferences, sending observers to each other's exercises, encouraging joint exercises in border regions, and negotiating reciprocal care agreements and a "no-border concept" for civilians in case of crisis-period migrations.[14] Despite evidence of cooperation, the Americans were reticent to share even with their closest allies, which led to duplication of research efforts. This was counterproductive, and the Americans knew it, as the President of Purdue University reveals in a plea to the FCDA in 1952: "It is . . . tragic from the point of view that our nation is spending literally billions in the attempt to strengthen, through the NATO organisation and the Mutual Security Agency, the free nations of Europe and then we turn around and refuse to collaborate with the British in matters involving the effect of atomic bombs on civilian structures. How foolish can we be?"[15] In 1954, Britain put pressure on the Americans to share more information about the hydrogen bomb. Evidently they had some but not all of the data and pressed for release of information on fallout's contamination contours, radioactivity's penetration of buildings, effect on human health, biological effects on flora and fauna, and methods of predicting contaminated zones.[16] In May 1955, the U.S. Senate agreed to the sharing of nuclear information (with some restrictions) between the United States and its NATO partners, and a tripartite conference on the topic was arranged in Ottawa in November 1955.[17]

The Effects of Atomic Weapons received a major revision as The Effects of Nuclear Weapons (1957).[18] Benefiting from a dozen years of empirical research, it offers physicists, engineers, and physicians guidance on the challenges facing them, while the key information for civil defense planners lay not so much in chronicling weapons damage as protecting people from it. Fallout was the new, openly acknowledged problem and distance, shielding, and time were the proffered panacea. With shorter attack warning times, it was less feasible to get people as far away from ground zero (GZ) as possible, and fallout complicated evacuation, so population dispersal was a controversial strategy. Early detection systems provided more warning than before, but how far could urbanites get in two hours if caught in horrendous traffic jams? Evacuation was impractical because there would be so few places to go, even in the United States, and so little time to get there. As the governor of California quipped, "Los Angeles cannot even evacuate itself on a Friday afternoon."[19] Shielding involved surrounding people with as much mass as possible, preferably in underground shelters, which would block gamma radiation. Most housing provided insufficient structural strength to be of much use

Chapter 1

against blast, but residential basements (beyond a specified distance from GZ) provided enough strength and could be modified to protect against radioactive fallout. The United States and Canada established guidelines from this data, developing shelter designs for home use, criteria for selecting public shelters in existing buildings, and recommendations for new construction. Coupled with advice on stocking food, water, and other survival supplies this became the backbone of civil defense policies. Planning in Britain strove for the same standards but, like parts of the United States, had to make adjustments for the absence of basements. Britain's estimates of the likely effectiveness of its housing stock were probably overstated.[20] High-rise housing built of reinforced concrete could be expected to offer significant protection from fallout in the central areas of middle floors, but such structures could be vulnerable to over pressures from the blast's shock wave or become deathtraps if ignited. When fallout protection was the only concern, subterranean locations were always preferred.

Based on data from tests in the South Pacific, fallout could be expected twenty miles upwind and over two hundred miles downwind of GZ, theoretically distributed in a cigar-shaped pattern up to forty miles wide but subject to infinite variation depending on conditions. Anyone in the central half of a downwind plume within approximately 140 miles of GZ could expect rapid fatal exposure if not shielded; in the remainder of the plume the lives of half the inhabitants would be threatened. At least 7,000 square miles would be in peril from each thermonuclear explosion, depending on weather conditions and the height of the detonation.[21] There are many by-products of the bomb, each of which decays at a unique rate, so over time the duration needed to accrue an equivalent dose decreases but some radiation remains. If the radiation intensity at a given site is 1,000 roentgens (r) per hour one hour after the blast, it would be 100 r per hour after seven hours (H+7), 10 r per hour after two days (D+2), and 1 r per hour after two weeks (D+14).[22] Recovery or rescue operations at a hot spot would not be attempted by civil defense workers. The maximum recommended exposure for American civil defense workers was 100 r, which meant that no exposure close to GZ should be chanced until a considerable time had passed, and even then it should be limited, for example only for the purpose of aiding escape. The two-day outdoor dose in the New York to Baltimore corridor could be 2,300 r and in Washington up to 19,000 r. In the latter case, even the best shelter would not save anyone.[23] As arsenals grew, more targets could be hit. In an "unlimited" war, the overlapping of fallout areas in Britain could make nearly the entire country uninhabitable; in Canada the populated band in the most southerly region would almost certainly be contaminated, along with parts of the Arctic territories down-

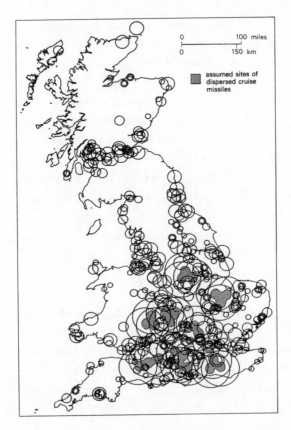

2. United Kingdom targets in attack on dispersed cruise missile sites, ca. 1983. Reprinted from Openshaw, Steadman, and Greene, 1983; courtesy of Blackwell Publishing Ltd.

wind from Alaska or stricken Distant Early Warning Line (DEW Line) sites; and in the United States the distribution of fallout from bombing counterforce targets meant that rural areas in the center of the continent were as subject to fallout as large cities and coastal population centers.[24]

As NATO prepared to issue its "New Assumptions" document late in 1954, its Civil Defence Committee warned "whereas the last war object was 'Business as usual,' the next war object must be 'survival'; and there is a wide gulf between them."

A "survival period," as conceived in this memorandum, means that the situation could become so difficult, not only in the areas attacked and their environs, but perhaps for the whole country if it is small, that everything would have to be temporarily subordinated to the maintenance of life and health; in other words, to the basic essentials of human existence. Conditions closely resembling a state of siege may therefore be experienced, and it will be a case of the country having to live off its own fat.[25]

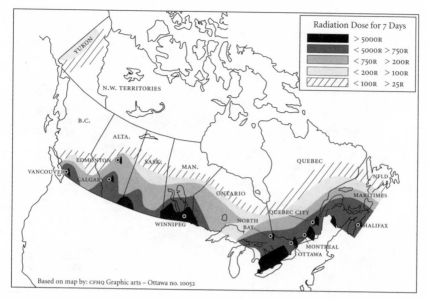

3. Anticipated radiation dose over seven days across Canada. Adapted from Canadian Forces HQ Planning document, 1970.

Civilian priority targets were assumed to be centers of government, industrial and communication centers directly supportive of a war effort, major ports, and large centers of population. The heaviest attacks were expected in the first three or four days of war, though the first thirty days would be critical. Peacetime preparations could mitigate the effects, but NATO cautioned that "thermo-nuclear weapons can create destruction and chaos on a scale exceeding anything hitherto contemplated."[26]

NATO recommended preserving the public in "tolerable living conditions" while securing utilities, food distribution, transportation, fuels and other essential commodities, ports, and medical and pharmaceutical supplies and facilities. In addition, it recommended special measures to maintain the authority of governments (including legislation for emergency powers), plans to transfer the essential elements of government and the civil service to less exposed areas, decentralization of responsibility to regional and local authorities, arrangements for maintaining communications between levels of government, and plans for close liaison between civil and military authorities.[27] This resulted in plans to relocate the highest echelons of the British, American, and Canadian governments to command and control centers in blast-proof bunkers and elements of the civil service in provisional accommodation of varying degrees of protection. They proceeded to construct or modify and equip premises, drill personnel in exercises, and prepare to occupy emergency facilities.

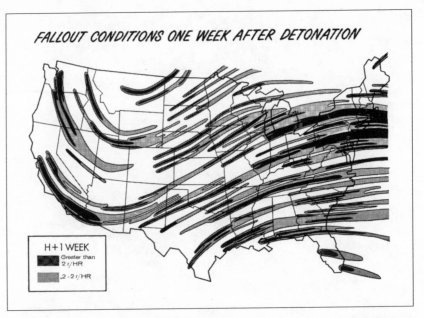

FALLOUT CONDITIONS ONE WEEK AFTER DETONATION

H + 1 WEEK

Greater than 2 r/HR

.2 - 2 r/HR

4. Fallout conditions at D+7 based on hypothetical pattern of 144 detonations over the United States. At D+6, 40 percent of the land mass would be effected; at D+7 one third would still be covered by significant fallout. Reprinted from *You and Civil Defense: A Guide for Teachers, Administrators, and School Board Members*, 1964.

The United Kingdom expressed the view that since NATO's commanders "had been authorised to plan for a nuclear war, the civilian sector could not base their plan on any other type of war."[28] Civil and military measures must be brought into harmony, yet the disparity was patent between blast-proof shelter for governance and makeshift provisions in residences for John Bull, Joe Citizen, and Johnny Canuck. The Canadian representative to NATO's Civil Emergency Planning Committee noted that the markedly different provisions for an inner circle and the general public would raise justifiable questions. The U.S. representative agreed that there was merit in this concern, but the responsibility of leaders to take such measures in order to continue to lead outweighed such niceties and to neglect this would indeed make them "very culpable."[29] A British Home Office (HO) lecturer looked back on "those days, almost happy days, when we had to contend with atom bombs only." He compared this, in 1963, to the new reality "where we could not expect a few hydrogen bombs to be exploded on this country but one hundred or more. The extent of the damage which would result from such an attack on cities and military targets and the widespread threat of fall-out led to the organisation of government in war being wholly recast."[30]

Britain called into being a nationwide Civil Defence Corps, the only NATO member to do so.[31] At any given time from 1950–68, there were several hundred thousand British volunteers giving up their weekends and evenings to train as wardens, firefighters, and rescue workers, in radiological monitoring, reconnaissance, and the welfare work of emergency housing, feeding, and registering the homeless. The National Health Service also maintained a reserve of physicians and nurses to augment the Civil Defence Corps. NATO's New Assumptions recommended adding to the highly localized civil defense efforts mobile columns of equipment and personnel that could be deployed as needed; Britain already had this as part of its army, but disbanded the columns in 1959. In the late 1950s, the idea began to be mooted by nuclear critics that civil defense was a con perpetrated on the British public. Skepticism grew over the government's inability to actually do anything in the event of war, and in 1968, in the face of growing public apathy, a calmer international situation, and financial pressures the British government put the Corps onto a "care and maintenance basis": a euphemism for stripping it of legitimacy, disposing of its equipment, and curtly thanking the volunteers for their interest.[32] Emphasis in the 1970s was upon providing a skeletal alternative machinery of government. Central government funding was never renewed for significant civil defense, though in 1983 Prime Minister Thatcher mandated that local councils make emergency plans for nuclear war. Few complied—despite threats from Whitehall—and those that did used the opportunity to highlight the monstrosity of nuclear weapons, the futility of civil defense, and their adamant stance as nuclear free zones. South Yorkshire, for example, wrote realistic plans on the best available data, comprising nine volumes, pointing out the HO's paucity of guidance and the local authority's marked preference for spending money on emergency services rather than war planning.[33] London, in its version of compliance, criticized the government's dual-use policy of "civil protection" encompassing all kinds of disasters when funding was only available for war planning.[34] By then, there was no active memory of the training received by the Civil Defence Corps fifteen to thirty years earlier, and even those with occupational responsibility for civil defense were woefully under-trained. As a consortium of local authorities in the northwest reported, "an exercise at Greater Manchester's war HQ in 1989 was held up for half a day because a group of scientific advisers was unable to find the switch to turn the teleprinter on."[35]

In Canada, responsibility for civil defense rested with the Department of Health and Welfare until the formation of the Emergency Measures Organization (EMO) in 1957. EMO was the most active from 1957 through 1963, when it was demoted from the Privy Council's orbit to the Ministry of Defence Production. It had never been successful in arousing widespread public support. In 1967, under the Pearson government, it suffered severe budget cuts which further eroded its staff and status. Three years later its brief changed from not only war but any threat to Canada's social, political, or economic structure: effectively everything from blizzards to oil spills to air crashes. Reconstituted as Emergency Planning Canada (EPC) in 1980, for the first time peacetime planning explicitly took precedence over wartime planning.[36] Like the United States, Canada promoted actions — such as nationwide surveys for potential shelter sites — that would protect everyone, but like the United Kingdom, Canada pragmatically and overtly recognized that efforts would need to concentrate on those who managed to survive an attack not those who *might* be protected in advance of it.[37]

The United States maintained its pretense of workable civil defense the longest. In the early months of the Truman presidency, just after wartime civil defense was disbanded, the United States Strategic Bombing Survey recommended shelter programs.[38] From 1950 to 1959 the Ground Observer Corps organized citizens to watch the skies for enemy bombers. These "plane-spotters" were superseded by the DEW Line and other air-borne and ground detector systems, but while the program lasted it had remarkably diverse volunteers among 389,000 members.[39] President Eisenhower endorsed private shelters, and President Kennedy also pushed stocking public shelters and labeling them at street level. Public efforts were curtailed under President Johnson. In 1969, the Nixon administration lowered the American civil defense budget, cancelling various programs that chronically lagged behind goals. The Office of Civil Defense (OCD) continued to mount exhibitions nationwide, produce new publications, and facilitate public education through home study courses and university extension classes, giving training in everything from shelter management to radiological monitoring. The public shelter program — a leftover from the Kennedy administration — officially remained but nothing had been put into the facilities since the early 1960s and not even the signage was renewed. In 1971, greater onus was put on local governments for emergency operations, an old ruse to shift the financial burden off federal authorities. Soon after, civil defense was replaced with "civil preparedness," a move toward "all-emergency planning" solidified in 1978 with the creation of the Federal Emergency Management Agency (FEMA) which endures to the present time with the broad mandate to cover everything from natural disasters to industrial safety, radiological accidents, nuclear attack, and terrorism.[40] The claim in such dual-use or all-hazard schemes "is that planning is generically similar across hazards so that to plan for the one is to plan for the many. Specifically, all hazards planning says that natural calamities are the same as technological, and especially nuclear, calamities."[41]

Civil defense was a domestic policy, yet sent signals abroad: the Kremlin was an implied spectator of rehearsals and Soviet assessment of efficiency was crucial to deterrence. As a National Security Council document commented in 1960, civil defense consisted of the national psychology as well as fallout shelters, and while "the lack of an effective civil defense has, so far, not been a handicap in the conduct of foreign affairs," with the advent of ballistic missile systems the "compensating effects" or massive retaliatory capacity "appears to be fading."[42] Pressure grew from some factions to address the presumed "gap" between civil defense in the United States and the Soviet Union, which was believed to have extensive protection in its residential blocks, factories, and subway system.[43] Under President Carter, planning for civil defense shifted to CRP, an ambitious scheme to shift the population away from urban and counterforce target areas as international tensions built up, so that if an attack came it would minimize effects on the population and economy. Instead of insurance against attack, it was thought of as deterrence.[44] Some experimental play with CRP occurred, reviving exercise practices that had waned since the mid-1960s. President Reagan proposed a $4.2 billion program to modernize civil defense, incorporating crisis relocation, blast shelters for essential workers, protection for strategic portions of industry, and a renewed bunker system for senior government. He did not get it.[45] By 1985, CRP was defunct: funds were instead channeled into SDI ("Star Wars"), a futuristic attack detection system of dubious feasibility.[46]

The Goals of Civil Defense

Cold War civil defense, as articulated in these nations, was not as broad as "home defense," which has connotations of the military's armed defense of the homeland. Sometimes the military was slated to take part in civil defense activities (notably in Canada and the United Kingdom), but it was primarily a civilian responsibility, involved civilian personnel, and addressed the needs of civilians, industry, and government. It consisted of the planning, practicing, and (if ever needed) the implementation of plans for protection of people, property, and government in the event of nuclear war. Some Cold War planning also addressed biological and chemical attacks but these were lesser concerns: modern warfare was assumed to be aerial, and biological and chemical attacks were usually treated in the civil defense literature as sabotage or fifth column (traitorous) activities. Either planners were naive about the effects of these other forms of attack or regarded the dangers of nuclear weapons as infinitely more deadly, as well as more likely to occur.[47]

Civil defense programs were the confluence of three kinds of concerns. These

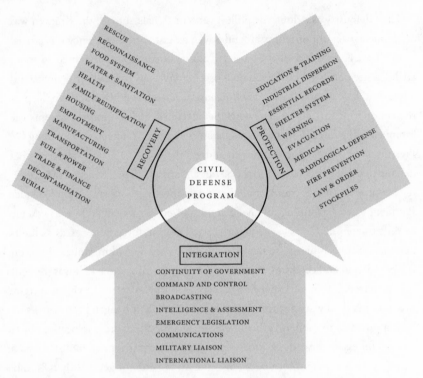

RESCUE
RECONNAISSANCE
FOOD SYSTEM
WATER & SANITATION
HEALTH
FAMILY REUNIFICATION
HOUSING
EMPLOYMENT
MANUFACTURING
TRANSPORTATION
FUEL & POWER
TRADE & FINANCE
DECONTAMINATION
BURIAL

RECOVERY

EDUCATION & TRAINING
INDUSTRIAL DISPERSION
ESSENTIAL RECORDS
SHELTER SYSTEM
WARNING
EVACUATION
MEDICAL
RADIOLOGICAL DEFENSE
FIRE PREVENTION
LAW & ORDER
STOCKPILES

PROTECTION

CIVIL
DEFENSE
PROGRAM

INTEGRATION
CONTINUITY OF GOVERNMENT
COMMAND AND CONTROL
BROADCASTING
INTELLIGENCE & ASSESSMENT
EMERGENCY LEGISLATION
COMMUNICATIONS
MILITARY LIAISON
INTERNATIONAL LIAISON

5. Civil defense responsibilities. Based on the *Ellis Report*, 1961; and Vale 1987.

were schematized in a report commissioned early in the Kennedy presidency as recovery, protection, and integration. This schema constitutes the agenda for developing policy and plans—thus the priorities for rehearsal—and is typical of concerns in all three nations. It is difficult to separate the protection component from the recovery component in terms of any sequential activity. Recovery needed to be prepared for in advance, and protection would continue after attack. Likewise, with respect to integrating efforts in an emergency, the continuity of constitutionally authorized government would be enabled through activity in command and control centers coming on-line as a crisis developed, but emergency legislation would need to be drafted long in advance for implementation post-attack. Trade and finance and re-establishment of the food system post-attack would be directed from command and control centers but facilitated by intervention of the police. But food could only get to the public if transportation was available, and transportation could only be sustained if petroleum supplies were assured, which in turn depended upon international liaison and trading partners abroad. Radiological defense consisted of determining the size of bombs, fallout patterns, and decay rates, which dictated where and for how long people could work in the open, when manufacturing could resume, and how long command and control functions would operate in special facilities. Industrial dispersion—the relocation of manufacturing plants away from dense concentrations and likely targets—could be undertaken in peacetime in order to lower the risk of destruction, while the caching of microfilmed essential records further hedged the bet, but these plans could only pay off if managers could continue to communicate over long distances, if utilities were operational, and if workers had housing, medical care, and other essentials of life. While few of these categories have clear-cut domains and not all civil defense activity can be coordinated, figure 5 conveys something of the scale and complexity of problems. Genetic and ecological damage are certainly germane to the recovery effort, but omitted here because, though they were speculated upon, they were not gamed as aspects of civil defense.

The important point about this schema is not the advisability of any civil defense policy but what it sets as an agenda for exploring civil defense through the limited empiricism of rehearsal. Rehearsal was the predominant (and yet historically uncelebrated) technique of exploring the viability of civil defense plans and policies. The political scenarios that rehearsals were predicated upon varied enormously, but that is not within this study's purview any more than an analysis of military strategy is appropriate; instead, it is what ensued from chosen scenarios in rehearsal that matters. The political science may seem, therefore, unsubtle but as such it is true to form. The ethical questions may be, therefore, skirted but the purpose is not a heuristic education in morality. The discovery of archival evidence of so many rehearsals in so many contexts is remarkable, and though rehearsing may not be unique to this realm the shibboleths of civil defense addressed matters of unparalleled consequence.

Theater did not dwindle in stature after the mid-twentieth century; it simply broadened its range of venues. Instead of relying on its customary pools of actors, directors, and scenographers, it drew on novel talent: physicists, economists, meteorologists, police, postmasters, wholesalers, tree-trimmers, nurses, truck drivers, bankers, psychologists, clergy, broadcasters, homemakers, and morticians. In their occupational capacities and in their domestic settings, everyone had a role to play.

Getting the Message Out

Billed as "the most far-reaching public-education project of its kind," the Alert America campaign set out in December 1951 "to awaken American men and women, boys and girls—no matter who they are, where they are, or what their station in life may be—to the urgency of their personal participation in a vigorous

6. Overhead view of a section of the Alert America exhibit, Washington.
Courtesy of NARA.

Civil Defense in their own city, factory and farm, and to encourage volunteers
for such specialized training as may be needed."[48] Three convoys, each with ten
thirty-two-foot trailer trucks, traveled 36,000 miles throughout the nation, at-
tracting 1.1 million people in eighty-two cities. Billed as "the show that may save
your life," it was displayed in exhibition halls, gymnasia, and armories.[49] The exhibit featured the peaceful uses of atomic energy as well as the changes wrought by
new biological, chemical, psychological, and incendiary weapons of modern warfare. Films of atomic explosions were shown, leading up to "the dramatic Atomic
Attack Room—mock air raid depicting devastating assault on typical American
city" followed by "the transition—with Civil Defense we can beat this menace."
Displays on local, state, and national responsibility for civil defense in the pre-
attack and post-attack periods were linked to a catechism on American freedoms
and the Communist menace. The chance to sign the "Alert America Pledge" to
acquire and implement civil defense training was featured in the last part, "the
pay-off room," geared to local needs and volunteering opportunities. Visits from
the convoy were frequently supplemented by related activities: parades, military
exercises, air raid siren tests, mutual aid exercises, mobile support demonstrations,
and mock raids by the Air National Guard to promote the exhibit and reinforce
recruitment messages.[50] The Alert America message was pressed upon groups rep-

7. Alert America convoy on Parliament Hill, Ottawa. Courtesy of NARA.

resenting women, industry, agriculture, labor, youth, schools, and veterans, the extravagance of its displays enabled through corporate donations. Smaller-scale exhibits at state and county fairs brought the civil defense message to millions of other Americans. Before the Alert America convoys were broken up and refitted with different displays for a new phase of touring aimed to reach four million people in 1953, one of the caravans was loaned to Canada, where it covered 10,000 miles in the "On Guard, Canada" promotion.[51]

Nothing like this was ever mounted in Britain in conjunction with its recruiting campaign for the Civil Defence Corps, which relied on advertising in print media, short films on the BBC and in cinemas, and exercises and demonstrations.[52] While Americans blatantly pressed Alert America upon children, encouraging schools and Scouting troops to attend as groups, Britain faced obstacles in enlisting the hearts and minds of youth groups. Scouts had been instrumental during World War II air raids, carrying messages, assisting in hospitals, helping with evacuees and billets, maintaining respirators, erecting air raid shelters, running public shelters, and helping to sandbag and camouflage vulnerable sites.[53] During the Cold War, some Boy Scouts (and their leaders) were taught about nuclear

Join your workmates in

CIVIL DEFENCE

In industry, Civil Defence has some 200,000 members, forming Units in thousands of firms. They would do many jobs—Rescue, First Aid, Control, Communications—all of them vital if war should come.
We have a Unit here. We need YOU
See the Civil Defence Officer about joining NOW

PRODUCED BY THE CENTRAL OFFICE OF INFORMATION FOR H.M. GOVERNMENT

8. Poster for British Civil Defense Corps recruiting campaign. Courtesy of PRO.

threats and trained in rescue techniques, but there was no official training. Scouts were not allowed to participate in exercises unless they were over age fifteen because the Home Office (HO) ruled school-age children were not covered by the Personal Injuries (Emergency Provisions) Act of 1939, and thus injuries could not be compensated; nor could Scouts join the Civil Defence Corps, which had an age limit of eighteen.[54] They sometimes participated as mock casualties, guides, or indoor messengers.[55] In Canada, however, Boy Scouts and Girl Guides participated extensively in exercises by running messages, serving as mock casualties, and swelling the crowd in registration practices.[56]

More active roles probably meant more thorough indoctrination. In the United States, Boy Scouts were casualties and stretcher bearers in medical exercises, volunteered in the Ground Observer Corps, cooked food for outdoor exercise participants, and Boy and Girl Scouts were message runners in command center exercises and conducted first aid demonstrations.[57] Civil defense was integrated into the family "be prepared" plan from 1951 and incorporated by Scouting headquarters into national "liberty" themes for Scout meetings until after the Cuban

Chapter 1

9. Boy Scout's family checks shelter emergency supplies, 1958. Courtesy of NARA.

Missile Crisis. Home preparedness, wilderness skills, troupe mobilization, and self-protection in atomic attack were inculcated in den meetings; the 2.75 million Scouts were then to take the message to their families, ensuring their parents had set aside essential documents, knew the CONELRAD (Control of Electromagnetic Radiation) emergency radio frequencies, and kept fallout shelters stocked.[58] Explorer Scouts (aged fourteen and above) emphasized a "ready" stance to assist in a wide range of emergencies, including natural disasters and nuclear war, and were the most frequent participants in field exercises.[59]

In 1956, Boy Scouts hand delivered a million civil defense posters within critical target areas, and in 1958 nearly three million Boy Scouts were recruited to distribute OCD's new "Handbook for Emergencies" to thirty-seven million homes. They had President Eisenhower's direct sponsorship and blanketed the nation's cities as well as rural areas.[60] During the Berlin Crisis, Scouts built and exhibited model fallout shelters and helped with the stocking of public shelters shoulder-to-shoulder with the Salvation Army and the National Guard.[61] Following the Cuban Missile Crisis, interest waned: in 1963, Cleveland, Ohio's civil defense was only able to recruit half the Boy and Girl Scouts it hoped to participate as mock casualties in "Operation Know-How."[62] Instead of weaning young people away from civil defense in the subsequent era of dual-use emergency planning, the Scouts added an emergency preparedness merit badge in 1972 requiring proficiency with warning systems, elementary shelter knowledge, and messenger experience.[63] There was an upsurge of interest in the early 1970s not only from the Scouts but Future Farmers of America, Boys' and Girls' Clubs, and 4-H Clubs.[64]

In the early 1950s, media blitzes increased public knowledge about the basics of bomb effects, immediate self-protection, and home preparation, while outreach through youth groups, service clubs, and other types of formal social affiliations provided conduits to reinforce, elaborate, and rehearse the messages. In the late 1950s, it became necessary to inform the public about protection against fallout, which led to programs encouraging people to build home fallout shelters and to know the routes to public shelters. Andrew Grossman, in a recent study of American civil defense, describes the "400 million pieces of civil defense literature . . . aimed specifically at the general public" as a "blueprint for social control."[65] The American government produced a prodigious array of free literature for mass distribution, most famously the "Bert the Turtle" cartoon book for children in 1952, and in 1955 another illustrated pamphlet for adults with a similar style of line drawings ("Facts About Fallout"), followed by the more specialized "Rural Family Defense" (1956), "Facts about Fallout Protection" (1957), and "The Family Fallout Shelter" (1959), among many others. In the early 1960s, as the public shelter campaign intensified, a prolific literature on school fallout shelters was instigated, including "School Shelter: an Approach to Fallout Protection" (1960) and "National School Fallout Shelter Design Competition Awards" (1963).[66] In 1968, as dual-use emergency planning came into vogue, "In Time of Emergency" was issued in an initial 5,235,000 print run ultimately reaching twenty-six million copies in English and Spanish by 1977.[67] The Canadian government also published general advice ("Personal Protection under Atomic Attack," 1951), rural advice ("Fallout on the Farm," 1961), and shelter designs ("Your Basement Fallout Shelter," 1960, and "Simpler Shelters," 1962).[68] However, just as the Canadian per capita output was dwarfed by the American, the British output was dwarfed by the Canadian.

The advent of submarine-launched ballistic missiles, the prospect of intercontinental ballistic missiles (which shortened warning times), and tension over Berlin and Cuba (which made the world situation appear imminently volatile) led the Canadian government to issue a mass-released booklet "Eleven Steps to Survival" early in 1961.[69] Initially distributing a print run of a million copies to a nation of less than twenty million people, "Eleven Steps to Survival" repeats the basic catechism about blast, fallout, shielding and shelter, emergency supplies, fire prevention, first aid and home nursing, water and sanitation, decontamination, and the meshing of municipal and family plans for survival. It ends with a checklist to encourage reiteration of knowledge as well as implementation of action-based measures. The booklet survived as the mainstay of Canadian advice throughout the Cold War, reprinted in 1971 and 1980. Like most civil defense matters that were strictly informational rather than policy oriented, it aroused no controversy and little public notice.

By contrast, the Kennedy administration had a fraught experience bringing out a new booklet of advice for contemporaneous nuclear war scenarios, including "last minute improvised measures" for fallout protection for those with limited resources, procrastinating natures, or the misfortune to be targeted by a sneak attack. Congress endorsed the plan for identifying, marking, and eventually stocking public shelters in July 1961. By October, Marcus Raskin (an expert in disarmament negotiations and White House adviser) warned that OCD, then part of the Department of Defense (DOD), had changed the concept "to something much more broad, comprehensive and frantic" as represented by the booklet the Pentagon drafted and planned to issue to all households. Raskin warned that the booklet, in tandem with an announcement by the president, amounted to premature statements, creating an impression that the administration knew what it was doing and where it was going when in fact it did not have the facts to make such judgments: "the state of our knowledge with regard to civil defense is very limited and the societal (legal, economic, technical) tools to be able to undertake a comprehensive program in the U.S. are almost nonexistent."[70] Carl Kaysen joined the chorus of inner-circle critics, pointing out that neither the DOD nor state and local civil defense agencies had approved plans and specifications for home shelters and had no mechanism to inspect and approve any home shelters that were built. The Pentagon's proposed booklet, he warned, would "create very strong political demands for a Federal shelter building program on a large scale such as was never contemplated in the original Civil Defense message" delivered by President Kennedy in May 1961.[71]

Arthur Schlesinger Jr. criticized the draft pamphlet for giving nothing with which the working class could identify.[72] John Kenneth Galbraith, one of a chorus of intellectuals who warned the administration of the untruths in the pamphlet and urged them to shelve it, wrote:

The present pamphlet is a design for saving Republicans and sacrificing Democrats. These are the people who have individual houses with basements in which basement or lean-to fallout shelters can be built. There is no design for civilians who live in wooden three deckers, tenements, low cost apartments, or other congested areas. . . . I think it is particularly injudicious, in fact it is absolutely incredible, to have a picture of a family with a cabin cruiser saving itself by going out to sea. Very few members of the UAW [United Auto Workers] can go with them.

Galbraith also criticized the draft pamphlet's explicit message that civilian protection was a matter for private enterprise, specifically through the home shelter
market. He called the administration's plans "a great helter skelter shelter program" based on "the social discrimination in survival" and chastised President
Kennedy with the words: "We don't want to pay the price of deep urban shelters
so we are writing off the slum dwellers." Galbraith argued that if do-it-yourself-
shelter cannot serve all kinds of urban residents, it should not be undertaken.
"We cannot tell the poor family in a big city which would like to live that the government has written it off. The present pamphlet if read by such a family without
the space or the money for a shelter would cause it to conclude that its prospect
was hopeless. It would alarm without giving hope."[73]

This was already an old argument: FCDA plans in the early 1950s wrote off
the inner cities and high density residential areas, inequitably imperiling African
Americans, Jews, and Catholics.[74] Creating sufficient shelter spaces would cost
$5.5 billion, and such appropriations were never going to be forthcoming.[75] Be-
sides, building shelters was a zero sum game: Edward Teller estimated that $50
billion would be needed to cover the cost of "digging deeper" as the megatonnage
of bombs increased.[76]

These suggestions from the president's advisers were largely ignored when the
pamphlet was printed at the end of 1961 and twenty-five million copies distributed.[77] It baldly sets out the case for the kind of destruction to be expected from
a thermonuclear weapon while peddling civil defense as the remedy.[78] It advocates community shelters as ideal, for they pool skills and resources that might
not be present in family shelters, but also directs readers to information helpful
for planning home shelters and for improvised measures that can be taken if there
is no warning of attack. Disease and radiation contamination can be problems
post-attack, but again the pamphlet stresses the importance of community efforts
in the recovery period. "The world and your community would be shattered by
a nuclear war. Normal services would be disrupted; essential skills could be in
short supply; equipment you had taken for granted might not be available. You
would face the aftermath of a catastrophe, but if there had been previous planning, you need not face it alone."[79] If already organized into community units
through their shelter experience, the next steps—hosing contamination into the
gutters or plowing under exposed soil—would be easier to accomplish.

This was the official advice that the American public had at their fingertips
when they were informed that the Soviets had placed offensive missiles in Cuba.
Evidently, the majority of the population agreed with Raskin that advice such as
" 'the communities that are well organized and have planned their decontamina-

tion actions will be able to return to *normal life* conditions' is very dangerous since the notion of normal living conditions is meaningless when compared to pre-nuclear attack." Its "hodgepodge grab bag series of suggestions and non-sequitur" was merely advocating "action *qua* action rather than anything which has to do with creative problem solving."[80] Even without Raskin's access to the scientific information, and knowledge of its gaps, many sensed that the advice was erroneous. The public did not, however, react with panic or agitation. Worse, from the point of view of civil defense advocates, most people disregarded it entirely.

The Kennedy administration reached out to the usual groups in promoting "Fallout Protection: What to Know and Do About Nuclear Attack"—Steuart L. Pittman, Assistant Secretary of Defense for Civil Defense, sent a letter to Scout leaders commending the booklet to their troupes' attention—and though Women Strike for Peace urged people to mail the booklet back to the president, demanding a different approach, the public as a whole took little notice.[81] Putting the DOD's imprimatur on it made civil defense part of the Pentagon's overall defense strategy, but Congress's failure to fund ambitious civil defense projects had a countervailing message. During the Cuban Missile Crisis, 60 percent of the population took no civil defense measures whatsoever. Whether they were in line with Office of Emergency Planning's (OEP) graduated level of ramping-up preparations or acute critics of the administration's long-term civil defense policies is uncertain.

In Britain, the HO issued a series of advisory pamphlets, beginning in the 1950s, targeted at Civil Defence Corps members and civil servants. The first booklet intended for general readership was "Advising the Householder on Protection against Nuclear Attack," issued in January 1963. Significantly, however, this too was bracketed as a training prop for the civil defense, police, and fire services informing them of the kind of general information that would be given to the public in the event of an emergency. Instead of being widely distributed to the public, it was made available for purchase.[82] Essentially the same advice as in the Canadian and U.S. versions, but without the overt politics of the Pentagon's booklet, "Advising the Householder" was tailored for standard British housing designs, introducing what became the notorious phrase "the cupboard under the stairs" as the preferred fallout shelter for anyone dwelling in a post-war semi-detached two-story structure, and explaining what instructions to expect in case of post-attack evacuation. Its successor, "Protect and Survive," substantially the same information with new graphics, was billed as the booklet that "tells you how to make your home and your family as safe as possible under nuclear attack."[83] It was issued in 1976 and 1980 as the foundation of a vast archive of prepared television spots, newspaper layouts, and sound recordings to be stockpiled and released along with millions of copies of the pamphlet in case of escalating tensions. In the meantime, the pamphlet sold for £3.[84] Instead of fulfilling the government's fear that it would lead to demands for increased civil defense expenditure, "Protect and Survive" became the butt of anti-nuclear activists, who noted the irony of the government's rhetoric that it cannot afford to spend money to protect the public while it allocated £5 trillion to the Trident nuclear missile program.[85] One critic of Britain's plans to survive nuclear war states that it is "the object of well-merited ridicule and scorn because of the huge gulf between its bland aseptic primary school style, with its neat little diagrams of paper tissues and teddybears, and what any half-way imaginative reader knows would be the reality—crouching in fear for days on end, in the dark, behind a couple of doors, with a bucket for a lavatory, perhaps with some of the shelterers injured or suffering from radiation sickness."[86] In its first year, "Protect and Survive" sold just 85,000 copies.[87] E. P. Thompson countered with "Protest and Survive" in April 1980, and the Campaign for Nuclear Disarmament (CND) gathered steam that continued into the era of Greenham Common and the other peace camps.[88] In the fall of 1981, the government responded with "Civil Defence: Why We Need It" arguing that civil defense was a credible aspect of deterrence.[89] Raymond Briggs's illustrated novella *When the Wind Blows* (1982), depicting a couple's attempt to utilize the advice in their preparations for nuclear winter, contributed to civil defense's disrepute.[90] Even Home Secretary Douglas Hurd admitted that everyone treated "Protect and Survive" with derision,[91] and the planned successor of 1986 did not materialize.

The American public was extensively surveyed on their opinions about the likelihood of nuclear war, their perception of local risks, knowledge of civil defense principles, and inclination toward participating. Despite the efforts of the government and the enormous publicity accorded to civil defense, few Americans built shelters, and even fewer considered moving to reduce their risk. For example, in the county containing Chicago and most of its suburbs, 260,000 copies of "Family Fallout Shelter" were distributed to 3.5 million people yet only nineteen shelter permit applications were filed.[92] At the time, building codes within Chicago (but not its suburbs) actually precluded the construction of home fallout shelters.[93] People worried—especially the young and women—but race relations, taxes, and education were at the top of their agendas.[94] Canadians polled in 1962 responded overwhelmingly that they thought preparations were worthwhile (69 percent), and though fewer knew what to do in case of attack (45 percent), they believed the government—not individuals—should provide bomb shelters (70 percent).[95] They believed this so strongly that only a tiny fraction of the population built shelters in their homes: in early October 1961, while tanks stood nose-to-nose in Berlin, only thirty-six households nationwide (.009 percent) had applied for permits.[96]

In contrast, millions in the United States and Canada participated in the "Operation Alert" (OPAL) and "Alert" exercise series—as many as a quarter of the U.S. population in 1960—by running to shelter, listening to the heads of government give instructions over the radio, or complying in evacuation exercises. In Britain, hundreds of thousands of volunteers were involved in the Civil Defence Corps, National Health Service Reserve, and industrial civil defense, yet not even these keen volunteers built shelters at home. Insofar as participation in civil defense is a significant historical phenomenon among the general public, it achieves this distinction on the basis of performed compliance in exercises, not their creation of built structures. This unites the three national case studies.

Compliance was performative, not material, but even this had limits.

In 1964, a boiler exploded in a New York telephone center: the five hundred employees nearby "thought an atomic bomb had struck, and several later confessed, 'I thought it was the end.'" According to pollsters surveying them, this proved "that the Cold War has affected the imaginations and perceptions of Americans."[97] But outside scheduled exercises, this conviction did not translate into compliant civil defense behavior. When the Chicago White Sox baseball team won the 1959 American League pennant at a game in Cleveland, Chicago's fire commissioner authorized the ringing of bells and sounding of air raid sirens in celebration. Two-thirds of Chicagoans—unsure of whether this was carnival or catastrophe—turned on their radios, the same number looked out into the street, some discussed the situation with others, and a few phoned public agencies to find out what was going on. But among the half-million households within reach of the sirens, almost none (only 2 percent) took protective action. Researchers concluded that even those who were frightened enough to want to take action did not do so because "there is no action known to them that is worth taking."[98]

Other false alarms had similar public responses. One fine morning in 1955, sirens went off for a few minutes in Oakland, California. This was a false alarm, though as far as the Air Force was concerned it was a legitimate activation in response to incoming planes. Most people who heard the alarm did not believe it could be real. Up to 10 percent tried to get confirmation of an attack on the radio, but no more than this percentage of the population tried to protect themselves by taking cover, the recommended response in such circumstances. Researchers studying the event concluded that if another alert sounded, more than 75 percent of people would either pay no attention or do the wrong thing unless confirmation of real danger could be ascertained from another source. But using sirens, not CONELRAD, was the protocol at this point in an emergency, assuming a "sneak attack." As soon as the attack warning was issued, radio stations were mandated to go off the air lest their call signs help bombers get their bearings and zero in on a target. Anyone with a conditioned response to seeking confirmation before rushing to shelter was intensifying their danger. "It would seem, then, that in order to attach a more appropriate and adaptive meaning to the siren, people must be encouraged or forced to go through adaptive behaviors every time they hear it. There should probably be no siren tests or drills without public participation. There should probably be repeated public announcements to the effect that the air raid sirens will never be blown unless it is 'for real,' that is, unless public action is wanted."[99] Yet even if the public was rehearsed more often, without a threat period (inclement weather, smoke, or other sign of danger), it seemed, unexpected warning signals would not be believed.[100] People looked to each other for guidance, seeking validation for their interpretation, and "when they were calm and casual the behavior was emulated."[101]

Federal employees might be expected to show a greater compliance rate. When air raid sirens were accidentally set off in several Washington government buildings in 1958, at the height of the Berlin Crisis, two-thirds of staff not only discounted the possibility that there could be a real air raid but most did not even know whether it meant they should evacuate or take shelter. The resulting behavior is revealing: about a quarter of surveyed employees thought they should continue what they were doing, and just as many decided to await further instructions, see what others were doing, or check the situation by other means. Thirty-four percent reported being curious, 18 percent confused, 16 percent uneasy, 13 percent unconcerned, 6 percent irritated, and 2 percent scared or excited. A few went out to their cars, turned on the radios and then, not hearing confirmation of an attack, returned to work. Among these employees of the Veterans Administration, Weather Bureau, and Departments of Health, Education and Welfare (HEW), Commerce, Treasury, and State—75 percent of whom admitted to having had civil defense training—20 percent went to shelter but not one responded as they were supposed to by evacuating the city.[102]

These alarms indicate how individuals' interpretation of circumstances interfered with translating their training (and ostensible habituation) into appropriate behaviors. This suggests that unless circumstances validated a high level of prealarm anxiety about war, the public would not comply, or compliance would be maladaptive. Perfection in rehearsal would only lead to compliance in an emergency if a form of performance anxiety, resulting from anticipating the need to perform, was felt. Being relaxed in rehearsal was fine, but too great a comfort level in ordinary circumstances would lead to the perception of a real emergency as a false alarm.

Women, Families, and Workers in Civil Defense

Interviewees in 1950 expressed derision about American civil defense efforts during World War II. A sixty-year-old insurance broker from Chicago stated "the things I saw, like the wardens chasing balloons, and just everything. . . . I just thought it was all foolish." A young stenographer from New York working on her master's degree said that civil defense "was generally looked upon with amusement more than anything else. . . . I don't think it was done with any strong conviction of its utility."[103] In the United States, persuading the public of the need for civil defense was not simply a matter of explaining the power of nuclear weapons; convincing them to become involved required persuading them that they, and what they cared about, were directly at risk. Coordinated recruitment of volunteers into various civil defense schemes in the 1950s and early 1960s involved tapping into many types of communities. Communities based on moral criteria (such as religious affiliations or service organizations), consumption patterns (middle-class households represented by stay-at-home mothers), memory (especially through direct wartime service), symbolic similarity (such as professionally based clubs or trades unions), and interpretive similarity (as with ethnic-based groups) augmented the primary organizing strategy of grouping volunteers together according to their geographical distribution.[104] Among women, the recruitment message featured private responsibilities of home and family allied to global politics and the public-mindedness of citizenship. Among men and working women, the normative roles of laborer and breadwinner were allied to public responsibilities arising from the corporate identity of the workplace, the civic identity of collective preservation, and the national identity forged from active patriotism. Membership, belonging, and fellowship were the ancillary benefits of taking part in the civil defense effort. Wherever individuals felt most comfortable—within exogenous communities, reaching out to coordinate with differently articulated portions of their community, or functioning reciprocally across communities—a role for them could be found.[105]

By 1958, Britain had achieved a rate of one in seventy adults, or 1 percent of the population, trained in civil defense: 350,000 volunteers in the Civil Defence Corps and 200,000 in industrial civil defense, the majority of whom were women (55 percent).[106] Women had a demonstrable value to the cause: they presented a large and otherwise untapped labor force in wartime, frequently possessed skills indispensable to various aspects of civil defense, and were a conduit between households and communities. In Britain, their recruitment built upon traditions established by the Women's Voluntary Service (wvs) in World War II, "the Army Hitler forgot," which addressed on a local level the consequences of bomb damage by providing rest centers, relocating, resettling, re-equipping, and clothing those whose homes were damaged by bombs, organizing salvage operations, and billeting refugees and repatriates.[107] As a wvs member stated, "It was the woman, doing her job, in her little house, in every street, who upheld this great responsibility of civil defense."[108] After the war, the wvs was as much a fixture at disaster sites as the British Red Cross, providing meals, emergency clothing, and blankets. Their mobile canteens (the "flying food squads") were frequently employed at civil defense field exercises, as they had been at bomb sites during the war and wherever there were gatherings of refugees, agricultural workers, the shipwrecked, dock workers, and men helping with reconstruction.[109]

The wvs promoted civil defense knowledge through its "One in Five" campaign from the mid-1950s through the mid-1960s. The idea was that "the nation would be strengthened if one-in-five women knew the simple things they could do to mitigate effects of nuclear warfare" and passed the information on to others. Women were encouraged to gather in homes and parish halls to hear talks on the effects of nuclear explosions, staying put rather than evacuating, precautions that can be taken at home, the extent of help offered by the Civil Defence Corps, how women's self-sufficiency can help their families, and home nursing.[110] Initially, housewives who were not club or guild members were targeted, but focusing on women who were outside typical women's networks made for slow progress in achieving the one in five goal. Attention shifted onto women's clubs and organizations, government departments, factories, companies, stores, hospitals, and banks. "During the days of the Cuban crisis there was an up-surge of interest, and wvs speakers were hard put to meet the demands for information. By the end of 1962 . . . Over 1,000,000 out of the national target of 3,000,000 women had heard the talks."[111] The one-in-five concept was borrowed by the peace movement as "One in Five Must Know," juxtaposing passages from wvs literature with quotations from John Hersey's *Hiroshima*.[112] This radical recontextualization of the message attests to its essential conservatism as well as its wide recognizability.

With sixteen million women and men eligible for civil defense service in 1950, the British government had ambitions of recruiting one in twenty of these citizens into the Civil Defence Corps, Auxiliary Fire Service, National Health Service Reserve, or Special Constabulary. This would have created a trained cadre of about 800,000 in the early 1950s.[113] Men and women over age thirty were eligible for all branches, along with younger men declared unfit for military service, and women over age eighteen in the Ambulance branch of the Corps. They trained for forty-eight to sixty hours per year and were compensated for their costs of travel and uniforms.[114] Patriotism was not to be construed as a gender-specific sentiment.[115] The Civil Defence Corps recruited by foregrounding the prominence of satisfied women volunteers. The "English Personality" advertisement series of 1952 featured a photo of "Housewife cum Instructor," Kathleen Mary Fensom of Coventry, a forty-four-year-old mother who worked for the ambulance service during the Blitz, experienced the destruction of her own home, and became an instructor in the Welfare section of the Corps. Likewise, the photo of a pretty woman captioned "Teacher-learner" featured Jean Mary Dunn, a twenty-seven-year-old grammar school teacher in Birmingham who had been an aircraft inspector and auxiliary firefighter in Bristol during the war and joined the Corps to help her make friends in a new town. Ads appealed to men ("This is a man's job. Join the Rescue Section") but also addressed women ("There's a job for women too!" and "Where a woman's help is needed. Volunteer for the Welfare Section").[116]

Without women neither the job nor the recruiting quota would be met. They may have been attracted by the camaraderie of volunteering or the challenges inherent to training and rehearsals. Neither wartime nostalgia nor a unifying ideology seems to have motivated them. By the late 1950s, the pattern of women's involvement in the Civil Defence Corps was established: they were outnumbered two or three to one in the Headquarters and Fire Fighting sections; signed up in similar numbers as men for the Warden section; were either close in numbers or slightly exceeded male recruits in the Ambulance section; and constituted 96 percent of personnel in the Welfare section.[117] Women were entirely absent from rescue work because they were precluded from training. When two young women from Sheffield tried to join the Rescue section in 1951 they were prohibited by the HO on the pretext that there would be no distinction between light and heavy rescue work, and every member of a team must be available to turn their hand to any task.[118] Women learned basic rescue techniques as part of Warden training, and in 1954 two of them who excelled tried to switch to the Rescue section. Some officials were prepared to welcome this, but the predominant position in the HO is characterized in this memo: "There is no doubt in the minds of anyone that the full work of the Rescue Section is beyond the capabilities of a normal woman and I hardly think it advisable for the Home Office to launch a campaign to recruit those who are not normal. It is surely getting things out of proportion to suggest that we should amend a generally accepted policy merely in order not to damp the enthusiasm of one or two extraordinary women."[119] Women demonstrated their capability during natural disasters, and their ambition to be full-fledged members of Rescue squads was often supported by male relatives in the Corps. Their eligibility for rescue work as members of industrial teams but not local authority units was a clear bias.[120] The point continued to be hammered into the 1960s, and while the official position remained that the work was not suited to "normal women," those who insisted on taking it on were tolerated, though they were not compensated.[121]

In the mid-1960s, one-quarter of London's Auxiliary Fire Service members were women. While men were trained in emergency firefighting, and handling pumps, ladders, and lines, women were trained in operating radios, manual and automatic telephone switchboards, teleprinter systems, walkie-talkies, field telephones, field cooking, first aid, and driving.[122] Following the disbanding of the Civil Defence Corps in 1968, the Royal Observer Corps continued to staff 870 monitoring posts throughout the United Kingdom. These cramped three-person concrete bunkers were equipped for occupants to measure the height and position of bomb bursts and to monitor basic meteorological data. This information was relayed to Group Control centers. The volunteers included a disproportionate number of women into the early 1980s.[123]

During the Korean War, Canada feared an attack on its west coast, and so stocked respirators, helmets, anti-gas suits, and other protective clothing. Instructions for dispersal, evacuation, and bomb shelter construction were published and over 100 English- and French-language radio stations from coast to coast broadcast instructions on what to do in an attack, along with one-act plays " 'Preparing for Atomic Attack,' 'Bombed Out,' 'Emergency Feeding in Disaster,' 'Panic,' 'Civil Defence in Schools,' and 'When Disaster Strikes.' " Women's and church groups were called upon to urge their members to be prepared.[124]

The Canadian warden system, instituted in the early 1950s but allowed to disintegrate a few years later, was based on the British model, where "from ration books to radioactivity the Warden is the servant of the community, concerned with the formidable task of maintaining the morale of the public. As the man up the road or the woman round the corner they must be guide, philosopher and friend."[125] The warden's job was to oversee reconnaissance on the block level and link local people with the whole civil defense organization. The earliest promotion for this in Canada stated that "it has been proven that there is a place for women in the civil defence services. In the Warden Service, at least fifty percent should be women. Because of their wealth of local knowledge and conditions, they will be most useful as wardens."[126] Women were also considered vital in the somewhat later plans for community shelters. Organizational material on Halifax's welfare

10. Woman rescue worker, posed at Arnprior Civil Defense College. Courtesy of the Diefenbunker—Canada's Cold War Museum.

plans, for example, encouraged liaison not only with the Red Cross, Salvation Army, and St. John Ambulance but also the International Order of Daughters of the Empire, Junior League, Catholic Women's League, Mizpah Rebekah Lodge, YWCA, B'nai B'rith, Canadian Association of Social Workers, and Halifax Club of Business and Professional Women.[127]

Women participated in civil defense training at Arnprior, Canada's civil defense school, from the outset. Arnprior offered rescue training courses exclusively for women beginning in 1954. Housewives, insurance salesladies, and a policewoman were among the sixty women in the first course.[128] Arnprior commemorated this with photographs of a comely rescue worker in various poses (figure 10). A year prior to this, Katherine Graham Howard, Deputy Administrator of the FCDA, invited a group of women's leaders to see the Rescue Street at Olney, Maryland, the United States' premiere civil defense school.[129] The guest of honor was Pat Nixon, wife of the vice-president, accompanied by Oveta Culp Hobby (Secretary of HEW), Senator Margaret Chase Smith, several congresswomen, President Eisenhower's secretary and social secretary, Dr. Martha Eliot (Director of the Children's Bureau), the editor of *Ladies' Home Journal*, and

11. Members of the FCDA National Women's Advisory Committee witness a Rescue Street demonstration at the National Civil Defense Training Center, Olney, Maryland. Left to right: Miss Annabelle Peterson, American Nurses Association; Mrs. Naomah W. Maise, National Council of Negro Women; and Miss Rosemary Schaefer, American Home Economics Association. Courtesy of NARA.

officers of the Red Cross, Salvation Army, Associated Women's Farm Bureau, American Nurses Association, American Home Economics Association, National Council of Negro Women, American Association of University Women, General Federation of Women's Clubs, and National Association of Deans of Women. Civil Defense drew extensively upon women's networks, including most of those represented on this visit.

The United States considered creating a civil defense force, but never did so. In 1953, the Department of Labor calculated that the people available for such work would be the 8 million men who were either students or retired workers and the 16.5 million women—mostly housewives—who were not employed outside their homes, did not have preschool-aged children, and were between the ages of twenty-five and sixty-four. This meant that in any peacetime mobilization, American women would bear twice as much responsibility for civil defense work as men.[130] The FCDA recognized the importance of setting policy conducive to women's involvement and strove to organize women nationwide as early as 1951, when the National Civil Defense Advisory Committee of Women was formed within the FCDA. Women had ready connections to youth groups—Girl Scouts,

4-H Clubs, Future Homemakers, and Campfire Girls—and in all of these organizations women urged that the civil defense message be incorporated into existing preparedness programs. Women were considered a natural conduit into churches, schools, and homes, encouraging shelter provision and purchasing, storing, and maintaining food stockpiles. Women were also expected to be receptive to first aid and home nursing training and to stimulate the organization of professional medical care.[131] In other words, they were the basis for implementing plans on the household level.

Direct appeals were based on gender stereotypes: "Many of you have special skills in office systems and general welfare work. All of you have the desire to alleviate the suffering and heartache of others. Lodging, feeding, clothing, registering and financial assistance will all be required by those directly affected by the disaster."[132] Civil defense was promoted to American women as a seamless part of modern life: "something which every family with a reputation for prudence and common sense works into their pattern of daily living, just as they buy life insurance and teach their children traffic safety."[133] Security, not scare tactics, was the message to women in the 1950s, and insurance was the most persuasive metaphor for Americans to opt into civil defense.[134] As the *Homemaker's Manual of Atomic Defense* stressed in 1951: "More is known about the effects of atomic bombing than is known about the common cold. If your child has a cold, you don't hesitate to take the precautions which protect his health. The problem of possible atomic attack is vastly different . . . yet there are many precautions—incredibly simple—which can be taken to strengthen our home defense and lessen the otherwise disastrous effects of enemy attack."[135] Women should instruct their children about what to do in the event of atomic attack, practice controlling and containing their pets, reduce fire hazards, learn first aid, and memorize the alert signals.

This message is epitomized in a program pursued by the Women's Activities Directorate throughout most of its existence. In 1953, during Howard's tenure as Deputy Administrator of Civil Defense, the FCDA developed the first Home Training Program based on the prototype "Home Protection Exercises" plan.[136] By March 1954, only 6 percent of Americans surveyed claimed to have done something (prepared a first aid kit, stored food, or fixed up a shelter area) toward their family's safety, yet 55 percent said they were willing to spend two or three hours a week learning what to do.[137] This workbook-style "family action program" set out exercises designed to reduce death and loss of property in peace or war. Addressed to women who were supposed to explain the concepts to their families and organize rehearsals, the workbook covers signals, shelter, fire prevention and fire fighting, emergency action indoors and out, rescue, safe food and water, sanitation, and first aid. Blanks in the workbook were to be filled in with specifics about who was to do what, along with the name of their helper or alternate. Women were to "talk over the rehearsals afterward and decide how each performance can be improved. Drill the lagging members of the family again."[138] The booklet went through three editions from 1953 to 1955, incorporating updates for H-bomb warfare, and in 1958 blossomed into a door-to-door nationwide campaign to sign up women and endorse those who had completed the regime by bestowing a sticker "This Home is Prepared" to be displayed in front windows. Exemplary participants received certificates of commendation.

Like many other manifestations of public civil defense, the "Home Protection" rehearsals relied on learning in which systematic desensitization produces reciprocal inhibition in a relaxed response when the participant is exposed to what would normally be a source of anxiety. In other words, practice would integrate a sensory stimulus (such as the sound of a siren) with gathering the family in the fallout shelter so that in the event of an actual attack they would respond exactly the same way. In theory, this would save lives. Certainly, it would make the public's behavior more predictable.

Potential support for this was impressive. Women participated in the Home Protection Campaign under many auspices: professions (home economists, insurance brokers, physicians, medical assistants, lawyers, nurses, dieticians, business owners, aeronauts, farmers, journalists, and secretaries); unions, veterans' groups, and women's auxiliaries (American Legion, American War Dads, Amvets, Veterans of Foreign Wars, and American Medical Association); and patriotic, social, and religious groups (National Council of Negro Women, Daughters of the American Revolution, Republicans, Democrats, Junior League, sororities, PTAs, Catholic Women, B'nai B'rith, Jewish Women, Seventh Day Adventists, and clubs of all kinds). As many as 60 million of the nation's 64 million women were represented by groups attending the OCDM's last national conference in 1961. The "Home Protection Exercises," casting housewives as directors of rehearsals, had one of the highest print runs of any civil defense publication and remained popular until President Kennedy cancelled the women's initiatives in 1962.[139] Dialogic skits directed at women, such as "Let's Get Together," totaled just a fraction of the "Home Protection" kit's print run.[140] Leo Hoegh reported to the Holifield Committee in 1960 that as many as 18 percent of women receiving the "Home Protection" kits completed the program.[141] This would suggest that by mid-1958 nearly 2.25 million households had undergone the rehearsals. Women's reporting of compliance was considered accurate, as Dorothy Pearl (Deputy Assistant

Director for Civil Defense, with responsibility for the women's program) emphasized to a general working in the Pentagon's OCDM: "I am sure that no woman, given this by the civil defense director of her organization, would [falsely] check those things off and sign it and give it back to her and accept this seal to put on her window—she'd no more do that than she would fly, because you know why? About next week one of the girls or two of the girls would drop in and what would they say? 'Oh, by the way, let's see where you've picked your safest place in your home.' Or, 'Let's take a look at that two-weeks food supply.' No, they wouldn't take a chance on that."[142]

The mandate to stock "Grandma's Pantry"—an evocation of self-sufficient homesteaders prepared for catastrophes as predictable and certain as a long cold winter—fell upon women. Their compliance was linked with industry and commerce. Creating dehydrated foods was a priority along with the shelf stabilization of everyday products, and Canada and the United States sent delegates to a conference and tour on these topics organized by the British Ministry of Agriculture and Food (MAF) in 1951.[143] Since 1937, Kraft, the American food processing firm, marketed its dehydrated macaroni and powdered cheese packages with the slogan "Make a meal for 4 in 9 minutes." Dehydrated soups, puddings, and instant mashed potatoes were staples of the post-war larder, along with Ragu spaghetti sauce, V8 juice, and Reynolds Wrap aluminum foil. Such products were well adapted for storage and use in family fallout shelters. Kraft began to market instant soluble coffee in 1946, Minute Rice in 1949, Cheez Whiz pasteurized processed cheese in 1950, and Tang in 1957, exporting these and other similar delicacies to Canada and the United Kingdom.[144]

In 1955, the department store chain Sears Roebuck placed five hundred "Grandma's Pantry" exhibits in its stores.[145] The success of the self-sufficiency message was mixed: Gallup polls from June–November 1961 showed that during a period of extreme tension over Berlin, a maximum of 21 precent of households stocked food in response to anxiety about world events.[146] A survey of over 11,000 American homemakers in July 1962 revealed that two-thirds of households could subsist on in-house food stocks for a week or less, which was the same as in 1956, but a third could hold out for up to nineteen days, which was up from 16 percent in 1956. The lower the density of housing, the better off people would be: farm households were the most self-sufficient, suburbs were about average, and households in the central parts of metropolitan areas were the least well-stocked.[147] But there is no reason to conclude that the higher self-sufficiency of farms was a result of the Grandma's Pantry message.[148] Nor is it certain how much of the estimated supply was based on frozen food stocks, including the notorious TV dinner introduced to markets in 1954, which would be jeopardized in the event of a power failure (a likely contingency in wartime). In the United Kingdom, where rationing lingered until July 1954 and women tended to shop daily, the idea of stocking up was a vision of unattainable plenty for most households.

Women—especially housewives—were also the cornerstones of any evacuation plan, not only through gathering up their own families but in taking care of dispersed populations.[149] They were supposed to soothe the suffering of those under attack, address the bodily needs of those who escape attack, and mitigate the social stresses of those thrown together because of attack. A member of the FCDA told women gathering in 1954:

> The last important thing to keep in mind is that evacuation will radically change the social, economic, and political patterns of many reception communities. When you evacuate a tremendous industrial area with a polyglot of nationalities, of religions, of different income levels, into a quiet, middle class, mostly agricultural town, things happen, unless people are prepared to sit down and say, "What are we going to do and how are we going to handle it?" [Planners need to consider] What is the racial breakdown, the religious breakdown? What are all the various parts that go to make up the city, so that when you start movement, to the greatest extent possible, people can be fitted as closely as possible into the kind of community structure to which they are accustomed.[150]

The American tradition, he urged, is to break down a mass into individuals and families as soon as possible, and to do so they need to be registered, rehoused, and re-employed. Women would undertake these tasks, and were also encouraged to act at all times to reduce the "social strains of bigotry and prejudice" to prepare their communities for an emergency.[151]

A survey in 1956 showed that 40 percent of Americans planned to evacuate in case of attack, and that this option was disproportionately favored by those with advanced education, women, African Americans, and lower-income households. Most people—93 percent from large suburbs, 78 percent from the urban fringe, and 88 percent from rural towns—were willing to temporarily house strangers fleeing fallout, regardless of the migrants' age, race, religion, or socio-economic status. But if the danger was not imminent, if there was only a warning of attack instead of homeless migrants resulting from an attack, the altruistic hospitality would only be extended by 76 percent of people from large suburbs, 66 percent from the urban fringe, and 85 percent from rural towns.[152] In a 1963 study, race was the only variable that predicted greater disposition toward civil defense. This did not mean that African Americans believed self-help efforts would be efficacious, or that they were more disposed to participate in community plans, but that ongoing social anxiety and fear predisposed a more consistent approval of civil defense compared to the general population, whose anxiety level rose and fell along with world events.[153] A 1963 University of Pittsburgh study showed that 14.6 percent of people sampled had been involved in civil defense, most during World War II, with post-war involvement peaking in 1960–62. Involvement of Republicans and Democrats was equal throughout the 1950s, with Republicans surging ahead in 1960–62 and then Democrats reversing this trend with equal vigor by 1963 and continuing to be more favorable toward evolving civil defense policies into the mid-1970s. Respondents who were male, white, upper income, professional, or Jewish were most likely to have participated. Respondents with the lowest rate of participation were female, African American, lower income, laborers, or Protestants.[154] Twice as many African Americans as Caucasians in the northeastern corridor thought the poor would be worse off in an attack.[155] Among eighth and twelfth-grade children surveyed in 1966, nonwhite children were much more likely to approve of private and public shelters and civil defense in general, and nonwhite girls unanimously approved.[156]

Women were pegged for welfare, mass feeding, and first aid work, but were also forewarned that in the post-disaster period they should expect that men will "find 'picking up the pieces' pretty dull work." Women, it was assumed in a manner that made cheerful agreement mandatory, would prove "more adept at doing the kind of everyday job that the average man soon finds monotonous."[157] Perhaps this is what would unite women across all racial, ethnic, and religious divides. But women worried about nuclear war more than men,[158] and for enterprising women willing to get involved in civil defense, volunteering was not entirely bleak. In addition to the gender-stereotyped roles, women were also encouraged to train and to assist as civilian pilots; radio operators, announcers, and dispatchers; telephone, teletype, and telegraph operators in control centers; fire guards and auxiliaries; and traffic controllers.[159] Women organized trade unions to build demonstration shelters from materials supplied by industry and served as plane spotters.[160]

Data on the religious affiliations of participants in civil defense is interesting. Those with no religious affiliation were as likely to participate as Catholics. Among Protestant denominations, Episcopalians and Congregationalists were most likely to be involved, which correlated to their incidence in higher-income groups. The lower incidence of Protestant involvement nationwide may correlate to their greater prevalence in rural America and the lower involvement from such areas. Despite the data that people without strong religious beliefs were more likely to get involved (28.6 percent) than those with very strong beliefs (15.2 percent), congregations were targeted for dissemination of the civil defense message. From 1964 to 1972, nonreligious people became less inclined to volunteer, and Protestants overtook Catholics and Jews in willingness to become involved.[161]

"The Clergy in Civil Defense" was published in 1951 and distributed to pastors throughout the United States, followed a few years later by "A Special Course for Clergymen."[162] In Chicago, there is direct evidence of the involvement of a wide array of religious groups in the provision of post-attack welfare: the African Methodist Church, B'nai B'rith Council, Lutheran Women's Missionary League, and North Shore Seventh Day Adventist Church, in addition to groups like the American Legion Ladies Auxiliary, Chicago Nutrition Association, Chicago Woman's Aid, Czecho-Slovak National Council, Illinois Public Aid Commission, Trailer Coach Manufacturers, and Women's Army for National Defense.[163] They were recruited, in part, through an explicit linkage between religious duty and anti-Communist fear-mongering: freedom is God-given, hence clergy and their flocks should rally in freedom's defense.[164] For example, the leaflet "The Church in Civil Defense" (1956) stipulated that "Communism is a substitute religion" and the conflict between the Soviet Union and the free world was religious in nature:

> The very existence of Western civilization is endangered. Our present state of culture, developed over centuries, is threatened with extinction. Not only democratic government, the highest form of political order yet evolved, which offers the greatest degree of individual and group freedom while guarding the rights of all, but religion itself, is challenged by a godless, totalitarian tyranny. The church cannot do its work effectively in a state which stifles it. If civilization is to continue to make progress and if democratic government is to exist, then the church must be free to continue its mission.[165]

This is typical of the message to church groups: the information kit on "The Church and Civil Defense" produced by the Religious Affairs Office of OCDM in 1958 not only included the "Congregation Disaster Plan" and "Spiritual Needs in Disaster Situations" but also "Christianity and Communism" and "Why Communism Appeals" (both by Fred Kern, a clergyman on retainer with the FCDA), "The Communists are After *Your* Church!" (by Herbert A. Philbrick), and "The Growth of Communism in the Control of People" (by the Religious Affairs Office).[166] It was a persistent, but not subtle, message. In a 1964 survey skewed to include shelter owners, even among those who had no faith in their own shelter's ability to give protection, 18 percent of respondents agreed that anyone who was against fallout shelters should be watched for Communist leanings.[167]

Just as women were a targeted group, the 300,000 American clergy were also singled out early in the civil defense campaign and encouraged to preach the civil defense message to the 100 million churchgoers in their congregations; take part in planning for mutual aid, mobile support, and evacuation contingencies; be available to provide pastoral care post-attack; and make religious buildings accessible for any needed purpose.[168] During the United Kingdom's Civil Defence Week in 1956, clergy were invited to incorporate civil defense into their sermons (despite the Quaker, Unitarian, and Methodist endorsement of CND).[169] Canada did the same in its promotions for Civil Defence Day in 1958, also reaching out to religious radio stations.[170] A pastor was to serve as a soothing balm in the atomic age, fortify people against incipient mass hysteria, tend to frightened souls in the event of war, bury the dead and cope with the bereaved, and through "his presence, patience, faith, and words . . . be the bread of life to many souls."[171] In a post-attack world, the clergy's special skills were regarded as vital parts of the work force, along with parasitologists, personnel managers, dentists, construction specialists, chemists, mechanics, embalmers, and dozens of other fields adaptable to life-saving and life-maintaining.[172]

Clergy were considered among the best-equipped civilians to be public shelter managers.[173] For those resorting to home shelters, religion was also part of the formula. The Home Preparedness program included information on the importance of religion in shelter life. The director of OCDM endorsed this, writing: "We of course recognize the vital importance of spiritual values in the recovery of this nation from a nuclear attack. We are aware also that, in the long hours of confinement in shelter that may be necessary until fallout abates families can draw spiritual strength and comfort from reading of the Bible and other religious practices, according to their beliefs."[174] Clergy were expected to work with the wounded, dying, and bereaved in field hospitals, and so ensured that these mobile units were equipped with Bibles and religious paraphernalia.

Methodists warned against "the blind alley of a fallout shelter" and recommended working for peace.[175] Even so, the involvement of Seventh Day Adventists, who are messianic, and Mennonites, who refuse military service, in civil defense is a significant factor indicative of the diversity of religious support for the concept of civil defense and the power of its message. In Canada, Mennonites trained in humanistic civil defense skills (welfare, health, and rescue) and first aid. They formed mobile units exclusive to their own membership but ready for deployment anywhere as part of their larger program of implementing disaster relief organization.[176]

Workplaces were the other main unit of civil defense organization. This was, in part, a daytime extension of shelter policies so that workers, like schoolchil-

12. Father Maurus Fitzgerald ofm and Fred Kern, director of ocdm's Religious Affairs Office, discuss the donation by the nation's three major religious faiths of 2,000 cartons of Bibles and prayer books for 1,931 portable emergency hospitals. Courtesy of nara.

dren, knew where to go in the event of an attack. Additionally, though, industrial civil defense sought to preserve facilities and labor in order to accelerate post-attack resupply, recovery, and restoration. Canada had industrial mobilization plans to gear up for war production but took few measures to protect industry in advance of an attack.[177] Railways would relocate as much rolling stock as possible between cities to protect cargos and transportation lifelines but industrial sites per se were not protected. Britain encouraged factories and other workplaces to organize their own Industrial Civil Defence Corps units, and something like 25 percent of sites with over two hundred employees did so (representing three million out of seventeen million employees). This included government departments, the nationalized industries (transportation, hospitals, coal mining, electricity, gas, atomic energy, and steelmaking), and private industry, which received tax incentives.[178] Early efforts concerned listing potentially relevant facilities—from power generating plants to bacon curing factories—to encourage membership.[179] Personnel were trained at ho facilities and became instructors in the usual specialties: fire fighting; rescue; ambulance and first aid; and radiological monitoring. The ho kept industry abreast of developments through regular bulletins and circulars; however, these were not sent free of charge.[180]

Most facilities in the fuel and power industries participated in civil defense, yet the British Electricity Authority, for example, balked at the expenditure of dispersing personnel so that if plants survived they could be staffed.[181] By the late 1950s, a civil servant wrote anonymously that it had become clear that evacuating these industries was not feasible because they would be swamped by the large civil evacuation and most normal functions would disappear under survival conditions.[182] The National Coal Board, however, conducted practical exercises to ready its divisional headquarters as well as table top command-and-control exercises, including taking part in NATO's "FALLEX 62."[183] Competitive tournaments were staged for the display of other civil defense skills such as rescue, emergency feeding, first aid, and warden posts; in the northwest, this involved participants from the Central Electricity Generating Board, Manchester Ship Canal, Royal Ordnance Factory, Gas Board, and the manufacturing firms of Van den Berghs and Jurgens (margarine), Imperial Chemical Industries (dyestuffs), Lever Brothers (cleansers), Turner Asbestos Cement, J. Crosfield (soap), and the Calico Printers Association.[184]

In the United States, industry also sent personnel to train at the civil defense schools and then disseminate the skills to fellow employees. Radiological Defense (RADEF) teams practiced monitoring and reporting fallout hazards, simulated radiological decontamination procedures, conducted rescue drills and firefighting exercises, and tended to mock casualties.[185] Some firms constructed on-site shelters, in which case movement-to-shelter exercises were practiced as well as, in some cases, shelter habitation and shelter management.[186] Power companies, transport associations, and telephone companies took part in OPAL 61 by implementing their emergency plans and testing warning signals. Some firms, including C&P Telephone, Baltimore Gas and Electric, Western Union, and marine and railway companies, participated in state command center exercises and conducted analyses of their capabilities post-attack.[187]

A RAND study estimated that 20 percent of American manufacturing could be protected in shelters at a cost of $30 billion.[188] Needless to say, the money was not spent. Industrial civil defense extended to a wide spectrum of measures beyond the safety of facilities and personnel, and many of these were considerably less costly: duplication of essential records; relocation of these records to bombproof facilities, such as caves; establishing alternate headquarters, preferably blast-proof and fallout-protected; creating succession lists for managers and executives; installing back-up communications between facilities; and practicing shut-down protocols.[189] Lacking industrial emergency plans for most conurbations, corporate America was expected to undertake these measures without sub-

13. Sleeping quarters in the personnel shelter at the Rohm and Haas Building, a Philadelphia chemical works, 1967. Courtesy of NARA.

sidy and shareholders were supposed to see such provisions as forward-thinking. Sectors of the aviation, steel, computing, precision engineering, petroleum, and telecommunications industries were the most likely to participate.[190]

Getting industry on board was not exclusively the government's task: corporate involvement was advocated by the Society of Industrial Civil Defense Officers in the United Kingdom and the American Society for Industrial Security in the United States. This was bolstered by the need to know how industry could bounce back after attack in order to input contingencies into computer analyses developing macroeconomic recovery models. But few companies explicitly responded to the most effective means of preservation, namely dispersal outside those conurbations likely to become targets or the pathway of heavy fallout plumes, even with the tax incentives passed by Congress in 1956.[191] Some companies such as the aeronautics firm Boeing, in the Seattle area, were so large that they were targets in their own right, and nothing would change that.[192] Most, however, could move to smaller cities in the interior and south of the nation or even into satellite-style suburbs around large cities and reduce their risk somewhat. This was less of an option in Britain, and ignored in Canada, but an idea that was advocated early on in the nuclear era in the United States.[193] Dispersion required providing new transportation networks to compensate for losing waterways and rail links, and this certainly developed with the post-1945 construction of the interstate system in the United States and the Trans-Canada Highway in Canada. But it is dubious that the transformation of North American cities—their evacuated inner cores, rusting industrial belts, suburban sprawl, corporate campuses, and out-sourcing of the industrial base—can be attributed to civil defense measures.

Dissenting Practices

Maladaptive responses to signals, resistance to recruiting, and indifference to the civil defense message are all distinct from the decision to opt out. Opting out could be a principled stance involving the theatricalization of civil defense: sometimes repudiating spectacle and sometimes turning it to a new purpose. Coventry was devastated by heavy bombing raids in 1940 and 1941; still reconstructing in April 1954, Coventry's Socialist-controlled city council decided to no longer fulfill its responsibility to coordinate and support the Civil Defense Corps' activities, asserting that in the wake of the new H-bomb's "devastating effects . . . it is a waste of public time and money to carry on with the Civil Defense Committee."[194] Despite the controversy that this caused, the Experimental Mobile Column went ahead with its planned demonstration and exercise in Coventry on 30 May, joining the three thousand civil defense volunteers from the area. The next day, Prime Minister Churchill wrote a personal memo to the Home Secretary expressing confusion and indignation at the reported spectacle:

> Where does the responsibility lie for organizing the demonstration of an atom bomb raid prepared for Coventry? Who thought of the blood-stained old woman with the birdcage? I hope there is not going to be any more of this sort of thing at Government expense. The Coventry City Council of course behaved as badly as they could. The newspapers made an absurd fuss. The one sensible feature is recorded in The Times, namely that only 100 adults and two or three hundred children were enticed to attend. This is creditable to the people of Coventry and puts things in their proper proportion.[195]

Churchill implicitly acknowledges the spectatorial nature of this exercise, but by querying the wisdom of incorporating "the blood-stained old woman with the birdcage" he is not taking the Socialist council's side in advocating that no more money be spent on such activities. Instead, he is arguing that money should not be spent on the overtly performative dimensions: on the enactment of characters and the theatricalization of the spectacle. The actor in question was a member of the Casualties Union, enacting a shocked and probably concussed citizen, and had done so before at an exercise in London.[196]

The tendency in Britain to welcome theatrical elements and to invite the public to spectate at exercises was intended to amplify the effect of propaganda, education, and support; however, just as the performative component attracted the prime minister's disapproval, the publicness of exercises also seemed to invite expressions of dissent directed at Britain's nuclear weapons policy. In 1959, an evacuation exercise, "Exodus I," was organized in north Staffordshire. Buses and lorries gathered to move up to three thousand evacuees recruited from the towns of Audley, Halmerend, Ashley, Maer, Wetwood, and Standon in advance of hypothetical fallout arriving from Lancashire. Only one-tenth of the volunteer evacuees showed up because CND had canvassed homes and persuaded local people to stay away.[197]

Civil defense was not usually on the top of peace activists' agendas; however it became a major issue for CND in conjunction with NATO's "FALLEX 63." Hundreds of local groups leafleted, put up posters, and interviewed people to attract media attention. This was the same year that Spies for Peace was formed to publicize the whereabouts of the Regional Seats of Governments (RSGs), Britain's network of bunkers for post-attack government operations. They located the air filters, electric cables, and radio masts of the Reading bunker but did not know what it was. Finding the door to the boiler room unlocked, they entered, grabbed some documents, and rushed out. Enticed by what they saw—remnants of two exercises, FALLEX 62 and "Parapluie," both held in 1962—they entered again, photographed what they found, and left with a suitcase full of papers. The evidence was documented in a pamphlet and three thousand copies were distributed to the media, clergy, civil servants, activists, and anyone listed as staff of the RSG. It condemned the RSG system as a military government.[198]

In addition to clandestine activists, peace and disarmament advocates utilized theatrical means to demonstrate the futility of civil defense. In 1955, a group of twenty-eight activists from the War Resisters League, Peacemakers, and Catholic Worker Movement protested the OPAL drill which required New Yorkers to move into shelter for a brief period on a weekday afternoon. Claiming "this air raid drill is but an attack upon the general population; a continuation of the program of Fear which has been successful in the loyalty oaths imposed upon teachers, union members, tenants of public housing projects, all with the disruption of traditional American freedom," they characterized civil defense as a limitation of civil liberties and sat conspicuously in City Hall Park during the drill, quietly holding pacifist protest signs until they were arrested. In their defense, the protesters raised the issue of "conscription of the civilian conscience" in conscientiously objecting to civil defense exercises. In preparation for the court case that ensued, the defense consulted a U.S. Supreme Court ruling on compliance with a flag salute ritual, which stated that infringements on freedom of speech and the press "are susceptible of restriction only to prevent grave and immediate danger to interests which the state may lawfully protest." Is there "grave and immediate danger" during an air raid drill? What factual evidence could be brought to bear proving that a *pretense* of a drill constitutes the *danger* of bombing? Given that twenty thousand baseball fans watching the Bronx Bombers play the Detroit Tigers were allowed to remain in their seats, would prosecuting the protesters constitute unequal protection under the law?[199] As an editorial in *Commonweal* asked: "to what extent may the Bill of Rights be suspended and the police power invoked against free speech and free assembly during a *mock* emergency?"[200] They not only refused to act as prescribed, their refusal was in the context of a rehearsal. Even so, they were found guilty of not complying with practices consistent with the peace or safety of the state.

At OPAL 56, the protesters were back. A coalition of the Catholic Worker Movement, Fellowship of Reconciliation, Quakers, and War Resisters League argued that "the promotion of such Civil Defense demonstrations (whatever the intentions may be) helps to create the illusion that the nation can devote its major resources to preparation for war and at the same time shield people from war's effects. We must not help to create this illusion."[201] Their emphasis on illusion suggests they understood how theatrical techniques produce belief; their intention was to disrupt the chimera through protest acts that breached illusion's sustaining logic. In so doing, the protesters were once again arrested and convicted.

Though these protests continued annually, the major focus of attention shifted to actions at weapons test sites and only in 1959 did the spotlight return to the East Coast. In New York state, parents and children organized against the mandatory participation in school civil defense drills as well as OPAL exercises.[202] Students in the Bronx were suspended from school for their failure to cooperate.[203] During OPAL 59, a young mother named Mary Sharmat and her screaming child sat down at Broadway and 86th Street and waited there as the sirens went off. She was ordered to take cover but refused, saying " 'I do not believe in this. . . . This is wrong.' " Hundreds of people watched as she was fined.[204] Sharmat allied with another young mother who was profiled in the press for participating in the City Hall protest and together they organized at least five hundred protesters—recruiting them at subway stops, playgrounds, and PTA meetings all year—to occupy

City Hall Park during OPAL 60. When the sirens sounded to take cover, they stood up: "Mothers with children, fathers with mutual deep concerns, bachelors who had hopes and a borrowed baby, maiden aunts who had no children but were taking care of the rest of us." Unwilling to herd mothers with babies into paddy wagons, the police selected twenty-six single men and trouser-clad women to be taken to jail.[205] The next year, protesters distributed fifty thousand copies of a leaflet urging people to refuse to go to shelter during OPAL 61.[206] As a result, twenty-five hundred gathered for the OPAL 61 protest at city hall, and there were parallel demonstrations elsewhere in New York, as well as New Jersey, Connecticut, Pennsylvania, Massachusetts, Illinois, and Minnesota.[207]

In 1962, the War Resisters League called upon peace groups to stage a nationwide "10-Megaton March" in conjunction with Congress's debate of the $500 million public fallout shelter program. They hoped to revive the principle of a march organized in New York in March 1959, with protesters marching centrifugally to Elizabeth, Paterson, New Rochelle, Manhasset, and Brighton Beach, twelve to fifteen miles away from GZ at Times Square:

> In each target city the marchers will form in four sections at the heart of the assumed target. After starting ceremonies, the sections will march away from the target center to the north, east, south and west, toward destinations marking the circle around the zone of complete destruction. At those points, new teams of marchers will then proceed to the next zone limits, covering the area of very heavy but less than total destruction. And so on, to the outer zone of attack effects. This means that towns and country areas usually downwind from the target cities will have marchers covering areas that would be affected by fallout from attacks on target cities and military installations.

They would carry signs indicating the kinds of damage and numbers of casualties to be expected in the region through which they marched.[208] Such tactics did not change civil defense policy, though CND's threat to expose the fallacies inherent in the exercise specifications for "Hard Rock" before it was conducted in 1982 probably led to its cancellation. Hard Rock would have activated the United Kingdom's system of regional and sub-regional headquarters, and protesters planned to set up peace camps outside bunkers; collect identifying information about people entering the bunkers; block vehicle access to facilities; disrupt communications; advocate local acts of civil disobedience; panic-buy selected items; dress up as survivors, Soviet invaders, officials, subversives, or film crews to distribute leaflets; stage die-ins and conduct mock memorial services; perform street theater; and build shelters in public places. Prior to the exercise, they urged people to press their local council to not participate, to publish their pitiful home defense budgets and any war plans, and hold classes, exhibitions, and bunker tours. Too many local authorities withdrew from Hard Rock and it was cancelled. It would have been the largest civil defense exercise in fifteen years. Whitehall proposed reviving it after the general election of 1983 but it never occurred.[209] In a sense, protest theater trumped civil defense rehearsal.

In civil defense rehearsals, corporeal presence and embodied action were intended to habituate life-saving behaviors. In protest theater, actions could be comparably symbolic. Sometimes, civil defense rehearsals deployed massed bodies in order to create real pressure on those whose job it was to rescue, transport, feed, or otherwise attend to them in a further spur to action. In protests, mass equaled testament to conscience: purely political pressure. As a pedagogy for spectators, however, live action always bears the limitation of access, visibility, and repeatability. Disseminating critical messages by print, film, or television, even in a fictional format, reduces these disadvantages. Three examples warrant mention because they were so formative of the public mind-set—and indicative of governments' anxieties—across the Cold War period.

Nevil Shute's novel *On the Beach* (1957) depicts Australia as the last bastion of life in the aftermath of a nuclear war.[210] Fallout heads toward the continent at a predictable rate as essential commodities disappear: knowledge of certain death drives the narrative. A hundred thousand copies sold in the first six weeks after publication.[211] When it was about to be released as a movie, the United States' Office of Civil Defense Mobilization (OCDM) director said it "constituted an obstacle to the shelter program since it made everything seem hopeless."[212] The film received unprecedented publicity, and President Eisenhower's Cabinet discussed it for weeks before its premiere. They despaired that it would counteract the administration's progress in generating support for civil defense.[213]

British officials had a tougher time deciding what position to take on Peter Watkins' *The War Game* (1966), a documentary cinéma-vérité style film with amateur actors.[214] It depicts a transition from the present into a post-attack future of complete social and cultural breakdown as Britons cope with massive loss of life, psychological trauma, and food shortages. Civil society dissolves—even the ordinarily decent middle classes resort to looting and petty theft—and summary justice is invoked. One historian calls it "one of the three most controversial films ever made," along with *Triumph of the Will* and *Birth of a Nation*.[215] It was commissioned by the BBC for the twentieth anniversary of Hiroshima but was rejected for airing after completion.[216] Roy Jenkins, then Home Secretary, described his concerns in the House of Commons:

No one has suggested that civil defence measures could prevent widespread death and injury in the immediate vicinity of an attack. The Government consider[s], however, that general adoption of efficient and sensible preparations could do much to save lives, relieve suffering, and help the nation to survive. That is why we are maintaining a limited but effective civil defence programme . . . the film deals with the situation in the immediate vicinity of an attack, where the results would undoubtedly be appalling. There might be a different situation some distance from the attack, and it is the duty of the Government to take that into account.[217]

Instead of being televised, it made the rounds of art cinemas, galvanizing critics of nuclear defense and generating enormous publicity that lasted through the spring, summer, and autumn of 1966. The HO was compelled to consider showing it at their training schools, if only to enable civil defense volunteers to handle questions on it, recognizing that its graphic depiction of damage and suffering had merit—no wonder, since it was partly based on Samuel Glasstone's *The Effects of Nuclear Weapons* (published by the U.S. Atomic Energy Commission), the 1954 Nevada tests, and reports on the bombed cities of Dresden, Darmstadt, Hamburg, Hiroshima, and Nagasaki—but instead decided to write a commentary on it and to encourage training staff to see it privately.[218]

The commandant of one of the HO's schools saw the film at the Bristol Arts Centre and reported "although I am a hardened and staunch adherent of Civil Defence, this film affected me very much. . . . It did not blink [at] the horrors although some of the facts were to a critical eye distorted." The main objection, from his perspective, was that it left nothing to be done by civil defense: restrictions, hardships, mob rule, and devastated morale were depicted as the daily lot of survivors.[219] Another HO staff person reacted to the film's negative emphasis on the numbers dying rather than surviving, yet he found it was "composed mostly of scenes which I think can be described as similar in style and impact as the opening scene of the Home Office training film, *The Warden and the Householder*."[220] (This 1961 film opens with archival and reconstructed footage of the attack on Hiroshima, emphasizing that lack of preparedness led to the high mortality rate. This is the framing story for a film-within-the-film about a warden instructing the public in a time of national emergency, predicated on information in "Advice to Householders.") But an explicit conclusion in *The War Game* is that no amount of civil defense preparation, and no civil defense cadre of any size, could change the outcome of a nuclear attack. *The War Game* became a mainstay of the anti-nuclear movement, and was shown by peace groups into the 1980s.[221]

In 1983, ABC broadcast *The Day After* on network television. Set in Kansas, the heartland of strategic defense missile silos and thus a first strike priority for a nuclear aggressor, it depicts the fortunes of a heart surgeon, farm family, another rural family with a silo just beyond their back yard, and an African American soldier on a missile maintenance team. Following escalating tensions in Eastern Europe, the United States detonates a few nuclear devices over Soviet troops. All hell breaks loose. For Americans, the first intimation of war comes with missiles zooming out of their silos. Voltage surges caused by electromagnetic pulse (EMP) stall all traffic. Slowly, the characters discover which communities are flattened. All livestock is dead. When the farm family emerges from shelter, they discover the extent of their losses. At a meeting of farmers, the civil defense spokesperson explains that they will need to scoop off four inches of topsoil before planting crops. But where will they put all this earth? The hospital at the University of Kansas struggles to cope with low supplies and a huge influx of casualties, while the nearby indoor stadium is full of patients succumbing to radiation exposure. After the credits, a voice-over states that what the film depicts is probably less severe than what would actually occur. A bibliography recommended by the American Library Association rolls across the screen.[222]

Anticipating broadcast in Canada, EPC staff previewed *The Day After* and briefed the Privy Council, stating "there is very little that we would take issue with, from a civil defence point of view."[223] Noting that it "plays into the hands of proponents of unilateral disarmament," and that Canada supported balanced armament reductions, questions were expected to arise for Prime Minister Trudeau and his Secretary of State for External Affairs. W. B. Snarr, director of EPC, reiterated Canada's expectations for nuclear war: if cities are targeted, half the population and most of the industry would be destroyed; no matter what the attack pattern, nearly all the population would be at risk from fallout, but fallout protection for many people could be provided at modest cost; and the continuity of government program would provide "the surviving population with the nucleus for continuation of organized and duly constituted government."[224] Canada was not going to be like Australia, far removed from the fracas and stoically awaiting the toxic dust, but right in the middle of the destruction. If anyone remembered *The War Game* they would be compelled to question whether even a constitutional government could impose order on a desperate, frenzied, and debased population, and indeed whether there would be anyone capable of aiding the best-intentioned recovery effort. *The Day After* was not propaganda so much as a barometer of how opinion had changed: no longer drilled in civil defense techniques, the baby boom generation looked on this dystopic scenario as the realpolitik.

REHEARSALS FOR NUCLEAR WAR

Wargaming is a simulation of war, a horror show without props. Actors, chosen for the real war, walk the stage in rehearsal, ad-libbing to a script that keeps them bound by reality.

—T. B. Allen

At the outset, nuclear civil defense planning adopted organizational characteristics and implementation assumptions of civil defense from World War II-era Britain and coastal areas of the United States. However, the practical means of improving Cold War plans and techniques also borrowed extensively from practices significantly earlier than the immediate pre-atomic era.

Civil Defense Exercises: Antecedents and Evolution

War games plotted on a grid (from which chess and Goh are modern descendants) were updated in Kriegspiel, developed by Baron von Reisswitz in 1811, with the substitution of a three-dimensional topographical relief model and free-moving wooden playing pieces representing military units. Lt. George Heinrich Rudolph Johann von Reisswitz substituted a topographical map for his father's model, which made play more transportable, and in 1824 set out rules based on battlefield experience, which made play more realistic, along with umpires to settle disputes. Following the Franco-Prussian War of 1870–71, such gaming techniques became widespread, both for training officers and deriving battlefield strategy. In 1908, the U.S. Army developed one-sided games, with the umpires playing the opposing forces.[1] Gaming evolved into a tool for professional soldiers as well as a pastime for middle-class amateurs. As H. G. Wells wrote in *Little Wars*: "Here is war, done down to rational proportions. . . . For my own part, I am prepared. I have nearly five hundred men, more than a score of guns, and I twirl my moustache and hurl defiance eastward from my home in Essex across the narrow seas."[2] In either setting, war gaming is play, for it "provides an opportunity for glory without gore and defeat without destruction," but it is also rehearsal for attack and defense.[3] There were emotional, material, as well as fiscal savings in such "clean" representations of warfare.

The chief advantage for the military was in exploring warfare strategies and tactics involving unprecedented forms of modern weaponry. However, the games could be cumbersome. For example, in the 1960s the U.K. Defence Operational Analysis Establishment developed a game based on British forces combating up to two Soviet armies. Six to eight weeks of elapsed play time was necessary to explore a six to eight-week battle: "A game cycle represents one hour of battle time. During each cycle each commander relays orders concerning fire and movement to Control. After assessing any interactions between the two sides, Control gives each side the relevant intelligence."[4] In this form of manual game, controllers are bound by rules, and rarely exercise executive judgment. Such games are time consuming, and in order to make any statistical analysis of outcomes they must be played repeatedly.

Aspects of manual games were successively mechanized in order to achieve greater complexity and efficiency. In the Navy Electronic Warfare Simulator installed at the U.S. Naval War College at Newport, Rhode Island, in 1957, an entire building was devoted to gaming equipment, including an auditorium where observers could oversee the battle on an illuminated screen with symbols for ships, submarines, and aircraft. Twenty command rooms were equipped like a ship's bridge, connected electronically so that a total of forty-eight ships or aircraft could be plotted, "together with devices for simulating electronic countermeasures, malfunctions of weapons, and the susceptibility of any unit to radar or sonar detection."[5] Instead of writing and passing along messages manually, they were relayed electronically. Instead of mathematicians calculating weapons damage, a computer did this. Formerly, umpires' tables of outcomes were input into stochastic games; this evolved into "operations research," whereby games with randomly determined play applied mathematics to help solve military problems; this, in turn, evolved during the Cold War into the "speculative fabrications of systems analysis" that included more and more variable elements into play.[6] Thermonuclear-era war gaming was transformed by new technological capabilities, and civil defense planning benefited from the same tools. The avid amateur war gaming community finds its current avatars in computer games; however, these games are indebted, in turn, to 1960s' experiments undertaken by the Pentagon, such as the U.S. Single Integrated Operations Plan played by computers against the Red Integrated Strategic Offensive Plan, and Theatrespiel which combined intelligence, military, and logistics with Cold War economics, sociology, politics, and psychology, mechanizing nearly all aspects of play. In war games, mechanized computation could reduce the level of dynamic play, though in civil defense exercises there continued to be a large degree of human-to-human interaction.

The literature on war games and their civil applications frequently applies gaming terminology in a contradictory and convoluted fashion. This confusion arises, in part, from variant usages in different countries as well as in different application communities (military, civil, amateur). In military terms, an "exercise" is training involving limited operations of actual forces, usually the lower ranks, undertaken to test their ability to carry out assigned tasks, whereas a "war game" is training to explore decision-making processes of various ranks' tactical, operational, or strategic planning in a simulated forum.[7] In these terms, exercises are reducible to muscle and gaming to brains; exercising is enactment while gaming is abstraction. This distinction does not hold for civil defense because, unlike war, it lacked an extensive empirical realm from which to extrapolate data and assess results and had no testing program for personnel and equipment short of the rehearsal paradigm.[8] So, for the sake of inclusiveness, all civil defense rehearsals are referred to here as exercises rather than games, inscribing embodied presence that necessitated abstraction projected to future "real life" applications in nuclear warfare. From both historical and sociological perspectives, however, the term "gaming" is as apt as "playing" with regard to the rehearsals.

Definitions derived by a 1964 joint committee of military and operations research organizations from the United States, Canada, United Kingdom, and Australia stipulate the following key concepts:

> *game*: A simulation of a situation of competition or conflict in which the opposing players decide which course(s) of action to follow on the basis of their knowledge about their own situation and intentions and their (usually incomplete) information about their opponents.
>
> *war gaming*: An operations research technique whereby the various courses of action involved in a problem are subjected to analysis under prescribed rules of play representing actual conditions and employing planning factors which are as realistic as possible.

player: A participant who represents or is part of a group representing one of the opposing sides in a game. In a war game, the players assume the roles of commanders
and staff officers of military units or formations.

manual (war) game: A game in which pins, pieces, or symbols representing the forces
involved are moved by hand by the players and control personnel, and in which
all decisions are man-made.

conference game: an open, controlled-play game in which the player is presented with
a sequence of situations for which he must determine the best course(s) of action.[9]

Though dependent upon war games for formal techniques or genres—such as
manual play and the conference—civil defense exercises never involved opposing
teams with operational (or symbolic) play incorporating an enemy's actions, apart
from noting the detonation of nuclear devices or incidental sabotage.[10] Beyond
registering an attack, further actions by an enemy are not a factor.[11] The "real life"
application of nuclear civil defense involves operations, not battles, regardless of
whether what is being explored is oriented to experiential or policy matters. When
multiple groups (or sites) are involved in civil defense exercises there is an imperative to create consensus-based decisions and cooperative action: the point is to
optimize survival, not to inflict damage in kind. Each exercise genre involved (1) a
basic set of rules involving the suspension of disbelief; (2) expectations regarding
role play; (3) the function of umpires (also known as referees or controllers) who
had their own rehearsals prior to exercises; and (4) the types of impositions undertaken by a director or directorate (such as suspending play, stopping the clock,
or injecting information otherwise unknowable by the players), which could be
tailored to any particular exercise event.

While the British military were suspicious of what they perceived as an American mania for war games during this period,[12] civil authorities did not have qualms
about applying the techniques in civil defense exercises. Civil defense exercises,
like war games, were used for training, operations, and research.[13] Different types
of games or exercises were beneficial for each purpose, but some had repercussions for all. Exercises with maps or models were common when educating civilian
personnel to understand the scale of damage, range of operations, and complexities of coordinating command over various types of field units. To convey neighborhood planning priorities, tabletop models and maps were utilized. Americans
used variations on the hypothetical town of "East Cupcake" to convey concepts
of the warden system and neighborhood-based relief to volunteers in civil defense
and workers in local services. Training for higher-level officials and professionals
in emergency fields (police, fire, medical, and so on) emphasized the complexities of mitigating a city-wide disaster. British films such as *The Atomic Bomb: Its*

14. A group of school officials studies the "East Cupcake" model town used in a day-long operational exercise at the United States' first African American staff college course, 1956. Florida teachers and community leaders learned how to minimize loss of life through evacuation and shelter; problems of caring for evacuees in rural reception areas; and protective measures against radioactive fallout, gas, and bacterial agents. Courtesy of NARA.

Effects and How to Meet Them (November 1952) postulated the consequences of an A-bomb on "Sheppington," a city of half a million, illustrating the contours of GZ and concentric damage rings, comparing them to London, Birmingham, Glasgow, and Liverpool. It also used models of various kinds of buildings to display anticipated effects.[14] The earliest evidence of a floor map on this principle dates from January 1951, when officials at Sunningdale, one of the HO's civil defense schools, patterned the effects of an explosion on London at a conference with participants from eleven nations. This schematization of space delineated the site for play and inevitably conditioned it. Maps cordoned off a playing field for ease of conception and manageable interaction. The Americans utilized the same concept in maps depicting "City X" and later "City Y," both based on Baltimore. Baltimore functioned as the prototypical American disaster site because of its moderate size (around 1,000,000 people), industrial capacity, port facilities, and strategic access by water and land.

Canadians utilized similar floor maps for theatrical skits as well as training purposes. At Arnprior, at the outset of many training programs, the staff staged a readers' theater presentation utilizing sound and light effects and a floor map of

15. A lecturer expounds the latest methods on which to base defense against atomic attack during an exercise at Sunningdale that utilized a zoned map of London, January 1951. British Information Office photo, reproduced courtesy of the National Archives Image Library, London.

the Ottawa area. According to the script, they narrated and illustrated the typical succession of county-wide activities from peacetime through pre-attack precautions, tactical evacuation, warning of imminent attack, and a simulated explosion (sometimes represented by a two-foot mushroom which would have been equally at home as the center of attention at a Brownie pack's meeting). As the damage is assessed, a narrator explains what corresponds to the concentric "bomb damage" circles appearing on the floor:

> NARRATOR I: The template (now being) placed on the map shows the areas of severe and moderate damage to average structures. In the green coloured circle, that is the area of severe damage, virtually all structures and other features were estimated to be unusable. In the moderate damage area, the clear area inside the red band, structures were likely to be unusable until major repairs had been carried out. Outside the limits of the template there was some light damage but buildings were usable after minor repairs.[15]

Forty-eight hours later, the survival period commenced and rescue work began. The compere explained that decisions about the future of the city could only be made after long study by people in many fields; this consultation was begun,

16. Three-dimensional map of "City X" used to train for handling civil defense problems in a large city. Principal buildings and vital public facilities were made three-dimensional in sponge rubber; the rest of the city was painted in. Courtesy of NARA.

in effect, during the question-and-answer period that followed among audiences consisting of mayors, firefighters, police, medical personnel, and engineers who, later in their training at Arnprior, would game a disaster on the same floor map using an array of moveable pieces representing ladder trucks, ambulances, field hospitals, and traffic controls to practice the evacuation, rescue, and protection of the population within the conurbation and in reception centers beyond.[16]

Maps were also crucial to command post exercises, as weapons strikes and spreading fallout plumes charted immediate needs for local, regional, and national civil defense. Thus, maps were conceptual aids to conceiving, prioritizing, and ordering remedial action. Command post exercises typically involved the in-putting of strike information (arriving by phone, teletype, or sealed envelopes opened by the referee at stipulated times), calculation of areas likely to be damaged by immediate effects and fallout, and accretion of data of "actual" damage (again, by phone, teletype, or referee input). This information was disseminated to government departments or ministries (in the case of central government exercises) or medical, fire, police, rescue, and welfare authorities responsible for dispatching personnel into the field (in the case of local or zonal command exercises). Throughout the 1950s, such exercises emphasized the flow of information

17. An instructor at the Canadian Civil Defence College Arnprior indicating damage rings on a floor map of the Ottawa area. Courtesy of the Diefenbunker—Canada's Cold War Museum.

in the attempt to achieve efficiency in a world still dependent on paper, pencils, and manual transfer for much of the in-house communication. At their most elaborate, command post exercises could involve multiple levels of government, as in the exercise "Tocsin 60," when the federal government was in touch with the provincial command center in Ontario, which in turn communicated with county emergency centers throughout the province, or in the exercise "Tocsin B 1961," when seventy-three municipalities in Saskatchewan were supplied with information in sealed envelopes and communicated with the regional command center in Alberta as well as federal central command. Command post exercises could involve multiple governments, as in U.S.-Canada exercises "Alert III" in 1956 and "Co-Operation I" in 1957, or the joint United Kingdom and Netherlands exercise "Dutch Treat" in 1957, which tracked fallout from thirteen bombs in war rooms situated in central Scotland, Newcastle, Leeds, Nottingham, and The Hague. NATO's FALLEX series in the early-1960s also involved several member nations in concert. Such exercises were conducted from ordinary offices or improvised in large spaces, such as armories, which afforded enough room to put all consulting parties in proximity. As specialized emergency centers equipped for fallout came into operation, exercise play tended to occur there in situ using the "real life" communication devices provided for nuclear emergencies, including maps for graphing nuclear strikes and fallout patterns. Like site-specific performance, these rehearsals can be regarded as "inseparable from their sites, the only contexts within which they are intelligible."[17]

Field exercises involved the positioning of civil defense personnel—and, in some cases, members of the public playing the role of evacuees or casualties—in settings that directly tested participants' proficiency and resources' optimization in simulated circumstances. If the goal was to understand whether evacuation policies could be met by existing road capacity, an evacuation was staged. (This exodus could produce data that could be utilized in subsequent mathematical modeling of the feasibility of tactical or spontaneous evacuation.) If the goal was to discover how long it took to set up a field hospital or determine how many patients a first aid center could receive before exceeding capacity, nurses, physicians, orderlies, ambulance drivers, trained first aiders, and "casualties" were mobilized to test this in real time. Some aspects of such an exercise were mimed or representative, while others were fully enacted and embodied. (Data derived from such an exercise could result in new policy not only on staffing but also on the supplying of such units, with repercussions for national stockpiles, stockpile distribution, and industrial prioritization.) If the goal was to train civil defense staff to do neighborhood reconnaissance, assemble data at warden posts, and relay information to local control posts, then legions of foot patrols and fleets of cyclists and motorcyclists conducted a door-to-door or block-by-block survey, reporting to the designated warden post (typically someone's garage or a neighborhood pub) and utilizing an array of technical means ranging from telephone and ham radio to note paper and shoe leather to report up the chain of command. Relatively little exercising of this kind was conducted in Canada, somewhat more can be documented in the United States, especially in conjunction with OPALS from 1954–61,[18] but a great deal of it was done in the United Kingdom utilizing the Civil Defence Corps, National Health Service Reserve, WVS, and Territorial Army from 1950 to 1965.

As it became more and more difficult to recruit the public for civil defense activities, and as the scale of damage became less "containable" with larger weapons, field exercises faded in feasibility, practicality, and desirability. They endured the longest in Britain, but there too gave way to command post exercises, big picture simulations, and continuity of government communications exercises. Throughout the Cold War, however, problem-solving conference exercises—"syndicates," as they were known in the United Kingdom—were organized. These involved the setting of a problem for a group of specialists to analyze and pose solutions.

In the United Kingdom, where the need for decentralized control was a recognized priority by 1953, representatives from the HO, Scottish Home Department, Ministry of Health, Department of Health for Scotland and Northern Ireland, local authorities, WVS, and army met to study the control and deployment of civil defense under different systems of operational control following a hypothetical attack with heavy explosives and an atomic weapon on Sheffield. They discussed the advisability of fixed sector posts with predetermined boundaries, predetermined sector posts without predetermined boundaries, and complete mobility and flexibility at sector level. Multiple syndicate groups worked on these problems, each initially playing the role of controller of Sheffield, then sub-controller of West Sheffield, and so on down the line of command. They were then provided with maps showing the situation at specific intervals after attack and decided how to handle the withdrawal of a sector post in the face of spreading fires. Next, imagining they were operating as sector controllers from a retrenched position in a warden's post, they described what would happen at such posts in light, medium, and heavily damaged areas from the time of attack onward. They then discussed how to deal with outside reinforcements at main and sub-control levels and how to deploy reinforcements including two mobile columns. This was aided by a large floor map of Sheffield depicting the damage.[19]

Syndicate meetings were sometimes held serially, with groups coming together to work out problems, then considering the implications back on home turf, and returning again to a centralized syndicate site for more consultation. In February 1955, such an ensemble from the Admiralty; Air Ministry; War Office; MAF; Ministries of Fuel and Power; Health, Housing and Local Government; Transport and Civil Aviation, and Works; the Scottish Home Department; Department of Health for Scotland; General Post Office; WVS; and regional directors of civil defense in England and Wales met under the auspices of the HO to consider the consequences of fallout. In February 1955, they discussed the effects of a 10 megaton (MT) ground burst in relation to warning, emergency evacuation, shelter, and public information. In May, they gathered again to determine which tasks were appropriate to the military acting in support of civil defense. In October, another meeting of the same group considered the problem of fallout in the Midlands, forty-eight hours after the explosion of two 10 MT bombs over Merseyside and Clydeside. They discussed how to determine the appropriate perimeter for operations; public control and evacuation; maintenance of water, electricity, food, and transport under fallout conditions; and the role of broadcasting. This syndicate work led directly to a later syndicate meeting, "Zeta," on the management of Z-zone clearance in the East Midlands and Lincolnshire.[20] The Z-zone is the area sufficiently distant from GZ to allow survival but close enough for there to be considerable damage to structures and fires. This would complicate rescue and evacuation.

Sometimes syndicates were combined with other types of rehearsal. "Clear-site" began with classroom instruction then convened a syndicate to consider localized problems of evacuation. It culminated with a practical exercise including the actual removal of the population from part of one patrol area and token clearance (using vehicles only) of the remainder of a warden post area.[21] More often, conference exercises diagnosed problems which would be explored in continuity of government exercises. Perhaps the most ambitious example of this occurred at the culmination of a ten-month course at the Industrial College of the Armed Forces in Washington, when participants formed committees to report on:

I. manpower losses; damage to facilities and productive potential; disruption to services and federal government; psychological effects; standard of living; time and resources needed to restoration;

II. current readiness measures to undertake restoration after nuclear attack;

III. discussion of I and II and identification of problems to be resolved to restore and maintain a war economy;

IV. development of a plan of action to support the post-attack situation, solve mobilization problems identified in III, minimizing the impact of the war economy, and securing public support;

V. the political and economic feasibility of IV.[22]

Sometimes employing case study methods, these discussion and critique workshops were rehearsals insofar as they represented the kinds of expertise that would be assembled to solve (presumably) similar problems in the case of emergency, utilizing the bunch-of-guys-locked-in-a-room approach to produce results under time pressures. Without the Internet, and possibly without any dependable communications, they could only rely on pooled knowledge, collective experience, and materials at hand. This is the essence of improvisation, whether in theatrical rehearsal or war.

After 1945, war gaming found a new niche with in-service training for industrial executives. When Robert McNamara, president of Ford Motor Company, became U.S. Secretary of Defense in 1961, he encouraged academic strategists, political scientists, and other civilian defense specialists to become involved in gaming the political behavior that goes alongside military engagements. RAND, a nonprofit advisory corporation with ties to the USAF, was central to the interdisciplinary modeling of such efforts, beginning in the late-1940s.[23] When President

Kennedy shifted authority for civil defense to the Pentagon, this helped facilitate a change in the types of gaming undertaken in civil defense from those based on maps, models, command post exercises, and field exercises to computer-based simulations. The distinction is qualitative as well as technological: whereas the traditional war game—and civil defense exercise—focused on human behavior and resource deployment, with experience derived through decisions made during play (and the post-play analysis of decisions' advisability), the introduction of systems analysis made the outcomes more random at the same time that they allowed for envisioning operations on a macro scale.[24] As techniques shifted from map exercises to in situ tests to systems analysis, more and more aspects of the economy and management science were factored in, with less and less reliance upon human behavior within rehearsals. But, in an emergency, if data was not forthcoming, everyone hunkered down together in a blast-proof bunker would have to resort to the syndicate mode.

Whatever form exercises took, they were invariably structured by three phases.[25] The pre-play period (phase 1) was when the purposes and objectives were determined, grounding what would happen in the subsequent phase. In pre-play, conditions of play were defined; necessary data was determined and assembled; rules were reviewed and distributed; data forms for use during the exercise were designed; maps or other graphics were manufactured; the team was chosen, invited, and instructed; computers were programmed; logistics for any maintenance (such as feeding and housing of personnel) were planned; and the scenario was written and approved. Particularly large exercises, such as NATO's "CIVLOG 65," required nineteen months to complete this work. Other exercises took somewhat less time, though with systems analysis just the structuring, programming, and keying in of data could take months.[26] Civil defense literature frequently mentions that the time needed for the pre-play planning was a disincentive to staging exercises. In the 1960s, the United Kingdom streamlined local and regional training by producing a standard exercise ("Zedroad") for training in zone clearance. And in the 1980s, FEMA followed the same pattern by starting to develop tabletop exercise kits for local use in Crisis Relocation Plans (CRP). Both eliminated the time and expense involved in repeating preparations of much of the pre-play activity, thus allowing for the scenario to be replayed multiple times by different players.

Once an exercise was underway, play (phase 2) could be punctuated by briefings that resembled activities of the pre-play period. Play would then resume, sometimes with the stipulation that an artificially lengthy period of time had passed. Exercises were followed by a final phase (phase 3), called post-processing, which featured evaluation to derive insights for future applications. Post-processing usually immediately followed play, though higher-level officials might gather again to prepare reports. Such reports are frequently the only surviving evidence that exercises took place. Learning about the "synthetic experience" of the postulated world occurred in all three phases.[27]

Post-processing identifies what was unexpected in an exercise as well as new hypotheses that can be incorporated into future exercises. As a diagnostic tool, exercises help to make problems explicit: rehearsal is a sort of language by which ideas are communicated while simultaneously being symbolically explored amid military, political, economic, and domestic complications of civil defense. By exploring processes, limitations of command structures become evident when players experience decision making under "what if" situations otherwise unreproducible in peacetime. Exercises facilitate practical application of existing skills in concert with new skills, and when participants have faulty knowledge play will either cease or falter, allowing for inconsistencies in preparation or perspective to be recognized and either repaired or prioritized for attention in future rehearsals. "Such exercises may encourage the application of sound tactics, permit experimentation with innovative tactics, develop intra-organizational confidence and esprit-de-corps, facilitate examination of intra-unit and inter-unit communications, serve to validate standard operating procedures and logistic and administrative preparedness, and foster an appreciation of anticipation."[28] Exercises should be conducive to creativity and thus innovation. Indeed, the stimulus to innovate while exploring the unknown was considered a strong motivator to create exercises.[29] Among infinite possible futures, exercises posed many possible solutions to problems, allowing means to be explored in relation to impediments to choosing a "best" future. This analytical function had real world application, and thus the rehearsal format was itself a research methodology.[30] This methodology made study of a problem visible, "introducing clarity into what is otherwise complex, chaotic, or confused."[31] While gaming in warfare and management applications provided more economical and safe alternatives to the "real thing"—namely the detonation of a nuclear device over a center of population—the mitigation of effects of nuclear strikes on civilian populations and sites could not be studied except in a simulated format. And the more realistic the simulation, the more it relied upon techniques of theater.

Realism

Civil defense exercise documents routinely stipulate that planners and players strove for realism, but what did they mean by realism, and what did they hope to achieve by being realistic? If one exercise is not realistic and another is, what terms would disallow the former and describe the latter?

In the theatrical tradition, realism's opposite is romanticism, the predominant aesthetic of the early and mid-nineteenth century, characterized by individual exaltation; human emotions equated to the moods of nature; and a premium placed on the uncivilized, exotic, and macabre. As James Joyce put it: "In realism you are down to facts on which the world is based: that sudden reality which smashes romanticism into a pulp."[32] But if realism was that easy to achieve, any exercise that addressed the consequences of two nations pointing their nuclear arsenals at each other would be realistic, and the idea that they would not set the warheads in motion might be considered romantic. Robert Boyer defines dramatic realism as "the set of artistic strategies designed to achieve verisimilitude on stage, to create the appearance of the life that is, with no discernible artifice, no self-justifying poesy, no pretty illusions, and most importantly, no lies."[33] This describes a movement in dramatic writing, beginning around 1880, which still finds adherents on the contemporary stage, yet the spectacle of actors in role reciting lines written by someone else, emoting in front of an audience whom they pretend to ignore, shows the fault lines between dramatic realism and something one might try to posit as theatrical realism, which cannot escape the phenomenology of presentationalism.[34] Realism is not synonymous with authenticity. Successive generations of playwrights, actors, and designers have claimed to produce a realistic aesthetic, but the results are as different as David Garrick playing Hamlet in a fright wig in 1754 and the offstage thud of an axe in *The Cherry Orchard* in 1904: both are outward reflections of characters' inner states but there is little else that unifies them.[35] Theatrical realism is relative and historically contingent; performance theory offers useful clarification of this practice.

Anne Ubersfeld describes stage space "as the point of conjunction of the symbolic and the imaginary, of the symbolism that everyone shares and the imaginary of each individual."[36] Stage space may be referential of "real space," or it might be almost wholly non-referential to something that actually exists and is recognizable to an audience. Recognizability is as likely to be based on something observed as something imagined, and no matter how referential to the real that the aesthetic may be, theater audiences consider the messages projected on a stage to be unreal—or, rather, untrue—merely appearing as concrete reality. Stage space— like the actors within it who assume roles—"exists under the minus sign" like a negative number in mathematics which reverses denial about its existence.[37] The closer the resemblance between the illusion presented on stage and the spectator's known world, the more alienation is produced toward the spectacle and the more the apparatus of theater comes into the spectator's consciousness. This is the paradox of theatrical verisimilitude, but it is equally applicable to anti-realist aesthetics (such as expressionism, constructivism, and epic theater, though not film), for all rely on the event status of theater as connecting with fragments of reality, mapping these fragments with narrative and images, and yet being discernable as not reality.[38] As Gay McAuley defines it, fiction and reality combine in theater for complex interaction.[39] So, theater cannot be "real" and it inevitably signifies the status of its unreality: the more it appears like the real the less a spectator may experience it as such, and resemblance to reality will at best be fragmentary and intermittent.

It was these moments of resemblance that exercise planners sought; when achieved, they functioned like anchors to legitimate "real world" applicability, translating the simulated experience to a possible future emergency. Exercise reporters often comment upon the realism thus achieved in an exercise. For example, in OPAL 60, an exercise monitor in Detroit's operations center knew in advance when the strikes were scheduled to hit the city. The dinner period for staggered shifts spanned 16:20 through 19:40, and he struggled with himself over whether to go for his meal because this would tip off the players about when to expect the simulated attack (or rather, when *not* to expect it). "When he finally did try to sneak out, a whoop and a holler went up in [the] control center: 'Pritchard's leaving, boys—we can relax till he gets back!'" This foregrounds the problem of whether the exercise was realistic, not just because the staff's exuberance indicates broken concentration, suspension of disbelief in the narrative construct of waiting for news, or reluctant belief, but also because effective attack on this epicenter of the automotive industry was believed to require several waves of planes or missiles. Pritchard's timing indicated the prior decision to space attacks within a half hour period rather than a more realistic span of several hours, for the whole purpose of having monitors in the control room was for them to see how staff responded to incoming bulletins, and Pritchard would not knowingly absent himself during the action.[40] Another instance of commentary about realism is in relation to OPAL 61. The 125 staff at the Maryland operations headquarters were served a meal made of dehydrated food and "it was explained to those eating just what the food was so as to increase their knowledge of how the Control Center personnel could survive if kept inside the center by fallout conditions."[41] In other words, bad food was realistic, and this detail was supposed to enhance participants' learning and experience through the exercise's resemblance to "locked down" conditions.

The example of the attack from 1960 is a strategic matter while the meal in 1961 is a quotidian aspect of embodied play, yet both of these anecdotes reveal how intermittent realistic details are constructed, how realism results from calculated decisions, and that though realism depends upon context and narrative for meaning, participants' awareness of constructed play breaking through exercise protocols was not fatal to the continuation of a rehearsal. As a planning document for OPAL 57 phrased it, there are degrees of realism, and so realism can be stepped up incrementally.[42] It was not so much an aesthetic—all or nothing—but a technique capable of selective deployment.

This demonstrates how "consensual reality" is not just at the discretion of planners but its deployment is also at the discretion of players who can selectively invoke it.[43] Planners made choices about contingent factors and plausibility that resulted in greater or lesser realism depending on the pedagogical goals for the exercise. There was a lot to juggle:

- Is an attack scenario too light in relation to the contemporaneous military-political situation? If so, this may be to allow for post-attack humanitarian exercise play, especially the lending of emergency services from intact cities to stricken zones.
- Is it assumed that emergency relief services can be in place too early, and that most of them survive unharmed? Otherwise they may have nothing to do, in which case nothing would be tested.
- Are weapon sizes too uniform across conurbations of different sizes? This may be because the purpose is to test communications across strata of government and not to project the destructive power of the assumed Soviet arsenal.
- Are fallout patterns based on favorable static weather conditions nationwide? Perhaps meteorological data has not been incorporated before and the plotters need this kind of experience.
- Are there too many command centers participating for exercise play to be manageable, or too few for it to allow challenging complications, with numbers of staff significantly below wartime levels? The exercise may be structured pragmatically around centers willing to appropriate funds to assign staff and limited by the overtime they can afford.
- Are resource requirement estimates demanded too early in an exercise to be organically derived, just for the sake of bringing other aspects of the civil defense infrastructure into play? The time frame that can be allotted for play is probably too short to allow the kinds of problems needing to be tested to arise organically.
- Is public information handled in a way that is cognizant of the likely challenges to communications following an attack, and are inter-player communications always deliverable and coherent? The cost, in human hours, of interrupting signals transmission may be too great, so outages may be announced rather than simulated or foregone altogether.

- Are welfare agencies underestimating the scale and unpredictability of human migrations? Welfare needs may be calculated solely on census data because there is no other way for municipalities to lobby for appropriations.
- Are on-site relief policies and practices based on empirical experience in natural or industrial disasters? "Dual-use" emergency services may be the mandate of funding bodies and the only way for an exercise to get approved.
- Does exercise play extend over a sufficient period to allow participants to experience the onset, crisis, and resolution phases of their work? The onset and crisis periods needed to be perfected before a later phase in the scenario could be posited, and unless players were proficient there was no point in going further.
- Do players have too thorough a knowledge of protocols and too predictable access to expertise? Planners tended to prefer competent rather than incompetent players to test their war books.[44]
- Are players overwhelmed by the workload or coping comfortably with demands? A happy median may be difficult to foretell.
- Do emergency economic measures keep supply and demand too perfectly in balance? Perhaps the exercise is trying to test their constitutional legality rather than marketplace viability.
- Are the military's demands for transportation and resources comfortably met alongside civilian needs? This can only be answered hypothetically if the military will not devote players and resources to an exercise.
- Do players work around the clock, making errors that arise from exhaustion and stress? While this can be useful for a unit to experience, its snowball effect on other units can undermine an exercise.
- Do field workers fulfill their shifts without regard to radiation levels? The priority is probably to give them rescue experience, not practice in dosimeter reading.
- Do simulated casualties resemble the victims of nuclear war in the particularities of their injuries but not their numbers? Medics may need to practice triage rather than crowd control.
- Is full public cooperation assumed? That is the responsibility of the Territorial Army, militia, and National Guard, not civil defense.
- Why is a command center slow to initiate a warning or respond to messages? A hurricane or bank robbery may redeploy players to actual emergency postings, as reality intrudes upon realism.

Realism is not only selectively deployed, it is selectively desired.

A historian of war games, Peter Perla, insists that along with the symbolic, partial world created in a game, an exercise must also "make its players want to suspend their inherent disbelief, and so open their minds to an active learning process. It must also be accurate enough and realistic enough to make sure that the learning that takes place is informative and not misleading."[45] What civil defense professionals call realistic, therefore, is not subject to scrutiny as a coherent aesthetic but is subject to analysis as elements that bear special meaning within the exercises, within historically limited time frames, and for specific cultural, institutional, or organizational participant communities. Recognizing these "realisms" (rather than true "realities") or "realistic" elements circulating around what is mere play—a section of a scenario that is gamed, like a play within a larger dramatic cycle—is key to how exercises were evaluated and valued. Realism's recognizability as a mimetic function created belief and ensured that play was not mundane. Realism was negotiated somewhere between the tendency for artificiality to make an exercise trivial and the "heightened reality" of what would be larger than life and out of proportion, which is also an element of human play.[46]

Harold Guetzkow, who pioneered political simulation games starting in 1957, encouraged his students to "think of a simulation as a theoretical construction, consisting not only of words, not only of words and mathematical symbols, but of words, mathematical symbols, and surrogate or replicate components, all set in operation over time to represent the phenomena being studied. As in the case of other models, a simulation represents its object in but partial or simplified form."[47] Players needed to know what was constructed, representational, or partial. While Guetzkow seems to suggest that the manipulable circumstances of a simulation exist around the single constant of time, in civil defense exercises temporal manipulation was frequently a factor in negotiating realism. Lags in exercise play—while indicative of what would probably transpire in a war situation—were regarded as inefficiencies in exercise design or failures of imagination in realizing how activity in one sector would have impact in another. Under controlled circumstances, however, time could be sped up or slowed down for the benefit of players. The passage of time could be one of the abstractions, but it could then resume naturalistically, just as when act 1, scene 3 of Othello concludes in the Duke's chamber in Venice and act 2, scene 1 commences on the battlements of Cyprus, the Moor having wrecked the Turkish fleet and sailed from one site to the other in the blink of an eye. This was done in order to aid the simplification or abstraction of other elements needed by the narrative or pragmatic circumstances of staging.

The arbitrary start is a factor in all exercises and involves stipulating at exactly what point in a scenario play begins. For example, in a 1953 syndicate study it was stipulated that war broke out in the Middle East on 4 April; a week later the conflict spread and on 12 April the United Kingdom committed troops. Controlled evacuation of prioritized British cities began. At dawn on 13 April, as a land war commenced in Europe, heavy explosives rained down on the southeast, London, Northampton, Coventry, and Bristol, and at dusk atomic strikes were reported on Southampton, Liverpool, and Glasgow. At 17:30 on 14 April, Rotherham-Sheffield, where 90 percent of the population was still in place, was devastated by an atomic bomb. The syndicate's task was to explain how emergency feeding could commence from that point.[48]

If exercises proceeded naturalistically from such a "go" time in the scenario, play could proceed too quickly or slowly to be realistic. This is the same problem as in drama, when a crisis develops and is resolved through unbelievably swift utilization of narrative devices (such as fortuitous recollection of information, restoration of long lost evidence, or the coincidental arrival of characters).[49] Conversely, a crisis may take longer to play out in real time than the narrative time specifies (such as a five-minute ultimatum that takes an hour to transpire on stage). This elasticity of time—its compression and expansion—is a convention on stage but can be facilitated in an exercise by setting a playing-to-time ratio. An hour of narrative time could equal two or more hours of exercise time, or a narrative sequence transpiring over a day could take just three hours of real time. For example, OPAL 59 involved an exercise for local and state civil defense personnel (and federal personnel with local responsibilities) who determined what local requirements would be, when outside support would be needed, if resources could be made available to out of state areas, and whether existing policies made such flexibility feasible. This concerned the two-week period following attack but the exercise was conducted in just two days.[50] This made it difficult to control the exercise tempo, and staff needed to be very skilled to adjust. The advantage was that it allowed for greater tension following the insertion of incidents into exercise play than would arise in a naturalistic playing-to-time ratio. The 1965 British exercise "Warpost" was designed for wardens to practice scrambling into position on the sounding of the attack warning: three minutes were allotted for the pre-attack stage, sixty minutes for bomb bursts through self-help arrangements and taking shelter from fallout, and forty minutes for radioactive drills at warden posts and reappraisal. The compression ratio was fifteen minutes of actual time representing each two-and-a-half hours of narrative time.[51]

Alternately, when the period to be exercised was greater than the time available, time could be phased: gaps could be specified for suspended or elapsing time and play recommenced at a particular hour or day in the scenario. Canadians adopted this for "TOCSIN 61" to compensate for civilian participants' inadequate training. The exercise was run over a twenty-four-hour period, beginning Friday, 5 May and running into Saturday. In the middle of Friday's schedule, a gap was inserted to "enable departments to discuss with each other and with their umpires the first half of the exercise and to clear up any confusion that may have arisen."[52] Play then resumed where it had left off, but if the umpires wished it could have resumed later in the scenario on the same "go" basis as at the exercise's outset. This sort of time-leap was best undertaken during a meal break during which clocks were moved ahead to reflect the new fictional hour.[53] This establishes an off-stage space and an on-stage space with two distinct temporalities, one with real time and the other with theatrical time.[54] Arguably, the pretext of the nuclear war scenario requires a third temporality—an anticipatory historicized time—and in the same way that stage space exists under the minus-sign, temporality "theatricalizes history" by being "neither history nor our lived time." And thus time is a process or convention, not a universal constant but one of exercise play's oxymorons with the real. It is reported time, mediated by signs.[55]

Finally, it may be useful to draw a distinction between the significations of realism incorporated into civil defense exercises and the non-narrativized or compartmentalized events Michael Kirby describes in the 1960s performative genre of Happenings. Happenings, noted for their absence of exposition, do not obey traditional ideas of dramatic structure. Instead, "compartmented structure is based on the arrangement and contiguity of theatrical units that are completely self-contained and hermetic. No information is passed from one discrete theatrical unit—or 'compartment'—to another." Happenings cohere the way that a three-ring circus or variety show coheres, a set of simultaneous or consecutive actions that stand alone, or together, without causal justification.[56] Civil defense planners usually prepared a narrative of precipitant events concerning international relations, military and civil preparedness, and antecedent actions, even though players may not specifically engage with these "situation assumptions" during the play phase. Happenings may bear a superficial resemblance to some civil defense exercises, especially when considering that different kinds of players might have higher levels of security clearance and corresponding briefings, and thus not all understand (or have access to knowing) simultaneous or consecutive aspects of overall play. What may appear Happening-like to a player or spectator of a civil defense exercise may be perceptible to an umpire, a general, or an agency director at the same moment as fully integrated into a contingent plot.

Event Phases

As President Eisenhower knew from his wartime experience, if too many problems are "laid on the same people in so short a time" an exercise will not be effective.[57] Rehearsal thrives on selectivity as competencies are accrued. A variety of activities came under the umbrella of civil defense, and these needed to be engaged in a meaningful order or else chaos would reign. The crucial step in exercise planning was determining what segment of this meaningful order would be rehearsed. If all the steps could be identified, and competency achieved through practice in rehearsal, ultimately they could be strung together in an unfolding simulated or real crisis. Emplotment mediated narrative and time in order to allow complicated relational configurations in what otherwise was represented as a simple succession.[58]

In the preparation of a play for public performance, the script is broken down into workable parts (such as duets, crowd scenes, major phases of action, or groups of technical cues) and allotted space in the rehearsal schedule. Certain types of rehearsals tend to occur early in the process: sit-down readings of the script prior to blocking sessions to establish movement patterns, and run-throughs of long sequences of action prior to dress rehearsals. The idea is to make a finite amount of rehearsal time both efficient and effective. This pragmatic structure does not respect the fictional elapsing of time within a play—Rosencrantz and Guildenstern's journey to England does not happen in "real time" any more than Ophelia's descent into madness—and units of action can be rehearsed in any order—Mark Antony can orate over Caesar's bier, the stage can clear, then Calphurnia can beseech her husband not to go to the Senate-house that day—without harm to the understood logic of the script. The same principles of selection, separation, and sequencing operate in civil defense rehearsals, though instead of rehearsing out of sequence, sometimes steps in a sequence were skipped over and the intervening action "assumed" as if it was being rehearsed and perfected elsewhere by others, or as if it was a plot element that could be reported and taken as done without being seen.

Guy Oakes accounts for the OPAL exercises "as a play, in the sense of both an exercise and a drama. The drama was framed as a grand national epic, in the style of the MGM movie epics so popular in the 1950s. Following the logic of nuclear crisis mastery, the plot of the drama moved from threat to crisis to resolution."[59] Oakes is not alone in noting similarities between civil defense practices and drama, but he is insightful in recognizing the structural resemblance. This mirrors Gustav Freytag's inverted "V" model of drama from 1863, in which exposition gives way to rising action and climax, which descends with the reversal of fortune and concludes with the moment of last suspense.[60] Something similar was taught to generations of American writers in a playwriting textbook by John Howard Lawson, who claimed that everyday experiences comprised a decision, grappling with difficulties, test of strength, and climax.[61] In civil defense

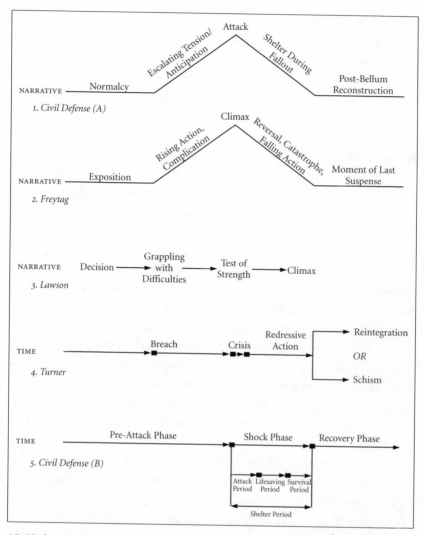

18. Nuclear Attack Narrative Structures. Based on Turner 1981; Lawson 1936; and Freytag 1863.

planning terms, these models correspond to a period of normalcy then escalating tension, attack, shelter during fallout, and postbellum reconstruction. Both are narratological models.

The anthropologist Victor Turner posits a similar structure for what he calls "social drama" with a breach, crisis, redressive action, then either reintegration or schism in the community.[62] The corresponding structural model for civil defense exercises involves a pre-attack phase followed by a tripartite "shock" phase (shelter during the attack and the lifesaving periods, possibly continuing into a survival period), followed by a distinct recovery phase.[63] This allows for a more temporal-based analysis, as the phases not only represent elements of the unfolding story but also function as units of time which may be taken up with inaction as much as with action, depending on the players' roles. Like Turner's model of social drama, events must occur in this order; however, the progression can be arrested at any point and remain indefinitely suspended. One could argue that the entire Cold War, for example, was the pre-attack phase, or that there were any number of breaches but they never reached a climax. In Turner's terms, the social breach occurs in the pre-attack phase, with the onset of the crisis coinciding with the instigation of the attack period. The post-attack "shock phase" continues the crisis and moves toward redressive action as the needs of the population are assessed and met (redressive action with a political enemy is beside the point in the social drama of civil defense, as distinct from the social drama of international politics). This is when all the medieval corporal works of mercy—feeding the hungry, giving drink to the thirsty, harboring the homeless, clothing the naked, giving alms, and burying the dead, which are called "welfare" in the civil defense literature—are implemented, including the rescue and recovery efforts of the life-saving phase and sheltering of the public for days or weeks. Turner's alternatives of reintegration or schism within a community correspond to the "Recovery Phase" of emergence from shelter, with the crucial unknowables of the success of law and order, preservation of government, and food supply remaining in the balance. Recovery per se may depend on the satisfactory accomplishment of reintegration. Schism would be prognosticated as failure to maintain continuity of government, social order, and national cohesion.

The way the event structure was described sometimes depended upon what was being exercised. Relocations of population prior to attack might, for example, be divided into three phases: international readiness (peacetime planning); mobilization (activating personnel and equipment and providing continual operation of essential industry and government in evacuated jurisdictions); followed by the period of evacuation itself (alerting and moving populations and preparing host areas).[64] Starting in the mid-1970s, with CRP, this was modified to a period of crisis resulting in evacuation and reception and care activities in host communities, a sheltered phase if attack warning is issued, and emergence from shelter. CRP then bifurcates: if there is a peaceful resolution to the crisis, the population would undertake a return movement to their homes, but if nuclear war occurred they would most likely undertake different post-attack activities.[65]

For the most part, Canadians utilized the same basic exercise structure as in the United States. In "TOCSIN 63," for example, planners nuanced descriptions of the shelter period into four phases:

Life-Saving: re-entry of civil defense personnel into affected areas; distribution of medical supplies, food, clothing, etc.; burial; control of manpower; resumption of civil authority over damaged areas; evacuation from fallout areas

Survival of the Nation: optimizing survival of uninjured in a disorganized country through distribution of food, fuel, currency, etc.; prevention of epidemics; provision of housing, hospitals, etc.

Restoration of the Nation: restoration of production facilities to meet war problems such as transport, communications, broadcasting, electricity; reconstruction of harbors and essential industries; development of government controls

Prosecution of the War: production and distribution of essential raw materials; repairs to war industries; assessment of production and processing capabilities; liaison with United States

While the strict sequencing of these phases is artificial, solutions to the earlier phases should have the final phase in mind: the purpose of post-attack analysis and reconstruction had the immediate goal of preserving the population but the ultimate goal of enabling Canadian forces to engage in a field war, probably in Eastern Europe.[66]

In the early 1950s, it was assumed that the population would shelter for about seven days. Later in the decade, this was extended to a fortnight, depending on local conditions. In the 1960s–80s, as weapons and damage assessments changed, electromagnetic pulse (EMP) was anticipated, and longer-term atmospheric and ecological effects became mainstream concerns, the shelter period was assumed to be three weeks. This extended the survival phase and deferred the recovery phase indeterminately.[67] The basic time line retained utility; however, its limitations as a realistic schema were addressed by more complex diagrams. In a 1968 report, a diagram derived from systems analysis recognizes civil defense preparation with and without a crisis status and allows for implementation of operations during a crisis to be phased differently in multiple locales, with the resultant distinctions in phasing of preparation, attack, and recovery work. In figure 19, 1 represents normal conditions, 2 represents the stepping-up of readiness undertaken in the historical circumstance of the Cuban Missile Crisis, and 14 represents all possible phases occurring simultaneously.[68]

A model derived for a Canadian exercise at the end of the Cold War, "Exercise Fifth Key," sets event structure both in relation to a time frame and a shorthand set of activities involving the government's response.[69] The familiar terms of the rising tension, crisis, and flashpoint are present, escalating into a conventional war then nuclear war; the encircled numbers correspond to the imposition of alert measures under the time frame (though not presented to scale). In this model,

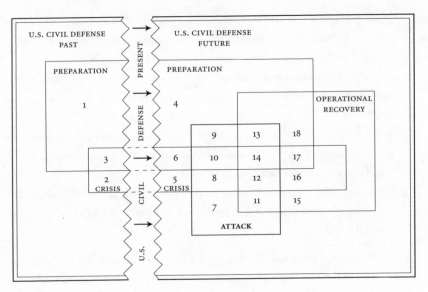

19. Phased diagram of U.S. civil defense. Reprinted from Haaland 1968.

there is not synchronicity of post-attack "normalization" procedures with the resumption of peace or the institution of a recovery period. This was thought to more accurately represent the complexity of central leadership authority in relation to what would likely be happening on the ground in communities across the country.

There were "obligatory scenes" in a nuclear civil defense scenario: specifically, the causal relationship between change in the political status quo and the launch of arsenals, arrival of weapons, estimate of the damage done, and ameliorative action. Nuances in understanding about event phases were sufficiently minor that the obligatory scenes in structural models can be regarded as a lingua franca of British, Canadian, and American civil defense communities. Considerable interaction between the three nations' training regimes and exercises suggests that despite the lack of affirmative evidence of British utilization of the narrative models this is not a barrier to assuming that they were considered equally valid in the United Kingdom. Variations in national zeitgeist did not alter how the basic scenario would unfold, though economic means, ideological preferences, exigent prioritization, and the electorate's tolerance determined what was proposed to be done in response to these obligatory scenes.

Because civil defense was predicated on the idea of the war at everyone's front door, it was important that the public grasped the basic event structure in order to participate effectively in their own defense. It was equally important that they

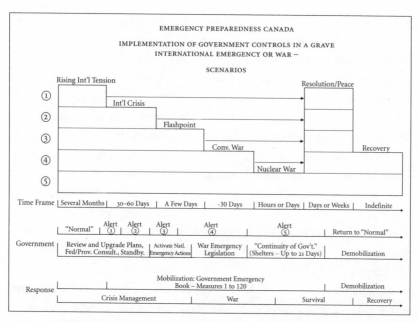

EMERGENCY PREPAREDNESS CANADA

IMPLEMENTATION OF GOVERNMENT CONTROLS IN A GRAVE
INTERNATIONAL EMERGENCY OR WAR —

SCENARIOS

| Time Frame | Several Months | 30–60 Days | A Few Days | -30 Days | Hours or Days | Days or Weeks | Indefinite |

| | "Normal" | Alert ① | Alert ② | Alert ③ | Alert ④ | Alert ⑤ | Return to "Normal" |

| Government | Review and Upgrade Plans, Fed/Prov. Consult., Standby. | Activate Natl. Emergency Actions | War Emergency Legislation | "Continuity of Gov't." (Shelters – Up to 21 Days) | Demobilization |

| Response | Mobilization: Government Emergency Book – Measures 1 to 120 | Demobilization |

| | Crisis Management | War | Survival | Recovery |

20. EPC civil defense event structure in crisis or war. Reprinted from DA, "Exercise Fifth Key General Reading Material," 16 November 1989.

grasped the distinction between calls for participation in a simulated activity and the imperative of rehearsed knowledge to be put into action in a real emergency. Even those who fundamentally disagreed with the doctrine of civil defense, arguing against the idea of effective measures of home defense as a deterrent to war, needed to be cognizant of pre- and post-attack priorities in order to participate effectively either in a rehearsal or wartime. Activities during the pre-attack phase were nuanced as the political analysis changed, for example during the early 1950s Americans were urged to be prepared to flee a target area by keeping the family automobile fueled at all times (the "Four Wheels to Survival" campaign),[70] which reflected the expectation that incoming bombers would be detected, allowing for a few hours' warning and thus evacuation from expected targets. Residents of the United Kingdom, who were much less likely to have automobiles, were urged to stay off the roads and instead would be evacuated by public transport in an orderly phased manner resembling the selected evacuations of World War II. In the late 1950s, "stay put" policies were adopted in all three countries, and household fallout shelters were especially urged upon the populations of Canada and the United States as their precautionary participation in the "normal" conditions of Cold War. If the situation became more critical, measures for providing improvised shelter would be urged. When it became clear that only a very insignificant percentage of the public would invest in home fallout protection, and that it was wholly unfeasible in Britain except in exigent circumstances, the American government began to stock public shelters; meanwhile, the Canadian government engaged in the first of three nationwide surveys of suitable shelter space, though the sites that were identified were never marked or stocked. The public was educated to understand that upon hearing the take cover warning, they were to move to shelter and remain there, listening to broadcast instructions until it was safe to emerge. In Canada and the United States, public information about the recovery phase consisted of authoritatively stated information about urbanites' expected participation in sweeping up fallout, farmers' need to scrape off the top layer of soil from their fields, and homemakers' need to take charge of the health of their families rather than burdening medical professionals with either minor or hopeless cases. In the United Kingdom, public information about the recovery phase was meager.

Mass public rehearsals, which were primarily phenomena of the United States rather than its allies, emphasized the pre-attack phase of operations, either through small-scale evacuations or running to shelter exercises. On a smaller scale, some households voluntarily rehearsed the shelter period by undertaking periods of living in corners of their basements or in shelters underneath their backyards. In Britain, the Civil Defence Corps facilitated various types of exercises aimed at the lifesaving period through rescue and field hospitals, evacuation of populations in radioactive Z-zones, and mass feeding. These occurred to a much lesser extent in the United States and rarely in Canada.

The "Deferred Event"

According to many scholars, everyday acts are performance, and indeed nothing or very little may escape the rubric of the performative.[71] However, rather than conceding that all is performance so there is no distinction between rehearsal and war—or that a civil defense exercise is ontologically the same as any other everyday act, ritual, or restored behavior—distinguishing between rehearsal and performance indelibly inscribes the significance of the particular contingency of anticipating war in each rehearsal for war and the politics of these events. Civil defense as practiced in the United States, Canada, and the United Kingdom was literally just that: practiced, and done so with conscious reference to the theatrical mode of rehearsal. Many recent historians of American civil defense argue that governments espoused nuclear civil defense to their citizens in campaigns of persuasion,[72] but persuasion is merely an intellectual function. The measurable, and reproducible, manifestation of persuasion is action: enacting a set of ideas through rehearsal imprinted behaviors upon the body, and in so doing created cognitive conditioning and a corporeal memory more likely to be reproduced in an emergency. Persuasion may have conditioned the public to *believe*, but rehearsal would enable the public to *behave*, not only in an orderly but in a constructively predictable manner. That was the theory, anyway.

Civil defense exercises were legion, but the nuclear wars posited in them did not "happen": no bombs were dropped, no one died, and the radioactive fallout strewn by stratospheric winds came from military weapons tests not civilian exercises. And yet, for the purpose of figuring out what to do if nuclear war did happen—for the course of minutes, hours, or days—dozens, hundreds, thousands, or sometimes millions of people behaved *almost as if* war was happening. Aided by exercise realism, they may have suspended disbelief in the fiction of an exercise precept sufficiently to participate in "playing out" the scenario. Alternately, participants "played along," displaying the same apparent behavior as those who suspended disbelief or became immersed to any degree in the "what if."

Because people acted out these scenarios something did "occur," yet this has a different epistemological status from the "performance" of similar actions in the event of war. To the extent that verbal and written messages were relayed, routine actions were executed, and circumstances demanded on-the-spot improvisation, real people did "real" things in real time: they worried over details, sweated over options, and made decisions, rehearsing as in theater. But if it ever seemed too real, or if the affective meaning of such destruction threatened to become too potent, they could remind themselves that no bombs were dropped, no casualties stricken, and no mass suffering occurred. They rehearsed nuclear war, they did not live it.

Postmodern performance theorists acknowledge the ephemerality of the object of their studies, an unreproducible fleeting moment of embodiment, and are cognizant of the " 'drift' between presence and absence" in its historicization.[73] Performance may leave frustratingly elusive "traces" which are as problematic as the epistemological status of rehearsal itself. Civil defense exercises foreground an important and related issue: mimesis, which Paul Ricoeur defines as the intersection and mediation between a textual (or postulated) world and the real world.[74] This is central to practices of embodied representation and crucial to rehearsals' status for a "deferred event."

Drama's etymology involves the duality of doing and a thing done: real and simulated action, both unfolding before witnesses and mimetically referential to something known beyond the fiction of a play and the confines of a theater. A mimetic act refers to an ideal "real" which can never quite be successfully invoked: theater is doomed (or blessed) by this failure. In the case of civil defense exercises, this "problem" of mimetic failure is foregrounded in order to draw a somewhat artificial but ontologically significant distinction between rehearsal and performance. This is faithful to the participants' sense that what they did was not commensurate with what they prospectively imitated: nothing quite like all-out nuclear war had occurred, so exercises, on an existential level, strove to anticipate a mimetic referent. Because this was anticipatory, they could not succeed in mirroring an unprecedented future: it is a variant on the classic mimetic failure to fully or successfully mirror a referent, though the unimaginability of nuclear war poses a special problem distinct from the usual ontological gap of mimesis. As Sharon Ghamari-Tabrizi puts it, "nuclear war couldn't be grasped because it was unreal. It could only be approached with the imagination born of a faith that leapt across the abyss between the present and the post-attack world."[75] Thus, drama's paradox of doing while simulating an action finds a corollary in the mimetic impossibility of performing something as unknowable as nuclear war while making a claim to knowledge through its rehearsal. It is difficult for actors to play "as if" with "if" material, and nuclear Armageddon may be the ultimate "if."[76] Civil defense rehearsal must fail insofar as it inevitably falls short in mimesis, so performance is the term reserved for the execution of similar actions during war, when horror on the fullest possible scale could be known for the first time.

In a poem famous for the lines "The best laid schemes o' Mice an' Men, / Gang aft agley," Robert Burns addresses a mouse losing its nest to a farmer's plough. Man and mouse alike may find that foresight is in vain, but whereas the mouse can only understand its plight in the moment, humans have the ability to reflect beyond that.

> The present only toucheth thee:
> But Och! I backward cast my e'e,
> On prospects drear!
> An' forward, tho' I canna see,
> I guess an' fear![77]

Civil defense rehearsals could do no more, or less.

In Richard Schechner's terms, "performance is the inverse of the workshop-rehearsal": in becoming a performance, coordinated action "becomes 'real,' part of history."[78] As the exercise methodology produces and accumulates understanding about what might be anticipated in war, these behavioral "strips" are integrated into a partial narrative looking forward to the potentiality of full understanding. In a Derridean sense, the exercises are "texts" made up of bits of knowledge grafted onto behavior; like other kinds of texts, these have precedents and so are mimetic acts, though in this case freely playing with doubling and substitution with respect to the "original" that they "mimic." Their referential basis could be conventional war, the A-bombs dropped on Hiroshima or Nagasaki, or data gathered from subsequent nuclear tests, natural disasters, or controlled behavioral experiments, but it could not be all-out nuclear war because that was unknowable, short of it actually happening. Exercises postulated future conditions but could not know them. The exercises were rooted in contemporaneous "cold" anxieties, never reaching their referential absent, which was an unprecedented form of "hot" war; consequently, the Platonic sameness of mimesis has no metaphorically certain or secure point of reference in an exercise.[79]

Plato and Aristotle call this "partaking in the idea of the other" methexis: literally, "participation," as in partaking of an idea or being contained or comprehended in relation to another concept.[80] The players' methexis in the future, as postulated by an exercise, reaches for an intelligible absolute but is, by definition, beyond experience. Separating three inter-referential mimetic acts illustrates this concept:

(1) Ordinary, ongoing levels of civil defense preparation in communities concerned about Cold War exigencies and seeking to increase survivability under a normal alert status (without addressing the causes of international tension);

(2) Civil defense exercises that are a consequence of the ongoing alert status of (1) but which rehearse actions anticipated during a higher degree of alert or outright emergency; and

(3) Executions of actions rehearsed under the lesser alert status of (2) but performed in wartime.

Acts undertaken in category (1) are not exercises. The distinction between rehearsal under (2) and performance under (3) is the difference between acts that are methexic and acts that are fully mimetic. The paradox rests on the idea that mimesis is inescapable, and so even methexis is enveloped by it. Just as (2) is mimetic of other rehearsals and war games, (3) is mimetic of rehearsals and the war-reality. At the same time, however, (2) participates through methexis as a likeness and an unlikeness of (3).

Performance calls something into being: by understanding that civil defense exercises are in the realm of rehearsal, nuclear war is not brought into being, but neither is its possibility excluded, and something about it *might* become known, though this is never definitive. Indeed, it is the fact of war's *possibility* and full knowability that the rehearsals portend yet hold at bay, for this kind of war is unintelligible. Rehearsal's epistemology calls attention to its own failings—its incompleteness in comparison to the real thing—and in this environment permissive of failure (even expecting it), the discovery of unanticipated failings, partialness, and oversights of imagination is the creative byproduct that improves subsequent exercises. Rehearsal can help to make an act complete and perfect, but only the execution of war—its performance—could make an "original" that could then be imitated with any certainty.

While scholarship in theater studies usually holds to the idea of a threshold relationship between rehearsal and performance (some intangible phenomenological line is crossed in the presence of an audience on opening night),[81] performance studies does not necessarily draw a distinction between a rehearsal and a performance (theater *is* performance but rehearsal may be seen *as* performance).[82] To historians, only some events matter (otherwise the task of constructing intelligible narratives and interpreting the past would be impossible) and so that which is analogous to performance is granted "event" status whereas the false starts and partial abortive attempts of rehearsal are not. My position between these three traditions is strategic and contentious. While I accept the theater scholar's claim that there is a threshold between rehearsal and performance, I take the performance scholar's part in asserting that rehearsals are events in their own right, and insist, in opposition to most historians, that rehearsal is a viable category for explaining an empirical testing-out, that play-acting a possible future is significant evidence of how civil defense planning is expressed through emplotment, and that producing "knowledge" about this particular kind of future through embodied exercises is an important aspect of Cold War history.

Civil defense exercises utilized a true/false dialectic, engaging participants in simulated action that took the form of embodied doing. Theater's ability to tacitly acknowledge pretense while continuing to sustain it—imaginatively and corporeally—was openly deployed in the exercises and helped to give them efficacy. Learning through doing, repeating for mastery, and improvising with given circumstances—the hallmarks of rehearsal—were intended to lead to a performance (someday, if necessary, but for the time being deferred) in the sense that performance is a naturalized execution of an uninterrupted unfolding sequence of actions. This does not require acting skill, but it is acting; this is not theater, but it is theatrical; this is not performance but it has a methexic relationship to what could someday be performed.

There is an epistemological distinction between rehearsal and performance and a politics in naming this distinction based on mimetic grounds. During the Cold War, civil defense was advocated either as a strategy of deterrence or a tactic of protective insurance: what it claimed to call into being was alternately prevention of war or lessening of its consequences. Meanwhile, pacifists denied any deterrent or protective function — thus rejecting the idea that exercises called anything into being except a rhetorical bamboozle — and regarded civil defense as a sop to the gullible or a way to hedge politicians' anxieties. By calling exercises rehearsals, the point is to simultaneously recall the advocates' and the pacifists' positions, destabilizing the advocates' claims, though not their nomenclature, reserving the term *performance* for the prosecution of war yet always recalling the signification — and potential — of mass death that gives exercises their potency within history. The etymology of "rehearsal" provides a convenient and apt reinforcement. The English word "rehearsal" is derived from the Old French term for harrow (*herce*), an iron implement for stirring up the soil. In the thirteenth century the term was borrowed for a similarly shaped elaborate framework for holding tapers over a canopied bier or coffin (hearse). In the fourteenth and fifteenth centuries, this accrued two new meanings. There are various military denotations of herse (all involving an upwardly placed object or formation that obstructs an enemy, thus either a battle array with archers backed by men of arms, or a portcullis). It also accrued the denotation of repetition or recitation (reherce or reherse). Theatrical connotations of "rehearsal" that we tend to recall derive from the latter meaning, but can be thought of conjointly with the term's ghosted links to the cycle of agricultural renewal and rebirth in raking over and breaking up the earth, as well as the elaborate decoration of corpses that run parallel both to the postures and fixtures of battle as well as the preparation to perform.

Jon McKenzie argues in *Perform or Else* that performance enriches notions of history through material inscriptions of temporal displacements. Anachronism is mixed up with past and present traditions, disparate media, and historical research, resulting in history's "multiplication and division, its generative and degenerative recombination."[83] Thus, in tragic theater, the court of Charles IX is displaced onto the end of the ancien régime and the exploits of Henry V onto Elizabethan England; postmodern theater and drama may take much greater liberties with sequencing, cause and effect, and the logic of action, but the principle is the same in contemporary dramaturgy. But what about non-theatrical performance? For example, does not a family of five descending into their fallout shelter for their two-week annual vacation also perpetrate a "generative and degenerative recombination" of history? They practice a familial rite simultaneously with an exploration of civic duty; closing the portal to everyday life, they enact in total privacy a temporal displacement "as if" fallout rained outside, striving to believe in the need for sheltering "as if" their lives depended on keeping away from radioactivity while, like stage actors, always knowing the difference. I argue that such a sojourn in a fallout shelter is not, in fact, a performance but a rehearsal for a performance; performance would transpire only if real bombs and fallout rained outside. The sojourn in the fallout shelter is history (as a paradigmatic and specific event in the Cold War) yet it was a conditional sort of event—a rehearsal for a feared future—which forestalled performance while inherently referring to its possibility. In so doing, there was "time out of time" and engagement with multiple simultaneous levels of reality and realism, or what NATO members referred to as the "scope of play" (*portée du jeu*) and the "play of decisions" (*jeu des décisions*). Being a rehearsal did not limit its gravitas, and indeed skeptics would say that such a family not only rehearsed their war plan but also conveniently assembled in a de facto crypt. Just because the family participated in a methexic "as if" does not mean the act comes within the purview of what J. L. Austin delineates as "performatives" that *do* what they *state*. Instead, like the infelicities Austin relinquishes to the extraordinary circumstances of theater, the family's sojourn in the fallout shelter (or the civil servant's in the emergency headquarters, or the politician's in the bunker) is "in a particular way hollow . . . . in ways parasitic upon its normal use."[84] Normal, in this case, would be the full performative use of the utterances and actions involved in taking shelter in an emergency. Going into the fallout shelter in circumstances short of emergency is not bad faith, it is good rehearsal. Nestled in their hollowed-out burrow, they contemplate biological, cultural, and political reincarnations, cognizant of death and the repetition of waiting.

Acting and Matrixing

Bert States's characterization of "the rehearsal atmosphere . . . [as] one of trial and error, seeking, interrupting, finding in general the best way to perform"[85] seems to suggest that the explorative experimental basis of a nuclear civil defense exercise is rehearsal's epitome. While there could be an unlimited number of opportunities to try out ideas there would be only one chance at actually implementing the plan. In rehearsal, actors experience the ever-latent breakdown of concentration as a result of error or interruption in order to become less susceptible to breakdown when infelicities arise in performance. Thus, in exercises, too, the point was to become as effective as possible at coping in a future wartime crisis by normalizing it into a routine while also practicing how to cope with the unexpected. Three examples of exercises serve to open up questions about important aspects of the theatrical dimensions of this work.

The earliest documentation for atomic-era civil defense exercises is British, though the most extensive documentation from the early period pertains to an exercise in Chicago.[86] In the 1950s, Chicago was the United States' second largest city: a vibrant transportation hub with 27 percent of the nation's railway workers and 7 percent of the nation's manufacturing workers, especially in metals and machinery, printing and publishing, petroleum and coal, and food.[87] It had over 20,000 city blocks in a 214-square-mile area, and a population density reaching 16,932 per-square-mile in some areas.[88] In response to the Civil Defense Act of 1950,[89] the mayor appointed a committee of more than one thousand people in forty-five areas of civil defense activity to work out a plan for the city. They had extensive cooperation from for-profit utilities companies.[90] Four years before the nationwide OPAL drills began, the city staged "Chicago Alert," involving two hundred delegates from fifteen states, Canada's coordinator for Civil Defense and several cabinet ministers, and delegates from the United Kingdom who gathered at the Field Museum of Natural History from 25–29 September 1950.[91] The National Security Resources Board assisted by sketching a hypothetical narrative for two air bursts seconds apart (one north of the city center, GZ at North Kedzie Avenue and Irving Park Boulevard, and the other to the south, GZ at West 107 St. and Prospect Avenue) followed by a ground burst several hours later in the rail yards west of the city center.[92] Chicago's eastern boundary stretches along Lake Michigan, so the exercise demanded consideration of damage and mobilization problems in the three other directions. Chicago Alert opened with the mayor's reactions to the strikes, followed by details of the hypothetical casualty rates (between 106,430 and 129,440 were dead and as many injured) and damage assessments by various city officials. Data was presented on solutions to problems, small-group conference sessions were held to brainstorm solutions, and reports on sanitary engineering, welfare services, shelter, feeding, clothing, salvage, cash assistance to victims, and case work assistance were made to the whole gathering. Each report was followed by a discussion period.

A highlight of the event was the forty-minute reader's theater dramatization of the water, bridges, and sewer services effected by the crisis, staged and presented to the assembly by the Department of Public Works. The dramatization incorporated sound effects and projected maps. Playlets are more typical of British exercises, several of which incorporated them to vary training formats; these were scripted mini-plays enacted by exercise organizers in order to introduce a situation and illustrate the dynamics of an operative scenario.[93] In Chicago Alert's playlet, the commissioner of Public Works was joined by the city engineer, assistant engineer, and colleagues whose regular duties made them responsible for water distribution, bridges and viaducts, and sewers to "bring to you, by way of simulated messages over the telephone, radio, and even by messenger if necessary, the manner in which we in the Department of Public Works think we will operate—should Chicago ever be attacked."[94] The off-stage narrator sets the scene: it is early in the morning, and Chicago's residents are still asleep. The mayor and civil defense officials have gathered at City Hall, summoned by federal authorities to put their plan into action. The characters—played by their real life counterparts—report their readiness status by telephone and detail the basic elements of their post-attack reconnaissance plans. The public receives just one minute of warning through the audible alarm network. Then, for a full minute of playing time, boards fall, sirens scream, and bells ring to indicate the detonation of the first two bombs. The narrator facilitates several temporal leaps. (1) An hour later in narrative time, emergency communications have been established and the commissioner receives oral reports from his chiefs; several pumping stations are out of order and measures are taken so that water can be supplied to firefighters at the expense of suburban services; sewer inlets are clogged by debris but causing few immediate problems; downed river bridges and highway and train overpasses are blocking access for emergency services trying to get to sites in north Chicago; and chlorine dosages are being increased in the domestic water supplies to guard against disease. (2) By late afternoon, roadways are being cleared and alternate routes established around downed bridges. Though pumping stations are considerably below capacity, they project steady improvement. (3) At 19:30, the third atomic burst is reported, complicating issues to the west of the city center. Another two-mile stretch in an important corridor is closed by downed bridges. Complete reconstruction of the sewer system will be necessary in the 1,000-foot diameter crater. (4) The next afternoon, services report on their plans for the following three days.[95]

This playlet produces the impression of a city that can assess damage to its infrastructure and calmly proceed to effect crucial repairs, despite the cumulative six-and-a-half-mile radius area of destruction and major damage and five-and-a-half-mile radius area of minor damage. It is wishful thinking, relative to the kinds of measures that existed; however, it served as a projection that modeled what delegates witnessing the playlet—including members of other city of Chicago departments, as well as the foreign visitors—should strive toward.

In contrast to transcriptions of question-and-answer sessions during other parts of Chicago Alert, the playlet's dialogic format utilizes presentational techniques—time compression, voice-over narration, and sound effects—to both inform and affect the spectators. The engineers recite tedious statistics while at the same time exemplifying the product of meticulous planning and training among city employees. The details lend realism and credibility while the efficiency represented in their dialogue models the type of activity spectators should bring about in their own work places and communities. While it is impossible to imagine this playlet captivating a theater-going audience, it was a bona fide performance: not just because of its aestheticized presentation of plot elements but because it was itself the culmination and finite product of rehearsals unseen by its audience.[96] Like a demonstration or exhibition of learned behavior, it rekeys "strips" of exercise activity into a cogent presentation.[97]

The distinction between rehearsal and performance is not based on participants' immersion in the simulated event or in spectators' "belief" in the integrity of what unfolds in front of them. Spectators "believe and disbelieve at the same time" and, as Schechner explains, it is as true for spectators as players that "the show is not real and not not real at the same time."[98] The aesthetic of performance and the fragmentation of rehearsal can both utilize variants on Michael Kirby's concept of the "matrix of time, place and character." Kirby distinguishes between (a) actors who are fully matrixed into a play and seem to deny the conditions of playing, (b) those who simultaneously or alternately embody the options of being matrixed and not being matrixed by taking on a character only some of the time and seemingly commenting or observing on the action at other points, and (c) those who are entirely nonmatrixed, such as stagehands who move furniture in a conventional play or participants in a Happening who make "no use of time, place, or character and no use of the performer's comments."[99] The nonmatrixed participant does not respond to stimuli with an assumed personality and is understood by witnesses to be outside the imagined time and place. This epitomizes the civil defense referee, umpire, or director keeping other players on task, managing time compression, and conducting the post-event analysis. Though the actors in the Public Works playlet played "themselves" in idealized form, they were matrixed into the event. While all participants in exercises are referred to as actors, matrixing provides a way to account for degrees of involvement in a wider array of aestheticized dramatic and quasi-theatrical formats along with the nonaestheticized war game techniques. While the playlet utilized time compression, its temporal arc of thirty-six hours compressed into forty minutes was too extreme to be analogous to exercise conditions. What more definitively distinguishes it from rehearsals, however, is that during the course of its presentation the onus for learning was not on the actors but on the spectators. Rehearsals are based upon the participants' explorations of skills, honing of techniques, and trial and error in approach; the playlet, by contrast, was a pedagogical tool to represent maximum efficiency already having been achieved (whether it had or not).

A more typical example of matrixing occurred in an early British exercise, "Medusa," under joint command of the Home Office and the army. Part I took place 7–8 December 1950 and involved two hundred representatives from the southwestern army command; Royal Navy; Bristol, Gloucestershire, and Somerset local authorities; central government departments; and other civil defense organizations allied to the new Civil Defence Corps. They considered the effects of an A-bomb detonation on Bristol, a city of 440,000 with an internal area of forty-one square miles. Though heavily damaged in the Blitz and still pocked with rubble in 1950, Bristol remained an important distribution center for goods via the Avonmouth and Portishead docks. In Part I of Medusa, small groups broke off for discussion of syndicate problems, then reassembled for general discussion.[100] Syndicates successively discussed the following problems over the two days: determining the best tasks for the military in support of civil defense services; considering how the military could assist civil defense services in the event that they were overextended by a period of heavy artillery raids followed by an A-bomb; coordinating control points to manage an exodus into the countryside; and utilizing a military brigade instead of civil defense services following attack by an atomic weapon (this assumed that civil defense forces were exhausted by several prolonged heavy explosive raids and depleted by deployment to South Wales). In the final syndicate, the last scenario was repeated but participants were asked to assume the role of the battalion's commander "and to explain how he would tackle the task allotted to him of doing what he could to succour the Knowle district, which had suffered severe damage and casualties."[101] Lectures and films were interspersed between discussion periods.

In this case, the assumed distinction between syndicate participant and spectator is blurred, for spectators contributed freely to discussions. During the final syndicate, role play encouraged participants to take on an uncharacteristic function—if not actually a character—for rhetorical purposes as well as to spark imaginative input. Participants were more likely to slip into a matrixed position in this period of play than in any other, though there is no direct evidence for this having happened. The personnel available for play were determined prior to Part I of Medusa, but the syndicates suggested how they might be effectively deployed in an emergency and this is substantially what was tried out in Part II. Part II is emblematic of the simultaneity that can complicate civil defense exercises. Multiple sites, and variable kinds of activity in each site, characterized the gestalt of Part II. The event phase was post-attack, and the "go" point was determined not by a naturalistically unfolding time schema but by the logic of training most of the participants on the first day, letting them rest overnight, then conducting the bulk of activities on the second day.

When Part II of Medusa was staged 10–11 February 1951, a variety of exercise techniques were incorporated: equipment tests, demonstrations leading to field exercises in firefighting and rescue, command post operations, and traffic control for a simulated evacuation. At 10:00 on Saturday morning, the Civil Defence Corps' Technical Reconnaissance Unit—dressed in full kit—conducted radiation tests in Wine Street, a busy destination for Bristol shoppers. Despite seeing these bizarre figures clad in long mufflers and tightly bound turned-up trousers and walking around with radiation gauges, the shoppers were "unmoved." While part of the point of staging this exercise in Wine Street was to attract public interest in the new Civil Defence Corps, the indifference of spectators—to the extent that they did not even look on—is incidental to the ontology of the rehearsal: the players were fully matrixed into a simulation of radiation testing and their failure to attract an audience changed neither the status of this as rehearsal nor the completeness of their matrixing.[102] An hour later, Commander Col. J. T. Gough arrived by helicopter at the Sea Walls: "during the course of his flight he attempted to get an aerial impression of the extent of damage that the City had suffered—it will be realised that this was pretence."[103] He was driven to the control room set up at the Regent Cinema (Castle Street), where he consulted with civilian commanders about the tasks that the military column of 1,300 converging on the city should carry out. These alternating demands of reality and exercise realism are conducive to his going in and out of matrixing: he actually was up in a helicopter, but during this trip he had to imagine the atomic bomb damage laid out on the ground below him, while at headquarters he consulted about how to deploy actual troops to address fictional problems at geographically specific sites. Meanwhile, troops at three assembly areas watched demonstrations and listened to talks on light rescue, stretcher bearing, first aid, and firefighting, which trained them for the tasks they would carry out the following day.

On Sunday morning, in the midst of a sleet storm, the troops and Civil Defence Corps converged at the grounds of a former chemical factory on Netham Road. Judge E. H. C. Wethered, a Red Cross civil defense officer and president of the Western Opera Players, supplied casualties and a make-up team to enable the "trapped" and "wounded" to appear realistic.[104] Eighty casualties were buried in wreckage. Evidence suggests they were fully matrixed into the situation and attempted through their acting to hold their rescuers in the matrix too, despite some inauthentic awkwardness in staging: "The tasks were made very realistic. Dummy casualties were buried under literally tons of debris all of which the troops had carefully to remove and as soon as they had unearthed a dummy casualty it was replaced by a 'live casualty' entered into a cellar by a backway and lay down in a safe void, screaming in a most unearthly manner as the soldiers cleared away

21. At Exercise Medusa, Bristol, February 1951, volunteer civil defense workers demonstrate to troops in the background how to clear debris and reach trapped casualties. Rubble has to be carefully removed by hand to prevent it from collapsing on buried victims. British Information Office photo, reproduced courtesy of the National Archives Image Library, London.

the debris above the void."[105] Once freed, casualties were carried to a makeshift first aid center and plied with tea. Other soldiers pumped water into plumes of dense smoke created by burning wood and smoke bombs. An urgent message of a second fire in Cumberland Basin caused some of the troops to be rushed to this secondary site, a plot twist unanticipated by their Unit Commander who was forced to improvise.

Meanwhile, police and military formed a cordon at twenty-three control points around entrances to the city, each staffed by a constable who could decide to control whatever traffic came along. Those whose radio communication devices worked were fed messages from time to time "about floods of homeless people leaving the City so that the Police and Military on the spot could exercise their minds as to what action they ought to take."[106] In other words, the situation set them up to have the option of being matrixed or nonmatrixed, and of moving in and out of matrixing, but technical failures may in some cases have left them unguided, idle, wet, shivering, and nonmatrixed.

During the 1950s, Canadian exercises were heavily dependent upon volunteer labor. As the federal government took more responsibility for survival planning, especially through the network of federal bunkers and communications systems ordered in 1959, a cadre of professionals needed to rehearse. On 3 May 1960, before any of the permanent federal sites came on-line, TOCSIN 60 tested procedures for a limited nuclear strike on Canada. This exercise helped to determine the kinds of space needed for provincial and regional control centers, but was primarily intended to test communications. One participant was the maritime province of Prince Edward Island, in the Gulf of St. Lawrence across the Northumberland Strait from New Brunswick and Nova Scotia. Prince Edward Island is just 2,185 square miles (.06 percent of Canada's land mass) and in 1960 had barely 100,000 inhabitants. As a mainly agricultural province, it was not a strategic target but it could become an important base if other parts of the Maritimes were hit. The exercise headquarters was set up in the Charlottetown Armory, with rooms set aside for federal departments, the Royal Canadian Mounted Police (RCMP), and the provincial premier. The civil defense staff assembled in a large room filled with tables for police, welfare workers, transport coordinators, fire officials, and command personnel who were in touch with volunteers in twenty civil defense communities throughout the province. Across the hall, the army operated communications equipment. At 15:00, the provincial EMO director briefed all personnel. When the simulated national attack warning sounded at 16:00, emergency communications were activated, followed shortly after by the take cover alarm. Nuclear bombs devastated the naval base at Esquimalt, B.C., both Edson and Banff Alberta (these were accidental bursts, presumably intercepted on their way to the United States), the rail hub of Winnipeg Manitoba, the nation's capital Ottawa, the steelworks at Hamilton Ontario, and the important manufacturing and transport center of Montreal.

Exercise play in Prince Edward Island focused on Argentia, a corner of Newfoundland leased to the U.S. Navy, which was hit by a 5 MT bomb, followed ten minutes later by a 5 MT bomb with GZ in Halifax harbor. The strike on the U.S. Strategic Air Command Base at Limestone, Maine, was also noted in Charlottetown but none of these incidents produced a fallout risk for Prince Edward Island. Compared to other provinces, players in Prince Edward Island had very little to do. Elsewhere in the Maritimes, message traffic indicated challenges in hypothetically controlling the flow of evacuees and feeding the homeless; there were panicked evacuees, false rumors of bacteriological agents released into the water supply, bridge outages, forest fires, and transportation challenges by land and sea. Prince Edward Island, by contrast, was to be a staging post to support army operations in Nova Scotia but was sent no other federal messages on any topic.[107] Local newspapers reported the hypothetical crash of an enemy bomber near Alberton, on the island's northwestern coast, producing a radiation risk that closed off the North Cape from the rest of the island. Local authorities requested evacuation of the population by boat, but instead Charlottetown sent orders to stay put and take radiation precautions.[108] This incident appeared to have been locally generated, for there is no record on this topic or anything resembling it in federal exercise planning documents. The local players may have been bored, or so matrixed into the scenario that they manufactured an incident that might keep them busy. A bomber crashing did not match the stated objective of testing federal-provincial communications so Charlottetown deemed it irrelevant to play.

Richard Schechner argues that when violence is acted out in theater, even though there is no physical violence, the activity is—rather than merely representing—dangerous and risky. "This danger is a mortgaged actuality indefinitely postponing the catastrophe. . . . the present moment is a negotiation between a wished-for future and a rehearsable, therefore changeable past. . . . The mortgaged future is always death; the past is always life-as-remembered, or restaged."[109] This condition is the essence of the principle of "restored" or twice-behaved-behavior which is the basis of Schechner's theory of performance.[110] Within the improvisation at Charlottetown there is a "quoting" of the past—or what is understood about the past, including instruction for the exercise—in the unfolding actions of TOCSIN 60. In the case of such an exercise, the negotiation may be between a changeable past and a dreaded future that in turn is ghosted in a wished-for outcome that rehearsal is supposed to optimize. If the experience of conducting civil defense rehearsals was a mortgaging of the future, this should have produced a sense of conquering—however provisionally—an impending death, akin to Schechner's concept of "dark play" that engages chance along with real danger.[111] But the considerable measure of bureaucratic oversight and dull inactivity inferable in the Charlottetown Armory, and perhaps even more so in the communities that had drilled in preparation for a disaster that did not even come in fictional form, must have created an experience markedly different from anything as stirring as conquering death. What remains unknowable was the extent to which reports of 5 MT strikes on neighboring provinces' ports would have registered in Prince Edward Island like a messenger's speech on the ancient Greek stage: messengers were doomed to carry bad news, created to produce tragic foreboding from the moment they stepped on stage, and existed to narrate the invariably violent plot elements that really move the story along. Those bearing witness to the messengers—the audience, protagonists, and chorus—could do little more than wail and draw the moral.

Listening to the messenger, or civil defense messages, stirs a dialectic between passivity and action. In a decision to ignore a message because it is intended for someone else, to act upon it, or to order inaction, there is a dissociation from the anguish that such a message implicitly represents. As Herb Blau puts it, "there are . . . performance events in which perception and participation are played against each other, or in which the activity of participation is an exercise of perception, further complicated (or distorted) by the sacrificial facsimile of the 'Real Presence' of pain. Sometimes participating, sometimes specular, the audience may be torn between the desire for symbolization and the nerve-wracking immediacy of the event."[112] What gets presented to players (and spectators) are variable kinds of demands, "from a state of beholding or contemplation to outright stupefaction," and what pulls one person in may leave another impassive.[113] Unlike the playlet in Chicago, TOCSIN 60 required that its players create an experience rather than being merely witnesses. Whereas the playlet aesthetically manipulated visual and auditory cues to try to produce a more uniform engaged result,[114] the players in Charlottetown relied upon the layout of the Armory, a trickle of incoming messages, and their imaginations to experience the event. The volunteers in Alberton and other outlying areas of the province had even less to go on. By contrast, the soldiers who found the dummies planted under debris, then "rescued" members of Bristol's Western Opera Players, were treated to a spectacle of grand guignol. They had to transport these screaming actors to the first aid post where the pretense of agony on a frigid morning was readily exchanged for hot tea. The rescuers would offload their stretcher and then go back to the rubble to seek another "victim." But everyone was safe. Pain was spectral, and though they were in its presence it was a signified intellectualized presence produced by acting and responded to with acting. This is what Eugenio Barba calls the sorting out of chaos and cosmos in rehearsal, not entirely subject to the actors' choices or intentions.[115] This is also what the small groups discussing disaster in Chicago and Bristol undertook, as much as the constables at Bristol's perimeter who waylaid Sunday morning churchgoers or the professionals in Charlottetown who told volunteers in Alberton to do nothing.

The designation "actor" is applied to all participants, regardless of what they do; however, there is theoretical justification for this. To theater historians, following the anthropologist Victor Turner, an actor is not so narrowly a person in a role as it is the function of enabling a shift in awareness from everyday life to a liminoid event.[116] A consensus has developed post-Turner that while typically a person is designated to cause this shift to the liminoid, once the shift occurs the function of "actor" may in some cases be interchangeable or simultaneous with the function of "spectator," accounting for the fluid matrixing and nonmatrixing of participants at different moments in play as actors spectate and then act again.[117] This allows for exercise participants to watch, during their own periods of idleness, colleagues who are busy, and thus observe more than they would otherwise see.

Sociologists have established the convention of using the term "actor" interchangeably with "individual," and so an actor is anyone who *does something* that gets on the radar screen of a sociologist. More specifically, for exponents of actor network theory, such as Michel Callon and Bruno Latour, "an 'actor'" is "any element which bends space around itself, makes other elements dependent upon itself and translates their will into a language of its own."[118] Note that actor is in quotation marks: the point being that the actor is someone "made to act," that agency is assigned not to an individual but to an effect of networks that exist a priori to individuals, and these "actants" coordinate a consistent effect.[119] The relationality of these actor/actant entities is so ruthlessly and indiscriminately deployed in actor network theory that an actual machine—such as a computer—falls within the purview of actor networks. Essentialisms are eroded not only in terms of scale, so "micro" and "macro" actors are the same "size," but also in terms of the human and non-human, the social and the material.[120] This insists upon the performative character of relations and objects as well as of individuals and destabilizes the idea of actor as agent in favor of a decentered structure.[121] By this logic, the helicopter used to deposit the army commander at Bristol's Sea Walls was part of the actor network, and perhaps also the smoke plumes that soldiers endeavored to extinguish. The enemy bomber crashing at Alberton, being entirely fictional, pushes the model to its extremes and suggests that plot elements themselves are actors. In theatrical terms this goes too far: an actor need not be human (animals act) or even animate (puppets act), but plots are what happen whereas actors are what tell these stories.

War games and civil defense exercises harden participants to the gruesome facts of death, but their effectiveness also comes by simultaneously engaging intellects and emotions in the rehearsed scenario.[122] While role play is important, designers of political games discovered that participants who were too immersed in their roles could be counterproductive to an exercise's goals: "we assumed that human players would respond only to a high-intensity crisis situation, on the grounds that anything less traumatic would fail to get them past the takeoff point into role-playing. But the result was that the control team improvised throughout with interventions that were unplanned and unmeasurable, thus running the peril of being unrelated to the main strategy, however imprecise, of the game designer."[123] In a theatrical situation, it is desirable that actors retain awareness of themselves and their job as actors while presenting a character or fulfilling a task, for to do otherwise can be dangerous to other actors, destructive of illusion, and counterproductive to the ensemble's task of presenting a play. This is true no matter how immersed or subsumed their acting technique encourages them to be.

Elly Konijn's study of actors who claim to use techniques involving correspondence between their own affective state or memory and the circumstances being portrayed in character, as well as those who claim to be purely presentational, suggests that they all simultaneously experience their role or function in the play along with their private self. In an exercise, this would mean that the people playing the commissioner of Public Works, brigade commander, stretcher bearer, checkpoint constable, switchboard operator, concerned citizen, or any other role, should maintain simultaneous awareness of themselves, their exercise function, discrepancies between their actual job and their function, and their execution of the exercise. In theatrical acting, this produces four eligible emotional categories:

Category	Corresponds to:
1) actor as person (private individual)	private emotions
2) actor as artist/craftsperson	task emotions
3) *modèle idéal* of how the character will be intended	emotions
4) character as presented by actor	character emotions[124]

Actors experience themselves as private individuals through their private emotions and they also experience themselves as actors with emotions relating to their tasks. But they may also have a *modèle idéal* of the role, and thus measure any discrepancy between intended emotions and task efficiency against what is actually experienced or achieved. For exercise players, absorption in the narrative is apt to fluctuate, just as it does for actors on the stage. Della Pollock calls this the performative mode, imagining "then" as now, what could be as if it were, and calling the future into the present as easily as if it were the past. This rehearsal into reality creates "real possibilities" or "possible realities" which "with a little coaxing . . . might as well be real."[125] They will not be real, but an emotional experience of them may sometimes feel like it. That is precisely the leap that exercises were supposed to enable.

While instrumental to the pedagogy of a civil defense exercise, an emotional experience is not the central objective as it may be in theater. Erving Goffman notes that in everyday life a role can be played "tongue-in-cheek . . . deliberately without inner identification."[126] If, instead of involvement, a player engages in deceit, this does not negate Konijn's four-part emotive model. The experience of "betweenness," ambiguity, rejection, and reabsorption is exactly what it allows, accounting for the interiorized experience of shifting from matrixed to nonmatrixed behavior, whether or not this is a volitional act. An actor—as much as a spectator—accepts a role and contracts for a consensual reality. Actors tend to cue each other into desired and effective behaviors, which reinforces the consensual reality.[127] This is not an entirely conscious process. The experience or the perception of such a moment may be what is called a "heightening" of scale—the larger-than-life sense often attributed to theater—but this is on a continuum and an exercise could as easily seem much, much smaller than life, especially if the pace slackened, as for those in the Charlottetown Armory and the shivering constables along Bristol's access roads.

Part II

ACT YOUR PART: The Private Citizen on the Public Stage

THE PSYCHOLOGY OF VULNERABILITY

NATE: How can you live like that? I mean, what if you found out you were
    going to die tomorrow?
BRENDA: I've been prepared to die tomorrow since I was six years old. . . .
NATE: Well, why since you were six?
BRENDA: 'Cause I read a report on the effect nuclear war would have on the
    world and it was pretty clear to me at that point that this was definitely
    going to happen.
NATE: When you were six?
BRENDA: And I wake up every day pretty much surprised that, um, every-
    thing's still here.
NATE: Well, I don't understand how you can live like that.
BRENDA: Well, I thought we all did.

— Six Feet Under

On 31 August 1946, John Hersey's ethnography of six Hiroshima survivors was published in its entirety as a single
issue of *The New Yorker*. Reprinted as a book, it was distributed
free to members of the Book of the Month Club and the entire
text read aloud on radio stations in the ABC, BBC, and CBC networks.[1] For the first time, Westerners were encouraged to empa-
thize with the victims of the atomic bomb and come to grips with
the human consequences of atomic weaponry. For Americans, in
particular, whose collective memory of air attack focused on the
naval base at distant Honolulu rather than their own neighborhoods, the details of shadows left by vaporized objects, testaments

by civilians suffering from horrendous burns and delayed radiation effects, and the devastation of whole cities were especially eye-opening. The collective sense of responsibility for releasing atomic bombs was assuaged by the American government's insistence that even more lives—American ones—would have been lost in an invasion of the Japanese homeland, but at the same time Hersey showed how A-bombs brought the potential battlefront to everyone's doorstep. Since it was believed that civilians' psychological response to disaster would likely determine the outcome of the next war, Western governments conceded that the public had to be a vigilant part of Cold War readiness, not to prevent conflict but to mitigate its consequences.[2]

This observation gave rise to two kinds of planning problems. The logistics of protecting the public in an attack focused civil defense efforts and was the overt goal of civil defense organizations. But, at the same time, the problem of securing public cooperation also preoccupied planners. This was approached primarily through education: in the United Kingdom and United States, advertising campaigns were coordinated through the mass media; direct leafleting was tried in Canada; and in the United States civil defense curricula were promoted in primary and secondary schools as well as adult education programs.[3] Governments hoped these efforts would result in behaviors compliant with civil defense planning. Home readiness, especially through reduction of extraneous combustible materials and, after the Soviets detonated an H-bomb in 1953, construction of domestic fallout protection, were the major thrusts. Community readiness, through the warden system, public shelter identification, and practicing shelter and dispersal drills were exercised to a differing extent in each nation at different points in time. However, solutions to an important problem remained unproven: even if a ready population could be achieved, would they behave as needed in an actual emergency? The views of the mental health community, who judged the likelihood that the public could buy into and rehearse civil defense, as well as the consequences if they did, weighed heavily in this matter.

Shock Proofing

Americans who attended public school during the administrations of every president from Harry Truman to John F. Kennedy remember how to "duck and cover." In August 1950, just after the outbreak of the Korean War, school civil defense drills began in major American cities.[4] By late 1952, civil defense training was present in 87.4 percent of elementary schools and 88.4 percent of secondary public schools.[5] From 1952, the drill procedure—in many places a fortnightly event—was promoted to primary school students by a comic book featuring a prudent

22. "Bert the Turtle Says Duck and Cover," from the comic book corresponding to the animated FCDA film. Author's collection.

turtle, Bert, who took cover in his shell whenever he saw "the flash." In January 1952, Bert was immortalized in an animated film.[6] Schoolchildren were supposed to follow Bert's example: drop to their knees, either hunch over as tightly as possible or lie flat facing the ground, and clasp their hands behind their necks. These postures were intended to make a human being a smaller target for projectiles, avoid retinal burns, protect the abdominal organs, and prevent the neck vertebrae from being severed. To duck and cover under one's desk gave added security. If sufficient warning permitted, ducking and covering in rows along schools' inner hallways kept the nation's youth even safer. With advance warning of attack, children could march in orderly fashion into school basements or windowless inner rooms and assume the turtle position there. On their way to school, they were to duck between seats on the bus. When playing at home, if there was no warning, children were to duck and cover under their beds or behind furniture. Out of doors, they were to duck behind trees, but they were to do it instantly! Humming the catchy jingle and keeping in mind Bert's jaunty upbeat attitude in the face of his nemesis, a mischievous firecracker-wielding monkey, American schoolchildren were drilled in these procedures year after year. With practice, the response became as ingrained as orderly exiting in a fire drill and taking cover for a tornado.

In 1961, all schools were assessed in the National Shelter Survey for their suitability in the event of fallout.[7] Under the Kennedy administration, new school architecture began to take shape to enable optimal ducking and covering. Some schools became community hubs for fallout protection. Successive generations of engineers and architects transformed the shape and materials of American suburban architecture to economically and unobtrusively offer maximum protection at minimum cost.[8] By remembering what to do when they saw "the flash," Americans grew shells—like the turtle's—affixed to their collective backs, into which they withdrew in times of trouble and instances of warning.

Meanwhile, Canadian children remained upright at their school desks.[9] The vast majority of them lived between the Pinetree Line and the Canada-U.S. border, in a geographic band likely to experience the consequences of U.S. intercepts of incoming missiles, though too far south for American defenses to destroy all the Soviet missiles targeted at Canadian cities, military bases, transportation hubs, power plants, oil refineries, and industrial centers; too far north to feel complacent that early warning would help them; and too far in league with NATO to do much more than hope for the best.

Neither the Canadian people nor their government were indifferent to the threats posed by the arms race. During the 1950s, there were numerous instances of civil defense rehearsals undertaken by communities, some in conjunction with the OPAL series as joint exercises. Canadian officials actively participated in joint committees to plan civil defense on both sides of the border. But from the early 1960s, discouraged by Canadians' rejection of the idea of building home fallout shelters, the federal government took upon itself the task of remaining vigilant by practicing for continuity of government but letting the public get on with enjoying and promulgating the fruits of postwar prosperity. Perhaps Canadians processed the threats of nuclear war differently from their southern neighbors. Perhaps their public exercises of the 1950s demonstrated to them the enormity of the problems of survival as well as the difficulties of expunging a limited population in a vast landscape. Perhaps the day-to-day challenges of survival in a forbidding climate already made Canadians look upon their structures, and especially their homes, as shelters against the elements and refuges from unpredictable forces, regarding every day they woke up warm and safe as a significant and sufficient triumph. Or perhaps the national ethos really was in accord with the armed forces' growing reputation for peacekeeping—following Nobel laureate Lester Pearson's example as president of the UN General Assembly and peacemaker at Suez—and granting a more tolerant perspective on Communism both abroad and at home.

Strapped by postwar shortages of food, consumer goods, and building materials for reconstruction, the United Kingdom deferred a sense of general prosperity in favor of trying to equalize opportunity. Nostalgia for the camaraderie garnered by wartime coexisted with embodied memories of civilian efforts to survive bombing campaigns and a rigid determination to move forward, not back. Less concerned about Communists at their gates than memories of buzz bombs in their skies, Britons kept the onus of responsibility for defense early in the nuclear age on those who protected more than just themselves: drafted soldiers and a Civil Defense Corps tailor-made for the nuclear age. So, while British children also remained upright at their school desks, and the public at large was very rarely inveigled to take part in their own defense, some adults were persuaded to join an active brigade of civil defense workers to learn skills and rehearse scenarios that put them to work in preserving others.

According to the medical director of the American Association for Mental Health, "one way in which every citizen can aid in civil defense is to shockproof himself through play."[10] He was referring to the importance of equipping shelters so that children would not get restless, but the principle applies to the practice of civil defense and shelter occupancy in general. During World War II, the British experienced an air raid on average once every thirty-six hours for five years.[11] They adapted shelters—both the steel, partially buried, back-garden Anderson type and the underground railway stations where thousands congregated—to accommodate the need for recreation. Anna Freud recommended equipping shelters so that children could *enjoy* the raid, storing games and toys inside or organizing impromptu orchestras. She advocated that families "make quite a confident ritual of air-raid precautions" by assigning everyone a task. This adds to everyone's sense of security. If a child's task is to collect his or her teddy bear on the way to shelter so it will be safe from bombs, that is all to the good. Reflecting on such precedents, Irving Janis commented:

> Although ritualistic observances of civil defense requirements would tend to be perfunctory performances, this type of conformity may prove to be a basis for maintaining at least some of the most essential protective activities among a large sector of the public. This would be especially useful if there were to be a long period during which an anomalous international situation required constant preparation for a surprise attack despite the absence of any definite signs of an imminent war.[12]

Nuclear preparedness, in other words, requires tolerance for repetition and waiting. Rehearsal does not evolve from ritual but rather ritual results from rehearsal.

Disaster planning is no good if it is merely on paper. An Eisenhower cabinet document observed: "Research has identified a number of human factors which contribute to failure to perform according to plan, important among which are lack of prior understanding or acceptance of the part one is to play."[13] The American Psychiatric Association noted that a warning may either have a disorganizing or constructive effect: like fear it alerts and prepares people to deal with what is coming. Undirected action will be useless and so tasks must be assigned to everyone and then practiced regularly: "There should be widespread public participation in practice drills providing effective patterns of behavior during the warning phase. Drilling is the only way to establish these patterns at a level at which they will be almost automatic under conditions of extreme stress."[14]

Curricula for the Nuclear Age

The state of Georgia's 1952 manual for civil defense in schools epitomized the slogan "*Preparation Prevents Panic.*" It specifies how to drill students to duck and cover but also advocates the initiation of action or service projects deploying students in community groups and ingraining pro–civil defense behavior into all aspects of civic responsibility:

1. Helping pupils to become sensitive to and concerned about the need for civil defense, reaching all [students], not creating fear, integrating with the curriculum, and involving community groups.
2. Helping pupils to identify and select civil defense problems in the community; holding symposia on American defense; making field trips to an observation post or shelter; attending invited talks; studying world events; surveying community resources and safety equipment.
3. Helping pupils to work out solutions to problems in home and school sheltering; posting information on school shelters; giving first aid demonstrations and courses; involving parents in cleaning up the attic; preparing a directory of local resources.
4. Helping pupils to evaluate procedures by preparing a glossary of atomic terms; studying nuclear scientists; studying nuclear war prevention; fostering democratic leadership; presenting radio programs on living in the atomic age; arranging exhibits for public library, store, newspaper, etc. on civil defense problems.[15]

The civil defense Staff College at Olney, Maryland, also recommended approaches for integrating civil defense into the curriculum. The idea, as taken up by the Colorado Department of Education, was "of converting the civil defense assets and virtues of self-discipline, sacrifice, service, self-help, and mutual aid to use as basic training in character building, citizenship development, social studies, and other areas of the curriculum."[16]

Oregon led the way in curricular reform, recommending strategies to integrate civil defense messages into all grade levels. In kindergarten and the first three years of school, social studies would emphasize the interdependence of residents in a community, including children's role and responsibilities. In the home this might involve learning how to use a flashlight; turning off the stove, lights, and furnace (disconnection from gas and electricity mains was recommended in the early 1950s in the event of imminent attack); how to open cans of food; and how to cover windows to reduce the velocity of flying glass and debris and make a home more resistant to heat flash. Children would learn to respect and observe safety rules and that under certain circumstances it may be necessary to make obedience mandatory. In science classes they would learn about the "peaceful applications" of nuclear energy in line with President Eisenhower's Atoms for Peace initiative. In health education classes they would study nutrition and how to maintain safe food and water, how to prevent accidents, very basic first aid, protocols in case of air attack, and the importance of cleanliness. Their mental health would be addressed through instruction to listen to the radio for directions in the event of attack, and writing about or drawing their fears. Songs, stories, and games would be used to allay children's anxiety about the bomb. Even simple arithmetical tasks served the civil defense curriculum: children would count as part of their protocols of safety and use oral arithmetic to pass the time. Fourth grade students would learn more about healthy eating, causes and prevention of disease, personal cleanliness, personal protection during atomic attack, the importance of not starting rumors, and of fireproof housekeeping. The next year children would study the composition and dispersal of nerve gas, nutrition under various atomic, biological, and chemical war scenarios, the bacteriology of biological warfare, and how to help others post-attack. In the sixth grade, students learned about contamination of foods by radiation, the role of blood and circulation, keeping fit for health, and more about helping others.

Middle-school children learned about the characteristics of fire, basic atomic physics, household safety, chemical laws in nutrition, how to dispel myths that cause panic, guarding against biological warfare, and the relevance of respiration and physiology for chemical warfare. In high school science, they focused on the behavior of living things and structure and function of the human body, complemented in social studies by lessons on the ideologies leading to World War II and then the Cold War. Grade eleven students learned advanced first aid and refined their knowledge of American history and world leadership along with the role of chemistry and the atmosphere in everyday life. Twelfth graders added to this the chemistry of heat and the structure of matter, along with international relations.[17]

23. High school girls on emergency mass feeding course prepare lunch in kitchen of a Portland, Oregon, underground civil defense operations center, 1958. Courtesy of NARA.

In Louisiana and elsewhere, the link between physical education and civil defense was also stressed through "teamwork, improvement of moral values, ability to follow directions, obeying of rules, and accepting decisions." In art classes, students learned to make civil defense displays. In industrial arts and vocational education, students were trained to develop shelters and make radio sets.[18] North Carolinian home economics classes also covered food preservation, a balanced diet during emergencies, large-scale food service as in canteens or hospitals, water treatment during nuclear attack, and raising one's own food supplies (vegetables, chickens, and pigs).[19] Michigan added to this the study of social and family problems, promotion of family togetherness, and homemaking skills related to emergency housing, safety, sanitation, care of the sick, and child care and development. Children were encouraged to "face dangers realistically" and learn by doing.[20]

So, American students at all levels could have a context in which to understand "duck and cover." Children were encouraged to take this curriculum home, while PTAs were encouraged to take an active role in schools' implementation of the basic curriculum. Not all school systems adopted such plans, but all urged the importance of the home-school link. "Why not let your children teach you what they have learned in school about protective measures? Let your children talk to

Chapter 3

you about their civil defense drills if they wish. Remember, they will be watching you closely to observe your reaction. Your attitude will largely determine theirs. If you are calm, they will be calm. If you are sensible, they will be sensible."[21] A study of Des Moines, Iowa, showed that householders who declared they would go to a public shelter in case of emergency, and had a definite *plan* to do so, were more likely to have children under age fifteen in the household. Having even younger children increased the incidence. There was no correlation between number of children, income level, religion, or gender.[22] Apparently, having children was a motivator, whether out of parental concern for their offspring or children's delivery of the civil defense message.

At the post-secondary level, civil defense was regarded with equal relevance across the curricular spectrum, enabling safety and survival in all kinds of situations.

> Problems of mass feeding under emergency conditions are valid subjects for home economics. Temporary and reconstructed housing involve engineering. The prevention and control of epidemics are the concern of biology, medicine, and nursing. Evacuation of a threatened or suffering population depends upon transportation. Physics and electronics are basic to many forms of communications vital in every emergency. The question of government in period[s] of emergency is an essential part of political science and public administration. Family welfare, delinquency, and penal control are the concern of sociology. Emotional reactions, hysteria, and acceptance of saturation bombing are topics for psychology. Group care of children is related naturally to the general field of education.[23]

Universities were to encourage faculty to undertake research relevant to civil defense (the University of Michigan and Michigan State, in proximity to the national headquarters for civil defense, are conspicuous in this regard, along with the University of Pittsburgh), to contribute expertise to their communities, and to offer extension courses for adult learners. Many non-urban campuses were designated relocation sites for federal and state agencies.

In the late 1950s, as national planning contingencies changed, aspects of the civil defense primary and secondary school curriculum followed suit. Oregon revised its *Instruction Guide* to include specifics about likely targets in the state. Portland and Klamath Falls were on the list of vital points (first-strike targets for incoming missiles), so instruction in evacuation routes and the role of welfare/relief centers were added to the curriculum. Schools in military target areas were even encouraged to store duplicate essential records off site. As television became a fixture of American life, PTAs were encouraged to sponsor programs on civil defense. As ham radios became popular, youth were encouraged to unify this interest with civil defense applications.[24]

The onus fell on schools nationwide to address two goals: to organize themselves to act in event of emergencies, and to implement curricula to build competent citizens.[25] Thorough preparation of facilities and briefing of children were supposed to prevent the shock effects of disaster.[26] The Indiana state superintendent of public education stated in 1960: "Today's world is a complicated one. A mighty struggle for the minds of men exists. Economic, diplomatic, scientific, psychological measures will be taken by both sides. It is up to the educators of today to prepare the next generation to meet all challenges."[27] The ethos was so well ingrained that the children's magazine *Jack and Jill* published an air-raid board game as the centerfold of its September 1961 issue—following a summer when President Kennedy initiated the stocking of public fallout shelters for fifty million Americans, and Germans constructed the Berlin Wall—without any contextualizing explanation whatsoever. The object of the game was for children to get from their classroom to the air-raid shelter, obeying appropriate signals along the way.[28] The nomenclature was blunt: this was an "air raid" not a "threat to our way of living" or "eventualities which may one day become actualities," terms which one historian of civil defense claims were frequent replacements in federal civil defense literature for schools circa 1951–65, replacing "technical words like *war, death, bombing, attack, battle, atomic warfare, atom bomb*, and *air raid*."[29]

After the mid-1960s, emphasis broadened to a wide spectrum of emergencies, locating nuclear civil defense among many possible natural and human-caused calamities. The American Association of School Administrators urged that "the old duck-and-cover position is not entirely obsolete" and given its utility in situations other than nuclear attack should be retained.[30] Yet whereas a study by the Office of Education in 1952 showed that 95 percent of 437 elementary schools sampled in cities with 50,000 or more population taught civil defense,[31] a poll of 20,000 teachers showed that by 1966 only 15 percent of schools still did duck and cover drills, 12 percent practiced moving pupils from school to their homes, and only 6 percent had mandatory shelter drills, averaging 3.9 per year. Despite 41.5 million children and 2.5 million employees in public schools, there were only about 5.5 million licensed and stocked spaces in school fallout shelters. Provision for 5,750,000 children and 250,000 staff in private schools was unknown. "What happened to the 'duck and cover' and mass community evacuation procedures that we rehearsed some years ago?," the National Education Association asked in conjunction with the National Commission on Safety Education in 1966. "What happened to your 1950 car? Some of us still have that model and find it useful for certain purposes."[32] Many students would hear about civil defense from other sources: 15 percent heard live speakers, 21 percent read about it in pamphlets or books, and 43 percent had seen a movie on the subject. But students exposed to civil defense—from any source—could recite more accurate information, more diverse facts, and actively use a wider spectrum of knowledge.[33] The question remained: would this knowledge help them in the event of war?

From Gross Stress Reaction to PTSD

Extrapolating from the behavior of seriously injured victims in Hiroshima, a Hudson Institute study of 1964 predicted that physically injured people would not cause disruption. Japanese A-bomb victims who made their way to hospitals showed gratitude for treatment, but were also reported to defer politely to others in greater need. Those unable to get to the hospital made modest requests for assistance but did not create any "administrative problem owing to bizarre behavior or demands for services that could not be supplied. . . . Even under these extreme conditions rationality was often maintained until consciousness left."[34] Ignoring the possibility of cultural difference between the Japanese in wartime and Westerners subject to a surprise attack, potential behavioral problems, therefore, lay with the little injured, uninjured, and the psychologically injured rather than survivors with grave physical injuries.

Considerable effort was devoted to studying the psychological effects of vulnerability, attack, displacement, and destruction of civil populations bombed in World War II, especially those in German, British, and Japanese conurbations. Running parallel to this empirical endeavor, other analysts focused on post-1945 peacetime disasters, particularly catastrophes caused by weather or industrial accidents, seeking to understand the emotional and behavioral responses among civilians that might complicate relief efforts by rescuers. Under President Eisenhower, the inferences drawn by these researches were funneled together to serve civil defense planning in the event of all-out thermonuclear war: the goal was to use motivational theory to channel emotional reactions into what the government regarded as constructive behavior.[35] The findings were not classified, and thus could be shared with the United States' closest allies, the United Kingdom and Canada. Massive public education campaigns were undertaken to persuade citizens to participate in a variety of activities for self-preservation and, ultimately, the preservation of national identities and cultures. In units as small as families and as large as nations, the public was exhorted to rehearse their responses to warnings of attack, becoming actors in a nuclear war scenario that was intensively practiced with minimal variation in plotting.

The RAND Corporation was the first to issue advice, publishing in 1949 *Proposals for Field Research on the Psychological Impact of Peacetime Disaster*, a document concerned with factors that precondition the spread of rumors or panic, proposing the types of empirical research necessary to adequately study the question. The same year, RAND also published *Psychological Aspects of Vulnerability of Atomic Bomb Attacks*, by Irving L. Janis, a Yale psychologist who expanded this work into a commercial imprint in 1951, extrapolating from classified U.S. data on the bombing of Germany and Japan.[36] A paper presented at the American Psychiatric Association conference in May 1949 by Dale C. Cameron of the National Institute of Mental Health advocated the importance of understanding group dynamics to curtail mass panic, for mass reactions would exacerbate preexisting personality disorders.[37] The emphasis in all these studies is on informing the public of the nature of atomic explosions so that, in the event of attack, it can react realistically and adaptively whether at home, work, school, or somewhere in between. Easily said but difficult to accomplish. In the United States, this implied the recruitment of fifteen million adults into civil defense training,[38] curricular reform for schoolchildren in kindergarten through grade twelve, and educating the public for a range of contingencies: nearby attack, remote attack, underwater detonation, attack when indoors, when out of doors, while traveling by automobile, with one's family, at work, in fair weather, foul weather, and so on. The entire U.S. budget for education was $3 billion — half a billion more than all other nations combined spent on education — and an unspecified portion of this would go to civil defense. Local authorities were reluctant to commit their funds, so from 1958 the National Defense Education Act made federal funds available for promoting civil defense in schools.[39] The United States, more than any other country, could afford to inform its population if it chose to do so.[40] But a delicate balance existed between giving the public accurate information about the realities of atomic attack and building morale that would motivate constructively compliant involvement. Feeding the mind with information was useless without also conditioning the emotions and body through practice.

The diagnostic and statistical protocol for psychiatrists, psychologists, and other mental health professionals (the *DSM-I* manual published in 1952) grouped response to disasters under what it named "transient situational personality disorders." Such disorders, specifically "gross stress reaction," arise in acute circumstances with extreme "physical demands or emotional stress, such as in combat or in civilian catastrophe."

> Under conditions of great or unusual stress, a normal personality may utilize established patterns of reaction to deal with overwhelming fear. The patterns of such

reactions differ from those of neurosis or psychosis chiefly with respect to clinical history, reversibility of reaction, and its transient character. When promptly and adequately treated, the condition may clear rapidly. It is also possible that the condition may progress to one of the neurotic reactions. If the reaction persists, this term is to be regarded as a temporary diagnosis to be used only until a more definitive diagnosis is established.[41]

This is the equivalent of "combat fatigue," a term that the Army Medical Service School recommended for such cases "since it fosters expectancy for a readily recoverable and transient benign disturbance due to logical situational conditions" rather than the alternatives: shell shock, psychoneurosis, concussion, or blast injury.[42]

Some of the early planning for nuclear disasters may seem both to mistake and underestimate the public's likely reactions to crisis; however, in the context of early 1950s' psychological knowledge it was on the mark. As the American Psychiatric Association Committee on Civil Defense and the director of the U.S. Civil Defense Administration noted, if a few people feel panic, blind flight can escalate into a crowd-wide reaction involving entire communities, cities, or other large population bases. Judgment is suspended and among some victims there is a desire to flee, uncontrolled weeping, and purposeless physical or verbal activity. Others may be numb and unresponsive. It was believed that some may unconsciously convert hysteria into a disablement—deafness, muteness, blindness, or paralysis—as debilitating as a real injury. The inability to focus on a task would make all these psychiatric casualties useless in rescue work unless effective psychological first aid was administered.[43] To avoid the escalation of fear and excitement into irrational acts, the U.S. federal agency responsible for public health (HEW) recommended education. Individuals' behavior would affect their families and whole communities, but to make constructive reactions possible during war, everyone needed to adjust to living "with uncertainty and some justifiable apprehension about their safety and survival as individuals, and as a nation."[44]

A 1956 report commissioned by the American Psychiatric Association predicted 10 to 25 "disaster fatigue" cases for every 100 physically injured casualties. Exposure to mangled bodies would exacerbate symptoms including muscular tension, sweating, stammering, trembling, nausea and vomiting (also symptoms of radiation exposure),[45] noise sensitivity, apprehensiveness, irritability, "stunned helplessness," docility, resentment, flight impulse, fatigue, euphoria, tearfulness, or restlessness. Those exposed to initial air attacks would be more likely to exhibit these symptoms than people already aware of the outbreak of nuclear war. Just a small number of cases (1–3 percent) would be severe, experiencing dissociation and inability to communicate, while 30–40 percent of cases would be moderate and 50–70 percent of cases would be mild.[46] In most instances, "giving 'effective activity'" would help as an "antidote to disorganized fear, depression, and apathy" especially with early on-the-spot treatment; thus, even ten minutes of psychiatric intervention with the sufferer isolated from others was believed to help prevent a pattern of behavior from coalescing.[47] Where the casualty toll was heaviest, survivors may be completely disabled by grief and shock: a study of four thousand survivors of the Normandy campaign found that all soldiers became incapacitated once roughly 75 percent of their companions had been killed.[48] In a West Virginia mining town devastated by a mudslide, 80 percent of residents still had traumatic neurotic reactions two years after the disaster. Traditional supports of kinship and neighborhood had been destroyed, and survivors were demoralized, disoriented, and disconnected from each other.[49] A 1985 report of the British Psychological Society, taking care to dissociate itself from anti-nuclear views and emphasizing the credentials of those who blind vetted the report, concluded that in a limited war, reconstitution was unlikely; effects of an all-out exchange of weapons would cascade, bringing about the end of British society.

> Five or six nuclear explosions on urban centres will so raise the level of psychological distress in survivors that the continued functioning of a recognizable social structure will be in question. A return to quasi-normal functioning is less likely, and it is more probable that there will be permanent and severe impairment, with a distortion and disintegration of the present social organization.
>
> A nuclear attack on the United Kingdom at the expected level of roughly 200 megatons will leave the 15 million or so immediate survivors severely and permanently impaired, and will destroy their capacity for productive social interaction. Given the further consequences which will follow upon the destruction of the economy, the capacity of the survivors to reconstruct any form of functioning society without massive and sustained outside help will be negligible. It is highly unlikely that a civilized society will survive.[50]

The problem was not just that things would be destroyed, or populations diminished, but that people could not retain mental health in the face of such devastation to the social fabric.

Until the late 1950s, the differences between individual adaptation and group behavior were not well articulated in the literature. In 1956, a group of sociologists sponsored by the United States' National Research Council's Committee on Disaster Studies noted that when Germans were under Allied air bombardment, disruption to public transport lowered morale more than interruption of any other utility service because this kept people from pursuing their usual forms of interchange, preventing normal contact patterns within social systems such as the family. Urban life is "characterized by conflicting loyalties and complex stratification arrangements" so that a person's response in disasters "is a function of his social identifications and his position in the various sub-systems . . . of his community or society."[51] This explanation took the focus off individual psychological reaction and instead accounted for patterns of social response.[52] Unlike gross stress reaction or disaster fatigue, sociologists argued, disruptions to social identifications are less likely to result in panic and flight; instead, the public is apt to converge upon the disaster site, in person and by telecommunications, seeking news of their loved ones or just satisfying curiosity. For example, the day after the deadly Waco, Texas, tornado of 11 May 1953, *in-bound* traffic was bumper-to-bumper on all routes and "airplanes buzzed over the ruins like buzzards, creating a sky-traffic jam."[53] Convergence could occur at different rates, as in Monte Cassino, Italy, where Allied forces attempted to breach the Gustav Line for five months in 1944, eventually reducing the fortress to rubble. "Within a few weeks of the end of active battle, people drifted back to live in caves, cellars, and dugouts, without food or means of livelihood, in an area infested with malaria and 550,000 mines."[54] Thus, both curiosity seekers and returning inhabitants could converge on a disaster site, the former hindering the work of disaster relievers, the latter without regard for personal safety. What may appear to an outsider as irrational convergence behavior can actually be social reestablishment, entirely different in fact from personal disorganization. Likewise, behavior such as mutual self-help at a disaster site may be ineffectual because it is uncoordinated, reckless, and short-lived (as in the counter-disaster syndrome)[55] yet at the same time it is purposeful because it therapeutically reestablishes social cohesion. Thus, according to a member of the Committee on Disaster Studies, "the central problem of disaster management is to broaden the focus of attention and re-establish general, co-ordinated action for this mass of individual and small group actions."[56]

A McGill University psychiatrist studying disasters ranging from the bombings of Hamburg, Hiroshima, and Nagasaki to the 1917 explosion in Halifax harbor[57] explained in the *Canadian Medical Association Journal* that for up to two days following a crisis "the destruction of physical facilities upon which social organizations and social cohesion depend, and the disorientation of the persons whose social roles give the society life" will result in social paralysis. "Individuals and small groups may be operating effectively at isolated points, but as a whole the community will be prostrate. . . . the social organization will be severely crippled and its immediate recovery will depend upon the introduction of social organizations from without."[58]

In these initial days, it is important that relief workers come from outside the afflicted community to offer aid (the cornucopia effect).[59] However, as nuclear attack scenarios grew from single-city events to nationwide and global patterns of attack, eligibility for outsider-ness dwindled. Leaders might emerge from within the afflicted population—individuals who never before took responsibility and, as in the case of natural disasters, may never again show civic spirit—but the co-ordination problems of a post-nuclear attack are complicated by the presence, movement, and dissipation of radiation, requiring specialized knowledge to con-trol migration and avoid further injury and thus are considerably less conducive to on-the-spot emergence of leaders than an event such as an earthquake.[60] Leaders who did emerge would have difficulty rallying followers.

Preparation and education were indispensable: people must understand a dan-ger in order to correctly process an escalation in level from normal to imminent threat.[61] Thus, on 24 October 1962, during the Cuban Missile Crisis, residents of San Antonio, Texas, dove to shelter when the air raid siren was accidentally activated, but when sirens sounded unexpectedly on 12 November 1961 most resi-dents in Oshkosh, Wisconsin, assumed it was not a real attack.[62] However, lead-ing up to and during an emergency it was also crucial to handle communica-tions appropriately: neither fanning over-anxious anticipation nor conditioning an attitude that would lead to denial of an actual threat.[63] Coordinating public response via the mass media was crucial in the event of imminent or on-going attack. This was much more difficult when emotions were engaged in an actual emergency than in a pre-announced exercise or drill; furthermore, the extent to which rumors and false reports could exacerbate problems was difficult to study in planned drills. An unplanned exodus of Port Jervis, New York, on 19 August 1955 provided more informative data about human behavior per se than the calm exodus of Portland, Oregon, in its civil defense drill a month later.[64]

The Port Jervis area, a triangle of land between the Delaware and Neversink Rivers, was inundated with water from Hurricane Diane, and at 02:05 on 18 Au-gust the mayor declared a state of emergency, putting the city of 9,000 in the hands of civil defense authorities. At 06:00 the river crested. The waters at Port Jervis then receded at the rate of six to eight inches per hour, yet a rumor that a large dam thirty-five miles upstream had broken spread rapidly on 19 August. Of the 107 people later sampled for interviews, nearly 75 percent had heard the rumor and evacuated, many without attempting to confirm the rumor's source.[65] Thousands in their nightclothes choked Route 6 trying to escape. The rumor was circulated by word of mouth and telephone, and some citizens rode around in cars shouting that everyone should flee. The fire department tried to deny the rumor using a loudspeaker, and the radio station went on the air after midnight, constantly repeating that the rumor had no basis. The majority, awakened from sleep or at home listening to the media, fled with their families. About a third of those fleeing first attempted to assist others or took neighbors with them. The flight could have caused a greater disaster than the flood itself had done.[66] It seemed that "residents had been so sensitized to the possibility of the catastrophe that the source of the message was relatively unimportant, and any alarm was sufficient to produce belief."[67] The original threat of flood from the hurricane raised fear levels; the subsequent rumor about the dam, though of uncertain veracity, increased the public's sense of vulnerability, resulting in an overly vigilant response.[68]

By the early 1960s, disaster planners were at least as concerned about people's behavior in crises as their reaction to repeated insistence in the media that a disaster *could* happen. The response to civil defense campaigns for home preparedness was disappointing to U.S. officials, despite years of effort and media blitzing. People were aware, but apathetic. The campaign of persuasion, it seemed, had resulted in two main undesired responses: "the 'endless euphoria' idea, or the feeling that nuclear war is so terrible it could not happen" and the " 'Armageddon attitude' which assumes it could happen, but if it does, whoever and whatever is left won't be worth saving."[69] Meanwhile, peace groups warned that civil defense would have a detrimental effect on national psychology as well as foreign policy, threatening the democratic process.[70] In testimony before the House Subcommittee on Government Operations, Herman Kahn argued that high morale and psychological training that conditions people against panic are of no use if they are not physically protected against fallout.[71] Most people knew they were not protected and did not feel sufficiently motivated to change this: the campaign of persuasion informed people of the dangers of nuclear war, and the people concluded that survival without quality of life was not worth seeking. As the recommended period of fallout shelter occupancy lengthened, public skepticism grew proportionately.

Research on survivors of Hurricane Audrey, which struck Louisiana 27 June 1957, revealed that isolated rural residents, surveying the watery expanse around them "obliterating the 'world' they knew . . . apparently could not conceive of anything ever being the same again."[72] A 1963 article in *Medical Times*, a periodical directed to physicians, explained the phenomenon:

> People can endure a great deal of hardship if they can sustain the hope that the hardship is not only a limited one, but that its end will come within a reasonable length of time. . . . After a nuclear catastrophe there would be no conceivable end to the kinds of suffering that survivors would have to endure. Those who fantasy [*sic*] that at the time they leave their shelters there would be a soldier at the entrance with a CARE

package would perhaps only then realize that they had been reduced to a primitive, chaotic way of life for a longer period of time than their imaginations might be able to tolerate.

Shelter occupants would fear radiation (an unseeable threat) as well as intruders. "There has been talk of equipping shelters with guns, yet little thought has been given to how well emotionally equipped the occupants would be to use such weapons."[73] If neighbors must be perceived as potential enemies, social cohesion has already frayed. As a staff member on the Peace Research Institute wrote, "When someone asks, 'should I shoot my neighbor?' he is asking, 'What are my aims in life? By what philosophy should I live?'" Such fears highlighted self-interest not collectivity.[74]

And imagine, one physician suggests, the psychological consequences of a death in a family fallout shelter. Occupants might not be able to dispose of the body out of fear that they could not go outside. The impact of cohabiting with the corpse—both on social cohesion and individual psyches—would be profound. Anyone able to cope with this, or the devastation that would await shelterees outside, might be people "whom we consider most primitive in their psychological makeup today." Almost anyone who is mentally healthy before an attack, he predicted, almost certainly would not be able to recover from the catastrophic damage, let alone assist their culture's recovery.[75] The national character itself could be irrevocably changed.[76]

Irving Janis's work showed that a high level of threat stimulates anxiety, which interferes with the ability to reason and problem solve.[77] In OPAL 56, 450 members of the Department of Commerce relocated to their emergency site, maintaining efficiency and high morale. But when this was discussed in a cabinet meeting, President Eisenhower "reminded the Cabinet that in a real situation these will not be normal people—they will be scared, will be hysterical, will be 'absolutely nuts.' We are simply going to have to be prepared to operate with people who are 'nuts.'"[78] The effects of confinement on efficiency in the event of nuclear war were impossible to test empirically, but the thinking was that if certain responses were pre-conditioned to particular stimuli, the overall outcome would be better: in other words, people would not need to think clearly and could revert to learned behaviors. So, for example, if the population could be persuaded to prepare home fallout shelters or practice getting to public fallout shelters in peacetime, they would cope better in the initial phase of catastrophe, if it ever occurred. But dissonance theory predicts that if people prepare for an event, they are more likely to believe that the event will transpire. Cooperation with civil defense policies, in other words, creates belief in the likelihood of nuclear war (but not necessarily

changes in political outlook or a sense of personal agency capable of intervening in politics). This dissonant effect needed to be psychologically counteracted.
Melvin Lerner found in a controlled experiment that high school students' exposure to civil defense literature explaining how to prepare against nuclear attack
enhanced belief that war would occur but also inclined students to believe that
civil defense preparation would increase survival rates.[79] What would happen to
the survivors remained at issue, with Nikita Khrushchev's famous prediction that
the living would envy the dead.[80]

A DOD report of 1971 proffered the sanguine view that in the recovery period,
"adaptive social behavior would be likely to outweigh the incidence of negative,
maladaptive antisocial behavior. . . . Simple fear emerged as the greatest psychological barrier to recovery, and communications appeared to be the key to penetrating that barrier," enabling the government to coordinate and advise survivors.
Aberrant and destructive behavior and the fragmenting of institutions would be
outweighed by the predominance of cooperative and constructive behavior in a
return to self-sufficiency and local resourcefulness.[81] Nevertheless, the *DSM-II*,
released in 1968, replaced the psychiatric diagnosis of gross stress reaction with
"transient situational disturbances" which allowed for "acute stress reactions" of
"psychotic proportions" in response to "overwhelming environmental stress."[82]
The assumption was that a person's pre-traumatic personality had no bearing on
the reaction,[83] the stress response was temporary, and (with early effective treatment) reversible. This view from the psychological community is at odds with the
military view that by overcoming people's fears with effective communication,
society would soon stabilize into a harmonious, cooperative whole.

The British Psychological Society's 1985 report acknowledged the depth of despair that was likely to exist. Extrapolating from other forms of disaster, the report
predicted that following nuclear attack, the bereaved would not be able to find
support and succor from others, prolonging the grieving process. "This will diminish their capacity to interact socially in a productive manner. Victims need
some form of acknowledgment of their suffering, but social norms may deny
them the right to express their grief and hopelessness. Fear and apprehension per-
sist, and many may feel that the catastrophe will recur. . . . Disaster persists as
a tormenting memory, and is relived again and again."[84] The psychiatric community's growing experience with treating Vietnam War veterans, prisoners of
war, Nazi death camp survivors, and other trauma victims prompted a major re-
evaluation of transient situational disturbances. *The DSM-III*, released in 1980,
named "post-traumatic stress disorder" (PTSD) for the first time, allowing for an
acute version as well as for its onset to be delayed by months or even years, and

for symptoms to be chronic. The symptoms are similar to earlier diagnoses—sleeplessness, hyper-alertness (hyper-vigilance), distraction, anxiety, irritability, aggression, and jumpiness—but its causes were expanded. The instigating trauma could affect groups (such as military combatants) or individuals (such as rape survivors). The bereaved, chronically ill, or sufferers from business losses or marital discord could experience PTSD. It could be brought on by natural disasters, transportation accidents, fires, as well as the effects of torture, genocide, or bombing, but "the disorder is apparently more severe and longer lasting when the stressor is of human design."[85] Sufferers from PTSD typically re-experience their trauma over and over again in sleep or full consciousness.

> Commonly the individual has recurrent painful, intrusive recollections of the event or recurrent dreams or nightmares during which the event is re-experienced. In rare instances there are dissociative states, lasting from a few minutes to several hours or even days, during which components of the event are relived and the individual behaves as though experiencing the event at that moment. . . . Diminished responsiveness to the external world, referred to as "psychic numbing" or "emotional anesthesia," usually begins soon after the traumatic event. A person may complain of feeling detached or estranged from other people, that he or she has lost the ability to become interested in previously enjoyed significant activities, or that the ability to feel emotions of any type, especially those associated with intimacy, tenderness, and sexuality, is markedly decreased.[86]

Extrapolated to a population surviving nuclear war, this radically changes the scenario away from a cooperative, adaptive population functioning well in family units and as communities, getting on with the job of happily reconstructing Western civilization.

With sufficient warning of catastrophe and sufficient provision of shelter—as predicated in Crisis Relocation Plans (CRP)—a majority of Americans could, theoretically, escape the horrors of witnessing the attack close-up and seeing its carnage firsthand by moving out of harm's way well in advance of attack. Yet residents of coastal Texas and Louisiana, areas prone to severe weather on an almost annual basis, overwhelmingly failed to heed warnings about Hurricane Carla in 1961. Fifty-five percent of the population stayed at home as this category five storm loomed in the Gulf. People less experienced with a given risk are less likely to respond to warning, yet residents along the Gulf of Mexico should have been able to see the purpose of avoiding this trauma.[87] People's fear level following a directive from the president about anticipatory evacuation prior to a nuclear onslaught *should* result in compliant precautions because of the magnitude of the danger, though lack of experience with any given disaster tends to diminish compliance.[88] The fewer people who were compliant, the greater the proportion of survivors who would incur PTSD.

The *DSM-IV*, released in 1994, further adds to the list of potential traumatic events that instigate PTSD, including diagnosis with a life-threatening disease; observation of serious injury or unnatural death occurring to someone else as a consequence of war, accident, disaster, or other violence; viewing a corpse or body parts unexpectedly; hearing of extreme stress occurring to a family member or close friend; sudden discovery of a family member or close friend's death; and learning that one's child has a life-threatening disease. In other words, the onset of PTSD can be caused by personally experiencing horror, witnessing someone else's suffering, or even a *report* of someone else's horror. No matter what the cause, the severity of symptoms can be identical, can occur to a person of any age, and may last for decades. PTSD sufferers are also at risk for developing major depressions as well as other anxiety disorders: panic disorder, obsessive-compulsive disorder, agoraphobia, and other phobias.[89]

So, as the Cold War concluded, it became evident that governmental solutions to protect the physical well-being of the population, to reduce their exposure to bombs and radiation, and to attend to their welfare in the long-term could not possibly protect people's mental health. As a psychiatrist testifying before FEMA in 1982 stated, civil defense encouraged people to not face up to danger:

> Civil defense is a psychological defense. Its most important function is to contribute to the system of belief that allows most citizens, including public officials, to *deny the realities of nuclear war*, and to *avoid* the anxiety of thinking about the deaths of ourselves and our families, the destruction of our Nation and of our civilization, the possibility of extinction of humanity, and even the possibility of the end of all life.[90]

It is indeed difficult to imagine anyone surviving an all-out nuclear attack without incurring an immediate danger of radiation sickness, a long-term fear of genetic damage, the shock of bereavement, exposure through personal experience or the media to devastated landscapes, the sight of carnage, or the knowledge of others' imminent demise through observation of their weakening or knowledge of ecological catastrophe. From a psychological perspective, therefore, civil defense defended not people, not their culture or way of life, but only concepts and institutions. It remained in doubt that there would be a population willing—but more importantly *able*—to return to their jobs, function in an economy, and preserve an ethnos. As sociologist Lee Clarke predicts, there would be post-attack panic, making it impossible to instigate institutional behavior. This was the paradox: "either the social order would not be destroyed, in which case civil defense was redundant, or social order could not get going again, in which case civil defense was impossible."[91] This was an emergent view, not one fully embraced by the mental health community until the dissolution of the Soviet regime, after relations between East and West warmed. However, the responsibilities accorded to private citizens to rehearse the realities of the weapons threat and act in the case of war trace the emergence of this viewpoint. It puts the onus on the individual to take a role on the public stage, but in doing so the citizen accepts part—and only ever part—of the consequences of nuclear war, just as an actor activates the "as if" of imaginative play, suspending aspects of reality in order to focus on a select scenario. Thus the campaign of persuasion—activated in a campaign of rehearsal—used one of the fundamental aspects of performative play in order to foster constructive belief. The remainder of part 2 focuses on the overt manifestations of the activated "as if" in the public realm.

SHELTERING

The question might arise as to the validity of information derived from testing only the supremely healthy, the well adjusted, well-oriented segment of the population through very careful screening and selection of subjects. This may not be realistic in terms of the real problem in time of eminent disaster when everyone, regardless of his health and personality characteristics, will seek shelter. Or will this "across the board" experiment come later?

—Paul Parrino

There were limits to the extent that post-attack shelter conditions could be simulated and reactions tested. Nevertheless, gathering data on people's physical and psychological responses to confinement was crucial to the credibility of survival planning. Shelter occupancy rehearsals in domestic and public settings offered an experimental context for deriving relevant data, testing people's tolerance for primitive conditions, and demonstrating that the actions recommended in the immediate aftermath of nuclear attack were viable. Isolation and privation structured rehearsals as ethical acts of the nuclear age. As site-specific stagings, they produced data about the bodily and emotional experience of confined living. Like time-based performance art, spatial habitat was inextricably tied to corporeal and psychological endurance. A few habitations, like the Mininsons who spent their two-week honeymoon in a bomb shelter, were stunts (in this case sponsored by the shelter's manufacturer).[1] Others were propagandistic, but some were scientifically monitored studies.

For years, while the Civil Defence Corps faithfully trained for a nuclear emergency, British civil defense officials and the government debated whether to inform the general public about what to do in event of an imminent nuclear threat. In January 1963, at last, the HO released "Advising the Householder on Protection against Nuclear Attack."[2] To prepare their homes in times of crisis, the public were to whitewash windows; remove flammable materials from attics and upper storeys; dispose of old newspapers, magazines, firewood, and rubbish; station buckets of water on each floor; and close all curtains and blinds. The booklet gives advice on how to choose a room to be the fallout shelter in standard houses, flats, and bungalows, none of which were presumed to have basements or cellars. These should be interior rooms without windows. Within the room, a "core" sandbagged to give further protection against fallout would be prepared. In a two-storey attached house design (i.e., row houses), this would necessitate using the cupboard under the stairs; the core should be sandbagged on the stairs that form its roof and along the hallway wall forming the outside of the cupboard. Alternately, a core area within a parlor or sitting room would be established by making a lean-to from doors, sandbagged on top and at both ends. Covers would be bolted over the room's windows and the resulting space filled with earth. Residents of one-storey bungalows and portable trailers should seek shelter elsewhere, for example digging a trench outdoors and sandbagging the roof. Whatever the form, householders were advised to equip their shelters with fourteen days' supply of food and water, a portable stove, radio, and other essentials.

Following the specifications in "Advising the Householder on Protection against Nuclear Attack," a group of civil defense volunteers in York converted a room adjacent to the Guildhall in 1964 and put it on public view. The shelter room had 120 square feet (9′ by 13′ usable space), furnished with a table, easy chairs, cupboards, bookshelves, linoleum, area carpet, and portable toilet. At one end, after several tests of materials, they devised a lean-to core consisting of two doors, battened at the bottom and top, covered with 130 sandbags weighing half a ton altogether. This " 'core' was 2′10″ from the wall at the base, 5′8″ at the maximum height up the wall, and 5′ long. The angle between floor and door was 66°."[3] Offering 80 Protective Factor (PF) shielding, the radiation protection mimicked residential shelter on the outer edge of Z-zones. The space was too cramped to allow occupants to move around comfortably, and large enough for only one adult to lie down.

At 10:00 on Saturday morning 20 March 1965, three friends—Margaret Jones, a housewife, Winifred Smith, a welfare officer with British Rail, and Mildred Veale, a civil servant—moved into the shelter. The civil defense van outside made seven simulated regional broadcasts at predetermined times. To signal that they had received the broadcast, the women pressed a buzzer. No other communication with the outside world transpired, except receipt of a written message which the warden pushed through the letter box at the experiment's end.

As per instructions, the women spent the early part of their occupancy in the core room, avoiding the worst of the simulated fallout. They huddled together, without heat or extra light, under conditions where "they could simply endure." When they emerged after seven hours, they fixed a meal on the primus stove and swallowed some aspirin to ease their headaches. At 22:00, following the last broadcast of the day, they bedded down, two outside the core and one inside. The paraffin heater had nauseated them and they turned it off overnight. By morning, the room was cold and humid, the wastebin smelled bad, and the women were dispirited. After twenty-four hours, according to the *Times*, "even that basic feminine impulse to make frequent cups of tea deserted them."[4]

> The experiment had taken on an air of reality that they would not have believed beforehand. So much so that when the 1.00 P.M. broadcast finished rather suddenly, due to a transmission error, they were fearful that the wireless had broken down and perhaps would not work again. This fear persisted for the next three hours. Some sewing and knitting was attempted but was abandoned and later the work had to be undone because of mistakes. . . . At 6.20 P.M. they started to prepare the second meal of the day, but after 10 minutes the lights failed and they finished the meal in the light of torches and candles. After the meal at about 7.00 P.M. they were cold, bored, fed-up and went to bed.[5]

But sleep did not come, even when they dosed themselves with Serenesil®, a tranquilizer. Monday morning, they were apathetic and proceeded in a lackluster manner to prepare breakfast and dress for their 10:00 departure. About forty members of the press greeted them as they emerged. BBC Radio covered it live. That evening, all three women were on Granada television's late-night show. The story was carried by all national papers the next day.

The exercise was a success insofar as the women's radiation exposure was deemed within acceptable limits. Assuming that a 5 MT bomb had been dropped seventeen miles away on the outskirts of Leeds, exposure outdoors would have been 1,000 r per hour, with a cumulative dose of 2,800 r in the forty-eight hours of the exercise. Within the shelter, the women who slept outside the core would have received a total of 68 r while Miss Veal, who slept in the core both nights, would have been exposed to just 48 r. No studies of air quality were undertaken, and some speculation occurred about whether an excess of carbon monoxide accounted for the women's malaise. But two of them were smokers and reported that the exhalations were clearly effected by drafts, so there were constant sources of fresh air.

In 1981, a British couple and their eleven-year-old daughter conducted a fourteen-day occupancy test of a shelter in Newbridge. In this case, the interior climate was monitored with scientific instruments.[6] Empiricism was not limited to the experiential components of endurance but also resulted in data to evaluate habitability. Other European nations also conducted shelter occupancy tests,[7] but it was the Americans who explored these endurance rehearsals to the fullest, despite debates over the viability of evacuation versus shelter (and the kinds of shelter that should be recommended).

Public Shelter Exercises

A 1957 study of metropolitan St. Louis, Missouri, predicted that with a minimum of fifteen minutes warning, 45–60 percent of the population could survive a large thermonuclear blast if they had access to shelters with at least 30 psi blast protection.[8] The emerging thought was that a national system of fallout shelters, coupled with tactical evacuation in an attack on fifty cities, could save twenty million lives if there were thirty to sixty minutes' warning, or sixty million lives with between three and six hours' warning. In an attack on 150 cities, the same strategy could save seventy-five million lives with a brief warning, or one hundred million lives with the longer period of warning. Implementation hinged on cost.[9] A 1965 study of Houston, Texas, showed that for $201 million, 100 psi blast protection could be provided in public shelters, saving 70 percent of people in surrounding counties from a 10 MT bomb; fallout protection alone would cost $104 million, for a 63 percent survival rate.[10] The cost of blast protection for the general public was considered prohibitive in the United States; home fallout shelters, which put the cost onto private citizens, were favorable as far as government expenditure was concerned. While Britain did nothing toward community shelter provision, Public Works Canada identified suitable buildings, stockpiled signage, but never marked shelters.[11]

To encourage planning for fallout shelters in new buildings, the Eisenhower administration's 1958 National Shelter Policy included provision for design and construction of prototype shelters in various climates and geographical areas.[12] Some shelter proposals were far fetched: Guy Panero proposed blasting shelters out of the rock eight hundred feet below the surface of Manhattan Island, at

24. Manhattan Island elevated to reveal proposed layout of 800-foot-deep blast and fallout shelters. Courtesy of NARA.

a cost of $28 billion (figure 24). Other proposals for different degrees of fallout or blast protection for urban as well as rural populations ranged up to $115 billion for the entire nation. Proposals that also provided blast protection averaging 100 psi brought the cost up to $528 per person. Achieving this would occupy the entire construction industry for years. There was hesitation over exactly what to do despite consensus that shelters could protect against fallout. The federal government favored, not surprisingly, surveying potential existing public shelter in target areas (estimating costs for this at just $13.6 million) and encouraging home owners to install their own shelters, using FCDA designs (for which training and education would cost the government merely $1 million).[13] More research was needed to lower construction costs, refine designs to protect against blast, fire, and immediate radiation, and improve livability: this is what the National Shelter Policy proposed to enable.[14]

It was all very well to design structures suited to the purpose, but how would people confined within them cope? A study of motorists stranded for up to thirty-six hours in a Howard Johnson's restaurant in Morgantown, Pennsylvania, 19–20 March 1958, is indicative of the kind of sociological research on shelters and confined populations that complemented the studies by engineers and physicists into structural issues. From the early hours of Thursday, cars and trucks within a twenty-mile stretch along the Pennsylvania Turnpike were immobilized by a blizzard. By 05:00, up to 150 people had arrived at the restaurant/service station. During the day, many more, totaling 800 in all, left their cars and proceeded to the same site, occupying facilities built to accommodate no more than 200 customers popping in for a quick meal and leaving in under an hour. One man died of a heart attack while on the trek. His widow continued, joining a cross-section of society including twelve employees of the restaurant and gas station, between fifty and two hundred truck drivers, several bus drivers, three physicians, two or three nurses, two ambulance drivers, four clergymen, a few nuns, ten servicemen in uniform, three Air Force helicopter personnel (two majors and an engineer), twenty rock-and-roll entertainers, college students, teenagers, and around thirty children under the age of twelve. There were many elderly and infirm and five ailing people among the group.

Early on Thursday afternoon a physician, Dr. L., began to organize the shelter. He was assisted by Mr. F. (a sales manager) and Mr. F.'s associate. Major T. and Major H. later assumed charge. To get things started, Dr. L. stood on the cashier's counter and began to speak. "Everyone turned and stopped talking at once; it was so quiet you could hear the snow falling." He asked for volunteers, and "the response was amazing; tremendous. We got cooperation from everyone. We asked for volunteers and we got 700 of them. Everybody came up and wanted to know what they could do."[15] The space was diagrammed and allocated. Dr. L. was concerned about disease spreading in the severely crowded conditions. He banned smoking and set up a first aid station. Truckers were dispatched to help people still stranded in cars. A diabetic stranded in an ambulance could not be freed, so a helicopter was summoned from Olmsted AFB. Dr. L. and his aides inventoried food in the facility and in trucks outside, concluding that they could survive for a week. Initially, as people were arriving, competition arose over food. Individual orders were eliminated from the restaurant's menu, and by evening a feeding line was formed to dispense soup, coffee, and eggs. Money was no longer collected, and the regular kitchen and wait staff were assisted by volunteers. A rumor circulated that a busload of children was stranded; this turned out to be thirty-four adults and just a few children. They decided not to evacuate, and sandwiches were delivered to them. Another rumor about motorists dead in their cars was proved false.

Overnight, food service was suspended, allowing restaurant employees who had been working nonstop for thirty hours to rest. A truck with 150 packing quilts stalled near the restaurant loaned its cargo to help bed down the travelers. The sick, including an accident victim and cardiovascular patient, were separated from

other shelterees. Mothers, small children, families, and single women were bedded down in the area nearest the milk dispenser. Single men occupied the less
desirable locations such as the gas station and lubrication bays. Friday morning
at daybreak the ailing were evacuated by helicopter. By noon the road was open
and people began to depart. It was two more days before electricity was restored
and the emergency generators could be turned off.

A week later, in interviews with eleven of the stranded motorists, the FCDA's
Disaster Research Group ascertained that leadership had been taken by persons
accustomed to supervisory roles, and "furthermore, each probably comes from
a middle socio-economic class background which emphasizes the need for order
and rational behavior."[16] No rifts emerged between groups of shelterees, and researchers found that the spirit of cooperation and harmony overrode prevailing
prejudices.

> There is no evidence in this situation pointing to the carryover of pre-existing preju-
> dices and conflicts between racial, ethnic, and social status groups. If anything, such
> cleavages seem to have been mitigated by the situation. Negroes were in the group
> but there were no signs of prejudice against them reported. A woman "dripping with
> diamonds" was observed helping a mother with her baby. A clergyman helped pre-
> pare food and a Doctor's wife put on a waitress' uniform and helped in the kitchen.
> These are some examples which indicate that social distinctions were pretty generally
> ignored.[17]

Despite the crowding, food and water were not in short supply and this may have
helped maintain decorum.[18] In debriefings, Dr. L. recommended that in any subsequent event everyone should be given a job. He also stressed the importance
of keeping people informed about what was happening outside. His wife recommended streamlining the food service by eliminating menu choice earlier and
setting restaurant employees to supervise rather than doing the labor themselves.
The Air Force major who took a leadership role in a few helicopter rescue missions
recommended strict control of movement as well as giving people responsibilities
in order to make them feel part of a constructive team, getting people information
in order to control rumors, and providing entertainment.

While no natural disaster could simulate the emotional circumstances of
people sheltering during nuclear war, such incidents were used to help understand some of the consequences of confined and constrained group living and
what could be done to help people to adaptively respond. The Morgantown
case, for example, shows the kind of " 'heroic' purpose" beyond mere survival
that Albert D. Biderman of the Disaster Research Group concluded that shelter

leadership needs. This purpose "may be mythical, rather than rational, if necessary. Ideally, it should represent some continuity with traditional activities and values. Defense against invasion, and the reconsolidation of the larger community and the nation, might serve as such values."[19] Studies of prisoners of war, civilian internees, and political prisoners also pertained in this field of inquiry. Some researchers branched out to use confinement studies of submarine personnel, polar scientists, and people stationed at remote radar bases.[20] Further study of historical incidents of slow starvation, the behavior of people in life boats, and besieged cities in wartime was recommended in order to better understand problems likely to face communities in shelters and following emergence.[21]

Civilian disasters were extensively considered, and some cautions were taken from history. For example, crowding proved an important factor in the *Londonderry* disaster of 1849: when a storm arose in the Irish Sea and two hundred famine victims en route from Sligo to Liverpool were forced into a hold 18' × 11' × 7' (where each person had 1 square foot, or 7 cubic feet, apiece). The hatches were closed and tarped, muffling their cries from the crew. Frenzied violence erupted in the darkness. One man fought his way out and alerted the ship's mate, by which time seventy-two were dead and more were dying. Crowding was also an issue at Fort William in 1756, at the incident made famous as the Black Hole of Calcutta. A survivor's version of the event—claiming that 146 East India Company officials were locked overnight in a cell meant for two, with just two small windows to let in air—has raised suspicion, but even the more likely case that sixty-four people were crammed into a room 24' × 18' at the height of the Indian summer, resulting in forty-three deaths, shows the effects of crowding, heat, and desperation. A DOD report on crowding in shelters cited both these examples as cautionary tales.[22] But as a planning document for shelter studies noted, "the problems of physical simulation are trivial compared to the problems of psychological simulation. Consider the ethical consequences of making a person believe that he may have been or may be exposed to an overdose of radiation, that his family and closest friend may have been killed, that the total fabric of his society is in jeopardy."[23] Studies on animals could show the effects of radiation's permeation of shelters but not psychological effects of sheltering per se and the stress of nuclear war; for this purpose, comparisons were made with terminally ill cancer patients.[24] The consequences of short-term crowding were extrapolated from civil disasters while the consequences of long-term confinement were extrapolated from military situations, though neither quite matched the psychological profile expected among the general population in nuclear war. As a British Ministry of Health official commented in 1965, "medically there are grounds for arguing that the emotional and psychological strains imposed upon people who have to remain under cover for long periods might well manifest themselves both in the shape of depression and lassitude that could not easily be distinguished from the effects of mild doses of radiation but also in the form of irritability and over-activity. It could well be that these psychological consequences would present greater difficulties for those attempting to maintain law and order than the physical health hazards" from radiation sickness which lead to depression and malaise, or massive illness among the population due to decreased resistance, breakdown of medical services, and people's inability to help themselves.[25]

A series of experiments using the U.S. Naval Radiological Defense Laboratory test shelter at Camp Parks, California, added considerably to the knowledge about physical responses to shelter confinement. In the first experiment, one hundred male volunteers inhabited the shelter for two weeks in early December 1959. The group consisted of three physicians, a trained shelter commander and his assistant, five deputy sheriffs, and ninety-two prison inmates from the Santa Rita Rehabilitation Center chosen from among four hundred volunteers. All "psychotics, homosexuals, enuretics, drug addicts, alcoholics, and compulsives" were eliminated, then the remaining 225 were screened for high blood pressure, chronic skin disorders, urinary-tract disease, digestive disorders, active or recent tuberculosis, asthma or hay fever, streptococci, heart disease, dental problems, convulsive disorders, and a history of trouble making. A group aged from seventeen to sixty-two was selected. They occupied a buried flexible-arch structure measuring 25′ × 48′ with double rows of canvas bunks stacked four high. During the occupancy period, all aspects of the interior environment were monitored as well as the actions and responses of the shelterees. Evening entertainments included recorded music, films, and talks about atomic weapons and fallout. Researchers tested four types of diet that required little or no heating or preparatory and serving equipment but which could withstand long-term storage. One diet consisted of a Planters Jumbo Block Peanut bar and a vitamin capsule, which met nutritional requirements for $.31 per person per day but gave some inmates diarrhea. Another menu consisted of a liquid diet of nonfat milk powder, dextrimaltose, vegetable oil, and water, a formula that could be digested by anyone including infants, at the cost of $.35 per day. A third group received the ration recommended by the Department of Agriculture (USDA) based on a canned wheat product eaten with reconstituted nonfat milk and sugar at breakfast, and other toppings such as gravy, chili, or spaghetti sauce at other meals, plus packets of cheese and crackers and peanut butter sandwiches, cookies, or candy, altogether costing about $.75 per day. Those receiving c-rations (canned protein and sweets), which cost $1.85 per day, considered them the preferred choice though they caused constipation.[26]

A follow-up study along similar lines was done in summer to test modifications to the facilities.[27] The Camp Parks subjects were highly uncharacteristic of the general population: the presence of the deputy sheriffs were a reminder that the shelterees were already incarcerated. By contrast, the study conducted in Pittsburgh by the American Institute for Research in November 1960 used a more typical cross-section of the public. Volunteers were screened for psychological and physical problems. Most were inclined to agree with the concept of civil defense. A series of four experimental groups including men, women, and children aged seven to seventy-two years occupied a simulated shelter. A major variable tested was climate, some groups experiencing temperatures up to 85°F.

The first three groups at Pittsburgh were each in the shelter for seven days. A final group experienced a week of hot temperatures followed by a week of moderate temperatures. Everyone knew the length of their occupancy period in advance. Volunteers were paid $50 per week and explicitly told that there had been no attack. The space allowed 8 square feet, or 58 cubic feet, per person (the conservative estimate of the Calcutta disaster calculates 6 square feet per prisoner, the Brandywine service station and restaurant permitted about 9.5 square feet per person during the maximum occupancy, and the Camp Parks experiments had allowed 12 square feet per inhabitant). One toilet served all thirty occupants of each group.[28] Researchers wanted to determine shelterees' response to space, internal layout, sound level, cooking facilities, and stocked supplies, and to study emergent leadership, organization, and activities mitigating the effects of habitation and preparing shelterees for emergence. Simulated CONELRAD transmissions were broadcast almost hourly. Researchers monitored inhabitants through one-way screens, closed-circuit television, automatic recording devices, and audio feeds. A telephone link to the researchers was available for emergencies. Inhabitants were aware of the monitors and also kept diaries, filled out a battery of pre- and post-shelter questionnaires, and submitted to interviews.

After an initial period of bumping into each other, inhabitants adjusted to the restricted space. New "movement folkways" emerged, involving increased tolerance for bumping in order to keep conflict to a minimum. Many people compensated by offering excessive warnings and apologies.[29] During the last experiment, an additional eleven people entered the shelter for the final forty-eight hours. They slept head-to-toe and instituted a hot bed system in order to accommodate forty-one people on the thirty bunks. Researchers concluded that a group of thirty inhabitants was small enough that they did not need to be further subdivided within the shelter. Shelters holding sixty to three thousand were recommended for subdivision to aid management.

A major report on the Pittsburgh studies emphasizes the interpersonal dynamics resulting from leadership. By and large, whether emerging from the group or being designated in advance, leaders tended to exhibit either exceptionally good or exceptionally bad adjustment to life in the shelter. The self-appointed leader of the first group, Mr. Black, a thirty-five-year-old unemployed youth director, earned the disrespect of other people through his officious, arbitrary, and sexist behavior. To counter potential threats to his leadership, he stayed awake night and day. By the fourth day, he nearly collapsed from fatigue. When a simulated CONELRAD broadcast described radiation exposure,

> Black jumped from his bunk and rushed to the emergency phone to report that he had radiation sickness. He then "dictated" his symptoms for the shelter log in a loud voice "so others will recognize radiation sickness if they get it."
>
> Black started to keep a large screwdriver hidden in his bunk and Mr. Knight, a 33 year old nuclear power technician [whose wife and three children were also in the shelter], started to carry a hammer in his pocket as a potential countermeasure. On the evening of the fifth day Mr. Knight made several emergency phone calls to request instructions concerning the care of the mentally ill. Several of the young men in the shelter were alerted by Mr. Knight in case any violence erupted and physical restraint was required.
>
> During that same night two notes were passed under the shelter door by one of the mothers in the group begging that Mr. Black be removed from the group for the safety of the children.

The project directors persuaded Black to leave the shelter, and though he tried to set the condition that three other inhabitants must leave with him to act as shields, he did eventually go alone. In debriefing he explained that he believed he was being irradiated through the one-way observation screens and that there were half a dozen employees of the institute planted in the shelter in order to challenge his leadership.

A friendly thirty-three-year-old housewife who had been Mr. Black's chief deputy assumed leadership for the remaining period. Many liked her—she had been Black's most vocal critic while he remained inside—but "reservations concerning her were generally vulgar speech, constant references to body processes and toilets, and a tendency to be noisy and active at night when others were trying to sleep."[30] She was evidently of lower social status than many of the occupants. Her nighttime activities added to the problems of lack of sleep among many in this group.

In the second group, a thirty-four-year-old professional civil defense instructor who had been briefed in advance on the experimental management program immediately assumed leadership. His deputy was a forty-one-year-old female disaster researcher who became the confidante of many, particularly girls and women. They followed a predetermined shelter management program, including "guided democracy," and there were no derogatory comments about them afterward.

Civil defense literature emphasizes the importance of establishing leadership in the first phase of shelter occupancy.[31] The third group elected a twenty-two-year-old airman on leave, Mr. Boyd, as their leader. This is how it transpired:

> Less than half an hour after shelter entry, someone said, "Let's have a meeting before we go out of our minds." A man having military experience and at the time a member of the United States Air Force introduced himself and suggested that a shelter manager be elected. The group agreed this was a good idea but impractical because they did not know each other. The military man suggested that they introduce themselves and made the introductions. Thus by identifying and solving the problem he emerged as the leader.[32]

Mr. Boyd took a more authoritarian approach than previous leaders, insisting on reserving water and food in case of an unanticipated length of occupancy, but surprisingly, apart from this, there was little complaint about his leadership and morale was high. He tried to maintain his status especially among a group of working-class inhabitants by boasting about his experiences in the Korean War, misrepresenting his age, for he was in fact only in school in the early 1950s. He was supported by a forty-one-year-old housewife who served as a big sister to many inhabitants and a twenty-two-year-old registered nurse, a member of the American Legion Auxiliary.

Another of Boyd's deputies was Mr. Carlos, a thirty-three-year-old professional gambler. Gambling occurred to some extent in every study group. Boyd opposed gambling at first, then acquiesced.[33] Boyd tried too hard to be accepted by the men, adopting their profanities and obsessing on topics of blood and guts. With women, he was friendly but reserved. Such dualities could not go unobserved in confined quarters. His leadership remained secure despite an unfortunate incident midway through the study when some residents were talking loudly an hour after curfew. Boyd, boiling over, leapt from bed and announced a group meeting. But the group could not reach consensus about what to do, and Boyd returned to bed without having resolved the situation.

The fourth group, which occupied the shelter for two weeks, was led by a fifty-one-year-old professional civil defense worker and, as his deputy, a twenty-one-year-old miniature golf course operator who also had been part of the first group.

A security guard with lots of experience in civil defense also assisted; he was in the shelter with his wife and three children and, as a big man, exuded an air of authority which many respected. During the second week, the leader had subgroups work on problems related to post-emergence from shelter. Their reports were then discussed by all the occupants.

This group, like the others with clear and effective leadership, gave a prominent role to religious observance via mealtime prayers and Sunday services. Mr. Black, the paranoid leader of group one, had delivered an impassioned sermon begging God's mercy for mankind, though his piety was considerably undermined by his predilection for making lewd remarks to women. Other sermons focused on hope through salvation or the story of Noah's Ark. Those objecting to religious services simply opted out of participating. Unlike exercise, religious services provided recreation without increasing the temperature inside the shelters.[34] By and large, lectures were regarded as ineffective means of disseminating information — especially civil defense training — except at the outset of an occupancy period. Shelterees reported "difficulty in concentrating and short attention span."[35] Discussion and group problem-solving proved more effective techniques.

When each subject was later surveyed, they rated the extent to which different factors bothered them. Many people had difficulty sleeping, complained of the lack of water (they were told they were allotted about one gallon per person per day, exclusive of toilet flushing, but in fact used much less), temperature and humidity, lack of exercise, food, crowding, and lack of privacy. The biggest problem, however, was the behavior of others. Two groups of subjects reported marked desire to leave the shelter from the fourth day of each confinement — these were the groups with the paranoid leader and the professional gambler — but the third group had a drop in desire to leave after the sixth day and the fourth group, which had a gradual increase in desire to leave over the two-week period, peaked considerably lower than the first two groups.

There was much nervousness and excitement on the first day of each study. Inhabitants worked out systems to prepare and serve food and distribute bunks. Women dominated in the kitchen in the first days, with more teenagers and children volunteering after the mid-point of occupancy. Each test group experienced a slump around the fourth day: most people were quiet, withdrawn, and had diminished appetites. After supper on the fifth day, higher levels of activity and noise were evident, with more group activities and conversations. During the last twenty-four to thirty-six hours, each group evinced increased tension, with temper outbursts, refusals to cooperate in collective tasks such as cooking or cleaning up, and aggressive remarks (this was known as the "stage of collapse").[36] A group of women accused someone of stealing cigarettes. A group of young men stole a woman's diary and read it despite her protestations. Such manifestations of hostility were otherwise rare. Usually, inhabitants confided in each other to vent their frustrations. Upon emergence, the tension almost immediately disappeared and subjects proclaimed the solidarity of the group and acceptability of their experience. Years later, an institute member who had been a plant in one of the shelter groups claimed that inhabitants were particularly resourceful in drawing on people's strengths: "One of the people in a shelter I was in, was a negro. They wanted to make him feel at home so they set him up as the choir leader and organized a choir in the shelter. He led the singing, and he had a special status the whole time he was there." This special status, in his recollection, was different from what would occur in everyday life.[37]

A woman with a phobia of enclosed spaces managed to stay the course, as did a male alcoholic. A few other inhabitants, however, were unexpectedly strained by their circumstances. One woman slipped into a mild depression and sought to leave the shelter early. Despite her constant negativity, other shelterees talked her into staying. She had also been excessively disturbed by teenagers' petting. A ten-year-old boy resident in the shelter without either of his parents was the only child to cause negative comment. He found the shelter unusually permissive and he became a mild discipline problem. A young man who kept the company of a withdrawn young woman became a problem when their amorous behavior turned into "violent wrestling, apparently by mutual consent, on the bunks."[38] One individual who had been very well-adjusted and popular in the first group, taking on increasing responsibility and entertaining the children, also joined the last group in a leadership role but failed utterly in this. He struggled to maintain his status and took on the role of agitator. The project investigators discovered that he had fabricated his background in screening interviews, though not as egregiously as Mr. Boyd.

A study of attitudes toward fallout shelters conducted in Wilkes-Barre, Pennsylvania, in May and August 1961, a period of considerable international tension, concluded that while many people saw the need for fallout shelters, they could not transfer this rational perspective to an emotional acceptance. Many people were deterred by the expense. Others expressed difficulty imagining a two-week shelter occupation. For example, in response to a question about what it would be like to use a family shelter, one interviewee responded:

> Five people for two weeks. Kind of—well deadly. Deadly if you are there and deadly if you are not (laugh). I don't believe that I have claustrophobia, but trying to think of being dead or wishing that you were while you were in it. I am just joking really. It

is hard to think of beyond the two weeks. Come out to devastation and this I would think of: What will I find in the way of food and shelter and activity?[39]

During a civil defense drill, most Wilkes-Barre respondents either stayed in their homes and continued with normal activities or, if at work, kept occupied as usual. Some went to their basements, one watched television, more listened to the radio. Very few went to a home fallout shelter or secure area at work, and many confused the sound of a fire siren with the civil defense warning. The study concluded that it would be an error to try to use fear to motivate people to build fallout shelters. This would paralyze them and then they would be unable to take any action at all. Information must be positive and encouraging, emphasizing survivability as a result of sheltering.[40]

A study conducted at Princeton University in a simulated shelter in the basement of the Psychology Department corroborated this outlook. The "Project Hideaway" shelter was actually an acoustical chamber with inner dimensions of 8′ × 9′ (72 square feet) buffered by 6″ concrete walls, an air gap of 5″, and another set of concrete walls 18″ thick. This conformed to an Office of Civil Defense Mobilization (OCDM) bulletin of 1959.[41] A family of two adults and three children (aged six, three-and-a-half, and twenty-three months) was paid $500 to remain there for fourteen days. Their body heat quickly increased the shelter's temperature from 70°F to 89°F, so to adjust for this, cool dry 50°F air was pumped in whenever the occupants operated the ventilator. Cooking was done in a chafing dish over a candle and prepared and served on TV tables. All lighting was with flashlights and candles. A chemical toilet without outside exhaust stood in one corner. They had no electricity, radio, telephone, or other means of communication except an emergency alarm button to signal the desire to emerge earlier than fourteen days. Researchers monitored and taped all daytime conversations and kept an auditory monitor on at night; there was no prior consent for this, and the family was given the option upon emergence to take all notes and tapes or to censor all usages. They declined both options and gave researchers free rein with the data.

The children brought their favorite toys, blankets, and stuffed animals into the shelter. The parents would let them play with one toy at a time then put it away for a few days to preserve its novelty. Modeling clay and other creative activities kept children and adults occupied. Everyone read books, and the adults found that the eleven they brought in for themselves were insufficient. Song books would have been a boon, as singing was popular but the family had a limited repertoire of lyrics. The middle child became withdrawn after a time, and reverted to bed wetting, but was administered a tranquilizer and returned to normal. As a whole, the

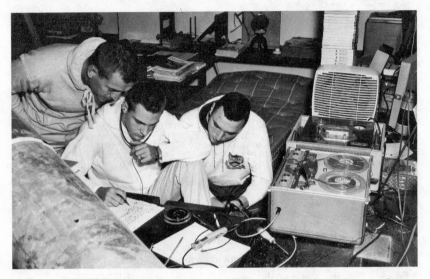

25. Princeton's "Project Hideaway" researchers monitoring shelter inhabitants. Courtesy of NARA.

family showed "a great deal of mutual pride in their achievement" and claimed to be strengthened as a unit.

> The most positive effect of the confinement was the integration of the family. The father of the family had an opportunity to get to know his children better and, as a consequence of the conditions, he came to have a new-found respect for the entire family. Both adults felt that the children actually profited by the experience. The youngest child's vocabulary increased a great deal more than it would have under normal conditions which was probably due to the attention she received. This attention came from the other two children as well as from the parents. The older children came to take on the responsibility of the younger which helped her achieve needed independence from the mother.[42]

They did not complain of excessive crowding, but did recommend slightly larger dimensions (10′ × 10′ and 8′ high) in any of the federally designed dual-purpose family shelters doubling as dens, game rooms, workshops, or music rooms.

The utility of this kind of research, beyond its scientific value, was that it seemed to prove the viability of shelter life. Not only could the public survive the bomb's blast, and successfully take refuge from radioactive fallout, they could survive and perhaps even flourish during the shelter period then emerge in cohesive social units, capable of tackling recovery and reconstruction tasks. Empirical tests proved this, in a manner of speaking. "Realistic" rehearsal undergirded the empiricism.

Optimizing Shelter Life

Most research on shelters was based on the study of adults and teenagers. The "Project Hideaway" researchers concluded that no special instructions should be given to children entering a shelter, and young children would find their parents' presence sufficient. Older children can understand the need to live in a shelter. "Parents should not view shelter life with children apprehensively. The presence of the children may provide the basis for sustaining the parents during the confinement. The children present an opportunity for the parents to engage in . . . productive activity. Not only will the parents spend some time entertaining the children, but they may profitably engage in actually instructing in such subjects as mathematics, reading, spelling, or whatever is appropriate." Shelter life, in other words, can be good for the family and good for the mind. The researchers recommended that families with shelters have trial occupancy periods to get used to them and to create positive associations through rehearsal. "To spend an occasional week-end in the shelter could hold much of the excitement of camping out and at the same time serve to show the family exactly what their needs will be. Once a given family becomes acquainted with their shelter they may be able to give helpful instructions to neighbors and others about shelter life."[43] A CBS television broadcast in the *Retrospect* series observed similar benefits from the shelter confinement of the Brown family in Topeka, Kansas: they emerged with a more resolute sense of themselves after this "exciting and wholesome form of entertainment for the entire family."[44]

Few of the experiments on shelter habitation would pass the ethical standards imposed by Institutional Review Boards today. And yet for all the "realism" shelter habitations incurred, it was a problem that the data collected might not be applicable in the event of nuclear war. A 1962 report emphasized the difficulty of predicting a community's behavior given variations in regional culture; local authority structure; ethnic, racial, class, neighborhood, occupation, and kinship groupings; local conceptions of leadership roles and their interaction with civil defense representatives; and local demography, including age, residential dispersion, differential growth rates of social segments, migratory turnover, day and nighttime populations.[45] A 1963 study on psychological stressors suggested that it would be interesting if subjects could be told that war is actually happening (or imminent), but either people might be hurt (or killed) or there could be irrevocable damage to property. Hypnosis was considered in order to make subjects *believe* an attack was imminent, with post-hypnotic suggestions to curb rage, aggression, and other violent tendencies, but unfortunately the effect was unlikely to last over several days. Mass hypnosis might sustain a prevailing attitude, but interruptions in the hypnotic state could be indistinguishable from stress reactions. It was proposed that hypnosis be used to tell a woman, as she rushed to shelter during an alarm, that she became separated from her husband and children. Her reactions would be measured. Additional stress could be imposed by telling her that she saw her son trampled by a panic-stricken crowd. Such an experiment could be "highly informative" and have innumerable permutations. But the moral objections to such applications of hypnosis could not be overcome in peacetime.[46]

When shelterees knew in advance the length of their inhabitation, they tended to exhibit anxiety with depression or apathy. But if the period of inhabitation was not known, or other stress factors were introduced, subjects were more likely to combine depression with maladaptation. The complications produced by realistic stress levels were particularly elusive factors, and researchers observed effects created by environmental circumstances, crowding, and population variables related to socio-economic grouping, age, gender, ethnicity, race, and religion.

Recommended preventive or corrective factors for inducing more harmonious shelter life included pre-shelter training; a positive and reassuring introduction to shelter life; well-defined, meaningful, and organized activities creating a sense of personal importance within the shelter community and for life after emergence; and perhaps group therapy within the shelter for those prone to creating problems.[47] Anxious people should be gathered together early in the habitation and, led by a person competent in psychotherapy, encouraged to express their feelings, release internalized pressure, and thus avert destructive behavior.[48] Aggression, anxiety, withdrawal, and fatigue due to little food or sleep were all conditions considered amenable to drug control. Tranquilizers (phenobarbitol or Compazine®) for "the chronically peevish neighbor" were endorsed as a standard part of shelter first aid kits.[49] Sleeplessness emerged as a chronic problem in shelter tests, and sedatives were considered options, even en masse, for a severely overloaded shelter. Amphetamines would suppress hunger. Barbiturates would make inhabitants calmer, more receptive to training, and more compliant toward leaders.

A DOD report proposed that "to calm a very anxious individual one might rapidly establish a strong fear reaction by surreptitiously cutting off power to the ventilation system and announcing that lack of oxygen will cause general suffocation in a short time. Panic may reign, but once the ventilation system was again operating the relief would be likely to take the form of an over-compensatory reaction resulting in a reduction of activity of those whose anxiety level increased during the crisis."[50] Something like this occurred in a 1960 test of the Camp Parks

26. Shelter habitability test for 100 civilians conducted at Camp Parks, California, 1960. During the test, half of the bunks were left in place for daytime lounging. The board to the right of the door holds 100 numbered drinking cups. Note that each person wears a number on his or her sleeve. Chairs and benches are fiber board and collapse easily for storage. Courtesy of NARA.

facility by a group of ninety-nine people from the general population aged three months to sixty-eight years, half of them children. A power failure was simulated and the shelter was plunged into darkness. Initially, people reacted well to instructions from the shelter commander. Those with flashlights turned them on. Others remained quiet and still. The shelter commander tried unsuccessfully to start the auxiliary generator but its carburetor flooded. The shelter became permeated with the smell of gasoline. One panicked child cried, and mothers gravitated toward their children. But before the situation could turn grim, a group of teenagers launched into a rendition of "I've Been Working on the Railroad." Others joined in, and mothers and children were soothed. After five minutes, lights were restored.[51]

Human subjects provided data on behavioral responses to various circumstances but despite numerous attempts at manipulating internal climate, the extent to which extreme temperatures could be tolerated was little understood. Subsequent experiments at Camp Parks were conducted on "human simulators," heat-conducting units arrayed on bunks and dining tables. Each heat-conducting unit consisted of a five-gallon paint pail with a nichrome wire heating

27. Second full-scale manned naval shelter test at Bethesda, Maryland, conducted under hot weather conditions. Men listen to a lecture by the shelter commander shortly after entering. Courtesy of NARA.

coil mounted in its base. The pails were draped in cotton flannel, which served as wicks, and water dripped onto the top of each unit, simulating the evaporation from perspiration in an enclosed space.[52] The objective was to determine the interaction of air temperature, humidity, and "bodies." Heat and relative humidity were monitored without anyone actually suffering, in contrast to human subjects tests at Gainesville, Florida; Reading, Pennsylvania; St. Louis, Missouri; Artesia, New Mexico; Tucson, Arizona; Lincoln and Omaha, Nebraska; and Fort Belvoir, Virginia.[53] A U.S. Naval test at Bethesda, Maryland, in 1962 exposed a hundred men to high temperatures and humidity (figure 27). The simulation at the University of Illinois Chicago campus in August 1967 also sought to simulate hot conditions for four hundred people, as researchers tested the effectiveness of a new generation of ventilation equipment. A five-week test of a family shelter in Bozeman, Montana, sought the opposite climatic challenges: in February and March 1964, sixteen people simulated winter occupancy in a partially buried shelter. But the weather turned out to be warmer than expected and the experiment was of negligible value.[54]

The Roberts' Dairy Farm, in Elkhorn, Nebraska, conducted a two-week trial of the shelter that combined accommodation for the farm's hired men and herd

28. Improvised fallout shelter for livestock in barn. Heavy concrete walls, with straw over the windows, and a deep layer of straw bales on the floor of the upper level, would protect livestock in pens on the barn's lower floor. A shielded room for caretakers, tractor-powered feed grinder, and automatic feeder complete the shelter. Courtesy of NARA.

of thirty-five cattle. Straw was the principle shielding for the livestock. Their care-takers dwelt in a concrete room, reporting on their condition to the civil defense van outside.

The University of Georgia conducted a series of studies involving members of the public in Athens. Simulating conditions in stocked public shelters, with civil defense biscuits and tinned water for sustenance but no blankets, cots, or bunks, people spread out as best they could to sleep on corrugated fiberboard pallets three-sixteenths of an inch thick, but "at 9 sq. ft. per person it is difficult for a person to lie completely out flat without touching somebody else, kicking some-body else, or hitting somebody else." Another test group was allowed to bring their own comfort supplies, and in this case air mattresses proved a big prob-lem, for people claimed whatever space their belongings occupied, whether or not there was sufficient room.[55] A third test allocated three hundred occupants seven hundred calories per day from survival biscuits and a carbohydrate supplement.[56] Sheltered life mimicked normal pastimes, including exercise, religious services, and a talent show.

Some businesses, particularly large corporations implicated in post-nuclear

29. Barn shielding enhanced with straw bales, exterior view. Courtesy of NARA.

survival, installed and tested shelters. During OPAL 55, the Chicago *Tribune* staff held their fifth full-scale test since 1947. The newspaper's microfilm storage room was the basic shelter area.

> Flashing lights and bells in the Tribune switchboard room brought the first warning at 11:04 A.M. When the city sirens sounded the "yellow" alert at 11:07, Miss Margaret Riley, chief telephone operator, pushed a button, sounding the internal horn warning system. Floor wardens, wearing fluorescent colored caps, helped evacuate those of the 3,000 occupants taking part in the drill. Elevators evacuated prescribed floors to the lobby where passengers continued the descent to the shelter by stairways. One employee walked down from the 24th floor to the shelter in seven minutes. . . . Tape recorded messages, followed soon by live broadcasts from the reel room control center, gave advice and warned that "this is a test." In the shelter specialized crews assembled with their medical, demolition, or decontamination equipment. Powered megaphones (bull horns) helped keep the traffic flowing at an even pace, and walkie-talkie radios maintained contact between various evacuation points and the control center.[57]

Telecommunications giant AT&T "maintained 20 key switching centers for DOD's Automatic Voice Network (AUTOVON) in hardened 25-foot-deep underground sites."[58] Like many utility companies, they rehearsed key staff in their emergency

30. Roberts Dairy shelter test, where attendants Dennis A. DeFrain and Arthur Ike Anderson Jr. kept busy caring for their cattle, cooking, making reports by radiotelephone to the civil defense trailer outside, and passing time reading and playing chess and cards. Courtesy of NARA.

roles. In 1963, Western Electric rehearsed forty-two staff, confined in a simulated emergency operating center at Princeton, New Jersey; they coordinated allocations between seventy-seven of its company's locations and government agencies, civil defense units, and telephone companies.

> Life in the shelter was as much like the real thing as possible. Participants lived on canned food (corn beef, beef stew, fruit and brown bread), drank instant tea and coffee or water from the HQ's own emergency water supplies, and slept on cots strewn in the hallways. Oil-run electrical generators powered the air conditioning and lights. Toilet facilities were chemical-filled GI cans. The absence of transistor radios and television confirmed the severance of ties with civilization, but the gray metal desks and swivel chairs looked familiarly like a WE [Western Electric] office.[59]

Six hundred messages were conveyed by teletypewriter, telephone, and shortwave radio during the twenty-four hour exercise, 350 in the first eight hours alone. Plant directors reported hypothetical employee casualties and damage to regional sites. One called in and said "there's not a living soul here." None apart from himself, presumably.

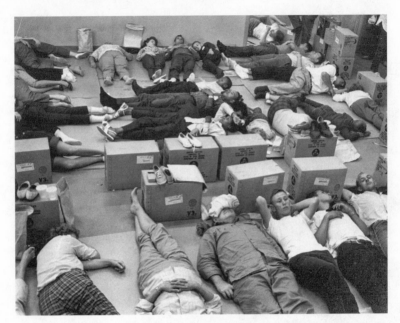

31. Crowded conditions within the University of Georgia's shelter; this test used only standard-issue public shelter supplies, so participants slept on cardboard sheets. Courtesy of NARA.

32. Isometric exercises attempted by participants in a weekend shelter study at the University of Georgia. Courtesy of NARA.

33. Church services during a University of Georgia shelter test. All prayers expressed concern that the stay in the shelter never be "for real." Courtesy of NARA.

Private Sheltering

While some families conducted their own occasional shelter rehearsals, unofficially and unobserved by scientists or the media, others made shelters a permanent fixture of their lives. For a few, this practice lasted as long as owners perceived a threat from missiles. An Arkansas family refitted a cave in 1983, capitalizing on its grand proportions, featuring a waterfall in the living room, and moved in.[60] Donald Hurt, who grew up in rural St. Charles, Missouri, began constructing a backyard bomb shelter with his father in 1956. He started with a sledgehammer, bashing through the basement wall then digging a tunnel using a shovel and five-gallon buckets. The tunnel connected to a 10′ × 8′ × 7′ concrete shelter built to government specifications. After six months of labor it was ready. "The day after construction was done, Dad and Mother moved a reasonable amount of clothing into the shelter, smiled at me and my sister, and were swept into the shelter about 10:00 P.M. every night for about twenty years! That's right, my folks slept in that shelter every night they were at home for the next twenty years! My sister started going to college very soon after the shelter was finished and she was very pleased about that."[61] The federal government's suggested plans for shelters frequently urged dual-use, but never with the prescience of suggesting an extra bedroom and haven from one's own teenagers.

Despite enduring skepticism among the public, the summer of 1961 was the height of the fallout shelter craze, sparked in part by President Kennedy's speech recommending personal shelters and huge appropriations for government spending on civil defense. The president's letter to the people in a September 1961 issue of *Life* magazine, printed over a picture of a mushroom cloud, emphasized the importance of the shelter survey program and his recommendation to Congress that the public shelters be stocked. He urged readers to seriously consider the articles in the rest of the magazine: they featured a test shelter built into a hill in Boise, Idaho, which families owned as shareholders; a prefab shelter distributed by Sears Roebuck erected by a family in Detroit, Michigan, for $700; an ingenious above-ground design in Orlando, Florida, erected next to the patio (the proud owner is shown lounging while his wife tends the garden on the shelter's roof and their children play shuffleboard); a corrugated metal shelter buried in the ground in Amarillo, Texas; a farm in St. Charles, Illinois, where a huge corrugated metal shelter has cattle at one end and the family at the other; and finally a teenager in Vega, Texas, pictured drinking Coca-Cola and talking on the phone in her clubhouse which doubles as the family's backyard shelter.[62] Most of the advertisements in the issue are complementary to shelter life, including first-aid supplies, aspirin, hemorrhoid cream, deodorant, recorded music, books, shelf-stabilized foods (corn flakes, dried milk, soup, Kool-Aid, and Tang), mattresses, cigarettes, alcohol, rifles, construction materials, and a plug from the National Lumber Manufacturers Association cooing about "treasured hours in your den."[63] Numerous advertisements for insurance stand out with impressive irony.

The *Life* issue was just the most prominent example of the media blitz. "From late September through November 1961, hardly a day went by when civil defense was not mentioned on the radio, in the newspapers and magazines," such as *Good Housekeeping* and *Popular Mechanics*, "and on television." In a similar period the previous year, civil defense was mentioned only twice, yet "from July 27, 1961, to the end of the year, civil defense was a major topic of interest. No fewer than twelve NBC-TV shows touched upon civil defense in that five-month period, and shelters became a frequent subject of discussion on the Jack Paar show."[64]

The United States' sense of potency was challenged by the imprisonment of American missionaries in China, the presence of Russian military experts in Cuba, the dispatch of American troops to address the Berlin crisis, and the Soviets' successful launch of Yuri Gagarin into space. A writer for the Peace Research Institute in Washington explained that civil defense

restored to the male his ancient masculine function of protecting the family. This is important in a society in which . . . there is a lack of masculine work. In addition, the role of the father and husband has undergone profound changes in mid-twentieth-century America. Marriages, especially among the educated middle class, are now equal partnerships. The home more resembles a cooperative farm than a man's castle. Civil defense provides useful and masculine work. The father is reinstated as the head of the family fallout shelter. It is he who is depicted in the advertisements and the government pamphlets as the one who builds, stocks, and supervises the shelter.

Civil defense became like a religion, complete with "salvation, redemption, afterlife, and good works." [65] Male adherents could heroically battle an enemy, embody chauvinistic strength, and fight their personal battle against Communism and the infidel. Female adherents could offer comparable gender stereotyped behavior, including maternal reassurance, caregiving, and submission.

After the Berlin Crisis, "Wall Street investors said the shelter trade could gross up to $20 billion in the coming year, *if* there was a coming year." [66] President Kennedy's May 1961 speech set off a frenzy of interest in prefab home shelters. The Peace-O-Mind Shelter Company in Stephenville, Texas, Atlas Bomb Shelter Company in Sacramento, and Chicago's Wonder Building Company were just a few manufacturers. " 'Survival stores' around the country sold air blowers, filters, flashlights, chemical toilets, plastic fall-out-protection suits, first aid kits, food and water." [67] General Mills and General Food marketed dehydrated meals. Piles of used frozen TV dinner trays were washed and stacked for use in shelters. However, the happy portraits of close-knit families did not persuade many Americans to build or equip home shelters. Americans were curious, but seldom matched curiosity with expenditure. It is reported that $938,000 was spent on a bomb shelter at the White House at the outset of the Eisenhower administration, [68] yet even President Eisenhower explained that he would not build a shelter on his Gettysburg, Maryland, farm out of concern that this would alarm his neighbors. A scandal erupted in New York state when the speaker of the state assembly, who had railroaded through legislation on shelters, turned out to be director of a company that made them. [69] Concerns were rife about shelter scams, hucksters who sold prefabs that offered little radiation protection, and fly-by-night companies that did not fulfill contracts to install shelters.

A *Life* cover story in January 1962 raised more skeptical questions about the shelter movement. It included comments by people from many walks of life expressing pro, con, and ambivalent viewpoints. Despite an editorial in favor of mass shelters, and a feature on the seven families in Tewksbury, Massachusetts, who each chipped in $1,000 to build a group shelter, *Life* also quotes Professor Thomas Martin from the University of Arizona who asks what good shelters would be in Tucson, which is ringed by eighteen Titan ICBM sites and a bomber base, for ini-

34. Fallout shelter built by Louis Severance adjacent to his home near Akron, Michigan, includes an entrance to his basement, special ventilation and escape hatch, tiny kitchen, running water, sanitary facilities, and a sleeping and living area for the family of four. The shelter cost about $1,000 and featured a ten-inch reinforced concrete ceiling with thick earth cover and concrete walls. Courtesy of NARA.

tial post-attack radiation likely would be between 20,000 and 100,000 r per hour. Other articles questioned the ability to farm successfully, explained the likely disappearance of forests, and pointed equally to the difficulties of restoring ecosystems and the national economy. This reflects the debate between Herman Kahn and Erich Fromm in *Commentary*.[70]

Performance Art of Endurance and Deprivation

On 30 September 1978, Tehching Hsieh sealed himself into his New York studio for the start of a year-long solitary confinement. He vowed not to converse, read, write, listen to the radio, or watch television for the duration of his confinement. This was a performance art piece, not a shelter exercise, though the similarities and contrasts with respect to isolation and privation are illuminating. The idea of confinement, coupled with deprivation, is ancient and in some traditions the setting for a spiritual quest. Hsieh was not embarking on a spiritual journey through his physical state, any more than participants in civil defense shelter exercises were doing so. Hsieh did not seek to make a metaphoric statement about his condition, only to endure it. Similarly, for shelter dwellers what emerged as knowledge from their confinements was incidental to any metaphoric meaning. Chris Burden imprisoned himself in a school locker for five days, and Lee Lozano based her final work of art on her pledge to refrain from talking with another woman for the rest of her life. The family in the Project Hideaway experiment and the women in the York refuge room agreed to isolation and limited communications for a specified period before emerging to a hail of media attention. The performance art pieces were probably intentional "meditations on the social conditions of isolation, homelessness, alienation, union and bondage" in contemporary life; the shelter exercises only coincidentally so.[71]

When Hsieh tied himself by a rope to Linda Montano, or Montano handcuffed herself to her husband, Tom Marioni, for three days the boundaries of public and private were inherently questioned, for the actions were on display and opened to critical and public commentary. However, like the shelter subjects observed by researchers, there was no inherent meaning in the linkages or even in bonding together individuals. The maintenance of a period of strict confinement—to withdraw into a more private space away from the everyday world—became for the shelter dwellers as well as the performance artists an ethical act. With the act came obligations created out of expectations: just as performance artist Chris Burden's invitation to witness himself being shot "established an obligation, or at least an expectation, that he would do something, for or with a group of people," a shelter inhabitation—even without media attention—blurred privacy with intimacy, seclusion with overt display, the researchers in such cases functioning as audience and expecting the shelterees to stay the course.[72] Hsieh, Montano, Marioni, and Burden were challenged by their circumstances, as the shelter dwellers were, and what arose from these challenges became in one case art and in the other case data. While the performance events had no aspirations to be social science, the shelter exercises do have provocative overlaps with performance art.[73]

Consider the projects of performance artist Stelarc, who is famous for threading metal hooks through his body and suspending himself, naked, in precarious positions. "Such a body, rhetorically defined as *only* an object to be controlled and manipulated" requires spectators to perceive its pain. This is its cultural power, "to provoke new ways of thinking about embodiment and subjectivity." There is no ostensible political content in this, only a demonstration of spectators' own surprise as a result of having their expectations challenged.[74] Vito Acconci's "Seed Bed" involved the "audience" walking up a ramp and speaking into a microphone; they were heard by the performance artist who was sealed under the ramp where he masturbated and ejaculated continuously for many days. Unlike sideshow acts—fire-eaters, glass chewers, or the blockheads who hammer nails through their tongues and into their skulls—there is no question about illusion or trickery. The feats in performance art are as authentic as they are ephemeral. For shelterees enduring excessive heat and humidity, unpalatable rations, cramped conditions, or psychotic neighbors there was also genuine discomfort and risk.

Another conceptual artist, Marina Abramovic, dwelt in three platforms/boxes affixed to the wall of a gallery without eating or speaking for twelve days beginning 15 November 2002. Spectators, who agreed not to speak or pass beyond a white line on the floor, observed her through a high-powered telescope. Abramovic's only way out of the platform/boxes was by falling or scaling the ladders whose rungs were constructed of butcher-block knives. Her vigil of "purification" corresponds to shelter-dwellers' vigils of isolation from a (hypothetically) radioactive world. The perilousness of Abramovic's ladders corresponds to the air locks and passageways between everyday life and shelter spaces, though in this case the space of confinement and person experiencing privation are in plain view, open to scrutiny like a proscenium stage.[75] One critic calls this Abramovic's "performative technique of 'living immobility' . . . a question of will and commitment" to the act itself, directing attention to both "interior awareness and into the exhibition space." Such live tableaux became a feature of experimental art in the 1970s and 1980s.[76] Like the shelter exercises, they "realize" bodily and social experience in a different way than everyday life. They call into question the principles governing these finite worlds and their bearing on the world at large.

For many Westerners, during the Cold War fallout shelters were imagined spaces, made concrete through the publicity surrounding a few exercises and the iconic popular culture function assigned to them. Given the tiny rates of shelter construction, relatively few Americans and even fewer Canadians and Britons could have ever been in one. In a sense, the occupancy exercises were symbolic public actions, demonstrating that shelters were livable and challenging the idea that they were merely tombs for those who plan ahead. Richard Schechner typifies performance art of the 1960s through the 1980s as embracing liminoid spaces for political-celebratory-ritual purposes. "It is most theatrical," he argues, "at the cusp where the street show meets the media, where events are staged for the camera."[77] Less so than the flamboyant street displays which he calls "direct theatre," these smaller-scale events share a ritualized ambiance. They are not willful death rituals—in contrast to performance artist Qi Li's *Ice Burial* in which he endeavored to lie naked on a block of ice until he succumbed to hypothermia[78]—but in a paradoxical sense assertions of life.

More like the first inhabitants of Biosphere 2, who planned to hermetically seal themselves into the Arizonan structure for two years, or later interpreters of this act who declared it a "living art form" and created time-based performances about it, the civil defense shelter dwellers made statements about experiencing time and space in a way inseparable from ecology and adaptive habitat.[79] Social action and cultural expression reverberate off each other, or merge. As long as the boundaries of what was "real life" and what was "exercise" (or "performance") were maintained, the events were comprehensible to artists and audiences, subjects and researchers.[80]

Site-specific performance may involve artificial barriers restricting movement, explicit rules imposed by site controllers, and behavior organized by tacit or communal agreement. This affects both the enactors who stay in the site and the spectators (including those who spectate in person, via the media, and as researchers) who agree to observe conventions about the integrity of the site and those performing within it. To the extent that shelter exercises were humane, sane, or culturally countenanced to have utility and relevance, the same can be said of them.[81]

As David Blaine continues to demonstrate when viewed in a glass coffin, encased in ice, suspended in a Plexiglas box above the Thames, or "drowned alive" for a week in a sphere, public witness to endurance affirms both the performer's authentic feat and the collective experience of marvel. And yet Blaine's invariable need for hospitalization following his performances also affirms the physical consequences of privation and constriction. Cold War shelter rehearsals are variations on this theme, substituting extremes of "what if" for performance's extremes of actuality, concentrating instead on confinement and group dynamics under stress and their intersections.

GET OUT OF TOWN!

The only alternatives that I can see for our great cities in the United States
are to dig, die, or get out.

— Val Peterson

A spectacular form of theater, involving streets as conduits
of escape, was staged in Britain, Canada, and the United
States at scattered intervals in the 1950s. As with shelter exercises,
the greatest amount of research and rehearsal via these population dispersals occurred in the United States; however, the scripting for such events is highly uniform and the characteristics of
the rehearsals are altered not so much by national idiosyncrasy
as geographic variance and transportation infrastructure. Land-
locked cities generally provided a spoke pattern of arterial escapes.
Cities in mountainous regions have proscribed alternatives for
egress that usually rely solely on road, not rail, routes. Cities by the
sea or large lakes must disallow at least one direction for dispersal.
In all cases, the direction of prevailing winds, and thus the expected movement of fallout, makes some directions less desirable
than others. The quality of roads, access to vehicles, and proximity
of other population centers varies the rate at which the dispersal can take place. If the dispersing public is to be processed by
welfare centers and moved to temporary housing in the receiving
communities, evacuation planning—and thus its rehearsal—ne-
cessitates a second phase.

Evacuation as Street Theater

The precedents for evacuation exercises were from wartime Britain. In advance of World War II, the Air Raid Precautions service executed evacuation plans for major British cities. Nearly 3.75 million people in priority classes—children, mothers of young children, pregnant women, the elderly or infirm, and teachers or helpers—were relocated in 1939. They trickled out of cities during the summer in self-instigated evacuations, but when the official evacuation commenced by train and boat on 1 September, almost 1.5 million were moved within three days. This was a selective "tactical evacuation," immediately preceding the expected onset of aerial bombing; in a nuclear scenario this would have to be accomplished in at most a few hours. With selective tactical evacuation, most workers remained close to their jobs; the idea was to spare the lives of persons not contributing to war production, especially the young. During the Cold War, the British maintained and updated the plans they had executed in 1939–45 for the removal of selected groups from vulnerable cities to the countryside and to Ireland. Canada and the United States, in contrast, expected to disperse all types of citizens if a tactical evacuation was ordered.

Many Canadian cities drew up evacuation plans in the early 1950s, but only a few ever tried them out.[1] Five months of planning for Calgary's "Operation Lifesaver" culminated in a trial evacuation of a portion of the city in September 1955; this case study is typical of the local logistics for evacuation exercises.[2] Calgary, the largest city in southern Alberta, was a strategic center for the administration of oil and gas production, but not its refining; an important center for wheat distribution and meat packing; and the Canadian gateway to rail traffic through the Rockies. In the 1950s, it was considered a secondary nuclear target and it was not until the TOCSIN exercise in 1960 that it emerged as a primary target, designated to receive a 5 MT direct hit.

In Operation Lifesaver, the civil defense subdivision "B," straddling Center Street north of the Bow River, was to be evacuated. One hundred and twenty wardens canvased practically every household in the area—presenting themselves as "guide, philosopher, and friend"—aided by Boy Scouts who urged everyone to "Be Prepared." All households were notified of their destination and route, and since Calgary had an exceptionally high number of automobiles per capita, evacuation was to take place by car. The twenty-first of September 1955 was to begin like any other Wednesday for workers, parents, and schoolchildren: all except civil defense personnel, who were to be at their posts by 09:30. No one knew exactly when the exercise would commence, and thus when they were to re-gather at home or at the collecting points for movement out of the city. House-holders were to match the color of the posted evacuation route signs to the color of the ticket provided for their car's dashboard to find their appropriate route out of town.

The plans were foiled by the Canadian climate, for in the hours before the exercise was to begin "a heavy snow fell in Calgary and surrounding districts." In the night, civil defense organizations in reception towns assumed the evacuation would proceed, and prepared to billet evacuees who might not be able to return to Calgary during the storm. But "at 9:30 A.M. the following morning with blizzard conditions prevailing, it was decided to postpone the Exercise for one week."[3] Instead of hosting Calgarians on a day out, Strathmore civil defense workers took in 100 travelers stormbound on the Number 1 Highway.

A week later, Operation Lifesaver was executed on a cold, windy, rainy, and sleet-filled day. The warning was sent from the province's capital, Edmonton, by telephone at 10:32, and Calgary's sirens sounded at 10:50. There were more volunteer cars and drivers than needed, and the RCMP force of thirty-two officers, plus forty-three civil defense auxiliary police, who stayed in the neighborhood to prevent looting, patrolled without incident. The auxiliary fire service made coffee and sandwiches, the Amateur Radio Association lent equipment to report on traffic flow, and a staff of thirty-two plotted communications and transport information. Among the visitors to the main operations center in City Hall were Alberta's lieutenant-governor and premier.

Meanwhile, traffic control was handled by 166 persons in twenty-three vehicles. Pedestrians moved to assembly points in an orderly fashion, and 90 percent of vehicles had passed the city limits within an hour of the alert, proceeding at 40 to 60 mph on main highways, with 1,200 vehicles passing any given point each hour. Officials estimated that fifteen to twenty times more traffic could have successfully exited, but other studies suggest this was grossly optimistic.[4] At 15:03 the "all clear" sounded and the evacuees returned home. While deemed a success, Operation Lifesaver also revealed that the warning sirens could not be heard in many areas, either indoors or outdoors, cross-traffic needed to be minimized, and uniting of families had to occur before departure if it was to happen at all. This set the agenda for subsequent planning.

Alberta's civil defense was comparatively advanced, yet as an isodemographic map of Canada correlating population distribution to area illustrates, the preponderance of the population was not in the prairie provinces, and so greater challenges for evacuating fell elsewhere (figure 35). Vancouver, tightly sandwiched between the Rocky Mountains and the Pacific Ocean, could evacuate some resi-

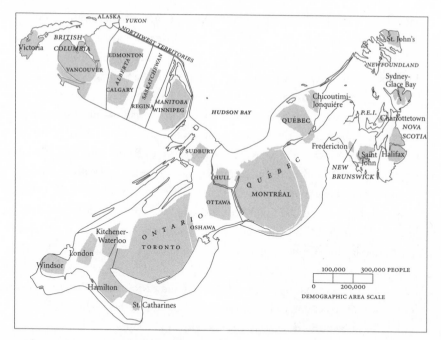

35. Isodemographic map of Canada, based on the 1966 Census. By correlating size of population to area, the nation's actual geographic contours are severely distorted. Courtesy of the School of Community and Regional Planning, University of British Columbia.

dents into the Fraser Valley, but most would have to go south into Washington state. Evacuation of Montreal, penned by the Laurentian Mountains to the north and with the U.S. border just thirty miles to the south, would be complicated especially since many escape routes depended on bridges across the wide St. Lawrence River that bisects the city and surrounds its islands. The greatest challenge of all lay in southern Ontario, the industrial heartland and most densely populated area of the nation. Ontario contains 11 percent of Canada's land mass but 34 percent of its population; the "golden triangle" in the province's southern portion squeezes 88 percent of these people into 12 percent of the province's total area, so one large center after another competed for rural areas into which people could retreat. Toronto, the most populous city, is located on the north shore of Lake Ontario. Some Torontonians could go north, toward the Muskoka district of lakeland cottages. A band of farmland to the east provided many egress, though downstream along the St. Lawrence River they would encounter evacuees from other prime targets, particularly after completion of the St. Lawrence Seaway in 1959. The greatest area of accessible land with an extensive road network lay to the southwest of Toronto, but here travelers would compete with evacuees from

Hamilton, Kitchener-Waterloo, London, Niagara (St. Catharines), and Windsor, squeezing between the area bounded by Lake Erie and Lake Huron. The only other egress from Toronto was toward Detroit or across the Niagara River toward Buffalo, both assumed to be first strike priorities for the Soviets.

In 1956, the Department of National Defence (DND) determined criteria for evacuating Ontario. Destinations were to be no more than 100 miles from target centers (five hours slow driving), and numbers of evacuees should not far exceed the population of reception areas. This was based on a British formula for building occupancy: "the British wartime evacuation scheme . . . was based on one person per habitable room for England and Wales, and one person over 14 years of age or two persons under 14 for Scotland. The assumption made here is closely in line with the Scottish policy since the person/room ratio among the resident population in the reception areas in Ontario is about 0.6, and about 27% of the population is under 14."[5] At the time, 30 percent of homes outside cities did not have telephones but 93 percent did have radios. Most rural residents would hear in advance, therefore, what was about to descend on them. It would be their responsibility to bury the expected 35,000 radiation fatalities.[6]

Voluntary dispersal was the official federal policy as early as 1957.[7] By 1959, Victoria, Vancouver, Calgary, Edmonton, Winnipeg, Toronto, Windsor, St. John, and Halifax had plans for evacuation. Hamilton, Niagara, and Montreal had studied the problem. Cities issuing instructions to the public included Victoria, Vancouver, Edmonton, Windsor, Quebec City, Montreal, St. John, and Halifax. Winnipeg went the furthest, issuing instructions to groups through its Block Officer Plan, and publishing assembly areas and evacuation routes in the telephone directory.[8] The federal government's 1956 plan clearly stipulates a policy based "on the development and testing of plans for the orderly evacuation on short notice of the main urban areas in Canada should the possibility of attack on such areas by nuclear weapons appear to be imminent," but the tests did not materialize.[9] Despite all this planning, no other large-scale evacuations from Canadian centers are documented following Calgary's Operation Lifesaver.[10] In 1961, as part of the TOCSIN B exercise, Charlottetown, P.E.I.'s evacuation plan was implemented but it was "literally carried out by a few selected families in an attempt to check its workability."[11] Canadian civil defense planners continued to game evacuations, but the public did not take part.[12]

Early planning focused on authorized evacuation, but by 1962 "changing methods of nuclear attack indicated the advisability of dispensing with Planned Evacuation of the Civilian Population" and instead recognized that people may spontaneously disperse in response to international tensions.[13] Fourteen 100-mile evacuation routes out of Toronto were determined, and officials planned to mark them with arrows and the yellow letters "EMO" (for Emergency Management Organization) on a blue background. Plans were also drawn up for Ottawa-area evacuation routes, but no markings were ever posted. Given that it would take sixteen hours to evacuate 600,000 vehicles out of Toronto on routes converted to one-way traffic, lives could only be spared in southern Ontario if road conditions were optimal and if the public did not wait until attack was imminent.[14]

In Britain, spontaneous evacuation was a serious concern. Officials were confident that it would occur, as the Labour MP for Coventry East observed in 1954, "there will be a mass trek out of the industrial areas. . . . From Coventry 100,000 people went away from the city on the night of the great raid [in 1940] and lay in the fields outside," and they would do so again.[15] This might spare them from blast effects but not radiation. If there was a period of tension building up to a nuclear exchange, Britain also anticipated being inundated with refugees from the Continent, compounding provision of welfare services for evacuees.[16]

The number of British evacuees out of London, eastern, and southeastern counties (roughly everything south of the Humber and east of the Severn) would make this area off-limits for reception of further evacuees.[17] The task of keeping areas needed for military purposes clear of excess civilians—at land bases, ports, and along traffic corridors—was a tremendous logistical challenge. Once bombing occurred, the best-laid plans would be overturned as a result of the specific attack pattern. An attack scenario from 1951 assumed twenty A-bombs and 40,000 tons of conventional explosives: this would result in 3.25 million homeless, almost half of whom would find no room in rest centers.[18] After 1954, when massive attack from H-bombs was expected, fallout was kept out of the equation in exercises because the government felt it should not "impress upon the public the dangers of thermo-nuclear war *until it can also tell them what measures to take against it.*"[19] Like continental NATO nations, the British recommended that the best policy for civilians was to "stay put." Of course, this would increase civilian casualties from blast as well as fallout but it would significantly ease military maneuvers and the routing of suddenly rare supplies to the fighting forces. In the early 1960s, the British government recommended staying put in combination with sandbagging homes' most vulnerable areas, calculating the number of sandbags needed to be around 3.4 billion but never stockpiling bags or explaining where the sand would come from.[20]

British civil defense personnel gained a lot of practice with theoretical clearance of Z-zones. "Exercise Review" in 1955, predicated upon two 10 MT H-bombs over Merseyside and Clydeside, looked at the problems that would occur over a 7,600-square-mile area. "Exercise Zeta" in April/May 1957 studied the problems arising in clearing the Z-zone surrounding Sheffield following an H-bomb attack.[21] Starting in the late 1950s, this theoretical knowledge was tested in practical exercises. In May 1959, "Exodus I" prepared to move two thousand evacuees from several Staffordshire towns in buses and army lorries. A thunderstorm immediately before the exercise is credited with lowering turnout, but it is also likely that door-to-door leafleting by the Campaign for Nuclear Disarmament (CND), calling civil defense "Civil Deception," also turned off some volunteers who had signed up. The exercise assumed the detonation of nuclear weapons in Lancashire fifty hours earlier. Evacuees were fed a lunch at Kidsgrove Town Hall and a boys' secondary school, shown a civil defense film, then a western, and taken home.[22] In contrast, "Exodus II," the following March, hypothetically cleared 7,400 from Herefordshire and Worcestershire but relied on a household register to evaluate need instead of incorporating live bodies. The variables tested here were aspects of the police and army's control of convoys.[23] Exercise "Clearsite" in October 1960 focused on the need to remove thirty thousand people from Stratford-upon-Avon, but rehearsed the practical part of the operation only symbolically by using two coaches for evacuees.[24]

"Zedroad," a standard exercise developed in 1961 and restaged in many locales until 1965, focused on clearance of a Z-zone by road but did not actually move the public. Cards, symbolic of people, were moved instead. The parts of drivers and their assistants in clearance vehicles were played by members of the Rescue and Ambulance and First Aid sections of the Civil Defence Corps in order to help familiarize them with clearance plans, directions of traffic, and convoy work. In all, fewer than two hundred participated. Token cards were collected from warden posts—actual homes, garages, or sheds—then taken to assembly areas outside the town. Wardens were advised to use bicycles among the twenty-five convoy vehicles to try to *simulate* the size of buses. Cars were used for messenger traffic, directing staff and umpires; motorbikes for dispatch riders; and Land Rovers for posting parties.[25] Exercise "Maybee," in 1960, involved the movement of five convoys (279 vehicles) by day and night through East Anglia.[26]

A small-scale exercise conducted near Hastings on 8 April 1962 attempted a local evacuation with live "evacuees." The entire coast of East Sussex, along the southern perimeter of Great Britain, was designated a Z-zone requiring clearance. Civil Defence Group 122 practiced road movement from assembly areas to the entraining station for convoys carrying "homeless" away from the Z-zone. This was coordinated with transport along the railway from Sheffield Park to Horsted Keynes (a distance of 4.5 miles), sending the evacuees on a half-mile walk from the detraining to the embussing point; coordinating eighty-five single-decker coaches and ten double-decker omnibuses between the embussing point and thirty-two rest centers staffed by Civil Defence Corps members from East Grinstead, Uckfield, Lewes and Chailey, and Burgess Hill and Cuckfield; providing emergency feeding at the rest centers; and marshaling and billeting the homeless for dispatch by road to symbolic host accommodations (actually, they were delivered back to their own homes). Called "Operation Bluebell" in honor of the vintage 1880 and 1882 locomotives that transported the homeless in five train loads, the exercise conformed to East Sussex County Council's "Homeless Movement Control (Provision)" issued in November 1961.

Bluebell was conducted on a cold day with outbreaks of heavy rain and gale force gusts. The 3,145 people who were moved included parties from old people's homes, family groups with children, and teens from youth organizations. There were forty-seven umpires and an untold number of spectators, whose cars choked the areas around rest centers. Parties of spectators, each accompanied by a guide, toured the area, learning about civil defense planning. The event was covered by national papers, BBC and ITV networks, and filmed by the Rank Organization, which toured the area in a forty-seat coach.[27]

While these exercises did not fully engage the problems that might arise from the public's involvement, they did sometimes get down to the nitty-gritty of practical logistics. In the Zedroad exercise conducted in Hornchurch in 1963, for example, debriefed participants asked how households without radios would know what zone they were in and what to do. Should wardens compiling household registers record whether or not homes have radios? Or should anyone without a radio make a point of visiting their home once a day during the shelter period to check for messages put through the letter box? What luggage will Z-zone evacuees be allowed? The new handbook "Advising the Householder on Protection Against Nuclear Attack" stipulated that evacuees would be allowed one suitcase each, but interpretation of this varied from "a 'gypsy's bundle' which will not even go through the door of a bus and a couple of large traveling trunks for a family of six as opposed to six suitcases." And what about pets? "It is understood they are not to be taken by Z-zone evacuees. Are they to be left behind whilst still alive and if so, are they to be left shut up in houses to starve to death or turned loose? What is the alternative? What is to be done about householders who refuse to leave without their pets?"[28] These unsettling questions did not all receive reassuring answers.

The purpose of testing evacuation plans was, in part, to find out if they were feasible. But part of the feasibility lay in how the public responded. As with shelter exercises, simulating the emotional valences of a real evacuation would be unethical and perhaps impossible, given that lives and property could be endangered. Without the emotional component, even Bluebell was more like a Sunday outing than a war-like simulation. Peter Watkins' film *The Journey* documents a Norwegian family living near a NATO base forcibly evacuated during a drill; they experienced tension while preparing to depart but especially when traffic clogged and no alternate routes were available due to the mountainous topography.[29] But this is not the sense that comes through in earlier American tests. A paper study of Milwaukee did projections for ideal evacuation in the dark, at night during foul weather, and by day under various conditions.[30] This was all predicated on perfect human as well as vehicle performance, even though in the early 1960s cars were expected to break down approximately once in every ten thousand miles traveled.[31]

In 1954, the National Academy of Sciences and National Research Council's Committee on Disaster Studies reported on three evacuation exercises conducted by the FCDA. The first, "Operation Walk Out," was staged in Spokane on 26 April 1954. The event had been heavily advertised through newspapers, radio, television, posters, and handbills. At 10:00 on Monday morning, with just fifty minutes warning, a simulated 50 KT bomb detonated over the central business district. During the intervening fifty minutes, the working population of fifty square blocks was to be evacuated without the use of private vehicles or public transit. Schools did not participate. People in residential areas were asked to draw their blinds, stay indoors, check their food supplies, and note potential hazards.

That day, only about half of the usual population was present in downtown Spokane, even though the press had encouraged people to "come to town to see the show."[32] Morning shoppers delayed their excursions. "At 10 A.M., to simulate an attack, a bomber dropped leaflets over the city, saying 'this might have been an H-bomb.'" But the bomber missed the central area and instead leafleted an outlying residential district. Nevertheless, the central area, where there were eleven thousand people, was substantially evacuated in twelve minutes. The emergency plan was for buses to meet people in designated areas and take them away. It is questionable whether the city had enough buses to move even 10 percent of the numbers amassing in the rehearsal, but this was not acknowledged as a problem. Police and auxiliary police patrolled the streets, and "to dramatize the civil defense exercise, National Guardsmen were posted at street corners; emergency civil defense and military vehicles moved on the streets; anti-aircraft and machine gunners fired their weapons from the roof tops of several buildings; jet fighter planes and bombers flew over the air" and control centers and aid stations were staffed, which pedestrians said "contributed to the apparent seriousness of the situation." The evacuation was orderly, but not necessarily realistic. Various participants, asked what they would do in an actual attack, said "I would high-tail it home, grab my family and get out quick," "Run like Hell," or perhaps the most honest of all, "I don't really know." [33]

The predominantly white and middle-class participants in downtown Spokane were perhaps the normative idea of who civil defense was designed to protect, but it was not the reality of who was imperiled. Inner-city residents were disproportionately poor and from minority groups. "Operation Scat" was conducted in Mobile, Ala., in 1954 specifically to test what would happen when a business district, wharf area, heavy industrial area, and an old inner-city neighborhood were evacuated. The area was predominantly inhabited by African Americans of limited means, though there were also 23,000 to 28,000 white residents and about 22,000 non-resident workers in the designated zone. Mobile was considered vulnerable to attack by bombers stationed in Communist Guatemala or elsewhere in Latin America, from aircraft carriers in the Gulf of Mexico, and from submarines sneaking into Mobile Bay. The presence of the Aluminum Company of America and an air force base contributed to its vulnerability. Egress from the evacuated zone is complicated by water toward the south and east.

The National Academy of Sciences and National Research Council sent a flock of ethnographers to the site to observe and interview people during the day of the exercise, hoping to discover what would succeed in getting the important message of evacuation to the population and, especially, to motivate African Americans to participate. The media was saturated with the news well in advance, and the local paper had carried an article on the topic every day for thirty days. Radio and television stations broadcast spot announcements. Despite all this, a large portion of the population was not reached because, as the ethnographers discovered, relatively few African Americans read the newspaper, not all had radios, and even fewer had televisions. Their participation was in doubt.

Organizers were ineffective in reaching appropriate members of the black community who could have provided leadership in the run-up to the evacuation: all the civil defense officials at a briefing the morning of the exercise were white, strongly representing contingents from the chamber of commerce. A rumor that an actual bomb would be dropped so that schools would not have to be desegregated attests to the level of distrust among the black community. At least one elderly African American man was convinced that a bomb would be dropped, and was concerned because he was sick and could not evacuate. Ethnographers recorded that "one Negro woman about 50 years old was observed walking down the evacuation street with two suitcases and a market bag. A young Negro couple stopped and picked her up. They were much amused at her. She said that she 'didn't want to get hit by that bomb.' A filling station operator on Davis Street said people had been leaving since daybreak, a good many taking all their personal possessions."[34] A taxi driver reported he had had a busy morning taking people to the bus station and outlying towns. A Greyhound bus leaving at 15:00 was packed. Other people, less certain of what hand-delivered mimeographed sheets of instructions meant, had "a certain amount of vague, unidentified fear" of what was taking place.[35] Many of the forty thousand African American residents from the inner city area had not left Mobile in nine or ten years and some businesses had never closed before and did not even have locks on their doors.

Despite the lack of black leadership, the majority of the population complied with the evacuation order, either by leaving earlier in the day or when the siren sounded just before 17:00. One of the participant observer researchers reported:

> About ten minutes before the air raid sounded there was a rush in the street. People started to come out of the offices. There was a certain amount of tension on the street. The traffic began to speed up, horns began to honk as if expressing a certain amount of irritability. I noticed two men, who probably were in the upper income bracket, come out to their cars, sit in their cars and wait until the alarm was sounded before they left, in an attempt to completely comply with the regulations of the practice air raid.[36]

Lower-middle-class workers, for the most part, complied with the late-afternoon evacuation. Clerks and office workers "seemed to be well informed on the reason for conforming—'so people would fall into the pattern they had rehearsed in case of actual attack.'" Many citizens were proud that Mobile had been chosen for the exercise—that it was important enough to be a target—and so took the exercise seriously and considered it worthwhile. One bookkeeper, asked whether the exercise would do any good, explained: "Well, maybe not if it were a real air raid, and then on the other hand, after the first few moments of panic maybe the people would fall into the pattern that they had rehearsed."[37] A department store clerk, however, expected a different outcome: "No, if it were real there would be panic. This wouldn't do any good at all. . . . I think they are trying to scare people into a war. Russia would like to see us panic. And this sort of thing makes you think that they know something that we don't. Kind of scares you a bit."[38] A white laborer was tempted to lie in bed reading but came along at the last minute. He told the researcher that the exercise was not a good idea, "that in case of a real attack there would be panic of all sorts, people would be injured more trying to get out of town than if they just sat tight and tried to get protection."[39] A young waitress knew to walk north and west, but could not point the interviewer to the routes or explain why those were the appropriate directions, though she was cheerful and helpful. Despite being well-represented among the event's planners, the professional class was subversive of the intent and uncooperative in the exercise itself. Physicians and lawyers closed their offices early. A judge was reported having said at a cocktail party a week earlier, "I wouldn't state this publicly, but we are among friends. My advice is for you all to do what I plan to do. Go home for lunch and stay there."[40]

Willingness aside, people's success in evacuating could depend on their race. A researcher walked six blocks and waited for a bus that never came before being picked up by a secretary and her husband, a lawyer, who had also collected an elevator operator and a newspaper boy. Though the secretary noted and complained that African Americans were not being picked up, everyone in her car was white. Black drivers were also observed passing by African American pedestrians. A police officer was asked whether white people would pick up African Americans in a real raid and, after expressing strong support for segregation, stated that if he observed that a black man had no chance of being picked up by any African Americans, he would give him a ride to save his life. The researcher got a clear impression from this that whites would always be given priority, or as the historian Laura McEnaney put it, "Jim Crow would survive a nuclear attack."[41] People who could get a ride on a bus were jammed together at twice the seating capacity. Despite this, segregated groups of evacuees waiting at the perimeter points for the signal to return were stalwart and positive. Even parents evacuating with eight to ten children were confident that leaving was the right thing to do.

One researcher summed up the views of citizens he encountered after the exercise: "It was interesting to see the opinions broken down class wise. Lower middle class a little suspicious, somebody else knew more than they did. Middle class real involved, and proud of the fact that Mobile might be hit. The professionals uninvolved, too much trouble, let other people do it."[42] As a café manager said, " 'if they want heavy traffic, then it is my job to be a part of it,' to which a manager of a finance company heartily agreed."[43] There was, in fact, a high degree of compliance from African Americans. As a researcher reported, "even one 'wine head' who came up to bum a cigarette said, 'If I had one more drink I'd go over and crawl under a house and play like a possum, but I guess they'd arrest me and throw me in jail so I might as well get on out.' "[44] An African American longshoreman, waiting with his wife and four children to return to town, was asked if he thought the exercise worthwhile: "He was very serious and a little alarmed that I would even raise such a question. He pointed out that you can never tell when 'they' would come and drop a bomb on you so you had to be prepared." [45]

One researcher concluded that though there was a high rate of participation and the exercise went smoothly (apart from the inadequate provision of buses and no attention to the problem of transporting people back into town), Scat was not indicative of how people would behave in a real emergency. More people would try to reach their families, or just seek shelter nearby when the alert sounded. The sirens were barely audible to many, and if they sounded without warning it was unlikely that everyone would heed them. This calls into question the viability of any evacuation except spontaneous dispersal.

"Operation Rideout," conducted on 24 June 1954 in Bremerton, Washington, a naval port on Puget Sound, also involved an evacuation by automobile, though it focused on a smaller population scattered over a larger area. Populations of 28,000 in the city and 40,000 in the urbanized area of fifteen square miles were to be evacuated. At 15:00 the police, state patrol, buses, medical, and communications personnel received the yellow warning alert. At 16:15 all incoming traffic toward Bremerton stopped. Dispersal began at 16:30 prior to the red alert at 17:00 and simulated bombing over the shipyard at 17:50. Evacuation maps for cars and ferries were published in the newspapers and Navy Yard bulletins, there was publicity on radio and television, and all roads were marked. More than two thousand cars and about fifty buses took part from Bremerton. A total of 9,559 pedestrians and 1,080 cars from the Navy Ship Repair Station were evacuated in twenty-two minutes.

Organizers were severely disappointed by the participation rate. "The merchants and business people were willing to withstand the loss of a low volume of business on the afternoon of the exercise, and were willing to close early. The remainder of the population, which was subject only to minor inconvenience and an automobile ride . . . did not participate to a marked degree." It was clear, in this case, which segments of the population were cooperative. Yet there was no doubt that such tactics were useful: "One secondary implication here might be that mass participation is not a successful means of conducting Civil Defense exercises"; however, it was deemed better to inform a public that does not comply than to have a public wholly ignorant when an emergency arises. [46]

Another exercise on 23 November 1954 involved evacuation of 25,000 people from offices in a twenty-block area of central Philadelphia. The public was instructed to walk to a distribution point about a half mile from the district. To avoid early walk outs, the timing of the exercise was not pre-announced, only that it would occur between 09:15 and noon. [47] In 1955, another exercise was held in Houston, involving evacuation of 175,000 people from the downtown area by car, bus, taxis, motorcycles, rail and marine transport over twenty-two routes.[48] This type of tactical evacuation, predicated on fairly low-yield bombs and focusing on moving people quickly to the periphery of likely target areas, was obsolete by the mid-1950s. The destructive power of new weaponry necessitated serious rethinking about the nature of preparations and the feasibility of evacuation.

As problems were reconceived, or newly recognized, planning took new forms. A detailed 1956 study of Washington, D.C., estimated that of the 1,677,000 people in the metropolitan area, only 330,000 might be expected to survive blast and thermal radiation, but even they would require medical attention. Taking into account other critical targets in a seven-state area (including New York City, Trenton, Scranton, Wilkes-Barre, Harrisburg, Lancaster, York, Wheeling-Steubenville, Pittsburgh, Johnstown-Altoona, Philadelphia, Allentown-Bethlehem, Reading, Baltimore, Wilmington, and Norfolk-Hampton) whose radiation plumes would effect potential evacuation routes, meant that the only feasible routes would be into northern and central Virginia. This was not a matter of walking a few blocks but moving approximately thirty miles from the Capitol. There would be severe damage to homes within twelve miles of GZ, and trees within six to eleven miles would block roads. All the Potomac River bridges within four miles of GZ would be down, and so the river would be an evacuation barrier for anyone fleeing the District of Columbia or Maryland for Virginia. Within eight miles of GZ, an area of high residual radiation, people would need rescue from basements where houses had collapsed and then transport to replace their destroyed cars. If two bombs detonated in the capital region — say, one downtown and the other in the northeastern part of the District of Columbia — all trees would be downed from Alexandria to Bethesda, and some as far as Falls Church and the Beltsville Research Center. Clearing these trees was essential to moving people out, yet would consume a lot of time and expose many workers to radiation. The solution? "Consideration should be given to replacing trees with smaller shrubs. Dual-lane highways with a grass strip provide the best access routes. Superhighways should have detouring facilities for destroyed overpasses."[49] One response was the Interstate Highway Act of 1956, to provide easier access between city centers and suburbs, and easier egress in case of nuclear attack.[50]

Preemptive attack gave no chance for tactical evacuation to succeed. However, thinking of evacuation in more strategic terms, and pushing dispersal backward in the time line to a point earlier in the period of rising tension, could give many a chance to escape the worst effects of the attacks. A computer model investigating evacuation of the New York City conurbation in the late 1970s concluded that with slightly more than three days' warning, 2 million cars with full fuel tanks and perfectly operating engines could carry more than half the 11.3 million population from 3.8 million households. The remaining 4.81 million without cars could be relocated by water, rail, bus, and air, "an effort that will require the use of 50 percent of the nation's inventory of Boeing 747s and 75 percent of the DC-10s and L-1011s, assuming twenty hours per day of plane use with 20 percent overloading," ferrying passengers as far away as Buffalo.[51]

In the 1970s, Americans began to seriously investigate these problems under the auspices of CRP. In the first phase of experimentation with CRP, "we took people from Birmingham, New York out to the little city of Deposit . . . and tried to get them into a shelter, right away into a private shelter. This worked well, and the people received them out there. . . . [but] There is not enough motivation in the country now in civil defence preparedness to try these kinds of exercises."[52] Unless actors are willing, rehearsal cannot proceed. Consequently, CRP planning was usually tested in tabletop exercises among civil servants rather than as public exercises (for more detailed discussion, see chapter 12).

Civil Defense as Lifestyle

By the early 1970s, the political situation suggested that "surprise" attack was unlikely, and instead a period of tension—possibly of several months' duration—would precede any nuclear war. Emergency planners adjusted their advice accordingly, and in the United States CRP was the most significant result. Two documented rehearsals of expedient shelter building demonstrate the techniques that remained for anyone who was not encompassed by CRP, was unwilling to relocate, or was determined to be resourceful with materials at hand, as well as those creating expedient shelters in CRP host areas.[53] These are essentially the same kinds of options that existed for Britons living in mobile trailers or one-storey homes without basements. The Soviet government offered similar advice to many of its citizens. As Thomas K. Jones, a Reagan appointee who studied Soviet civil defense, quipped: "Everybody's going to make it if there are enough shovels to go around."[54]

One rehearsal involved the family of F. LeRoy Hoffner. Under the auspices of research funded by the Defense Civil Preparedness Agency (DCPA) and sponsored by the University of Colorado, they built an expedient shelter near their home in Mechanicsburg, Pennsylvania. First, they excavated a trench several yards in length and deep enough for the adults to stand in at about chest height. They laid wooden doors side-by-side across the opening, stretched plastic sheeting across

36. Expedient backyard trench shelter being excavated at home by Mr. and Mrs. LeRoy Hoffner, son Michael, 16, and daughter Kathleen, 14, near Mechanicsburg, Pennsylvania. Doors are placed over the trench. Courtesy of NARA.

the doors, then layered the excavated dirt on the plastic. Lengths of plastic protruding at each end of the trench, held in place by sandbags, were tented to provide ventilation and egress. The Hoffners demonstrated that a family of four, including two healthy teenaged children, could complete the shelter in a day and huddle inside without benefit of extensive amenities. Being below ground level, the shelter offered significant protection from a shock wave and counter-wave, but its radiation protection depended on the depth of the dirt piled on the plastic sheeting and its retention during the extreme winds that would result from the blast.

In another case, an Oak Ridge, Tennessee, couple with one teenage son and a supply of dull rusted tools excavated an 11′ × 28″ trench in six and a half hours. This involved hard pick work through the heavy yellow clay. The overhead shielding in this case was provided by their compact car, a 1970 Ford Maverick two-door sedan, which they parked directly above the trench. Carefully covering the upholstery with plastic that extended outside the car doors, and using bed linens in a similar fashion clamped underneath the hood and trunk and angled toward the ground, a foot of earth was shoveled into the car, on top of the hood, and into the trunk, and then banked alongside the vehicle. Ingenious placement of sheeting

37. Plastic sheeting covered by earth increases shielding over the Hoffners' trench shelter. Tented flaps for air circulation would later be constructed at each end. Courtesy of NARA.

allowed rain to run off the car's roof gutter and away from the underground shelter, permitting a dry storage shelf between ground level and the under-chassis, all along the perimeter of the trench. One foot beyond the end of the hood, an entrance was provided through a narrower twenty-inch portion of trench covered with a plastic awning and ringed with sandbags. Once the family had entered the shelter, the sandbags were arranged to hold down a wooden plank and an inverted car seat covered with earth was arranged to give added protection. Flaps at front and back allowed for air circulation. The whole project took nine hours to complete.

The DCPA proclaimed that a family of four could dwell in such a shelter for up to ten days without emerging. This may be difficult to imagine, especially in hot weather, and was not tried. On the day of the Oak Ridge shelter's construction, when the temperature rose to 80°F, humidity made it uncomfortably warm even with both ventilation flaps wide open. Nevertheless, the idea was that once the trench and car were in place, the shelter could be slowly and safely deepened to about 5′ if time allowed, and earth banked alongside at the last minute. Given Oak Ridge's concentration of nuclear research and uranium processing sites, the "last minute" might be a very tense one indeed.

These tests were intended to prove the feasibility of last-minute measures and

38. Car-over-trench shelter prepared by a rural Oak Ridge, Tennessee, family. Excavating the 11′ × 28″ trench. Courtesy of NARA.

39. Car-over-trench shelter with 1970 Maverick two-door sedan in position over trench. Earth is shoveled into the car's trunk, floors, and seat areas. Courtesy of NARA.

40. Car-over-trench shelter showing plastic sheeting extending from the inside of the car to the ground so that earth can be banked around the vehicle. At each end of the trench, ventilation is provided. Courtesy of NARA.

41. Car-over-trench shelter
occupied after nine hours.
Courtesy of NARA.

to determine whether ordinary Americans could interpret the schematic plans
published by civil defense authorities. Some doubt remained on the latter point,
and even if expedient shelter-building was feasible its effectiveness may have
been a question in many people's minds. In the 1970s, a sub-culture of survivalists emerged in the United States, Britain, and Canada who believed wholeheartedly that with the proper preparation and the latest in gadgetry, they and
their families would emerge intact from a nuclear war. They published magazines which demonstrated the extent of the industry that existed to support their
views.[55]

R. D. McCann of Regina, Saskatchewan, not only had a fallout shelter built
and stocked in his urban home but also had plans to evacuate to the northern part
of the province in the event that Regina received fallout from a strike on Montana's missile bases. Having taken into account "communications, food shortables
[*sic*] for a prolonged period, water purification problems, radiological defense including high & low level counters, and EMP proofing the evacuation vehicle by

reverting to a standard ignition," in all about a $20,000 investment, he gave himself a fifty-fifty chance of survival, assuming that Regina itself was not hit. But he needed to know how much worse nuclear winter would be than a regular winter in the north country, and wrote to Canada's Coordinator of Operations for Emergency Planning in 1985 expressing his concerns that recent revelations about nuclear winter might complicate his preparations.

> Like any other menace or threat from nuclear war, I am optimistic that *some* steps could be taken to *increase* survival chances even if that horrific event should materialize [*sic*]. If Eskimos can survive in total darkness through a 6 month winter in the Arctic (I have been there) then, in a fallout free zone, it should be possible to do so, provided the period does not last too long and provided adequate food is either stored or could be found. The problems after that would not be insurmountable . . . provided one made ones [*sic*] way south to areas that had sufficient light etc. to support plants and wildlife or sealife.[56]

Disavowing an identity as a survivalist except in the matter of nuclear war, McCann proclaimed fear as the greatest barrier to others' self-protection.

John M. Hoffman, a physician who chaired an American Medical Association committee on Emergency Medical Defense, gave a lecture on Home Preparedness to colleagues in Salem, Oregon, in 1959. He recommended specific things they could do now to survive later:

> Go camping at least one week a year, away from civilization and your car. Plan in advance for all you will need, put it on your back, and walk five to ten miles. This is especially feasible in the Pacific northwest. — Stop putting things off: get that hernia fixed, learn to control your diabetes if possible, improve your circulation and weight, get an extra pair of glasses, get that sore tooth pulled, and that ingrown toenail removed. — Keep your immunizations up to date. — Learn to swim. — Walk at least a mile a day. — Keep up with the news. — Establish a second residence, whether with friends or otherwise; certainly somewhere you can send your kids. Know how long it takes to get there and alternate routes. — Renew your knowledge of first aid and home sanitation. — Build a shelter that you can enter at a moment's notice. Encourage your neighbor to do the same.[57]

Most of this sounds like good sense, but taken as a whole it integrates civil defense preparedness with lifestyle, dictating leisure (nobly — or rationally — organized), wellness regimes, and social networks.

A more detailed instance of this is supplied by a pair of former university professors who relocated in the late 1950s to Bucks County, Pennsylvania.[58] Charlotte and George Dyer, founders of the Dyer Institute for Interdisciplinary Studies, sought to counter the defeatism that attended so many people's thinking about nuclear war. They advocated and tested practical programs for families to prepare for disaster, especially nuclear attack. This included home fallout shelters, or having the materials at hand to build them quickly (such as concrete blocks set into an outdoor fireplace without mortar), and also extended to a much more imaginative set of exercises than civil defense authorities concurrently endorsed for the public. Inspired by Operation Plumbbob, a series of atmospheric tests in Nevada during the summer of 1957, their exercises all involved moving out of areas of danger, in family and group-based evacuation units. Like Hoffman, they advocated camping as the basis of their practice.

The Dyers made very specific recommendations about the contents of personal survival kits in the form of a haversack or duffle (doubling as the ideal camping outfit) and group kits (tents, cooking gear, and a canoe) which should be kept ready at all times. Their first excursion, "Operation X," involved just their family. A two-and-a-half day exercise in May 1960, "Operation Great Egg!," involved thirty-four people in eleven canoes paddling down the Great Egg Harbor River in New Jersey. These "training" exercises incorporated a broad curriculum, covering survival skills as well as radio communications, problems of assembling together in the country, the logistics of travel by station wagon and canoe, map reading, and camping skills. While on "Operation Great Egg!" they pretended to be in tropical climes. Out of this, they recommended more detailed assignment of responsibilities to group members and more practical ideas about menus and shelter.

The Dyers set themselves up as leaders of a loose affiliation of families prepared to take action in case of threat or attack. Their rehearsals sought stimulation from the kinds of scenarios that emergency planners themselves imagined. They recognized that if the government announced an evacuation in anticipation of nuclear attack, roads would become extremely congested, resulting in pandemonium. In these cases, waterborne (or equine) transit would be the preferred options. "Operation Ready? Alert!" in spring 1961 practiced a pre-dawn alarm and rally, with loading of the station wagons done in the dark. Aiming to launch canoes in Lake Oswego at 07:00, they established canoe-to-canoe radio contact until the group assembled down river. The Dyers explained that two essential aspects of the nuclear age were demonstrated by colleagues on this exercise:

a. *Leff* had prepared, with great thoroughness and skill, an elaborate exposition of how the techniques of the "Situation Map" could be adapted to warn an evacuating party in the open of the probable approach of dangerous radioactive fallout.

This was begun (as it would likely be under "for real" circumstances) beneath the cloudy windy sky above the Assembly Point on the Oswego; and clinched with a radio-reenforced exercise in the Recreation Room at "Chip's Folly" on the Wading River, just before the Group broke up the next afternoon. The latest color film on "Radef" ("Radiological Defense," No. N-210, 28 min., sound) was also shown.

b. *Mac*, with equal skill and effectiveness, explained the two best-known types of radiation-detection equipment (1) the professional survey Geiger counter and (2) the Bendix ratemeter-dosimeter set. . . . This presentation was also started in the open at the Assembly Point, illustrated with a surprizingly [*sic*] heavy piece of actual uranium borrowed for the occasion from Mac's university physics lab; and was reenforced at "Chip's Folly" by comments on the motion picture and "Situation Map" exercise.[59]

Building on this knowledge, the Dyers projected "Operation F" for August 1962, eight months after the handbook in which it is described was published. Operation F would be precipitated by delivery of seventeen H-bombs and twenty-one A-bombs on the United States. They planned to stay underground for two weeks, inferring details of fallout patterns from CONELRAD. Close study of their geological survey maps would lead them to discover a little radiation-free island four miles off the Atlantic coast. When fallout in their area decayed enough for them to venture above ground for one hour, they would don personal dosimeters, assemble their gear, and move out toward their objective. They practiced what would be necessary to execute this: getting to a site, reconnaissance to determine if the site was uninhabited, and crossing in locally available boats.[60]

Evacuees might need to cover a long distance, hence the Dyers' "Operation Run for Canada," which focused on provincial parks in Ontario. They could not be certain that this area would be free of fallout, but inferred from weather patterns that it might. They recommended paying attention to Canadian radio in case of emergency. Families'

"situation map" should certainly carry every scrap of reliable information received as to conditions in all areas north and west of their location. They might very well find that Ontario, for instance, was clearing up far faster than their own neighborhood — and this more especially since the Province of Ontario is much larger than most Americans south of its borders are prone to realize. If it were plain to them in two or three weeks that their home territory would not be steadily habitable for full-time reconstruction for several months — the stage would be set for serious consideration of the "Run for Canada."[61]

This was practiced by four adults and three dogs who headed northwest in two station wagons laden with canoes. In their rehearsal, the roads were perfect and they traveled swiftly, but in order to simulate disaster conditions they broke the journey from Pennsylvania overnight in a New York state park. An ordinary tank full of gas proved enough to get into Canada; however they carried jerry cans of gas just in case. Planning to cross the Niagara River near Buffalo, they concluded that if bridges were out they would canoe into Canada. Canadians might dispute the wisdom of entering southern Ontario at such a time: in a real emergency it would be teeming with evacuees from Toronto, Hamilton, London, and Windsor. The Dyers, apparently unaware of the Ontario wilderness that stretches west and north of Sault-Ste-Marie, were prepared to consider western provinces, and even Alaska, if southern Ontario was too radioactive.

The Dyers understood the importance of planning, communications, and especially the discipline that comes from practice. President Eisenhower had recognized the importance of the public learning to discipline itself as early as 1953, though very few took the kinds of measures the Dyers or even Dr. Hoffman advocated.[62] The long-term trend was toward professional first responders taking charge of herding the public in any kind of emergency. As a 1994 HO paper argues: "As with all emergency management, the existence of a command and control system coupled with an existing and rehearsed emergency plan has been found to enhance the effectiveness of the management of the evacuation. We have argued that the importance of the preparation of an emergency plan is as a rehearsal and a socialization exercise rather than as a plan." Whether the plan entailed seeking (or digging) shelter close at hand or evacuating, the recommended means to bring a plan to fruition—through performance—in a real emergency was socializing family or community groups through activity: in other words, rehearsing. But as the Dyers' exercises demonstrate, communication and accurate fallout data were critical in improvising upon a plan or choosing between pre-rehearsed options. Governments, and through them broadcasters, were the source for such information so they too had to plan, rehearse, learn from rehearsals, revise plans, and rehearse some more.

COMMUNICATIONS

To recognize the possibilities of nuclear war in the missile age, without our citizens knowing what they should do and where they should go if the bombs begin to fall, would be a failure of responsibility.

—John F. Kennedy

A RAND report of 1949, commissioned to help civil defense authorities understand how people were likely to behave in the event of an A-bomb attack, predicted that there would be a huge population who "will be extremely disturbed by the appalling sights about them, by the fear that they have been exposed to lethal amounts of radiation, and by the intense suspense of not knowing the fate of their families and their friends." They will likely show disorganized and maladaptive behaviors: they may not help others or not take obviously needed precautions. This could be rendered less likely by training the population prior to an attack, though there was a distinct danger that training might be forgotten in the throes of emotionality resulting from actual war. To control for this, "perhaps the most effective device" in an emergency "would be a calm, familiar, authoritative voice giving both reassurance and directions as to what should be done," for example through public address systems, an underground communication system that could withstand the bomb damage, or mobile radio broadcasting units.[1]

Various communication systems were tried in exercises, such as the "Warning Voice from the Sky" over Cape Elizabeth, Maine,

42. A warning voice from the sky supplemented CONELRAD emergency radio, sirens, and other devices to spread civil defense warning of impending attack or post-attack fallout to threatened communities. Based on an exercise conducted over Cape Elizabeth, Maine. Courtesy of NARA.

that spread the word about impending attack for those who were out of range of air raid sirens (figure 42).[2] British authorities used public address systems mounted in automobiles and roved around neighborhoods instructing people when it was safe to emerge from their fallout shelters.[3] These met local but not national needs and fell short of the goal to disseminate official instructions from centralized authorities. Americans concluded by 1953 that it would be vital to keep the public regularly and accurately informed, and planned to do this through continuous post-attack CONELRAD broadcasts.[4] Canadian and British planning also relied on the radio waves. Ensuring that the plans would be effective entailed rehearsing broadcasters as well as the public, so protocols and scripts were developed to do precisely that.

Prime Time

Media theorists have observed that "media influence the political agenda and public opinion not necessarily in terms of *what to think* but rather what to think *about*. That is, the media have the capacity to 'prime' audiences."[5] A paper from the *Canadian Medical Association Journal* urged in 1957 that "previous to disas-

Chapter 6

ter. . . . it is not enough to communicate a warning. Once this has been given, communication must continue. . . . the guidance, reassurance and social cohesion provided by good communication can prevent the disorientation and confusion that leads to impulsive, irrational behaviour on the part of individuals and groups."[6] Thus, priming needed to be appropriately coordinated with several event phases: pre-attack, warning of attack, the duration of attack, and post-attack.

Assuming that the public would be on the move to assembly points and shelter, often in cars, radio was the preferred medium of communication during an impending nuclear attack and in the period immediately following it. Battery-powered radios, and particularly the popularity of transistor radios after 1954, made it feasible to tune in almost anywhere en route to shelter, and then once again inside domestic or public facilities.[7] In the United States, civil defense authorities broadcast on CONELRAD stations, banning all other simultaneous commercial transmission in order to avoid giving enemy aircraft the opportunity to discern their location from local call signs.[8] In 1964, CONELRAD was replaced with an Emergency Broadcast System of three hundred participating stations; by 1971, the system could only reach 9 percent of the population. The United States still had no nationwide plan on a par with its closest allies.[9]

In Canada and the United Kingdom, the CBC and BBC (nationalized radio networks) would be used for broadcasting instructions to the public. Where the population was thinly dispersed, radio was a more effective means than sirens to disseminate warnings as well as specific information.[10] Until March 1968, Canada maintained twenty-four-hour-a-day broadcasting capacity at thirty-two radio stations across the country; stations remained under contract for operation and maintenance of emergency broadcasting equipment for such a purpose until 16 May 1991.[11] In an emergency, commercial AM, FM, and television stations would be alerted (except Frobisher Bay, in the eastern Arctic); they would then cease normal programming, and CBC radio would begin emergency broadcasting within three to five minutes. Every station had a collection of recordings to play in case they received word from the Emergency Measures Organization (EMO) and Department of National Defence (DND) that missiles were in-coming. About fifteen minutes would remain before ICBMs arrived in southern Canada.[12] Post-attack, the continuity of the nation would be ensured by government relocation in the regional and central emergency government headquarters (REGHQs and CEGHQ), where the CBC maintained special studios and where, in a growing emergency, civilians would relocate to staff the Emergency Public Information Service and Emergency Broadcasting System.[13]

43. CBC radio broadcast booth in Canada's CEGHQ. Courtesy of the Diefenbunker— Canada's Cold War Museum.

Similarly, the British planned to station BBC personnel in each Regional Seat of Government (RSG) bunker. Despite this, for two days post-attack they anticipated that most areas would be without broadcast capacity.[14] This was extensively gamed in the NATO exercise "CIVLOG 64."[15] Documentation from a later British exercise from 1967 asserts:

> The ability to broadcast . . . would constitute one of the most powerful instruments in the hands of the Regional Commissioner. . . . In the very early stages after attack the morale of the public would inevitably be at a very low ebb; they would need reassurance from the highest level. Through the medium of broadcasting the Regional Commissioner would be able, personally, to introduce himself and to let it be known that a pre-planned system of emergency administration was in existence. Through this medium, too, news of national importance would be promulgated, together with details of any special measures of importance that it might be necessary to introduce in the interests of the community. It would provide, too, by far the best means of advising the public as a whole on matters concerning fall-out.[16]

But, as civil defense officials frequently noted, plans were not worth anything unless they stood up to testing.

Relying on commercial stations, and thus having to be much more public about its plans, the United States tested its system regularly from 1954 through 1961 in the OPAL exercises. In 1955, a five-minute program was broadcast coincident with the simulated attack warning, and another five-minute program was broadcast coincident with the simulated attack imminent stages, including running news accounts of the simulated evacuation.[17] Media executives recommended that President Eisenhower make a broadcast early in the exercise to demonstrate that he is alive and working, that democracy is preserved, and that government goes on.[18] In 1956, it was assumed that following the simulated attack, only 35 percent of the country—mostly in the southeast, because it would suffer fewer strikes—could be covered by radio, but within four hours 90 percent of coverage could be restored, rising to 100 percent within twenty-four hours, provided that stations could get electrical power. These would be addressed from High Point (the presidential bunker in the Blue Ridge Mountains, near Berryville, Virginia) and signals relayed station-to-station.[19] During the drills for this, all AM, FM, and television stations were mandated to leave the air and remain silent unless they were part of the National Defense Emergency program, in which case they switched to broadcasting on 640 or 1240 kilocycles at 15:10 EST. Everyone was requested to monitor their radios from 15:10 to 15:25 EST.

Testing communications and broadcasting to the public was a regular part of Canadian nuclear civil defense exercises from the late 1950s through the mid-1960s. A ninety-minute coast-to-coast-to-coast broadcast hosted by CBC personality Byng Whitteker during Exercise TOCSIN B in 1961 specified what the public would hear at each stage of an emergency, and included a three-minute live broadcast by Prime Minister Diefenbaker and taped messages (broadcast regionally) from provincial premiers and territorial commissioners.[20] The live portion gave the public the flavor of an unfolding nuclear war emergency:

TAPE: BEEP WARNING

WHITTEKER: We rejoin the national network now at the Emergency Headquarters of the Federal Government for Exercise Tocsin, and for the next three minutes I am going to describe to you some of the activities in this centre. (AD LIB DESCRIPTION FOR THREE MINUTES, BASED ON PREVIOUS BRIEFING) Now, I have with me (NAMES TWO CABINET MINISTERS AND THEIR POSITIONS) Mr. _____, could you tell the Canadian people of the reasons for sounding National Take Cover just 12 minutes after the Alert Warning? I have understood that we would have two hours' warning of attack by aircraft and that the Take Cover would be sounded in each regional [*sic*] separately when aircraft approach a major city.

MINISTER: That's what would happen in an attack involving only manned aircraft.

However, in this exercise the assumed enemy is also using missiles, and these have been identified by the BMEWS system.

WHITTEKER: BMEWS—That's the Ballistic Missile Early Warning System.

MINISTER: Yes, the one that has been set up in the North for the detection of missiles. For purposes of this exercise, apparently enough missiles have already been launched against North America to justify warning people in all of our likely target areas to take cover.

This was followed by reports from each regional emergency control center until Whitteker was interrupted by a report from the army.

WHITTEKER: I have just been informed that exercise missiles have exploded in Canada in the general area of Courtney, B.C., Edmonton, Alberta, North Bay, Ontario, Chatham, New Brunswick, and South West Newfoundland. We now take you to Regional Headquarters [REGHQ] at Camp Shilo, Manitoba, for the first report.

TAPE: BEEP WARNING

SHILO: I have just been handed an Army report of an exercise nuclear detonation in Alberta. It reads as follows: "A nuclear weapon exploded in the Edmonton, Alberta area at 5:35 P.M. Edmonton time."

TAPE: BEEP WARNING

WHITTEKER: "Everyone within 20 miles of Edmonton take shelter against the fallout which will start to come down in that area within 30 minutes."

TAPE: BEEP WARNING

WHITTEKER: "A much larger area will eventually be affected as the upper winds will cause the fallout to drift southeast from Edmonton toward Saskatoon at about 22 miles per hour."

TAPE: BEEP WARNING

WHITTEKER: "The estimated times at which fallout will reach localities Southeast of Edmonton will be broadcast in a few minutes. The situation will be easier to follow if you have a road map at hand."

Federal Exercise Headquarters then reported additional detonations, followed by instructions about how to equip emergency shelters and cope during fallout. On-the-spot interviews were held with a prescient man in Esquimalt, B.C., who built a shelter in his home, and a farmer in Alexandria, Ontario, who made accommodation for his livestock as well as his family. The lesson is drawn as the ninety-minute broadcast script concludes:

WHITTEKER: If this were a real attack we would, of course, be staying on the air till the immediate danger was over and the All-Clear Message was issued; and there is no doubt that many thousands of Canadians, roused by reality, would be rushing to make preparations for the next attack.

Whitteker then outlined the advice in the government's standard booklet "11 Steps to Survival," and regional correspondents signed off with updates on local fallout forecasts.

The centralization of broadcast information and regular exercises including public broadcasting had several purposes: by habituating the public to tune to these stations, they could be better informed. Otherwise, as was gamed in Chicago in 1956, eight days after the attack "incipient panic" arose "due to erroneous and alarming information being broadcast over radio" as news reporters relayed information from numerous arms of the federal government—army, Red Cross, and USDA—instead of the official versions passed through the civil defense public information office. Saboteurs, it was thought, could take advantage of this confused situation.[21] Keeping the public tuned to official conduits of information made their behavior more predictable; the point was to inform but also to manipulate. Planners recognized this could go both ways. In OPAL 59, for example, all commercial broadcasting and telecasting ceased in the United States while 1,200 stations transmitted Civil Defense Director Leo Hoegh's address from the presidential bunker. A quarter of the U.S. population tuned in, but this left many susceptible to being mislead by other sources, such as the mobile radio stations that simulated broadcasting clandestinely from Manitoba (Canada) and Coahuila (Mexico), beaming psychological warfare propaganda into the United States "urging revolt against authority and surrender."[22] In at least one British scenario, the tracking down and closing of such illegal broadcasting stations is detailed.[23]

In North America, cross-border cooperation would be crucial, not only to avoid subversive broadcasting but also in order to coordinate public action. A joint 1965 exercise involving nuclear strikes twenty-five miles southwest of Regina, Saskatchewan (with fallout headed toward South Dakota), and twenty-five miles east of Minot, South Dakota (with fallout headed toward Minnesota and Manitoba), posed the problem succinctly: if people are moving toward shelter but they still have some time before fallout danger strikes, what should they do? Should people in North Dakota and Minnesota know of Saskatchewan's strike and take measures to avoid its fallout? Will Minot's strike be known to residents of Saskatchewan and Manitoba, and if so by what means? The CBC's signal could be picked up across the border, but for whom, exactly, does the CBC broadcast? Do stations broadcast predictions of fallout trajectories and instructions as to what all people in fallout paths must do? Who is responsible for instructing them? What

44. Dennis R. Kunkle, news director at WSBA-TV in York, Pennsylvania, simulates telecasting emergency survival instructions to the public using emergency information scripts and visuals supplied by the DOD, OCD. Courtesy of NARA.

if instructions for border regions conflict? Do the two governments agree on what the audiences for different radio networks should do at this point?[24]

Hypotheticals came into play in all civil defense exercises, but it was crucial to distinguish between the hypotheticals of fact (such as detonations and fallout paths) and the condition of simulation upon which an entire exercise was predicated. For example, thirty-eight pages of sample scripts were produced for official broadcast during OPAL 59, and all four radio networks in the United States (ABC, CBS, NBC, and the Mutual Broadcasting System) linked up to carry FCDA Director Hoegh's address from High Point.[25] Like all the OPAL broadcasts, this was punctuated with reminders that this was just a drill and there was no attack.

> ANNOUNCER: This is a CONELRAD drill. . . . We cannot close our eyes to the possibility of attack. That is why the radio and television industry has given up valuable time to help make this exercise successful.

The attack alert and take cover signals were described, and actions that should be taken upon hearing them reiterated. Listeners heard descriptions of the typical kind of information that would be broadcast: instructions regarding shelter supplies, evacuation procedures, and warning times along with details of the mili-

Chapter 6

tary's detection system for early warning, how the United States was striking back at enemy forces, and the function of the North American Aerospace Defense Command (NORAD). Fallout and shielding principles were explained, along with procedures for taking shelter.

> ANNOUNCER: As you leave the city, your government officials will be moving to relocation centers outside the target area in order to maintain government operation and leadership. Under national emergency conditions, local governments will have an immense responsibility. It is here that the attack will first strike — it is here that plans for survival of the people will have to be executed. . . . The threat of nuclear weapons does not end with the explosion of the bombs.

The pretext was simultaneously that all was functioning well at the point of the broadcast's origin, and the situation was dire enough that Newspoint—the journalists' enclave located in rural Virginia, removed from High Point but directly in touch with it—was staffed and reporting official information. Another announcer drew a verbal picture of what Low Point (in Battle Creek, Michigan, at that point the FCDA's headquarters and crossroads of information between the military, regional authorities, and federal government) looked like (figure 45).

> ANNOUNCER #2: This is _____ reporting from one of the secret relocation centers of your government. . . . away from Washington. During an actual attack your government would operate from places like this. We are in the operations room. . . . Young ladies on step-ladders are working at the enormous map of the United States. . . . They are plotting attack information on the map with colored plastic markers attached to tiny magnets . . . the markers indicate which places are being evacuated. Later they will show which have been hit. . . . which spared. Across the room is a smaller map covered with clear plastic. A weatherman charts the predicted movement of fallout across the nation . . . historic decisions for the United States . . . and the world . . . will depend on the information reaching this room . . . for the men sitting around me here today . . . in a training exercise . . . are the men who would make the decision . . . in case of attack. The information with which they work comes over a gigantic emergency communications system . . . from the military and from civil defense installations which relay reports from cities . . . states . . . territories . . . and from other secret government headquarters similar to this one . . . Man cannot handle this tremendous flow of information fast enough . . . so there are great banks of electronic equipment. . . . the brains of the computer . . . ready for use by the men who must make the decisions for survival . . . This room is the core of Operation Survival. . . . in many other rooms at this hidden headquarters . . . hundreds of experts keep track of . . . how many

45. Low Point Operation Room, Battle Creek, Michigan, with film crew during OPAL 55. Courtesy of NARA.

> Americans would have died if this attack were real . . . how many injured . . . how
> much is left in stockpiled food . . . fuel. . . . clothing . . . medical supplies . . .
> blood. Transportation experts get reports on which railroads can operate and how
> many locomotives and cars they have . . . the number of buses . . . trucks . . .
> aircraft and other vehicles available for the recovery effort . . . medical men get
> reports on the number of doctors and nurses who survived . . . they also are told
> how many hospital beds are available and where they are . . . how much medicine
> is left and where it is . . . the condition of the nearly two thousand emergency
> hospitals civil defense has spotted strategically around the nation . . . all of this
> information . . . and much more . . . is fed into the Operations Room.[26]

Exhortations on cooperation and the need for public involvement in civil defense followed. This comprehensive overview of civil defense planning and rehearsal is noteworthy; what the public did with this information can only be conjectured, especially as they were repeatedly reminded "this is a CONELRAD drill."

The National Damage Assessment Center, part of High Point, received data on defense conditions, warning times, aircraft tracks, submarine locations, and missile reports which in turn were translated into public warnings. After an attack, the National Damage Assessment Center was fed data on areas of heavy destruction, radiation intensities, and protective action which in turn was translated into information for dissemination to the public. CONELRAD could then give instructions on nuclear, bacteriological, and chemical attacks, personal care, the evacuation situation, and radiation.[27] In a war, they anticipated relaying this information to Low Point which would in turn issue press releases on meteorological and radiological information to Newspoint.

Britain and Canada had similar, though more centralized, systems. In Exercise "Dustbath," 7–8 November 1964, scripts with information about fallout were written for the BBC. Scripts were short, and telegraphically informational, not unlike the daily shipping forecasts in style. At H+4, the proposed text read:

> This is the B.B.C. Regional Service for the Counties of AYSHIRE, BEESHIRE, CEESHIRE and the West Riding of DEESHIRE. Alvan Fiddell reporting. Between one o'clock and three o'clock this morning a number of attacks were made on this country by nuclear weapons. The main attack has been directed against London and the Home Counties but this Region has been subjected to attacks on West Middlepoole, Nottington and Darlingham. Serious fires are raging in these places and there are very many casualties. Civil Defence and other rescue services are doing everything they can to rescue survivors. Immediate retaliatory measures were taken by our own forces and there have been no further attacks since 3 o'clock. Radioactive fall-out already affects part of our region and will affect other areas later. If you have not already been warned to go to your refuge room, listen for the public warnings. As soon as you hear maroons [loud explosive devices, used as warnings in areas unequipped with sirens] or are instructed by your Civil Defence warden or police go at once to your refuge room and remain there until you are told you can come out. This station is now closing down. A further transmission will be made at 7 o'clock.

Twenty-four hours after the attack, Alvan Fiddell was scheduled to broadcast again, reporting that:

> Rescue work is proceeding in the towns of West Middlepoole, Nottington and Darlingham and many casualties have been removed to hospital. Many fires have been brought under control and reinforcements of rescue services are on their way to these areas. Apart from the very north of AYSHIRE radioactive fallout covers almost the whole region. It is particularly heavy in the areas around LIVERTON, SOUTHSHORE, STOCKPORT AND NORTHCAPE, and along the REED VALLEY. Do not leave your refuge room. The civil defence authorities are aware of the situation and are keeping a constant check on it. Your warden will tell you when you can come out but it may not be for some considerable time. There will be a further news bulletin in one hour. Switch off your radio to conserve the battery and tune in again at 3 o'clock.[28]

This was meant to resemble a news broadcast, not a play: informational and non-dialogic. Yet this does not alter its status as a dramatic script. It is precisely because it is part of a speculative exercise that it is *more*, not less like drama, for it super-imposes one pretext (blatantly untrue: there is no war) over another (manifestly true: there could be war). The real time and the real radiological situation in which the broadcaster exists is in tension with but does not negate the unreal time and reported radiological situation of the simulated post-nuclear war scenario. These particular scripts were not publicly broadcast; this further enhances their status as "what ifs" with respect to rehearsal and the real thing. Dramatic scripts are action-in-potential, whose existence implies the need for rehearsal. Rehearsal, in turn, is a practice that lends credibility within the boundaries of simulated action.

The Real Thing

Equally intriguing are the related texts—sometimes pre-recorded, sometimes held on deposit in typescript form—that were cached in case nuclear war actually broke out. These have never been broadcast—yet—but like all scripts have the status of events-in-potential, postulated futures capable of making the transformation to something transacting in time. In this case, it would be an apocalyptic time. For these reasons, they have more value than as mere historical curiosities.

In the United States, CONELRAD pre-attack broadcasts would typically focus on what to stock in shelters, evacuation procedures, warning times, the military's detection system for early warning, NORAD, and the capacity to strike back.[29] In Canada, most post-war objectives would be enhanced through communications: the highest priority would be "public education on self-help in first aid, firefighting, and personal survival." The preservation of life and property would also be supported through second-tier objectives such as continuity of government and broadcasting of fallout information, and through third-tier objectives including the conservation of resources, stabilization of the economy, and resumption of governmental peacetime programs.[30] In each case, media primes listeners to be prepared for certain actions.

Just as exercises repeated phrases of disavowal—such as "this is a drill"—in order to distinguish the rehearsals for nuclear war from the real thing, authenticating scripts were devised in order to distinguish the real thing from drills. In any other circumstance, "authenticating scripts" would be an oxymoron, but in the case of wartime broadcasts they existed to affirm the distinction between rehearsal and the no longer deferred status of civil defense performance. In the event of an attack warning, regional CBC stations would repeatedly broadcast the following text, interrupted only by a speech by the prime minister or acting prime minister.

SOUND EFFECT: Undulating sound of sirens for a few seconds.

ANNOUNCER: This is _____ (well known announcer) speaking. The Canadian Government has declared a national emergency. An enemy attack on North America has been detected. This is a real emergency. Sirens are now sounding or have sounded the "ATTACK WARNING." . . . Take cover immediately in the best available protection against blast and heat, do *NOT* worry about fallout now. Here are some instructions:

If you are at home go to the strongest part of your house or building which offers the best protection against flying objects such as glass, wood or bricks.

Take your battery radio with you, or turn up the house radio so that you can hear it while under cover.

Stay away from windows.

Lie down and protect yourself from falling debris.

Shut your eyes and shield them from the flash of an explosion.

If you are away from home, at school or work, take cover where you are.

If you are in a car, truck or bus, stop and take cover in a building, culvert or ditch.

If you are only a few minutes from a known safer destination proceed and take cover as quickly as possible.[31]

These instructions would be familiar to anyone who had paid attention to the civil defense catechism in peacetime. It was necessary, therefore, to authenticate their urgency as wartime imperatives.

A set of ten draft typescripts from 1962 indicate the content of the taped messages that were stored across Canada. The scripts relate to the stages of attack warning, take cover, instructions for those whose areas came under attack, fallout reports, evacuation, and emergence from shelter.[32] These were developed by a working group with input from the CBC, army, Emergency Health Services, Emergency Supply Planning Branch, and EMO, revising scripts used for TOCSIN B the previous year. Attack warning messages were printed on pink paper and kept on file until at least the mid-1980s.[33] To avoid playing messages pertaining to stages of the survival period in the wrong order, they were combined on a single tape.[34] Purely educational and instructional material about sheltering and mitigating the effects of fallout, which would also be broadcast prior to an attack if time allowed, were produced on video and stockpiled at television stations,[35] though in addition the CBC retained scripts for live broadcast on personal decontamination, water, food handling, disposal of garbage and human waste, disease prevention, and first aid.[36]

The British government also produced videos and audio recordings intended to be broadcast in the pre-crisis period: the infamous *Protect and Survive* series.

Twenty-four-hour-a-day broadcasting would be devoted to the twenty videotapes lasting a total of forty-seven minutes and audiotapes lasting thirty-seven minutes.[37] Once war broke out, there would be a single BBC Radio sound program, and no television. The public would be urged to tune in continuously for the first twenty-four hours, then to conserve battery life by only turning on the radio at specified times or when they heard sirens or maroons. Generic texts allowed for more specific guidance emerging from localities throughout the nation.

> The following areas are under Fall-out Warning Black. This means that radioactive fall-out is imminent, or has already arrived, in the area(s). You must therefore take cover immediately and remain under cover until you receive further instructions. This broadcast may not include all areas where there is danger of fall-out and you should therefore act immediately on any warning which has been or will be given by maroon or whistle which you may hear, whether or not your area is included in this broadcast.

Alternately, for regional broadcasts, proposed texts read:

> This is a broadcast to (South-Eastern) Region. Radioactive fall-out is now affecting the whole of the counties of A, B and C and the following areas in county D as well as parts of adjoining Regions. Stay under cover, and if you have a refuge room, stay in it as much as possible. Do not come out until you receive further instructions. Keep your radio tuned to this station. This broadcast may not include all areas where there is danger of fall-out and you should therefore act immediately on any warning which has been or will be given by maroon or whistle which you may hear, whether or not your area is included in this broadcast.[38]

The resemblance to Exercise Dustbath scripts is notable. RSGs would also broadcast international, national, and regional situation summaries; the end of the nuclear exchange; forecasts of when broad areas are likely to emerge from cover; specific instructions for emergence applicable to smaller areas; instructions to the public that they will be transported to other regions; instructions that those with transport should travel, along with specific instructions on destination and routes; instructions about rations, food stocks within fallout zones, and local food, including contamination dangers; how to use one's time in the open, especially for workers such as nurses, public utility maintainers, slaughter men, and farmers; medical guidance on caring for radiation victims; and advice on decontamination.[39]

As archival objects, these scripts demonstrate the ideologies and tactics of civil defense programs during the height of the Cold War. Does their nature change if we think of them in the light of their real utility: to instruct at the outbreak of nuclear war, a performance coincident with the cessation of life for hundreds of millions of people? If indeed the exercise scripts are dramatic because they superimpose a real-time referent (the exercise) over imagined-time referents (the fiction of war) in dialogue or monologue form, would the same script being broadcast to millions in the midst of crisis *cease* to be dramatic?[40] What does this reveal about threshold events and the standard form of evidence for history, ritual, and theater history?

Anne Ubersfeld argues that every performance references three domains: the dramatic text, the performance itself (reflexively), and the natural world.[41] In the case of the civil defense scripts stored in-potential, the relationship of these domains to each other becomes particularly interesting. Existing only to be broadcast in the event of wartime, these texts provoke questions about the circumstances under which the domains of reflexive performance and the natural world collapse in order to eliminate the domain of a dramatic text.

During exercises, the public was urged to take shelter: the same shelter they would take if the attack were real. The context was serious, though the enactment was fundamentally playful: an "as if" of nuclear war, with the radio repeating this essential fact. But closing the shelter door, though the same gesture, might not always have the same reflexive relationship to the natural world. For example:

> We interrupt our normal program to cooperate in security and civil defense measures as requested by the United States Government. This is a CONELRAD Radio Alert. Normal broadcasting will now be discontinued for an indefinite period. . . . In the interest of national security, radio silence *may be prolonged*. If this happens, don't use your telephone. Be patient. Official information will be broadcast as soon as possible.[42]

Delivered in an exercise, this rehearses possibilities for a future. Delivered in wartime, it would become an apocalyptic script describing what would then be the present.

What, precisely, is the difference in terms of performance theory? As dramatic scripts, civil defense instructions compress narrative, stimulate unconscious drives, and call a mise en scène into being; in other words, they rely on realism in their fundamental fictionality. Their purpose in peacetime is to habituate auditors' responses, rehearsing reactions—soothing emotions and constructively activating behaviors—so they can be reproduced in war.[43] As long as the world's first thermonuclear war was merely anticipated, broadcasts of the scripts could only be realistic, not reality. Only if they were broadcast without the exercise caveat did they forfeit realism. After the bombs hit, well-habituated citizens listening to their radios in places of relative safety would, it was thought, seek reliable news in order to stem off the negative effects that would incur from unreliable information. They would seek to correlate their experiences to local and world events, integrating themselves into a broader narrative. Under these circumstances, according to the British Psychological Society, "monitoring the news serves as an attempt to reconstruct a comprehensible set of explanations, and to reduce the uncertainty brought about by uncontrollability." This was not only socially adaptive but psychologically healthy.[44] The Eisenhower administration regarded the two most important instruments of social planning for a post-disaster period to be the supply of food and other essential items and maintaining communications (preferably two-way) between the government and the people. This would emphasize national solidarity and facilitate long-term recovery and rebuilding.[45] A British report also emphasizes the importance of mitigating the isolating confinement of taking shelter: "The longer individuals remain isolated the greater the likelihood of group collapse, and society as a whole is only a group composed of subgroups."[46] So, post-attack such scripts would constitute sanctioned national narratives of solidarity, the will to survive, and the authority of government. The truth (or otherwise) in their particulars was not the issue so much as an implied conversation between those broadcasting official messages and those who received and acted upon them. It is another instance of how, through civil defense, audiences are turned seamlessly into actors, trading on the imagination for transformative purposes.

During the 1938 radio broadcast of *War of the Worlds*, a discrepancy occurred between auditors' belief and broadcasters' repeated insistence that there was no invasion from Mars. Invading Martians were posited in the dramatic text and depicted in the performance, but they did not exist in the natural world. Panicking auditors, however, did not heed the disclaimers, ignored the fact that they heard a dramatic text being performed, and became absorbed, believing that Martians were invading Earth. To grasp the story's pretext, listeners needed to be alienated from the content, to engage cognitively not just emotionally, and thus realize that their planet was truly safe. Not everyone could do so, and subsequently *War of the Worlds* has become synonymous with this error.[47]

Conversely, in the event of nuclear war, the exercises' disclaimers of rehearsal status would be replaced with disclaimers utilizing a form of double negative canceling the mimetic pretense (or falsity) of the rehearsal condition. Thus, "this is not a test; radar stations have detected incoming Soviet missiles; take cover immediately" spoken in performance would be as true in the script as in the world.

A change in the world beyond the script (namely, the failure of diplomacy to pre-serve peace) changes the status of the scripted words and the hermeneutics of their delivery from rehearsal to performance. It was crucial that the exercises condition credibility, and though estrangement is vital to this process, performance must not retain the effect of estrangement excessively.

Any performance, and any preparation or rehearsal for performance, is a unique combination of variables, never wholly repeatable. The spectators' construction of meaning in response to what they see, hear, and experience is part of this dynamic instability.[48] By changing one variable, a crucial distinction would be drawn. The difference between rehearsal and performance would be signaled not by a wholesale substitution of the text or players but merely through a change of disclaimer: from this is not true, to this is not false. It is the status of the "this is true" while it is patently false that tends to delineate the usual terrain of theater, but the scripts warehoused for apocalypse would change ontologically in the moment of their performance. As exercise scripts, they *propose* a future; as apocalyptic scripts, they *describe* a present. When the three domains of scripted text, reflexive performance, and natural world make an identical claim, dramatic contingency dissolves. Methexis, as participation in an imagined mimetic postulate, is defunct. Whereas the peacetime exercise relies on auditors to accept the alienation of an illusion broken—the "correct" response to *War of the Worlds*—wartime auditors would need to *not* be estranged, and instead to be absorbed.[49] Alienation—the affect that allows spectators to cognitively evaluate a performance's ideology—also enables analysis of the conventions that give theater its potency. Laying bare the mechanics of realism in exercises is an aesthetic trick. Performances of nearly identical scripts under rehearsal and wartime circumstances may deploy the same aesthetics, but the onus for auditors' belief is changed from the meta-message to the message itself: dig, duck, cover, or get out of town, but do it, or else.

ACTING OUT INJURY

I would use the entire civil defence budget, if I had it, to buy morphine.

—Anonymous physician

If repetition of an action or series of actions in peacetime could breed automatic responses in an emergency, not only the public but emergency workers too needed to be drilled in order to deal with human carnage on a scale proportionate to a nuclear calamity involving thousands, tens of thousands, and perhaps millions of injured. Part of the problem was technical: how to get people out of wreckage and to a site where their injuries could be assessed. Another part was logistical: how to triage the patients, ensure that adequate medical supplies were on hand, and cope with the influx of serious, critical, and morbid cases. Rehearsing this involved three interconnected types of civil defense workers: rescue personnel who knew how to safely approach ruined or damaged structures and extricate victims; first aid and ambulance personnel who could stabilize victims for transport; and medical personnel who could prioritize casualties and treat the wounded. Countless practical exercises were conducted involving one or more of these groups. A fourth group—the casualties themselves—added an especially intriguing aspect to rehearsals.

Many exercises involved the setting up and operating of mobile civil defense emergency hospitals: fully self-contained 200-bed hospital units complete with radiology equipment, surgical suites, labs, pharmacies stocked for over sixty therapeutic categories, and expendable supplies for thirty days. All that was needed was a couple of trucks to deliver the hospitals to an indoor venue with space to set up areas for triage, admitting, wards, surgery, central supply, and maintenance. Many exercises involved the setting up and operation of these units, training personnel in austere medical care.[1] Additional training emphasized the skills needed for dealing with mass casualties. But before any victim would reach such a facility, many would presumably have to be rescued and then handled by a first aid worker. For the purposes of training rescuers and first aiders as well as the nurses and physicians in the portable hospitals, added realism was provided via a technique developed by British civil defense forces in World War II: simulated casualties who *looked and behaved* as much like real victims as possible.

Acting, Faking, and Staging

In the spring of 1941, during the latter days of the London Blitz, St. Andrew's Convent School in Leatherhead, Surrey, was badly damaged by a parachute mine. The nuns evacuated, turning the ruined building over to the county. The mine exploded in the bend of the elbow-shaped building leaving "a mixture of totally destroyed, unstable but shorable and secure ruins."[2] In these ruins, Surrey established a Rescue School where civil defense workers went to practice techniques for safely extricating victims from bombed-out structures. Squads came down from London and surrounding regions to become proficient in handling ropes and tackle, shoring up precarious debris to allow workers access and victims egress, and removing stretcher cases from hazardous positions. The school's superintendent, an engineer who in peacetime had inspected the county's bridges, routinely lay down in the rubble and observed students' proficiency as they delivered him from beneath collapsed walls and out of cellar basements. Eric Claxton later admitted "I pretended a nonchalance I did not always possess that their knots were properly formed when they hoisted me out from a third storey window opening! It made them more careful and gave them confidence to feel that I had faith in them."[3]

A year later, during a lull in bombing, Claxton prepared a special course for the heads of the Rescue Service, all trained engineers. He wanted to increase the rescuers' consideration in handling stand-in victims and Brenda Whiteley, a local ambulance driver who "dabbled in the make up of wounds" was recruited. She "introduced some acting" into their first aid practices and in subsequent courses the rescue scenarios staged by the School became more elaborate. In one, Whiteley was placed under the joist of a collapsed floor, her leg apparently crushed.

She was scared by her predicament—the dirt, the dust, plaster, soot, the pain in her leg, the terror of being held in a vice by the beam. Her dog had run off or was, perhaps, another victim. Her husband did not come, when she called. She had renewed pain when the beam was lifted off her leg, was profoundly grateful to her rescuers, frantic about dog and husband, and distressed that lunch would not be ready when the children came home from school. The rescue men had entered a new world. Here was a person with problems as well as injuries, and there was a need to care for the person as well as for the broken leg. This person was part of a community with responsibilities—not just another statistic.[4]

Within months, the Leatherhead Rescue School became noted for such innovative use of "acting casualties."[5] Dr. W. J. Maelor Evans taught the actors medically accurate signs and symptoms of injury so that they could simulate both the appearance and behavior of casualties. They filled in the rest of the situational narratives themselves.

Twenty years earlier, through the innovations of a Swedish sculptor, first aid began to be consistently taught with the use of moulages (prosthetic simulations of wounds and fractures applied to the skin).[6] But this had been a mere gimmick. What Claxton, Whiteley, Evans, and their collaborators pioneered—apparently uniquely—was the addition of explicitly theorized principles of acting and staging to enhance the experience of realism for the rescuers and first aid workers.[7] After each rescue, resuming their own personas, the actors critiqued the rescuers and medics on their work: which is to say, on the response that resulted from the realism of the casualties' acting. This approach led to practices that increased the proficiency of extraction, appropriateness of first aid, and the comfort and survival of the Luftwaffe's real victims.

The Leatherhead School had a winning formula. On 22 November 1942, Claxton held an open meeting for anyone interested in the approach. Over 100 new volunteers signed up, charter members of what was dubbed the Casualties Union. Considered a vital part of Home Defense efforts, these volunteers included a boy with an amputated arm and a man with a silver plate in his head, who incorporated their unique physicality into the scenarios. Women were especially valued as members, for their involvement tended to produce more careful handling by the rescuers.[8] A member who had undergone a mastectomy offered particularly valuable scope for incorporating practice in dressing and bandaging chest wounds in what would otherwise be delicate circumstances.[9] Most of the Casualties Union's members were ordinary citizens who utilized lessons in anatomy to craft moulages from linseed oil putty tinted with grease paints, rubber built up with automobile enamel, cold cream and powdered whiting, and their characteristic "bread plastic" made from white bread moistened with petroleum jelly and held in place with wallpaper paste to approximate severed limbs, im-

46. Casualties being made up for an exercise at the FCDA school, Olney, Maryland: standing left a woman with amputated arm and prosthesis and seated center a man with head and wrist injuries. Courtesy of NARA.

palements, hemorrhage, displaced organs, and other mutilations from the mild to the severe.[10]

As impressive as the illusion of injury might be, it was behavior that created the urgency for treating the trapped and injured. Implemented under the principle of "controlled acting," the Casualties Union drew a distinction between "faking," its technical term for the application of makeup and moulages, and "acting," which signified characterological behavior responsive to the unfolding situation. This is a crucial distinction between the fully theorized aesthetic practice of the Casualties Union and the French theatrical genre of grand guignol, as nauseating as the effect of squirting blood or protruding bones may be to spectators of both.[11] At a time when training elsewhere utilized dummies or sandbags for rescue practice and mannequins for first aid practice, the students at Leatherhead encountered live people whose own basic preparatory curriculum involved how to "act" an injury, react to being handled, and partake in incident planning and staging for fractures, traumatic amputations, burns, blows to the head, asphyxia, and abdominal wounds.[12] Perhaps most importantly, however, the Casualties Union was able to address the complexity of wartime injuries: almost all real-life bombing victims suffered from shock, no matter what the extent of their other wounds, exacerbated by the effects of the blast itself and the cold nighttime conditions; most victims were covered in dirt and grime, which could obscure penetrating wounds; while the most frequent injuries—from falling masonry, bomb fragments, and flying splinters—were typically compounded by sprains, bruises, and fractures of no attributable cause.[13] The Casualties Union actors needed to evoke this complexity and to remember not to exceed the scope of what could be done by persons with their assigned injuries. If asked to do the impossible, they would try but fail. If urged to continue trying, they would collapse, exhibit fear, or panic. They would react to stimuli such as loud noises, the smell of gas or smoke, rough handling, exposure, or neglect just as they would try to rally when well-treated or offered encouragement. When they overheard careless remarks about other casualties or were roped up into a stretcher and tilted helter skelter for transport they would exhibit the suffering that was proportionate. And particularly, when they expressed concern for family, neighbors, friends, and pets but could not get definitive reassurance, they not only provided vital clues to the extent of the scenario being enacted so that the rescuers took measure of their task, but their own quota of shocked symptoms might expand, complicating the work of their first aiders.[14]

Casualties Union members began with their own personae, and as their experience and proficiency increased they branched out. Actors' briefing slips perfunctorily stated their injuries and symptoms and the posted General Narrative indicated the wider context of the incident. Beyond this, actors were encouraged to incorporate observations from everyday life to flesh out a character and *become* the part while maintaining some distance from it; they sought to portray "the *appearance* of emotion and sensation, not to feel the emotions and sensations as such."[15] Concentration and a sense of proportion were key.[16] Actors visualized themselves in distressful circumstances, tried to capture the outward symptoms, and practiced. Technical advice also helped. For example, they were advised that in acting pain their eyes "will almost certainly be puckered up, from the cheeks upward. . . . it helps the sensation of being tensed up, and also gives the appearance of flinching—or trying *not* to flinch." The mouth will be tight or twisted, teeth clenched, forehead knitted, and head inclined. Hands can indicate the type of pain: "the sudden agony will cause a sudden clenching, the steady pain, a steady grasping or pressing on or near the injury, the fidgety 'discomfort-pain' will cause restlessness, plucking at the blankets, and so on." And the fear of pain may produce the most overt of all signs.[17] Tutored in falling, vocal intonation, and relaxation, practice led Casualties Union actors to have "a perfectly clear mental picture of one's thoughts at any given moment of the performance" and equally clear exhibition of symptoms.[18]

47. One of the casualties from the Olney, Maryland, exercise in position among debris, awaiting rescue. Courtesy of NARA.

Practiced episodes extended from thirty seconds to many hours. A long episode might be punctuated by "fainting" or "exhausted collapse" to give an actor time to rest.[19] With all injuries, but especially where casualties enacted unconsciousness, first aiders relied on what the Casualties Union called "staging" for vital information about the nature of their malady.

> When we speak of staging we mean any location, or object, which is or could have been the primary or indirect cause of an accident, or to which some reference could be made in explanation of an accident. This definition applies equally well to the kettle of boiling water as to the overturned 'bus. Staging can be anything from a banana skin to a mountain, a bumble bee or a battleship. Its importance lies in the relationship between the staging and the casualty, and its influence on the atmosphere of an "accident" and the decisions of the first-aiders. Whatever else may be a fake, the staging must be actual.[20]

So, staging is scenographically contextual, and together with acting led to "performance chaining": rescue and first aid workers' immersion depended first on casualties' creation of illusion so, in a sense, acting was "contagious." If, for whatever reason, the staging was violated or the safety procedures were inadequate and the umpires did not catch what had happened, casualties were instructed to recite specific lines in order to break the performance chain. If casualties got hurt they would indicate this by saying "Acting stopped, genuine casualty." If they got into the hands of non-matrixed medical personnel in error, they would say "Exercise. Acting casualty."[21] Presumably, this would hasten treatment in the first instance and prevent a psychiatric diagnosis in the second.

In 1944, the Leatherhead School was wholly turned over to training Allied army personnel, which effectively spread knowledge of the Casualties Union's techniques to the French, Belgians, Dutch, Poles, Americans, and Canadians.[22] In the nuclear era, it became the standard technique internationally for rehearsing rescue and medical scenarios.

Nuclear Casualties

Immediately after peace was declared in Europe, the Casualties Union reconstituted itself to provide volunteers trained in acting, faking, and staging for demonstrations, competitions, tournaments, and exercises involving first aid workers of the police, St. John Ambulance Service (and in Scotland the St. Andrew's Ambulance Service), British Red Cross, and the Scouting movement. The scenarios provided scope for imagination at events depicting road accidents, industrial disasters, and home safety. At large-scale competitions, teams of first aid workers were deployed in rotation to assess and treat casualties on a station-by-station basis. Large numbers of spectators were accommodated in stands, for "gruesome as it sounds, blood and twisted limbs seem to attract people like a magnet."[23] Branches of the Casualties Union sprouted up all over southeast England, and by 1949 had spread to Ireland, Wales, and South Africa. By the mid-1950s, membership was close to 1,500 in thirty branches throughout Great Britain and the Republic of Ireland, and there were additional branches in Norway, Belgium, Malta, New Zealand, and Canada. The Casualties Union averaged participation in twenty-five British events each week, about half being first aid training, a third competitions, and a sixth demonstrations and lecture illustrations.[24] By the mid-1960s, it had five hundred affiliate groups worldwide, and it still thrives.[25]

Beginning in 1950, the Casualties Union became a significant part of Britain's federally organized, but officially volunteer, efforts in civil defense against nuclear war, an auxiliary to the Civil Defence Corps. The first intimation of the Casualties Union's interest in faking the effects of atomic weaponry shows up in a 1950 article in the *Casualties Union Journal.*[26] The union avidly acquired literature that would help members expand their repertoire of acting burns and shock in proportion to what would be incurred from an A-bomb.[27] Extrapolating from Hersey's ethnography of Hiroshima survivors, the Casualties Union imagined scenarios with 100,000 dead and as many crushed by buildings, lacerated by flying debris,

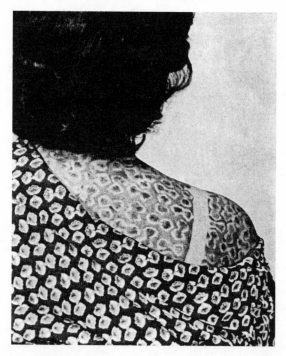

48. Make-up for a flash burn victim, based on Japanese A-bomb survivors, demonstrated in *Casualty Simulation*, published by Canada's Department of Health and Welfare, 1965. Courtesy of the Library of Congress. Instructions read: "White material reflects light rays and black absorbs them. Colors within that scale absorb light in varying degrees. Therefore, in simulating a flash burn through clothing, the skin beneath white or very light-colored material will remain its natural shade; under colored material it will be reddened. . . . Method of Preparation. 1. Apply a very thick coating of cold cream to the area, as a basis for make-up. 2. Outline the pattern of the printed material on the skin . . . 3. Mix vermilion and brown grease paint diluted with cold cream in the palm of the hand. 4. In the areas where burning is indicated, apply the grease paint with a fine paint brush."

and burned. The burns are particularly relevant: there would be ordinary burns from fire as well as flash burns (figure 48). In severe cases there would be "raw skin-surface and hanging shreds and strips of dead skin. Eyebrows . . . burned off; sometimes the features . . . almost wiped out, with the eye-sockets empty and the fused eye-substance trickling down the cheeks." Radiation victims "would be sitting on the pavements, or lying where they had fallen, retching and vomiting, and then suddenly dying without a sign of warning. . . . Within 12 to 15 hours, whole areas of skin are liable to slip off the body if any force is applied." Later, there would be "headache, tiredness and depression, indigestion and diarrhoea, fever and nausea" indistinguishable from classic shock.[28] The greater the area of effected skin surface, the greater the loss of nerve endings and advancement of shock, loss of fluids, and falling blood pressure. Actors were advised: "All these symptoms will tend to increase if no treatment at all is given to you, or if rough handling and tight bandages aggravate the pain. Pressure on a burn will give added distress, and protest must be made by saying; 'Oh, don't touch it!' 'I can't bear it!' 'Just leave me alone,' or by prolonged moaning if your condition is supposed to be really severe and the degree of shock limits your vocal expressions to weak noises rather than words."[29]

As Britain entered the Korean War, the Order of St. John began to instruct members in how to treat A-bomb casualties.[30] Late in 1950, the Casualties Union incorporated a flash burn victim into a large-scale demonstration at Hay's Wharf.[31] Early in 1951, at the joint army and Civil Defence Corps exercise Medusa, sixty casualties took part as A-bomb victims (see chapter 1). However, a major compromise to Casualties Union protocol was incorporated due to the army's lack of training: "Rescue work was made more realistic by burying sandbags for the military to dig out, the actual casualty standing by, made up ready for treatment [by Civil Defence Corps] when the token was brought to light."[32] Of course, this substitution was not "realistic" at all. Following this event, the Civil Defence Corps noted the importance of staged casualties, calling the Casualties Union "a council of perfection," and in subsequent exercises the union's orthodoxy for staging prevailed.[33] Within two years, they participated in countless courses at the Home Office training grounds as well as large-scale exercises in London, Liverpool, Exeter, Glasgow, Newcastle, Altrincham, Stroud, Middlesbrough, Hull, and Halifax, where it was admitted "some of our members may have thought they were acting in Hell."[34]

The Cold War era work of the Casualties Union is significant because of what it illustrates about the role of acting in circumstances far from playhouses. This poses a "context problem" for understanding the reach of theater into everyday life, given that the Casualties Union explicitly disavowed the glamour of theater and the egocentrism of actors while publishing a fascinating commentary on the important acting teacher Richard Boleslavsky, a Russian émigré to the United States, echoing his credo that "inspiration and spontaneity are results of calculation and practice" and extolling the importance of concentration, observation, "beads of action," and rhythm.[35] The author of this commentary, Helen Nicholson, noted similarities not indebtedness. The Casualties Union's work was neither a wholesale importation of theatrical ideas nor a pastiche of theories: cognizant of professional theater, no doubt, Casualties Union members nevertheless articulated and practiced a set of principles resulting in autonomous activity. The degree to which their work can be understood through knowledge of theater is likely more significant than their reliance on contemporaneous theater to derive their ideas. They deployed theatrical comparisons usually to make distinctions between their practices and the theater, to show their separateness, to contextualize not by analogy but by contrast. They believed that casualty simulation could "at its highest be a work of art," not through its resemblance to theater but its quality as an emotional experience for anyone in the performance chain, including spectators.[36]

Dramaturgy of the Casualties Union

The Casualties Union was an experimental prototype. Its practices became, over the course of three decades, the international standard for fully-enacted medical emergency drills. The Casualties Union's protocols are significant insofar as they represent an elegantly simple pattern for improvisation within a thriving genre that Gary Izzo calls interactive performance and that Richard Schechner names direct theater.[37] The contrasts in different participants' levels of immersion and the different protocols for responsiveness to simultaneous fictive levels in scenarios are significant given human beings' conditioned disposition for responding to illusion. The Casualties Union's protocols took a critical stance within culture only insofar as they sought to improve the skills of first responders and contribute to the evolution of sophisticated triage protocols for field hospitals and emergency rooms. What forced these reforms, as much as anything, was the scale of casualties attended to by the Civil Defence Corps and its corresponding arm in the National Health Service in the context of war exercises in the age of thermonuclear weaponry.

The report of the 18th International Conference of the Red Cross, held in Toronto in 1952, acknowledged "how significantly the position had altered" since 1945. "Adapting themselves to the situation," the Red Cross now was "visualizing help to the armed forces only in the sphere of social assistance and moral comforts with their main activities directed towards supplying the maximum aid to the non-combatant victims who would be most in need of it."[38] Of course, health and emergency services could not protect the public, but only ameliorate the effects of war. The consequences of radiation from a nuclear attack complicated the job of the emergency and health services so extensively that it was difficult to calculate—never mind exercise—its consequences. Nuclear attack exercise scenarios from the late 1950s and 1960s only indirectly acknowledge the importance of fallout for human life; instead, the effect of immediate radiation and blast remained the more manageable problems and so these were tested extensively.[39] By necessity, the exercises' scale was better suited to local, natural, or industrial disasters (not nuclear war), and the overlapping aspects of disasters rather than the uniqueness of radiation effects was usually gamed. Even so, the consequences of fallout gradually made their way into exercises. "Bull Ring" (30 May–1 June 1956), a syndicate exercise, predicted that 48 percent of British hospital beds would be lost or inaccessible; 225,000 would be usable but 900,000 would somehow be provided.[40] A Working Party report of 1962 predicted nearly 8 million Britons would die early in a war but only 350,000 casualties could be accommodated in hospitals.[41] There would be, as a civil defense recruiting poster of 1955 stated, "No mere spectators."[42] In the life-saving period—the seven days immediately post-attack—the scale of the disaster would inevitably strain rescue services past the breaking point, never mind the demand on devastated health providers in the subsequent survival period when countless millions with radiation sickness would emerge from shelter with symptoms of advancing illness. Practical exercises could help establish what such a strain may produce.

Rescue and first aid workers could not come in close proximity to the zone where damaged buildings were likely to trap casualties until a significant period after the attack. By the time rescue workers could put in an eight-hour shift in a zone radiating 10 r per hour, anyone they could rescue would have terminal radiation exposure. A rescue crew could recover one trapped person per hour, on average, so they could expect to save eight lives per shift before their own health became endangered.[43] A city receiving a 1 MT bomb would need to place its emergency field hospitals—Forward Medical Aid Units (FMAUs)—a minimum of five miles upwind of GZ, with ambulance teams shuttling victims out to this line. Increase the bomb's strength to 10 MT and the FMAUs would have to be at least eleven miles upwind of the blast's epicenter. The greater the distance to be traveled, the more road clearance would be required, the more evacuees would be streaming along cleared roads, and the longer the turnaround time would be for the precious few ambulances and drivers transporting the wounded to care.

In exercises up and down the country, Casualties Union members represented a range of anticipated injuries. Among 250 stretcher cases for "Exercise Battledore" in 1959, for example, there were patients who were only slightly injured and could benefit from treatment at the FMAU, serious cases including some who would benefit from immediate hospital treatment, and others who were beyond medical aid. The total arriving at hospitals for a single civil defense area in wartime was calculated at 7,000 to 14,000. The majority of cases were made up with second- or third-degree burns or severe flesh wounds; others would suffer from broken limbs, blast injuries, crushed chests, disembowelment, internal bleeding, or gas poisoning. To round out the picture in "Exercise Shuttlecock," there was

49. An ambulance collecting point in a London exercise. British Information Office photo, reproduced courtesy of the National Archives Image Library, London.

a woman in labor, a dazed but ambulatory victim in shock, and a handful of cases beyond all hope.[44] Among the wounded and homeless casualties taking part in "Exercise Gory" in 1960 were three hundred Casualties Union members and seven hundred cadets who cycled through an FMAU two or three times each to extend medics' experience with routine injuries.[45]

The actual injuries expected were equal proportions of major lacerations, uncomplicated burns, and either injuries to the extremities or other wounds. Those with lacerations, closed fractures of small bones, or 10 percent burns, which add up to a third of all expected casualties, would be treated at FMAUs or by first aiders. Those with more serious injuries but a high chance of survival—patients with respiratory obstructions, accessible hemorrhage, traumatic amputations, or open fractures—would receive immediate treatment at FMAUs, including surgery, provided this took little time to carry out. Others who could remain alive with antibiotics, intravenous fluids, or naso-gastric suction, or who had closed fractures of major bones, no more than 30 percent burns, large muscle wounds, and treatable abdominal, thoracic, head, or spinal injuries would be designated for non-immediate surgery. A third of all traumatic cases would have complica-

50. FMAU during a London exercise. British Information Office photo, reproduced courtesy of the National Archives Image Library, London.

tions of thermal burns and/or radiation exposure, exacerbating their treatment needs. Anyone whose injuries were severe enough to require immediate, time-consuming, or complicated treatment, or who was unlikely to survive rough evacuation—in other words those who would be regarded as priorities in peace-time—would "in a war situation . . . not be allowed to enter and encumber the evacuation routes but should receive appropriate supportive treatment locally" in FMAUS only if supplies and staffing permitted. Thus, anyone with extensive burns, multiple problems, severe head or spinal injuries, or high radiation doses would be administered morphine, as long as it lasted, and offered comfort, as long as someone else had strength to give it, until they died, probably never reaching a hospital and perhaps not even an FMAU.[46] This outlines the full briefing range for Casualties Union participants and the logic of those responding to them.

Initially, victims may be apathetic, dazed, grateful for help, and concerned for others. Later they may be worried, aggressive, and dissatisfied. Observers of large natural disaster survivors note two types: those who combine their own physical fatigue, apathy, and helplessness with intense preoccupation about their own or family needs, and those who have suffered a near miss and are a lot less easy to control, in which case their "apathy, hopelessness, and sleeplessness are accompanied by quick temper, excitability, vague but imperative fears and lack of adaptability." Civil defense workers were trained to try to channel ambulatory survivors' energies into constructive work and to assume a confident attitude when managing disruptive people. The mentally distressed were channeled to rest centers, the physically injured to FMAUs. The burden of caring for psychological trauma would fall to relatives or friends, so civil defense workers were drilled to stress that survivors were experiencing merely *temporary* responses ("mental shock," "fatigue," or "exhaustion" rather than "psychiatric illness," "neurosis," or "nervous breakdown"). There was to be no such thing as a British "psychiatric casualty."[47]

Practice showed that one ambulance party (consisting of rescuers and first aiders) could process twelve seriously injured people per hour, for a maximum of 100 on their shift. Thirty ambulances would be necessary to transport these injured to FMAUs for triage. A 150-person FMAU could handle 120 seriously injured casualties per hour (approximately 1,000 per shift), so ten ambulance parties would be required to keep the FMAU running at capacity. Forty more ambulances would be needed to transport the 40–60 percent of casualties warranting further care (sometimes higher for exercise purposes) to the even more distant hospital of bricks and mortar.

To test this model using a single FMAU, about 150 National Hospital Service Reservists, 70 ambulance drivers, 10 parties of rescue and first aid workers (up to 80 Civil Defence Corps members), and 270 casualties would be needed in the pipeline at any given moment in addition to the exercise umpires and constables controlling traffic. To keep the entire system busy in the middle hours of an eight-hour exercise, casualties would need to multiply: if most cycled through the system twice in an eight-hour day, around 500 casualty actors would be needed. To add the additional step of hospital triage, more than one FMAU would be required, as several FMAUs funneled patients to a single hospital: the need for casualty actors approaches 1,000 very quickly. Exercise "Triad" (April 1959), for example, operated with 1,000 volunteers from the National Health Service and Civil Defence Corps combined with nearly 1,000 casualties in a FMAU test staged by the Birmingham Regional Hospital Board. A similar number of casualties gathered for a demonstration exercise and recruiting drive in New Cross Hospital parking lot on 25 September 1960.[48] In such tests, the special abilities of Casualties Union members helped to create the sense of urgency that came from more realistic practice than would otherwise be suggested by a time and motion study.

The presence of acting casualties helped to establish that FMAUs, as planned, were inadequate in layout. The "Operation Fall" series of exercises, staged by the Welsh Hospital Board from 1960 to 1965, illustrates the range of operational play and how this discovery was made. The first exercise was predicated on a surprise nuclear attack involving seven bombs (totaling 10 MT) dropped on London, Bristol, Cardiff, Birmingham, Leeds, Manchester, and Glasgow. In Stage I, six FMAUS were (theoretically) dispatched to western Cardiff, but only one was actually set up and tested. The exercise involved processing casualties through the FMAU; each person cycled through three times. At 11:30, the FMAU received news that 900 casualties were expected in the next four to five hours. Within the first hour, the 4,232 square feet of floor space proved inadequate and the 800-square-foot holding bay was already full of moribund cases. The FMAU handled 415 casualties in four hours, averaging 104 casualties per hour. Calculating the needs for round-the-clock operation, if the death rate was 50 percent of cases, 50,000 square feet of space would be required, over ten times more than what was made available. From handling these casualty actors, it became apparent that for every square foot allocated to reception and sorting, another square foot was needed for evacuation, twice that was needed for light treatment, and six times as much for emergency and supportive treatment.[49]

Using acting casualties also established the load that medics could handle. Stage III of Operation Fall was conducted in Flintshire and involved a much heavier bombing pattern. Civil defense columns took part from as far away as Liverpool, along with 1,600 people from the Territorial Volunteers, army, National Health Service Reserve, and the Women's Voluntary Service (WVS). To prepare the victims, the Casualties Union supplied 108 faking specialists in sixteen teams to prepare over five hundred adults and cadets. The Casualties Union developed a production line system for faking teams. Dividing injuries into six categories — unconsciousness, burns, fractures, hemorrhages (internal and external), minor injuries (cuts, lacerations, bruises, incised wounds, etc.), and open wounds including the presence of foreign bodies — a production line of three or four fakers, each dealing with a specialty, could prepare about ten casualties per hour. A couple of floaters, assisting with bottlenecks, kept the system flowing.[50] Casualties were briefed in groups, and each pinned on a 1.5-inch color-coded cardboard disk with their serial number, blood pressure, pulse, and other clinical data. Casualties were not trapped in debris but awaited collection by ambulances at fourteen staging posts. First aid parties administered help then dispatched casualties to the two working FMAUS. After treatment, 10 percent of cases were mild enough for release to a rest center to join other homeless persons while 90 percent went to a checkpoint for further routing to acute hospitals. There were five designated hospitals, one of which was fully staffed for exercise purposes with 150 beds. Those arriving at token acute hospitals were processed by nurses then

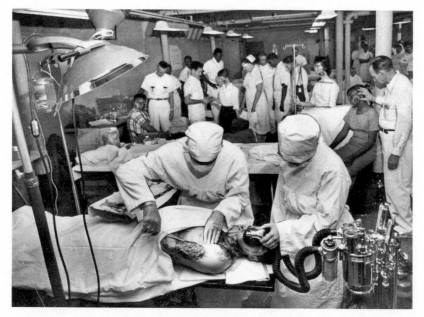

51. Moulages in use during a surgical training exercise for mobile hospital personnel at the U.S. Civil Defense Staff College, Battle Creek, Michigan, 1960. Courtesy of NARA.

released. Those arriving at the activated acute hospital were triaged for further treatment by awaiting nurses and physicians who simulated treatment on faked injuries.

The strain resulted in compromises to health care. Each FMAU saw about 120 patients per hour: too many to be provided with intravenous care, to apply limb splints, or control bleeding, all treatments expected at this stage; 75 per hour would be more realistic. "Assuming that 50% only needed these treatments the remaining 50% being only slightly injured, or so severely injured that nothing could be done for them, other than alleviate pain and make comfortable [*sic*], one cannot see 60 patients requiring these treatments being treated at the rate of one per minute."[51] Exercise "Life Line II," held in Worcestershire 16 June 1963, initiated play at H+9, which is later than most casualty exercises. In this case, the FMAU could handle eighty-nine cases per hour over a nearly five-hour period. Of these, around a quarter were lightly injured, and similar proportions were moribund, in need of immediate hospital treatment (in which case they were transferred to the two thirty-bed hospitals involved in the exercise), or could wait for treatment.[52] In nuclear war, it was unlikely that there would be enough dextran and plasma substitutes to administer to so many patients. Realistically, only minimal care could be administered: applying pressure bandages, tourniquets, morphia,

52. Radiation casualties at a decontamination area during "Operation Survival," a civil defense exercise conducted by the Humbolt County, California, civil defense organization at Fortuna, California, 1962. Courtesy of NARA.

and strapping fractured limbs to bodies. Staffing in the acute hospital was wholly inadequate to deal with the casualties requiring orthopedic, abdominal, and thoracic surgery, and a mobile blood bank was desperately needed.

The presence of acting casualties tended to make errors and deficiencies of all kinds more apparent. In Operation Fall Stage III, triage for patients going from the FMAU to hospital was inadequate, and one case was transferred already "dead."[53] This wasted transport resources as well as medics' time. At some point, if an exercise was realistic enough and if it went on long enough, the effects of injury and radiation would become more critical even though the pace of new incoming patients would slacken. At first, moribund cases in holding units might only constitute 20 percent of casualties, but by H+48 this figure might double or triple. Rehearsing showed that as the inward flow of cases begins to lag, staff—especially nursing staff—should be reassigned from critical to terminal cases. These are major considerations in medical and palliative planning. While medical exercises focused on injuries, the consequences of nuclear warfare also suggested the need to address the presence of radiation on victims' skin and clothing from the moment patients arrived at FMAUS. One U.S. exercise simulated casualties' radioactive decontamination. This is a major consideration impinging on the effectiveness of subsequent care and recuperation as well as workers' safety.

Psychological Acting

For argument's sake, let us take it for granted that the Casualties Union's faking of displaced intervertebral cartilage, fractured kneecaps, open pneumothorax, dislocated jaws, and skull fractures, as taught through its *Atlas of Injury*, was optimal. Also take it for granted that the acting of burns was so routine from staging household accidents, chemical fires, and electrical mishaps that symptoms of these injuries were well ingrained in the actors. In nuclear war exercises, casualties must sustain the authenticating conventions of their acting matrix throughout handling by successive teams of medics with different responsibilities and skill levels, for many hours at a time, necessitating that the emotional shock of disaster be portrayed along with physical trauma. Whatever the Civil Defence Corps' expectations regarding the un-Britishness of psychological trauma, the Casualties Union believed in it wholeheartedly. Again, the *Atlas of Injury* provides guidance. Casualties may exhibit stupor, slowing down movements and responses so as to appear "vacant, helpless and bewildered." They would behave dazed and listless, and respond to questions with a shrug of the shoulders or a blank gaze, remaining otherwise still amid any amount of mayhem. If urged to get on with things, they would become even more confused and indifferent. Other casualties may be emotionally excited, thrashing their limbs, sobbing noisily, and calling out for pity. These actors were cautioned against overdoing hysteria, though "tense muscles, refusal to be touched, noisy sobbing, biting at a handkerchief or your fingers, are all part of the behaviour of a highly strung person faced with an unpleasant or scaring situation." Casualties who were isolated from the scene of disaster and who were spoken to calmly would relax. Those scolded or treated unsympathetically would not improve. Other casualties would become aggressive as a response to fear, criticizing caretakers and acting out on repressed hostility. Many would be overcome by panic, noisily resisting help and showing terrible judgment.[54]

Ted Aldridge specialized in such symptoms and did pioneering work at Netherne Psychiatric Hospital, training Casualties Union members to display psychological symptoms. They practiced in groups and were assessed by student nurses. In the 1960s, this was an increasingly important aspect of psychiatric nurses' training. The more Casualties Union members who became experienced in this, the more diverse the range of psychological maladies that could be incorporated into nuclear exercises.[55]

Little explicit evidence incorporating these techniques is available. However,

53. "Carolina IV" psychiatric casualty undergoing prompt treatment. Courtesy of NARA.

one instance of an American exercise documents how such casualties would be treated. On 1 November 1973, an incident involving a bomb was staged at the campus of the University of South Carolina in Columbia. Soldiers from Fort Jackson served as injured casualties to test helicopter evacuation procedures while more than two hundred students provided the psychiatric dimension for the Richland County civil defense workers. A psychological triage team sorted trauma victims arriving at the hospital. Psychotherapy was provided for disaster casualties "aimed primarily at opening the emotional flood gates to enable victims to 'talk out' their feelings of guilt at having survived when loved ones were lost, remorse at the loss of loved ones, inability to face an uncertain future, and other acute anxieties." Another group of social workers fielded telephone inquiries about relatives and friends, checking lists, and alleviating the emotional shock of informing people of fatalities. A photographic series shows a casualty separated from the throng and aided in "talking out" his trauma at the Columbia Area Mental Health Center.[56] In nuclear war, demand for psychiatric services would be high: a Canadian manual of 1953 predicated that 5–10 percent of casualties from an A-bomb would suffer from psychiatric conditions (some in combination with other injuries) and half of them would require care in a psychiatric facility;[57] in OPAL 59, the expected need for in-patient care was assumed to be 40 percent neuropsychiatric cases.[58]

The Casualties Union proselytized tirelessly and its techniques were disseminated far and wide.[59] The techniques were explicitly recommended, though without credit, by the Canadian Department of Health and Welfare in a manual of 1965 and incorporated in rescue exercises at Arnprior from 1954.[60] The Leatherhead Rescue School's techniques for staging were adopted by the United States in the early 1950s, incorporated at Olney, and widely admired.[61] Meanwhile, in Europe, Britain maintained its leadership in the acting of casualties. In nuclear war exercises, casualties which had been scrupulously faked—for example, with an abdominal wound that could actually be stitched—had to be prepared to be "dismissed with little or no apparent treatment" in the FMAU because in the simulation of wartime conditions such injuries could not be afforded treatment.[62] In principle, then, Casualties Union actors were prepared to give as realistic responses to neglectful exercise protocols as actual errors in treatment; to react to the breakdowns in orderly triage as well as to act out post-attack civil (dis)order; to show medics, the government, and army personnel who set up exercises and members of the public who came to watch the consequences on this small scale what happens when pharmaceuticals, splints, blood plasma, other medical staples, and personnel are under-supplied; to portray what the scene would look like when the morphine runs out, as it surely would in the earliest days of the life-saving period; to stand in for the bodies that pile up and will soon begin to putrefy; and to demonstrate how the initial conditions of disaster create a mobile and desperate population on an unprecedented scale.

The aesthetics that went along with the protocols of Casualties Union practice show, on these quintessential stages of emergency, a rehearsal of what citizens should expect when their governments' plans for them were put to the test. By necessity, practical rehearsals could not be on the scale of nuclear war—the CRP-2 scenario from 1984, for example, projects 23 million Americans with radiation sickness, and estimates that they would require 780 million units of platelets and 390 millions of white blood cells[63]—but exercises could be extrapolated to scale. Actions were repeated in an attempt to get things right, though full success was eternally elusive.[64] Within the playing spaces of these stages of emergency, explicit exercise protocols ensured that a certain degree of order reigned, as players acted out their designated roles. Everyone was required to think and react in character, to demand believability of each other while operating within the scope of play.[65] Though non-matrixed, even the exercise umpires were in character, as themselves, as witnesses, as officials charged with enforcing the rules of play, remembering what transpires, and recommending improvements in subsequent planning. This decorum of structured improvisation within a complex set of conventions differentially assigned to various players is explicitly theatrical, and enables a safe zone for discovery. In civil defense exercises, players necessarily locate their function in relation to the overall narrative; by continuing to act their roles, Casualties Union members, rescue workers, physicians, and nurses make a conditioned choice to enhance mimetic illusion through their methexis in accident, disaster, and war scenarios projecting the circumstances of post-nuclear attack.

Spectators found this enthralling. By recognizing the theatricality, audiences participated in the dissociation necessary to understand the event. The audiences at British civil defense exercises experienced different degrees of physical containment: sometimes they were in bleachers or behind barriers, sometimes they wandered at will. When permitted, they congregated around arriving ambulances, making it difficult for stretcher bearers to do their work, and crowded other sites where the casualties and workers were most evident.[66] While Dennis Kennedy argues that to assist in any spectacle, audiences necessarily surrender some of their agency, Baz Kershaw stipulates that there is no such thing as a 100 percent passive audience: spectators authenticate the "real" in what they observe and actively construct meaning from it.[67] In civil defense exercises, much happens that is unplanned, improvised, and inadvertent, with the different valences these terms imply. In this "dramaturgy of changing states" (to use Eugenio Barba's term), spectators find meaning, each perceiving differently and each perception distinct.[68] To become immersed in the Grand Narrative—to believe the participants to be actual casualties of nuclear war—would require spectators to also believe themselves to be nuclear war survivors. This would violate the "performance consciousness" of not/but/not that separates realistic play from that which it projects to simulate.[69] This must not happen to casualty actors, medics, or civil defense workers (for it would mean psychosis under circumstances of manifest pretense), and it must not happen to spectators either. The event must be maintained as a rehearsal but exists in order to produce "collective reflexivity."[70]

With the enabling effects of active dissociation, alienation, or self-reflexivity in standing aside from the scenarios of suffering, players and spectators could experience a self-possessed critical stance so as to "draw the lessons" from their experience. The Casualties Union's faking, acting, and staging is emblematic of what set the process into motion. It is this same principle of imagination and acting in rehearsal that, it was thought, might enable citizens to take their part—intellectually prepared and emotionally in control—without succumbing to the psychological devastation projected in actual nuclear war. Role-play and acting in repeated rehearsals during peacetime was integral to governments' recommended preparations for their citizens' survival in wartime. Thus, acting was not only the method but also the ontology for the populace to preserve life, the ethnos of their nation, and the fabric of their culture. It was the bulwark against nihilism, the motivation for belief, and the insurance of survival. Acting was the way to buy into the idea that civil defense could be efficacious; it was also, at the same time, the means to see how it did not work.

Part III

CRISIS PLAY

This exercise again posed the dilemma which faces the decision maker in an emergency short of war, namely, how far can the government go, in initiating controls piecemeal, without being drawn into what amounts to a comprehensive mobilization of resources before actual military conflict. In turn, this raises the issue of the relationship of one set of controls to others, as well as the judgmental problem of how long we should wait to mobilize in a clearly deteriorating situation.

—Edward F. Phelps, Jr.

The last of the OPAL civil defense exercise series, indeed the last nationwide public civil defense drill in the United States and possibly any NATO nation, was held in April 1961.[1] Instead of having the public scramble for shelter, henceforth exercise resources would be put into continuity of government planning. This was coordinated at the federal level by the newly restructured Office of Civil Defense (OCD) in the Pentagon and Office of Emergency Planning (OEP) in the executive branch, leading toward exercises involving key civil service employees, officials of federal agencies and departments, and the White House. The degree of publicity that the civil service attracted during the OPAL series would be a thing of the past: future exercises involving the federal government were rarely noticed in the press. While the Boy Scouts, American Legion, Teamsters, and service clubs across the nation gained a sense of involvement and agency by volunteering time and equipment to put federally purchased supplies into marked public shelters in 1963, the federal government literally went underground in its parallel efforts. Planning for continuity of government in the event of nuclear war involved provision for relocation sites and their staffing, storage of duplicate records, and communication with other levels of government. For the duration of the Cold War, civil servants in all branches of the federal governments of the United States, Canada, and the United Kingdom rehearsed their wartime functions in their regular offices or alternate emergency relocation premises (for further details, see chapter 11).

The paradigmatic instance of how the "what ifs" of a continuity of government exercise took on real world significance is "Operation Spade Fork," an exercise that concluded less than three weeks before the onset of the Cuban Missile Crisis; as such, it was truly a dress rehearsal for what could have happened if Americans' worst fears were realized. Spade Fork provides a unique instance of how the simulated corresponds to the real, and how the purview of a civil defense exercise (risk management) illuminates the compass of international relations (risk abatement). While most civil defense exercises have an empirical element, the Cuban Missile Crisis was a bona fide emergency; because of its peaceful conclusion it became, in turn, data for refinement of planning, just like Spade Fork. When the Kennedy administration revised the Eisenhower-era *National Plan for Emergency Preparedness* in October 1963,[2] the revisions arose not just from what was learned during routine tests and exercises like Spade Fork but also from direct experience of actions taken by the OCD in the Pentagon and by the OEP under direct presidential authority during the Cuban Missile Crisis.

Countless civil service exercises were undertaken in the United States, United Kingdom, and Canada, but only the Cuban Missile Crisis forced the issue beyond the hypotheticals of rehearsal and toward performance in an authentic crisis. Records from the John F. Kennedy archive reveal the relationship between civil defense crisis planning and the unfolding missile crisis of October 1962, allowing this aspect of the domestic situation to be written into history for the first time.

The State of Emergency Planning and Preparedness

By Executive Order of President Truman, each federal department and agency was required to "prepare plans for maintaining the continuity of its essential functions at the seat of Government and elsewhere during the existence of a civil-defence emergency."[3] Continuity of government planning involved establishing lines of succession, preserving essential records, and designating protected locations for federal, regional, state, and local operations in communication with each other. But, as the director of the Office of Civil Defense Mobilization (OCDM) observed, "plans are worthless if governments do not survive to execute them."[4] American government was not in good shape to survive, either at the federal level or below, at the outset of the Cuban Missile Crisis. Though all fifty states and more than 2,500 county and city governments had developed survival plans, few were operational. There was no attention to post-attack resource management in the plans, even though state and local governments were responsible for provisions (including food) following an attack.[5] As of February 1961, only thirty-eight states and just a few counties or cities with populations under 50,000 had legislated for lines of succession. Duplicating and storing essential records was all very well, but they had to be maintained and kept current; no state operated a fully adequate program. All states and many large cities had alternate sites for emergency governments, but virtually none were in blast-proof or even fallout-protected facilities. Few government employees at any level were trained beyond what they had experienced in OPALs,[6] which confined exercises to just a few days following nuclear attack and never rehearsed the reconstruction or emergence from shelter phases of a post-attack world. Without improved readiness at all levels of government, the effective operation of the executive branch's Classified Location ("High Point," at Mt. Weather, Virginia, also referred to as "the Hole"), which had been on continuous activation since 22 September 1958,[7] would be fruitless.

The "Basic Report of Civil and Defense Mobilization," issued in February 1961 to apprise the new president of the defense situation, points out that with the development of Soviet missile systems the United States not only became more susceptible to surprise attack but active defense became increasingly vulnerable. Passive measures—population and resource dispersion and mobility, hardening of facilities, and concealment—were what remained.[8] The short warning times for missiles and unpredictability of attack patterns no longer made evacuation of cities a sensible option. Instead, President Kennedy encouraged citizens to provide their own shelters and endorsed schemes to locate and mark public shelters, leaving the private sector to bear the burden of these costs. With the proliferation of nuclear warheads, increased speed and accuracy of their delivery, and escalating number of anticipated hits, arrangement for continuity of government was a growing concern. Yet the federal relocation arc—involving sixteen sites located between thirty and three hundred miles from Washington and 35,000 designated personnel—utilized few, if any, hardened sites and their provision was not accounted for in the 1962 budget allocation.[9] The State Department, for example, had been stalled for ten years in its desire to make the cave designated for its use at Front Royal, Virginia, viable for emergency occupation (or, alternately, to install steel prefab shelters at the site) so that the department could safely occupy it under fallout conditions.[10] In any case, the viability of the arc was dubious in the age of missile delivery because it was less likely that staff could successfully relocate in a rapidly accelerating emergency.

Most federal agencies and departments had field offices throughout the nation, and thus their staff was always decentralized. Many federal departments incorporated field offices into their continuity plans; however, the capital's concentration of federal agencies and personnel made its potential destruction central to the issue of continuity of the government—and thus the nation—and some key functions were directed solely out of Washington-area headquarters. The president's Science Advisory Committee warned that 95 percent of the District of Columbia's population would become casualties in an attack. "From these data, OEP concludes that all National Government headquarters in Washington, D.C. are virtually certain to cease to exist." Because most executive federal field personnel were based in fourteen large cities that were also vulnerable to attack, "federal offices and field personnel will sustain much higher proportions of casualties than the population in general."[11] To avoid such a scenario, an OEP report of 11 June 1962 emphasized the practicality of prelocation (transporting key officials and staff—whose work related to emergency functions—before an emergency had been declared) over relocation (which occurs later in the crisis time line).[12] In order to ensure that the existing structure of government was in place after nuclear war, planners believed that the arc had to be staffed continually throughout an emergency, not waiting until the situation was about to erupt into war.[13]

At the next level of operations, Steuart Pittman (assistant secretary of defense for Civil Defense) envisioned the network of eight regional civil defense headquarters (at Harvard, Massachusetts; Olney, Maryland; Thomasville, Georgia; Battle Creek, Michigan; Denton, Texas; Denver, Colorado; Santa Rosa, California; and Everett, Washington) as the loci for pre-attack planning and of survival operations immediately post-attack. Post-attack, the OCD regional headquarters would become communication conduits, gathering data on damage assessment based on radiological monitoring; authorize distribution of local stockpiles and federally owned survival items; serve as clearinghouses for demands to help with mass feeding; coordinate evacuation, utility repairs, decontamination, debris clearance, and rescue; provide support to the states for radiological defense and decontamination; and liaise with state governments on survival needs. The regional hardened shelters would also serve as record repositories and communications links to aid in the control of resources. But none of the regions had their purpose-built sites by the time of the missile crisis. Indeed, only one (in Denton,

Texas) had been authorized for construction, and it would not be ready for another year.[14]

Dispersed sites exacerbated the need for reliable communications. In his memoir, the White House Press Secretary Pierre Salinger writes that on the morning of 21 October 1962 he met with an official of the OEP to set in motion a plan for emergency information procedures for the Cuban Missile Crisis, and "to place on standby alert a nation-wide communications system, most of it underground."[15] Salinger avowed that there had already been twenty-two months of meetings to update emergency procedures, including communications, but he may have been misinformed about realities. The extent to which there was a system with any likely utility following nuclear attack is called into question by a report of 20 August 1962. Four categories of requirements were identified, as follows.

CATEGORY I

The national military command would provide the president with information on warning, threat analysis, enemy capabilities, damage assessment, and recommendations for action. It was necessary, therefore, to link the Pentagon, Raven Rock, Pennsylvania ("Site R," designed to provide communications if Washington is destroyed),[16] and airborne and ship command posts as well as field posts by secure voice and television transmission to the secretary of state and the war room, presidential and State Department successors, the CIA, and DOD. In addition, communications with selected allies, all nuclear-capable enemies, NORAD, and regional and state civil defense headquarters needed to be accessible by expeditious means.

CATEGORY II

Priorities at this level involve survival operations. The transmission of 750,000 words a day was anticipated between the OEP/OCD headquarters at Mt. Weather, Virginia, and the eight regional headquarters, federal field offices, and military emergency sites. Contact pertinent to weather information (Department of Commerce), rural fire control (Forest Service), and air traffic control (Federal Aviation Administration) were as crucial as internal security (FBI) against counterespionage and in aid of state police. For allocation of medical supplies and services for post-nuclear operations as well as biological and chemical warfare, HEW would need to be in communication. The president's capacity to address the nation, particularly by radio, was crucial. At this level, international links to heads of governments in the Communist Bloc were also prioritized, along with neutral nations (Sweden, Switzerland, India), allies with which the United States had multilateral or bilateral arrangements (NATO, ANZUS, and Japan), NATO in Paris, U.S. ambassadors abroad, and State Department regional supervisory posts in Ottawa, Mexico City, Rio de Janeiro, London, Rabat, Accra, Beirut, New Delhi, Pretoria, and Manila.

CATEGORY III

Summaries on electrical power, communications, transport, food, fuel, and housing would come in via agency heads in the Washington area. Information on agriculture, food, and mass feeding (USDA), manpower and equipment (Post Office and Labor), transportation (Commerce and Inter-State Commerce Commission), and emergency shelter (Housing and Home Finance Agency) would come in from across the nation. Commerce anticipated a high volume of communications—around 300,000 words daily—with agencies such as the Weather Bureau, Maritime Administration, Employment and Training Administration, Business and Defense Services Administration, district offices, and ships at sea. Key points in nets of commercial communications companies would facilitate contact within the United States, and U.S. Information Agency transmitters would facilitate broadcasting to enemy, potential enemy, and key neutral nations abroad.

CATEGORY IV

Reports would funnel upward to the president from federal, regional, and state authorities on population migrations and relocations, medical facilities, transportation resources, power and fuel availability, housing, communications, industrial capacity, military control, agricultural facilities, and morale. Reports would be needed on control of shipping, reconstitution of production and distribution systems (Commerce); fuel and energy production (Department of Interior and Federal Power Commission); manpower planning and allocation (Labor, Selective Service, and the Civil Service Commission); registration (Post Office); reconstruction of the banking and financial systems and emergency action for the Bureau of Customs (Treasury and Federal Reserve); reactivation of power generating facilities (Atomic Energy Commission and Federal Power Commission); civilian air traffic (Civil Aeronautics Board); housing facilities (Housing and Home Finance Agency); and hospitals (Veterans Administration). Communication with relocation centers for Congress and the Supreme Court were also needed in order to reconvene Congress and reestablish the judiciary.[17]

Not much of this could be counted on, assuming destruction of existing land lines. But to set priorities, agencies and departments were asked to identify the time after the outbreak of nuclear war by which information must be available to them. Connecting state and regional facilities to each other would be of higher priority in the early days than connections between them and either Washington's relocation arc or the president. At the time of the missile crisis, headquarters for Region One (the northeast) had no communications with federal agencies' relocation sites, no funds to allow for teletypewriter exchange (TWX) installation, and no way to make existing communications secure.[18] The situation at other regional sites is unknown, but since the northeast was a critical priority it should not be assumed that facilities elsewhere were any more sophisticated. Failure to provide even the facilities specified in Category I had a serious effect on the unfolding Cuban Missile Crisis, as the ExComm (the ad hoc committee hurriedly convened to advise the president) communicated by teletype to the U.S. embassy in Moscow, which relayed communiqués to the Kremlin and then awaited translation and reaction, taking a minimum of four hours.[19] The cumbersome nature of this communication was not as dire as the effects of precipitate counterstrikes might have been, when delays of minutes could be catastrophic, but even the lack of communication requirements specified in Category II would cause delays of up to an hour, significantly increasing casualties.[20]

The OEP's 11 June 1962 report was promptly endorsed by the president on 25 June.[21] It recommended greater versatility, austerity, and specificity in planning. For example, too much responsibility lay with the OEP (civil defense planning for the executive branch), so whatever could be divested to other agencies should be shifted, at the same time that the OEP should improve its capability to control and allocate resources such as consumer supplies during an emergency. The presidential line of succession—all personnel based in Washington—were vulnerable to elimination in a single attack, and the report strongly urged that this be addressed either through expansion of the line of succession or dispersal of the successors at all times. It also noted that a survivable national communications system linking the president, civilian leaders, diplomatic and intelligence personnel, DOD and the military was lacking for emergencies of any kind, and the National Military Command System (in the planning stages) should be adapted for this purpose. The readiness of the proposed survivable communications system by the autumn of 1962 is highly dubious.

Plan C and Plan D-Minus

Civil defense planning in the executive branch was based on *The National Plan* of October 1958 and coordinated under documents titled *Mobilization Plan C* (the blueprint for civil defense measures during build-up to nuclear war, first drafted in mid-1950s and applied to an emergency situation short of nuclear attack, specifying actions to be taken under statutory authority) and *Federal Emergency Plan D-Minus* (also drafted in the mid-1950s as the plan for the aftermath of nuclear assault not preceded by other hostilities, specifying actions to be taken initially under emergency presidential powers until legislative approval could be garnered).[22] They were the basis of federal tests such as "OPEX 61-1" (6–7 April 1961).[23] In January 1962, McGeorge Bundy and Frank Ellis updated *Plan C* and *Plan D-Minus*, recognizing new situation assumptions and a broader range of emergency possibilities.[24] From 6–27 September 1962, Spade Fork—rehearsed in conjunction with NATO's Fallex 62 and the joint chiefs of staff "Exercise High Heels II"—tested the federal government's ability to implement *Plan C* and *Plan D-Minus*.

Plan C had two major thrusts. Upon declaration of a civil defense emergency, each federal agency or department would occupy its relocation arc site with skeleton staffs who would "prepare sites and facilities for occupancy by personnel required to conduct all essential functions," the remainder of staff continuing as normal in Washington.[25] Relocation of some personnel would be immediate, but most operations would be phased in over a period of up to ninety days following declaration of a civil defense emergency. In addition to mobilization of federal agencies and departments, *Plan C* stipulates pre-attack planning for the implementation of rationing; wage, rent and credit controls; requisition of industrial facilities; and the curtailment of all activities of HEW except mitigation of the emergency.

Plan D-Minus ran consecutively with *Plan C*. It is predicated on the deaths of over 48 million Americans and the injury of 12 million more, not all of whom would receive adequate care. The survival of 120 million others—as yet uninjured by exposure to residual radiation, consumption of contaminated food, or contagious disease—was believed to allow recuperation efforts to be feasible.[26] *Plan D-Minus* assumes that Washington is so severely damaged that no operations are possible there. Most sites in the federal relocation arc escape direct hits but some personnel within them are assumed to have fatal radiation exposure; in any case, they are inadequately staffed to perform all essential functions. It is assumed that an attack would not only impair government functions but also their control, "seriously reduce military strength . . . disrupt industrial and agricultural production and endanger the existence of the nation and the free world."[27] Reestablishing communications is assumed to be hampered by "casualties, sickness and confusion, the fear of radiation, and lack of food and water," which prevents surviving workers from executing repairs to power, telephone, and telegraph facilities. "Consequently there are long delays in placing all but the most urgent telephone calls as well as in the delivery of telegraph messages." International communication capability is all but destroyed due to damage within the United States and abroad, electronic jamming, sabotage, and lack of personnel.[28] In addition, the attack would have "almost completely paralyzed the functioning of the economic system, causing disruption of organized governmental activities, fragmentation of society into local groups, deterioration of our social standards, breakdown in our financial system, and complete disruption of normal production processes. The proportion of human casualties exceeds the proportion of material losses."[29]

Plan D-Minus was predicated on an attack of realistic magnitude yet one which was considered survivable, in time. However, when the attack scenario was read aloud at a National Security Council meeting in 1957, the minutes state "the President interrupted to ask . . . why . . . it was necessary to go any further, since by this time we would all be dead (laughter)." Mirth aside, President Eisenhower went on to note that "all our initial effort would have to be devoted to keeping a government running."[30] *Plan D-Minus* specifies policies and actions designed to maintain the form and authority of government, support military operations and alliances, ensure survival of the remaining population and recovery of the nation, encourage effective use of resources, and maintain the unity of the free world.[31]

The OEP's 11 June 1962 report recommended replacing *Plan C* and *Plan D-Minus* with comprehensive plans for the executive branch, "representing a spectrum of measures from which those appropriate to the situation can be selected" depending on the level of tension.[32] Until that point, civil exercises assumed the worst—full nuclear exchange—which did not prepare civil servants for differential phase-ins short of full emergency. Immediate implementation of such recommendations could have resulted in preparation of new plans in time for testing during Spade Fork in September, but this did not come to pass. Instead, the 11 June report helps highlight aspects of planning where implementation difficulties were expected during Spade Fork, and thus where they were also unavoidable during the Cuban Missile Crisis.

Prior to attack, the OEP was responsible for developing understandings, plans, and procedures among all federal elements, suppliers, and distributors of consumer supplies in order to permit effective post-attack consumer rationing. During a nuclear exchange and continued hostilities, the OEP was to immediately decentralize administration of its programs, authorizing direct state and local control actions such as freeze and release orders, anti-hoarding and requisition orders, and conservation and limitation orders. The OEP would determine rationing policy and allocations but their administration would devolve to other entities. Post-attack, the OEP would order phase-in of direct economic controls, extending control back through the distribution chain to the producers, and institute ways to legally enforce any needed procedures.[33]

Post-attack, most functions would be executed by existing agencies; however, a number of emergency agencies would come into being to address economic stabilization, public information, economic warfare, psychological warfare, and censorship. Secret emergency designees, chosen from outside government, would take charge of these agencies (though as of June 1962, only one designee—for censorship—was current, all others having resigned or been terminated). Their staff would come from the 1,700-person Executive Reserve, public sector workers who received training for these emergency assignments.[34] Falling under the auspices of the OEP, these agencies (with the exception of economic warfare) increased the OEP's burden beyond already unmanageable levels, so it was recommended that they be put under the control of other agencies and that the OEP focus on telecommunications management and initial resource control and allocation. This recommendation appears not to have been put into effect by September.

Rehearsing Crisis: Operation Spade Fork

Spade Fork involved six hundred civilians from twenty-seven federal departments and agencies, many of whom moved into emergency relocation sites that operated on an austere basis, though no aspect of this was apparent to the public.[35] The nuclear attack postulated thirty-four million dead and seventeen million injured: a somewhat lower casualty count than *Plan D-Minus* stipulated.[36] It rehearsed a two-week pre-attack phase, during which participants received a daily simulated newspaper detailing the escalating international and domestic crises in addition to intelligence reports from the Exercise Directing Staff. This triggered activities to increase readiness according to predetermined emergency actions specified in *Plan C*. For example, the Department of the Interior established emergency agencies for administering electricity, minerals, solid fuels, petroleum and gas, and fisheries. The State Department organized a committee including members from Treasury, Interior, Agriculture, Commerce, Labor, and HEW to handle foreign trade. The Treasury Department issued a regulation to curb runs on banks and tightly control credit prior to attack (though the measure was designed to be implemented following an attack). The Defense Resources Act was submitted to Congress, and simulated presidential approval gave authority for rationing, wage, rent and credit controls; requisitioning, condemnation, allocation, and plant seizure; and the establishment of emergency agencies.[37]

DEFCON 5 was the normal Cold War condition of military readiness. Spade Fork's pre-attack period simulated actions through the escalating military alert phases of DEFCONS 3, 2, and 1. The highest level of alert achieved during the Cuban Missile Crisis was DEFCON 3 (from 22 October 1962), involving review of readiness, relocation of an advance cadre of personnel, activation of the emergency communications system, and twenty-four-hour shifts for civil defense personnel in the White House.[38] During Spade Fork's simulated DEFCON 3 a few weeks earlier, federal civil defense agencies also distributed rations, radiological instruments, and survival stockpiles to public shelters; increased information broadcasting; recalled personnel from leave; prepared for further relocation of personnel; moved essential records to relocation sites; and ordered the use of shelter sites for the public. During DEFCON 3, it is stipulated that "no measures will be taken that could be considered provocative or that might disclose operational plans. Readiness actions should be accomplished without public notice, if possible."[39] On Spade Fork's simulated declaration of DEFCON 2, the assistant secretary of defense (for Civil Defense) and other emergency personnel were (hypothetically) relocated, the president was requested to declare a civil defense emergency, emergency action documents were reviewed, and reservists and governors were alerted. On simulated declaration of DEFCON 1, more personnel were relocated, emergency action documents readied, and executive reservists assigned to duty stations. The exercise revealed that further inter-agency coordination was needed at this stage. For example, while the OEP prepared economic controls to prevent hoarding, the USDA recommended that the public stockpile food and gasoline.

In Spade Fork, one of the first simulated bombs to arrive "detonated" over Quonset Point Naval Air Station, across Narragansett Bay from the president's simulated location in Newport, Rhode Island. He was "safe," as were all successors to the presidency and department and agency heads.[40] The attack on Washington came nearly six hours after instigation of war, so key federal officials were presumed to relocate and survive. This delay was tactically unrealistic, but allowed for more play than would otherwise be feasible in the post-attack period. State governments were not so fortunate: half of all state capitals were severely damaged and only a few were able to carry out limited emergency operations. The District of Columbia lost its emergency headquarters and its government was inoperable. Regional OCD headquarters at Thomasville, Georgia, and Denver, Colorado, incurred damage and were declared inoperable for ninety days; responsibility was transferred to adjoining regions.[41] During the attack, the OCD headquarters focused on monitoring reports of nuclear detonations; updating war room displays; assessing damage to the population and civil defense organizations, supplies, equipment, and facilities; and implementing legislation that designated broad authority to act in an emergency of this kind.[42] Regional OCD authorities focused on requirements for emergency housing, food, medical supplies, and gasoline. By this time, *Plan D-Minus* was being rehearsed.

A forty-eight-hour attack period emphasizing damage to 355 military targets in the United States and Canada was followed by a five-day post-attack period when exercise time was devoted to assessing remaining industrial production capability (without regard to transportation capabilities). The military assumed losses of 22 percent in the army, 40 percent in the navy, and 42 percent in the air force. Civilian losses were particularly high in the railroad industry, and there was a 75 percent reduction in productive capability of air, ordnance, motor transport, and other industries.

Civilian exercise play focused particularly intensely upon shortages of health resources, medical manpower, and petroleum but was by no means comprehensive. HEW liaised with regional offices to handle food, shelter, and medical crises, especially where evacuees congregated. Ships at sea carrying essential survival items were recalled. Other commodities were presumed to be sufficiently supplied, though not always located where they were needed.[43] Simulated presidential actions included consulting with Congress on new legislation and preparing an address on the state of the nation. Examples of other decisions included the Federal Reserve Board's issuance of schedules for redistributing currency, part of a package of emergency banking measures.

Following such massive loss of human life and dislocation of populations, labor supply interacted with other factors to determine the feasibility of many recuperative, industrial, and military operations. *Plan D-Minus* stipulates:

> In many localities there is a surplus of manpower in certain skilled occupations which could be used if necessary equipment and supplies were available. Difficulty has been encountered in trying to contain evacuated populations in relocation centers around cities which have been attacked. . . . As a consequence, the size of the labor force and the skill distribution within the relocated area change continuously. . . . Effective use of manpower is further reduced by the unavoidable effects of lowered resistance, psychological shock, and varying degrees of exposure to radiation.[44]

The Department of Labor planned to channel employment opportunities from nonessential fields to survival and recovery efforts. These controls were made ready in case of need but not authorized by the OEP until voluntary systems were evaluated; the question was still under study at the conclusion of the exercise.[45]

The Defense Resources Act was used to requisition surplus federal personnel, materials, and facilities for civil defense; reimburse states for civil defense assistance to other states; provide essential financing to victims; and employ temporary personnel outside normal civil service regulations. On D+3, the OEP established provisional post-attack rehabilitation and production goals for various business and industrial sectors, based on quarterly estimates of gross national product.[46]

The global political situation that eventually led to the missile crisis hampered the civil service's ability to participate in Spade Fork as fully as hoped. According to the military exercise report, "due to the critical international situation which was developing during the two-month period immediately prior to the exercise, the Exercise Director advised" that civil play "would be carried out on a 'low key.'"[47] The State Department kept all exercise wire messaging from having any bearing upon current events: this was deemed a necessary measure but led to skepticism about applicability. Interplay between the military and civil agencies lacked realism: "many problems injected locally by the military did not have time to become issues of national consideration. The failure to receive military force tables and requirements, key items in meaningful resource analysis, disappointed many civil agencies."[48] Several agencies "reduced the planned scope of their exercise participation and likewise cut back the amount of exercise activity planned for their most senior officials. There was little participation at the regional, state and local levels."[49] Too much emphasis was put on "response to player actions" as distinct from "simulation" of state, regional, and national leadership. Spade Fork's "low key" may have reduced players' commitment to serious participation in finding solutions to problems and led directing staff to sometimes determine solutions to the problems that they themselves had written for exercise play.

The five-day post-attack period left little time to game damage assessment, industrial production, or residual capability. While the military exercised its requirements for movement in the first phase following nuclear war—for example, utilizing alternate port designations for sea and air traffic—it was not able to coordinate with the national transportation system's reaction to increased civil or military demands. The military's test of emergency communications was compromised: military participants were supplied with a list of just seventy-seven selected hypothetical outages representing disruptions from thirty minutes to forty-eight hours, none of which involved critical circuits.[50]

Insufficient time elapsed between the end of Spade Fork and escalation of the Cuban emergency for participants to fully evaluate the exercise, recommend changes, and significantly amend policies. Circular 9410.1A (13 September 1962) provided guidance to departments and agencies under escalating DEFCON declarations, and Executive Order 11051 (2 October 1962), written in the immediate aftermath of Spade Fork, clarified the roles of the OEP and OCD during an emergency.[51] The existence of the first and readiness to draft the second proved important in the missile crisis of October 1962. Basically, however, the actions taken during the Cuban Missile Crisis were predicated upon the same planning assumptions rehearsed during Spade Fork under *Plan c* guidelines. In particular, important areas of paper planning that preoccupied the OEP during the missile crisis were also gamed in Spade Fork: the human welfare problem and economic continuity problems including manpower management, economic stabilization and recovery, and resource allocation.

The Cuban Missile Crisis: Covert Preparedness

The ExComm, chaired by Attorney General Robert Kennedy, held its first meeting at 11:50 on Tuesday 16 October 1962, the same morning that President Kennedy was informed about the missile installations in Cuba. While the ExComm deliberated, the OEP moved into action: by 19 October, it formed an Interagency Emergency Planning Committee to update the *National Plan* and supporting documents and work on readiness for continuity of government in the event of nuclear war. This was not a test. On Saturday, 20 October, upon President Kennedy's return from an aborted campaign tour, he met in the White House with ExComm members and decided to impose a naval quarantine on Cuba.[52] According to Salinger, Edward McDermott (director of the OEP) was present at this meeting.[53] By Monday, 22 October, the OEP had appropriated funds to enable it to direct and coordinate readiness efforts within Washington and across all regions.

That was the same day that the navy ordered 180 ships into position throughout the Caribbean and the USAF put nuclear-ready B-52 bombers into the air and dispersed the Strategic Air Command to civilian airfields in order to reduce the squads' vulnerability to attack.[54] President Kennedy briefed former presidents and met with the National Security Council, his cabinet, congressional leaders, and Soviet Ambassador Dobrynin.[55] Around the world, NATO and allied leaders were briefed by U.S. ambassadors.[56] Finally, early that evening, 55 million Americans listened as John F. Kennedy described the detection of Soviet missiles and his intention to impose a naval quarantine around Cuba beginning on Wednesday morning.

At this time, unbeknownst to the ExComm, sixteen missile launchers were operational in Cuba. Within a week, by which time the missile crisis had ended, Soviet forces working at full tilt had readied all twenty-four of the medium range ballistic missile (MRBM) launchers on the island.[57] In a sense, the public had spent seventeen years preparing for this and had steeled themselves for nuclear war.[58] In another sense, however, the exigencies of the nuclear age had not sunk in: to the extent that the public had not embraced a shelter-building program, it had not accepted what President Kennedy's adviser Charles Haskins called the "realism" that "would dispel the concept 'it can't happen here.'"[59] Despite nearly a decade of skywatching by the Ground Observer Corps, Boys Scouts calling door-to-door with civil defense pamphlets, civil defense curricula in schools, the Home Preparedness Program espoused by women's groups, and a blizzard of information in all mass media, the Cuban Missile Crisis made nuclear war a tangible and immediate possibility for the first time. Even so, while 30.5 percent of Americans who were later surveyed about the crisis said they had discussed the situation with their families, and half of them made some kind of shelter plan and took steps toward preparing shelter space at home, only 5.5 percent thought of getting in touch with local civil defense authorities for instructions. So, while the ideas of civil defense got through to many Americans, civil defense in an organizational sense was largely ignored.[60]

Under the auspices of DEFCON 3, the Pentagon readied the U.S. Marines, army, and air force to take the next steps if the naval quarantine of Cuba failed to keep the peace, positioning troops and equipment throughout Florida, mobilizing units throughout the southeast, and calling in American firepower from bases as far away as the Philippines, though trying to attract as little notice as possible. On 24 October, Salinger directed the press not to cover any of this or the DEFCON stance of the armed forces.[61] The keynote of this tense week was preparedness without public involvement or, if possible, public knowledge.

Between Spade Fork and the start of the missile crisis, the OEP clarified what civil actions would correspond to defense conditions. DEFCON 3 entailed "*moderate* step-up of readiness within the Executive Branch . . . strictly intraorganizational in nature and limited to administrative measures to increase the organization's preparedness posture." As long as the military stayed at DEFCON 3, the federal apparatus was a long way from mobilizing even the compromised civil defense posture which the upper echelons of the civil service had rehearsed in Spade Fork. DEFCON 2 entailed "substantial step-up in readiness of the Executive Branch" and the public moving into an emergency stance. Only if the president declared DEFCON 2 would OCD warn governors to expect "unfriendly actions," put emergency plans into effect, and activate emergency operation centers.[62] At DEFCON 1, the Executive Branch would be prepared to execute emergency plans and sound public warning signals.[63] On 21 October, the OEP contacted the eight regional civil defense directors by telephone. They were advised that the nation would be going to DEFCON 3 and that they should prepare to staff their offices on a round-the-clock basis and convene the regional civil defense and defense mobilization boards.[64] Regional civil defense offices were charged with *reviewing* readiness but not taking "substantial public actions to improve readiness." Regional directors would, for example, find a pretext to contact governors and discuss civil defense responsibilities and encourage each one to review continuity of government programs in each state but not take "substantial public actions to improve readiness."[65]

In Washington, the OEP was taking steps laid out in *Plan C* to ready the federal apparatus. (In terms of the time scheme in figure 19, this marks the jump from step 2 to step 5.) The Department of Labor and the Post Office finalized proofs for the rationing system: these were to be in governors' hands by 26 October. While the OEP pondered where to establish an economic Stabilization Agency, the Department of Commerce "set in motion a more sensitive price-watching mechanism with respect to basic materials and industrial price movements" dating from 20 October, to create a daily picture of the economic impact of the unfolding situation.[66] The Treasury Department considered closing the stock and commodity exchanges to prevent panic as tension escalated; the Securities and Exchange Commission would probably be responsible for implementing such a decision, but it was unclear who had the authority to make such a call. Treasury also revised and amended Emergency Banking Regulation No. 1, to curb runs on banks and non-essential or speculative withdrawals; this measure, designed for implementation post-attack, was instead being contemplated for use "during a period of grave tension," as in Spade Fork.[67] (This regulation put tight controls on credit, which was undesirable in a period of mobilization; this is an instance of how the need for greater coordination and inter-agency communication was discovered.)[68] Other measures to deal with foreign financial transactions, the debt limit, emergency financing, general versus defense lending authority, and measures to prevent speculation and price movement on defense-related materials and products were contemplated. These are exactly the sort of concerns a Stabilization Agency would take over if the crisis escalated. The director of Industry and Finance in the OEP advised on 24 October that unless the crisis improved in the next day, operational responsibility for "guiding and coordinating the fiscal and monetary operations of the financial agencies" should quietly be given to the secretary of the Treasury, but not by an Executive Order, which would attract publicity. This would free the OEP to concentrate on direct controls as the crisis worsened: stabilization legislation and freezes on prices, wages, and rents. Geoffrey Baker, vice-president of Ralston Purina, was appointed head of the Price

Control Agency, but someone had yet to be named from the Executive Reserve to head the emergency Stabilization Agency.[69]

By 24 October, transportation agencies met almost continually at the Department of Commerce, their key personnel on alert and actively reviewing internal preparedness relating to DEFCON 3's mandate to make emergency operations capable of implementation. They issued instructions to the Bureau of Public Roads, Civil Aeronautics Board, and Federal Aviation Agency.[70] Jurisdictional grey areas were clarified; for example, the Interstate Commerce Commission agreed to give authority over ports to the Maritime Administration in an emergency. The movement of people as well as goods was at stake, and they studied a hypothetical evacuation of Florida based on actual hurricane experience.[71]

James Hagerty, vice-president of ABC and formerly press secretary to President Eisenhower, was quietly asked to steer the Office of Censorship if an emergency occurred; this office was intended to coordinate information for the media and suppress stories the administration deemed unconstructive.[72] Communication logistics within the federal system were more difficult to address. The State Department called meetings on 24, 25, and 26 October to discuss linking each U.S. diplomatic post to Washington. Robert McNamara is quoted as saying: "Go do it, I don't want to see you until you are finished. Money is no object."[73] The president's difficulties in communicating with Chairman Khrushchev are well known. But direct links with foreign posts, such as a TWX system, would also ensure that instead of suffering up to ten-hour lapses in message relay, any major policy release by the president could be in the hands of all U.S. ambassadors and selected heads of state by the time a release was made public. The General Services Administration advised that the intra-U.S. communications system would be operable in seventy-five days. Links with Latin American governments were especially crucial during the Cuban Missile Crisis, and while telephone service to Mexico City was good, AT&T was asked on 26 October to look into using private equipment, transportable military equipment, or cable such as was being laid to Panama in order to link Washington with South American governments.[74]

States attempted to comply with the OEP's recommendations of 22–23 October, establishing emergency planning committees, checking the status of relocation sites, reviewing lines of succession to key department and agency positions, locating duplicate records at emergency sites, and allocating space for civil defense operations in capitals, but their ability to fulfill reporting expectations up the chain of command following a nuclear attack was doubtful.[75]

Steuart Pittman briefed the ExComm on civil defense at the 23 October 18:00 meeting, though what he was able to present was sketchy.[76] The next day, he drafted more specific proposals to protect areas of the United States vulnerable to attack by conventional weapons launched from Cuba, requiring coordination with the regional civil defense office in Thomasville, Georgia, and gulf coast governors, mayors, and civil defense directors. This involved plans to relocate federal emergency supplies (equipment to pump, repair, and purify water supplies; two-hundred-bed portable hospitals; processed food; and medical stockpiles); activate and train auxiliary police, fire, and rescue personnel; activate emergency mass casualty care centers surrounding target areas; call up and station the National Guard to maintain civil law and order; and develop selected evacuation plans (not mass evacuation) for Florida and New Orleans. A second plan, extending in a 1,000-nautical mile arc from Cuba and effecting half the population of the United States,[77] proposed to expand shelter capacity by lowering the standards of fallout protection from 100 PF (protective factor) to 40 PF; undertake a crash campaign to identify and mark public shelters and caves, stock them with three-day supplies of food, and publicize procedures for entering, occupying, and emerging from them; inform rural populations of low-cost do-it-yourself shelter methods; crash train 14,000 architects, engineers, and contractors on shelter location and building; accelerate distribution of radiological monitoring equipment to double the number of stations to 14,000 and undertake a crash training program for their use; relocate food stockpiles, especially at New Orleans, closer to targets; use stand-by reservists to help civil defense efforts; and step-up distribution of ten million specially printed copies of the federal booklets "Fallout Protection" and "Family Shelter Designs" which would be ready at the end of the month. This was in addition to improving emergency operations centers augmented by federal communications equipment.[78] These are exactly the sort of measures that were thought about and planned for, but not implemented, at DEFCON 3.

A written inquiry from Pittman to Bundy on 25 October asks whether there would be objection to discussing the civil defense situation with the public.[79] Pittman was confident that guidance on life-saving capabilities could be provided, but this was in the context of his apparent enthusiasm to capitalize upon anxiety prompted by the missile crisis to double the number of marked shelters to accommodate 100 to 120 million people by lowering their PF ratings; suspend the requirement that every building owner sign a written agreement for their property to be marked and stocked as a public shelter; and utilize the Agricultural Extension Service to advocate an intensive drive for $75 to $250 rural home shelters. These measures, Pittman advocated, could be launched in connection with the Saturday, 27 October, long-planned civil defense meeting of governors, mayors, and county commissioners in Washington, and conclude around the time when Congress would reconvene in January. "Federal, state and local government officials would cooperate in creating the impression that the only connection between the Cuban situation and this three month undertaking is that the public has been reminded of the dangers of our times and a new receptivity to civil defense has been created which makes possible civil defense activities which are long overdue." Otherwise, the federal leadership's resolve would appear weak and the chances of accomplishing the president's objectives would be "greatly reduced."[80] Pittman's proposal seems to assume that the true crisis would soon dissipate while a bounce-back effect from it could be opportunistically turned to create greater preparedness for the long run. His ambitions accord with the OCD position throughout the Kennedy administration.

Some of the documents dated 24–28 October pertaining to acceleration of civil defense have been removed from the National Security Files at the Kennedy Library, however a great deal of the mundane day-by-day activity can be discerned from inter-office memoranda of the OEP. It continued to make progress in readying the federal apparatus for a deteriorating situation. *Plan C* and *Plan D-Minus* were reviewed by key executives and short-term revisions sent to McDermott with the goal of replacing all the documents with new drafts on Wednesday, 31 October. Lines of succession to emergency committees were designated[81] and agencies were contacted regarding plans to move three or more personnel (ideally including one person in the line of succession) from each agency to High Point prior to DEFCON 2, with at least one other more senior successor assigned to each agency's own relocation site.[82] And yet at the worst point of the crisis, Saturday, 27 October, when the British Bomber Command stepped up to full operational capability to launch its nuclear arsenal with less than fifteen minutes warning,[83] just seven U.S. federal departments had fully complied with OEP recommendations on lines of succession.[84] Agencies planned partial prelocation upon declaration of DEFCON 2, but McDermott instead advised that they should wait for specific instructions from the OEP before prelocating. In the meantime, employees anticipating prelocation should make arrangements for their families, who would not be able to go with them.[85] Readiness procedures for transporting personnel to alternate sites were refined, particularly pick-up points for Congress, Supreme Court Justices, and defense coordinators of agencies.[86]

Planning under McDermott's authority clearly distinguished between orders for immediate implementation and actions that could be recommended as the situation escalated toward war. If the president declared DEFCON 2 or 1, HEW, for example, would submit recommendations for emergency health and welfare legislation; implement the emergency medical procurement program; recommend an export embargo on medical supplies; ready the medical stockpile for allocation and distribution of supplies and arrange for movement of narcotic painkillers from federal stores (in coordination with the FBI and Bureau of Narcotics); establish procedures for requisitioning shelter, food, and clothing; arrange with the Veterans Administration to use medical facilities; and request that states prepare to receive and distribute medical supplies and alert state health departments to be ready to mobilize operations. In order to have the personnel to carry out emergency preparations and post-attack plans, HEW would alert professional medical, dental, and nursing organizations for assistance in mobilization, preparing plans for the work force, and alerting emergency and volunteer welfare organizations. Emergency immunization programs would be readied, and the Red Cross would be instructed to establish emergency blood collection. Finally, HEW would notify the public on medical self-help measures via television and radio. Under DEFCON 3, however, HEW, the most important federal department for post-attack amelioration of human suffering, could only review these policies but not act on them.[87]

Likewise, the Department of Labor, already working at "a high degree of emergency," was reviewing measures to compel employment and in an escalating situation would undertake various organizational tasks pertaining to workers: review mobilization lists of critical occupations and essential activities; select personnel for Labor-Management Manpower Committees in all major market areas; and collaborate with the National Science Foundation to utilize the Register of Scientific and Technical Personnel to place scientists and engineers in essential roles.[88] The Department of Labor would work with the USDA to issue policies on agricultural labor and the use of migratory workers and collaborate with HEW to issue policies on using older workers, men rejected for military service, the handicapped, women, and minorities. Labor and management Manpower Committees would be coordinated with employment stabilization plans. Thinking ahead to the post-attack period, the Department of Labor would need to prepare programs to meet civil defense needs by establishing payment rates and death and disability compensation for civil defense workers; issue regulations for employment ceilings, limitation of employment to priority activities, fixed hours of work, mandatory worker registration, compulsory assignment, and job freezes of very critical skills; establish re-employment rights for workers required to take emergency assignments; and assess labor supply data for military and civilian requirements.[89] At DEFCON 3, however, they reviewed such plans and waited.

Planning looked ahead to a deteriorating situation. At DEFCON 2, the Post Office would staff its Emergency Relocation site with damage assessment and radiological defense officers. On declaration of DEFCON 1, other designated staff would relocate. Following nuclear attack, the Post Office would maintain a registry of national locator files on dislocated populations and assure delivery of mail to displaced persons, which in the event of significant evacuation and urban damage would be a considerable task. An inventory of registration forms was already at 39,000 post offices, but selection and training of staff to handle postal concentration centers was not complete.[90]

McDermott recommended that the Department of Justice prepare to implement emergency instructions to U.S. attorneys and marshals. In an escalating situation, the attorney general would recommend that the president issue a proclamation declaring a national emergency, convene Congress, and enact Executive Order 10501 authorizing federal agencies to classify defense information.[91] Only if a national emergency was declared would civil defense preparations escalate to their maximum achievable readiness.[92]

A war mentality was settling in, though there was no consensus on the urgency for implementation of most measures. As the missile crisis worsened on Friday, 26 October, telecommunications staff struggled to supply basic communications equipment in emergency sites and mobile equipment for ranking OEP staff in the White House.[93] Efforts were accelerated to develop emergency planning priorities for the use of computing equipment.[94] McDermott reviewed emergency procedures for the Supreme Court with Chief Justice Earl Warren, but the problem of relocating records for the court remained undecided: did they want to establish a fully implemented operational capability in a relocation site, or could just a few essential items be relocated?[95] In the medical field, health mobilization officers were being sought but were not ready for assignment to the states. The Public Health Service had secured funds for 10,000 kits to train nurses but would have no curriculum until December.[96]

Plans were refined for rationing inventories of food, petroleum, and other essential consumables and controlling items such as drugs that would experience critical shortages post-attack.[97] These measures were not just contemplated for the aftermath of nuclear attack: the Council of Economic Advisors warned that even early in a mobilization for limited war, "direct controls might be necessary . . . to cut across *psychological* inflation. This kind of economic problem can arise even though we have substantial unused capacity and only moderate total mobilization demand."[98] This continued to be under review on "Black Saturday," 27 October.

On 28 October, despite having accepted Chairman Khrushchev's promise to withdraw the missiles—cooling the political crisis—President Kennedy approved "discreet consultation with state and local authorities" in relation to the 24 October plan to step up civil defense measures in areas vulnerable to conventional weapons launched from Cuba, presumably in accord with the continuing military crisis. Regional civil defense directors were encouraged to assess and evaluate their recent experience, just as in any exercise,[99] but until the missiles were removed from Cuba civil defense readiness continued to incrementally increase. The president approved Pittman's plan pertaining to areas within range of MRBMS provided it could be accomplished "without undue public impact" and that "regional acceleration be limited to the period of the present emergency."[100] Pittman was quietly dispatched to Florida, ostensibly to consult with local civil defense officers and the director of the regional headquarters in Thomasville, Georgia.

The missile crisis was somewhat successful in improving readiness at the executive level, though it also reveals what remained undone. On Monday, 29 October, all federal departments and agencies reported their readiness to go to DEFCON 2 and 1. Many plans, such as transportation for approximately 35,000 non-military employees assigned to emergency headquarters, were still inadequate.[101] Many deficiencies in supply became glaring inadequacies: only 20 percent of the goal for identifying emergency hospital beds was reached, and the nation had just 29 percent of the needed supplies to cover the period up to six months after attack.[102]

On 21 November, the president ordered the end of the naval quarantine. On 27 November, when the commander-in-chief of NORAD declared DEFCON 5, the crisis was officially over.[103] The materiel and logistical problems encountered during Spade Fork also pertained during the missile crisis: cryptographic equipment was obsolete, causing serious delays at the regional level, and resource data for computing was inadequate, incomplete, and in some cases obsolete; for example, aeronautical facilities data was based on information from 1955 despite considerable growth in civil aviation in the intervening years.[104] Branches of NATO's civil emergency agencies had not yet been established in the United States and could not even be activated in skeletal form. The State Department formed an ad hoc International Resource Committee to bridge the gap but in the event of nuclear war this suggested that the United States would have had few ways to coordinate information flows or distribution of fuel, transportation, food, or other essential resources with European allies and no means to coordinate the international refugee crisis arising if Europe, too, came under attack.[105] Studies of the pre-attack and post-attack information and analysis essential to survival planning, operations, and resource evaluation arising from Spade Fork were the preliminary steps that set the civil defense planning and exercise agenda for the remainder of the decade, especially with the growth in applications for computing and improvements in communications. Initiatives such as PARM (Program Analysis for Resource Management), then in the final phases of development but not yet implemented, would "provide estimates of the attack effects on the economy in depth," including "interrelationships and interactions of these effects on the various industries" and "development of feasible production goals and programs responsive to priorities and within the limits of available resources."[106] In Spade Fork, however, participants needed to collect data in order to execute the exercise; after the missile crisis, this would be done as part of normal staff work in readiness for either exercises or political eventualities.

The Line Between Rehearsal and Performance

Nineteen days after Spade Fork ended, before significant post-exercise analysis could occur, President Kennedy was presented with conclusive evidence that Soviet nuclear missile launching bases were in advanced stages of construction just 100 miles off the shore of Florida. During the Cuban Missile Crisis, he stopped short of calling for public participation, did not mandate widespread civil service involvement, and authorized minimal relocation of civil personnel to emergency facilities. Spade Fork's implementation of an extended pre-attack and post-attack scenario simulated much more drastic measures, even within the scope of *Plan c* alone. The similarities between Spade Fork and the missile crisis center upon continuity of government preparation and diverge in terms of civil defense by the public. One was a rehearsal, the other a full-fledged performance, yet in the longer historical sense they share a significant ontological characteristic.

The missile crisis was notably more conservative — or preliminary — in its civil defense readiness posture, even though it has sometimes been historicized as a situation so tense that the invasion of Cuba was predicted for 29 or 30 October, nuclear war was thought to be imminent, and the public displayed widespread signs of alarm and preparation.[107] McNamara and Bundy later claimed that utilization of nuclear weapons was only a remote possibility, even at the tensest point in the crisis. Comparison with Spade Fork suggests that perhaps this is correct, not only for the United States but also the American perception of the Soviets' likelihood to deploy their arsenal.[108] It is certainly more consistent with the Kennedy administration's orders regarding civil defense.

Even though the civil defense work during the Cuban Missile Crisis was preparatory, its referential urgency surpassed anything undertaken during planning or exercises. By the time the ExComm gathered for its first meeting, the threshold was crossed from rehearsal to performance: unlike an exercise which might also unfold in real time, this performance was underway without any civil servant declaring "go." Neither the OEP nor the OCD could "rehearse" any action for the duration of the crisis; they could only "prepare" and as such "perform."

If DEFCON 2 was declared, the performance would have become more apparent to the public, but this does not alter its status as performance under the auspices of DEFCON 3. The exclusivity of witnesses does not preclude an event from being a performance; the presence of designated witnesses is not even needed. The significance lies in the distinction between anticipation through contingent practice (rehearsal) and actions undertaken by legislative or policy mandate (performance). OEP administrators met with members of federal departments and agencies to debate their best course of action, and in this respect the thirteen days of the missile crisis resembled exercises, but there was no playing.

Scholarship on the Cuban Missile Crisis is preoccupied with "the lessons learned." Putting civil defense preparedness into the mix reveals one lesson more. Exercises groped for a mimetic referent in the unimaginable complexity of nuclear attack. The civil defense preparations during the missile crisis reflected several military options including amphibious invasion of Cuba, foreign land war, and domestic nuclear war. As the crisis precipitated military mobilization and civil defense implementation, it looked toward a seemingly undeferrable event of awful magnitude, the antithesis of a rehearsal posture.

The importance of this distinction lies not in the novelty of recognizing a correspondence between Spade Fork and the Cuban Missile Crisis but in authorizing a historiographic assertion that even without the missile crisis the methexis of rehearsals, in readiness for war, gives exercises authenticity on their own terms. Before the Cuban Missile Crisis, exercises rehearsed a pre-attack "real" that had not yet existed but which was based on an extrapolated model of "real" (with increasing levels of inference and assumption as the weapons delivery systems became more complex and the contingencies gamed took on greater inter-elaboration). On one level, they functioned as analogs to the Cuban Missile Crisis. On another level, as Spade Fork shows, they rehearsed crisis. But just as the aftermath of the Cuban Missile Crisis brought about a decrease in international tension and a change in the situation assumptions that could lead to nuclear war,[109] it too became a rehearsal for an incomplete performance, not just metaphorically (whew! we can go back to our urban homes now) but ontologically, too (whew! no one pushed The Button). Because the Cuban Missile Crisis did not erupt into nuclear war, it too could become a warehouse of data from which lessons could be drawn. This has been the principle focus in the historiography, without exploration of its mimetic pedagogical precursors. For civil defense planners, the Cuban Missile Crisis—like Spade Fork—also became data pertinent to future planning. When war was averted, it became (with hindsight) a scarier rehearsal.

INTERNATIONAL PLAY

> To say that there will be "30,000,000 casualties" in an America of
> 160,000,000 is one thing, but to many a friendly or neutral country abroad,
> a casualty figure of 30,000,000 would mean extermination.

> —John Foster Dulles

Spade Fork and the Cuban Missile Crisis help reveal the extent of contingencies gamed by the American government and sketch an impression of how federal agencies and departments would coordinate with regional and state authorities to try to anticipate and solve problems. The objective is to take a "big picture" view and be cognizant of needs in the most comprehensive way possible. By their nature, such exercises focus on administrative and structural solutions, envisioned within the cloistered precincts of government relocation sites. The magnitude of challenges for governors is even more complex in multinational exercises, both in terms of the human welfare problem and economic stabilization.

All NATO member nations endorsed the principle that "civil defence is an essential, integral and continuing part of their national and collective defence planning and preparations," but the organization was slow to do much on behalf of civil planning.[1] When Lord Ismay became secretary general in 1952, NATO had begun to study only two areas of civil emergency planning: mobilization and control of merchant shipping, and petroleum requirements and distribution. He regarded planning for the control of the civil population and direction of civilian activities equally important as military preparedness in the event of thermonuclear war, and promptly established additional civil committees on European inland surface transport, civil defense, refugees and evacuees, food and agriculture, industrial raw materials, coal and steel, and manpower in order to plan for wartime needs. From 1955, they were coordinated under a single Senior Civil Emergency Planning Committee, chaired by the secretary general.[2]

NATO's "FALLEX 62" (September 1962), using a mobilization period of three work days and war phase of twenty-four consecutive hours, was the first NATO exercise to incorporate international exchange of simulated fallout information among civilian staffs. Though each nation undertook paper exercises on manpower availability, international play on civil defense did not extend beyond radiological dispersal.[3] "FALLEX 64," played two years later, added simulations of public alerts, evacuation of shipping and aircraft, government relocation, and aspects of welfare (particularly supplies distribution) to international play.[4] Planning for wartime refugees, projected in 1952, was apparently little evolved a dozen years later. Refugee problems were interjected in FALLEX 64 to develop and test reporting procedures, though even this, like many aspects of civilian play, was curtailed due to the heavy workload of planning for CIVLOG 65.[5]

The Scale of International Play

CIVLOG 65 was a new departure for NATO, involving the full range of civil planning committees without simultaneous military play. The situation assumptions and operational scenario—which detail the background political, military, and civil narrative from the outset of tension, through the exchange of nuclear arsenals, and up to D+120—is the most extensive unclassified scenario written for a civil defense exercise. It details the global implications of a full exchange of nuclear arsenals (NATO, Soviet, and Chinese), skimping on details for military play but fulsomely investigating the consequences for civilian sectors, including the worldwide economy (transportation, labor supply, and key commodities) and demographics (survival rates and migration patterns), involving NATO Civil Wartime Agencies for air, water, and surface transport; petroleum; food; and refugees. Exercise planning began in September 1963 and took nineteen months. Play began on 19 May 1965 at NATO's Supreme Headquarters Allied Powers Europe (SHAPE, located in Paris) and member nations' capitals and lasted thirty days, compressing a ninety-day scenario into one month. Some nations extended exercise play on their own military and civilian scenarios.[6] Canada, for example, revived narratives used in TOCSIN 63 to also play the pre-attack, life-saving, and survival of the nation phases,[7] and Britain used CIVLOG 65 as preparatory work for a subsequent exercise that would activate all RSGs.[8] Multinational play, however, skipped the pre-attack, attack, and shelter phases, and instead concentrated play on the restoration of the nation phase (D+30 through D+120), following which prosecution of the war by conventional means would commence. This was, in other words, the hiatus between nuclear and conventional war campaigns during which civil problems would take focus in order to restore order, assert governmental authority, and do what would be necessary to mobilize and equip the military for conventional battle. Final reports were submitted by 1 December 1965.[9] CIVLOG 65 traces the state of planning for the post–Cuban Missile Crisis realpolitik, in the period when France still participated in NATO's Defence Committee but before multiple warhead delivery systems were fully operational.

These are the situation assumptions leading up to war.[10] On D-19, "Orange" (the Soviet Eastern Bloc) moves missile launchers to Spitzbergen and steps up naval activity in the North and mid-Atlantic. Small skirmishes are fought along the Greek-Bulgarian border. Industrial tension mounts in West Germany (FRG). By D-8, the situation is hot enough for NATO to declare the condition of Military Vigilance.[11] Over the next three days, from D-7 to D-5, industrial tensions mount in the FRG, Orange forces enter Austria, and there are increases in Bulgarian troop concentrations along the Greek-Thracian-Turkish borders. On D-5, NATO declares the condition of Simple Alert. The following day, border incursions are made into Norway and the FRG, threatening stability there. The death of the Yugoslav leader precipitates a crisis in that satellite nation. On D-3, a coup d'état is executed in Austria, establishing a Popular Democratic government. Orange makes further troop offensives into the FRG, and Romanian and Bulgarian troops advance into Yugoslavia. On D-2, Orange captures the Hanseatic port of Lubeck and the Barent Sea port of Kirkenes, and advances into the Norwegian Sea. A surprise air-sea attack is launched against "Blue" (NATO) forces' Strike Fleet in the Atlantic. Orange continues its conventional attack in Central and Southern European regions as Blue counters by land and air. A Reinforced Alert is declared, invoking food rationing, call-up of forces, regulated labor markets, and compulsory work. As far as possible, Blue nations evacuate harbors of civilian and military craft, mobilize airplanes away from metropolitan and major military airports, and shift railways' rolling stock into the countryside. There is mass movement of civilians as NATO and non-NATO nationals try to repatriate to their homelands. Major urban centers in Europe and North America are ordered to evacuate nonessential personnel. On D-1, Orange, somewhat slowed by Blue, launches more aggressive attacks. Blue resists. Orange halts its offensive and calls for diplomatic action. This is a ruse.

From D Day to D+2, Orange launches chemical attacks on NATO's Army

Groups in Northern and Central Europe and the Greek and Turkish forces defending the Turkish Straits and Eastern Turkey. There is extensive sabotage to electrical transmission stations, bridges, and oil refineries. Most importantly, however, Orange launches an all-out nuclear attack against NATO nations, and Blue retaliates in kind. By D+5 the nuclear exchange ends, exhausting capabilities on all sides. The United States and Canada receive over 400 strikes on military and civilian targets (most in the 1 to 5 MT range, some up to 10 MT); the United Kingdom receives 80 (most in the 1 to 3 MT range), while continental Europe—where the strike rate was criticized by players as being unrealistically low in incidence and severity, but which was established at this level in order to permit further operational play—receives approximately 230 strikes (most in the 200 KT range).[12] In the aftermath of nuclear attack, CIVLOG 65 dispensed with the realistic idea of heavy European bomb damage in order to facilitate more extensive civil play as easily as it postulated a nuanced international background for setting resource and trade problems. Artificiality does not give rise to counterfactuals: this is necessary to enable plot elements pertinent to the exercising agencies. Just as *Hamlet* does not begin until the king is dead, the queen remarried, and the prince returned from university (narrative elements that could have been dramatized but are instead relegated to exposition), CIVLOG 65 utilized the strike scenario and subsequent month of developments as background leading up to its main arena of study and concern, particularly the international problems that could be addressed only after damage had been assessed, the shock of attack dissipated, and the surviving population emerged from shelter.

European powers are unable to conduct extensive military operations due to losses of materiel and personnel, the scale of the civilian catastrophe, and disrupted supply lines. Both Orange and Blue suffer extensive loss of ground forces; their air power is negligible (almost all combat planes are destroyed, and only some reconnaissance, transport, and training craft are able to be put into service); and with the complication of ongoing submarine activity and underwater mining, only light naval vessels remain, and many of these are required to escort merchant convoys. Damage to ports, railroads, bridges, major oil pipelines, and power and fuel storage facilities is critical throughout Europe but heavier in North America and the Soviet Union. Both Blue and Orange lose most of their major cities, yet Eastern bloc governments are intact. In the following weeks, Orange and Blue struggle to establish government control and order, to supply citizens and refugees with the basics of life, and to mitigate shortages of fuel, power, transportation, clothing, and shelter. By D+25, NATO arranges for Venezuelan and off-shore refineries to ship oil to North America and Western Europe, while the

Persian Gulf begins to resupply Western Europe via the Horn of Africa (the Suez Canal has been sabotaged and will be impassable until D+50). The Straits at Marmara (Turkey) and Gibraltar are open but the Panama Canal is impassable until D+90.[13]

At D+30 the Republic of Ireland, Switzerland, Sweden, and Finland remain neutral but Finland's borders are threatened and Switzerland is increasingly cut off. Orange forces are reduced in Austria and Yugoslavia and pre-war governments are re-established. Borders between Orange and Blue nations are closed, and some negotiations on the exchange of refugees have begun but their repatriation is impeded by problems of transport, pockets of radiation from fallout, and outbreaks of disease. Except for sabotage at ports, Central and South America, Australia, and New Zealand are untouched. The Central Treaty Organization (CENTO), South East Asian Treaty Organization (SEATO), Australia, New Zealand, and the United States defense pact (ANZUS), Organization of American States (OAS), British Commonwealth nations, and French colonies pledge support to the West but are struggling with civil relief and hoarding at home. The Middle East is largely unchanged though Pakistan, India, Iran, and Afghanistan are occupied with internal problems; Iraq experiences Kurdish uprisings in the north; and oil production is slowed because workers flee in panic. Much of Africa is plagued by labor strikes. Much of Southeast Asia is stable, though civil uprisings in Laos, Vietnam, Cambodia, and Indonesia make approach in territorial waters impossible. All the U.S. bases in Spain, Japan, and the Philippines are lost. China is severely damaged by nuclear strikes but is not considered a threat to NATO.

Though rich in narrative detail, this is all exposition for the play that was about to commence. Exercise play was sparked when each NATO capital received data detailing their nation's nuclear strikes, casualty rates, impediments to resupply, and resultant shortages in commodities. As they calculated the scale of civilian catastrophe, they reported in to SHAPE by teletype and telephone.[14] It was the task of NATO's Civil Wartime Agencies in Paris to respond to this information, interject new data, and indicate common problems to be worked out between nations. For the most part, immediate resupply of food was not as critical as the restocking of coal where depots were burned out, the provision of aviation fuel, and the restoration of electrical transmission equipment. In the long run, however, importation of key commodities like coal and iron ore to restore military materiel, wood to rebuild housing, and food to compensate for loss of domestic production needed to be negotiated with non-NATO nations. In southern Europe, much of the spring harvest was effected, but in northern Europe, Canada, and much of the United States spring sowing was interrupted, presaging a meager fall harvest and in turn suggesting long-term supply problems. Neither pre-war levels of production nor importation could be achieved, sometimes for logistical reasons, sometimes for political ones. In the case of powdered milk, demand significantly exceeded pre-war levels because fresh cow's milk was unfit for consumption due to the shortage of uncontaminated silage and fodder; dairy herds were turned out on pastureland but much of this was also compromised by fallout. Sources needed to be found outside Europe and North America. Argentina, which formerly supplied Europe with meat and flour, held stocks ransom until it could be guaranteed uninterrupted oil supplies.[15] Commodity shortages interrelated with loss of industrial facilities and competition for raw materials came from markets that had not previously been a factor. The United Kingdom, Turkey, and Norway all needed wheat but lost much of their capacity for milling it into flour; they had to compete with India while struggling to restore processing facilities. France, Luxembourg, Germany, the United Kingdom, and the Netherlands all clamored for potatoes; Greece offered some surplus but not enough; Egypt and Malta were ruled out as sources, and North African export capacity was reduced by 50 percent. Denmark's supply of meat was secure through D+120, but the Netherlands and France only through D+30; Norway and Turkey faced long-term difficulties at D+60 and D+120 respectively when Italy too expected critical shortages. Sugar supplies, controlled by rationing, held out but could not be resupplied from within the alliance. Severe problems arose in the stockpiles of fats and oils in Germany, the United Kingdom, and elsewhere, but Norway could be self-sustainable if its fish oils could be processed. Luxembourg, where civil defense ensured that all households had fifteen-day supplies, lost 75 percent of its other food stocks, and with inland surface transport infrastructure destroyed its problems were urgent.[16]

Theatrical Play

Around four hundred NATO personnel engaged in daily play in Paris, joined by representatives from various industries; cumulatively many times this number played in national capitals. The dramatis personae at SHAPE included an impressive array of personnel: NATO's Secretary General Lord Coleridge was chair and exercise director. He was assisted by Danish, American, and French officials serving as higher control staff and senior directing staff from NATO's food and industrial divisions; oil and petroleum boards; agencies for inland surface transport, overseas shipping, and civil aviation; the European Space Agency; and the Refugee Agency. National advisers were joined by commanders of NATO military operations in Europe, the North Atlantic, and English Channel, and legions of translators and typists.[17] Many of the planners who wrote the exercise scenarios doubled as players who coped with the effects of the devastation and worked out the consequences in time and space before scrutinizers in Paris and at home.

While the "prequel" scenario for this exercise is particularly well documented, most of what is knowable about what transpired during the exercise itself must be inferred from how the event was set up in planning documents and the post-event critiques and self-evaluations undertaken by NATO agencies in the months following completion of CIVLOG 65. In many exercises, much can be inferred about the scope of improvisational play from the message traffic interspersed by directing staff, but in this case it is not available; neither are the daily reports issued by participating agencies, industries, and nations which usually enable inferences about the kinds of "scripting" that occurs as an exercise unfolds. So, while the set-up is fulsomely in evidence, and reports show what was judged less than optimal post hoc, what occurred during the event itself cannot be directly known. (This is analogous to any rehearsal or performance neither witnessed by a theater historian nor extensively logged by participants. Neither absence from an event nor lack of first-hand accounts of what transpired prevents analysis based on other evidence that does exist.)[18] Obviously, there was an event and some of the rules by which participants engaged in the event are known. What scope does this leave for understanding what happened?

The NATO Planning Board for Inland Surface Transport and the Agency for Coordination of Inland Transportation in Central Europe (ACTICE) listed a set of "lessons" that resulted from the exercise. For example:

> Lesson 13: ACTICE participation was on a scale never before reached, even during FALLEX 62; 57 persons (12 in the Executive Secretariat and 3 on the Directing Staff) took part in the Exercise (out of a planned theoretical total of 100).[19]

This restates the principle that the exercise was a rehearsal, not a performance: in a performance there would be one hundred participants from ACTICE, but in the exercise there were only fifty-seven. Though barely half the full performance complement, this was an increase from earlier exercises. In recommending the institution of rehearsals qua rehearsals prior to such an exercise, the idea that CIVLOG 65 was a rehearsal may seem to be contradicted:

> Lesson 23: Others expressed the wish that in future there should be exercise rehersals [sic] some days before the exercise itself or that the experts should at least be summoned a few days in advance, the better to prepare them for their duties.[20]

In other words, they were under-prepared, and the exercise put stress on participants precisely because of this. This is what rehearsals typically do: they create a situation where participants strive to demonstrate proficiency but cannot fully do so; the inevitable errors lead to diagnosis of remaining problems and identification of the technical elements that remain to be provided or perfected in order to optimize proficiency and effectiveness. Further rehearsals allow participants to show increased competence and fuller integration with others' contributions. This is, in fact, what CIVLOG 65 enabled, even though some players impatiently wished for greater competence earlier on.

Rehearsals have different framing devices than performances: they are engaged with the accrual of competence, not the full demonstration of it. In both, an artistic rendering "coaxes into being something which has not previously appeared. . . . it is action at the limit of the already controlled and understood; it is risk."[21] However, in rehearsal the rendering is incompletely realized, according to the judgment of its creators. This does not preclude an impression that a segment of what is rehearsal may be flawless, yet it is crucial in the context of nuclear war exercises to emphasize that full engagement, full immersion, and uninterrupted universal "belief" in the scenario being played (all associated with a sustained, fully realized performance) must not occur. Like a Diderotian or Brechtian actor, the participants in the exercise should remain capable of simultaneous consciousness of the fictive scenario and the conditions of actuality.[22] In rehearsal this simultaneity may be especially fluid while the boundaries, relatedness, and interchangeability of each is synecdochically explored. In the aftermath of a real nuclear exchange, the behaviors and rationales upon which national officials would draw—though still based upon a mixture of embodied practice and rote learning—could not indulge in the unreal pretexts of "what if," and therefore would sacrifice essential aspects that make rehearsals so malleable, fluid, and playful. But this does not mean that activity in an actual post-war situation would not be improvised.

NATO calls undertakings in this type of exercise "play," the participants "players," the problems to be tried the "scope of play" (*portée du jeu*), and the events that transpire the "play of decisions" (*jeu des décisions*). But just because something employs performative language does not mean that it is inherently performative. NATO utilizes vocabulary that is theatrical, applying it to civil and military exercise protocols, but in this case it is not merely metaphoric; it is *functionally* performative.

In an attempt to provide characteristics for a wide range of phenomena, Richard Schechner describes six conditions as the template for "play acts."

1. *Structure*: viewed synchronically, what are the relationships among the events constituting play acts?
2. *Process*: viewed diachronically, how are play acts generated and what are their phases of development?

3. *Experience*: what are the feelings or moods of those participating as players, directors, spectators, and observers? A spectator is often directly involved in the play act—such as fans who root for their teams or their favorite performers—while an observer is, for example, a scholar who in studying a phenomenon attempts to maintain a non-involved distance from it.

4. *Function*: what purpose or purposes do play acts serve?

5. *Ideology*: what values do play acts enunciate, propagate, or criticize either knowingly or unknowingly? Are these values the same or different for every player, director, spectator, and observer?

6. *Frame (or net)*: how do players, directors, spectators, and observers know when a play act begins, is taking place, and is over? Is being "over" the same as "concluding" or "finishing"? What metaplaying is framing the playing?[23]

The first condition is met through the careful negotiation over the hours of play: in the case of CIVLOG 65 they would work from 09:30 to 17:30 with an hour and a half break for lunch during which play would be suspended.[24] If players in Paris needed to go between the rooms designated for CIVLOG 65 and their ordinary offices, they would suspend play. The second condition is met through the scrupulous planning, occurring over nineteen months, that preceded the exercise; each of the planning documents would be reviewed and responded to diachronically in national capitals, just as the exercise itself was diachronically played between Paris, London, Washington, and Ottawa due to time zone differences. Military exercises necessitated adherence to Zulu time (coordinated with Greenwich Mean Time); this civil exercise, seemingly, did not. Schechner's third condition is not knowable from the declassified records. The fourth condition is indisputable: the exercise served to test readiness to respond and the thoroughness of relevant data collection for a post-war scenario written in accordance with conditions expected at D+30. This period had been tested at least twice before, and this repetition was a cause of some complaint, but the function is nonetheless clear.[25] Priorities revealing compliance with condition five include acceptance of the preeminence of military prerogatives in civil planning, belief in the just cause of democratic governments, affirmation that survival is feasible following war on this scale, and the conviction that a nuclear holocaust would not have insurmountable long-term biological consequences. These tenets likely varied in strength and relevance for different players according to perceived national threats and priorities. Finally, the temporal frame for rehearsing is clear-cut: play began at 09:30 Paris time on 19 May 1965. It ended thirty days later, without regard for the conclusiveness of any acts or the completeness of any plans. A fact predicated on "work" rather than actual "survival" frames the play of decisions.

Schechner's conditions may be criticized for being predicated on Western forms of theater and performance and therefore not universals for a "play act." However, the Nigerian playwright and theorist Ngũgĩ wa Thiong'o stipulates five ingredients for performance that are also evident in this exercise: *place* (there is a mise en scène in Paris, too small as it happened, but definitively delineated); *content* (the scope of play); *audience* (arguably, nations were audiences for each other, but certainly the exercise directors observed the NATO agencies and national players from their aerie at Paris); *time* (there are clear temporal delimits); and the *goal* (a reformative effect of some kind, in this case directed to all players improving their readiness and effectiveness, and diagnosing shortfalls in planning).[26]

Play has other transcendental characteristics: though there is indeterminacy there is also order that brings harmony to the actions through the "unique rationale" of the rules which establish play. Players strive "to resolve something, or achieve something difficult, or somehow end a tension" which entails "a heightened reality, a situation larger than ordinary life."[27] Within the protected environ of play, safety reigns: there have been no thermonuclear detonations, so players can proceed without fear. No actual damage is incurred, so the projected extent of (fictive) damage has no permanency, and players can think without anxiety. This conforms to Gary Izzo's concept of "interactive theatre," which may be predicated on a contest to achieve something (as in a game) or representational play where the goal is to move beyond ordinary selves without losing consciousness of ordinary reality (like actors).[28] In the case of CIVLOG 65, both pertain.

There are other paradigms that also explain aspects of the exercise. Civil defense exercises bear some resemblance to improvisational theater, especially the type where audiences shout out elements which the actors then must incorporate into a scenario.[29] However, Michael Kirby differentiates Happenings (the site-specific genre of non-linear unplotted performance) from improvisation. In improvisational theater, Kirby argues, players adjust the qualities of their performance in order to be in keeping with others' input, adhering to causal logic. In Happenings, however, performers' actions are neither wholly predetermined nor do they explicitly respond to each other's spontaneity: they are "often *indeterminate* but not improvised in nature."[30] There is something of each type in CIVLOG 65. How else could geographically disparate units of players (e.g., Belgians, Norwegians, Italians, and Canadians) be said to participate in the same rehearsal? They were not even in direct communication with each other: information from national players flowed into SHAPE but very little information from the nations was in turn channeled out of Paris to all national capitals. Players in Happenings know they are part of a larger canvas, like the CIVLOG 65 participants in Luxembourg, Athens, and London who pursued distinct non-convergent purposes yet were cognizant of each other from time to time. The master narrative was encompassing enough to permit nations to proceed selfishly, willfully ignoring others' perhaps greater needs, trampling the political idea of an interdependent alliance as cavalierly as they acted without regard to the whole ensemble.

With the development of new media, particularly Web-based interactive game play, many of the classic characteristics of war games are recycled from exercises such as CIVLOG 65. Without the speed, simultaneity, or interactivity of computer-based play, the civil defense exercises cannot be credited with innovations leading toward Multi-User On-Line Role-Playing Games such as Asheron's Call, or Live-Action Role-Playing Games (LARPs) such as Dungeons and Dragons.[31] However, there are characteristics in common. In LARPs, characters "might be given a set of small sealed envelopes, or 'packets,' marked with instructions on when to open them."[32] This finds an equivalent in predetermined instructions issued periodically from SHAPE to participating capitals. In some exercises, actual physical envelopes are pre-planted which exercise directors open periodically. As such, exercise directors stimulate events in the same manner as game masters. Players have freedom to accomplish their goals in response to the events, and game masters/exercise directors must step back and let this transpire, remaining aloof unless rules are violated. However, in both LARPs and CIVLOG 65 the players maintain interaction beyond, outside, and after the game or exercise concludes.[33] As in many contemporary mediated interactions, they are "acting for distant others" and their actions may have unforeseen implications, but while acting they are matrixed into a fiction à la theater, separated from everyday life.[34]

Theater historian Bruce McConachie describes theater performances as "'condensational events' in which certain primary metaphors, condensed from cultural-historical interaction, emerge as significant."[35] One way to study condensational events is to recognize performance details (spatial relationships, costuming details, communication modes, discursive features, or structural elements in narrative, plot, and action) and then identify other events which have the same features. In CIVLOG 65, the preponderance of evidence features details about structural elements. For example, there is a sequence of actions resulting from the prequel narrative, but no "story" per se that develops after D+30, only more narrative details of theme (basically, how will a nation cope with shortages of fuel?), motif (such as statistics on casualties and the crisis in medical care), and gaps in narrative (for example, we cannot know what transpired when 150,000 Austrians and Yugoslavs hypothetically arrived at Italy's border, only that they were moving through mountain passes toward Italy and the Italians had no intention of admitting them). The theater poses narrative gaps routinely: every dramatic script is full of provocative information about characters, setting, and action but this is at best schematic. What happens in the preparation of a production is what narrative theorists call "over-reading" in order to decide upon specifics of locale, appearance, and mood in a production design, resulting in an impression of even greater specificity in the mise en scène through the choices made by the actors, designers, and director, but never all-encompassing depiction of eligible details.[36] CIVLOG 65 does not go this route, yet it does depend upon chains of events recorded in log format. Nations can only discover the consequences of their chained events when they log information with Paris, not as plot but as action.[37] In order to make sense of the exercise directors' response, and in order to synthesize domestically based data with their instructions from Paris, players needed to "over-read" an inherently imaginative act. There simply could not be enough information to scientifically "interpret."

The participants could all recognize the unfolding action because they agreed upon context from the beginning, namely the aftermath of catastrophic nuclear war.[38] This is the case in many theater events. In murder mystery theater, for example, audiences arrive knowing the context of the event and this permits them to recognize plot elements as they are presented. Otherwise, the discovery of the candlestick in the conservatory and the guilty expression on Colonel Mustard's face would just seem random. The popular performance event *Tony n' Tina's Wedding*, focused around another highly recognizable ritual-structure, operates in the same way, as audiences witness a "wedding" then participate in the structured improvisation of the "reception."[39] In CIVLOG 65, the content is radically different, but the incitement to rehearse is comparable.

On arrival, the members of the agencies were briefed by agency directors on their functions and then attended a general briefing by civil and military staffs. They were then presented by the directing staff with commodity figures relating to national requirements extended to D+120 and remaining resources at D+30, and with certain military problems, principally for the transportation agencies. These latter agencies had to examine the effect of these problems on available transport resources, thus giving them some immediate work to do while they were waiting for the supply agencies to prepare their programs with their consequent transport requirements.[40]

It did not matter that it was unrealistic to have such complete data by D+30: the four hundred participants at Paris suspended disbelief and proceeded to game the problems. Despite extensive preparation, in a phenomenological sense the exercise only transpires once it is declared underway and so, as in social rituals (weddings, reunions, parties, crime investigations), there is no difficulty recognizing what is unfolding as the exercise per se, whether or not any particular participant is immersed in the fiction and temporarily forgets the boundaries imposed upon action.[41] Not all participants would be matrixed into the fiction during all moments of play; some industry representatives observing the NATO agencies at work, for example, would probably have had a learning curve that initially distanced them from belief in the unfolding action. It is typical of many kinds of performance to have a mixture of matrixed and non-matrixed participants and a continuum of matrixing.[42]

Thus, complying with the genre that Schechner calls "direct theatre," it is less important that CIVLOG 65 is "about" the aftermath of nuclear war than that it is "made" of the events and decisions that attempt to ameliorate the effects of nuclear war. This "making" involves actual actions as well as ritual symbolic actions; indeed the whole thing is predominantly symbolic rather than representational.[43] The tallies of European refugees, for example, indicated a *masse de manœuvre* as populations fled political turmoil, shortages, and fallout, accentuating crises in their host nations. One hundred fifty thousand West Germans fled into the Swiss Jura and taxed the Swiss economy and its supplies of food, fuel, and medicine.[44] Forty thousand refugees from Aachen needed to cross Belgium en route to France, instigating negotiations between a third-party nation. The FRG, coping with 12,000 Hungarians at Lake Constance, sought overseas destinations for them but boats were scarce. France was asked to accept 150,000 women and children from the Palatinate and Rhineland who faced malnutrition and epidemic, but moving them increased the likelihood of spreading disease. Norway had 16,000 refugees in Finnmark, small numbers relative to other areas but catastrophic in this Arctic zone.[45] Canada and the United States, which unlike most European NATO partners had standing agreements to treat each other's refugees on a par with their own citizens,[46] exchanged 145,000 northward, particularly in the central and prairie provinces, while 20,000 Canadians from Montreal and Vancouver were in upper New York and Washington states. These are symbolic exchanges, merely ritualistic crises, which challenged ethicists, economists, public health specialists, and jurists to make symbolic solutions that constituted the rehearsal.

These are problems for exercise play similar to the assumed ability to dispose of the nearly 55 million bodies that accumulated in NATO nations or the nearly 46 million injured who still required medical attention at D+30. Only imaginary graves were dug, and no tangible stocks of plasma or morphine were disbursed. The figures gave rise to symbolic action, a claim to truth that was known by all not to be true, a willful blindness to truth that came with suspending disbelief yet bearing a compelling relationship to an imaginable truth.[47] Like Spade Fork, CIVLOG 65 drew on collective understandings of policies and data in order to methexically derive the play of decisions. This was merely representational, and belief *must* be suspended: after all, amelioration of the consequences of all-out nuclear war is not a scenario that can be experimented with, merely projected and rehearsed. There is limited latitude for empiricism with Armageddon, and this is why the theater, which has been addressing the conduct and consequences of war since Aeschylus' *The Persians* in 427 BCE, is itself a condensation crucial to the gaming of CIVLOG 65. Theater is inherent to such cultural explorations, and in this case rehearsal was the methodology.

As human beings, we "think with narrative"[48] and are conditioned to use it to negotiate between deterministic forces and our own will, or agency, in history. Despite its logistical complexity, CIVLOG 65 is in many ways typical of civil defense exercises which gamed survival and continuity of government in the post-war phases, using narrative to establish the circumstances of crisis then symbolically setting players in medias res to anticipate, conceive, juggle, and solve problems. Closure, or the final resolution of difficulties, was always denied, which may be why some players were frustrated to be gaming the same time period over and over, or antithetically, were desirous of more rehearsals before this "real" rehearsal transpired. In this sense, players worked with the given circumstances to derive details of the action—the specifics of the narrative implications—then posed solutions, the viability of which was tried out, to a degree, in rehearsals but only to a degree because it was rehearsal. What matters more than closure, as Anton Chekhov argued, is "the correct setting of a question" to be fulfilled by thinking with narrative: that was the task of the artist and, it seems, civil servants.[49]

Chapter 10 **DISASTER WELFARE**

> No city, no family nor any honourable man or woman can repudiate this duty and accept from others help which they are not prepared to fit themselves to render in return. If war comes, great numbers may be relieved of their duty by death, but none must deny it as long as they live.
>
> —Sir Winston Churchill

In a 1913 manual for a children's battlefield game of war set in a model village, H. G. Wells explained how to enhance realism by utilizing miniature adjustable cannons to fire wooden cylinders that topple lead soldiers.[1] Despite Wells's attention to detail, his model Kriegspiel lacked civilians. No wonder, for at that time war was perceived as hazardous to soldiers and sailors, not noncombatants. Early twentieth-century wars saw the advent of aerial bombing, which was perilous for civilians, and the ratio of military deaths to civilian fatalities—twenty to one in World War I— equalized in World War II. In subsequent nuclear warfare, the firepower leveled against just one large city would likely exceed the equivalent tonnage of all the TNT employed in both world wars. With thermonuclear weapons, the death toll of all major twentieth-century conflicts could be doubled in a few hours without creating a single military battlefield of the traditional kind or losing a single soldier in combat. This made the stakes of planning for civilian survivors, as well as their dead, very high indeed.

Displacement: The Scale of the Human Welfare Problem

Civil servants who gamed nuclear war scenarios had beds waiting for them at the end of the day, especially if they rehearsed in blast-proof bunkers. When they left SHAPE in Paris, the relocation arc around Washington, RSGs in Britain, or REGHQs scattered across Canada, the highways and streets that they traveled toward their homes were not filled with either corpses or swarms of evacuees. Combating rush hour traffic was nothing compared to the scale of the human welfare catastrophe that the thermonuclear war civil exercises posited.

CIVLOG 65 provides explicit documentation of possible refugee movements within Europe, as well as the need for relocating European populations overseas (see chapter 9). Internally, too, each nation would have population flows, whether predicable as a result of directed relocations, unpredictable as a consequence of spontaneous evacuations, or chaotic in the aftermath of bombing and in the face of fallout. In order to try to correctly anticipate human behavior in such circumstances, civil defense planners looked to historical precedents. During the Allied bombing of Hamburg in 1943, 900,000 people left the city within a forty-eight-hour period; in the first week, nearly one million reporting and search cards were filed by and about them, a number that doubled within a few months.[2] Such examples helped planners envision the kinds of problems that would arise in nuclear war but not necessarily their scale. Vast as the displacement was in 1939–45, no historical diaspora, even forced diasporas, came close to the extent of movements anticipated in nuclear war, and no post-war dislocation presented problems on the magnitude of what would result from using nuclear weapons. However, by utilizing these precedents, nuclear civil defense exercises posited a template for sketching diaspora in demographic, political, and narratological terms, including the conflicts arising from recombining cultural idioms, the loss of geo-cultural folkways, and the pain of no return.

Prioritizing basic bodily needs for food, clothing, shelter, and medical care was paramount, but parallel efforts to catalogue relocated populations and cross-reference them for survivors seeking loved ones were daunting tasks in an age without desktop computers, the Internet, or cell phones.[3] During the Blitz, casualty lists were posted at town halls and enquiry bureaus for missing persons. When just 100 people were killed in a raid this was manageable, but an A-bomb could easily increase the mortality a hundredfold. Each A-bomb would generate about 250,000 inquiries.[4] A 1953 British committee anticipating A-bomb attacks describes the problem:

Let us suppose . . . that the lists are to be confined to 10,000 dead. This means that about every day for ten days a thousand names must be sorted into alphabetical order and these names must then be typed on to sheets which must be [rolled] off on duplicating machines, stitched together, placed in envelops and sent out to the various enquiry points. To do this, even for a 1,000 names a day, would occupy a staff of some 10 people (all of whom would have to be able to use a typewriter) something like half a day; how the work would be done at the rate of 20,000 a day in an improvised office, baffles the imagination. Nor is it clear how those daily casualty lists are to be used when they reach the various enquiry points: are the public to file past, looking up each list in turn until they find (or fail to find) the entry for which they are looking? It will be a very slow process and the lists will soon be thumbed to pieces.[5]

This would certainly keep post office workers and other local authority employees with relevant skills (such as tax assessors) occupied during a period when normal delivery of mail or property assessment was impossible due to fallout and destruction. A Canadian trial using trained volunteers to fill in registration forms, however, showed that people could only complete five or six forms per hour, so the information input into the process would be cumbersome.[6]

Each nation anticipated massive dislocation of citizens and tried to imagine how to ameliorate pressing needs in order to abate despair, get the able-bodied back to work, and stabilize the economy. The anticipated presence of foreign nationals complicated things. There would be untold displacements, but the legal rights of the displaced turn upon the agent of change: voluntary movement, forcible removal, persecution, genocide, ecological disaster, or war. Migrants, technically, undertake voluntary movements. Exiles are those who cross borders but have reason to believe they can return. Refugees are those who cross national boundaries under pressing exigent circumstances and whose return would likely bring about their persecution. Someone who moves purely for economic reasons can be a migrant, a migrant in exile, but not a refugee. Someone who flees fallout—a form of ecological, political, and social disaster—may be none of these.

According to the 1951 UN Convention on the Status of Refugees, a refugee is "a person who is outside his/her country of nationality or habitual residence; has a well-founded fear of persecution because of his/her race, religion, nationality, membership in a particular social group or political opinion; and is unable or unwilling to avail himself/herself of the protection of that country, or to return there, for fear of persecution."[7] Apart from citizens of Soviet satellite countries pressing into the FRG, Italy, Finland, and so on, this does not anticipate the kinds of migrants resulting from nuclear war. Certainly, it would not account for the western Europeans likely to land at British ports, the British pouring toward the Republic of Ireland, or the Canadians and Americans relocated because of the exigencies of topography that determine routes of escape. The UN's position on refugees disqualifies the victims of civil wars, as well as many circumstances arising between nations. NATO's European members understood refugees as foreign nationals "who, through fear of approaching enemy troops, take refuge, in a disorderly fashion, in an allied country."[8] These definitions were finessed in 1969 by the Organization of African Unity Convention which defines refugee status as also applying "to every person who, owing to external aggression, occupation, foreign domination or events seriously disturbing public order in either part or the whole of his country of origin or nationality" is dislocated from their usual country of residence.[9] The Cartegena Declaration of 1984 is even more comprehensive in its recognition of the circumstances of dislocation, specifying that refugees are "persons who have fled their country because their lives, safety or freedom have been threatened by generalized violence, foreign aggression, internal conflicts, massive violation of human rights or other circumstances which have seriously disturbed public order,"[10] allowing for a generalized threat to substantiate asylum claims.

In nuclear war, people would move not only because they feared persecution under changing regimes, not only because of civil disorder arising from internal strife or foreign domination, and not only because of human rights violations. Forcible removal, ecological disaster, destruction of the physical and social infrastructure, starvation, and epidemics would combine with the loss of housing and nearly universal unemployment to set people in motion on what remained of the roads. The task of determining whether people's reason for migrating was bona fide according to international law would probably be impossible, not least of all because many people would not have identification documents due to loss, destruction, or the haste of flight. In conventional refugee situations, individuals' claim to identity (and therefore their history or likelihood of persecution) is subject to rigorous standards of proof: the taking of refuge in another nation is not equated to the giving of refuge either by the receiving nation or a prospective third nation for resettlement. Legal processes of resettlement depend upon demonstration of bona fide identities and histories, taking years to determine and work through.

Field workers assigned to these problems following nuclear war would face circumstances radically unlike the decision-making processes for those adjudicating the fate of conventionally displaced persons, the juridical, rational, and empirical process that determines which citizens are homeless, which exiles are refugees, which displaced persons are prima facie refugees, and which are merely de facto refugees tolerated on humanitarian grounds.[11] It is the difference between CIVLOG 65's disaster and other historical conflicts that makes the distinctions so stunning. And yet, within Europe, civil servants needed to estimate the scale of this political, military, social, ecological, and human disaster—and the population dispersal that would result—then rehearse their response to the extent that was possible.

British regulations dating from 1949 stipulate that the care of the civil population prior to and during hostile foreign action was the responsibility of local authorities.[12] A 1951 working group on care of the homeless in nuclear war noted that "the position of foreign refugees would require special consideration": they would be clothed from stocks held by the Women's Voluntary Service (WVS) and billeted.[13] By 1953, it was clear that the coastal towns of Kent, Sussex, and East Anglia could expect a large number of refugees from the continent and that this would overload a system already strained by internal migrants.[14] Despite the official "stay put" policy, British authorities always expected a mass exodus from cities. The Phoenix Five exercise of 1967 anticipated a heavy burden around London and Medway towns, with the police and army unable to control the flow of people on the roads even before bombing occurred. Following bombing, a second wave of migrants further strained southeastern towns.[15] Telexes sent by Essex County Control during the 1978 "Scrum Half" exercise "stressed the problem of 'attempting to keep zombies separate from clear local residents.' The 'zombies' in question were largely the half million refugees from bombs on London and southeast Essex who were tramping northeast, away from the havoc. Other requests in the same set of telex messages from the control advised that a particular route was 'passable but difficulties with refugees (so) inadvisable to send unprotected food convoy by this route.'"[16] Hundreds of thousands of these British refugees were (theoretically) relocated in Scotland. Assuming that the ports survived, the exodus was expected to be compounded by refugees finding their way from the Low Countries and France and pressing into Harwich, Felixstowe, Ipswich, Southend, and Clacton. Meanwhile, British citizens would also press westward to Ireland. Duncan Campbell speculated that the Irish government had not considered this possibility, and records of the Irish Department of Foreign Affairs seem to bear this out.[17] Lancashire, which had 13 percent of the United Kingdom's population (more than Scotland) and a high agricultural output, was to lead the recovery effort in part through helping evacuees from targeted metropolitan centers. By 1989, this had "faded because of conflicts with government policies, coordination problems, and the government's failure to provide a regional government headquarters."[18] British authorities extensively tested exodus problems in practical and paper exercises, never resolving the issue of how to handle simultaneous uncontrolled nationwide mass movement. Relocation to Commonwealth nations was ruled out early in the nuclear era as "the economic consequences of such a policy are such as to put it outside the pale of practical politics."[19]

Canadian and American authorities assumed that migrants from each other's country would be temporary visitors and agreed to treat them on a par with their own citizens. Cross-border flow in the Detroit, Michigan, and Windsor, Ontario, area, two heavily industrialized cities facing each other across a river, was studied in detail.[20] For the most part, though extensively discussed, refugee problems in North America were not the subjects of exercises.[21]

Helping the Living

When President Eisenhower was informed of the situation assumptions in OPAL 55 (8.5 million were assumed dead, 8 million were injured, an undetermined number of future fallout casualties would swell casualty figures, and 25 million homeless were in need of federally supported food and shelter programs) his sole comment was "staggering."[22] Exercise play in OPAL 56 included the need to locate accommodation for 4 million people fleeing New York City, Newark, Trenton, Elizabeth, and Bridgeport at D+4. Trained medical personnel were urgently needed throughout the northeast and east central areas. In OPAL 57, 10 million dwelling units in the New York/New Jersey area were destroyed in the attack, resulting in 25 million displaced persons in need of shelter in that vicinity.[23] In OPAL 58, a similar number were made homeless, but less than 20 percent of the area of the northeastern states was safe to inhabit, and what remained safe was mostly near the Canadian border.[24] Health workers struggled with shortfalls of 10 million doses of penicillin at D+30 and a deficit of nearly 19 million doses of smallpox vaccine at D+90.[25] Lacking basic medical supplies in OPAL 59, drastic measures were enforced. Antibiotics were reserved primarily for post-surgical patients and those with extensive radiation or gastrointestinal injuries, marrow damage, or burns: only 10 percent of patients needing antibiotics received them. Hospital labs attempted to extract penicillin from patients' urine, and cadavers were drained for blood plasma.[26]

Canada ran a series of exercises to complement the United States' OPALs. One of these, Exercise "Co-Operation II," conducted in two phases in May 1958, tested communications and messaging on a wide variety of topics for nationwide play at all levels from federal through municipal control centers. The first part was a two-day exercise based on the immediate aftermath of an attack pattern of twenty-one nuclear bombs. For five days following Part I, federal staffs were expected to study the situation and determine problems that provincial staffs would play during the next part, a one-day exercise involving only federal and provincial players which resumed play at D+5 ½. Welfare problems in Part I show communiqués between provincial and target area control centers that were devised to necessitate deviations in reception plans, salvaging of food and other survival supplies, and manpower and materials allocation (for example, in order to assist a relocating clothing manufacturer, and to identify specialized personnel to run group homes for teenagers). Rural areas receiving random bomb bursts had not ordered households to store food, as they were not designated target areas, and so the indigenous sheltering population was in urgent need of allocations. People who hurriedly fled their homes, schools, and offices needed warm clothing in place of garments contaminated by fallout. Reception areas accustomed to low population density and without police were inundated with evacuees who faced unsanitary conditions and shortages of food, medicine, and heat. Some private householders refused to take evacuees unless guaranteed payment, but no voucher system existed. (Britain specified responsibility for sheltering and billets in statutory instruments, but there was no official provision for this in Canada.)[27] Wealthy evacuees paid exorbitant rents to ensure they had commodious living space, while the poor had no means to secure even basic shelter. Thefts were compounded by violence that increased in intensity by the hour. Orderly reunification of families was hampered by various causes: lack of registration cards in some areas made people restive and despondent at the delayed prospect of reuniting; parents who heard an unfounded broadcast that hundreds of unidentified children were billeted set off on frantic searches; and areas receiving evacuees from Maine had no idea where to send the American citizens' registration cards because there was no protocol for this contingency. Coastal areas needed advice about fallout in order to decide whether fishing boats should go out in search of new food stocks, and ranchers wanted to know what to do about range cattle. Provinces puzzled over whether inmates in provincial and county jails would be released while zonal authorities were challenged to find space for hundreds of elderly people evacuated by railway to their areas. On a micro level, welfare reception areas queried zones and provinces about what specific commodities should be designated for control; on a macro level, provinces indicated to federal authorities that they had seized stocks of food, clothing, and blankets to control distribution, giving rise to issues about authority over retail versus national stocks (such as stored grain and foods undergoing processing) and the mechanisms for instituting rationing and currency controls.[28]

Welfare problems in Part II of this exercise continued to be logged and (hypothetical) action consisted of bringing additional commodities to bear on the situation. Questions proliferated. Stocks of lumber and other construction materials were in urgent demand, but who controlled the dispensation of such survival items? Furniture factories offered to adapt their manufacturing to produce utility items, prioritizing bunk beds, but the logistics of planning for implementation were unclear in this sector, as they were in the reactivation of many industries involving redirection of labor and availability of raw materials. The public was uncooperative on many fronts: demanding extra payment for billeting aged, infirm, and handicapped persons; wanting to retain items for their own future use and thereby making clothing drives for those in urgent need unsuccessful; and supporting a flourishing black market; for example, a bank manager suspected of stuffing his car with the bank's money paid $4,200 for a child's snowsuit. Law enforcement was inadequate to protect a reactivated clothing factory from having its first day's production violently seized. Basic food items ran out in many places, which was substantially a transportation rather than supply challenge. Where registration cards were available, the system went awry because either post offices were out of stamps or people were out of money, and postmasters refused to transmit unstamped cards. Many parents who discovered the location of their children could not secure transport to reunite with them. Other families were on the move indiscriminately. Medical staff and supplies were needed at temporary auxiliary hospital facilities, which had difficulty coping with the glut of psychiatric cases and could not control the onslaught of lightly injured patients who should have gone elsewhere. Hospitals also needed welfare feeding teams for staff and patients and lacked instructions for disposing of the dead. Early signs of disease presaged big headaches later on: some water supplies were not chlorinated; dysentery, scarlet fever, and polio had been diagnosed; and bed bugs proliferated at rest facilities.[29]

In "Co-Operation III" (1959), players dealing with welfare issues assumed the populations they would aid suffered nearly complete loss of personal effects and income. They took as fact that a third of the Canadian population (5.7 million out of 17.5 million) would be evacuated and all survivors would require at least some welfare assistance. The normal distribution system would not operate due to loss of equipment, personnel, storage space, and transportation and there would be no prior stockpiling of essential goods or relocation of industry.[30] This exercise is unusual because, among its many aims, it explicitly gamed radiation sickness as a health problem. Provincial or zonal players were told that half the population of a town of several thousand people experienced symptoms of nausea, vomiting, and weakness within four hours of a fallout plume's arrival. They had been exposed to between 250 and 350 r of whole body gamma radiation. The town's population included two hundred trained civil defense workers who would be ill for weeks; how could they be replaced? A set of problems ensued. Players received instructions that the sick should be rescued, evacuated, and treated but needed to strategize how to minimize exposure of civil defense personnel active in the operation; despite best efforts, rescuers were exposed to 100 r within a twenty-four-hour period, and so preventing their future radiation exposure became a consideration. The casualties had to be accommodated in already overflowing medical and reception areas, safe water and food supplies secured, an immunization program instituted, and disposal of excreta and garbage arranged in light of an outbreak of an acute communicable disease among patients already in one reception area.[31]

The Co-Operation series exemplifies how there were really no discreet areas in welfare services. The problems arising in one category necessitated action from personnel ostensibly assigned to other functions. This was intended to make players use all available channels of communication, think about which level in the hierarchy should be consulted or directed for action, and explore how problems move up as well as down (and often both) the hierarchy of control, decision-making, and implementation.

A 1949 British working group on civilian morale concluded that "the British type of society would react best to a difficult situation when it was convinced that the worst was known and unpleasant truth was not being kept from them."[32] It was assumed, therefore, that not only the workers in control centers but also civil defense workers in the field and the people they were assisting would know the basic facts of their plight. Effectiveness and pragmatism went hand in hand. Elderly people in Derby and Joan clubs would be encouraged to see their responsibility to "stay put" as an essential contribution to social stability; for example, they could help look after a working son-in-law if a daughter (and her children) were evacuated to the countryside.[33] It was thought that in the early 1950s, if there was sufficient warning, the British would order evacuation of 5 million city dwellers (two million of them from London), increasing the population of reception areas by 25–33 percent even before any homeless or unplanned evacuees arrived there.[34] (Only one million people were evacuated in 1939.) The London County Council estimated it would take three months to complete plans, print documents, and train staff, but if needed some sort of evacuation could be cobbled together with just two weeks' notice.[35] Without the public's willing cooperation, the situation could be made very much worse. The public—largely indifferent to civil defense per se—needed to have experience in peacetime that was relevant to what might be required of them following nuclear war; however, this did not necessitate public exercises. For example, a British committee observed that holiday camps gave people experience of community life which could be helpful in the event of evacuation, while youth and Scout camps gave even more valuable experience of country life.

By the early 1960s, the number of designated evacuees was increased to 9.5 million (and another million from Scotland) with the addition of Bristol, Southampton, and Plymouth to the national evacuation priorities, but the advisability of having an explicit plan was debated. Its existence might heighten international tension or lead to local chaos when residents discover that they are told to stay put in what were expected to be dangerous areas. Yet the absence of a plan could be perceived as dereliction of duty on the government's part, alarming NATO and fueling the arguments of nuclear protestors. Planning of this kind had to be made known to local authorities if it was to have any chance of success; decentralization was planning's best hope in an emergency and its greatest downfall in other circumstances.[36] If evacuation could not be carried out in advance, large numbers of homeless people would congregate in open spaces for hours at a time awaiting transport and welfare services. According to the police, civil control would compound the inherently challenging logistics of feeding, clothing, sheltering, and moving the homeless to safety.[37]

The scale and complexity of evacuation, with the complicating needs for welfare pre- and post-attack, were perceived very early in the Cold War era. Exercise "Britannia" in 1949 was probably the earliest syndicate to consider the problem.

> [It] postulated the pre-war evacuation of all non-essential inhabitants from a strip of London along the Thames from Fulham to Barking, 15 miles long and 3 to 3 ½ miles wide. This would involve evacuating some 1,100,000 residents, leaving behind only about 100,000 essential workers (for whom shelter would be provided) to operate vital services such as docks, railways, public utilities, central and local government, police, &c. It was [a]greed that, whilst the problem was not peculiar to London this proposal might be studied as an example of what might have to be contemplated. . . . The Chairman . . . suggested that no Government would be willing to invite or order an area evacuation of the magnitude of the Thames-side proposal, in anticipation of an attack which might never materialize, if it were certain that widespread unemployment and disruption of normal life, with consequent damage to morale, would result.[38]

Neither the targeting nor precision delivery of a bomb was ever assured. Residents could be evacuated only to become victims—and burdens—somewhere else. Thinning out a densely populated area was considered, at this time, a better option than wholesale evacuation. It would preserve industrial output just when it was most needed, keep the maximum number of people in employment, reduce the congestion on essential service routes, and keep the enemy guessing about vital points.[39]

The Home Office gathered wvs members and two dozen high-ranking civil servants from England, Scotland, and Northern Ireland at Sunningdale in early 1953 to review exercises and pilot studies on welfare that had occurred up to that point. The priority was to safeguard the population, thinking ahead to imminent as well as long-term needs: "Under a war of survival 'stay put' priority must go to those on whom the continued ability of the population to exist depends. All other production, even munitions, unless special instructions to the contrary have been issued, must take second place. The phrase 'the survival of the population' must, in fact, be interpreted literally." This group determined that the homeless must be accommodated in existing buildings (not huts or tents) and utilize existing water and sanitation in these earmarked premises. When capacity was reached, the next resort would be to billet in private homes and garages. "It is hoped that by using existing cover of every sort and kind, no matter what temporary inconvenience is caused, it would be possible to absorb the homeless, even on the scale antici-pated. If these heroic measures still left a balance then any remaining expedients would have to be adopted." They would exhaust resources within target areas first, and then turn to surrounding areas. Each properly equipped and staffed rest center would be ganged with up to seven other designated or improvised sites for administrative purposes.[40]

Documentation of this welfare study warns that civil defense organizers needed to prepare themselves and the public psychologically as well as physically if plans were to work, but timing was crucial. "Action as drastic as is contemplated must not be made public at this stage . . . . the public have no conception of what such a situation would mean; neither, of course, does it accord with the tenor of ministerial announcements. This does not mean that plans cannot be made or exercises held. It is obvious that both are essential."[41] This was the British civil defense catch-22: the public is ignorant, the public needs to understand, yet the public must not be told now. Until this cycle was broken, even the best-prepared Civil Defence Corps could find their efforts were in vain in aiding an unprepared public.

A series of emergency feeding studies in 1952 and 1953 reveal the kind of prag-matic thinking that prevailed among British planners during this period, in part due to the living memory of providing wartime welfare relief for the homeless. The Leeds study (20–21 October 1952) involved around seventy-seven participants including personnel from county council education services, school meals organizers, welfare and civil defense officers, police, town clerks, and the Ministry of Agriculture and Food (MAF). Leeds was presumed to suffer a wave of heavy explosive bombardment followed by an A-bomb burst centered over Leeds Bridge. About 130,000 homeless streamed out of this city of 503,030. Sheffield was also struck, and though civil defense units were in short supply Leeds received reinforcements from the West Riding of Yorkshire, Wakefield, and Dewsbury. Stockpiles provided for 1 million servings of tea but only 40,000 servings of canned beef in the immediate area of Leeds. The first priority was to establish sites three or four miles outside the city boundary where improvised kitchens would be set up. Shelterees would be given sweet tea, supplemented later with broth or soup and biscuits. The ministry forecast providing an additional three tons of sugar, eight tons of milk, forty-nine tons of biscuits, five tons of margarine, six tons of preserves, six tons of soup powder, three tons of Mexican canned beef, five tons of canned carrots, seven tons of canned beans, and sixteen tons of raw potatoes to the Leeds area, with approximately fivefold these supplies going to the rest of the West Riding. The keynote was "flexibility."[42]

The Kingston-upon-Hull study three months later was posited on about 200 surviving personnel in the East Riding of Yorkshire trained to handle emergency feeding (assisted by 400 additional staff). The syndicate considered how to advance the readiness condition for a nuclear war emergency. Hull carried out a partial evacuation, but 210,000 remained within the city. Hull received a barrage of heavy explosives on the port area followed by an A-bomb centered close to the Corporation Depot off Stepney Lane. Within an hour, a general exodus of 120,000 homeless was underway. The syndicate debated how to provide for the evacuees and rescue workers remaining closer to GZ. They would seek practical help from the WVS, police, Scouts and Guides, Grocers' Association, Farmers' Union, transport authorities, commercial haulers, and firms with mobile canteens to control, care for, and feed the homeless, but pragmatic considerations like provision of cooking, serving, and eating utensils had to be solved along with choosing sites for feeding centers.[43]

The last of the feeding studies concerned Rotherham and Sheffield. Participants in the syndicate included 100 personnel from the county council education services, sanitary inspectorate, Ministry of Labour and National Service, as well as school meals organizers, welfare officers, restaurant managers, police, and town clerks from surrounding areas. Receiving considerable warning of Britain's involvement in the war, orderly pre-evacuation was assumed, though 70,000 remained in Rotherham and 392,000 in Sheffield. A thousand tons of heavy explosives fell in a mile-wide strip from Rotherham Borough boundary at Dalton to the Brightside railway sidings in Sheffield, followed by an A-bomb centered over Sheffield's St. Philip's Church. Peacetime civil defense welfare contingents of 2,190 were presumed to have swelled to 6,570 persons. Syndicates focused on maximizing catering resources and utilizing improvised cooking methods in the absence of gas and electricity. Water was plentiful. Conversion of gas and electrical equipment for hard fuels was deemed impractical, and instead open fires would be improvised with bricks. Adaptability, again, was the keynote, and "a Syndicate member thought we were under-rating the British housewife, who could be depended on for ingenuity in improvisation and assistance in other problems." They anticipated needing to feed 168,000 at rest centers, private homes, improvised shelters, and in the open, though twenty-three emergency meals centers with the capacity of seating 26,000 people (at one sitting) had been destroyed in Sheffield. Rotherham had just one central kitchen remaining, with capacity for providing 6,000 light meals every three hours. Street parties would need to be organized (this assumption is without regard to fallout) and meals sent in to workers in damaged areas.[44]

Rationing and effective distribution of essential supplies would be instrumental in staving off chaos. A later study, "Short Commons" (20–21 November 1959) held at the Priory Theatre in Whitley Bay, posited that after nuclear attack it was likely that "the contents of the national larder might be approximately halved," there would be virtually no overseas supply for three months, home production would be seriously impaired, and existing arrangements for distribution disrupted. Those surviving attack were in grave danger of starvation, and to maintain morale a fair system of distribution must be sought. Participants from the HO and Ministry of Agriculture and Food and Fisheries (MAFF) were joined by county and borough officials from throughout the north of England and Scotland; the army; RAF; Newcastle Regional Hospital Board; Ministry of Works representatives from water, gas, and electrical utilities boards; the National Coal Board; British Red Cross; and Imperial Chemical Industries. They assumed a best-case scenario of pre-war survival preparations: most households heeded instructions to lay in a seven-day stock, and there was enough food in the distribution chain to last fourteen days. But 50 percent of food regularly consumed was produced abroad, which meant an immediate reduction of the supply chain by one half. In addition, two-thirds of the raw and processed foods held in bulk could be lost in an attack and stocks currently on farms would be immobilized for weeks due to fallout. An immediate cut in the basic ration to half of peacetime consumption would be essential. Local food officers would need to come into being as soon as the precautionary period commenced in order to prepare for rapid implementation of major commodities rationing post-attack. Milk for expectant mothers and children would be the only priority ration, and even this might need revising later.[45]

A Sunningdale working party, "Janus 63" (19–21 November 1963), examined the previous decade's work on welfare services and integration into the functions of regional, sub-regional, and county/borough headquarters as they in turn related to central government, the armed forces, operational services, and public utilities. Syndicates were assigned to concentrate on food and water; housing and health; communications and transport; industry; and law and order, using the same attack pattern gamed in FALLEX 62. Water would be needed both for fire services and survival; syndicates determined that demand and supply should be assessed, radiation tests conducted, and provision made for emergency supplies. Food rationing should be implemented. Emergency sheltering of the homeless would be followed by redistribution of the population. Repairs to dwellings with minor damage could be conducted with salvaged materials; some heavily damaged properties would have to be sealed. Public hygiene to control for epidemics would be essential, along with assessment of the likelihood of radiation sickness, broadcasting to the public, and provision for future production of medical supplies, drugs, and blankets. This exercise, like others, identified issues that needed problem-solving, but also came to pessimistic conclusions acknowledging the interdependence of welfare with non-economic issues. Without continuity of government, effective communication systems between levels of government, and public broadcasts by the BBC, the working party suggested, it was unlikely that any of the welfare goals could be accomplished. Even if it did all somehow come to pass, "doubts were expressed about the ability of the police and the armed forces to cope with the problems of law and order after attack; the magnitude of the task in some areas would be likely to be so great as to be beyond the control of the limited number of uniformed men available."[46]

"Janus 64," held four months later, focused on the order in which measures should be taken to preserve health, revive industry, and prioritize use of resources, giving a more brutal prescription than earlier studies: "if it were necessary to discriminate in applying measures for providing food, water and medical aid, efforts should be concentrated on keeping alive those likely to survive." Thus, repair factories before houses. Move people to supplies, not supplies to people. This depended upon effective—which is to say discriminatory—policing. Some matters should be highly localized, such as handling food ration systems and emergency feeding, while restoration of the food industry and control of stocks should be handled by sub-regional headquarters.[47] This sounds easy enough, but the Ministry of Power, based in London—which regulated coal, electrical generating and distribution, and petroleum refining, storage, and distribution—had no regional organization to which it could divest decision making. Water was a local service but not always under the auspices of local authorities. Unique solutions were needed for almost every commodity and service. While the emphasis for planning was on continuity of government, post-attack realities in Britain would demand that the government reorganize into a different, much less centralized, form. For a time, each county might have to operate semi-autonomously, "but if organisation stopped there, the result would be the creation of city states fighting each other for such supplies as had survived the attack."[48] If maintaining continuity of government suggested the best means to preserve the national ethos, as well as survival of the greatest number, maximizing efficient functioning and survival of the population dictated that new forms of managing the post-war government's work would be required immediately. This effected not only welfare but its integral partners, the economy and policing.

"Minerva 65," also a Sunningdale study, questioned other formerly sacred aspects of British civil defense planning: the assumptions that people would stay under cover if ordered to do so and that Z-zones should and could be cleared to remove at-risk populations from severe fallout. With the realization that there would be overlapping fallout plumes from multiple strikes, Z-zones might be so far inside radioactive areas that not everyone could be reached. This intense study of Northampton resulted in a recommendation not to move the population. "The accommodation and stocks of food in the accessible fall-out free areas might be so limited that to clear people from Z-zones would only be to transfer a disaster from one geographical point to another at the cost of many radiological lives and the wasting of thousands of gallons of precious fuel." The syndicates concluded that most people would obey orders to stay under cover for between five and ten days. Where fallout conditions permitted, emergency feeding in the open air could be facilitated by bulldozing over the grass of playing fields, turning under surface radiation. Retaining mass feeding stations for homeless and emergent populations in situ meant that it would be easier to inform targeted local populations and to recruit labor. This, presumably, enhanced their safety and saved resources. Shelter, public control, and supplies of food, water, and fuel would be interlocking problems for all zones, and the syndicates recommended prioritizing tasks as follows: (1) establish communication with public, including telephone service, (2) restore water, and (3) distribute food to certain families. Of a less urgent order were (4) emergency feeding, (5) medical care for radiation exposure and other illnesses, (6) restoration of electricity, (7) movement of the public, (8) establishing a transport system for distributing food and other essentials, and (9) law and order.[49] It was a radical re-prioritization from the early nuclear era as well as the first decade of NATO's New Assumptions of thermonuclear warfare.

A follow-up study, "Minerva 68," was planned to look again at the merits of organized movement of people out of fallout areas versus self-evacuation, and other problems with the Z-zone clearance scheme. It was cancelled when the British government put civil defense on a "care and maintenance" basis.[50]

The American exercise "Operation Sentinel II" examined the post-attack food problem in 1957 and attempted to assess the likely provision of labor and food stocks, along with the system's ability to meet caloric needs for the surviving population, by gaming the command and control needs for localized areas within each region's authority. In Region 3, for example, players focused on a 220-mile diameter area of northeast Georgia, western North Carolina, northeastern Tennessee, and western South Carolina, with GZ at Spartanburg, S.C., an area with mixed industry and agriculture. Harvesting was 95 percent complete at the time of attack, with food processing at the seasonal peak. Players arbitrarily assumed that each survivor could forage one pound of unconventional food (fish and game, the internal organs of animals and fowl, roots, and herbs) per day for six months. Even if those in the immediate area lived solely on such sources, they could survive fifty to sixty days.[51] In the corresponding exercise for Region 6, the focus was on Salina, Kansas, which suffered heavy fallout. This area is known for farming and ranching. Two million pounds of food was hypothetically distributed for emergency feeding. Beyond this, there were stocks of wheat, meat, milk, and eggs. The governor recommended an austerity diet of 2,000 calories per day, which extended the longevity of stored supplies for the entire state from thirty-eight days to sixty, yet "someone must decide whether we will eat hamburger or oatmeal." Here, too, unconventional sources of food could extend the supplies. They calculated that the state of Kansas had nearly 11 million man-days in rabbits, 5 million in other rodents, 10 million in wild birds, 5 million in fish, 3 million in grasses and plants, and 20 million in pets, though none of these were to be used "unless deemed essential for morale." Vitamins were to be confiscated and controlled like medical supplies. The surviving twenty-eight-day supply of coffee could prove important in maintaining morale; on the other hand, perhaps it should be reserved for civil defense personnel?[52]

Sentinel II involved a great deal of data on the regular food supplies of the nation, extrapolated to the surviving population post-attack. Still, the exercise came under criticism from Ernest V. Holmes, brigadier general (ret.) and emergency planning coordinator for the Department of Commerce.

Frankly, I don't think we are ever very realistic in our approaches or our conclusions. . . . I tried to make the point several times, without too much success, that when we came up against a problem for which we had no answer, usually because "we could never get the public to accept such a premise," we tried to assume ourselves out of the predicament. Assumptions are great little solvers of problems. There are answers to most of our problems, of which the majority of us engaged in this program are aware, but we won't even mention them publicly because they violate some of our most sacred ideals and traditions. Until now we haven't had to even contemplate the conditions which would exist throughout the nation following a thermonuclear attack and even the most sanguine of us are somewhat loathe to put our thoughts into words. We bicker about "confiscation," the use of the word, and disregard the actual conditions which would make such actions mandatory. . . . I realize fully the need of being practical in our approach to the public and in the development of our plans, but we are continuing to procrastinate in many areas on the grounds that it is not "politically expedient," "unacceptable to the public," or "not our way of life."[53]

Realism was always selective: the Department of State for example, complained that by dismissing the international situation and going on as if "the war is over" ignored an important part of the over-all problem. The method, too, came under scrutiny. Holmes observed that if the exercise was conducted at Battle Creek under austere conditions (i.e., in the basement fallout shelter of FCDA's HQ) the results may be different; on the other hand, many participants would not have agreed to show up.

In general, protection systems were more effectively gamed with empirical field exercises, and recovery systems other than medical care (including long-term housing, restoration of systems, and decontamination) which could not be realistically "tested" were more effectively explored through discussion-style formats. These syndicate exercises constitute a repertoire of practices exploring welfare problems after nuclear attack. As discussions, workshops, and talks they are not reproducible—nor can they be substantially reconstructed—yet as explorations of the scenarios of the human casualties of war they proved capable of transferring discovery from the moment of intellectualized exploration to an archive of knowledge, belief, and speculation just as with the field exercises involving explicit enactment. Scenarios, as described by performance scholar Diana Taylor, are "meaning-making paradigms that structure social environments, behaviors, and potential outcomes. . . . The scenario makes visible, yet again, what is already there: the ghosts, the images, the stereotypes" from archived knowledge. This is carried forward to the next event as the setup's range of possibilities and action, framing ensuing explorations. Delimited by "localized meaning," scenarios may "attempt to pass as universally valid" in establishing what is a "predictable . . . seemingly natural consequence of the assumptions, values, goals, power relations, presumed audience, and epistemic grids established by the set up itself" while also being fundamentally receptive to change.[54] Change is precisely what allows for policy to be suggested and, in some cases, adopted as a result of the syndicates.

As a mechanism to develop narratives, syndicates generated "received knowledge" and then passed it down to successive syndicates. This live story-telling format, whereby scenarios are derived and evolve, was the most prominent method chosen for exercises on welfare topics. This kind of exploration is not historiographically different from the more pragmatic public field exercises explored in chapter 7 or time-bound role play of exercises like Spade Fork and CIVLOG 65 (chapters 8 and 9). Role play in the syndicate-type meetings is not usually demonstrable, but an "as if" still prevailed in problem-setting and problem-solving. Communication was conducted as dynamic interactivity within the parameters of the "as if" scenario, though with less apparent "eventness" or playful pretense than a field or bunker exercise. Empirical exploration was possible, on a limited scale, with some of the welfare problems—registration, relocation, billeting, rescue, triage, and medical treatment—and the emphasis in such exercises fell upon training through embodied experience. The syndicates, by contrast, could investigate the problems not as scaled-down practicums but as explorations of the theoretical dimensions of crisis, leading toward planning or revision of existing plans. For example, an evaluation of Sentinel I, a command and control exercise at the FCDA headquarters in Battle Creek, emphasized the desirability of talking in problem-setting groups: "A 'think' exercise of this nature . . . divorced for the moment from the perplexing operational problems . . . could well prove to be highly productive."[55]

This productive tension between empiricism and abstraction, or temporary relief from pragmatic pressures, was helpful in imagining some welfare problems—handling the dislocated masses and supplying the essentials of life—but especially important in planning for disposal of the dead. As President Eisenhower reminded his cabinet following OPAL 56, "Who is going to bury the dead? Where would one find the tools? The organization to do it? We must *not* assume that we are going to handle these problems with calmness. Any such assumption would be completely unrealistic."[56] The aggregated corpses, even more so than streams of needy citizens, triggered emotional reactions in planners, yet this needed to be imagined in order to set policy. Planning for the dead on this scale suggests a more circumscribed methexis with post-attack circumstances than in embodied exercises, and yet it was so affectively loaded that psycho-physical reactions were likely even in syndicates.

Burying the Dead

Nuclear war would produce millions of dead. Recovery, centralization, identification, and burial of bodies would be allied problems. What precedents did planners draw upon for dealing with this? What problems were recognized as part of the need to bury the unprecedented number of civilians who would perish? Could solutions be rehearsed?

Following Allied raids on Hamburg in 1943, recovery of bodies from streets and squares was prioritized; however, two years after these raids officials estimated that 10,000 corpses were still trapped in the debris. Many remained where they had been roasted alive in bunkers. This was, in part, a labor problem. The Germans had to resort to using concentration camp internees reinforced by the SS and soldiers to tackle the job.[57] In a scarcity economy following nuclear war, food may have to be offered as an incentive for "volunteer" corpse collectors and grave diggers; in Britain, they would come under the jurisdiction of the officer for burial of the dead, who in peacetime was the director of recreation.[58] But persisting with the task was also, in part, a psychological problem. A 1946 HO report on the Hamburg raids cautioned that "the mental and physical strain on the men employed was quite exceptionally severe, especially in view of the indescribable condition of many of the bodies."[59] Though there would be many unemployed following nuclear attack, authorities anticipated difficulty in recruiting people to perform the dispiriting task of preparing and conducting mass burials.

Depending on weather conditions, burying decomposing corpses could be difficult. If it was too cold the frozen ground could not be broken; if it was too warm the need for haste would be accentuated. Following Allied efforts to recapture Manila in 1945, 39,000 American troops died, and in the intense heat they putrefied and disintegrated quickly. Soldiers recovering bodies for centralization and burial handled corpses with meat hooks, yet many were overcome with nausea, vomiting, depression, nightmares, and insomnia as they pursued the gruesome task of collecting the dead. Interment began a week later and presented another logistical challenge. In cemeteries and public parks, bulldozers dug trenches 197′ × 10′, two hundred bodies were dumped in each, and earth was compacted over top. It took eighty men eight weeks to complete the burials.[60] The Manila example led British researchers to conclude that in "ideal conditions, one person working as part of a team can bury 50 corpses in a week. In post-nuclear conditions, 25 would be optimistic. . . . If 1 uninjured survivor can bury 100 bodies in four weeks, and if one uninjured survivor in 10 will be available for the work, then the manpower exists in principle to carry out mass burial in any district where the ratio of corpses to uninjured survivors is less than 10 to 1."[61]

In Nagasaki, squads collected the 25,761 corpses that resulted from immediate A-bomb effects, but some areas were inaccessible for three days due to heat. Initially, seventy morticians reported for duty; when support came from neighboring cities, four hundred morticians aided this work. Crematoria could not cope with the load, so bodies were burned in groups of five using combustible debris from the wreckage.[62] Cremation was not the preferred option in North America. In 1942, an official from Detroit Civil Defense expressed horror at the crude interment practices he observed in Europe and stressed the inappropriateness of cremation if the United States or Canada experienced mass death.[63] In the event of all-out nuclear war, tens of millions of human corpses and perhaps hundreds of millions of domestic and farm animal carcasses would require disposal. Cremation would accentuate the shortage of combustible fuel. One local government estimated resources needed to bury the dead from just one large British town with a high casualty rate: "26,000 railway sleepers or equivalent wood, 5,850 tons of coal and other materials in similar quantities for cremation, and 14 bulldozers, 2,800 gallons of diesel fuel and 9,800 burial workers for mass burial."[64] Where equipment could be spared from road and housing clearance, and where petroleum could be found, deep trenches were the best option. It was estimated that it would take an excavator twenty-five hours using twenty-five gallons of petrol to dig a pit 50 × 4 × 2.5 meters capable of holding 1,000 bodies layered five-deep.[65] U.S. officials calculated that collection and interment teams would require forty people per shift: 700 labor hours for each 1,000 bodies, or 17,500 labor hours for 25,000 dead, not including truck drivers and grave diggers. "If conditions permit, mechanically dug continuous trenches offer the best solution to the burial problem. If the machines available are capable only of digging narrow trenches, bodies can be placed head to foot instead of side by side."[66]

Centralization of bodies for disposal provided economy of effort but it exacerbated problems of identification, whether for legal purposes of proving a death or addressing the emotional needs of survivors. In the first days of World War II, the British Ministry of Health prepared for anticipated air attacks by providing local authorities with a million burial forms along with stacks of paper shrouds and papier mâché coffins. Trench graves, deep enough to accommodate five rows of coffins, were prepared to receive bodies.[67] This requires a bureaucracy for matching a corpse to documentation and documentation to a specific resting place. In 1949, the year of the first Soviet nuclear test, the British again planned for mass burials.[68] A Ministry of Housing and Local Government report of 1952 recommended digging trench graves in the event that war broke out.[69] Local authorities earmarked sites such as country parks, golf courses, and nature reserves where decomposition would not leach into water supplies and estimated that between 5,000 and 7,000 coffins could be accommodated per acre.[70] A tactical study group gaming the problems of burial recommended that in the event of attacks on London, a four or five-acre area of Wanstead Flats could be used to accommodate just 17,500 shroud-wrapped corpses, but such estimates are predicated on pre-apocalypse proprieties.[71] To save space and resources, a report by the Ministry of Housing and Local Government recommended a Dutch system of using either coffins with detachable tray-like bottoms or coffins modified with hinged bottoms so that after they are lowered into a grave bodies could be discreetly released and the coffins removed for re-use.[72] Both Canadian and American procedures included working with clergy to arrange funerary rites, but recognized that niceties like caskets, lying in state, and individual ceremonies would have to be foregone. "Bereaved families and persons will want private attention and the clergyman must be prepared to serve them without depriving others of his time and comfort."[73] The clergy were regarded as integral to civil defense teams that included coroners, police, representatives from departments of health and vital statistics, funeral directors and licensed embalmers, and transportation coordinators.[74] In OPAL 58, New Orleans civil defense had its mortuary unit make plans for mass burial and the religious unit for joint services.[75]

Instructions from the FCDA advised that an absolute minimum of laborers should be devoted to disposing of the dead: the living should instead concentrate on caring for the sick and wounded. "Those killed at some distance from ground zero will have been identified by survivors in the same area and their names entered on emergency medical tags for use in mortuary records. Furthermore, these individuals could also be later legally proven dead by the direct testimony of surviving witnesses." Rescue workers who came upon corpses would apply tags marked with a large X, though very badly maimed or burned bodies might not be tagged. Meanwhile, closer to GZ, "legal identification by personal recognition will not be possible because of the large number of dead, wide dispersal of the population after a disaster, and lack of necessary space, time, and labor." Assuming that ambulances, hearses, and panel-bodied trucks were used to assist the injured, flatbed or dump trucks could be used to collect the dead and take them to a mortuary area as close as possible to the burial site. Mortuary teams were instructed to wrap each body together with its personal effects in a mortuary bag, recording the sex, height, weight, age, color of hair and eyes, and physical markings. If six minutes were spent by each three-person identification team, a total of ten identification teams should be able to handle 100 bodies an hour (800 bodies in an eight-hour shift).[76]

In 1953, the Canadian Ministry of Health developed punctilious instructions for handling corpses following a nuclear attack. Bodies were to be taken to mortuaries, where physicians would confirm death. If a physician was not available, this task could fall to a mortuary director. Serial numbers would be affixed with wire around the necks of corpses and all known details logged: location of recovery and identification documents or, in their absence, vital statistics, descriptions of teeth, deformities, clothing, laundry marks, jewelry, and contents of pockets. Logs would be copied and sent to local registration offices, but families would want to scour morgues, not just official records. The ability to accommodate them would depend on the scale of the disaster.

> Indiscriminate viewing of bodies by friends and relatives should be discouraged, but if necessary, separate rooms should be provided for this purpose. Bodies should be adequately covered at all times and sheets, blankets or clean wrapping paper can be used for this purpose. Bodies too mutilated for possible identification should not be viewed. If identification appears possible, body preservation procedures of a minor nature would be undertaken. This would be by body cavity injection with a mixture of formalin and alcohol. These bodies could be held longer for identification if mortuary space permitted. . . . Unclaimed unembalmed bodies should be held a maximum of 48 hours before burial. . . . burials should be in an established cemetery if possible and it may be necessary in this emergency to provide body covering by wrapping in a blanket or shroud. . . . It is extremely important that a chart should be made of each common grave showing the position of bodies by mortuary accession number. If the disaster is so great that bodies could not be cleared through area mortuaries in the manner described, but were still in the disaster area some days after death, it might be necessary to waive the routine suggested above and transport them directly to a common grave site. In this event as much as possible of the mortuary record and identification procedure, together with a chart of the common grave area, should be completed.[77]

No special measures were deemed necessary for handling bodies exposed to radiation. Identification would sometimes happen through these measures; however, relatives would want a chance to claim the bodies of their dead, and the Americans made plans for tackling this contingency. "Ten thousand unidentified bodies would require over 5.5 acres of space (250,000 square feet) for adequate display. A person would walk five miles between the rows of bodies before all were seen, and for each 25,000 identifiable bodies probably 10,000 would be unrecognizable because of disfigurement by injury or fire."[78] The likelihood that ailing, hungry, and shocked survivors could file past tens of thousands of bodies arrayed across miles of aisleways might be disputed. It certainly was not tested.

With the likelihood of a dispersed population and the need to get corpses into the ground, there probably would be no way for survivors to claim their dead except through recognition of characteristics formally listed and posted in designated locales. This might preclude legal recognition of their demise, and thus leave survivors without the ability to claim insurance, pensions, or other death benefits, assuming that such provisions still existed. Would wondering about a loved one's fate be worse than knowing? The difficulties of identification would inevitably compound the psychological toll of the disaster. In the aftermath of the 2004 Indian Ocean tsunami, in which at least 270,000 died in a ring extending from Sumatra to Thailand, Sri Lanka, and Somalia, many communities posted pictures of their dead—taken with digital cameras and printed on computers—but during the Cold War there was no comparable technology to facilitate this expedience, let alone allowing electronic distribution of the likenesses to additional communities.

Burial problems were gamed at all levels of government. Though civil defense literature for the public avoided graphic images and explicit information regarding scenes of destruction, corpses, and gore in order to forestall panic and despair, the civil service was not so sheltered.[79] They identified the linked planning problems of setting operational priorities as well as the linked manpower problems of welfare and burial. A British syndicate exercise of 1955, "Beagle II," posited a situation in the Midlands in which, in the midst of 900,000 homeless civilians in Warwickshire and Staffordshire, there were an estimated 600,000 bodies in need of immediate burial to prevent epidemics. The lingering presence of the dead was a factor in the mental health of survivors as early as D+48.[80] In 1954, eight western states plus Hawaii, Alaska, and three western Canadian provinces participated in "Operation Second Phase" along with federal agencies and the Sixth Army. They tested the load of public information messages likely to arise in a post-nuclear war situation. TWX and radio communications were tested for nine hours commencing at D+48, incorporating issues such as sabotage and heavy explosive damage to water systems, dams, and other electrical generation facilities; destruction of utilities; forest fires; sabotage to railway bridges; logistics of supplying stranded motorists with petrol and food; controlling the traffic of evacuees streaming from the coast toward the interior; setting up improvised hospitals; disbursing critical supplies of food, equipment, personnel, and medicine; bacteriological warfare in rural areas; and mass burials.[81]

The city director of Baltimore, participating in "Operation Sentinel I," complained that no local government could handle the requirements to feed, clothe, and house its devastated population even if officials had found safe haven outside the target area and the line of succession was intact. Their responsibilities were too enormous: survey needs and equitably distribute consumer goods; ensure that the necessities of life are met; continue medical care; clear public ways and important industrial sites; begin to decontaminate essential areas; reestablish utilities; resume education for children; demolish or render safe public and private structures; assist in restoring essential industrial plants; provide manpower and allocate specially skilled workers; provide shelter; assist other local governments; determine the whereabouts of citizens and reunite families; and recover, identify, and bury the dead.[82] The viability of this list ran counter to the findings of a ten-month course at the Industrial College of the Armed Forces which predicted that for the first week after attack the entire labor force would be occupied with cleaning up, rescue, caring for the injured, and burial. For at least a month following attack, two people would be needed to take care of each injured person, severely reducing the available labor supply. And if burial was the *only* task, this *alone* would be a massive problem. "If it is summertime . . . what does it really mean to bury 600 million pounds of the rotting meat of our problem?"[83] Just burying the human dead of the District of Columbia would require a ditch 6 feet wide and 92 miles long.[84] Many bodies would disintegrate in time, but these figures do not also account for the putrefying vermin, pets, livestock, and formerly frozen food that would compound the tonnage of rotting meat. OPAL 58 posited the deaths of over 2.5 million cattle in the plains states up to D+30 (equivalent to 3 billion pounds).[85]

Exercises conducted to account for NATO's New Assumptions of thermonuclear warfare show that officials were able to envision circumstances necessitating sharp distinctions from ordinary conduct and peacetime squeamishness. The nationwide Canadian exercise, Co-Operation II (May 1958), set a sample problem for the welfare service that involved estimating the number of people dead from exposure on the highways. Survivors stripped the dead of clothing to keep themselves warm. Burial shrouds were in short supply at the same time there was a desperate need for blankets for the living. Welfare services dispatched clothing and supplies, and recommended salvaging all garments before burial.[86] In OPAL 59, Connecticut and Rhode Island urgently requested assistance with burial of their dead. They had nearly 1.5 million corpses at D+30, mainly around Hartford, New Haven, and Providence. Most were slow-dying radiation casualties, and the states could not keep up. The U.S. Corps of Engineers declined to help, claiming that digging burial trenches was not a task for which it was well trained or adapted, referring the states to HEW and instead sending two divisions of Engineers to clear harbors and waterways.[87]

Despite all this, Defense Secretary Robert McNamara insisted in 1965 that "normal, but austere, practices for burial of the dead could be followed." He explained that 2 percent of the land area in the United States would be so devastated that fatalities near GZs would not be approached by survivors anyway. In surrounding areas, with mixtures of dead, injured, and healthy, the healthy survivors would simply take care of the others.[88] In other words, a communal ethos would kick in and neither shock nor self-serving survivalism would hinder this function.

Nothing could be more austere than the expedient disposal of 6.5 million ruminant animals slaughtered in Britain during the 2001 foot-and-mouth disease epidemic. This presented an enormous logistical challenge. Some animals were buried or incinerated in the fields where they grazed, but a large number were taken to one of five mass burial sites dotted around the country. At Great Orton airfield in Cumbria, teams of vets and slaughtermen toiled day and night for a week in order to dispose of 120,000 sheep, just a quarter of their half million quota. Brigadier Birtwhistle, overseeing this site, described it as "an apocalyptic task."[89] In the aftermath of nuclear war, there would be concentrations of human corpses at first aid and reception centers; however, the adaptations for efficiently dealing with cattle and sheep could hardly be applied. While the 2001 foot-and-mouth epidemic allowed for an empirical test of mass burial procedures, it also strained resources, had a huge impact on the economy, and pushed the sensibilities of the largely cooperative British public to the limits. McNamara may have been too sanguine.

Perhaps, more than most aspects of the post-nuclear war clean-up, human burial could have been practiced on a simulated basis through activities such as gathering animals and digging trenches for their disposal. However, any empirical analogs to mass human interment overtly practiced would not only have constituted an admission of the cost of nuclear warfare but also traumatized participants and risked damning coverage in the media.

In the casualty exercises described in chapter 7, the mass "dead" did not really pile up: in syndicate exercises they could, but only theoretically, which was not quite so distasteful. Though likely to be a pressing problem in the recovery phase of operations, and integral as it was to other issues of health, resources, and labor, mass burial was not usually even mentioned as a need in planning, and it is rarely documented as playing a factor in discussions. Even so, in the occasions when its precedence was weighed, the manner by which the logistics of death and burial were calculated tie nuclear war to the most sobering scenarios of modern memory: expedient mass interment, epidemics and disasters, and war on a cataclysmic scale. Instead of imagining a callous regime dumping victims in pits, picturing a localized outbreak of a devastating disease, or thinking of the casualties of a single battle or campaign, nuclear civil defense planners projected scenarios where the dead accrued from the equivalent of all these factors, all at once, everywhere in their jurisdictions and the jurisdictions of their regional, national, and international colleagues.

CONTINUITY OF GOVERNMENT

Came back to DC on the Airborne Command Post — and they staged a briefing and a test exercise. Pretty scary. They went through the whole intelligence & operational briefings — with interruptions, etc. to make it realistic. . . . Fascinating plane — with command room set up — all kinds of communications, display boards, rear projection, etc. Took P. [President Nixon] a while to get into the thing (his mind was on the [Vietnam] peace plan) but he finally did — and was quite interested.

— H. R. Haldeman

Impediments to realistic simulation arose from multiple, complex, and inter-related factors. The evidence shows, over and over again, that civil defense exercises were limited by the cost of resources, both in time and material; concurrent real emergencies that pulled participants away or split the focus of politicians, professional planners, and emergency responders; the complexities of communication and coordination; and intangible obstacles such as ethics, psychological barriers, and the limits of imagination. Even in optimal circumstances, the parameters of civil defense exercises were compromises to practicality, recognizing the overarching impossibility of encompassing the gestalt of disaster planning and response. The ultimate value of an exercise for real-world applicability depended not only upon whether it addressed a pressing problem with sufficient complexity but also upon how accurate the assumptions behind it would prove to be in the event of war. This relationship of testable problems to background assumptions is the foundation of civil defense exercises in continuity of government, as in all else.

One of the chief ways in which civil defense engaged realistically with post-attack conditions was through rehearsals in site-specific emergency headquarters. Just as the public was urged to prepare home shelters and know the whereabouts of public shelters, designated civil servants and elected politicians expected to perform — but for the time being only rehearse — in fallout shelters or, in some cases, hardened blastproof bunkers fitted up with office space. These exercises were not only referential to the conditions following attack but also relocated personnel into the facilities where they would actually operate post-attack to maintain continuity of government. Such embodied testing by civilians took on a heightened degree of realism. Diana Taylor argues that "every performance enacts a theory, and every theory performs in the public sphere,"[1] but she did not anticipate the contingency of acting on behalf of the public in secret and unbreachable facilities, nominally "public" because they existed for civil servants and elected officials with the highest security clearances but also "private" in the sense of being hidden, classified, or clandestine. Yet here, too, performance enacted theory that was stated as problems yielding to effort.[2] Numerous exercises touched upon in earlier chapters were to some extent conducted in such facilities, including Spade Fork, the OPAL series, CIVLOG 65, FALLEX 62, and the Co-Operation series. These continuity of government rehearsals mirrored military exercises in situ at command headquarters remote from battlegrounds.

Each nation determined its emergency sites based on a combination of geographic, political, and defensive factors. Americans built bunkers for the various branches of federal government (executive, legislative, and administrative) as well as in designated regions, encouraging states to do the same, and reserving the alternative of putting their commander in chief up in the skies in the event of emergency. With comparatively little airspace, the British derived a land-based plan of central government bunkers whose specific roles were not assigned in advance, allowing for flexibility depending on the attack pattern. Canadians had plenty of airspace but in a sense that was the problem: the distribution of the population across the vast land mass made a combination of centralized and disbursed control centers advisable so that regions could function autonomously, if necessary. The federal government was highly localized in Ottawa, yet wielded fewer constitutional responsibilities than in Britain, which led to a bunker system for federal and provincial governments utilizing both centralized and dispersed facilities.

Through the ingenuity of engineers, these built environments are not only testaments to belief of biological survivability within their walls, and beyond, but also concrete (and steel, lead, and tungsten) confirmation of the tenet of cultural survivability because of what would be harbored inside and thereby nurtured outside. During civil defense exercises they served as consummate multi-disciplinary rehearsal sites, but their primary purpose was to shield decision-makers and ensure the flows of information that would preserve nations and ideologies (and thus the *will* to fight) as they enabled operations related to welfare, industry, and resupply that were intended to preserve and revive communities in the first thirty days following an attack.

Evidence of embodied rehearsals' ability to engage participants emotionally as well as intellectually in the hard realities of nuclear warfare comes from no less a testament than the diary of H. R. Haldeman, President Nixon's chief of staff, a few months after Nixon took office. On their way back to Washington from Florida, they rehearsed airborne protocols for the Single Integrated Operational Plan, a counterforce strategy predicated on massive nuclear attack on Soviet and Chinese capabilities. There, with the actual visual aids and communications equipment, in the site-specific locale for instigating World War III, President Nixon realized "that when the Russians appear to be launching an attack our options are pretty limited," and was moved to ask "a lot of questions re our nuclear capability—and kill results." Haldeman's comment that Nixon "obviously worries about the lightly tossed-about millions of deaths"[3] is reassuring to posterity, and may be the seed of his insistence, along with Henry Kissinger, that the Pentagon derive strategic alternatives, escalation control, and selective targeting.

For officials on the ground—or if they were lucky, underneath the ground—who could only try to carry out continuity of government plans, nuclear strikes would be treated as facts to graph post hoc, not potentialities to try to limit as a matter of political strategy. The maintenance of peace between NATO, the Soviet Union, and China for the duration of the Cold War meant that the primary purpose of the emergency headquarters network was never fulfilled. Yet the bunkers were important factors in training and exercise activity, and as such also served as research sites to test the viability of civil defense plans. As built environments, they were engineered to function as hermetically sealed-off sites for decision-makers while most of the population had a more personal encounter with the grim aftermath of attack. Their materiality provides evidence of what was considered feasible for post-attack continuity of government operations, and therefore what was available to be tested and who needed to rehearse. Their principal interior areas—Nuclear Detonation (NUDET) plotting, operational control, maintenance of life, and sleeping quarters—define priorities, determine the scope of relevant action, and suggest the dramatis personae of staff allocations. The sites that survive are monuments in concrete to the scenography of civil defense rehearsals, defying the ephemerality of embodied enactment.

Bunkers' Physical Layout and Function

Britain was probably first to recognize the need: as early as 1947, it set aside a World War II-era facility for an emergency seat of government command center for A-bomb defense.[4] By the early 1980s, it had designated Hawthorn (ninety miles west of London) as the Central Government War Headquarters; in addition, a network of bunkers to disperse operational personnel hedged against this central facility being destroyed.[5] This network evolved over the intervening decades. Regional War Rooms—above ground or partially sunken two-storey windowless blockhouses—were built in the early 1950s. In July 1957, following the first British H-bomb test, local authorities were informed about a new system of regional and group control revolving around twelve emergency Regional Seats of Governments (RSGs), supported by sub-RSGs.[6] Some RSGs were purpose-built, but many were adapted from RAF operations centers, radar stations, and other kinds of buildings.[7] Their operational assignments have a convoluted history, and the lack of clarity about the RSGs arises, in part, from the attempt to keep the facilities secret and the decision around 1967 to wait to assign any given facility definitive RSG status until after a nuclear attack occurred, when the site for the central seat of government would also be determined.[8] Two of these larger sites are open for public viewing.

Kelvedon Hatch (Essex) was a likely candidate for central government emergency headquarters because it is just twenty-five miles northeast of London. It started out as an RAF site in 1953, where information was centralized from subregional radar facilities. Bawburgh (Norfolk) was built at the same time, and Box (Wiltshire) and Shipton (North Yorkshire) are the other comparable facilities. The entrance for personnel is masked by a farmhouse bungalow which obscures a massive structure consisting of three underground storeys capable of accommodating six hundred staff. Its lowest level is approximately 100 feet below grade. To make it blastproof, construction is of ten-foot thick concrete reinforced by tungsten rods, in turn covered by an outer brick skin with netting and pitch, all enclosed within a wire mesh Faraday cage to ground the facility. Layers of concrete "burst caps" are placed around the upper level of the facility to reduce damage if hit from above. A grassy hillock with an enormous communications tower tops the 27,000-square-foot bunker. In its capacity as an RSG, it was refitted to provide office space, kitchen and dining areas, living quarters (two dormitories

54. Kelvedon Hatch bunker, Essex, equipment entrance tunnel. Photo by M. K. Shapey; reproduced courtesy of J. A. Parrish and Sons, Kelvedon Hatch Secret Regional Government Nuclear Bunker, Kelvedon Hatch, Essex.

and several private suites for Cabinet ministers), a medical room, BBC studio, a map room for plotting fallout, and situation room.[9]

The headquarters for Scotland's northern zone at Anstruther was built in 1951 as a radar station serving the navy's Rosyth docks and RAF Leuchar. The entrance is obscured by a steel and concrete-reinforced guardhouse posing as a traditional Scottish stone farmhouse. Bunkers like this are underground because it makes them less subject to detection but also because by burying a building the mass needed to provide blast protection is significantly reduced. The engineering challenges — providing flexible connections to services coming into the building, keeping the atmosphere comfortable in ordinary circumstances and pristine when closed-up — pertain whether a building is above or below ground, but the materials needed for construction are reduced by a significant degree if earthworks, rather than walls, can take the brunt of a shock wave. Set in a 150-foot hole on gravel for shock absorption, the Anstruther bunker consists of a ten-foot deep outer shell of concrete reinforced with one-inch tungsten rods set vertically and horizontally at six-inch intervals. This is encased with brick and netting soaked in pitch, covered with earth then a "raft" of concrete, and dirt piled on top and landscaped. In the conversion from RAF site to RSG bunker, Anstruther was refitted as an underground two-storey facility including living accommodations for up to three hundred people in six dormitories, a suite for the secretary of state, and

55. Kelvedon Hatch Operations Room, with reconstructed arrangement of facility. Photo by M. K. Shapey; reproduced courtesy of J. A. Parrish and Sons, Kelvedon Hatch Secret Regional Government Nuclear Bunker, Kelvedon Hatch, Essex.

accommodation for military staff. Civil defense operations were aided by banks of communications equipment, operation situation maps, desks for vital services personnel on the central command floor, and a BBC studio.[10]

Declassified evidence of RSGs' use during exercises is scanty. The sub-RSG at Shirley (Warwickshire) was a World War II-era war room, re-designated as a Regional War Room in the early 1950s. In 1960 it was used for the command and control exercise "Mercian Trump": staff crowding together to rehearse activities from H to H+9 included representatives from the HO; army; Admiralty; Air Ministry; MAFF; ministries of Housing and Local Government, Health, Transport, and Works; the Regional Hospital Board; Post Office; Scientific Office; fire services; and police.[11] Eight months later, in May 1961, a follow-up exercise was held at Drakelow (Worcestershire), the new facility for the West Midlands. Modified to accommodate 325 staff, this 250,000-square-foot facility near Kidderminster was adapted from an underground site built in 1941–43 as a bombproof factory for making Rover aircraft engines.[12] For a number of months in advance of "Mercian Trump II," participants underwent a training course and attended talks by the regional director, L. Pendred, who reported that "these discussions were followed up by rehearsals in the RSG and SR [situation room] during the week prior to the exercise and the rehearsals were interspersed with demonstrations of various procedures and talks on the more abstract aspects of the organisation. This method

56. Kelvedon Hatch Situation Centre. Photo by M. K. Shapey; reproduced courtesy of J. A. Parrish and Sons, Kelvedon Hatch Secret Regional Government Nuclear Bunker, Kelvedon Hatch, Essex.

of indoctrination proved to be satisfactory." The rehearsal program for three days prior to Mercian Trump II included:

— plotters and staff officers: 20-minute demonstration on the use of projecting equipment and the preparation of transparencies;

— plotters: 40-minute demonstration and practice on the reception of scientific information over closed circuit telephone system, including fallout contours, bomb bursts, and distant fallout threat messages;

— staff and liaison officers: 45-minute talk and discussion on "Information in a Sub Region" then a 30-minute demonstration on message procedures and writing;

— following lunch, a 2-hour mini-exercise.[13]

During Mercian Trump II, the team was responsible for coordinating everything in the region except lifesaving. The plotters' radiological mapping would provide the primary point of reference for all decisions. Staff officers worked in an open office format intended to stimulate discussion and consultation. Participants monitored the flow of homeless and the strain on local authorities outside the damaged area, and drafted the regional commissioner's broadcast.[14]

The United States separated its relocation bunker for federal lawmakers (annexed to a luxury hotel in rural Greenbrier, West Virginia, in 1957) from the presidential and executive branch bunker (completed at Mt. Weather, Virginia,

57. Anstruther bunker, Fifeshire, Guard House covering staff entrance tunnel. Courtesy of M. K. Shapey.

in 1958) and the eight regional headquarters (completed in the mid-1960s).[15] The Greenbrier was elaborately maintained but did not host exercises and, as such, is of peripheral importance to the history of civil defense rehearsal. Mt. Weather, by contrast, involved the civil service and probably several presidents in exercises on a par with a military command post. It was designed for total occupancy of around 2,500 people working in two or three shifts. The cafeteria and auxiliary snack bars provided meals. Depending on their role, each person was assigned 55 to 100 square feet of space. Agency heads had combined office and sleeping space, partially divided between the three-quarter bed and desk area. Sixteen of these suites had semi-private bathrooms. Eleven additional suites for cabinet members, consisting of three connecting offices and a bedroom with bath, were installed. Other personnel slept in male or female dormitories, each holding more than two hundred persons per shift in double bunks. In the build-up to war, staff could be working indefinitely in the facility. After the breakout of hostilities, a closed-up period of at least a month was anticipated, so measures were taken to make life in the facility bearable: "Pastel shades of paint are used throughout the installation. With the exception of the lack of windows, the rooms are no different from those above ground. Good lighting, air conditioning, ventilation and heat control are essentials. Modest effort has been made to make the installation more livable. Pictures, maps and charts have been mounted on the walls by various agencies."[16] Such design touches "normalized" windowless bunkers, creating continuity with

58. OPAL54 Emergency Operations headquarters for OCD at Battle Creek, Michigan. Courtesy of NARA.

ordinary offices of the period. Internally, space correlates to function and the assignments of specialists and "experts" in post-nuclear war survival. The operational parts of the facility include the War Room, where decision-making officials and their staff concentrated. Contiguous with this area in its early years were the message center and rooms for groups working on attack analysis, resource evaluation, and presentations. OPAL exercises probably served as experimental sites for developing these rooms. Additional areas addressed communications needs for liaison to the media, civil defense headquarters in the regions, and agency headquarters in Battle Creek, Michigan.[17]

Mt. Weather is now a FEMA facility, fully operational and still accessible only with a high level of clearance; archived records pertaining to it in the United States remain classified and nothing is accessible regarding its use during exercises. By contrast, not only can the physical structure of Canada's Central Emergency Government Headquarters at Carp, Ontario (CEGHQ or "The Diefenbunker," a pun on Prime Minister Diefenbaker who commissioned it) be scrutinized (it is now Canada's Cold War Museum), but copious documents relating to its design, engineering, and operational period are available for study. Thus, Canada provides a unique opportunity to discover the relationship between the site explicitly designated and built for the federal government, the conduct of exercises held within the central HQ, and rehearsals involving the network that supported it.[18]

Comparisons of Carp with descriptions of Mt. Weather in its earliest days suggest how the Diefenbunker bears the American facility's imprint. The Montreal-based architects consulted not only with the National Research Council and Defence Research Board in Canada but also with the U.S. Army and Navy and American design consultants and architects, relying on data from the Nevada and Pacific testing programs as well as submarine design and testing. As the CEGHQ's chief engineer remarked, "this project has necessitated a more or less complete departure from the normal fields of design experience in many phases of the work."[19]

Canada's basic continuity of government plan was settled in August 1958.[20] Late in 1959, it was determined through meetings at Camp David, Maryland, that the years 1961–63, when Soviet missiles were expected to come on-line, would be "the most likely period of attack on the North American continent," and so plans for a central government relocation headquarters received heavy investment in order to aim for completion by mid-1961.[21] In the meantime, concerns about the prospect of a flare-up in Berlin led the Emergency Measures Organization (EMO) to cobble together an interim facility at Canadian Forces Base (CFB) Petawawa, Ontario, code named RUSTIC, where an exercise involving 135 Ottawa civil servants was held in 1959 in order to familiarize them with the facility.[22] TOCSIN B 61 utilized RUSTIC and another facility at Borden, Ontario: the solicitor general and ministers of Defence, Health and Welfare, and Defence Production went to RUSTIC, and Ontario's Premier Frost went to Borden.[23] Both these facilities joined the network of six Central Relocation Units (CRUs) adapted from existing buildings in Ontario; together they were designated to house 829 staff from federal government departments and the province of Ontario.[24] Canada's network of the CEGHQ, CRUs, plus six regional two-storey underground government headquarters (REGHQs) was planned and implemented in the early 1960s.[25]

The army's cover story—that Carp was merely a signals site—was exposed in newspaper reports while the CEGHQ was under construction, so its secrecy was compromised from the start.[26] The site was chosen because it is close to rail lines and a landing strip but access does not depend on any bridge within five miles. Rushed into production, the shell was under construction while the interior was still being designed. Nothing could withstand a direct hit, but architects wanted the bunker to survive a nearby hit, so it is designed to take the shock of a 5 MT weapon detonating within 1.1 miles and producing overpressure of 100 psi (the equivalent of 7.5 tons per-square-foot) at ground level lasting three or more seconds, as well as ground shock of 15 GS capable of displacing the massive structure by up to three inches. Such a blast would produce winds of over 1,000 miles per hour. It is rated at 1,000 PF and designed to withstand thermal radiation that

59. Canada's CEGHQ Carp Ontario under construction, revealing the Bank of Canada vault in the foreground connected by tunnel to the base level of the main bunker. Three more storeys were added to the bunker then the entire site was mounded with earth. Courtesy of the Diefenbunker—Canada's Cold War Museum.

would combust everything else within a five- to ten-mile radius. The bunker is 154 square feet with roughly 100,000 square feet of interior space, and rests on 3.5 feet of compressed gravel laid over 40 solid feet of limestone bedrock. The base and roof are 5 feet thick and outer walls are 2 feet thick, comprising 32,000 tons of concrete over a 5,000-ton steel frame.[27] Each of sixty-two interior support columns is approximately 4 feet in diameter, flaring out to 10-foot shear heads at top and bottom in order to spread overpressure loads into the floor and roof slabs. Its 56-foot height is obscured by a 10-foot thick grassy mound, contoured to displace a blast wave. During its operational period, a forest of microwave towers above the roof was linked to the separate signals-sending facilities at the CEGHQ and each REGHQ.

Like all blast-proof nuclear bunkers, the CEGHQ is entered through a long tunnel—constructed out of corrugated plate pipe tested in Nevada—set at right angles to the building to displace shock. The tunnel leads to blast-resistant freight doors of lead and steel, alongside air-locked main doors for personnel. The top level includes decontamination chambers, medical and dental suites, accommodation for the Royal Canadian Mounted Police (RCMP) and governor general, a centralized control monitoring desk, telecommunication equipment, a computing center, radio room, and escape hatches. The next level houses the war cabinet room, military information center, situation room (SITCEN) for radio-logical monitoring and civilian assessment, prime minister's and cabinet minis-ters' offices and bedrooms, computing area (added in the late 1960s), and CBC studio. The third level features the cafeteria and kitchen, senior officers' quar-ters, laundries, dormitories, and mufflers for the diesel generators. The lowest of four levels houses most of the dormitories for the approximately 535 staff and the generators and air filtration equipment needed to run the facility and pre-vent radiological, biological, and chemical contamination. In closed-up mode, it was fueled from a 10,000-gallon underground tank attached directly to the base slab in order to protect it from shock and overpressure. Emergency water sup-plies came from two deep artesian wells that geologists predicted could not be fouled by radiation, which pumped into 32,000-gallon storage tanks. One hun-dred and fifty thousand gallons of water were needed daily because of the burden on cooling equipment for partially recirculated air. All heavy equipment is shock mounted, plumbing fixtures are designed to spring under shock, and furniture is non-combustible. The flooring was chosen for its ability to withstand 3 GS of force, reducing the effects of extreme shock pressure on personnel. Deep freez-ers for food (or, if needed, a morgue), refrigerated garbage storage, an isolation ward, laundry rooms, and small arsenal are some of the adaptations installed for closed-up use. In addition to the life support facilities, a secure room measur-ing 47,880 cubic feet jutting off from the rectangular structure of the building at the lowest level was constructed to hold the bullion supply of the Bank of Canada. Canada went off the gold standard, and this space was later reassigned for national art treasures and records storage. Above the vault, at ground level, is a helicopter pad.[28]

The CEGHQ at Carp became operational in December 1961, and from then until 1994 was occupied by military staff stationed to CFB Carp. At the end of its operational life, emergency staff allocations were 57 percent civilian and 43 per-cent military, the latter mainly in signals and site administration.[29] The bunker's architectural details help reveal what was expected from the staff if the site ever needed to be locked down. And yet because it was one in a chain of sites where government prepared to perform during a crisis, these dispersed locales are critical to the operational "go" moment for the CEGHQ's legislative authority. In an in-flammatory international situation, the governors-in-council would preside from Parliament Hill for as long as possible. Meanwhile, a second team replicating their authority and administrative responsibilities would move into place at the CEGHQ and remain there for days or weeks, working in cooperation with colleagues still in Ottawa. A third team, replicating the authority of the other two, would move into a CRU. Only when an attack was imminent would the team still in Ottawa transport by bus or helicopter to the CEGHQ. If they were stricken en route, the second team would assume leadership of the government. If the first two teams were stricken or cut off from communications with the REGHQs, the third team would assume authority from the CRU.[30] This redundancy system resembles the British plan insofar as the line of succession is based on rank within the party in power, rather than the United States' constitutional succession based on the office held. Unlike Britain, Canada's bunkers are in centers with small populations, and most are distant from concentrations of industrial targets. Doubling as communication hubs, the CEGHQ and REGHQs were military vital points, though except for Carp they were not likely to warrant enemy targeting.

In Canada, the signature of the governor general (as the Crown's representative) is required to enact legislation, call elections, and convene constitutional government, and so someone holding this office is a vital—though symbolic—part of the continuity of government. Justices of the Supreme Court could assume this role if the governor general did not survive.[31] Lieutenant governors serve the same function in the provinces and so would be relocated in REGHQs. The presence of lieutenant governors would allow Orders in Council to be issued under provincial jurisdiction, though not every province had a regional headquarters, and members of the legislative assemblies from Saskatchewan, New Brunswick, Prince Edward Island, and Newfoundland might have difficulty accessing neighboring facilities on short notice so instead would operate in or near their capitals. Each REGHQ's regional commissioner, appointed by the governor general in council, would coordinate joint federal-provincial operations. If communications with Carp were not possible, regional commissioners, assisted by a committee of senior federal and provincial officials and a military adviser, would also assume the powers of the federal government under emergency legislation and deal directly with other regions and the United States concerning manpower and resources. Staffing for each regional headquarters mimicked Carp's, including federal and provincial civil servants; provincial premiers or commissioners; military Radiological Defense (RADEF), intelligence, communications, household site managers, and command staff; meterologists; RCMP; and medical personnel.[32] Military personnel would conduct operations in support of the population in damaged or seriously contaminated areas under direction of civilian authorities housed in regional headquarters. This was considered the primary function of armed forces stationed within Canada, and no declassified Canadian exercise was gamed over a long enough time line to see their redeployment to an overseas war zone.

Exercises to maintain operational readiness were periodically conducted, such as "Wintex 73" (7–16 March 1973), including two days when, for the first time in many years, the CEGHQ facility operated in closed-up mode. "Wintex/Prime Rate 75," taking place 24 February through 14 March 1975, involved extensive interaction between military and civilian players. This was useful insofar as the military discovered that they did not have sufficient personnel to provide necessary communications support to Carp and the CRUS, to deploy base support staff for CFB Carp, or to give logistic support to Carp's civilian staff, even with reserves in play during a total recall of personnel 12–13 March. (Military contributions involved physical security, housekeeping services, maintenance of the site, accommodation allotment, radiation monitoring, decontamination measures, and feeding of personnel in shifts, starting at 05:00 hours and ending at 00:45.) Inexplicably, the strike pattern (NUDET) script was drastically modified in the later phase of the exercise; the consternation that this caused military reporters indicates that the SITCEN had meaningful interplay with the military side.[33]

SITCEN

Carp's SITCEN staff included some military, but for the most part personnel were drawn from civil defense professionals from the EMO (later Emergency Planning Canada [EPC]) in Ottawa. SITCEN had two shifts with a chief, deputy chief, RADEF Section, reports and briefing section, damage assessment and casualty estimation section, and duty officers. Figure 60 provides a plan view of the room, and a set of photographs from a 1986 exercise in the Diefenbunker shows the SITCEN in action. The SITCEN includes two operational areas: figure 61 shows the status boards reporting the overall national situation of medical, shelter, survival, information, and morale; in the other half of SITCEN (figure 62), there are several map displays indicating nationwide locations of nuclear detonations and fallout zones.[34] SITCEN staff received, processed, displayed, and disseminated information to senior and subordinate emergency personnel and civil authorities involved with policy or decision-making at the CEGHQ.[35] Each of these departments and agencies in turn performed resource analyses for their areas of responsibility. Early in an exercise, great importance was placed on interdepartmental staff conferences and verbal briefings. Later, memoranda, circulars, and minutes were substituted. A closed-circuit television system monitoring the SITCEN kept the cabinet room and more distant locales within the facility informed of the unfolding situation. Departments and agencies were designated to produce written reports between 18:00 and 20:00 daily, while SITCEN would produce a summary of the nationwide situation at 20:00 each day. The CEGHQ would also

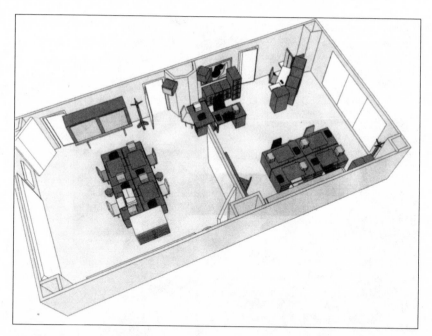

60. Three-dimensional plan view of Canada's CEGHQ SITCEN. On the left are maps to display NUDET and fallout contours. On the far right are the status boards and above them in the upper right corner is the closed-circuit TV control desk. Courtesy of the Diefenbunker—Canada's Cold War Museum.

summarize the situation in regional and zonal HQs (ZEGHQs)[36] every six hours from the start of operations during the first twenty-four hours, then daily at 23:00.[37]

As the sites where blast and fallout data was centrally collected, SITCENs prefigure all civil defense decisions. Design of the SITCENs of Canadian and British bunkers was influenced by World War II RAF flight operations control centers, such as the one on display at the Imperial War Museum (Duxford, Cambridgeshire). The two-tier design with a platform for visual overview (or three-storey overview, as originally built at Kelvedon Hatch) is less practical in an underground installation where cubic footage is at a premium, though it survives in Anstruther's Nuclear Command Control Center. Because of their evolution from different kinds of facilities, the British rooms for NUDET plotting show a greater degree of variation in layout, dimensions, and construction than the purpose-built Canadian facilities. Through trial and error, standardization developed—for SITCENs and facilities for operational personnel—in facilities of variable size. U.S. facilities such as the Du Page County, Illinois, continuity of government center, built in 1958, include most of the same interior elements as Canadian sites,

61. SITCEN status boards during a 1986 exercise at the CEGHQ SITCEN. On the right are operations officers; rear left shows closed-circuit TV controls; and left foreground is the safety officer. Courtesy of the Diefenbunker—Canada's Cold War Museum.

even though Du Page set its emergency operations facility underneath the Highway Department building, with some fallout protection but no blast resistance. Facilities either centralized SITCENs and operational controls into a single room or, if more complex staff interactions were necessary, partitioned functions into separate offices. Smaller facilities, such as Du Page County's, tended to cluster everyone together; larger facilities such as Canada's CEGHQ had office suites for each government department. Breakdown of space into many small rooms was thought to ease claustrophobia.

A journalistic account of what happened in a Canadian SITCEN during the process of NUDET plotting narrates a scenario involving the receipt of strike information:

"It's Chapleau, sir," says the corporal. Major Wenzel wheels abruptly and leaps up onto a small aluminum stepladder to mark the spot of the Nudet on a large map of Ontario. "Where the hell is Chapleau?" he mutters. Tension mounts. "I can't find Chapleau." Finally he locates it and draws intersecting lines on the map [north of

62. Scientific officers' desks with fallout plotting map in the background during 1986 exercise at the CEGHQ's SITCEN. Courtesy of the Diefenbunker— Canada's Cold War Museum.

Sault Ste. Marie], explaining that the area around the Nudet would be destroyed. If it was a ground burst, destruction would fan out for seven kilometers, with multiple fires in the area. Half the population would be dead and the rest injured. The Major moves to another map and plots wind direction and fallout. Timmins, he notes, is about 150 kilometers from the blast. What should people in Timmins do? "If they have enough sense they'll be down in their basements with water and cans of food." How long should they stay down? "As long as they can." Having informed North Bay of his calculations well within the allotted time, he sends a teletype message to the CBC's main control room.[38]

The CBC would instruct the public. Damage reports would come in next. To ameliorate the effects of blast and fallout, survival, health, and welfare operations would take priority, though their interdependence with resource and economic stabilization, and the capacity for transport, made these elements integral for all practical purposes.[39]

Military personnel assigned to these facilities would have become inured to the cheerfully muted pastel decor and windowless rooms that were their daily work-

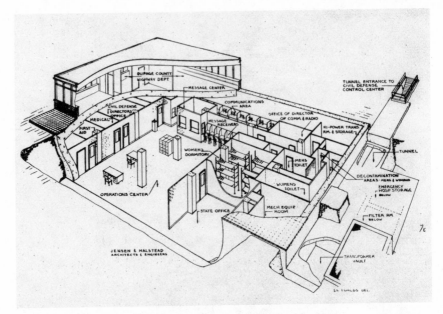

63. Schematic cutaway drawing for the Du Page County control center near Wheaton, Illinois. Courtesy of NARA.

places. Yet being accustomed to the facilities did not insulate everyone from the affective content of exercises. One informant for this study, Corporal Bob Biggs, was stationed in Ottawa when he participated in a nuclear attack simulation exercise in the early 1970s. The first part took place in Ottawa, and the second part inside the CEGHQ. Biggs's responsibility was to plot the detonations onto maps in the SITCEN. He recalls that after a week or so in the bunker, the officers gathered together in the SITCEN. The commander put on a video clip of the CBC National News (though to Biggs and his fellows it appeared to be a live feed), hosted by its regular anchorman Lloyd Robertson, who stated that Ottawa had been hit by another explosion. This was in addition to the rapid and numerous detonations already plotted in the SITCEN. Corporal Biggs recalls that there was an audible intake of breath and the commander himself was "white as a piece of paper": it had been his street that was hit and "he was totally in shock." The exercise directors—all military—then said the "exercise is over and everyone can go home," but the confusion that arose at this juncture over whether this was an exercise or real existed because of the CBC clip. Doubt was confounded by the secrecy under which the exercise was conducted and the lack of an exercise code printed on incoming teletype messages, which is highly unorthodox and dangerous for an operational emergency facility.[40] The commander's shock reflects his inability to

64. Close-up of fallout contours ensuing from a strike on Chicago during OPAL 55, Low Point HQ at Battle Creek, Michigan. Courtesy of NARA.

continue suspending belief as he became immersed in the exercise pretense. He suddenly shifted from dutiful contemplation of strangers' demise to a scenario implicating his own family and property. He ceased being an actor and reverted to his own persona: father, husband, and neighbor.

This is a chilling story, and the details about lacking exercise codes and the realistic CBC clip might sound like bad practical jokes if their affective context were not so consequential. It attests to the idea that even with training, even with the experience the commander no doubt had to fulfill his duties, a verisimilitudinous detail within an exercise could cause reality to intrude upon realism. The commander, it is important to recall, was thunderstruck not by the mere "fact" of the NUDET but by the report of his neighborhood being destroyed. No personnel assigned to the bunkers could take their families in with them. Men and women with these assignments were urged to make other arrangements for their loved ones when they received their assignment. Not being in touch with families while undergoing the isolation of an exercise would be a source of worry, but concerns could be set aside by the alternate "as if" narrative of the exercise as long as the suspension of belief prevailed. This illuminates the human face of what is otherwise conveyed as dry reportage in countless exercise analyses. For the commander—who turned on the video—the "destruction" of his street produced physical and psychological shock. For the other staff, the looming referentiality of exercise play—politics, beyond mere duty—was foregrounded in their commander's reaction, though they themselves retained consciousness of their role as simulators and the CBC clip's function as a mere realistic device. Yet it makes one wonder whether, in a real attack and even with the best-trained personnel, the CEGHQ's psychiatric holding cell might become the most important room in the building.

Coast-to-Coast Continuity

Canadian records provide the best documentation of nationwide continuity of government rehearsals. Canada's REGHQ system was announced by Prime Minister Diefenbaker in January 1961 but until the new sites could be completed, interim sites such as basements were used. TOCSIN 60 was conducted from these facilities with the participation of three hundred municipalities.[41] An account from Charlottetown describes the improvised quarters:

> At the Armory, rooms had already been set aside for the various department officials. The doors were labelled "transportation," "health and welfare," "agriculture" and so on. One large door carried a sign which read "premier." Off to the side the teletypes were clacking out reports from across the nation and soldiers in uniform were carrying messages to the three major headquarters. In one large room, loaded with tables, the province's civil defense team assembled. Police, welfare workers, transport people, [and] fire officials took their places. At a lead table the operational chiefs took their places.[42]

In such facilities, exercise participants imagined the arrival of bombs and fallout, made decisions based on damage estimates, advised players standing in for government leaders, and generally translated their peacetime expertise into simulated wartime utility. They imagined "what ifs" yet were not bound by them. In TOCSIN 62, for example, which coordinated NORAD's headquarters in North Bay with makeshift REGHQs, Penhold's staff did not get out of Edmonton before their city was "destroyed." A ninety-minute drive then awaited these "corpses."[43]

Following completion of the REGHQs, efficiency at all levels was worked on for two years, culminating in "TOCSIN 66," the fourth exercise designed to improve Canada's capability of recovering from a nuclear attack at *all* government levels and the first nationwide exercise since 1961. (The military played "FALLEX 66" concurrently.) TOCSIN 66 was two weeks in duration, though the emergency governments at central, regional, zonal (ZEGHQ), and municipal (MEGHQ)[44] sites played for just one day. During the pre-attack phase, the deteriorating international situation was monitored from peacetime locations during normal working hours. A limited Responding Cell of Ottawa-based players issued bulletins on these incidents and approved alert measures and actions. Staff reviewed emergency plans, updated warning lists and emergency staff cadres, and prepared for actions as specified in departmental war books. The day before attack, a telephone fan out exercise was conducted involving all departments in order to practice alerting players.[45] Exercise orders for staffing emergency facilities were issued, but not acted upon. For one day during the attack phase, the exercise central site (at Arnprior) and other CRUs were fully occupied; allocations of exercise instructions suggest that at least 550 civilians participated in Ottawa and the CRUs and as many again in REGHQs. They received briefings on the situation up to H+48, orientations to a model of the Carp site, and studied typical problems arising from attack through D+30. Ministerial staff received special briefings in syndicate rooms, led by their departments' emergency planning officers. Activity in CRUs was similar. Players were asked:

First Do I fully appreciate and understand my role or part?
Secondly Am I qualified or ready through briefing or training to fulfil my function?
Thirdly Is the organization of which I am a part properly designed to meet the task?
Finally Have I, regardless of appointment, the departmental planning documents policies, directives, references, etc., available?[46]

These four reminders resemble Konstantin Stanislavsky's acting principles of representation (*predstavlenie*) and experience (*perezhivanie*, sometimes translated as "living through") which enable creativity. Because actors make demands of themselves that are not "real" they must create a "logical, motivating and emotionalizing context" that will "function *as if* it was a real demand." Knowing one's role, being thoroughly ready to execute it, and having colleagues who are equally prepared to engage in play, enables the mind to produce the "impulse to action" that makes the body follow through. To produce this "unreal" demand requires training to amplify and vitalize the paradox of rendering an extreme situation despite the mundane reality.[47]

Determining staff for exercises was always tricky. No sitting member of parliament—and certainly not the prime minister—was likely to take time for practical exercises, especially once the threat level abated after the Berlin and Cuba crises of the early 1960s or during the fragile tenure of a minority government. The military stuck by its cover story that the Carp facility was a signals site, and so attention could not be drawn to it through high-profile visitors. As plans were made for TOCSIN 66, a major joint military and civilian exercise, not even the

Parliamentary Committee on Defence was approved for a site visit. A privy councillor suggested that parliamentary assistants could substitute for their bosses at Arnprior CRU during TOCSIN 66 and brief their ministers afterward. However, in a real emergency these assistants would not be called into action, so training them was of dubious value, and briefings would not truly substitute for experienced ministers. Seven months before the exercise, plans for ministerial participation in TOCSIN 66 went ahead at Arnprior, with the understanding that parliamentary assistants might go in their stead. A ministerial expedition to the CEGHQ following the exercise was proposed but not conducted.[48]

The national situation shortly after attack in TOCSIN 66 involved estimates of 1,100,000 Canadians dead, over 800,000 injured and as many trapped in wreckage, and 2,800,000 people in the path of fallout. At least 160,000 Americans had migrated into bordering provinces. Civilians experienced critical shortages of drugs, clothing, footwear, and blankets. Communication capacity was reduced by 50 percent, destruction of power stations in Ontario resulted in a complete blackout in its western half, some areas were short of food, and industrial capacity in most sectors, including food processing capacity, was reduced by half. Players were briefed on regional problems, emphasizing the need for inter-regional consultation to solve problems. Records include an evocative coast-to-coast summary of the exercise scenarios for all levels of play:

> Strikes on Victoria and Vancouver have created a situation beyond the immediate capability of the military and civilian rescue forces available and additional support is required. The Regional Commissioner in British Columbia has asked for a major force of soldiers and civilians. The Regional Commissioner of Alberta, when approached on the intention to move this force by air, stated that all military forces in the province were needed to maintain law and order and he wished to have them available should a further attack take place.

Inter-provincial allocations such as this required intervention at the federal level. Meanwhile, in Saskatchewan, municipalities refused to lend their firefighters and police to other communities, arguing that they were needed at home to deal with refugees; this was dealt with at the regional level. Manitoba and Ontario generated another conflict requiring federal intervention:

> The Federal Emergency Health Services plan to move their pre-positioned medical supplies from Manitoba to Ontario where they are urgently needed for casualties from fallout and evacuees from Western Ontario. Manitoba regional authorities object to this proposal as they feel that the movement of these supplies will create critical shortages in that province.

Ontario and Quebec were badly hit, and could offer no support to the Atlantic provinces. Consultation between several provinces and the federal government was needed to determine priorities.

> The relative geographical location of the four Atlantic Provinces place them in a special situation where outside assistance is difficult. . . . Prince Edward Island stated that the province can accept up to 20,000 refugees from other provinces, or, alternately, they can provide food and clothing for 20,000 for six months if this is needed. . . . In Quebec and in Nova Scotia, major harbours have been evacuated and there is an urgent requirement for loading and discharging facilities at smaller river or seaboard ports or emergency anchorages. This problem would involve the General Transport Controller, War Supply Agency, Public Works and Manpower to decide what can be built or supplied to certain ports so that they can be expanded on short notice.[49]

The exercise presumed that at D+30 the federal government operated from a combination of unharmed emergency headquarters and improvised facilities. Provincial governments could operate in situ in Saskatchewan, Quebec, New Brunswick, Prince Edward Island, and Newfoundland, but five other provincial capitals were struck and their governments operated from emergency facilities. Devastating economic effects were felt by New Westminster (Vancouver), Edmonton, Winnipeg, Sault Ste. Marie (St. Lawrence Seaway locks), North Bay (Trans-Canada pipeline and NORAD), Toronto, the Windsor-London area, Montreal and Chambly County, Chatham in New Brunswick, and the Halifax-Dartmouth area. Over 16 percent of the population was dead, still too ill to work, or missing. Rationing was imposed in some municipalities, but not nationally.

In the regions, the scope of play varied from study groups to embodied exercises, but full staffing was encouraged in order to exercise the national communications system. Nanaimo in British Columbia conducted an exercise fan out, staffed the regional HQ, carried out a study group based on the common exercise setting, and exchanged radiological information with U.S. Region 8 (headquartered in Everett, Washington). Penhold conducted an exercise fan out and fully staffed the regional HQ for operational consideration of the situation from H+48 to H+56. Zonal emergency headquarters and relocation units for the War Supplies Agency, federal and provincial departments of Agriculture, and provincial Department of Health and Welfare were staffed, and municipal HQs in Calgary and Edmonton had skeleton crews. Saskatchewan conducted a study group on reception problems. The regional HQ at Shilo was staffed, along with three zonal HQs in Manitoba; they tested the emergency communications system via line loading with exercise message traffic. Study groups in Ontario and Quebec examined how regions and the Department of National Defence (DND) would address the immediate rescue problem in these provinces. The Atlantic provinces conducted briefings and staffed facilities where available, focusing on self-help and mutual assistance within the region.

Exercise officials were in place to give realistic responses when full staffing was not possible. They simulated invoking the National Survival Attack Warning System (without raising the alarm in public) and rehearsing the stages of alert, government action arising from alerts and war plans, emergency communications, national survival problems, and the exchange of fallout information with the United States. During the post-attack phase, the exercise directors' Responding Cell continued to provide input as if from the DND, consulting with departmental colleagues as needed. They utilized the same attack pattern as TOCSIN 63, plus data on Victoria, and based resources on the document "Resources in Canada 48 Hours after a Hypothetical Nuclear Attack—November 1963."[50]

"Exercise Rainex 2," conducted in 1970, occurred in three phases. The first involved checking of radiological detection equipment and implementation of a recruiting and crash training program for use by municipalities. During the next phase, which began six weeks later, advance parties prepped regional and zonal HQs for use, prepared evacuation plans for areas at high risk from fallout, and installed and tested emergency communications. Six weeks after that, regional and zonal HQs were fully staffed, and municipal HQs were staffed on a skeleton basis.[51]

Evidence from "Exercise Minor Key" in September 1991 indicates that the central and regional HQs and provincial warning centers (for provinces without bunkers) engaged in setting message traffic for a challenging array of post-attack problems. The devastation caused floods, fires, and power and transport disruptions, compounded by bubonic plague in British Columbia, a stricken nuclear power station in Ontario, biological attacks on the Maritimes, and the obliteration of broadcasting capability in Newfoundland.[52]

By this time, Canada's continuity of government program had existed in the same basic form for three decades. New facilities were not being added, and the existing sites were not updated. Communications equipment used by the military at the CEGHQ was maintained and modernized (notably the state-of-the-art computer in 1976, which took several more years to become operational),[53] but the program had no powerful advocates. Provincial Warning Centres collaborated with the CEGHQ on exercises two days a month every month until 1994, but these were military communication exercises rather than embodied civil defense rehearsals.[54] In 1988, REGHQ Nanaimo was occupied four hours a day on weekdays, but bringing any of the regional sites to a functional level would take up to a week.[55] It would take "upwards of a *month* of major effort and the commitment of significant personnel and materiel resources being necessary to raise this posture to a 'ready' level."[56] EPC advised parliament that "the readiness of the present network of emergency government facilities to fulfill the functions for which they were intended is questionable, especially at the lower headquarters level. The original system was never completed; communications and other equipment are for the most part antiquated; plans and procedures need confirming, updating and exercising on a system wide, regular basis." This accounted for working accommodation for about 8,500 people in twenty-three facilities, 40 percent of the originally planned number.[57] In the early 1990s, Canada decommissioned the emergency HQs, and several were sold or destroyed.

A similar fate befell British facilities as the Cold War ended. Emergency government relocation sites continue to come onto the market and present ideal secure accommodation for computing operations, air-filtered premises for pneumo-restorative centers, damp caves for mushroom or marijuana growers, and unstormable hideouts for motorcycles gangs. Only in the United States have post–9/11 security concerns produced the opportunity to breathe life back into these sites, hosting a new generation of players, scenarios, and rehearsals predicated on new theories, drawing on an old archive with evolving repertoire.

Chapter 12 **COMPUTER PLAY**

Where is your data? Give me something I can put in the computer. Don't give me your poetry.

—Robert McNamara

Computers had vital roles to play in both military and civil defense, coordinating vast amounts of data which, by implication, organized legions of workers into an intricately orchestrated whole. In the 1950s, the SAGE computer pooled data from radar posts, aircraft flight paths, and the Ground Observer Corps, processed it in real time to enable simultaneous calculation of multiple bomber or missile intercepts, and set into motion the personnel of NORAD and the Ballistic Missile Early Warning System (BMEWS).[1] In civil defense gaming, computers came within the purview of staff exercises from the late 1950s. As with all computer applications, electronic replacements for human calculating functions enabled greater speed as well as improved coordination of interrelated tasks. The two most notable uses of this are in calculating the economic aftermath of nuclear attack and gaming how to evacuate areas at risk.

While computer gaming allowed for greater calculating capacity, perhaps more than any other exploration of civil defense it relied upon the "manufactured" expertise that had become the basis of planning. Experts drew upon a body of knowledge, but as the sociologist Lee Clarke states, the empirical basis of civil defense was thin compared to the huge assumptions and extrapolations, "indeed, fanciful stories," that were the basis of rehearsals for survival, ame- liorating effects, and recovery. Notwithstanding the pigs dressed as soldiers that were exposed to radiation; transplanted Ponderosa pines that swayed in the blast and counterblast; trains, planes, and buildings buffeted by the tremendous forces of atom-busting; or iconic families of mannequins that survived nuclear may- hem at the Nevada Test Site, it simply could not be known whether people, for- ests, cities, or households would survive nuclear attack.[2] A metonymic chain of assumptions created the impression that problems could be identified and an- swers honed. "But not just any problem," Clarke argues, "rather a problem that yielded to reasonable effort."[3] This gave rise to the shibboleths of civil defense planning, empirical (in a sense) but extrapolated to serve many analogical pur- poses. Beyond test site observations, civil defense was predicated on data that had nothing to do with nuclear weaponry: responses to natural and technological disasters, psychological experimentation, sociological observation, and incidents from World War II. Beyond this, there was surmise and homology, yet without such abstractions there could be no civil defense. In this sense, methexis in a con- tingent future was possible only through constructions about the past but this, like all shibboleths, was subject to mispronouncing, misunderstanding, and mis- knowing: who, in all honesty, could say they spoke the language of the future? Rehearsals, whether embodied or computer-aided, were predicated upon a chain of analogies derived from weapons testing, and on homologies derived from social observation, correlated to assumptions dressed up as metonyms, whether empiri- cally "scientific" or qualitatively psychological.

It was the best they had. Or the best they decided to have, as Lynn Eden's recent revelations patently reveal how firestorms were systemically discounted as nuclear consequences.[4] Or the best that computers could output, given the models programmed into them. Gaming insisted upon feasibility; if the odds were too long, the data was adjusted. Computed "facts" are as subject to disproof as the "realism" of any embodied rehearsal: indeed, there is an uncanny resem- blance between these conditions. Contrary to McNamara's desire, there was not such a clear difference between "data" and "poetry."

Economic Recovery

During World War II, a new profession arose for the analytic study of military problems via mathematics. Originally called operations research, in the 1950s it also came to be known as systems analysis.[5] This is defined as economic analysis in which "the planner [is] seeking the best allocation of limited resources among a variety of competing military [or other] demands. The starting point of any systems analysis is the concept of a particular system and a variety of alternative systems, and the environment in which they will operate" in order to maximize outcomes such as preservation of life, government, or economic resources.[6] It allowed gaming of many variables which, in theory, led to flexibility with unforeseen contingencies.[7] This practice grew in popularity as corporate in-service training after 1956, and received a big boost when Robert McNamara, formerly the president of Ford Motor Company, took over the DOD in 1961.[8] The best evidence of its use is based on American exercises from two periods, the late 1950s and after the mid-1970s.

Exercises utilizing data or descriptive modeling resulting from systems analysis were sometimes called simulation-games, recognizing the hybridity of simulations and war games. Simulations could be so mechanized as to dispense with human players,[9] however the variant discussed here might be more accurately termed "interactive simulation" exercises. Still reliant upon the shibboleths for initial conditions that are input into the model, with systems analysis exogenous variables result in a technologically fancier form of analogy. Even so, the complex interactions of models' endogenous variables allowed for significantly more sophisticated exercise play. Permanently lacking controllable economic experiments, civil defense planners relied upon systems analysis to explore post-attack economic structures.

There are many examples of computer forecasts of the number of living, injured, and dead following hypothetical nuclear attacks. Their variety is enormous, depending upon the number and precise location of GZs, size of bombs, height of detonations, proximity to centers of population, and destruction of firefighting capacity, hospitals, and stockpiles of essential commodities.[10] When longer-term forecasting was attempted, additional variables were brought to bear on the situation, such as the ability of neighboring areas to lend support, the cascading effect of nationwide shortages, impediments to transportation, restoration of industrial production capacity, provision of labor, and effects on morale. What was input into computer models directly belies concepts and beliefs about recovery as much as anything that could be postulated as fact. The electronically computed aspects of scenarios for survival and recovery are not what Diana Taylor would call "necessarily, or even primarily, mimetic," but they set the parameters for what ensued as corporeal methexic activity in some exercise situations.[11] In a few instances, deeply ingrained ideas were resisted as a result of this data—by suggesting, for example, that a welfare system might have to supercede government guidance of the free market—as ways to demonstrate the severity of catastrophe, but such heresy was rare inside the feedback loop of U.S. government-commissioned reports.[12]

The need to recognize the interdependence of people alongside the economic system was addressed through a combination of tactics. Though gaming out problems was instrumental in training, the ability to combine it with the abstraction of simulations, particularly computer-modeling, led to greater realism. OPAL 59 provides an elaborate example of how this was attempted. Planners realized, for example, that it was insufficient to determine the number of hospital beds that survived (or could be improvised) in an area post-attack if medical personnel did not have the necessary supplies to perform their work. So, a list of essential items was drawn up and data gathered on their stocking and distribution in peacetime; this was correlated to the bombing pattern and assumed destruction, and a final data set predicted the level of demand and supply that would pertain under the hypothetical circumstances. This enhanced the likelihood that players at the regional as well as local level could conduct the exercise simulating the realistic problems they wanted to anticipate and try to solve. This "man-machine form of gaming-simulation" became the norm for operational exercises that attempted to teach, predict, develop new concepts, and coordinate research.[13]

Even with practice, interactive simulations could not be made perfect, and the accuracy of forecasting was highly dubious. As a proponent of the practice stated in 1972, "at present, the major use of simulation models is to educate the intuition of economists. The main benefits of simulation lie in exploring the properties of systems for which analytic solutions are difficult or impossible and in revealing incongruities in the behavior of a simultaneous system when individual equations are plausible. There is much to be learned from tracing through the reasons for and remedying these incongruities."[14] Despite the limitations, a historian of military simulations stressed that where "death is merely rows of numbers in the millions or tens of millions," the interactive simulation is incomparable training, for "what appears to be the *unreality* of gaming—the vise of time, the lack of solid knowledge, the dominating influence of Control [the directing staff]—is the *reality* of crisis."[15] This is a critical observation, rationalizing the value of rehearsal. War games—and by extension the civil defense games that used their techniques—"can help the professional commander and staff officer experience decision making under conditions that are difficult or impossible to reproduce in peacetime" and at their core "provide a unique forum for communicating ideas in vivid and memorable ways, and for discussing the validity and applicability of those ideas in a more empirical and less abstract way than the exchange of scholarly papers."[16]

OPAL 58 included attempts to examine production, labor, and output potentials in each region, utilizing calculations of losses in major industrial sectors.

Based on the attack pattern, the larger Federal Reserve banks and commercial banks were considered inoperable in many regions. The provision of money for consumers, employers' ability to meet payrolls, the clearance of checks, and satisfaction of credit demands came into play as complicating mechanisms for the restoration of the economy.[17] Yet even where such resources were not directly damaged, pressures would grow. As one participant commented, the unity of the entire national system became apparent.

> Our only solution to keeping the banks and financial institutions functioning would be to establish a moratorium until such time as currency payments could be resumed. It is reasonably safe to assume that in a condition of crisis such as imposed in the attack, the banks and financial institutions in the so-called undamaged communities would be immediately subject to the demands of depositors to withdraw all or substantial portions of their accounts. From a standpoint of banking and financial matters, there would actually be no such thing as an "undamaged community." The national economy would be severely damaged and this, in turn, would call for immediate and drastic financial controls.[18]

The entire economic system would also be subject to inflationary pressures. The guidance furnished for the exercise helped players recognize problems, especially the pressing need for even more guidance before theoretical problems and solutions could be posed. Homology was the recourse, with the recommendation that historical data from World War II and the Korean War be brought to bear on the post-nuclear attack situation for OPAL 59.[19]

Players who sought definitive solutions were destined to be frustrated, for as Sidney Winter observed "what is fundamentally at issue in planning for a nuclear emergency is not the desirability of coping with the problems, or the desirability of trying to cope, but the feasibility of coping effectively," and historical precedents can never ultimately satisfy.[20] Computations of resource supply and requirements in OPAL 59 predicted major shortfalls up to D+90, but this could not be addressed independent of labor supply. Computers allowed players to test hypotheses during play; for example, solutions to labor shortages were sought by broadening the definition of the labor force. The Midwest region found "there was no way we could supply the requested labor, even if utilizing very young groups."[21] In the southeastern United States, by extending the work week and expanding the labor force to include all able-bodied persons aged ten to seventy, labor shortfalls were met by D+30.[22] But some labor problems could not be solved by inputting new numbers into the computer. One Midwestern agency's solution, when considered within the scope of the whole systems analysis, was found to create insoluble problems for other areas: the Railroad Retirement Board hypothetically called up experienced former workers to help get rail transportation operating at optimum levels, telling pensioners to report to local employment offices, but employment offices would either be swamped with people from every other walk of life or bereft of laborers because they were unwilling to leave the relative safety of their own basements.[23] Getting people back to work meant prioritizing industrial expansion in areas with acceptable levels of fallout, reconstructing workplaces, addressing the housing shortage, identifying skilled laborers, and finding ways to place people in the right jobs. Problems were interlinked, and both cultural and historical knowledge helped players recognize the limits of the computer models. As Annabelle Heath of the Housing and Home Finance Agency remarked when told there would be no shortage of materials for housing in the southwest, "in World War II, there was a housing and building materials shortage even though this continent was not attacked so I still come back to the belief there would be unprecedented housing and construction materials shortages in such an emergency." On top of the material problems, she insisted, were related problems of race and, in the meantime, billeting.[24] Presumably, she meant that disproportionate damage to inner cities would result in higher rates of death among African Americans, particularly in the north, hitting the heavy manufacturing industries in which they were employed. Even if this was not the case, relocating available labor to optimize output assumed the absence of color bars and the viability of completely integrated housing.

The OPAL 59 group working on Treasury problems in the Midwest focused on keeping banks, savings and loans, credit unions, and postal savings offices open in order to keep currency circulating and a money economy operating. This assumes that as long as money is available people will not worry, but if it becomes scarce they will make it scarcer. The Federal Reserve undertook to honor checks written on non-operating banks in order to keep money in circulation, but of course this could be calamitous if not done properly. Evacuees would generally have only pocket cash and no proof of assets. Before the advent of automatic teller machines, even multi-branch banks could not necessarily discover a person's bank balance without presentation of a deposit book or their latest statement. People with appropriate documents would produce heavy demands for cash withdrawals, cashing of government savings bonds, and payment of life and property insurance claims, pushing the system to the point of collapse.[25] What would other people, without documents, do?

H. E. Hemmings of the Federal Reserve Bank of San Francisco proposed ways to get to unharmed vaults, extract currency, and distribute it with the help of post office vehicles but developed doubts about whether this would be effective to the economic situation per se. He conjectured a scenario that could make the Federal Reserve irrelevant:

> I am not so sure money is going to be the answer to all these problems. Survival is the most important thing. Money is not a survival item particularly if there is nothing to buy. If I had $20 in my pocket and my friend had nothing, we could stand in line and both get a free meal. Under the assumption that measures will be taken to keep our monetary and credit system solvent Federal Reserve plans contemplate that credit will be given for checks even though drawn on inoperative banks. Under this system, currency per se may not be of too much importance. But we of course can't make a dry run on anything like this.[26]

Maintaining confidence in the currency, or its surrogates, was crucial and OPAL 59 did game dry runs for a variety of related financial problems. What if holders of vital consumer goods refused to accept Federal Reserve notes or state-issued script as currency: would workers in Michigan starve because Texas ranchers or Kansas farmers refused to ship their products? Could citizens use savings bonds as a medium of exchange? If HEW provides the general public with direct relief, should insurance, retirement, and veteran benefits be withheld from those who were ordinarily entitled? Should private insurers make payments to policyholders? How could evidence of assets be ascertained when two-thirds of banks were destroyed or inaccessible? With half the population experiencing loss of assets, should a moratorium be granted on pre-attack debts? What would happen if states did not honor each other's ration schemes: would hoarding, inflation, black markets, and theft lead to civil chaos? Would the government try to collect taxes, and if not how much revenue would it lose?[27]

Let the economy go unregulated for as long as ten days after an attack and a cascade of problems for prices, credit, transfers, and taxation would be set in motion.[28] Assuming that all banks are insolvent, inflation is rampant, state rationing and price controls are ineffective, hoarding has caused widespread hunger, remaining currency in banks is in the hands of unscrupulous manipulators, credit is non-existent, and large areas of the United States approach anarchy, players drew a relationship between economic stabilization and law and order resulting in a list of new fiscal concerns. The stakes went to the core of the American republic. Confidence in the credit system needed to be restored, but the propaganda effort was daunting. To begin this process, war losses must be indemnified, but on what basis and by whom? How could stocks, bonds, mortgages, bank promissory notes, and other paper tokens of value reduce the need for currency? Because the only way to support indemnification and welfare relief was through taxation, what should be taxed and when? Inflation is best controlled by reducing the need for money, but players admitted "this means we must consider various forms of modified socialism." Meeting payrolls with a high percentage of rationing currency rather than cash would help control income levels, but could this be implemented beyond the civil service? To make rationing viable—with coupons replacing money—the government must seize and control all retail outlets for essential commodities, but this meant suspending the profit motive.[29] Documents from these exercises do not pose the next logical question, but surely it was on players' minds: if the basis of wealth was overturned, it followed that the symbolic value of capital and the free market economy were voluntarily suspended, in which case what, exactly, would constitute winning a war against a Socialist adversary?

Interactive simulation exercises are predicated on computer-generated models and analysis but place the emphasis on human decision-making about this data. The learning derived from them "comes both from the experience of making decisions (playing) and from the process of understanding why those decisions are made (game analysis)."[30] Role play propelled players into a mimetic scenario beyond their everyday jobs, sometimes into extraordinary circumstances, lending the exercises an aura of "eventhood." This encouraged suspension of disbelief in order to permit the necessary improvisatory exploration leading toward discovery of further useful, but sometimes uncomfortable, scenarios.

Until the late 1950s there was insufficient information to derive a formal model for simulation, and so exercises tended to be more loosely structured. "Formal models, simulations, and completely computerized games are normally used when someone is convinced that the phenomena under study can be accurately described. . . . Such games stress explorations into the unknown as a means of clarifying and correcting misperceptions about the aspects of the actual world replicated by the game." This is subject to fallacies which may or may not come to the fore during play,[31] yet abstraction for the sake of scientifically replicable play did not necessarily compromise the applicability of rehearsal. Indeed, the interactive simulation could be an astute diagnostic tool for discovering policy alternatives and outcomes, and generating and testing new hypotheses about crisis management.[32] According to the assistant secretary of defense for management of military and civilian manpower, playing "Nifty Nugget" led directly to the creation of FEMA in 1978. In this extensive three-week exercise involving the Pentagon and thirty-one civilian departments and agencies simulating the transport of 400,000 troops and 350,000 tons of supplies to a nuclear-devastated Europe, "refugees would all be coming back from Europe. HEW . . . was supposed to sort

them out, but HEW didn't even know it had the responsibility to handle refugees."
The president needed to double the number of military reservists but players discovered that there was no legal system for calling them up without declaring a
national emergency.[33] An integrated agency with total responsibility for coordinating all-occasion disaster relief was the outcome.

Strategic Crisis Relocation Planning (CRP)

In the early years following Soviet development of atomic weapons, the capacity
to effect a sudden and decisive attack abroad gave rise to civil defense planning
that revolved around reducing losses of population and domestic manufacturing potential. This is evident in the earliest large-scale rehearsals such as the 1949
exercise Britannia involving evacuation of East London from Fulham to Barking
and the 1951 Chicago Alert involving the impact of multiple bombs on Chicago's
industrial and transportation centers. As the Soviet ability to produce an arsenal
of A-bombs was demonstrated, scenarios involving nearly simultaneous attack on
multiple cities were gamed. The challenge of removing as many people as possible
from harm's way was, in some respects, just a matter of transportation and organizational logistics: utilize the most efficient means to move the most people to
the right places in the least amount of time. Moving industries was another matter. This had to be done as a peacetime measure, reducing the attractiveness of
industrial targets by dispersing factories, refineries, utilities, and transport lanes
as much as possible from their traditional heavy concentration in centers such as
metropolitan Birmingham, Toronto, and New York. Though recommended for
nuclear war planning as early as 1949, to be implemented over the course of the
next two decades, dispersion was never substantially successful: some corporations put new facilities in far-flung suburbs or urban locales not traditional for
their industries, but the overall impact on industrial vulnerability was negligible.[34]
The population could be saved, to some extent, but neither their livelihoods nor
means of economic recovery were subject to preservation measures per se.

With the advent of thermonuclear weapons, the increased damage from individual hits cumulatively worsened the overall industrial outlook. It was no longer
a question of whether a bomb hit Dearborn, Detroit, or Windsor, for the North
American automotive industry would be devastated in any case. Likewise, a direct
hit on Birkenhead would be as effective as one on Liverpool insofar as shipping
traffic in the Mersey was concerned. The anticipated short warning times suggested that people could not evacuate far enough out of conurbations, and the
new geographic realities of nuclear warfare shifted emphasis from avoidance of
damage to determining what would remain functional and who would be alive

to work it, then calculating the new industrial capacity on this basis. Evaluative studies such as the 1955 "Baltimore and the H-Bomb," which is unabashedly pessimistic about this metropolitan area's ability to cope with minimally 47 percent losses in population and 53 percent loss of industrial production capacity, paint a bleak picture but do begin to broach the problems related to interconnected regional economies, multiple stricken conurbations along the Atlantic seaboard, national resupply problems, and the global impact on raw materials, markets, and shipping.[35] Systems analysis exercises took up some of these issues, with emphasis falling on calculating the damage and optimizing the outlook following attack, but without considering what the consequences would be in areas not directly hit yet responsible for initiating recovery. The authors of the Baltimore study posited: "after attack small cities and towns which had previously functioned as satellites of larger centers would then become the substitute centers of economic activity. How well could these surviving but fragmented facilities, with impaired transportation and communication facilities, shoulder the main burden of production for public and private needs after sudden loss of their former production centers?"[36] This is a different way of stating the macroeconomic problem of fulfilling the needs of survivors, of thinking about those whose immediate environment escaped the bomb blast, and whether a clear demarcation could be drawn—in economic terms—between the dispossessed and their hosts.

In the mid-1950s, the three options for evacuation were seen as (1) tactical, involving temporary removal of most people from target areas, warranted for sudden attack or in response to attacks upon other areas; (2) partial strategic evacuation, involving the long-range evacuation of non-essential personnel, especially mothers and children, when hostilities seemed imminent; and (3) strategic evacuation of essential and non-essential personnel during imminent threat of attack.[37] In the early decades of the Cold War, the United States and Canada planned and tested only for the first option, while Britain had detailed plans for the second. Crisis Relocation Planning (CRP), which is the third type, departed from tactical reactive thinking and took a proactive stance. CRP redefines the pre-crisis period with new complexity. Finessing the line between business as usual and all-out crisis, CRP allows for a build-up of international tension while the public is moved away from likely targets, before the precipitating event for a thermonuclear exchange occurs. This mobilization, if undertaken nationally, was seen by some as a deterrent to Soviet aggression, for the damage to the American population would be reduced.[38] Some CRP documents contemplate what would be done to also get the population back to their customary abodes following threat resolution, and a few posit multiple cycles of relocation and restoration.

With the United States' existing roads in 1956, it was estimated that 36 percent of the total population of 161 target cities (32.4 million people) could be evacuated to a fifteen-mile line in ninety minutes if five people rode in each automobile. To be able to evacuate everyone to that point in that time frame would cost $9.9 billion in capital improvements, and to take them to a twenty-five-mile line in two hours would cost twice as much.[39] Over the next two decades, metropolitan areas grew, both in square mileage and population, and along with them the road transportation infrastructure grew as well as the demands upon it. More people had access to automobiles, compounding congestion, which made the situation more difficult rather than less. Despite this, the automobile became the chief instrument of CRP, and at least 80 percent of evacuees were expected to relocate in private automobiles, effectively putting most of the cost of transport onto evacuees themselves.[40] Through effective implementation of CRP, a computer model from 1976 predicted that 89.6 million people could move from blast risk areas to host areas nationwide, sparing about 90 percent of the population.[41] Their travel distances were supposed to be less than 250 miles, the assumed range for a car with a full tank of gas.[42] Over a three-day mobilization period, CRP projected that 40–50 percent of the Californian population residing in risk areas could be relocated by private automobiles and buses, and an additional three to four days would be needed to complete the relocation.[43] Over the same period, it was estimated the capacity for relocating people in the Boston to Washington corridor by highway, air, and rail (including freight) would fall short by 5,211,000.[44] Once the relocation was underway, and as long as it was sustained, essential workers—a broad definition encompassing utilities maintenance and law enforcement as well as grocers and aerospace factory employees—would commute back into target areas on extended shifts. Outlets for essential services—gasoline, food, medical care, and schooling—would be reoriented to serve the relocated population. This meant temporary unemployment for many, but the impact on the economy was considered worthwhile if war casualties could be reduced, and especially if war could be averted through the reduced attractiveness of bombing depopulated cities.

Computerization was central to linking active defense to civil defense planners' ability to comprehend the situation's growing complexity and write CRP scenarios.[45] By 1975, American civil defense planners were using data compatible with accurate military expectations of bombing patterns. This is when the DOD published an atlas showing what they anticipated as attack priorities: military installations; supporting industrial, transport, and logistics facilities; basic industries significantly contributing to the U.S. economy; and population centers over 50,000 that presented counterforce targets with strategic offensive capability, high military value, and high-risk urban/industrial complexes. Maps indicating areas at risk from direct weapon effects and radioactivity show that not a state in the union would be spared.[46]

CRP, an idea rejected in the aftermath of the Cuban Missile Crisis,[47] arose again in the 1970s and 1980s as a distinctively American option to consider a different economic equation along with the fundamental problem of preservation of life through mobilization. It represents a shift in the planning basis for civil defense from the assumption that centers of population may be first strike targets to a pattern acknowledging the targeting of missile sites and many military installations in addition to population centers.[48] Based on new assumptions that an attack would only be likely following a period of explicit diplomatic tension—and that the Soviets had workable plans to relocate their population to shelters[49]—CRP posited a phased evacuation of non-essential personnel over a three-day or longer period into rural and low-density urban parts of the country surrounding risk areas. Those who had holiday homes, friends, or families in host areas were encouraged to take advantage of these opportunities. Host communities would billet other evacuees in their homes and create temporary shelters in buildings identified through the community shelter plan, including churches, schools, and businesses, improving their fallout protection rating where possible. Hosts and evacuees would also work together to construct expedient shelters, digging trenches if other protection was not available. Recommended fallout precautions relied upon plans for community shelters written in the early 1960s and personal shelter designs from the 1950s, augmented by a variety of improvised group shelters to accommodate swollen populations in all kinds of buildings. An early version of this kind of thinking was applied to Detroit in 1968, identifying 3,671,000 vulnerable people. "Under this system, people and many social and economic activities are moved in advance . . . to outlying areas. The objective is to reduce population vulnerability while at the same time maintaining GNP at the highest possible level." This would require billeting at a ratio of six evacuees to each permanent resident (6:1) in surrounding counties.[50] The average ratio in the northeast would be nearly 4:1, though parts of New Jersey could be as high as 44:1 and Connecticut 31:1.[51] Whereas in the 1950s emergency welfare in evacuation planning was largely a post-attack and early-recovery activity, in CRP emergency welfare began with the arrival of the first evacuees in host communities and continued either until the relocation was cancelled or war conditions made it impossible to continue services. In effect, CRP made welfare services and sheltering inseparable and moves them up in the event structure.[52] In 1973, the Defense Civil Preparedness Agency (DCPA) surveyed fifty high-risk areas for suitable shelter; these were extended to full-scale prototype CRPs for Richmond, Virginia, and San Antonio, Texas; initial field tests were conducted in Colorado Springs, Colorado; Dover, Delaware; Duluth, Minnesota; Great Falls, Montana; Macon, Georgia; Oklahoma City, Oklahoma; Springfield, Massachusetts; Tucson, Arizona; and Utica/Rome, New York, and operable plans were developed for some of these areas.[53]

Industry, too, was part of CRP. While some essential workers would remain in risk areas, many others would commute daily into the risk areas for extended shifts then back to the relative safety of their host communities. This kept the highways clear of non-essential traffic during an extended evacuation period, which was advantageous for military mobilization as well as pre-planned routing for wholesale distribution of consumer necessities—food, building materials, and medical supplies—away from their customary destinations in target areas and instead to the host communities. Tabletop exercises, a variation on syndicates though with more structured gaming, were used by emergency operations center staff responsible for overseeing the exodus, hosting, and local functioning of CRPs in small and large communities. They gamed responses from the first spontaneous voluntary evacuations through the presidential order to relocate and the start of nuclear war. Uncooperativeness, lawlessness, traffic congestion, and health problems arising from overcrowding were discussed.[54]

Communicating the imperative to relocate and persuading people to do so in an orderly and constructive manner was always a concern in these plans. The tabletop format allows for debate around specified issues—some generic and others specific to local institutional or industrial factors—by the people who would be on site to direct and monitor progress, typically in a group of just five to twelve players actually responsible for CRP implementation on a local level. Participants in a Morgan City, Missouri, exercise in 1983 included not just the county's civil preparedness director and planners but the presiding judge, mayor, and local sheriff, police, fire, rescue, health department, and newspaper officials. In three hours they received an introduction, overview of evacuation plans, orientation and discussion of the scenario, review, and critique.[55] Participants in the tabletop exercise "Fast-Forward" in 1981 dealt with routing and access problems, price gouging, anti-war demonstrators attempting to turn evacuees back from checkpoints, looting, and a dog breeder who arrived in a host city in the Pacific Northwest with four trucks full of large canines.[56] The disposition of pets and other animals is a recurrent theme in the relocation literature. They were not to be taken into shelters, and this became a factor in many people's refusal to cooperate with relocation directives.

Assuming that CRP was made viable, would the public follow orders to evacuate? Concerns about white suburbanization and black urbanization in the United States led FEMA to commission research on minority compliance with relocation orders in 1981. Minorities were expected to suffer disproportionately in a relocation because of a larger number of one-parent households, more young children, and fewer transportation options. In a sampling from Atlanta, 88 percent of whites and 45 percent of minorities had contacts in host areas; having such contacts improved the likelihood of complying with relocation orders, but obviously with disparate racial outcomes. Data derived from group discussions with residents of Atlanta, El Paso, San Francisco, and Harrisburg, Pennsylvania, showed a much lower level of trust in officials and police among African American, Hispanic, and Asian American participants, resulting in credibility problems for civic leaders.[57] British research corroborated these findings, noting that "sheltering runs against both socialisation and familiar behaviour patterns." The public may self-evacuate when taking shelter would be more appropriate: "unless the individual regards the threat as an inconvenience rather than a real threat. . . . there will be a diversity of response by the public: some will leave when advised to shelter; others will shelter when advised to leave."[58] A study of compliance attitudes toward presidential-directed relocation among 1,620 Americans in 1978 indicated that 35 percent of those surveyed would remain behind, a figure that does not seem to be correlated to race or class but is disproportionately representative of people living in cities with greater than 100,000 population, the fully employed, and women. As many as 23 percent of other respondents had maladaptive responses, with 14 percent saying they would go from one risk area to another and 8 percent indicating they would go from a low risk area to a high one.[59]

Another series of desktop workshops on reception area management was held in 1978 in Kansas City, Missouri, Shreveport and Minden, Louisiana, and Glens Falls, New York; these involved emergency planners, parish and local government officials, and in one case also military and naval representatives. Clearly, at this time few local officials had any prior knowledge of CRP concepts or plans and the private sector was no better informed. In New York, the researchers were told "no one here really believes in crisis relocation."[60] The workshops revealed that host area authorities were hostile toward the plans, asserted the political impossibility of accepting authority over neighboring risk areas, and doubted their ability to fulfill other allocated responsibilities. There was "universal (variously stated) anticipation of intractable problems with special groups of relocatees" and skepticism that the evacuees would obey local authority under harsh conditions.[61] Nevertheless, major concerns centered on acquiring needed resources (radiation monitoring, communications, goods, and services) rather than controlling operations. The burden suddenly befalling host area local governments would be enormous, not in any way comparable to the onslaught that a holiday weekend can bring upon a picturesque town. This would involve hordes of people, anxious and uncertain, imposing without invitation for an indefinite period upon localities whose existing fallout shelter facilities were probably inadequate for their own permanent residents. Conflicts were inevitable, and the conclusion in Glens Falls was "they might just as well stay and die in New York City." Participants advised that except for personnel with a few key skills, evacuees should not be integrated into the host area's economic structure. "Except for church activities, they felt that any inclusion would merely aggravate problems. Relations will become more strained as time goes on."[62]

Host populations were not the only ones liable to find the situation irksome. Dutch researchers studying the population evacuated and billeted during flooding in 1953 described the five stages experienced by evacuees:

1. Spontaneous reception (first few days): sympathy and altruism
2. Occasional frictions: attempts to adjust such as territorial divisions and schedules for use of common facilities
3. Trial and error efforts at adjustment: tensions from sub-cultural differences (urban vs. rural origin; religion; socio-economic class)
4. Modus Vivendi established (one to three weeks): mutual adjustment pattern entrenched
5. Evacuation fatigue[63]

In other words, tolerance for being evacuated, even when a threat was undeniable, had a limited span. Other factors might exacerbate the discontent. Upon arrival in the host areas, CRP evacuees would be directed to report to designated schools for registration and billeting, but as one study of the plans for New York State revealed, schools were never informed that they had been selected for this purpose. (While CRP plans were never classified, knowledge about CRP was kept low-profile, emphasizing the technical planning effort and very little public involvement. If the potential for implementation arose, information would be disseminated early in a crisis, but short of a crisis would not go much beyond public officials, community leaders, and professional disaster planners.)[64] Staff were supposed to allot three minutes to registering each arriving family, though a trial run showed it took on average seven minutes to complete the task.[65] In Herkimer county, a reception area for Utica, New York, one ton of dirt (approximately one cubic yard), would need to be moved per person for each shelter site in order to upgrade facilities to a uniform 40 PF.[66] As daunting as this might be for a town of 1,700 trying to accommodate 8,000 evacuees, in Louisiana the problem was compounded by the unavailability of dirt due to exceptionally high water tables, low-lying terrain, and a propensity for flooding. A study of a community shelter plan in Dayton, Ohio, suggested further factors intensifying the impracticality of sheltering: even if the public had been informed of a community shelter plan, few could recall their designated shelter or read a map to decipher their instructions.[67]

A 1975 series of tabletop exercises with civil defense personnel, county welfare and emergency response representatives, Red Cross personnel, planners, and traffic engineers for six California counties known to be friendly to emergency planning explored hypotheses about what would prompt local officials to action and how computing technology could be used to coordinate crisis management. They used a program developed by Richard Laurino called "Dial-A-Scenario" that enabled automatic generation of scenarios for nuclear war as well as natural disaster training. Integrated human-machine simulation training was conducted using terminals for data access and to monitor and update events. Computers were far more than dumb data reservoirs for remembering shutdown procedures or lists of other scheduled actions, but they were not intended to replicate human thought. Instead, they simulated responses of allowable actions, performance rates, locations, and resources. For example, a player could input when an ambulance was dispatched and the computer would output its arrival time. Computers could utilize remote scheduling and resource allocation to compare the availability of resources with demands in real time, or compare resources available in various locations and give alerts of actions or support responsibilities which human players were then expected to incorporate into play. Most of these functions had previously been assumed by referees. The adoption of Dial-A-Scenario did not automate play so much as make rehearsing more accessible to communities that did not have the planning experts who were otherwise needed to monitor play. While this is an important democratization of gaming, the report on these simulations concludes that "experience has shown that crisis relocation plans, once made, will probably tend to become shelf items subject to obsolescence. As local personnel change, the participating experience of developing the plans may be quickly lost. Periodic simulation exercises can indoctrinate new personnel and motivate planners to update their data to reflect changes in resources and capabilities," but authorities must be vigilant to insist on constant retraining.[68]

Computer modeling (with TEMCRIS II) of the economic impact during a period of crisis concluded that the annual GNP would fall by 1 percent each week the population was relocated in host areas. Assuming a peaceful conclusion to the crisis, moving the population back to their customary locales would also be hard on the economy; this would take at least a month and result in a minimum of 0.5 percent loss of GNP for each week spent in the transition.

> The rationale for this estimate is that about three-fourths of GNP is generated in the risk areas but that a small portion of it, perhaps 10%, will be continued as essential production, and that some net increase of host-area activity will occur. Host-area product[ion] may increase to about a third of current national GNP because of some transfer of activity from risk areas, some augmentation of host-area work force by evacuees, and greatly increased demand in host areas for conventional services. The attendant general confusion in economic activity will lower net productivity, which will somewhat offset the other increases in host-area output and limit the net gain. Moreover, confusion and delays in start-up will similarly lower productivity in the risk areas during CR reconstruction.[69]

Results were highly sensitive to the particular scenario that was being played out; however, additional complications could arise from uncertainties about whether there would be moratoria on debts, if the federal government would underwrite the costs of shelter construction or cover losses incurred from shelter conversion, and whether the costs of feeding and sheltering evacuees would be free, sold for cash, or vouchered. Losses were expected to be $12 billion a week (in 1976 dollars), though pressures on the economy would not just come from disruptions in commerce but also from consumers. Prior to an ordered relocation, nervous consumers were expected to withdraw $70 billion (in 1977 dollars) anticipating the need to cover a two-week relocation by using personal savings, though one-third of households were presumed to have no liquid assets to draw upon. And what if peace broke out? Any relocation period lasting longer than twenty days was likely to cause crises in the money supply as well as in personal and business liquidity. If multiple relocation periods were ordered, compliance with relocation would probably fall but the economic effect would compound. A single relocation event would reverberate throughout the economy for a year, though the computer modeling does not fully consider the ramifications of bankruptcies likely to result from suspended business dealings and personal debt or broach the economic problems beyond the United States. As a key study of CRP concludes: "a crisis of this severity, which involves the United States and the Soviet Union in a direct confrontation, would affect [sic] economies throughout the world. Thus, the impact of CR on the U.S. economy cannot be considered in isolation."[70] Recognizing the artificiality of isolating one factor from another was always the conundrum, the fate, and the Achilles heel of computer modeling. Exercises were designed to combine the advantages of mathematically derived representative schematic data with the hands-on experience of role training. The human players could only identify the next problem if conditions were right.

Systems analysis made exploration of an extended time line more feasible in syndicate or tabletop exercises as well as simulations involving embodied role play, such as continuity of government exercises. As OPAL 59 shows, this enabled exploration of the relationships between monetary scarcity and the evolving economic picture of labor, industry, and the need for government-imposed controls. As later CRP modeling also shows, these investigations of financial systems — invariably based on the hypothetical abstractions of Cold War marketplaces — assumed that whenever possible, bureaucrats would return to their desks, tellers to their cages, and farmers to their ploughs. It was not until late in the history of Cold War that concerns about the viability of post-attack biological ecosystems came sufficiently to the fore to question the validity of all other systems analysis. What good would it be to have continuity of government, a restored manufacturing base, and an intact population if the earth did not cooperate in growing a simple sheaf of grain? Indeed, one condition could not be possible unless all were possible.

A historian of Cold War computing, Paul N. Edwards, stresses that computing was a discourse knitting fictions, fantasies, and ideologies to "connect technology, strategy, and culture." The Cold War itself, he argues, was "literally fought inside a quintessentially semiotic space, existing in models, language, iconography, and metaphor."[71] Civil defense exercises substantiate this observation, both with respect to their methodologies and, ultimately, their utility as pedagogical and planning aids. Recent historians of war game techniques refer to a related policy exercise as "The Day After" games: "the players do not implement moves, but give statements identifying the essential decisions parameters and the decision recommendation in each situation."[72] In such games, the problem of recognizing appropriate variables upon which to base decisions was, in part, a matter of scientific knowledge and technological know-how, and in part the consequence of imagination and exploratory play. What *was not* gamed that should (or could) have been? The key lay in combinations of known and imagined elements, or in Edwards's term "recombinant theater" abstracting and engineering "panoptic management."[73]

Thinking about problems with more complexity, and with the added variable of elapsing time, brought about novel intuitions. This could put exercise efficiency at odds with reality. For example, one OPAL 59 player commented: "a great deal we did was unrealistic. We walked in with Guidelines and Federal Registers. We walked in with figures on so many needed and so many available. In a real situation that would be trickling up for a long period. Our big job will be to tally these things up as they accumulate rather than take totals."[74] Being prepared for an exercise was not necessarily the equivalent of being able to cope in an emergency if preparedness itself, as one of the given circumstances, was unrealistically enhanced by computer play. In other words, a more complex exercise did not necessarily rehearse what some players imagined to be the inevitability of a chaotic post-attack world.

The advantage of theatrical pretense and the dramaturgy of safe play was also its chief drawback: "as ifs" are always silently partnered by "as if nots" that overlook, deny, or willfully trample equally plausible scenarios. In the "recombinant theater" of exercises, and especially in those invoking the illusion of fulsome complexity that arises with systems analysis, both the sense of a complete overview and competent control can be heightened. Though some of the exercises document how rehearsal parameters raised doubts, it is noteworthy that documentation of dissent (or even skepticism) about civil defense per se is extremely rare among participants. It may have been that civil defense gaming communities were self-selecting, weeding out the naysayers both from exercises and report writing. It may have been that exercises made converts out of doubters. Or, ominously, it may have been that the exercises (or their work milieu) were either hostile or not conducive to honest critique.

But what if theater itself was the culprit? What if using its techniques and the ontology of rehearsal created a sense of false security, the millennia of dramatic tradition seeming to create satisfactory closure despite unresolved time lines or chaotic plot lines? What if acting insufficiently enabled participants to get intellectual distance from the problems being explored, or proximity to problems being ignored? What if the ingenuity of theatrical play—its very distinction from sober toil—is what made civil defense appear reasonable, feasible, and efficacious?

When I see a piece of duct tape holding something together, it strikes me as funny because it's obvious that it was a quick fix by someone who neither had the patience nor the ability to fix it correctly. . . . Come to think of it, that seems to be the American way lately.

—Tim Nyberg

At the end of the Cold War, a new day seemed to dawn. In 1993, Ken Farrell, a civil engineer who had worked on public shelter issues for thirty years, was asked by Public Works Canada to come out of retirement and write a textbook and curriculum on the fundamentals of radiation shielding in order to "mothball" the technology in case of future need.[1] This was prudent: texts on the topic were decades out of date and Farrell had no lieutenants to succeed him. And yet, with intervening events, the 7 July 2005 attacks on London transport were instantly touted as "the surprise we expected," though non-nuclear. On the very same day, a thousand-person terrorism exercise on the London Underground, conducted by Visor Consultants on behalf of a corporate client, coincided *exactly* with the detonation of the real bombs.[2] As Ian McEwan describes that dreadful day, "a man in a suit pulled a fluorescent jacket out of his briefcase and began directing traffic with snappy expertise."[3] Did he think he was still in a rehearsal, or a performance?

Aircraft crashes in New York, Virginia, and Pennsylvania on the morning of 11 September 2001 propelled emergency services into an unscheduled performance. In the days that followed, a new era of civil defense was launched, which is to say a new roster of rehearsals, both public and covert, massive and quotidian. On 8 October 2001, the day after the United States began to bomb Afghanistan in Operation Enduring Freedom, the Office (later Department) of Homeland Security (DHS) came into being to advocate, orchestrate, and oversee these rehearsals. This includes a grassroots campaign to integrate preparedness into everyday routines. Citizen-actors remove jewelry, belts, and shoes in order to travel, and forgo the convenience of metal cutlery in airport restaurants, scissors in on-board luggage, and portable electronic devices during take-offs and landings. Citizen-actors remain seated when approaching Washington's airspace, submit to scans when entering sporting arenas, and practice vigilance anywhere the public gathers, reporting suspicious packages. Noncitizen-actors give their thumbprints to enter the United States and are required to report regularly to police while they study in U.S. universities. Ready.gov, a Homeland Security program, urges householders to prepare emergency kits and family plans for any contingency. Businesses are advised to plan for evacuation as well as shelter-in-place, and to hold tabletop exercises and walk-through drills for staff, then to "evaluate and revise processes and procedures based on lessons learned in training and exercises."[4] As a *Bulletin of the Atomic Scientists* article puts it, a new "silly season for civil defense" has commenced.[5] But exactly what is silly: the rehearsals themselves or the justification that is given for them?

Civil defense scenarios, briefly archived in the 1990s, are current again. In February 2003, the DHS began to urge Americans to designate a "safe room" at their homes and workplaces and set aside a survival kit including duct tape and plastic sheeting. Embracing the legacy of Bert the cartoon turtle, FEMA's "spokescrab" Herman was invented to promote disaster-preparedness among children, sending them on home scavenger hunts looking for stored water, high-energy foods, sets of spare clothes for each family member, flashlights, battery-operated radios, and chlorine bleach.[6] The American Red Cross, not to be outdone by legions of entrepreneurs, sells survival kits over the Internet, joining the plethora of other emergency gear—hand-held Geiger counters, inflatable plastic rooms, and potassium iodide capsules—recommended to the American public as their props in the event that rehearsals become performances.[7] Phone books urge families to create a communication plan and to keep their cars fully fueled in case of sudden evacuation. Mental health professionals are offered free training in the psychosocial management of a radiation attack,[8] and colleges have jumped on the bandwagon by publicizing their emergency response plans.

On 11 September 2001, 100 senior civil service managers were hurriedly relocated outside Washington.[9] Subsequently, Congress quietly updated its emergency relocation plans "to deal with a doomsday scenario."[10] In exceptional circumstances such as this, or when an errant civilian plane flies over the U.S. capital, pedestrians and bureaucrats scramble to shelter, and the president is whisked to "a more secure location," do we recognize that their behavior as well as the infrastructure for their safety is based on Cold War planning? For the rest of us, September is designated National Preparedness Month, reviving a practice similar to the 1950s coupling of National Civil Defense Day (7 December) to commemorations of the attack on Pearl Harbor.[11] The direct legacy is undeniable. Starbucks, a U.S. corporation emblematic of global capitalism, urged customers in September 2004 to "Be Prepared" with a "ready kit checklist" and fill-in-the-blanks family communication plan.[12] Such messages compound dozens of warnings from the DHS inveighing the public to take care when traveling, be conscious of surroundings, and report suspicious activity. Personal safety, minor sacrifices, and vigilant preparation are civilians' responsibility: security through collective rehearsal ensures cultural preservation. Yet by the summer of 2004, psychologists observed that Americans had settled into "a long-term relationship with catastrophic risk," and the three-year trend showed that people had come to experience anxiety in an inverse relationship to periods of heightened DHS-declared alert.[13] Were they psychologically maladaptive, distrusting of the information source, or experiencing rehearsal fatigue in the War on Terror?

In a car bomb exercise outside the Pentagon, casualties act the part of victims, emergency responders triage and tag them, and firefighters douse the scene while witnesses on their lunch breaks stroll by without slackening their pace.[14] Ian McEwan's 2005 novel, *Saturday*, offers a parable of what might be understood post–9/11 that could not be grasped during the Cold War: we assume we can recognize a threat, but over-determine the wrong signs, misread overt cues, and fail to coexist peacefully within our own neighborhoods.[15] Thus, the new generation of civil defense exercises addresses a wide array of problems, must adapt for each newly acknowledged risk, but may rehearse in vain or in error. Pneumonic plague in McAlester, Oklahoma, a chemical attack on Seattle, Washington, and a radioactive leak in North Castle, New York, have once again become routine kinds of exercises, making headlines because of the high profile of the DHS.[16] Fears of an influenza pandemic step up rehearsals for animal disposal, biological containment, and hospital triage.[17]

Canada and Britain also rehearse for disaster preparedness. After 9/11, research priorities were assessed and public outreach and education highlighted.[18] Canada's EPC calls for all-occasion readiness, not only for radiological incidents but also natural disasters and cyber-sabotage. Nevertheless, American exceptionalism—asserting that it is the bulwark of democracy, revered by the just and despised by the unworthy—feeds domestic confidence that the United States is perpetually beyond reproach and uniquely blessed, as well as paranoia that it is especially targeted by terrorists. President George W. Bush persistently touts nuclear proliferation by "rogue states" as the ultimate threat to us all, and those who already control massive arsenals (or are political and military allies of those that do) must prevent others from joining the nuclear club. The rhetoric of non-proliferation is mobilized as the justification for neo-imperialism. In the midst of this, the rehearsals go on. All the elements in rehearsals are recognizable, but do they focus on the biggest threats to Americans? What about poverty, racism, lack of medical access, crumbling urban infrastructure, and the crisis in public education: the same problems, not incidentally, that plagued the United States during the last flowering of civil defense?

Everyone is right to want to prevent the use of nuclear weapons. In 1913, H.G. Wells depicted in his novel *The World Set Free* that the West would revive, phoenix-like, from devastating "atomic bomb" warfare. Wells's bombs devastate Europe for a generation, emitting poisonous rays that make cities uninhabitable, but eventually this gives way to a world republic, responsible consumption of non-renewal resources, flourishing artistic expression, the elimination of avarice (and along with it capitalism), and a civilization where religion dwindles to insignificance but charity and public works are the dominant aspirations.[19] But in the early 1980s, all remnants of such post-attack Pollyannaism faded when additional validity was brought to concerns about nuclear war by *Ambio*, the *Bulletin of the Atomic Scientists*, and Physicians for Social Responsibility, which emphasized the long-term consequences from communicable diseases, genetic mutations, a worldwide blanket of ash, marine ecosystem destabilization, food scarcities, and contamination of fresh water.[20] Versions of these concerns had been voiced for decades but finally, it seemed, the fears of the public and the theories of the scientific community coalesced around "nuclear winter."[21] What remained of public sympathy for civil defense was dismantled in the face of newly articulated overwhelming odds. Nuclear winter meant that an ecological balance could not be restored, and without that how could an economy, or even a government, be preserved? From the early 1950s, civil defense rhetoric supported blindness to some factors in order to claim the optimism of survivability, just in case it could be made true. It emphasized the rapid decay of some isotopes so that people could be active again in a matter of weeks, and ignored other isotopes with half lives equivalent to or greater than the earth itself. It claimed that fallout would only be a problem where it landed, overturning basic bioscience by ignoring radioactivity's mobility once taken up by plants or animals, if only through the effect of concentrating in blown seeds and wayward proliferating insects. It assumed universal access to radiological monitoring so that people would know where to farm. It recommended scraping back the uppermost layer of earth, never asking if crops could do without that topsoil or if farmers could work next to mountains of this stuff without harmful effects. Even if crops could grow, reduction of petroleum supplies might mean ploughs would be drawn by oxen on fields whose productivity would be vastly diminished by the lack of chemical fertilizers and pesticides. Only third-world countries retain the agricultural know-how to function under such circumstances.

In the face of latter-day scientific insights, the civil defense exercise narratives are scaled down: one or at most three cities, not an entire nation or hemisphere, are under attack at any given time. The bombs are not always 10 MT warheads carried by ICBMs (Weapons of Mass Destruction), but are "dirty" radioactive dispersal devices, in suitcases or duffel bags (Weapons of Mass Disruption). Damage on this scale is "containable," restoration can be achieved through community effort, and nothing so diminutive can set off nuclear winter. While this may seem a more modest and perhaps a more realistic threat scenario today, the problems set out in today's exercises are actually on a scale commensurate with many of the field and syndicate exercises of the 1950s and early 1960s when all-out nuclear war was the presumption.

Cold War civil defense has several things in common with the new generation of security rhetoric. The enemy is demonized, its leaders inscrutable and elusive, and its followers unreasoning ideologues. Patriotism is the measure of active resistance, and short of actual involvement, expressions of patriotism are an incontrovertible assertion about a common national, or even international, purpose. Though there is now an expanded professional cadre of first responders, every member of the public also has a role to play in being prepared. As an ABC documentary put it, "the fact is that you are your own first responder."[22] This means, minimally, protecting ourselves and our households through basic steps but can extend to community volunteerism. On Halloween 2002, Britain created its Civil Contingency Reaction Force, organizing 7,000 volunteer military reservists for emergency mobilization nationwide.[23] The Citizen Corps, a DHS initiative, aims to involve communities in the nationwide effort to enlist volunteer firefighters and law enforcement officers, improve first aid knowledge, strengthen neighborhood watch programs, and support the Medical Reserve Corps.[24] The DHS passes money down to local jurisdictions so that things can be seen to improve by the voting citizenry right where they live.

When FEMA was created in 1978, its director Bardyl Tirana emphatically excluded the possibility of public participation in simulations; such activity was to be limited to key state and local officials responsible for implementing FEMA's plans. "There is one way to familiarize key officials with their responsibilities to make plans work in the real world," he wrote, "and that is to conduct exercises involving these officials, based on a simulated evacuation. The public, in contrast, need not participate in drills or rehearsals. In fact, this could be counterproductive, as a rehearsal would be apt to be quite artificial or contrived, and thus not reflective of the 'way it would really be' if plans were actually implemented."[25] Instead of fearing such a disconnection between reality and rehearsals' realism, the DHS and Home Office now insist that rehearsals are commensurate with the new realpolitik. Indeed, vigilance may prove crucial. Only time will tell. In the meanwhile, the shibboleths of Terror are reflected in the new rehearsals, and the rehearsals themselves help to form the public's conception of "risk" as well as "risk management." Standing patiently while being scanned, producing identity documents, and calmly detouring around HAZMAT trailers, we rehearse "risk abatement."

With time and distance from 9/11, public anxiety is reduced in proportion to behaviors that become ingrained. Instead of questioning authority, the new orthodoxy of fear is expressed as patriotism within the United States and "setting people free" abroad. This is not so readily or widely accepted in Canada or the United Kingdom, perhaps the result of a greater consciousness of integral, reciprocal, and fragile relations with a globalized community. Embodied rehearsals are conducted in all three nations, and there may even be an equal legitimacy to danger, but there is not a uniform sensibility about the rationale that to conduct a War on Terror is to preserve peace. In each nation, an up-to-date version of duck and cover is conducted moment by moment in airports, while in the United States the rhetoric of risk leads additionally to fears that anyone photographing federal sites ipso facto plans to sabotage them, that the press should not report openly on defense matters, and that scrutinizing financial transactions, conducting data mining, and demanding libraries' lending records are duties that supersede concerns of racial, ethnic, or religious bias. The Canadian Security Establishment also spies on private communications post–9/11, as the arrest of terrorist plotters in June 2006 brought to the fore.[26]

Does what we do in conjunction with rehearsing civil defense now make sense? Do we realize when and how it is vestigial of Cold War behaviors, shibboleths, or politics? When we squeeze our cars in beside Hummers—the dressed-up military vehicles General Motors sells under the motto "like nothing else"—are we the puny peasant beside the draft horse of a crusading knight whose hegemony (or righteousness) must not be challenged? When we scrutinize the handwriting on our post, look twice at a neighbor's chador, or sign up for a national identity card, is this the modern counterpart to building a family fallout shelter? Do we wonder how an "enemy" arises, is defined, devised, and inculcated into our consciousness?

Just because the public memory of extensive involvement in civil defense rehearsals has faded does not mean that 9/11 or London's 7/7 "changed everything." Perhaps the most compelling evidence that what we rehearse or perform does not disappear in the moment of its execution is the continuity of civil defense scenarios—and practices—over so many decades. In the twenty-first century, considerable onus for preventing attacks falls on the public, while professional first responders train to ameliorate the consequences of terrorism after it occurs. Will there ever be a rehearsal—and at last a performance—of peace? Would that be the ultimate breach in the—as yet—unbroken tradition?

APPENDIX   *Cold War and Civil Defense Time Line*

1945

8 May: VE Day ends war in Europe
6, 9 August: A-bombs detonate over Hiroshima and Nagasaki, leading to end of World War II
24 October: Establishment of the United Nations (UN)

1946

U.S. Air Force initiates guided missile research
1 July: First peacetime atomic explosion (at Bikini Atoll)

1947

Soviet Union consolidates Eastern European satellites by controlling Romania in addition to
    Poland, Hungary, and Bulgaria
United Kingdom establishes its first emergency seat of government for A-bomb warfare
April: Bernard Baruch coins the term "Cold War"; it is subsequently popularized by journalist
    Walter Lippmann
June: *Bulletin of the Atomic Scientists* initiates "Doomsday Clock" to register prospects of nuclear
    war, starting at seven minutes to midnight

1948

United States terminates guided missile research due to lack of funds and technological data
January: Soviet Union annexes Czechoslovakia
25 February: Communist coup in Czechoslovakia
22 June: Berlin blockade begins
September: North Korea founded
October: Canada appoints coordinator for civil defense (General Worthington)
November: Permanent office for civil defense in United States recommended

1949

United Kingdom resumes planning for mass burials

3 March: United States transfers civil defense functions from DOD to National Resources Planning Board

4 April: NATO formed

12 May: Berlin blockade lifted

23 May: Occupying powers establish Federal Republic of Germany (FRG)

June: First documented nuclear-era civil defense exercise, "Britannia," is held in London

29 August: First Soviet nuclear test (announced 23 September)

1 October: Proclamation of People's Republic of China by Communists

1950

Britain institutes the Civil Defence Corps

U.S. Public Law 920 allows for civil defense in case of attack

Casualties Union incorporates first flash burn case into exercise

31 January: President Truman orders development of H-bomb

9 February: Senator McCarthy begins anti-Communist hearings

14 April: U.S. National Security Council calls for active containment strategy and military build-up (NSC 68)

1 June: Ground Observer Corps founded

25 June: Korean War begins

July: United States doubles defense budget

16 December: United States creates Office of Defense Mobilization

1951

January: United States revives long-range guided ATLAS missile project

12 January: United States creates Federal Civil Defense Administration (FCDA)

23 February: Canadian civil defense placed under Department of National Health and Welfare

2 April: NATO activates integrated command

1 August: Construction on Pinetree Line beings along 50th–53rd parallels (initially 256 sites, reduced to 80 by 1983)

1952

First Pinetree site activated at Lac Ste-Denis, Quebec

7 January: Short film *Duck and Cover* is released in the United States

22 April: First televised broadcast of A-bomb test

14 July: Operation Skywatch (Ground Observer Corps) officially commences

October: *Project East River* published, recommending a broad agenda for U.S. civil defense planning

3 October: Britain tests its first nuclear bomb

1 November: "Mike," the first H-bomb test (10.4 MT), detonates in the Pacific Proving Ground (information withheld until 1954)

1953

16 January: U.S. Executive Order 10427 extends civil defense to natural disasters as well as wartime acts

5 March: Death of Josef Stalin

17 March: Televised broadcast of "Operation Doorstep" showing a-bomb's effects on sample homes, cars, and furnishings

19 June: Execution of Julius and Ethel Rosenberg

27 July: Korean War ends

12 August: Soviet Union announces detonation of H-bomb; Doomsday Clock moves to two minutes to midnight (the closest point ever reached)

September: President Eisenhower launches "Atoms for Peace" plan to put all nuclear stocks under international control; rejected by Soviets

November: Canada decides to build Mid-Canada Line (on 55th parallel)

14–15 December: White House conference of mayors on national security

1954

Guided missile program accorded top U.S. Air Force priority

Pinetree Line becomes fully operational

January: Canada establishes civil defense training school at Arnprior

12 January: U.S. Secretary of State Dulles announces policy of "massive retaliation"

February: Focus of Cold War concern shifts from Europe to China due to French troubles with Indo-China

2 February: President Eisenhower admits to Congress that United States exploded the first full-scale H-bomb at Eniwetok in 1952

1 March: H-bomb test at Bikini Atoll drops radioactive fallout on residents of Rongelap Atoll and crew of Japanese fishing vessel *Lucky Dragon No. 5*; worldwide awareness of fallout hazards begins

7 May: United Kingdom and United States reject Soviet Union's bid to join NATO

14–15 June: First OPAL exercise involves all U.S. states, territories, and Canada

18 November: NATO's "New Assumptions" asserts that thermonuclear weapons will be used in response to Soviet aggression

December: W. Strath forms U.K. cabinet committee to study implications of thermonuclear weaponry

2 December: Senator McCarthy censured by the U.S. Senate

1955

January: United States considers using nuclear weapons to defend Nationalist-held islands in Formosa Strait

21 February: DEW Line construction publicly announced

March: Strath Report recommends widespread change in U.K. civil defense due to fallout potential from thermonuclear weaponry

6 May: FRG joins NATO

14 May: Formation of Warsaw Pact

15 June: OPAL 55 features civilian exercises across United States

September: Guided missile program given highest priority by U.S. National Security Council

1956

April: Canada commences planning for a survivable national communications system

26 July: Egypt nationalizes Suez Canal

23 October: Beginning of Hungarian revolt

5 November: United Kingdom and France begin brief occupation of the Suez Canal zone ("Suez Crisis")

1957

Robert Panero studies the feasibility of evacuating the population of Manhattan into a mass underground shelter

10 April: Suez Canal reopens

15 May: Britain tests H-bomb at Christmas Island

June: Linus Pauling and 11,000 other scientists call for a global nuclear test ban

June: Canada creates Emergency Measures Organization (EMO) within Privy Council Office while Civil Defence Organization remains in Department of National Health and Welfare

24 July: Neville Shute publishes *On the Beach*

31 July: DEW Line completed on 69th parallel, giving United States four to six hours warning of Soviet air attack, but with the development of missiles (presaged by Sputnik) tactical warning time is anticipated to be as little as thirty minutes

August: Plan to locate NORAD within Cheyenne Mountain is mooted

26 August: Soviets test first ICBM

12 September: NORAD is established

19 September: First underground test by United States in Nevada

1 October: United States puts bombers loaded with H-bombs into the air twenty-four hours per day

4 October: Soviets launch Sputnik I, the world's first artificial satellite

4, 7 November: Gaither Committee secretly reports to President Eisenhower on vulnerability to attack and fallout

15 November: National Committee for a Sane Nuclear Policy (SANE) launched

1958

FCDA and Defense Production Administration merge in Executive Office of the President as OCDM

United States and Soviets deploy first ICBMS

United Kingdom consolidates RSG network

January: Ballistic Missile Early Warning System (BMEWS) authorized to supplement DEW Line

1 January: Mid-Canada Line becomes operational (8 sector stations and 90 unstaffed Doppler detection stations)

31 January: First successful satellite launch by United States

17 February: Campaign for Nuclear Disarmament (CND) formed in United Kingdom

7 May: President Eisenhower announces National Policy on Shelters

12 May: NORAD Command Agreement signed by United States and Canada

1 August: Operation Teak H-bomb test at Johnston Island blacks out radio communication to and from Australia, New Zealand, Hawaii, and the North American west coast, the first widespread electromagnetic pulse (EMP) observation

27 August–6 September: Argus high-altitude tests off the Falkland Islands create an artificial ionosphere against which radar can be bounced for spying

22 September: Continuous activation of the bunker for the executive branch and OCDM begins at Mt. Weather, Va.

1 October: Civilian space agency NASA established

31 October: U.S.-Soviet nuclear test ban talks begin after unilateral suspension of testing by United States

10 November: Berlin Crisis

1959

Canada implements plans for constructing Central Emergency Government Headquarters (CEGHQ)

Following the Graham Report, Canadian EMO organizations combine in Privy Council Office while government departments such as Health and Welfare and Justice assume some functional responsibilities

1 January: Fidel Castro comes to power in Cuba

31 January: Ground Observer Corps terminated

October: Turkey and the United States sign agreement to place fifteen Jupiter nuclear missiles in Turkey

17 December: *On the Beach* premieres in cinemas in sixteen countries

1960

Israel begins nuclear program

13 February: France tests a nuclear weapon

17 March: President Eisenhower authorizes Operation Mongoose (covert operations against Cuba)

1 May: Francis Gary Powers' U-2 spy plane shot down over Soviet Union

3 May: Joint U.S.-Canadian exercise OPAL 60 and TOCSIN

31 May: Prime Minister Diefenbaker announces Operation Bridge emergency relocation plans and six Regional Emergency Government Headquarters (REGHQs) in Canada

October: Cuba nationalizes American-owned assets worth $1 billion

October: BMEWS comes fully on line; four days later a Greenland station erroneously reports a full-scale Soviet attack

10 November: Moscow Summit with 81 Communist countries

13–14 November: TOCSIN B exercises held throughout Canada

15 November: United States launches first submarine with ballistic missiles

1961

3 January: United States and Cuba sever diplomatic relations

12 April: Yuri Gagarin becomes first man in space

17–18 April: Aborted Bay of Pigs Invasion of Cuba

May (and September): President Kennedy recommends individual fallout shelters

3–4 June: Vienna summit with President Kennedy and Premier Khrushchev

20 July: President Kennedy assigns responsibility for civil defense to DOD (OCD) while policy and planning functions for emergency mobilization fall under OEP in Executive Office of the President

25 July: Congress authorizes $207.6 for public fallout shelter program for 50 million Americans

12 August: Construction begins on Berlin Wall

18 August: President Kennedy orders reinforcements to the Berlin garrison

19 August: Civil Defense Bill signed by President Kennedy

21 September: U.S. National Intelligence estimate downgrades size of Soviet ICBM arsenal to 10–25 warheads, though in reality the Soviets have just 4 working ICBMs

23 October: Soviets detonate 58 MT bomb, the largest to date

27 October: Tank-to-tank standoff at Berlin Wall commences

1 November: Women Strike for Peace stages protests in sixty U.S. cities

30 November: President Kennedy endorses Operation Mongoose

December: Canada's CEGHQ becomes operational

1962

U.S. above-ground nuclear testing peaks

31 January: Organization of American States (OAS) votes to exclude Cuba and President Kennedy orders almost complete stoppage of trade

April: Jupiter missiles in Turkey become fully operational

29 May: Soviet Union approaches President Castro about placing nuclear missiles in Cuba

July: United States eliminates Women's Activities Director for civil defense

9 July: EMP causes massive electrical disruption 930 miles from the test site

July–August: Cuban Defense Minister Raul Castro visits Soviet Union and agrees to accept nuclear missiles in Cuba

10 August: John McCone (director of CIA) informs President Kennedy that Soviet missiles are en route to Cuba

24 August: U.S. sources reveal thousands of Russian technicians (many military) in Cuba

4 September: President Kennedy warns President Castro not to use Russian arms offensively

6–27 September: Operation Spade Fork rehearses *Plan C* and *Plan D-Minus*

7 September: President Kennedy asks for emergency authorization to call up 150,000 reserve troops

16 October: U-2 spy plane photos presented to President Kennedy reveal nearly operational offensive missile launching bases in Cuba

22 October: President Kennedy addresses the nation about the Cuban situation and increases the military alert status to DEFCON 3; the civil defense program is stepped up but no public actions are ordered

24 October: Naval quarantine of Cuba commences; Strategic Air Command goes to DEFCON 2 for the only time in its history

25 October: Adlai Stevenson presents evidence of Cuban missiles to the UN

28 October: Premier Khrushchev capitulates

2 November: President Kennedy announces that the Russian bases in Cuba are being dismantled

1963

Canada EMO moves out of Privy Council to Ministry of Defence Production

3 February: President Kennedy orders resumption of underground nuclear tests in Nevada after test ban talks with Soviet Union collapse

April: Ipswich Anarchists break into Regional Seat of Government (RSG) in Essex and publicize their findings in the "Spies for Peace" scandal

20 June: United States and Soviet Union agree on a "hot line" telephone

5 August: After 235 atmospheric nuclear tests, the Partial Test Ban Treaty is signed and future tests are underground; Doomsday Clock moves to twelve minutes to midnight

22–23 October: Operation Big Lift transports 14,500 U.S. soldiers to Europe to demonstrate rapid deployment of NATO support

22 November: Assassination of President Kennedy

31 December: Bomarc-B nuclear warheads deployed in Canada at La Macaza and North Bay

1964

U.S. Secretary of Defense McNamara outlines doctrine of Mutually Assured Destruction

Responsibility for OCD moves from secretary of defense to secretary of the army

January: Western half of Mid-Canada Line is closed

29 January: *Dr. Strangelove* premieres in cinemas

7 August: Gulf of Tonkin Resolution gets U.S. troops into Vietnam War

16 October: People's Republic of China tests its first A-bomb

1965

Canada's EMO moves to Ministry of Industry, Trade and Commerce

April: Mid-Canada Line is fully closed

6 April: First U.S. commercial satellite launched

May–June: CIVLOG 65 played by NATO

1966

United States brings multiple warhead delivery systems on-line

Peter Watkins' film *The War Game* shown in United Kingdom

May: France withdraws from the Defence Committee of NATO

1967

U.S. nuclear arsenal at all-time high (32,500)
6–10 June: Six-Day War in Middle East
17 June: People's Republic of China tests its first H-bomb

1968

Soviet multiple warheads deployed
Canadian Prime Minister Trudeau cuts back civil defense spending and moves EMO to DND
6 January: British Prime Minister Harold Wilson disbands Civil Defence Corps, dismantling
    all elements except those geared to emergency control centers
20–21 August: Soviet invasion of Czechoslovakia

1969

20 July: Apollo 11 moon landing

1970

5 March: Nuclear Non-Proliferation Treaty limits nuclear weapons to United States, Soviet
    Union, United Kingdom, China, and France
19 August: United States deploys first missile with MIRVs (a missile with multiple warheads)
13 October: Canada establishes relations with the People's Republic of China

1971

Canada phases out Bomarc missiles and renounces a nuclear weapons role
Greenpeace founded in Canada
29 July: United Kingdom cancels Black Arrow program, opting out of the space race
6 November: United States tests nuclear bomb in the Aleutian Islands off Alaska
3–16 December: Indo-Pakistani War

1972

January: Pakistan begins nuclear program
5 May: OCD reconstituted as Defense Civil Preparedness Agency (DCPA) within DOD
26 May: SALT I and Anti-Ballistic Missile Treaty signed by United States and Soviet Union
October: Canada's Dare Report recommends reorganization for civil emergencies of all kinds

1973

29 March: United States begins withdrawal from Vietnam
3–26 October: Arab-Israeli Yom Kippur War

1974

Crisis Relocation Planning (CRP) gears up substantially in United States
18 May: India tests nuclear weapon
9 August: President Nixon leaves office in disgrace following Watergate scandal

1975

Soviets deploy MIRVS
Emergency Preparedness Canada (EPC) succeeds EMO
30 April: Vietnamese War officially ends with the fall of Saigon

1976

9 September: Mao Zedong's death marks end of Cultural Revolution

1977

21 September: Nuclear Proliferation Pact signed by 15 nations including United States and
   Soviet Union

1978

19 June: President Carter announces reorganization of Federal Civil Defense Administration
   (FCDA) to become Federal Emergency Management Agency (FEMA), creating an all-disaster
   agency
29 September: President Carter issues directive to upgrade defense and include civil defense in
   the strategic balance

1979

1 January: United States establishes diplomatic relations with People's Republic of China
16 January: Shah flees Iran, sparking Iranian Revolution
28 March: Three Mile Island, Pa., accident leads to U.S. moratorium on building nuclear re-
   actors
2 June: Pope John Paul II becomes first pontiff to visit a Communist country
18 June: SALT II signed by presidents Carter and Brezhnev (though never ratified by U.S. Senate)
4 November: Occupation of U.S. embassy in Tehran begins (Iran Hostage Crisis)
12 December: NATO decides to deploy Cruise and Pershing missiles in Europe
25 December: Soviet Union invades Afghanistan

1980

First Nuclear Freeze resolutions passed in United States (Massachusetts)
July: United States boycotts summer Olympics in Moscow
31 August: Solidarity Union founded in Gdansk, Poland
3 November: Comprehensive review of Canadian federal emergency planning policy

17 November: First Women's Pentagon Action

1981

January: Doomsday Clock moves from seven to four minutes before midnight

March: Nuclear Weapons Freeze Campaign holds founding convention in Washington

September: Women's encampment at Greenham Common founded

24 October: Largest CND rally to date in London (other demonstrations throughout Europe)

21 November: Huge anti-nuclear rally in Amsterdam (one in thirty of The Netherlands' population attends)

13 December: Martial law declared in Poland to contain "Solidarity" movement (lasts until 22 July 1983)

1982

4 March: United Kingdom announces new Home Guard unit to help in crises

21 March: Mass protest at Greenham Common

June: President Reagan's European tour sparks massive demonstrations

12 June: 1,000,000 gather in New York City demanding end to the arms race

29 November: UN demands Soviet withdrawal from Afghanistan

12 December: 30,000 women form a human chain around Greenham missile base

1983

Prime Minister Thatcher mandates that local authorities draw up civil defense plans for nuclear war

23 March: President Reagan announces Strategic Defense Initiative ("Star Wars")

15 July: Prime Minister Trudeau agrees to Cruise missile testing in Canada

26 September: A Russian colonel detects a massive incoming strike from the United States but assumes it must be a computer error, preventing World War III (not revealed until 1998)

October: Conference on the World After Nuclear War publicizes the concept of "nuclear winter"

20 November: Made-for-television movie *The Day After* airs in North America

23 November: Ground-launched Cruise missiles installed in United Kingdom

Soviet Union breaks off strategic arms reduction talks (START)

1984

5 March: Iran accuses Iraq of using chemical weapons

8 May: Soviet Union announces boycott of summer Olympics in Los Angeles

1985

Glasnost begins in Soviet Union

6 August: President Gorbachev announces unilateral Soviet nuclear testing moratorium

7 September: Canada invited to join Strategic Defense Initiative but after cross-country hearings Prime Minister Mulroney declines

19 November: Presidents Gorbachev and Reagan agree in principle on 50 percent reduction in strategic nuclear forces

1986

Soviet arsenal reaches all-time high (45,000)

28 January: Space shuttle Challenger explodes

19 February: Soviet Union launches Mir space station

26 April: Chernobyl nuclear reactor accident in Ukraine

1 October: President Reagan orders massive reorganization of DOD

12 October: At Reykjavik Summit, presidents Reagan and Gorbachev nearly agree on elimination of nuclear weapons

1987

15 January: President Gorbachev proposes phased elimination of all intermediate range ballistic missile (IRBMs)

11 February: United States conducts nuclear test in Nevada

June: President Gorbachev announces economic restructuring plans (perestroika) for Soviet Union

8 December: United States and Soviet Union sign Intermediate-Range Nuclear Forces Treaty banning land-based intermediate range weapons

December: President Reagan agrees not to undertake SDI tests in violation of the Anti-Ballistic Missile Treaty

1988

Al-Qaeda established by Osama bin Laden

15 May: Soviets begin withdrawal from Afghanistan

1989

18 January: Soviet Union announces reduction in forces, defense spending, and arms production; other Warsaw Pact nations follow suit

2 February: Soviets complete withdrawal from Afghanistan

3–4 June: Tiananmen Square uprising in Beijing

4 June: Solidarity wins Poland's first free elections

26 July: First U.S. prosecution for releasing a computer virus, a new form of civil disruption

October: East Germans begin emigration via Hungary; Hungary adopts democratic constitution

9–10 November: Opening of Berlin Wall

17 November: Velvet Revolution begins in Czechoslovakia

22 December: Ceauşescu regime falls in Romania

29 December: Vaclav Havel elected president of Czechoslovakia

1990

United States deploys Trident II missiles on submarines (highly accurate "first strike" capacity)

March–May: Baltic nations declare independence from Soviet Union

2 August: Iraq invades Kuwait

3 October: German unification

9 December: Lech Walensa elected president of Poland

1991

17 January: Gulf War begins (Operation Desert Storm)

28 February: Kuwait liberated

March: United States completes withdrawal of missiles from Europe

1 July: Collapse of Warsaw Pact

31 July: START I signed; Doomsday Clock moved to seventeen minutes before midnight (the farthest point ever reached)

19 August: Coup attempt in Soviet Union; President Gorbachev restored but substantially weakened

27 September: Presidents G. H. W. Bush and Gorbachev agree to one-third nuclear arsenal reductions, both withdraw mid-range missiles; United States withdraws airborne nuclear bombers for the first time since 1957

November: President Yeltsin bans Communist Party throughout Russian Republic

26 December: Soviet Union officially dissolves

NOTES

Archival sources are cited in full in the notes. Other sources are cited in abbreviated form, with full details in the Works Cited.

Introduction

1. There is a fast-growing literature on this topic, indicated but not bounded by Auerswald et al. 2006; Ranum 2004; El-Ayouty 2004; Baudrillard 2002; and Dudziak 2003.

2. In retrospect, many civil defense measures seem inadequate, and perhaps even ludicrous. The historiography features much of the information disseminated about them—based on popular media, populist tactics, and populism—in a conjunction between pop culture iconography and post hoc dismissive reductionism of what was, at the time, often experienced as the terrifying imminence of death. Kitsch history displaces attention from the causes of civil defense, namely an arms race of unprecedented destructive power, huge investment in the military-industrial complex, and technologies of paranoia propagated by the ideological opponents.

3. Oakes 1993: 348.

4. Associated Universities, Inc. 1952; and U.S. President's Science Advisory Committee 1976.

1. Civil Defense Concepts and Planning

1. US FCDA and Safety Commission 1952.

2. Conway 1954: 65.

3. Kaplan 1984: 78.

4. NARA RG 396 Entry 1009 41/32/04, Box 1, "Address by Governor Val Peterson Before the Canadian Civil Defence College Arnprior, Ontario, Friday, July 8, 1955."

5. NATO MC 48, 18 November 1954; rpt. in Pedlow [1997]: 231–50. See also Trachtenberg 1999: 158–76.

6. See, for example, Jackson and Harker 1969; and Harker 1970.

7. Northwestern University Special Collections, Stage for Action Collection, Robert Adler and George Bellak, *Open Secret*, performed in the 1947 season of this community-oriented leftist group's Chicago company. For the short story, see Ridenour 1962: 280–88.

8. See also Grossman 2001: 72, 88.

9. National Military Establishment 1948; and Hopley 1948.

10. Laurence 1950: 68, 73, 75, 106. Edwin J. Grace and David Bradley were rare among nuclear commentators to warn against fallout in this early period. P. Boyer 1998: 65–74.

11. PRO AB 6/471, UK Atomic Energy Authority [Atomic Energy Research Establishment Harwell], Exchange of Information with USA on Atomic Weapons Effects: Civil Defence Aspects, J. D. Cockcroft (AERE Harwell), carbon memo via diplomatic air bag to F. N. Woodward (British Commonwealth Scientific Office, Washington), 15 November 1948; J. D. Cockcroft, "Exchange of Information on Service and Civilian Protection against the Radiation of Atomic Bombs," 12 July 1948; and M.W. Perrin (Ministry of Supply, Shell Mex House London), letter to John Cockcroft, 8 July 1948.

12. PRO AB 6/471, UK Atomic Energy Authority, Exchange of Information with USA on Atomic Weapons Effects: Civil Defence Aspects, John A. Derry (Executive Officer, Division of Biology and Medicine, US Atomic Energy Commission), letter to A. K. Longair (Assistant Director, UK Scientific Mission, British Commonwealth Scientific Office, Washington, DC), 7 April 1950; A. S. Hutchinson (HO Civil Defence Department), memo to M.W. Perrin (Ministry of Supply), 27 April 1950; and BJSM [British Joint Services Mission] in Washington, telegrams to Cabinet Office, 14 and 15 June 1950, and 8 and 28 July 1950.

13. Hirschfelder et al. 1950. Initially published by Los Alamos Scientific Laboratory in cooperation with the DOD and the U.S. Atomic Energy Commission in June 1950 and reissued in August by the Combat Forces Press.

14. NARA RG 396 Entry 1013 650 41/32/07, Box 1 and 2; RG 396 Entry 1029 650 42/05/05, Box 1; RG 396 Entry 1015 650 41/33/05, Box 7; RG 397 Entry 39 650 42/26/06–07, Box 1 and 2; and RG 396 Entry 1050, Box 1, "Discussion Topics Noted in letter from C. R. Patterson to Darrell Trent—April 5, 1973."

15. PRO AB 6/451, UK Atomic Energy Authority, Liaison with the HO: Civil Defence Policy 1948–53, Frederick L. Hovde (President, Purdue University), copy of letter to Lloyd Eno (FCDA), 4 December 1952.

16. PRO AB 6/1422, Exchange of Information With USA on Atomic Weapons Effects: Civil Defence Aspects, Lt. Col. K. Stewart (BJSM), memo to Paul W. McDaniel (Atomic Energy Commission), 13 August 1954; Cabinet Office, telegram to BJSM Washington, 30th September 1954; BJSM Washington, telegram to Cabinet Office, 1 October 1954; J. D. Cockcroft, carbon memo to Frederick Brundrett (MOD), 6 October 1954; and R. R. Powell (MOD), memo to Gen. Sir John Whiteley (BJSM Washington DC), 9 November 1954.

17. PRO AB 6/1422, Exchange of Information with USA on Atomic Weapons Effects: Civil Defence Aspects, 1954–55. This relationship continued: in 1969, the Americans sought a cooperative program with Britain—and technically all NATO partners—to share plans for accommodation, transportation, civil manpower, engineering, and medical facilities and for effective use of mutual resources such as personnel, materials, and communications which might survive after an attack in order to support U.S. facilities and bases in Europe. PRO FCO 46/378, M. H. C. Warner (MOD), letter to R. E. L. Johnstone (Foreign and Commonwealth Office), "United States Proposal for Integration of their Installations as part of a UK Civil Defence Organisation," 3 April 1969; and John C. Fahringer (Col. USAF), letter to Mr. Stoddart (Political Military Affairs, US Embassy), 26 May 1969.

18. Glasstone 1957.

19. Quoted in Rose 2001: 219.

20. Diacon 1984.

21. NATO AC/23(CD)D/106, NATO Civil Defence Committee, "Civil Defence and Thermo-Nuclear Weapons. The Problem of Fall-Out," 28 May 1955.

22. In 1962, the roentgen was replaced by the more precise rad as the measure of radiation. Roentgens are cited here in order to reflect the data presented in the 1950s. Vale 1987: 29.

23. Bentz et al. 1956: 7.

24. Openshaw, Steadman, and Greene 1983; US DOD 1966; US DOD *High Risk*, 1975; US FEMA 1980; and Canada Department of Public Works 1974.

25. NATO AC/23 (CD)D/98 Civil Defence Committee, "Civil Defence and Thermo-Nuclear Weapons Memorandum by the Senior Civil Defence Advisor," 25 November 1954: 5, 3.

26. NATO C-M(55)48 (Final), Note by the Secretary General, "The Application of the New Assumptions to the Work of the Emergency Planning Committee," 27 May 1955.

27. NATO C-M(55)43, Deputy Secretary General, "The Application of the New Assumptions to the Work of Emergency Planning Committees," 21 April 1955.

28. NATO C-R(55)14, NATO Council, Summary Record of a Meeting of the Council held at the Palais de Chaillot, Paris XVIe, 27 April 1955 [document dated 29 April 1955].

29. NATO AC/98-R2, NATO Senior Civil Emergency Planning Committee, "Maintenance of Governmental Control," 26 and 27 April 1956.

30. PRO HO 322/309 Janus 63 Draft Report, "Machinery of Government in War," 17 October 1963.

31. Vale 1987: 123–51. Grossman documents a well-developed civil defense organization in New Jersey as of 1952, with 231,000 members, a quarter of whom were trained as wardens. Though he cites one defense drill in Glen Ridge, the training of members in specialties such as transportation, fire, police, rescue, welfare, and public works, and the fate of the organization overall, are obscure (79–90). The extent of civil defense volunteering in the United States in the 1950s is not well documented; however, in 1958 New York state alone claimed to have held 420 command post exercises, 43 state-directed exercises, 1,298 demonstrations, and dozens of mobile hospital exercises. NARA RG 396 Entry 1029 650 42/0505, Box 4, NY State Civil Defense Commission, "Annual Report for 1958," 1959: 4, 24.

32. Crossley 1985.

33. South Yorkshire Fire and Civil Defence Authority 1988b.

34. London Boroughs 1989: 21–22.

35. Poole, Lloyd, and Hally 1989a: 99.

36. Canada EPC 2000.

37. See Canada EMO 1968b; and Ken Farrell, interview with the author, 2000. Public Works Canada initiated its first survey in 1964, identifying all buildings in the province of Alberta that could offer a minimum of PF 10 and 1,000 square feet. See Canada EMO 1968a and Department of Public Works Development Engineering Branch 1964. This pilot study was followed up in 1965–70 with a nationwide survey identifying 72,759 structures (EMO and DND, 1970). Highly detailed provincial community shelter plans followed (Nova Scotia 1975; Prince Edward Island 1976; Quebec 1983; New Brunswick 1985; Ontario, Manitoba, Saskatchewan, and Alberta 1992; British Columbia and Newfoundland 1993), which

are available in the Public Works Canada Collection at the Diefenbunker Archive. The Territories were not surveyed. In 1966, the U.S. Census included questions about respondents' homes that were intended to enable federal officials to remotely determine the best location for a fallout shelter and provide this as follow-up advice.

38. Boyer 1985: 319.

39. Ghamari-Tabrizi 2005: 98–103; Grossman 2001: 79; and DDEPL, Files of Special Assistant Relating to the Office of Coordinator of Government Public Service Advertising (James M. Lambie, Jr.), Ground Observer Corps—Air Defense Command Reports, 1955.

40. US FEMA 1979: iii.

41. L. Clarke 1999: 74. See also Kincade 1980; and NARA RG 397, Box 8, #55, Shane E. Mahoney for DCPA, "Civil Defense and American Federalism: a Pre-Primer," June 1978.

42. Lay 1960: item 54.

43. See Vale 1987: 152–92; Rees 1984; US FEMA 1983e: 1–32; and Yegorov, Shlyakhov, and Alabin 1970.

44. Vale 1987: 55, 73–78.

45. Pike, Blair, and Schwartz 1998: 321; and P. Boyer 1985: 352–67.

46. Vale 1987: 85, 91; P. Boyer 1998: 175–81; Sherry 1995: 405–6.

47. This was originally referred to as "ABC warfare" (atomic, biological, chemical) and flagged by the Hopley report (1948). Concern revived in the late 1970s, so NORAD developed the Nuclear, Biological, Chemical Warning and Reporting System. See NORAD Headquarters, 1978.

48. Oakes 1994: 82; and Valley Forge Foundation and FCDA, 1951: n.p.

49. US FCDA 1952a: 15.

50. Valley Forge Foundation and FCDA, 1951: n.p.

51. US FCDA 1953: 52; and FCDA 1954a: 74–75.

52. PRO HO 322/111, "Civil Defence Week: Visits by Home Secretary and by Parliamentary Under-Secretaries of State," 1956.

53. Boy Scout Association 1941; Scout Association Archive, Chief Executive Commissioner, letter to J. M. Ross (HO), 23 October 1953; and A.W. Hurll, "For Information on the Committee of the Council for their Meeting on 27th September, 1950."

54. Scout Association Archive, Ministry of Education Confidential Note, 1953; Ministry of Education Minutes [meeting on the Role of Juveniles in Civil Defence], 2 October 1953; HO Civil Defence School Easingwold, Special Course for Leaders of Youth Organisations, 1956; Civil Defence Corps, Bucks Division, Rescue Section basic and advanced courses for Senior Scouts, 1966; and T. G. Martin (County Commissioner), letter to A.W. Hurl (Scout Association), 1 July 1967.

55. Crossley 1982: 58; and PRO HO 322/141, Command and Control Exercises by Midland Civil Defence Region, "Exercise 'All Together Heave,'" 1960, and "Exercise 'To and Fro,'" 1962.

56. DA, PEI Scrapbook, unattributed clippings, "Individual is Called Key in Nuclear Raid Survival," 6 May 1961; "Arnprior Scouts Assist CCDC," ca. May 1954; and "'Exercise Confusion' at CCDC," 5 August 1954. See also Salopek 1989: 78.

57. US FCDA 1956a: 9; Pritchard et al. 1956: 3–5; Chicago Civil Defense Corps 1955: 7–8; NARA RG 304.2 RI & 2, FCDA, OPAL 56; RG 396 Entry 1029 650 42/05/05, Box 6, "Evaluation Report Civil Defense Alert Exercise April 17–18, 1959"; and RG 396 Entry 1063 650

42/13/01, Box 1, Regional Director OCDM Region 7, letter to Assistant Director Plans and Operations at OCDM National Headquarters, 2 June 1960.

58. Boy Scouts of America 1951a; Boy Scouts of America 1951b; Boy Scouts of America 1951–64; and NARA PARA PN 10.50.

59. NARA RG 396 Entry 1009 41/32/04, Box 1, Albert C. Tilley (FCDA Regional Administrator, Denver), letter to Val Peterson [Director FCDA], 24 February 1955.

60. DDEPL, Files of Special Assistant Relating to the Office of Coordinator of Government Public Service Advertising (James M. Lambie, Jr.), Box 27, Public Affairs Office of FCDA, memo to Advertising Council, 20 February 1956; NARA RG 396 Entry 1015 650 41/33/05, Box 7 of 82, "OCDM Central Files," Leo A. Hoegh, memo to General Goodpaster (White House), 6 March 1959; and RG 396 Entry 1025 650 42/04/06–42/05/01, Box 2, Women's Activity Subject Files, "Shelter Policy. Point One Information" [ca. 1960].

61. NARA RG 396 Entry 1025 650 42/04/06–42/05/01, Box 5, Women's Activity Subject Files, "National Organizations and Civil Affairs Progress Report," June 1961. See also US DOD OCD 1963a:15.

62. McIlroy 1997–98: 82.

63. Boy Scouts of America 1972.

64. US DOD 1975b: 35.

65. Grossman 2001: 37, 54.

66. US FCDA, "Bert the Turtle," 1952b; FCDA, *Facts About Fallout*, 1955a; FCDA, *Rural Family Defense*, 1956e; FCDA, *Facts about Fallout Protection*, 1957b; DOD OCD, *The Family Fallout Shelter*, 1961b; DOD OCD, *School Shelter: An Approach to Fallout Protection*, 1960; and DOD OCD, *National School Fallout Shelter*, 1963b. See also OCDM, *Index to Publications*, 1960; DOD OCD *Publications Catalog*, 1972, 1974, and 1976; and FEMA, *Publications Catalog*, 1985.

67. US DOD OCD 1968b.

68. Canada Department of National Health and Welfare, Civil Defence Canada 1951; Canada, Department of Agriculture 1961; Canada, Central Mortgage and Housing Corporation 1960; and Canada EMO 1962.

69. Canada EMO 1961.

70. JFKL, National Security Files, Box 295 CD 10/1/61–10/27/61, Marcus Raskin, memo to McGeorge Bundy, 23 October 1961.

71. JFKL, National Security Files, Box 295 CD 10/28/61–11/12/61, Carl Kaysen, memo to McGeorge Bundy on Secretary McNamara's Memo and Attached Civil Defense Booklet, 3 November 1961.

72. JFKL, National Security Files, Box 295 11/22/61–11/30/61, Arthur Schlesinger, Jr., "Reflections on Civil Defense," [November 1961].

73. JFKL, National Security Files, Box 295 CD 10/28/61–11/12/61, Ambassador [to India] John Kenneth Galbraith letter to John F. Kennedy, 9 November 1961.

74. Grossman 2001: 95, 101.

75. JFKL, National Security Files, Box 295 11/22/61–11/30/61, Carl Kaysen, memo to the President, 22 November 1961.

76. JFKL, National Security Files, Box 295 12/61, McGeorge Bundy, memo to the President, 1 December 1961.

77. Figures on the print run vary from 25 to 35 million copies. The pamphlet was released to

the public on 2 January 1962. Five million copies were set aside for federal, regional, state, and local civil defense headquarters; 5 million for the OCD at Battle Creek and the Pentagon; 15 million were placed in post offices; and 5 million were held in reserve for resupply. JFKL, Presidents Office Files, Box 85 OEP 7/61–12/61, Carl Kaysen, memo to the President, 27 December 1961.

78. US DOD OCD 1961a: 6–7.

79. Ibid.: 38.

80. JFKL, National Security Files, Box 295 CD 11/13/61–11/19/61, Marcus Raskin, memo to Carl Kaysen, 15 November 1961.

81. Stanford University Libraries, Boy Scout Collection M0855, Steuart L. Pittman, letter to "Dear Scout Leader," [1961]; and Wittner 1997: 252.

82. UK Departments of State and Official Bodies and HO 1963.

83. UK HO 1976.

84. BL typescript BS.18/796, HO and Scottish Home and Health Department 1983: 26.

85. Bolsover 1982: 34, 150, 156. See also Poole, vol. 2, 1989b: 18–21; and Churcher and Lieven 1983: 117–32.

86. Openshaw, Steadman, and Greene 1983: 222.

87. Tyrrell 1982: 53.

88. E. P. Thompson 1980. Greene et al. 1982 attempts an even-handed analysis.

89. Crossley 1985: 76.

90. Briggs 1982.

91. London Boroughs 1989: 11.

92. Cited in Vale 1987: 65.

93. Mack and Baker 1961: 63.

94. Levine and Modell 1964: 112.

95. DA, Privy Council Office, EMO, Telepol Results, 1962.

96. "So Who's Worried," 1961: 7.

97. Levine and Modell 1964: 48.

98. Katz 1960: 68, 63.

99. Scott 1955: 13.

100. Mack and Baker 1961: ix, 7.

101. Ibid.: 11.

102. Williams and Baker 1959; Mack and Baker 1961:17–23.

103. University of Michigan Survey Research Center 1950: 32, 58.

104. The categorical distinctions are drawn from Fuoss 1995: 79.

105. Ibid.: 91–92.

106. NARA RG 396 Entry 1025 650 42/04/06–42/05/01, Box 4, Women's Activity Subject Files, Patricia Honsby Smith, MP, Speech to National Women's Advisory Committee, Washington DC, 23 September 1958: 8.

107. Lady Reading, quoted in Howard 1977: 308. See also Isaacs 1954; and Fitzpatrick 1950.

108. Mrs. Frances Clode, director of the Civil Defense Department for the WVS, quoted in US FCDA 1954b: 26.

109. Women's Voluntary Service for Civil Defence, WVS for Civil Defence 1963: 7; and Westwood 1998: 3–5.

110. Women's Voluntary Service for Civil Defence, wvs for Civil Defence 1957; and PRO IR 80/43, Board of Inland Revenue, "Civil Defence Recruitment, etc. 1950–1968."

111. Women's Voluntary Service for Civil Defence, wvs 1963: 14.

112. James Cameron's article appeared in *Peace News*. See Crossley 1985: 25; Berenbaum 1960: 292; and Hersey 1946.

113. "Pageant of Civil Defence," 1950: 3.

114. Baker 1951: 3.

115. PRO RG 40/42, Social Survey, "Civil Defence Survey II: Originating and Financial Sanction," 1950. Some women's anti-nuclear groups played on the same stereotypes, presenting themselves as middle-class housewives and mothers in order to claim the high ground and moral authority of motherhood (Wittner 1997, vol. 2: 252).

116. PRO INF 2/118, Civil Defence Recruitment, 1952 Campaign. There is evidence that such campaigns were not successful. Following the 1950 print campaign, neither the awareness of Scottish respondents was substantially increased nor were their attitudes toward civil defense altered. RG 23/539 "Civil Defence Publicity in Paisley and Dumbarton County. An Enquiry into the Readership of Civil Defence Advertisements and Posters," 1950.

117. PRO HO 322/120, War Planning: Progress Reports to Permanent Under-Secretary of State, Nos. 1–6.1956–1958, "Draft Report 30 April–1 September 1958"; HO 322/111 Civil Defence Week: Visits by Home Secretary and by Parliamentary Under-Secretaries of State, "Programme for Northumberland County Civil Defence Corps 'Annual At Home,' 6 October 1956 at the Civil Defence Training Centre, Porteland"; and "Civil Defence Department. Progress on War Planning. Report for the Period 1st October, 1956 to 31st March, 1957" [3rd report].

118. PRO HO 322/110, Recruitment of Women to Civil Defence Corps Rescue and Pioneer Services, J. R. Hutchings, memo to Flt. Lieut. L. Eardley-Wilmot (HO, Leeds), 21 February 1951.

119. PRO HO 322/110, Recruitment of Women to Civil Defence Corps Rescue and Pioneer Services, F. L. F. Devey, memo to C. C. Hutton, 11 November 1954.

120. PRO HO 322/110, Recruitment of Women to Civil Defence Corps Rescue and Pioneer Services, John Hays (Town Clerk of Sheffield), letter to Regional Director of HO Civil Defence at Leeds, 20 July 1962.

121. PRO HO 322/110, Recruitment of Women to Civil Defence Corps Rescue and Pioneer Services, G. H. C. Pennycook (Chief Training Officer), memo to Mr. North (HO, London), 14 September 1962.

122. Greater London Council 1966.

123. Crossley 1982: 20.

124. Salopek 1989: 80–81.

125. Poulter and Willesden 1957: 8–9.

126. Canada Department of National Health and Welfare and Civil Defence Canada 1952: 3.

127. Director of EMO for Halifax 1964.

128. DA, Arnprior Scrapbook unattributed clippings, " 'Bombing' Applauded," [ca. May 1954]; and Suzanne Brady, "L'Homme Libre," 7 October 1954.

129. Howard was the first woman deputy in any federal department or agency, and served in the FCDA 1953–54. She was responsible for FCDA publications and women's participation,

congressional liaison, NATO affairs, and sat in on National Security Council and Cabinet meetings when the director, Val Peterson, was out of town (Howard 1977: 282–84).

130. DDEPL, Civil Defense Campaign 1953 (1) Correspondence, Seymour L. Wolfbein (Chief of the Division of Manpower and Employment Statistics), letter to James Lambie (White House), 11 May 1953.

131. NARA RG 396 Entry 1025, Box 4, "Notes on History of Women's Activities in Civil Defense, FCDA." See also Northcutt 1999: 129–39; and McEnaney 2000: 88–108.

132. NARA RG 396 Entry 1025 650 42/04/06–42/05/01, Box 2, Women's Activity Subject Files, Barent F. Landstreet, "Community Organization for Government in Emergency," talk delivered to National Women's Conference on Civil Defense, 29 September 1959: 4. See also Beck 1975: 22–23.

133. NARA RG 396 Entry 1025 650 42/04/06–42/05/01, Box 2, Women's Activity Subject Files, Edward B. Lyman (Deputy Assistant Director National Organizations and Civil Affairs, OCDM), "The Role of the National Organizations in Support of the National Plan," talk delivered to National Women's Conference on Civil Defense, 29 September 1959: 4.

134. Nehnevajsa, Brodie, Krochmal, and Pomery 1964.

135. Columbia Broadcasting 1951: n.p. Ellipses in original.

136. Howard 1977; Oakes 1994: 110–19; and McEnaney 2000:109–10.

137. Withey 1954: 81, 100.

138. US FCDA 1955b: 8.

139. By May 1958, 12,287,000 copies of *Home Protection Exercises* had been printed. This is just half as many as *First Aid*, but close to the indispensable *Six Steps to Survival* (17,942,000) and *Between You and Disaster* (15,255,000). NARA RG 396 #1025, Box 2, table showing publication tallies, [May 1958]. *Home Protection Exercises* was still being distributed in 1968. US DOD OCD 1968a: 86.

140. Several skits totaled just 15,000 copies.

141. NARA RG 396 Entry 1025 650 42/04/06–42/05/01, Box 1, Home Preparedness Awards Program, "Summary of Awards as of April 1, 1960."

142. NARA RG 396 Entry 1025 650 42/04/06–42/05/01, Box 1, Mrs. Dorothy Pearl, "The Time for Decision," talk delivered to the General Session Women's Advisory Council for Civil Defense, 27 June 1960: 7.

143. PRO MAF 99/100 Defence Conference Between USA and UK on Food Aspects of Civil Defence, 1951.

144. Kraft Foods website, http://www.kraft.com/100/timeline/time_1940s.html and http://www.kraft.com/100/timeline/time_1950s.html, accessed 29 November 2005.

145. US FCDA 1956a: 8, 78–79.

146. Atkinson 1968: 307–8.

147. US Department of Agriculture 1964: 30; and FCDA 1956c: 22.

148. In 1954, 62 percent of rural Americans surveyed were willing to participate in civil defense, compared to 48 percent of suburbanites and 37 percent of city dwellers. Withey 1954: 100.

149. Address by Barent Landstreet (Operations Control Services, FCDA) in US FCDA 1954b: 13–14.

150. Ibid.: 18.

151. Marjorie Child Husted in ibid.: 31.

152. US FCDA 1956c, vol. 2: 5–6.

153. Wallis 1963: 128, 133; Simulatics Corporation 1966; and Atkinson 1968: 290–311.

154. Anderson 1964: 4–12; Nehnevajsa 1976; and Nehnevajsa 1975.

155. Levine and Modell 1964: 83.

156. Greenberg, Pettersen, and Kochevar 1966a: i–viii; and Greenberg, Pettersen, and Kochevar 1966b: 24.

157. *Michigan's Upper Peninsula*, 1953: 6. See also McEnaney 2000: 77.

158. Levine and Modell 1964: 68.

159. Washington (State) Department of Civil Defense, 1952.

160. DDEPL Civil Defense Publications by Organizations and Associations 1958–61 (17), Address by Katherine G. Howard in Minneapolis, 20 September 1960: 5.

161. Anderson 1964: 10–22; and Nehnevajsa 1976: 81.

162. See, for example, HWLC Chicago Civil Defense Corps *Information Bulletin #4*, 3 October 1956.

163. HWLC Chicago Civil Defense Corps, *Key Personnel Directory*, 1953, 1958, and 1961 edns.

164. NARA RG 396 Entry 1025 650 42/04/06–42/05/01, Box 3, Women's Activity Subject Files, "Religious Affairs Program Regional Offices," Draft for Mrs. Norton H. Pearl's speech to Seventh Day Adventists Conference, 8 April 1958.

165. FCDA 1956b: 2.

166. NARA RG 396 Entry 1025 650 42/04/06–42/05/01, Box 3, Women's Activity Subject Files, "Information Kit on the Church and Civil Defense," [1958].

167. Levine and Modell 1964: 161, 205–8.

168. NARA RG 396 Entry 1029 650 42/05/05, Box 3, Frederick D. Stanton, Chairman Resolutions Committee, "Resolutions. United States Civil Defense Council Fifth Annual Conference October 9–12, 1956 Atlanta, Georgia," 1956.

169. PRO HO 322/111, "Recruitment Publicity for the Civil Defence Corps and Auxiliary Fire Service in Northern Region. Civil Defence Week, 1956. Report of Conference held on Thursday, 17th May 1956, at . . . Newcastle upon Tyne." See also Wittner 1997, vol. 2: 50.

170. Canada Department of National Health and Welfare, Information Services Division, 1958.

171. US FCDA 1956b: 4.

172. NARA RG 396 Entry 1075, Box 2 of 2, Inter-Agency Committee Files, Manpower, OCDM, "Civil Defense Occupations," 20 July 1960. Versions of this go back to 1957.

173. Based on the *Attack Environment Manual*, cited in Zuckerman 1984: 119.

174. NARA RG 396 Entry 1015 650 41/33/05, Box 8 of 82, "OCDM Headquarters Central Files, 1959–60," Leo A. Hoegh, letter to Reverend Dean S. Collins (District Secretary, American Bible Society, Pasadena CA), 10 December 1959.

175. NARA RG 397 Entry 12 650 42/19/04, Box 5, Testimony of Herman Will, Jr. (General Board of Christian Social Concerns of the Methodist Church) before Subcommittee No. 3 of the House Armed Services Committee [Hebert Committee], 21 June 1963.

176. NAC RG 29 National Health and Welfare, Vol. 34, file 30-1-1, Edgar F. Bevis (Civil Defence Co-Ordinator for Ontario, Department of Planning and Development), letter to Dr. G. F. Davidson (Deputy Minister Department of National Health and Welfare, Ottawa), 26 June 1959.

177. DA, Canadian Commercial Corporation, "Memorandum of Understanding: U.S./Canada Mobilization production Planning Arrangements," signed by J. S. Glassford (Canadian Commercial Corporation) and Barry J. Shillito (Assistant Secretary of Defence for Installations and Logistics), October 1970.

178. PRO HO 322/221, "Civil Defence Industrial Advisory Committee. Future Policy on Industrial Civil Defence. Note by the HO," 17 June 1968; and "The Future of the Industrial Civil Service," 16 December 1965, CDA 175/3/7.

179. PRO MAF 85/175, Civil Defence in Industrial and Commercial Premises, 1951–55.

180. PRO HO 322/247, "Civil Defence in Industry," [ca. 1968].

181. PRO POWE 14/1173, Annual Statistical Return of Industrial Civil Defence, 31 October 1963; POWE 14/664, Ministry of Power, A. G. F. Farquhar (Central Electricity Authority, London), letter to A. C. Campbell (Electricity Division, Ministry of Fuel and Power), 25 November 1956; Henry Self (British Electricity Authority), letter to Sir Donald Fergusson (Ministry of Fuel and Power), 31 January 1952; and Sir Donald Fergusson, letter to Henry Self, 16 January 1952.

182. PRO POWE 14/477, "Civil Defence Evacuation Policy, Dispersal of the Administrative Elements of the [Electricity] Industry," note at beginning of file, 12 August 1957.

183. PRO COAL 74/850, National Coal Board, "Exercise 'Felstead'—East Midlands Division Timetable," [December 1962]; and "Civil Defence Autumn Exercise," 24 August 1962.

184. PRO AB 8/414, UK Atomic Energy Authority, Lt. Gen. E. N. Goddard (Regional Director for Civil Defence, Manchester), memo to the industrial working party, 24 February 1959.

185. Minnich 1960: 70–74.

186. New England Telephone and Telegraph Company 1964.

187. NARA RG 396 Entry 1063 650 42/13/01, Box 1, "Test Exercise Study Files," 1961.

188. Cited in Rose 2001: 118–19.

189. US OCDM 1961: 293.

190. See civil defense issues of *Industrial Maintenance and Plant Operation* 22, no.10 (October 1961), and *Industrial Security* 6, no.3 (July 1962). This extended to commercial films such as *Communications for Civil Defense*, sponsored by Bell Telephones of Canada in the early 1950s, produced in the United States and endorsed by the federal civil defense coordinator of Canada. The US FCDA's *Rehearsal for Disaster* (ca. 1956–57) calls for the trucking industry's support, and OCD's *The Day that Made a Difference* (1964) commemorates the work of port and overland transport industries in Oakland and New Orleans to help stock public shelters. OCD's *Memorandum to Industry* (1966) is the classic of this subgenre, with footage on Iron Mountain, New York (a deep shelter leasing 600,000 square feet of documents storage); IBM, Shell, and Standard Oil's corporate shelters; shut-down procedures at Jones and Laughlin's Steel plant; and decontamination protocols at a Chattahoochee, Georgia, textile mill.

191. Rose 2001: 119.

192. Dierst 1962: 31–33, 123.

193. P. Boyer 1985: 273–77; and Rose 2001: 124–26.

194. PRO HO 322/136, Town Clerk of Coventry, letter to HO Under Secretary of State, 7 April 1954.

195. PRO PREM 11/607, Prime Minister Winston Churchill's Personal Minute to the Home Secretary, Series no. M.96/54 (1 June 1954).

196. PRO PREM 11/607, Home Secretary D. Maxwell Fyfe's original typescript memo to the Prime Minister, 4 June 1954.

197. PRO HO 322/141, Command and Control: Exercises and Studies by Midland Civil Defence Region, 1957–1964," and clipping "Nature Marked Start of North Staffs. C.D. Test," [Stoke] *Evening Standard* 11 May 1959.

198. *Guardian* 9 April 1966; Walter 1963; and PRO HO 322/651 and 652, "Regional Government in an Emergency, Pamphlet published by 'Ipswich Anarchists' ('Spies for Peace') and Details of Public Demonstrations," 1966–67.

199. SPC WRL Series B, Box 8f, Conrad J. Lynn, David I. Shapiro, and Harris L. Present (representing law firm of Dickstein Shapiro & Friedman), "Memorandum to Provisional Committee," 1955: 14, 19; "Analysis of the American Civil Liberties Union, Answering Questions Raised RE: Arrest of Persons Refusing to Take Shelter During Civil Defense Drill, June 15, 1955," 1955; Catholic Workers, "Statement in Court," 1955; Provisional Defense Committee, "What Happened on June 15?," 1955; and War Resisters League, "Urgent Memo: Civil Defense Drill Protest Friday April 17 at 1:30 pm in City Hall Park (Broadway and Park Row)," 1955. See also "The Demonstrators' Statement," *WRL News* 73 (1955): 3; Bennett 2003: 207–16; Garrison 2006; Malina 1972: 82; and Malina 1984: 368–73.

200. "The Rights of Non-Conformity," 1955: 363. Italics in original.

201. SPC WRL Series B, Box 8f, Dorothy Day, Ralph DiGia, Robert Gilmore, and Kent Larrabee, letter to Hon. Averill Harriman (Governor of New York), 17 July 1956.

202. SPC WRL Series B, Box 8f, Civil Defense Protest Committee, "The Truth about Civil Defense," 1960; and Mary Sharmat for Civil Defense Protest Committee to Friends, October 1960.

203. SPC WRL Series B, Box 8f, War Resisters League, "Minutes of Meeting of Civil Defense Protest Committee," 13 October 1961.

204. Quoted in Garrison 1994: 211.

205. A. J. M. 1960: 3–5; Garrison 1994: 216; and Wittner 1997, vol. 2: 250.

206. SPC WRL Series B, Box 8f, "Brave Men Do Not Hide," 1961; and letter from David McReynolds and Mary Sharmat, 20 April 1961.

207. Garrison 1994: 218.

208. SPC WRL Series B, Box 14, Arnold B. Larson, memo to All Peace and Disarmament Organizations, 1962. I am grateful to Scott Bennett for elaboration on the 1959 "Act for Peace," in which convoys of cars circled the blast perimeter while protesters walked from ten suburban sites toward a rally near Times Square.

209. Peace Data Association 1982; Bolsover 1982: 62; D. Campbell 1982: 21–47; Crossley 1985: 94; and Poole 1989a: 33–35.

210. Shute 1957; filmed as *On the Beach*, 1959.

211. Wittner 1997, vol. 2: 58.

212. DDEPL, Cabinet Series, Box 14, 6 November 1959 (file 1).

213. DDEPL, Cabinet Series, Box 14, 6 November 1959; 11 December 1959; and Memorandum for Vice President 10 December 1959 re Cabinet meeting 11 December. The film's debut was 18 December 1959.

214. *The War Game*, 1966.

215. Welsh 1983: 33.

216. Tracey 1982: 38–54.

217. PRO HO 322/203, BBC Film *The War Game*: HO Assessment and Policy, Extract from Official Report, House of Commons, 23 June 1966.

218. PRO HO 322/203, BBC Film *The War Game*: HO Assessment and Policy, Extract from the Commandants' Conference held at Horseferry House, 17 May 1966.

219. PRO HO 322/203 CDS/280/FAL, "Note on viewing of the film *The War Game* at the Bristol Arts Centre on 2nd May, 1966."

220. PRO HO 322/203 CDS/280/FAL, [Opinion] 31 March 1966.

221. Peace Data Association 1982: n.p.

222. *The Day After*, 1983.

223. DA, W. B. Snarr, "Memorandum for the Hon. Yvon Pinard. Television Drama: 'The Day After,'" 17 November 1983.

224. Ibid.: 15 November 1983.

2. Rehearsals for Nuclear War

1. Lee 1990: 40–51.

2. Wells 1913: 99.

3. Perla 1990: 4.

4. Wilson 1968: 70.

5. Ibid.: 72.

6. Ghamari-Tabrizi 2005: 47. See also Hausrath 1971: 5–8; and Perla 1990: 23–33.

7. Perla 1990: 281. Even Perla acknowledges that command post exercises can be an exception to the rule with respect to mobilization (277). See also Dunnigan 1997; Miller and Duke 1981: 214–15; and Brewer and Shubik 1979: 10.

8. Arguably, other forms of disaster (landslides, hurricanes, industrial accidents, and floods) served as an empirical realm for testing and training in civil defense. The relevance is undeniable, and was explicitly called upon again and again. However, if these are rehearsals for civil defense exercises, it does not change the status of the civil defense exercises as rehearsals for nuclear war, or nuclear war's status as performance.

9. Hausrath 1971: 310–19.

10. For comparison, see Bloomfield 1982: 199–200; Graubard and Builder 1980: 3–4; and Perla 1990: 126.

11. When H-bombs proliferated, the enemy's physical presence in Canada, the United States, or the United Kingdom was not even postulated for civil defense planning purposes.

12. Ghamari-Tabrizi 2005: 173, 178.

13. Brewer and Shubik 1979: 8.

14. *The Atomic Bomb: Its Effects and How to Meet Them* 1952.

15. DA, EPC, [script] "Disaster Readiness Education. Concept of Emergency Operations (War)," 22.

16. A version of this map and its accouterments are in the Diefenbunker's collection.

17. Pearson and Shanks 2001: 23.

18. On the fate of wardens in the United States, see NARA RG 1025, Box 3, E.B. Lyman (Director, Industry Office, FCDA), memo "Staff Paper—Warden Service for Civil Defense," 27 January 1960.

19. PRO HO 322/191, Staff College Exercises and Studies: Control and Deployment, 1953. Arn-

prior's chief of instruction took part in this exercise, so the technique was certainly known in Canada at this early date.

20. PRO HO 322/185, Exercises "Review" and "Zeta": Public Control, Establishing Zonal Boundaries, Clearance of Z-zones, 1954–57.

21. PRO HO 322/141, Command and Control: Exercises and Studies by Midland Civil Defence Region, 1957–64, "Exercise 'Clearsite,'" October 1960.

22. Industrial College of the Armed Forces 1954: 1–4.

23. Ghamari-Tabrizi 2005: 51–54.

24. Perla 1990: 109–10, 275–76; and Wilson 1968: 55–56.

25. Hausrath 1971: 86–90, 203; and Kraake, Helling, and Huber 1993: 135.

26. Mandel 1985: 487.

27. Ghamari-Tabrizi 2005: 164–65.

28. Mandel 1985: 488.

29. Hausrath 1971: 10.

30. Brewer and Shubik 1979: 6; Perla 1990: 9; Seliger and Simoneau 1986: 3, 180; Wilson 1968: 58–59; and Hausrath 1971: 18.

31. Raser 1969: 15–19 cited in Greenblat 1981: 41–42.

32. Cited in Richardson 1996: 3.

33. R. D. Boyer 1979: xvi.

34. States 1996: 19.

35. Roach 1993: 58–59.

36. Ubersfeld 1999: 100.

37. Ibid.: 24, 114–15.

38. Ibid.: 25–26; and Shoef 2004: 360.

39. McAuley 1999: 274.

40. NARA RG 396 Entry 1063 650 42/13/01, John Pritchard, "Narrative Report of Monitor Operation Alert 1960 at Detroit Office of Civil Defense," 25 May 1960.

41. NARA RG 396 Entry 1017 650 42/03/07, Box 1, Maryland Civil Defense Agency, "Report Operation Alert 1961," 10.

42. NARA RG 396 050 42/0505, Box 3, Memo to Heads of Executive Departments and Agencies on Public Information for Operation Alert 1957, 15 April 1957: 2.

43. Contrast Hare and Blumberg 1988: 47.

44. See note 22 to chapter 8.

45. Perla 1990: 8.

46. Izzo 1997: 12; Blau 1990: 217; and Murray 1997: 110. The aestheticization of performance, no matter how "realistic," utilizes elements Erving Goffman identifies as the theatrical frame: artificial activity strictly bounded within a designated space; a pretense among actors to selectively ignore, as characters, the spatial "exposure" of the stage; angular "cheating" to aid the audience's ability to see actors; selective and successive giving of focus; taking turns speaking and hearing each other out; dialogic exposition; and elevated tone and elocutionary manner or, alternately, mundane conversation masking matters of great importance. Goffman 1974: 139–44.

47. Guetzkow 1967: 203.

48. PRO HO 322/194, Regional Exercises and Studies: North Eastern Region: Emergency Feeding, 1952–1953, "Rotherham/Sheffield Emergency Feeding Study, 14–15 April 1953."

49. For example, see how Phillip Pullman's 1,300-page trilogy was compressed into six hours of stage time in Butler 2003: 72–73.

50. NARA RG 396 #1029 Box 6, Robert L. Treanor, memo to Director of Test Office, "Operational Alert 1959," 15 May 1959.

51. PRO HO 322/193, Staff College Exercises and Studies: Central Exercise Staff Standard Exercises, "Exercise 'Warpost,'" 1965.

52. NAC RG 24 National Defence, Acc. 1983–84/215, Box 250, file C-2001-91/T18, pt. 1, R. B. Curry (EMO Director), letter to Major-General A. E. Wrinch (DND), 4 August 1960.

53. DA, EPC, *Emergency Government Headquarters Operational Procedures Planning Guide*, EPC 7/78, 1978 edn.: 29–30. This advice is repeated in EPC, [DRAFT] *Planning Guide for Emergency Government Headquarters. EPC Manual #7,* 1 November 1989.

54. Compare McAuley 1999: 18–25.

55. Ubersfeld 1999: 128–38.

56. Kirby 1965: 13–14.

57. DDEPL, Cabinet Series Box 5 A75–22, Cabinet Meeting Minutes, 10 June 1955: 4.

58. Ricoeur, vol. 1, 1984: 53, 65.

59. Oakes 1994: 85.

60. Freytag 1968: 114–40.

61. Lawson 1960: 245.

62. Turner 1981: 61–82.

63. DA, Task Force on War Planning and Concepts of Operations, *Wartime Public Protection in the 1980s* (Unpublished: Canada, 1985), fig. 1; and de Kadt 1964: 97–99.

64. US DCPA, *Operations for Population,* 1973.

65. Chenault and Davis 1975b: 7.

66. NAC RG 24 National Defence, Series C-1, Acc. 1983–84/215, Box 252, file S-2001-91/T21, pt. 2, "Exercise TOCSIN 63 Preparation of Incidents," 27 August 1963.

67. DA, Task Force on War Planning 1985.

68. Haaland 1968: 36–38.

69. DA, "Exercise Fifth Key General Reading Material," 16 November 1989: Appendix C.

70. HWLC Chicago Civil Defense Corps, *Information Bulletins,* 23 February 1956.

71. McKenzie 2001; Schechner 1986; Schechner 2002; Goffman 1959; and Dent 2004: 109–34.

72. J. Brown 1988: 68–90; Garrison 1994: 201–26; Mechling and Mechling 1991: 105–33; and Oakes 1994.

73. Diamond 1996: 1. See also Phelan 1993; and McKenzie 2001.

74. Ricoeur, vol. 1, 1984: 53.

75. Ghamari-Tabrizi 2005: 84.

76. Schechner 1982: 73.

77. Robert Burns, "To a Mouse," 1785 in Henley and Henderson 1896, vol. 1: 116–17.

78. Schechner 1982: 72, 39, 66.

79. Gebauer and Wulf 1995: 195–96, 300–303. See also Procyshyn n.d.

80. Plato 1921: 255–6; and Aristotle 1966: 19–20 (987b).

81. Breaking down the rehearsal-to-performance threshold has occupied aspects of the late-twentieth-century avant-garde, but such efforts attest to the idea's entrenchment. See Wolford 1996.

82. Schechner 2002: 41–42.

83. McKenzie 2001: 249.

84. Austin 1962: 22. For a commentary on this, see Jackson 2004: 182.

85. States 1996: 25.

86. "Exercise Britannia" in 1949 posited the pre-attack evacuation of 1,100,000 people along the Thames from Fulham to Barking, in a strip fifteen miles long and up to 3.5 miles wide, leaving only 100,000 essential workers to operate docks, railways, utilities, central and local government, and policing functions. Nothing is known about how this exercise was conducted, and the records may be confused with "Medical Britannia" which was a training exercise for 500 military and civilian doctors in radiological defense. PRO HO 357/9 Pt. I, Working Party on Civilian Morale, letter from S. G. Ransford, Royal Naval Medical School, [ca. January 1950]. See also PRO HO 357/14, Ministry of Health. Working Party on Evacuation and Care of the Homeless, 1948–1951, memo of meeting 8 June 1949. "Operation Foil," held 3 July 1949, was concerned with spotting and reporting bomber traffic over Cambridge and East Anglia, apparently involving field operations but nothing more is known about its conduct. PRO HO 322/130, Warning System Exercises "Foil," 1949.

87. Chicago Civil Defense Corps 1951: 8.

88. HWLC Chicago Civil Defense Corps, *Information Bulletins*, 1 February 1953; *Chicago Alert*: 237.

89. US Public Law 920, Federal Civil Defense Act (1950).

90. For example, the Commonwealth Edison [Electric] Company donated space for the civil defense headquarters from 1950 through 1956. HWLC Chicago Civil Defense Corps, *Information Bulletins*, 15 February 1957.

91. There had been earlier exercises in Seattle and Washington, D.C., but the Chicago event was considerably more elaborate, involving a large area and more than one state, but not an area large enough to be self-sufficient, so mutual aid pacts were formed with counties beyond the Chicago Metropolitan Area (*Chicago Alert*: 237). See also NLM MS.C 278 Warren Palmer Dearing Collection, Box 4, W. Palmer Dearing, "Personal Memo of Telephone Call from Mr. Eric Biddle of National Security Resources Board," 1950.

92. *Chicago Alert*: 10–11. Planning for this is detailed in NLM MS.C 278 Warren Palmer Dearing Collection, Box 5, National Security Resources Board, "Civil Defense Planning. An Hypothetical Narrative (September 18, 195_) for Chicago, Illinois," 1950; and Dr. H. N. Bundeson et al., "Chicago Civil Defense Organization Report of the Division of Emergency Medical Services, Public Health and Welfare," 1950.

93. Reader's theater makes less use of stage conventions than chamber theater, and so is the preferred term for this playlet: see Bacon 1966: 319. The British utilized playlets as early as 1953, in "Damage Control," to dramatize "The Problems in a Warden's Post Area" along with a staff discussion, followed by a syndicate, part of a Port of London Authority Exercise that gamed the devastation of a GZ at the outlet of Bow Creek, the fifth atomic hit on London within a week (PRO HO 322/189, Staff College Exercises and Studies: Damage Control, 1953; and PRO HO 322/196, Regional Exercises and Studies: London Region: Effects of Nuclear Explosion Over River Lea on Port of London, 1953–1954). It was also used for "Torquemada" and "Second Lap" (both 1959), and "Phoenix Five" in 1967 (PRO HO 322/187, Staff College Exercises and Studies: Torquemada: Deployment of Police and

Fire Service Mobile Columns After Nuclear Attack, 1958–1959; PRO HO 322/209, Regional Civil Defence Exercises and Studies: Reports, 1963; and PRO HO 322/35, Phoenix Five Hydrogen Bomb Exercise, 1967).

94. *Chicago Alert*: 155.
95. Ibid.: 154–59.
96. Sauter 2000: 98.
97. Goffman 1974: 59–60.
98. Schechner 1982: 76. See also McAuley 1999: 40.
99. Kirby 1965: 17.
100. BCL B20585, South Western Regional Office, HO (CD Department), "Report on Exercise 'Medusa'—Part I," July 1951: 1.
101. Ibid.: 14.
102. " 'Medusa' Men Toiled in Sleet Storm," 1951: 4.
103. BCL B20585, South Western Regional Office, HO (CD Department), "Civilian Report on Exercise 'Medusa'—Part II," May 1951: 26.
104. " 'Medusa Men,' " 4.
105. "Civilian Report on Exercise 'Medusa'—Part II," 26–27.
106. Ibid.: 27.
107. NAC RG 24 DND Series C-1, Acc. 1983–84/215, Box 250, file 2001-91/T17 pt. 2, EMO, "Exercise TOCSIN Sequence of Events," 1960.
108. DA, P.E.I. Scrapbook, unattributed clipping, "Civil Defence Emergency Exercise is Carried Out," 4 May 1960.
109. Schechner 1993: 259.
110. Schechner 1986: 35–116.
111. Schechner 2002: 106–8.
112. Blau 1990: 163–64.
113. Ibid.: 237.
114. Compare Brooks, Bahn, and Okey 1967: 396.
115. Barba 2000: 60.
116. "In the so-called 'high culture' of complex societies, liminoid is not only removed from a *rite de passage* context, it is also 'individualized.' The solitary artist *creates* the liminoid phenomena, the collectivity *experiences* collective liminal symbols. This does not mean that the maker of liminoid symbols, ideas, images, etc., does so *ex nihilo*; it only means that he is privileged to make free with his social heritage in a way impossible to members of culture in which the liminal is to a large extent the sacrosanct" (Turner 1981: 52). See also Denzin 2003: 4.
117. Blau 1990: 237; Graham-White 1976: 322–23; and B. Kershaw 1992: 16.
118. Callon and Latour 1981: 286, cited in Boyne 2001: 29.
119. Sismondo 2004: 72.
120. Law 1999: 7–8.
121. Ibid.: 5.
122. Ghamari-Tabrizi 2005: 162, 164.
123. Bloomfield and Gearin 1973: 1027.
124. Konijn 2000.

125. Della Pollock, lecture delivered at Northwestern University, 20 October 2000.

126. Described in Berger 1975: 14.

127. Hare and Blumberg 1988: 49.

3. The Psychology of Vulnerability

1. Hersey 1946.

2. Cameron 1950: 587.

3. Grossman 2001: 40, 83.

4. J. Brown 1988: 80.

5. Grossman 2001: 81.

6. US FCDA 1952b; also the FCDA film *Duck and Cover*, 1952.

7. Maryland Department of Education 1964: 17–18.

8. Vanderbilt 2002: 96–127.

9. There were exceptions: Louise Fox recalls participating in duck and cover drills in her school, a suburb of Toronto, during the Cuban Missile Crisis. Interview with the author 2004.

10. George S. Stevenson, quoted in National Recreation Association 1951: 8.

11. National Recreation Association 1951: 8.

12. Janis 1949: 35.

13. DDEPL, White House Office, Cabinet Secretary, Box 22, CI-55, "Human Behavior in Disaster," Cabinet paper, 22 April 1958: 9.

14. American Psychiatric Association 1956: 16.

15. Georgia Department of Public Defense 1952: 20–27.

16. Juchem 1953: 15. See also US FCDA 1952c.

17. Oregon Civil Defense Agency 1952: 13–39.

18. Louisiana Civil Defense Agency 1953: 33–35.

19. North Carolina Department of Public Instruction 1953: 13.

20. Michigan Office of Civil Defense 1955: 11–12.

21. US FCDA 1952c: 27.

22. Klonglan, Beal, and Bohlen 1964: 50–64.

23. American Council on Education 1954: 3.

24. Maryland Department of Education 1964: 28.

25. Oregon Civil Defense Agency 1958; and Lamers 1959.

26. Kentucky Department of Military Affairs 1964: 29–30, 37–39.

27. William E. Wilson, quoted in Indiana Department of Public Instruction 1960: iii.

28. Christiansen and Wickham 1961: 34–35.

29. J. Brown 1988: 79.

30. American Association of School Administrators 1966: 26.

31. Cited in M. J. Carey 1982: 116.

32. National Education Association 1966: 33–40, 6–7, 20.

33. Greenberg, Dominick, and Razinsky 1968: 2.

34. Rockett 1964: 58.

35. DDEPL, Administration Series, Box 14, A75–22, Val Peterson (FCDA), memo to the Presi-

dent, 2 August 1956, proposing members of the committee to investigate human behavior in disaster. See also Oakes 1995: 275–96; and Oakes 1994: 33–77.

36. Janis 1951. The reports on which this is based are still classified.

37. Cameron 1950: 588.

38. Janis 1949: 3.

39. Tuthill and Ludden 1961; and J. Brown 1988: 68.

40. Address by Dreyfuss 1951: 15.

41. American Psychiatric Association 1952.

42. Glass 1957: 266–68.

43. American Psychiatric Association 1954.

44. Erickson et al. 1953: 18. See also V. Peterson 1953. (This article was republished as a booklet and is preserved in DDEPL Civil Defense Campaign 1953 (1) General, Box 3, FCDA PA #96).

45. These are classic fear responses. A survey of over six thousand U.S. Pacific War combat veterans in 1944 showed that 52 percent experienced trembling, 47 percent felt nauseous, 18 percent vomited, and 11 percent lost control of their bowels. Stouffer et al. 1949: 201.

46. American Psychiatric Association 1956: 8–10. See also NLM MS.C 278, Warren Palmer Dearing Collection, Box 5, *Disaster Fatigue: the Cause and Treatment of Psychological Disorders in Civil Disasters*, 1955.

47. American Psychiatric Association 1956: 20–21.

48. J. Thompson 1985: 19.

49. Ibid.: 20; and Erikson 1976: 302.

50. J. Thompson 1985: 42.

51. Form and Loomis et al. 1956: 181.

52. Quarantelli and Dynes 1977: 23–49.

53. Fritz and Matthewson 1957: 8. A decade later, psychologists understood that different panic responses occur for people directly in contact with a disaster agent than for those at greater distance from a disaster, though the effect had received little study. Disaster Research Group 1962: 18–19.

54. Grebler 1956: 463–69, quoted in Fritz and Matthewson 1957: 33.

55. Rockett 1964, vol. 4: 64–65.

56. Fritz and Williams 1957: 46.

57. The disaster at Halifax was the largest human-made explosion until the bombing of Hiroshima in 1945. On 6 December 1917, a ship laden with munitions collided with another ship at the narrows leading into the harbor. Two square kilometers of Halifax were flattened; the damage was exacerbated first by a tsunami, then by fire, and finally by a blizzard that blew in later that day. More than two thousand people died.

58. Tyhurst 1957: 387–88.

59. The term "cornucopia" in this context was coined by Fritz 1961: 678, cited in Rockett 1964, vol. 4: 65–66.

60. Tyhurst 1957: 388.

61. National Opinion Research Center 1954: 502, cited in Rockett 1964, vol. 4: 25.

62. "Civil Defence," January 1963: 13, cited in Rockett 1964, vol. 4: 26; and Forman 1963: 285–90.

63. Tyhurst 1957: 389.

64. Danzig, Thayer, and Galante 1958: 1.

65. Ibid.: 26, 49.

66. Ibid.: 8–11.

67. Ibid.: 55.

68. This is Irving Janis's "sensitization hypothesis." See Baker and Chapman 1962, cited in Rockett 1964, vol. 4: 24.

69. McDermott 1962: 5.

70. Waskow and Newman 1962: 103–4.

71. Herman Kahn, "A Rational Basis for Decision Making on Civil Defense Policy," 23–51, taken from testimony before Subcommittee on Government Operations, House of Representatives, U.S. Congress, 1961. Testimony 7 and 9 August 1961, quoted in Baker and Cottrell 1962: 49.

72. Fogleman and Parenton 1959: 131.

73. Grinspoon 1963: 518, 519.

74. Waskow and Newman 1962: 91.

75. Grinspoon 1963: 519.

76. Rockett 1964, vol. 4: 72–73.

77. Janis 1962: 55–63.

78. DDEPL, Cabinet Series Box 7, "Notes on the Expanded Cabinet Meeting held from 2:30 to 3:45 P.M. on Wednesday, July 25, 1956."

79. Lerner 1965: 225–31.

80. "The Moscow-Peking Conflict: Differing National Interests Come to the Fore," 1963: 4.

81. Allnutt 1971.

82. American Psychiatric Association 1968: 133.

83. Keiser 1968: 22–23.

84. James Thompson 1985: 15.

85. American Psychiatric Association 1980: 236–37. See also Schnun 1991: 1–8. This is almost identical to the list of symptoms observed in professional first responders: see Canada EPC 1983.

86. American Psychiatric Association 1980: 236.

87. Rogers and Nehnevajsa 1984: 143, 148.

88. Ibid.: 174.

89. Saigh and Bremner 1999: 6–11. Patients who do not develop PTSD may still be incapacitated by psychosocial and environmental problems under the *DSM-IV*'s multiaxial assessment criteria of Axis 4.

90. Jeffrey Klugman testifying before FEMA, "Oversight: Will US Nuclear Attack Evacuation Plans Work?" 97th Congress, 2nd session, 22 April 1982: 51; quoted in L. Clarke 1999: 144; emphasis added.

91. L. Clarke 1999: 40.

4. Sheltering

1. Geerhart 2001.

2. UK Departments of State and Official Bodies, HO, *Civil Defence Handbook no. 10*, 1963.

3. UK HO, *York Experiment*, 1965: 3–4.

4. "Lethargy Troubled," 1965: 16.

5. UK HO, *York Experiment*, 1965: 8–9.

6. "The Newbridge Experiment," 1981: 18–19.

7. Holmström 1976: 123–41; and "One Week After," 1984: 4–5.

8. US FCDA 1957c: 8–9.

9. DDEPL, J. S. Bragdon, Facilities Survey-Education, Box 29, Captain Tily, memo to General Bragdon reviewing a RAND Report, 14 August 1958.

10. Eastman 1965: xi–xii.

11. Interview with Ken Farrell, 18 August 2000.

12. DDEPL, Eisenhower Diary Series, Box 33, Toner Notes May 1958 (2), "Special Legislative Note," 9 May 1958: 3.

13. DDEPL, J. S. Bragdon, Facilities Survey-Education, Box 29, memo from the Director of the Engineering Office to the Assistant Administrator of the Technical Advisory Services, 12 April 1954.

14. DDEPL, J. S. Bragdon, Facilities Survey-Education, Box 29, Captain Tily, memo to General Bragdon on House Subcommittee hearings on atomic shelter tests, 15 August 1958.

15. US FCDA and National Academy of Sciences 1958: 24–25.

16. Ibid.: 24.

17. Ibid.: 33.

18. Gross and Collins n.d., cited in Miller 1960: 53.

19. Biderman 1959: 74. See also Rayner 1960: Appendix.

20. D. Miller 1960: 51–57.

21. Committee on Behavioral Research 1962: 19.

22. Hanifan 1963: 2–3.

23. J. W. Altman 1960: 157–66.

24. Garrett 1976b: 136; and Hanifan 1963: 213.

25. PRO HO 322/340, Minerva 65 Study: Reports, 1965.

26. Etter, Pond, Schultze, and Strope 1960.

27. Strope, Henderson, and Rainey 1960.

28. Researchers concluded that since the lavatory was in use only a third of the time, one toilet would have served as well for seventy occupants. Altman et al. 1960: 49.

29. Ibid.: 17.

30. Ibid.: 34.

31. District of Columbia Office of Civil Defense 1960s.

32. Altman et al. 1960: 63.

33. Ibid.: 37.

34. Garrett 1976b: 139.

35. Altman et al. 1960: 44.

36. Hanifan 1963: 199.

37. Garrett 1976b: 139.

38. Altman et al. 1960: 75.

39. Opinion Research Corporation 1961: 36.

40. Ibid.: 63–64.

41. DOD OCD 1961b. See also McEnaney 2000: 68–9; and Rose 2001: 144–45.

42. Vernon 1959: 12, 20.

43. Ibid.: 28–29.

44. Oakes 1994: 127.

45. Committee on Behavioral Research 1962: 10–11.

46. Hanifan 1963: 265–66.

47. Ibid.: xx.

48. Ibid.: 248.

49. Ibid.: 252.

50. Ibid.:189.

51. Etter et al. 1962: 39.

52. Heiskell 1963.

53. Fairchild and Gonzalez 1963.

54. Flanigan 1964.

55. Garrett 1976b: 140. See also Hammes et al. 1963.

56. NARA RG 397 #36, Box 3, "Fact Sheet. University of Georgia to Conduct Fallout Shelter Occupancy Test for 300 Persons July 31–August 2," 27 July 1964.

57. NARA RG 396 Entry 1048 650 42/08/01, Box 1 of 2, "Transportation Survey Records," Clipping, "649 at Tribune Reach Shelter in 7 Minutes: Fifth Full Scale Test Held in Tower" *Chicago Daily Tribune* 16 June 1955.

58. Little, Pattak, and Schroeder 1998: 24.

59. Wolfenbarger 1963: 5.

60. Walton 1994: 46–58.

61. Interview with Donald Hurt conducted by Melissa Hurt, 21 April 2003; additional correspondence between the author and Donald Hurt, 23 April 2003.

62. "Fallout Shelters," 1961: 95–108.

63. Ibid.

64. Waskow and Newman 1962: 30.

65. Ibid.: 45.

66. Walton 1994: 54.

67. Ibid.: 54.

68. Winkler 1984: 16–22. Winkler cites FCDA records in the Truman Library: Box 19, John A. De Chant to Governor Caldwell (April 4, 1952); Box 32, Howard R. H. Johnson to Bess Landfear (April 23, 1951); and Box 1527 "Survival under Atomic Attack."

69. Marzani et al. 1962: 19, 26.

70. "Drive for Mass Shelters," 1962: 34–43; and Fromm, Kahn, and Maccoby 1962: 1–23.

71. Heartney 2002: 47.

72. Ward 2001: 114–30.

73. Heartney 2002: 66–70.

74. Jones 2005: 104, 101; see also Baraibar 1999.

75. Carr 2002: 57; and Westcott 2003: 129–36.

76. Fisher 1997: 28–33. There is a vast range of relevant art pieces, though I would caution that neither repetition nor minimalism per se are in themselves characteristics pertinent to the comparison.

77. Schechner 1998: 199.

78. Heartney 2002: 47. He survived after losing consciousness and being taken to the hospital but succeeded in committing suicide six months later.

79. Klein 2002: 74–81.

80. Compare Westlake 2002: 29–38.

81. Wilkie 2002: 248.

5. Get Out of Town!

1. By 1956, Calgary, St. John's, and Halifax had conducted evacuation tests, along with a few smaller communities. NAC RG 29, National Health and Welfare, Vol. 34, file 30-1-1, Memo Prepared for the Dominion-Provincial Conference, October 6–7: 4.

2. Alberta Civil Defence 1955; Alberta Civil Defence 1950s; and Salopek 1989: 75–88. See also *Operation Lifesaver*, 1956.

3. Alberta Civil Defence 1955: 12.

4. FCDA and Department of Commerce 1956.

5. Chaput and Groves 1956: 6.

6. Ibid.: 29.

7. This was made public in 1959. DA, Office of the Prime Minister, "Policy Concerning Evacuation and Shelter for Civil Defence Purposes as announced by Right Hon. J. G. Diefenbaker Prime Minister on November 20, 1959." See also NARA RG 396 Entry #1013 650 41/32/07, Box 1 of 2, "FCDA-OCDM Special Liaison Files of L.C. Franklin [Canada-US Joint Committee]," Barent F. Landstreet (Director of Survival Projects Office), memo to Executive Assistant Administrator, 17 July 1957.

8. DA, J. F. Wallace, "Status of C.D. Program in Canada [Memo to all instructors at the Civil Defence College]," 1959.

9. NAC RG 29, National Health and Welfare, Vol. 34, file 30-1-1, Department of National Health and Welfare Civil Defence, "Memo Prepared for the Dominion-Provincial Conference October 6–7," 1959.

10. NARA RG 396 Entry #1013 650 41/32/07, Box 1 of 2, "FCDA-OCDM Special Liaison Files of L. C. Franklin [Canada-US Joint Committee]," Dr. K. C. Charron (Director Civil Defence Health Services [Canada]), letter to Dr. John M. Whitney (Director of Health Office, Battle Creek) 5 November 1956. See also NAC RG 29, National Health and Welfare, Vol. 34, file 30-1-1, Civil Defence, Memo Prepared for the Dominion-Provincial Conference, 6–7 October 1959.

11. NAC RG 24 DND, Series C-1, Acc. 1983–84/215, Box 252, File S-2001-91/T19 pt. 1, DND Army, "Report Exercise TOCSIN B 1961," Charlottetown P.E.I.

12. See, for example, NAC RG 24 DND, Series C-1, Acc. 1983–84/215, Box 250, file 2001-91/T17 pt. 4, [Ontario Messages sent in TOCSIN 60] 1960.

13. DA, EMO, *Voluntary Dispersal Routes From the Metropolitan Toronto Area to Destinations in the Province of Ontario*, 1962: 1.

14. Ibid.: 10, 29; and DA, EMO, "Voluntary Evacuation Routes for Ottawa Carleton Eastview," n.d.

15. Republic of Ireland National Archives, NAI 341/89 Department of Foreign Affairs, R.H.S. Crossman quoted in "Extracts from Minute to Dr. Rynne from Mr. Seán Ó Héideáin Re-

garding Evacuation Arrangements as Part of Civil Defence Programme in Great Britain," 1954: 2.

16. PRO DEFE 7/722 MOD, Official Committee on Civil Defence, Evacuation and Care of the Homeless, Copy of a Minute (Ref. UKLF/14) from Secretary (Commanders-in-Chief Committee) to Secretary (Chiefs of Staff Committee), 14 January 1953.

17. PRO DEFE 7/722 MOD, Official Committee on Civil Defence, Evacuation and Care of the Homeless, A. J. Newling, memo to Secretary, 18 December 1952.

18. PRO DEFE 7/722 MOD, Official Committee on Civil Defence, Evacuation and Care of the Homeless, First Draft, "Civil Defence Joint Planning Staff. Care of the Homeless in Phase III Conditions," memo by the Civil Defence Joint Planning Staff [1951].

19. PRO DEFE 13/45 MOD, Memo to the Prime Minister, "The Defence Implications of Fall-Out from a Hydrogen Bomb," (D.[55] 17 and 18), 21 April 1955. Emphasis in original.

20. PRO HO 322/166, HO, *Inter-Departmental Committee on Shelter Against Fall-Out.* "Assistance to the Public in Self-Protection Against Fall-out," Drafts 21 October and 9 December 1964.

21. PRO HO 322/185, HO Regional Civil Defence Exercises and Studies, "Exercises 'Review' and 'Zeta': Public Control, Establishing Zonal Boundaries, Clearance of Z-Zones," 1954–1957.

22. PRO HO 322/141, HO Regional Civil Defence Exercises and Studies, "Command and Control: Exercises and Studies by Midland Civil Defence Region," 1957–64.

23. PRO HO 322/141, HO Regional Civil Defence Exercises and Studies: Reports, "Command and Control: Exercises and Studies by Midland Civil Defence Region," 1957–64.

24. Ibid.

25. PRO HO 322/193, HO Regional Civil Defence Exercises and Studies, Staff College Exercises and Studies: Central Exercise Standard Exercises, 1958–66.

26. PRO HO 322/193, HO Regional Civil Defence Exercises and Studies, Staff College Exercises and Studies: Central Exercise Staff (CES): Coordination and Administration of Central Government and Regional Exercises, 1958–67.

27. PRO HO 322/209, HO Regional Civil Defence Exercises and Studies: Reports, Report, Exercise "Bluebell," 8 April 1962. See also East Sussex Record Office, DH/B 51/6, Hastings County Borough Council's Civil Defence Committee, minutes of meeting 25 January 1962.

28. PRO HO 322/209, HO Regional Civil Defence Exercises and Studies, Reports, 1963.

29. *The Journey*, 1983–85.

30. Smith and Associates 1954.

31. W. M. Brown 1963: V-C-9.

32. Livingston, Klass, and Rohrer 1954: 2.

33. Ibid.: 3, 5.

34. Ibid., Participant Observer J: 4.

35. Ibid., Participant Observer B: 5. See also McEnaney 2000: 138–41.

36. Livingston, Klass, and Rohrer 1954: 8.

37. Ibid., Participant Observer W: 1–2.

38. Ibid.: 3.

39. Ibid., Participant Observer D: 9.

40. Ibid.: 8.

41. McEnaney 2000:150.

42. Livingston, Klass, and Rohrer 1954, Participant Observer W: 12.

43. Ibid., Participant Observer J: 3.

44. Ibid.: 1.

45. Ibid.: 2.

46. Livingston, Klass, and Rohrer 1954: 11.

47. Danzig and Siegel 1955: 3.

48. NARA RG 396 Entry 1048 650 42/08/01, Box 1 of 2, "Transportation Survey Records, 1955–58," 1955.

49. Bentz et al. 1956: 41.

50. Winkler 1984: 18.

51. Beres 1983: 9; and Henderson and Strope 1978.

52. Garrett 1976a: 137.

53. Plans for several expedient shelter designs (car-over-trench, tilt-up doors and earth, above-ground door-covered shelter, log-covered trench shelter, above-ground ridge-pole, door-covered trench shelter, and the crib-walled shelter above ground) are included in US DCPA and in US DOD, *Preparing Crisis Relocation Planning*, 1977.

54. Quoted in Rose 2001: 218.

55. For example, *Journal of Civil Defense, Survive*, and *Survival Tomorrow* from the United States; *British Civil Defence News, Practical Civil Defence*, and *Protect and Survive Monthly* from the United Kingdom; and *Lifeline* from Canada.

56. DA, R. D. McCann, letter to David Peters (Co-ordinator of Operations EPC), 24 July 1985.

57. Hoffman 1959: 1151, 1153.

58. Dyer and Dyer 1962.

59. Ibid.: 96.

60. Ibid.: 74–78.

61. Ibid.: 101.

62. DDEPL, Cabinet Series, Box 2, 1 May 1953.

6. Communications

1. Janis 1949: 38.

2. This was not an isolated incident. During OPAL 58, two State Emergency Information staff broadcast loudspeaker warnings of impending fallout from a private plane over Readfield, Maine, NARA RG 396 Entry 1029 650 42/05/05, Box 4, "State and Local Participation in OPAL 58. Presentation to the NASTD Conference, Colorado Springs, November 10, 1958," DRAFT, 3 November 1958: 4.

3. PRO HO 322/185 Exercises *"Review" and "Zeta": Public Control, Establishing Zonal Boundaries, Clearance of Z-Zones*, 1954–57.

4. DDEPL, White House Central Files, Official File 133-B-1 Air Raid Shelters, Box 658, 133-B-3, Conference of National Information Media Executives (Proposed), Val Peterson, memo to Sherman Adams, 28 April 1953.

5. Krajnc 2000: 25. Emphasis added.

6. Tyhurst 1957: 390.

7. Transistor radios were first marketed in the United States in 1954 (the Regency TR1); by 1959, half of the 10 million U.S. radios made annually were transistors. With external aerials, they could be used in most basements and buildings with frames of steel or reinforced concrete. PRO HO 322/336, Working Party on Broadcasting Fall-Out Information: Meetings and Interim Report, 1964–65.

8. Such techniques were used by each side in World War II. A missile's homing instruments could be adjusted to guide it down the path of a broadcast toward a radio transmitter. The only effective countermeasure was to cease broadcasting altogether or not differentiate broadcast frequencies. NARA RG 396 Entry #1013 650 41/32/07, Box 1, "FCDA-OCDM Special Liaison Files of L. C. Frankling [Canada-US Joint Committee], Meeting 7–8 January 1953."

9. US DOD OCD 1971: 18; and NARA RG 397 Entry #39 650 42/26/06–07, Box 1, JRCC D/34–65, "Report on Working Group on Emergency Public Information," 1965.

10. "Present plans provide for the rapid dissemination of attack and fall-out warnings to all centres of population down to the smallest villages, and that isolated communities outside audible range of warning device will be able to receive *attack* warning messages broadcast by the B.B.C. Consideration is being given to the possibility of broadcasting *fall-out* warnings by the B.B.C. which would cover isolated communities, but many practical difficulties have yet to be overcome." PRO HO 322/192, Staff College Exercises and Studies, Central Exercise Staff (CES): Coordination and Administration of Central Government and Regional Exercises, "Central Exercise Staff Bulletin January 1963."

11. DA, EPC, *Wartime Public Protection in the 1980s. Final Report of the Task Force on War Planning and Concepts of Operations*, 1985; see also "Public Protection Measures," 1991.

12. DA, F. P. Johnson (Director of Special Projects Canadian Broadcasting Corporation), letter to J. F. Wallace (Director National Civil Emergency Measure Program), 1 July 1969.

13. DA, "The Evolution of the Civil Situation Monitoring and Briefing Capability at the CEGHQ, Canadian Forces Stations Carp (the Diefenbunker) from 1961 to 1992," 1992; and "Readiness Status Summary [RGHQ Nanaimo]," 1988.

14. PRO HO 322/336, Working Party on Broadcasting Fall-Out Information: Meetings and Interim Report, "Interim Report for Period To D+5," February 1965.

15. PRO HO 322/336, "Working Party on Broadcasting of Fall-out Information. Exercise CIVLOG Attack Pattern: Immediate Effects upon Regional Broadcasting. Paper by A.1 Division," July 1964.

16. PRO HO 322/351, Phoenix Five Hydrogen Bomb Exercise, 1967.

17. NARA RG 396 Entry 1029 650 42/05/05, Box 2, Brig. Gen. Don E. Carleton, "A Report of Participation by the City of Milwaukee in the National Civil Defense Test Exercise of June 15–16, Operation Alert 1955," 1955: 6.

18. Oakes 1994: 88–89.

19. NARA RG 396 Entry 1029 650 42/05/05, Box 2, FCDA Emergency Control Division, Emergency Operations Office, "Intra-Agency Report on Operation Alert 195," 12 September 1956: 29–30.

20. NAC RG 24 DND, Series C-1, Acc. 1983–84/215, Box 252, Files S-2001–91/T19 pt. 1, CBC, "Radio Script Exercise TOCSIN B 1961 7:00–8:30PM EST November 13th, 1961. All Canadian Stations," Executive Producer Thom Benson, Producer Norman McBain. It is un-

clear why Byng Whitteker was chosen for this task: he was known mainly for hosting jazz broadcasts, so perhaps the fact that his voice was not associated with news programming was a precaution against the public making erroneous conclusions about the authenticity of the attack.

21. NARA RG 396 Entry 1029 650 42/05/05, Box 2.

22. NARA RG 396 Entry 1029 650 42/05/05, Box 6; and RG 396 Entry 1029 650 42/05/05, Box 2. See also US OCDM, Executive Office of the President 1960: 12.

23. D. Campbell 1982: 76–77.

24. NARA RG 397 Entry # 39 650 42/26/06–07, Box 1, "U.S./Canada Cross-Border Seminar Exercise January 27–28, Minneapolis," 1965.

25. NARA RG 396 Entry 1029 650 42/05/05, Box 6; and RG 396 Entry 1063 650 42/13/01, Box 1, "[Operation Alert 1959] Test Exercise Study Files," 1959.

26. NARA RG 396 Entry 1029 650 42/05/05, Box 6. Ellipses in original.

27. DA, OCDM, "Draft Plan for Operations at the Classified Location," 1960.

28. PRO HO 322/336, Working Party on Broadcasting Fall-Out Information: Meetings and Interim Report, "Broadcasting of Fallout Information. Report by South-West Region," Dec. 1964.

29. NARA RG 396 Entry 1029 650 42/05/05, Box 6.

30. DA, Public Works Collection, EMO, *Canada Survival Plan*, 1966: 3–4.

31. DA, "Emergency Broadcast—Attack Warning," 1967. This closely resembles two other documents: DA, Public Works Collection, Deputy Chief Reserves, *Civil Emergency Operations—War. Militia Training Material and Guidelines*, 1968: Annex C, Part 2, Sec 1: 36–37; and NAC R06059, CBC and EMO, *Nuclear Attack Clips. Public Service Radio Announcements*, ca. 1964.

32. DA, "Emergency Broadcasts No. 1–10 (Draft)," 1962.

33. Steed 1985.

34. DA, EMO, "EMO Working Group on Emergency Broadcasts for the Public Second Progress Report," 1962.

35. Canada EPC 1979: 4.

36. DA, "Health Maintenance Survival Instructions for the Public," 1962.

37. Crossley 1982: 85–86.

38. PRO HO 322/336, Working Party on Broadcasting Fall-Out Information, "Interim Report for Period to D+5," February 1965.

39. Ibid.

40. Pfister 1991: 246–47.

41. Ubersfeld 1999: xvi.

42. US DOD OCDM 1961. Emphasis in original.

43. The central point about transitivity and intrasitivity is drawn from discussion of mimetic fiction and poetry in Lane 2003: 450–69.

44. J. Thompson 1985: 14.

45. DDEPL, White House Office, Cabinet Secretary, Box 22, CI-55 "Human Behavior in Disaster," Cabinet paper, 22 April 1958: 4.

46. M. Clarke 1982: 29.

47. *War of the Worlds*, 1938. See also Cantril 1940.

48. McAuley 1999: 15.

49. Messinger, Sampson, and Towne 1975: 38. Rpt. from *Sociometry* 35 (September 1962): 98–110.

7. Acting Out Injury

1. Parrino 1964: 780–82; and Brantl 1958: 1550–51.

2. Claxton 1943: 101.

3. Claxton 1990: 31.

4. Ibid.: 38.

5. In May 1942, the magazine *Illustrated* featured the school. Gaumont British and Pathé Gazette included it in newsreels. Claxton 1990: 45–46.

6. Casualties Union 1963: 34.

7. See Wilkie 2002: 257.

8. Claxton 1943: 121.

9. Claxton 1990: 92–93.

10. Casualties Union 1963: 34–36.

11. Claxton 1943; and Gordon 1988.

12. Claxton 1990: 58–59.

13. NLM MS.C 187 Elizabeth G. Pritchard Papers, Box 22, C. F. W. Illingsworth, "Surgical Organization in Air Raids," 1941.

14. Claxton 1943: 107.

15. "Response and Responsibility," 1946: 13.

16. "Make Up Your Mind!" 1951: 134; and "Acting and Reacting 6," 1951: 83.

17. Realist, "Acting and Reacting. 3," 1949: 7–8.

18. From John Stevens's notes on the contributions of Miss Frances Marsden, a dramatic arts teacher, to a conference on the future of the Casualties Union held in June 1945 (Claxton 1990: 116–17).

19. Ibid.: 116.

20. Nicholson 1955: 152.

21. Claxton 1955: 143.

22. Claxton 1990: 107.

23. Groom 1953: 132.

24. Casualties Union 1957b: 10; and Casualties Union 1957c: 2.

25. "Study Circles," 1964: 47. The Casualties Union Web page now proclaims itself "Original and Best" and proudly boasts that it is "the only union allowing its members to lie down and be trodden on." The curriculum continues to adapt to modern warfare injuries and terrorism-related concerns. See www.casualtiesunion.org.uk, accessed 29 November 2005.

26. Claxton 1950: 26–27.

27. These include, in addition to John Hersey's *Hiroshima*; Hirschfelder 1950; UK Civil Defence Department 1950; and training manuals for medical corps and surgeons. "Casualties Union Library," 1955: 198.

28. "Research News," 1949: 12–15.

29. Casualties Union 1957a: 76.

30. Claxton 1950: 27; see also Towle 1950: 7.

31. "Hay's Wharf 1950," 1951: 61–62.

32. "The Army Joins," 1951: 4.

33. Ibid.: 4.

34. "Civil Defence, 1953," 1953: 5–6.

35. Nicholson was the Casualties Union's leading spokesperson for acting per se in the postwar period, writing about and deriving numerous activities for development of character and concentration for use in training. Compare Nicholson 1951: 68–70; and Boleslavsky 1933: 119.

36. Casualties Union 1962: 26–27.

37. Izzo 1997: 26; and Schechner 1993: 82.

38. Republic of Ireland National Archives, NAI 1937 B/3/61 Department of the Taoiseach, Aodh Mac Brádaigh, "Letter to An Cathaoirleach, Cumann Croise Deirge na hÉireann [Red Cross of Ireland]," 1958.

39. A navy exercise conducted by personnel from HMS *Ganges*, for example, in the derelict village of West Tofts in the Brecks region on Norfolk, gamed rescues from dilapidated buildings and medical services for the fully-faked injured. But "for the purpose of the exercise, and observing that the supposed bomb had been air burst [over Norwich, twenty miles to the north] the fall out problem was to be ignored" (Gent 1959: 119).

40. PRO HO 322/186, "Staff College Exercises and Studies: 'Bull Ring' Casualty Services," 1956.

41. PRO HLG 120/921, Ministry of Housing and Local Government, "Civil Defence: Tracing of Missing Persons in Event of Nuclear War," handwritten note on CIVLOG Figures [ca. 1962].

42. PRO INF 2/118 Folio 254, Ministry of Information, Civil Defence Recruitment Posters and Pamphlets, 1950–57.

43. The "Pikadon" study held 18–19 February 1959 concluded that even if the FMAU was correctly positioned, first aid rescue parties could maximize their wartime emergency dose in a single eight-hour shift. PRO HO 322/190, "Staff College Exercises and Studies: 'Battledore': Casualty Services," "Problems and Assumptions," 1959.

44. "In the News . . . Exercise 'Shuttlecock,'" 1958: 21–22; and PRO HO 322/190, "Staff College Exercises and Studies, 'Battledore': Casualty Services," "Problems and Assumptions," 1959.

45. "In the News . . . Exercise 'Gory,'" 1960: 165–66.

46. Costley 1983: 66–67.

47. Ibid.: 78.

48. PRO HO 322/141, "Command and Control: Exercises and Studies by the Midland Civil Defence Region," 1957–64, Report on "Exercise 'All Together Heave.'"

49. PRO BD 2/16, Welsh Hospital Board, Reports, August 1966; and PRO BD 51/73, Welsh Hospital Board, Civil Defence Hospital and Reports on Forward Medical Aid Exercises "Operation Fall" 1960–65.

50. PRO HO 322/192, Staff College Exercises and Studies: Central Exercise Staff (CES): Coordination and Administration of Central Government and Regional Exercises, "Central Exercise Staff Bulletin January 1965."

51. PRO BD 2/16, Welsh Hospital Board, Reports, August 1966.

52. PRO HO 322/141, Command and Control: Exercises and Studies by Midland Civil Defence Region, 1957–64, "Exercise 'Life Line II.'"

53. PRO BD 2/16, Welsh Hospital Board, Reports, August 1966.

54. Casualties Union 1957a: 119–21.

55. Claxton 1992: 250.

56. Clanahan 1974: 12–15.

57. This is from the proposed "Civil Defence Manual No. 7," which exists in typescript: DA, National Ministry of Health and Welfare, Civil Defence Health Planning Group, *Civil Defence Health Services Manual*, 1953: 25.

58. NARA RG 396 Entry 1029 650 42/05/05, Box 7, OCDM Battle Creek, "Operation Alert 1959 Report, Region 4."

59. For example, McGrath (1997: 99–101) argues that made-up casualties should be used in emergency room staff training, and that when makeup is skillfully applied it can be appropriate for high-level professionals.

60. Canada Department of National Health and Welfare 1965.

61. Medical emergency exercises were routinely staged in the United States from the late 1950s, yet the military literature on the subject stresses what the Casualties Union called "faking" rather than also adopting the aesthetics of acting and staging (Hack 1959: 193–95). Larger evacuations tended to be paper exercises, such as the evacuation of thirteen hospitals (including 4,202 patients and 1,249 staff) from Cincinnati, Ohio, to Miami University Hospital in Oxford, Ohio, along "with 3 days' supply of perishable foods, 57 days' of nonperishable foods, 7 days' supply of intravenous solutions, 12 days' supply perishable medical supplies, and 58 days' supply of nonperishable medical supplies" (Ransohoff 1959: 108). A city-wide eight-hospital disaster exercise in Boston in 1964 involved two hundred soldiers made up with moulages, but there is no evidence they were given acting instructions (Walker, Raker, and Voboril 1964: 605–10). by the 1980s, Casualties Union techniques (again, unaccredited) were standard (Seliger and Simoneau 1986: 196–97, 201).

62. Welbrock-Smith 1960: 169.

63. Abrams 1984: 23–26.

64. This is the "utopic" dimension of rehearsal. See Dolan 2001: 455–79.

65. Izzo 1997: 29.

66. PRO HO 322/190, Staff College Exercises and Studies: "Battledore": Casualty Services, "Paper 2. Home Office and Ministry of Health. Study Battledore," 1959.

67. D. Kennedy 2001: 277; and B. Kershaw 1992: 257.

68. Barba 2000: 60.

69. B. Kershaw 1992: 257. Diamond 1997: 49 describes the Brechtian "not . . . but" as a theatricalized "zigzag of contradictions." I include the additional "not" as a further paradoxical signification of methexis and the potential for a future played out in the exercises.

70. Davis 2003: 127–55; and Schechner 1993: 83.

8. Crisis Play

1. This nationwide readiness and attack exercise was Phase I of OPAL 61; Phases II and III (the follow-up exercises for state and federal field staff D+2 through D+28 and federal and headquarters staff after D+28, emphasizing resource management) were cancelled by President Kennedy. JFKL, White House Central Subject Files, Box 114 FG 11–6, Frank B. Ellis, memo to Frederick G. Dutton, 14 June 1961. See also DDEPL Cabinet Paper, 28 November 1960

CP-60-111, White House Office Cabinet Secretary, Box 4; and NARA RG 396 Entry 1017 650 42/03/07, Box 1, Assistant Secretary of Defense, memo to Secretaries of the military departments, Director of Defense Research and Engineers, Chairman of Joint Chiefs of Staff, Assistant Secretaries of Defense, General Counsel, [etc.], 15 February 1961.

2. JFKL, National Security Files Box 283A, OEP, *The National Plan for Emergency Preparedness* [DRAFT], ca. 11 October 1963: 11.

3. U.S. President, Executive Order 10346 (1952): 3477.

4. JFKL, Presidents Office Files, Box 84A, Frank B. Ellis, "Basic Report of Civil Defense and Defense Mobilization: Roles, Organization and Programs," February 1961, V: 68.

5. Ibid., VI: 67.

6. Ibid., V: 69–70.

7. DDEPL, Dwight D. Eisenhower Diary, Box 36, Toner Notes September 1958; and JFKL, "Basic Report" VII: 127. See also DA, Jack Scott (Classified Location Director OCDM), letter to P. A. Faguy (Assistant Director of EMO), 14 December 1960.

8. JFKL, "Basic Report" III: 35–36.

9. JFKL, National Security Files, Box 333A NSAM 127 2/61–1/62, Joe E. Walstrom, memo on "Possible Hardening of Department's Relocation Site at Front Royal," 16 May 1961; and NATO AC/98-D/26, Senior Civil Emergency Planning Committee, "Review of Measures to Ensure Maintenance of Governmental Control," 3 November 1956: 19. David Krugler details the emergence of the arc, which evolved to include ninety-six sites (2006). See DA, [EPC], *Extracts (on Continuity of Government Aspects) from a 1990 Comparative Study of Some Other Nations Civil Defense Programs*, 1992.

10. JFKL, National Security Files, Box 333A NSAM 127 2/61–1/62, William Y. Elliot, "Action Steps which the Department [of State] can take at once to Improve its Plans and Programs for Emergency Relocation," 22 May 1961.

11. JFKL, National Security Files, Box 295A Report by the PSAC Panel 7/16/62, President's Science Advisory Committee, "Report by the PSAC Panel on Civil Defense," 16 July 1962, VI: 13.

12. The OEP favored prelocation of civil servants over government leaders, such as cabinet officers—whose absence would attract notice and might occasion alarm—to a federal relocation arc with twenty to thirty sites equipped with fallout protection, equipment, and communications for minimal emergency operations. JFKL, Presidents Office Files, Box 94 Emergency Planning Committee on Assumptions for Non-Military Planning, "Report to the President on a Re-examination of Federal policy with Respect to Emergency Plans and Continuity of Government in the Event of Nuclear Attack on the United States," 11 June 1962. Portions of this document remain classified.

13. JFKL, "Basic Report" 2: 28.

14. Construction of the $2.4 million facility began in June 1961. JFKL, White House Central Subject Files, Box 597 ND2, Executive Office of the President, OCDM, *Annual Report of the Office of Civil and Defense Mobilization for the Fiscal Year 1961* (1962), 8; and Eriffin B. Huey, letter to John F. Kennedy, 14 November 1963.

15. Salinger 1966: 257.

16. This is the Alternate National Military Command Center blasted out of Raven Rock Mountain, Pennsylvania, six miles north of Camp David, in 1950–53. See Blair, Pike,

and Schwartz 1998: 210–11. "Communications Facilities at National Level" 27 February 1961 [evidently revised 1 March], details links between DOD facilities (Fort Ritchie and Raven Rock), High Point, and the federal relocation arc; see "Communications Facilities at National Level," Defense Communications Agency secret briefing for the Secretary of Defense, March 1961. Available at the website "A Secret Landscape," http://coldwar-c4i.net/index.html, accessed 3 December 2005.

17. JFKL, Presidents Office Files, Box 85 OEP 7/62–12/62, Tazewell T. Shepard, Jr., "Report of the Task Group on the Survivable Communications Requirements of the President and Top Civil Leaders," 20 August 1962. See also National Security Files, Box 283A.

18. JFKL, OEP, Box 1, [TWX Regional Reports to OEP], 23 October 1962.

19. Salinger (1966: 270) asserts that this was why Premier Khrushchev, seeking a swift resolution, broadcast his decision on Soviet radio on 28 October rather than relaying a communication through the Soviet embassy to President Kennedy.

20. JFKL, "Report of the Task Group."

21. JFKL, National Security Files, Box 337 NSAM 166, John F. Kennedy, National Security Action Memo No. 166, "Report on Emergency Plans and Continuity of the Government," 25 June 1962.

22. U.S. Executive Office of the President, OCDM 1958; DDEPL, White House Office Cabinet Secretariat Series, Box 4, Executive Office of the President, Office of Defense Mobilization, *Mobilization Plan C*, 1 June 1957; and DDEPL, White House Cabinet Secretaries Series, Box 18, Executive Office of the President, OCDM, *Federal Emergency Plan D-Minus*, June 1959. In Canada and the United Kingdom, comparable plans were known as war books. Each government ministry and office kept their own version, periodically updated. See DA, Public Works Canada, *War Book* [n.d.]; Privy Council Office, *War Book*, 1948; Privy Council Office, *Government War Book*, 1948; and NAC RG 57 EMO, Acc. 1984–85/658, Box 38, file 2615-1 pt. 1, EMO, Exercise Tocsin 66, Exercise Instructions (EXTOCS), 1966. As civil defense measures evolved, the EMO drafted *Crisis Management Plans* (1968). These were still undergoing revision and consolidation in 1989 but were never issued due to the changing political situation in Eastern Europe. See DA, EPC, [typescript] "Planning Guide for Emergency Government Headquarters, EPC Manual #7," 1 November 1989.

23. NARA RG 396 Entry 1017 650 42/03/07, Box 1, Regional Director Region 4, memo to Director OCDM, "Summary Report and Evaluation of OPEX 61-1," including Emergency Operations Log, 31 January 1961.

24. JFKL, National Security Files, Box 283A OEP General 6/1/6–8/19/61, Frank B. Ellis to McGeorge Bundy, 17 January 1962.

25. DDEPL, *Plan C*: 81–82.

26. DDEPL, *Plan D-Minus*: 11, 14.

27. Ibid.: 13, 5.

28. Ibid.: 18.

29. Ibid.: 11.

30. DDEPL, National Security Council Series, Box 9, Memo of Discussion at the 330th meeting of the National Security Council, Thursday 11 July 1957 [dated 12 July 1957]: 1, 2.

31. DDEPL, *Plan D-Minus*: 6.

32. JFKL, Presidents Office Files, Box 94, Emergency Planning Committee on Assumptions

for Non-Military Planning. Emergency Planning Committee, "Report to the President on a Re-examination of Federal Policy with Respect to Emergency Plans and Continuity of Government in the Event of Nuclear Attack on the United States," 11 June 1962: 3.

33. Ibid.: 10.

34. Ibid.: 21. Seventeen hundred personnel is an Eisenhower-era figure, though there is no reason to believe it would be smaller under the next administration. See NATO AC/98-D/26, NATO Senior Civil Emergency Planning Committee, "Review of Measures to Ensure Maintenance of Governmental Control," 3 November 1956: 19.

35. In the concurrent Fallex 62 and High Heels II, 29,000 military personnel also took part.

36. JFKL, National Security Files, Box 283A General 10/25/62–10/10/63, OEP, Program Evaluation Office, *Exercise Spade Fork September 6–27, 1962, Civil Evaluation Report*, 30 January 1963: 2.

37. JFKL, *Exercise Spade Fork . . . Civil Evaluation*.

38. JFKL, OEP, Box 1, memo to William B. Rice on "Developments during Cuban Crisis," 13 March 1964. The Strategic Air Command went to DEFCON 2 at the initiation of the quarantine, but this was not an all-services status. Sagan 1993: 63.

39. Sagan 1993: 64.

40. In fact, at this moment, the real successors were all in Washington (except for the secretary of commerce, en route to Chicago) and they would have been obliterated (JFKL, *Exercise Spade Fork . . . Civil Evaluation*: 9). Implications of Spade Fork for the general population are compared to the Holifield Committee's casualty data in Heer 1965.

41. JFKL, *Exercise Spade Fork . . . Civil Evaluation*.

42. US *Statutes at Large*, 1952: 1245–57.

43. See JFKL, *Exercise Spade Fork . . . Civil Evaluation*: 3.

44. DDEPL, *Plan D-Minus*, 23.

45. NATO AC/36(M)D165, Manpower Planning Committee, 18 July 1963.

46. JFKL, *Exercise Spade Fork . . . Civil Evaluation*.

47. JFKL, National Security Files, Box 283A General 10/25/62–10/10/63. Military Exercise Director DOD, *Evaluation Report Exercise Spade Fork* [September 6–27, 1962], 1 February 1963: 5.

48. NARA RG 396 Entry 1040 650 42/08/01–02, Box 3, Office of Defense Mobilization, E. L. Keenan (Director OEP Exercise Directing Staff), "Exercise Spade Fork OEP Directing Staff Evaluation Report," 28 September 1962.

49. JFKL, *Evaluation Report Exercise Spade Fork*, 5.

50. Ibid.

51. U.S. President, Executive Order 11051 (1962): 9683–9689; and JFKL, OEP, Box 1, OEP Circular 9410.1, 13 September 1962.

52. May and Zelikow 1997: 199.

53. Salinger 1966: 252–53.

54. Sagan 1993: 63.

55. R. Kennedy 1969: 30–31.

56. Haydon 1993: 227.

57. Freedman 2000: 199.

58. George 2003: 93; Henrikson 1997: 237; and Rose 2001: 192–209.

59. JFKL, National Security Files, Box 295 CD 1/61–3/61, memo from Charles A. Haskins to McGeorge Bundy, 21 February 1961: Addendum.

60. Mast 1966: 12.

61. Salinger 1966: 290–91.

62. JFKL, OEP, Box 1, W. P. Durkee, wire from OCD to the attention of Regional Directors, 24 or 25 October 1962.

63. JFKL, OEP, Box 1, OEP Circular 9410.1, 13 September 1962.

64. JFKL, OEP, Box 1, Albert G. Swing (Director of the Region 8 office), memo to Deputy Director of OEP, 25 October 1962.

65. JFKL, OEP, Box 1, Ralph E. Spear, OEP Bulletin 9300 (To Executive Staff and Staff), "TWX Message to OEP Regional Directors Governing Immediately Emergency Actions," 22 October 1961.

66. JFKL, OEP, Box 1, Edward F. Phelps, Jr., memo to the Director [Edward A. McDermott], 23 October 1962.

67. JFKL, OEP, Box 1, Edward F. Phelps, Jr., memo to the Director [Edward A. McDermott], Monetary and Fiscal Issues for Today's Meeting, 22 October 1962.

68. JFKL, *Exercise Spade Fork . . . Civil Evaluation Report*, 5.

69. JFKL, OEP, Box 1, Edward F. Phelps, Jr., memo to the Director of OEP, 24 October 1962.

70. JFKL, OEP, Box 1, Paul Revelle, memo to Edward F. Phelps, Jr., 24 October 1962.

71. JFKL, OEP, Box 1, Edward F. Phelps, Jr., memo to the Director [Edward A. McDermott], 26 October 1962.

72. JFKL, OEP, Box 1, John F. Kennedy, letter to James Hagerty [hand delivered in New York City by Col. Justice Chambers, deputy director of the OEP], 24 October 1962. Salinger claims that the Censorship Advisory Board consisted of fifteen prominent news executives and that Hagerty agreed to steer this advisory board, rather than become the censor per se. If a full-fledged censorship was needed, Byron Price would have been approached to take the job (Salinger 1966: 257, 289–90).

73. JFKL, OEP, Box 1, E. R. Saunders, Memo for the Record, National Communications System, World-wide, 2 November 1962 [covering meetings 24–26 October].

74. Ibid.

75. JFKL, OEP, Box 1, Ralph E. Spear, OEP Bulletin 9300 (To Executive Staff and Staff), "TWX Message to OEP Regional Directors Governing Immediate Emergency Actions [sent 22 October]," 23 October 1962.

76. May and Zelikow 1997: 338–39.

77. The president announced that Soviet MRBMs had a 1000-mile range, though previous intelligence estimates indicated a 400- to 700-mile range. B. H. Ross 1971: 119.

78. JFKL, National Security Files Civil Defense 10/1/61–10/27/61, Steuart L. Pittman, memo to John F. Kennedy (via McGeorge Bundy), 24 October 1962.

79. JFKL, National Security Files, Box 339 NASM 200, [Steuart L. Pittman], memo to [McGeorge Bundy], 25 October 1962.

80. JFKL, National Security Files, Box 295, Steuart L. Pittman, memo to McGeorge Bundy on Acceleration of Civil Defense Activities, 25 October 1962.

81. JFKL, OEP, Box 1, Edward A. McDermott, letter to Robert S. McNamara, 25 October 1962.

82. Personnel designated to go to High Point include seven from the State Department, six

from Commerce, four from Justice, and three each from Agriculture, the Atomic Energy Commission, Budget, CIA, Civil Aeronautics Board, Civil Service Commission, Council of Economic Advisors, Farm Credit Administration, Federal Aviation Authority, FBI, Federal Communications Commission, Federal Deposit Insurance Corporation, Federal Home Loan Bank Board, Federal Power Commission, Federal Reserve, General Services Administration, HEW, Housing and Home Finance Agency, Interstate Commerce Commission, Labor, NASA, National Security Council, Post Office, Securities and Exchange Commission, Selective Service System, Small Business Administration, Treasury, U. S. Information Agency, and Veterans Administration. According to the document "Continuous Activation of Relocation Site" (August 1958), 306 personnel were stationed at High Point during periods of tension, the largest proportions being from Commerce (75), HEW (150), and the General Services Administration (14). DDEPL, White House Office Cabinet Secretariat, Box 2.

83. Sagan 1993: 97–98, 111–12. Prime Minister Diefenbaker, for his part, refused a full NORAD alert, preventing U. S. bomber squadrons from dispersing to Canadian bases.

84. JFKL, OEP, Box 1, Robert Y. Phillips, memo to Edward A. McDermott, 29 October 1962.

85. JFKL, National Security Files, Box 283A, Edward A. McDermott, memo to Heads of Departments and Agencies Having Nonmilitary Defense Responsibilities, 25 October 1962.

86. JFKL, OEP, Box 1, Robert Y. Phillips, memo to Edward A. McDermott, 25 October 1962.

87. JFKL, Sorensen Papers, Box 50, Emergency Planning, Edward A. McDermott, memo to Theodore Sorensen, 25 October 1962.

88. JFKL, OEP, Box 1, E.L. Keenen, Status Report to Edward A. McDermott, 25 October 1962.

89. JFKL, Sorensen Papers, Box 50, Emergency Planning, Edward A. McDermott, memo to Theodore Sorensen, 25 October 1962.

90. Ibid.

91. Ibid; and U.S. President, Executive Order 10501 (1953): 7049, 7051–7054. Further information on plans for law and order remain classified.

92. This is defined as invocation of the provisions of Title III of the Federal Civil Defense Act, 1950 (Public Law 920), a presidential proclamation or congressional resolution declaring that attack has occurred or is anticipated threatening the national safety.

93. JFKL, OEP, Box 1, memos from F. C. Alexander to Eugene J. Quindlen, 26 October 1962; and R. M. Obermiller to F. C. Alexander, 29 October 1962.

94. JFKL, OEP, Box 1, Joseph D. Coker, memo to Edward A. McDermott, 26 October 1962.

95. JFKL, OEP, Box 1, Edward A. McDermott, letter to Earl Warren, 30 October 1962.

96. JFKL, OEP, Box 1, J. K. Shafer, memo to Edward A. McDermott, 26 October 1962.

97. JFKL, OEP, Box 1, Edward F. Phelps, Jr., memo to the Director [Edward A. McDermott], 26 October 1962.

98. JFKL, OEP, Box 1, Edward F. Phelps, Jr., memo to the Director [Edward A. McDermott], 26 October 1962. Emphasis in original.

99. JFKL, OEP, Box 1, Edward A. McDermott, memo to all Regional Directors, 29 October 1962.

100. JFKL, National Security Files, Box 339, McGeorge Bundy, memo to Secretaries of State and Defense and Director of OEP, National Security Action Memorandum No. 200, 28 October 1962.

101. Though 35,000 personnel is an Eisenhower-era figure, there is no reason to believe it would be smaller under the next administration. It most likely refers to the nationwide contingent of federal employees, rather than just the Washington-area relocation arc. NATO AC/98-D/26, NATO Senior Civil Emergency Planning Committee, "Review of Measures to Ensure Maintenance of Governmental Control," 3 November 1956: 19.

102. JFKL, OEP, Box 1, memo from Leonard L. Reese, Jr. [acting director, Program Evaluation Office], 29 October 1962.

103. JFKL, OEP, Box 1, [author's name redacted], memo to William B. Rice, Developments during Cuban Crisis, 13 March 1964.

104. This issue was debated during planning for Spade Fork. Calculating the manufacturing data on 25,000 separate available points would take more than six weeks' machine time, if all other work was dropped. RISK II data was more authoritative, but RISK I data had the advantage of being available. PARM models could calculate requirements to any actual or hypothetical situation, but pencil and paper probability estimates would be substituted instead. NARA RG 396 Entry 1054 650 42/08/04, Box 4, Office of Defense Mobilization, OEP, Central Correspondence Files, Robert W. Stokley, memo to Deputy Director, 3 May 1962.

105. JFKL, *Exercise Spade Fork . . . Civil Evaluation.*

106. Ibid.: 17.

107. Robert Kennedy opened his memoir of the missile crisis by writing that it "brought the world to the abyss of nuclear destruction and the end of mankind" (Kennedy 1969: 1; see also 109). Apparently, this view was held on both sides. When the crisis was over, Nikita Khrushchev wrote to Fidel Castro: "In your cable of October 27 you proposed that we be the first to launch a nuclear strike against the territory of the enemy. You, of course, realize where that would have led. Rather than a simple strike, it would have been the start of a thermonuclear war. . . . we have lived through the most serious moment when a nuclear world war could have broken out . . . There's no doubt that the Cuban people would have fought courageously or that they would have died heroically. But we are not struggling against imperialism in order to die, but to take advantage of all our possibilities. . . . Now, as a result of the measures taken, we reached the goal sought when we agreed with you to send the missiles to Cuba. We have wrested from the United States the commitment not to invade Cuba and not to permit their Latin American allies to do so. . . . We consider that we must take advantage of all the possibilities to defend Cuba, strengthen its independence and sovereignty, defeat military aggression and prevent a nuclear world war in our time" (National Security Archive, Nikita Khrushchev to Fidel Castro, 30 October 1962).

108. Opinion remains deeply divided on this point. See Nathan 1992: 17; and Trachtenberg 1990: 241–47.

109. Trachtenberg 1999.

9. International Play

1. NATO AC/23(CD)R/4 NATO Civil Defence Committee, [Extract from Report of Meeting], May 1954: 8.

2. NATO Text of Lord Ismay's Report to the Ministerial Meeting of the North Atlantic Council, Bonn, May 1957.

3. NATO AC/23(CD)D/456, Civil Defence Committee, "Experience Gained in the Field of Civil Defence From 'Fallex 62' in The Netherlands," 14 November 1963: 1–2.

4. NATO AC/64/40, "Future Participation NATO-wide Exercises," 21 September 1964.

5. NATO AC/23(CD)R/26, "Statement by the Refugee Adviser," [Extract from meeting 6–7 October 1964]; AC/98-R/12, "Minutes of meeting 12 November 1964": 35–37; and CD.3–16–01 Refugees-Ex.4, NATO Refugee Agency, "Summary of Developments as of 25.1100Z," 25 September 1964.

6. NATO AC/134(CIVLOG)D/18, NATO Exercise CIVLOG 65, "A Summary of National Comments and Recommendations," 24 September 1965.

7. NATO AC/134(CIVLOG)R/3, "NATO Civil Emergency Planning. Summary Record of Meeting 16 July 1964," ca. 16 July 1964. See also NAC RG 24 DND, Series C-1, Acc. 1983-84/215, Box 252, file S-2001-91/T21, pt. 2, "Exercise TOCSIN 63 Preparation of Incidents."

8. PRO HO 322/309, HO, Janus 63 Study: Post Nuclear Attack; Government and Local Government Functions, "Machinery of Government in War," 17 October 1963.

9. NATO ACI34(CIVLOG)D/7 (Revised), NATO Civil Emergency Co-ordinating Committee, "Working Group on Exercise CIVLOG 65. Sequence of Planning and Timetable," 16 October 1963.

10. NATO AC/134(CIVLOG)Ex/Inst.1 Annex to Serial 2, NATO Civil Emergency Co-ordinating Committee, "Exercise CIVLOG 65 Exercise Instructions. Summary of Scenario Employed in Exercise Fallex 65," 5 October 1964.

11. These alert terms appear to have been created for FALLEX 64. Correspondence with Anne-Marie Smith, NATO Archives Section 2005.

12. NATO AC/134(CIVLOG)D/11, NATO Civil Emergency Co-ordinating Committee, "Exercise CIVLOG 65 Nuclear Incident List," 6 March 1964.

13. NATO AC/134(CIVLOG)Ex/Inst-1 Serial Two, NATO Civil Emergency Co-ordinating Committee, "Exercise CIVLOG 65 Detailed Instructions Concerning Exercise Pre-Attack, Attack and Immediate Post-Attack Phase Situation," 15 April 1965.

14. NATO AC/134(CIVLOG)Ex/Inst.1 Serial Eleven, NATO Civil Emergency Co-ordinating Committee, "Civil Emergency Co-ordinating Committee Exercise CIVLOG 65 NATO-Level Opening Narrative Summary of Situation as at D+30 (Extracted from National Narratives)," 15 April 1965.

15. NATO AC/134(CIVLOG)D/16, NATO Civil Emergency Co-ordinating Committee, "Exercise CIVLOG 65 Planning Committee. Summary Record of a Meeting of the Board of the Central Supplies Agency held . . . 21st May, 1965," 23 July 1965.

16. NATO Civil Emergency Planning, "Conclusions Following Meeting of the Food Directing Staff (CIVLOG) on 4th March, 1965," 8 March 1965.

17. NATO AC/134(CIVLOG)D/17, NATO Civil Emergency Co-ordinating Committee, "Working Party on Exercise CIVLOG 65. Summary Record of a debriefing Meeting, at the Conclusion of Exercise CIVLOG 65, held at the Permanent Headquarters . . . 22nd May, 1965," 6 July 1965.

18. Performance criticism is more likely to result from first-hand observation of a production; this later becomes fodder for performance historians. The typical array of evidence for performance historians is reviews, iconography, memoirs, post-hoc interviews, architecture, designs, and any other iconographic artifacts.

19. NATO AC/15(CD)N/48, NATO Planning Board for Inland Surface Transport (PBEIST), "Preliminary Report by the Chairman of ACTICE and the Members of the Directing Staff Following Exercise CIVLOG 65," 21 June 1965: 6.

20. NATO AC/15(CD)N/48, PBEIST, "Preliminary Report by the Chairman of ACTICE and the Members of the Directing Staff Following Exercise CIVLOG 65," 21 June 1965.

21. Crease 1993: 110, quoted in States 1996: 22.

22. Diderot 1957; and Brecht 1964.

23. Schechner 1993: 25–26.

24. NATO AC/134(CIVLOG)R/4, NATO Civil Emergency Co-ordinating Committee, "Summary Record of Meeting held 18 December 1964," ca. 18 December 1964. This document specifies that play would continue to 18:30 each day; this was later revised.

25. NATO AC/15(CD)N/48, PBEIST, "Preliminary Report by the Chairman of ACTICE and the Members of the Directing Staff Following Exercise CIVLOG 65," 21 June 1965: 5.

26. Thiong'o 1997: 12.

27. Izzo 1997: 11.

28. Ibid.: 13–14.

29. Foreman and Martini 1995.

30. Kirby 1965: 18–19. Emphasis in original.

31. Abbott 2002: 32.

32. Murray 1997: 116–17.

33. Ibid.: 151.

34. J. B. Thompson 1995: 100.

35. McConachie 2001: 583.

36. Abbott 2002: 82–83.

37. Ibid.: 33–34.

38. Izzo 1997: 49.

39. *Tony n' Tina's Wedding* was created by the improv comedy troupe "Artificial Intelligence" in 1988. Originally produced in New York by Joseph and Dan Corcoran, and directed by Larry Pelligrini, it has enjoyed simultaneous runs in many major North American cities.

40. NATO AC/134(CIVLOG)D/18(Draft), NATO Civil Emergency Co-ordinating Committee, "Working Group of National Exercise Advisors. Exercise CIVLOG 65—Draft Report," 10 September 1965.

41. Sauter 2000: 98.

42. Kirby 1965: 16–17.

43. Schechner 1993: 88–89.

44. NATO AC/134(CIVLOG)DS/11, "NATO Exercise CIVLOG 65. Exercise CIVLOG 65 Supplementary Narrative No. 11," 28 April 1965.

45. NATO AC/134(CIVLOG)DS/12, "NATO Exercise CIVLOG 65. Incidents for the Play of the NATO Refugee Agency," 6 May 1965.

46. DA, W. W. Butterworth (US Ambassador to Canada), letter to Paul Martin [Sr.] (Canadian Secretary of State for External Affairs), 1963; this proposes revision to the 27 March 1951 agreement to protect persons and property "as if there were no border" and is accepted by Martin. See also "Statement of Principles Concerning United States-Canada Cooperation on Civil Emergency Planning," 1967, where the provision regarding citizens

is qualified to read that each nation "will treat each other's citizens equally with respect to welfare and health for the purposes of emergency relief."

47. McKenzie 2001: 129. McKenzie develops ideas from Crease 1993: 181–82.

48. Abbott 2002: 156.

49. Letter from Anton Chekhov to A. S. Souvorin, 27 October 1888, quoted in Abbott 2002: 169.

10. Disaster Welfare

1. Wells 1913: 99–100.

2. PRO HO 357/18 20, extract from Report by the Police President and local Air Protection leader of Hamburg regarding raids in July and August 1943 [report dated 1 December 1943], quoted in Working Party on Post-Raid Information About Individuals, April 1953.

3. For details on Canadian and American plans for change of address and registration and inquiry card systems, see NARA RG 396 Entry #1013 650 41/32/07, Box 1, "FCDA-OCDM Special Liaison Files of L. C. Franklin [Canada—U.S. Joint Committee]," Report, 5 October 1956. Canada, unlike the United States, had provision for "missing" persons.

4. PRO HO 357/18, Working Party on Post-Raid Information about Individuals, draft letter from J. M. Ross to twelve local authorities, 22 October 1953.

5. PRO HO 357/18, Working Party on Post-Raid Information about Individuals, memo by the Chairman [J. M. Ross], 20 April 1953.

6. PRO HO 357/18, Working Party on Post-Raid Information About Individuals, "Precis from Report of Registration and Information Conference held at Washington in July 1953," circulated to working party 25 February 1954.

7. UN Conference of Plenipotentiaries on the Status of Refugees and Stateless Persons, convened under General Assembly resolution 429 (v) of 14 December 1950, Chapter I, article 1 (2) (1951).

8. NATO AC/23-DI4, NATO Working Group on Civil Organisation in Time of War, "Report by the Luxembourg Government on the Problems of Civil Defence and the Evacuation of Refugees," 9 October 1952.

9. Organization of African Unity, Convention Governing the Specific Aspects of Refugee Problems in Africa, 1001 UNTS 45, Article 1(2) (1974).

10. Cartegena Declaration on Refugees, Article III(3) (1984).

11. According to the UN, prima facie refugees are persons granted temporary refugee status based on group rather than individual determination. De facto refugees are persons not granted asylum under the convention but given provisional permission to remain in a country on humanitarian grounds.

12. PRO HO 322/204, Regional Exercises and Studies: Staff College and Training Schools Historical Notes [1948–]1953; and UK 1949b: 654.

13. PRO HO 357/16, Ministry of Health, Working Party on the Care of the Homeless, "Conclusions," 2 October 1951.

14. PRO DEFE 7/722, MOD, Official Committee on Civil Defence: Evacuation and Care of Homeless, "Copy of a Minute (REF. UKLF/14) Dated 14th January, 1953 from Secretary, Commanders-in-Chief Committee to Secretary, Chiefs of Staff Committee."

15. PRO HO 322/351, Phoenix Five Hydrogen Bomb Exercise, "Study 'Phoenix Five' Regional Narrative up to D+30," 26 June 1967.

16. D. Campbell 1982: 63.

17. Ibid.: 75; and National Archives of Ireland NAI 321/2/4 and NAI 341/89.

18. Poole, Lloyd, and. Hally, vol. 2, 1989b: 41.

19. PRO DEFE 7/722, MOD, Official Committee on Civil Defence: Evacuation and Care of Homeless, "Brief," 26 May 1950.

20. NARA RG 396 Entry 1029 650 42/05/05, Box 1, "Summary of the United States–Canada Standing Planning Group Meeting, Battle Creek, Michigan May 14–15, 1959."

21. See, for example, NARA RG 397 #39, Box 1, from JRCC D/5–64, Department of National Health and Welfare [Canada], Emergency Welfare Services, "Evacuation Across U.S./Canada Border. Study of Possible Movement of Canadian Refugees," Annex E [7 October 1964].

22. DDEPL Cabinet Secretariat, Box 5, "Special 'Cabinet' Meeting of June 17, 1955."

23. NARA RG 396 Entry 1029 650 42/05/05 Box 2, FCDA, "Operation Alert 1956"; and DDEPL Emergency Actions Series, Box 5, "OPAL 57 (Bomb Damage Assessment)."

24. NARA RG 396 Entry 1029 650 42/05/05, Box 4, OPAL 58, A. D. O'Connor (Administrator for FCDA Region I), memo to heads of Federal Agencies, 27 June 1958.

25. NARA RG 396 Entry 1029 650 42/05/05, Box 4, OPAL 58, "Opal Health Agency Resources Board Papers."

26. NARA RG 396 Entry 1029 650 42/05/05, Box 7, OCDM, "Operation Alert 1959, Final Report Region 4."

27. See UK 1949b; 1951: 258; and 1952: 581.

28. NARA RG 396 Entry 1029 650 42/05/05, Box 4, Canada Civil Defense, "National Text Exercise May 3–4 and 9, 1958 Co-Operation II," 1958, "Amended Directing Staff Instructions."

29. Ibid.

30. NARA RG 396 Entry 1029 650 42/05/05, Box 7, Federal Civil Defence Headquarters, Ottawa, "National Test Exercise Co-Operation III: Co-Operation III Operating Staff Instructions," 1959.

31. Ibid.

32. This conclusion was based on data from the U.S. Strategic Bombing Survey's *Overall Report (European War)*, cited in PRO HO 357/9 Pt. I, "Working Party on Civilian Morale," Minutes of Meeting, 19 December 1949.

33. PRO HO 357/9 Pt. II, "Working Party on Civilian Morale," Minutes of Meeting, 10 December 1951.

34. PRO DEFE 7/722, MOD, Official Committee on Civil Defence, Evacuation and Care of Homeless, memo to A. J. Newling, 15 December 1952.

35. PRO CAB 21/5327, Cabinet Office Civil Defence Ministerial Committee, "Progress of Evacuation Plans, Note by the Ministry of Housing and Local Government," 4 June 1952.

36. PRO CAB 21/5182, Cabinet Office, carbon copy memo on "Evacuation Policy" from Michael Cary to the Prime Minister, 30 January 1962.

37. PRO MEPO 2/9487, Metropolitan Police, "Marshalling of Large Numbers of People Congregated in Open Spaces: Responsibility of the Civil Defence Assisted by Police to Maintain Public Order," memo from G. Payne (Chief Superintendent), 28 October 1953.

38. PRO HO 357/14, Ministry of Health Working Party on Evacuation and Care of the Homeless, memo of meeting, 8 June 1949.

39. PRO HO 357/14, Ministry of Health Working Party on Evacuation and Care of the Homeless, "The Industrial Aspects of Area Evacuation Memorandum by the Ministry of Labour," 4 July 1949.

40. PRO HO 322/188, Staff College Exercises and Studies Welfare Section, "Chairman's Summary of Discussions at the Welfare Study [6–8 January 1953]."

41. Ibid.

42. PRO HO 322/194, Regional Exercises and Studies: North Eastern Region Emergency Feeding, "Leeds Emergency Feeding Study, 20–21 October 1952."

43. PRO HO 322/194, Regional Exercises and Studies: North Eastern Region Emergency Feeding, "Kingston-Upon-Hull Emergency Feeding Study, 14–15 January 1953."

44. PRO HO 322/194, Regional Exercises and Studies: North Eastern Region Emergency Feeding, "Rotherham/Sheffield Emergency Feeding Study, 14–15 April 1953."

45. PRO HO 322/209, Regional Civil Defence Exercises and Studies Reports, "Short Commons," 20–21 November 1959.

46. PRO HO 322/309, Draft Report, "Janus 63 Study: Post Nuclear Attack; Government and Local Government Functions," 1963.

47. PRO HO 322/308, "Janus 64 Study: Post Nuclear Attack; Local Authority Functions; Report of Study," 1964.

48. Ibid. from "Aim of Study," introduced by R. L. Jones.

49. PRO HO 322/340, "Minerva 65 Study: Reports," 1965. Participants included representatives from the HO; air commander of Home Defence Forces; U.K. Land Forces; Post Office; MAFF; Ministries of Health, Housing and Local Government; Labour; Pensions and National Insurance; Power, Public Buildings and Works; Transport; Scottish Home and Health Department; police and fire services; WVS; government of Northern Ireland; Canadian EMO; and American OCD.

50. PRO HO 322/688, Operational Studies: Minerva 1968, "Problems of Survival in Fall-Out Areas, Arrangements; Cancellation Due to Government 'Care and Maintenance' Policy," J. L. Durward (HO), memo to all members of Directing Staff of A1 division, 23 January 1968. (A second file, HO 322/689, is closed.)

51. NARA RG 396 Entry 1029 650 42/05/05; Box 1, OEP, "Operation Sentinel II 1957, September 18, 19, 20 Thomasville Georgia."

52. NARA RG 396 Entry 1029 650 42/05/05, Box 1, OEP, "Operation Sentinel II, October 1-2-3, 1957. The Post Attack Food Problem. A Report and Analysis, FCDA Region 6, Denver Colorado."

53. NARA RG 396 Entry 1029 650 42/05/05, Box 1, OEP, "Sentinel II Replies."

54. Taylor 2003: 28–29.

55. NARA RG 396 Entry 1029 650 42/05/05, Box 1, OEP, "Operation Sentinel [I] Comments, March '57."

56. DDEPL, Cabinet Series, Box 7, "Notes on the Expanded Cabinet Meeting held from 2:30 to 3:45 P.M. on Wednesday, July 25, 1956."

57. PRO HO 322/100, Consideration of Report to CD Joint Planning Staff (CDJPS) by Minister of Housing and Local Government Working Party on the Disposal of Civilian Dead

in War, "Report of the Working Party on Disposal of Civilian Dead in War," 4 November 1952.

58. Poole, Lloyd, and Hally, vol. 5, 1989b: 22; and Civil Defence (Planning) Regulations of 1974, announced by HO Circular ES.1/1972 of March 1972, rpt. in Thomas 1977: 8.

59. PRO HO 322/210, Impressment of Labour for Civil Defence Purposes, 1953–54, quoted in Crossley 1982: 38, 14.

60. London Boroughs Association 1989: 19; and R. Clarke 1986: 171–72.

61. Poole, Lloyd, and Hally, vol. 8, 1989b: 12–13.

62. Stanford Research Institute 1953: 80.

63. NLM MS.C 187 Elizabeth G. Pritchard Papers, Box 24, Clarence E. Otter (OCD Detroit Metropolitan Area), letter to Major Victor H. Vogel, 16 October 1942.

64. Herts and Essex Nuclear Free Zone 1991: 137.

65. London Boroughs Association 1989: 19.

66. US FCDA 1956d: 14.

67. Greater London Council, Public Relations Branch 1985: n.p; and London Boroughs Association 1989: 19.

68. *Statutory Instruments 1949 No. 2145, The Civil Defence (Burial) Regulations* (UK 1949a: 648) states that local authorities will make plans to be put into effect in the event or threat of hostile action that will facilitate identification and disposal of bodies; determine buildings and land to be used, and plan for provision of personnel, vehicles, material, and equipment needed; estimate expenses; designate officer in charge; and train staff. See PRO HO 186/2301, Rescue School, 1942–45.

69. PRO "Consideration of Report."

70. South Yorkshire Fire and Civil Defence Authority 1988a.

71. PRO "Consideration of Report" "Group 2 Tactical Study, Serial II," 9.

72. PRO "Consideration of Report."

73. US FCDA 1956b: 4.

74. US FCDA 1957a: 3; FCDA 1956d: 11–13.

75. NARA RG 396 Entry 1029 650 42/05/05, Box 5, OPAL 58, "Report on Operation Alert 1958 New Orleans, La.," 1958.

76. US FCDA 1956d: 1–2.

77. DA, Civil Defence Health Planning Group, National Ministry of Health and Welfare, *Civil Defence Health Services Manual* [Typescript from Civil Defence Manual No. 7,1953]: 6–10.

78. US FCDA 1956d: 1–2.

79. Weart 1988: 130.

80. PRO HO 322/184, BEAGLE II: Functions of Civil Defence Forces and the Army after Nuclear Attack, 1955, "Summary of Syndicate Discussions on the Questions Posed at Study 'BEAGLE II,' held at the Civil Defence Staff College from 3rd–6th October, 1955."

81. NARA RG 396 Entry 1029 650 42/05/05, Box 2, "Report of Joint State–FCDA Regional Office Planning Conference on CPX, 'Operation Second Phase' December 7, 1954."

82. NARA RG 396 Entry 1029 650 42/05/05, Box 1, OEP, E. J. Quindlen (FCDA), "Operation Sentinel: A Report and Analysis," sub-report by George B. Hotchkiss, Jr., "Some Attack Effects for Operation Sentinel," II: 47–48.

83. Industrial College of the Armed Forces 1954: 38–39.

84. Ibid.: 80–110.

85. NARA RG 396 Entry 1029 650 42/05/05, Box 4, OPAL 58, ODCM Region VI, "Emergency Operations Plan for the OORO [Office of OPAL Resources and Operations], Region VI," July 1958.

86. NARA RG 396 Entry 1029 650 42/05/05, Box 4, Canadian Civil Defense, Amended Directing Staff Instructions, "National Test Exercise May 3–4 and 9, 1958 Co-Operation II," 1958.

87. NARA RG 396 Entry 1029 650 42/05/05, Box 7, "Operation Alert 1959. Extracts from OCDM Region I Report of the Regional Phase, July 8–9–10, 1959"; and NARA RG 396 Entry 1029 650 42/05/05, Box 6, A. C. O'Connor (Regional Director Region I), memo to Division Engineer (US Corps of Engineers), 7 July 1959.

88. U.S. Congress 1965: 257.

89. Quoted in Scudamore et al. 2002: 775–87. See also UK, Health Protection Agency 2001.

11. Continuity of Government

1. Taylor 2003: 27.

2. L. Clarke 1999: 99.

3. National Security Archive, Haldeman Diary.

4. McCamley 1998: 246–47. Canada explored a similar possibility in July 1947, later abandoning the plan after the Russian H-bomb test. Maloney 1997: 43.

5. Diacon 1984: 51–53.

6. Walter 1963: 19–21. The system was refined in 1963. At this time, locations are reported as: RSG-1 moved from Newcastle to Catterick; RSG-2 moved from Leeds to York; RSG-3 Nottingham; RSG-4 Cambridge; RSG-5 presumably in London, but probably not still in the Geological Museum in Exhibition Road; RSG-6 moved from Reading Gaol to Warren Row; RSG-7 moved from Bristol to near Kingsbridge; RSG-8 moved from Cardiff to near Brecon; RSG-9 moved from Birmingham to near Kidderminster; RSG-10 moved from Manchester to near Preston; RSG-11 Edinburgh; and RSG-12 moved from Tunbridge Wells to Dover Castle. In addition, there was a new facility at Armagh and the Scottish RSG at Anstruther. Subterranea Britannica, an organization for enthusiasts of all sorts of underground sites, maintains a Web site and links to useful information on Cold War facilities. See www.subbrit.org.uk, accessed 17 December 2005.

7. Ozorak 1998: 167.

8. PRO HO 322/651, Regional Government in an Emergency: Pamphlet Published by "Ipswich Anarchists" ("Spies for Peace") and Details of Public Demonstrations, 1966–67. See also Laurie 1979; and Greene et al. 1982: 82–84.

9. J. Cowan 1994. Kelvedon Hatch is the site of the 1963 film *A Hole in the Ground*.

10. Anstruther Defence Establishment Preservation Trust 1994.

11. PRO HO 322/141, HO, Command and Control: Exercises and Studies by Midland Civil Defence Region, Exercise "Mercian Trump," Report.

12. McCamley 1998: 219–26.

13. PRO HO 322/141, HO, Command and Control: Exercises and Studies by Midland Civil Defence Region, Exercise "Mercian Trump II," Rehearsal Programme for 4 May 1961.

14. PRO HO 322/141, HO, Command and Control: Exercises and Studies by Midland Civil Defence Region, Exercise "Mercian Trump II," Report.

15. DA, "Copy of Classified Location Information Paper Prepared in February 1960 for the Honorable R. B. Curry (Director, EMO, Privy Council Office). This is bound in with OCDM, "Draft Plan for Operations at the Classified Location," 1960. For a basic description of Greenbrier, see Vanderbilt 2002: 135–39.

16. DA, "Copy of Classified Location Information Paper," Tab L.

17. FCDA headquarters was moved from Washington, D.C., to Battle Creek, Michigan, in 1954 on the assumption that it was a safer location. Decentralization proved very inefficient for peacetime functioning and the Kennedy administration moved operations back to the capital, retaining Battle Creek as the Region 4 headquarters and Staff College.

18. While there are examples of federal, regional, state, and local cooperation in OPAL exercises, exercise information does not extend higher than Low Point. Canada's CEGHQ undertook the tasks assigned to Low Point (particularly radiological monitoring) as well as High Point (Mt. Weather) and the presidential HQ aloft.

19. DA, [A.T. Jeffrey], Foundation of Canada Engineering Corporation Limited for DND, "Project EASE Survival Capability Study," ca. 1960: 21. OCDM offered its full support on design matters. See NARA RG 396 Entry 1015 650 41/33/05, Box 7, "OCDM Headquarters Central Files," Leo A. Hoegh, memo to General Goodpaster (White House), 6 March 1959.

20. Maloney 1997: 44–46; and DA, John G. Diefenbaker, Cabinet Document 204/58, "Memorandum to Cabinet," 21 July 1958.

21. DA, Privy Council, EMO, R. B. Curry, Cabinet Committee on Emergency Plans, 26 November 1959: 2; see also DA, Privy Council, EMO, R. L. Beatty and J. C. Morrison, "Summary Record of the Dominion-Provincial Conference on Civil Defence Arrangements," 20 May 1959.

22. DA, R. B. Curry, Cabinet Committee on Emergency Plans, 4 June 1959; and DA, EPC, "Rustic Plan," EPC 1/82 (supersedes EPC 1/80 ed.), 1982. See also Maloney 1997: 44–46.

23. Maloney 1997: 53.

24. DA, EPC, "Central Relocation Unit Operational Procedures and Administrative Functions," EPC 17/81, 1981. CRU No. 6 is the largest, with an operations area measuring approximately 625 square feet.

25. The original plan to build ten sites, one per province, was abandoned. REGHQs were constructed on military bases stretching coast to coast: in 1961 Debert, Nova Scotia; in 1963 Valcartier, Quebec, and Borden, Ontario (also the site for the Joint Nuclear Biological and Chemical Defensive Warfare School); and in 1964 Shilo, Manitoba; Penhold, Alberta; and Nanaimo, British Columbia. Only Debert is not fully underground. Valcartier's proximity to Quebec City necessitated that it be built to withstand 15 psi, but other sites were not considered blastproof. Like the Diefenbunker, they had high fallout protection, equipment to regulate interior conditions and exclude radiation, emergency water supplies, back-up power, radio and telecommunications reception and transmission, satellite meteorological links, decontamination equipment, and medical facilities. Each REGHQ was approximately 68,500 square feet, capable of housing between 293 and 387 staff. DA, Privy Council Office, EMO, "Data for use in Design of Main BRIDGE Headquarters," 31 October 1960.

26. N. Campbell 1961; "This is the Diefenbunker!" 1961; and DA, R. B. Bryce, "Memorandum to the Cabinet Committee on Emergency Plans. Accommodation for Ministers and Officers on Stand-by Duty for War Purposes," 9 November 1960.

27. At 650 pounds of steel per cubic yard, this is nearly five times the standard in ordinary reinforced structures. The walls of the Diefenbunker are thinner than the tungsten-reinforced early British bunkers; this reflects what was learned in the interim from empirical testing of nuclear devices. All metal in the structure—reinforcing rods, doors, pipes, subfloors, etc.—is grounded.

28. Based on information from the film *Nuclear Roof*, 1961; DA, "Building Statistics and Other Information CFS Carp," 1968; DA, David McConnell, Staff Historian at Historic Sites and Monuments Board of Canada, "'The Diefenbunker': the Central Emergency Government Headquarters at Carp" [ca. 1990]; DA, "Details of Receiver Building R-I Carp"; DA, "Memorandum to the Cabinet Committee on Emergency Plans, Progress Report on the Long-Term Physical Arrangements in the Ottawa Area for Emergency Government (Project EASE)," 7 May 1959; DA, Foundation of Canada Engineering Corporation Limited for the Department of National Defence, "Preliminary Report, Projected Facilities at EASE," 6 July 1959; and DA, [A.T. Jeffrey], Foundation of Canada Engineering Corporation Limited for the Department of National Defence, "Project EASE Survival Capability Study," ca. 1960.

29. DA, [typescript] "The Evolution of the Civil Situation Monitoring and Briefing Capability at the Central Emergency Government Headquarters, Canadian Forces Stations Carp (the Diefenbunker) from 1961 to 1992," 1992.

30. DA, "Continuity of Government Program Review Background Discussion Paper," 1989.

31. For their part, the British planned to send the Queen to an undisclosed bunker and then abroad, possibly to Canada. Day 2004: A8.

32. Maloney 1997: 51; and DA, EPC, "Fact Sheet, Continuity of Government Program: Emergency Government Facilities," 1989.

33. DA, DND, "Historical Report—CFS Carp," 1976.

34. A sample script for a circuit TV briefing during an unknown exercise in 1985 augments interpretation of these photographs. DA, filed with "Exercise Fifth Key General Reading Material," 16 November 1989.

35. DA, EMO, [Draft] "Manual of Staff Procedures in Emergency Government Headquarters," 1970; and "Planning Guide for Emergency Government Headquarters. EPC Manual #7," 1 November 1989.

36. The continuity of government program called for thirty-one ZEGHQs, but only nine sites were ever renovated or built and equipped. Each province had several zones, based on geography, transportation access, and population. Sparsely populated rural zones could be vast. Zones coordinated municipalities, which were responsible for traffic control; water; shelter programs; communications utilizing local resources such as ham radios, taxis, and police; radiological defense drawing on local scientists and teachers; public information; evacuation for institutionalized persons, and care of evacuated children and dependent adults; recruiting and training auxiliary fire, police, and volunteer workers; mutual aid planning for neighboring municipalities; plans related to warning times; reception accommodation, registration, and feeding; sanitation, garbage, sewage, and vermin control; epi-

demic control and immunization; and maintenance of law and order. DA, EMO, "A Guide to Civil Emergency Planning for Municipalities," 1964.

37. DA, EPC, "Joint Standing Orders and Operational Procedures for Central Emergency Government Facility (Provisional)," 1979.

38. Steed 1985.

39. DA, EMO, "Regional Emergency Government Headquarters," 1964; and [Exercise Fifth Key] "Regional Commissioner—Terms of Reference," 1988.

40. Corp. Bob Biggs (ret.), interview with author 2004.

41. DA, R. B. Curry (Privy Council Office), "Memorandum to the Cabinet Committee on Emergency Plans. Subject: Regional Centers for Government in War," 1960; and "History of Civil Defense in Canada 1936 to 1968," 23 July 2003.

42. DA, PEI Scrapbook, unattributed clipping, "Pleased With Civil Defense Exercise Held in Capital Yesterday," 4 May 1960.

43. Maloney 1997: 54.

44. Of around five thousand municipalities in Canada, only a few hundred established any emergency capability. DA, "Canada EMO Bulletin No. 14: Decentralization of Government Emergency Government Zones," 1 May 1973; and "Exercise Fifth Key General Reading Material," 16 November 1989.

45. A fan out is a calling pyramid: A calls B, who calls C, and so on.

46. NAC RG 57 EMO, Acc. 1984–85/658, Box 38, File 2615-1 pt. 1, EMO, "Exercise Tocsin 66: Exercise Instructions (EXTOCS)," 1966, Serial IV (DS): 3.

47. Carnicke 1998: 112–23.

48. NAC RG 57 EMO, Acc. 1984–85/658, Box 38, File 2615-1 pt. 3, B. P. O'Connell (EMO), "Memo to Chief, Training and Exercise Division. Exercise TOCSIN 66 and FALLEX 66—Ministerial Participation," 9 February 1966.

49. NAC RG 57 EMO, Acc. 1984–85/658, Box 38, File 2615-1 pt. 1, EMO, "Exercise Tocsin 66: Exercise Instructions (EXTOCS)," 1966, Serial IV (DS): 19–21.

50. NAC RG 57 EMO, Acc. 1984–85/658, Box 38, File 2615-1 pt. 1, "Exercise Tocsin 66. Exercise Instructions (EXTOCS)," Serial 1: 3.

51. NAC RG 57 EMO, Acc. 1984–85/658, Box 38, File 2616-3 pt 1, Exercise RAINEX 2, 1970.

52. DA, "Exercise Minor Key [at FWC Carp]," 4–5 September 1991.

53. DA, DND, "Historical Report—CFS Carp," 1976.

54. DA, Diefenbunker footage, 1994.

55. DA, Privy Council Office, EMO, "Data for use in Design of Main BRIDGE Headquarters," 31 October 1960.

56. DA, "Exercise Fifth Key General Reading Material,"16 November 1989. Emphasis in original.

57. DA, "Input to EPC Annual Report to Parliament Continuity of Government," 1988.

12. Computer Play

1. Edwards 1996: 104.

2. L. Clarke 1999: 129.

3. Ibid.: 99.

4. Eden 2004.

5. Hausrath 1971: 8; and Edwards 1996: 114–16.

6. Wilson 1968: 48.

7. Peter Nordlie, cited in M. Clarke 1982: 32. Nordlie regards these factors, along with preservation of basic cultural values, as the sine qua non of national "survivability."

8. Hausrath 1971: 80; Light 2003: 41–42; and Edwards 1996: 125–34.

9. Hausrath 1971: 12.

10. Clark 1958; Lowry 1966; Sullivan, Guthe, Thoms, and Adelman 1979; NARA RG 396 Entry 1029 650 42/05/05, Box 2, FCDA Memo, "Damage Printout for Operation Alert 1956," 20 April 1956 [produced by the Stanford Research Institute using the Universal Transverse Mercator (UTM) Grid System]; and DA, [typescript, source unknown] Lloyd B. Addington, US Army Office of Chief of Engineers, "Postattack Viability of the United States — 1975," 1970.

11. Taylor 2003: 32.

12. W. M. Brown 1971. See also Winter 1967.

13. Miller and Duke 1981: 216.

14. Adelman 1972: 222.

15. Allen 1987: 248, 246. Emphasis in original.

16. Perla 1990: 9.

17. NARA RG 396 Entry 1029 650 42/05/05, Box 4, OPAL 58, "Annex 'C': Operations Plan OPAL Office of Resources and Operations OPAL Stabilization Agency [Region V]," 1958.

18. NARA RG 396 Entry 1029 650 42/05/05, Box 4, "OCDM Region 7 Evaluation Report," 1958.

19. Ibid.

20. Winter 1967: 4.

21. NARA RG 396 Entry 1029 650 42/05/05, Box 7, Operation Alert 1959: Extracts from OCDM Region IV Report of the Regional Phase, July 8–9–10, 1959, Joseph Borus, "Manpower Task Force Report": 4.

22. NARA RG 396 Entry 1029 650 42/05/05, Box 7, "Operation Alert 1959: Extracts from OCDM Region III Report of the Regional Phase, July 8–9–10, 1959": 7.

23. NARA RG 396 Entry 1029 650 42/05/05, Box 7, Operation Alert 1959: Extracts from OCDM Region IV Report of the Regional Phase, July 8–9–10, 1959, Joseph Borus, "Manpower Task Force Report": 3.

24. NARA RG 396 Entry 1029 650 42/05/05, Box 7, "Operation Alert 1959: Extracts from OCDM Region VII Report of the Regional Phase, July 8–9–10, 1959": 34.

25. NARA RG 396 Entry 1029 650 42/05/05, Box 7, "Operation Alert 1959: Extracts from OCDM Region VI Report of the Regional Phase, July 8–9–10, 1959": 15.

26. NARA RG 396 Entry 1029 650 42/05/05, Box 7, "Operation Alert 1959: Extracts from OCDM Region VII Report of the Regional Phase, July 8–9–10, 1959": 33.

27. NARA RG 396 Entry 1029 650 42/05/05, Box 7, "OPAL 59 — Relocation Phase August 24–28, 1959, Problems — Financial Area: Part I."

28. DDEPL, White House Office Cabinet Secretariat Box 4, OPAL 60, "Director's Staff — OPAL '59 — Problem No. 17, Indemnification Announcement (OCDM R[egion] 7 Stabilization)."

29. NARA RG 396 Entry 1029 650 42/05/05, Box 7, "OPAL 59 — Relocation Phase August 24–28, 1959, Exercise Problems Stabilization Area Part II": 1–4; and DDEPL, White House Office Cabinet Secretariat Box 4, OPAL 60, "Director's Staff — OPAL '59 — Problem No. 15, National Rationing System OCDM (Region I and Stabilization)."

30. Perla 1990: 276.

31. Brewer and Shubik 1979: 16, 52.

32. Wilson 1968: 58–59.

33. Allen 1987: 261–63.

34. City planners, scientists, and others (notably Project East River) argued for dispersal and new urban forms. Some dispersal occurred, but it is debatable whether this was due to defense concerns. See Dudley 2001: 52–63.

35. University of Maryland, College Park 1955.

36. Ibid.: 9.

37. Iklé and Kincaid 1956: 3–4.

38. Kahn 1984: 183–86.

39. US Department of Commerce 1956: 11.

40. Billheimer, Bullemer, Simpson, and Wood 1976.

41. This is the Adagio computer model, predicated on an attack of 6,559 MT nationwide, the largest blasts (20 MT each) on ICBM fields, with fallout 86 percent of the land mass receiving at least 10 r per hour. Haaland, Chester, and Wigner 1976.

42. Strope, Henderson, and Rainey 1977: Sec. 2–2.

43. JHK and Associates 1977.

44. Strope, Pond, and Schultze 1976: 59.

45. Systems analysis results in symbolic models, which can be rendered in descriptive form (textual or diagramatic), mathematically (analytic, with exact numerical solutions), or simulations "that may be used to converge on solutions to very com[p]lex problems involving uncertainty (probabilistic occurrence) and risk." Civil defense exercises often utilized a combination. White and Hendrix 1982: 105.

46. Earlier scenarios often contain the proviso that their bombing patterns do not reflect military expectations; this protected the secrecy of defense plans. See US DOD 1975a. A 1980 pamphlet giving the same information in digest form disseminated the news even more widely: US FEMA 1980. The DOD had additional lists of Military Vital Points covering property under their jurisdiction and Vital Material Contractors who provided essential supplies. In Canada, comparable civilian resources were chronicled in the *Vital Points Manual* of 1987, first developed as a plan in 1970 (for peacetime) and 1978 (for war). See Canada EPC, *Vital Points*, 1987. Canadian population distributions made something like CRP less feasible except perhaps in southern Ontario. In the United Kingdom, the size of the land mass ruled out a CRP-type solution. For a political analysis of the United Kingdom's vulnerability, see M. Clarke 1982: 102–62.

47. Stone 1963: Annex I.

48. US DCPA, *Fact Sheet*, 1974.

49. FEMA argued that the USSR had a survival capability of 90 percent compared to the United States' 40 percent. US FEMA 1981c. Supposedly, the more disciplined Soviet citizenry were better adapted to following the kind of authority necessary to make emergency relocation *en masse* feasible. Chester, Cristy, and Haaland 1975.

50. Harvey and Hubenette 1974.

51. Strope, Henderson, and Rainey 1977: Sec. 2:6.

52. Chenault and Davis 1975b: 7.

53. US DCPA, *Fact Sheet*, 1974; *El Paso County Crisis Relocation Plan*, 1976; JHK and Associates

1973; Chenault and Davis 1975a; Henderson and Strope 1978; *Guide for Crisis Relocation Contingency Planning*, 1976; and Leavitt 1974.

54. US FEMA 1983a, 1983b, and 1983c.

55. US FEMA 1983d.

56. US FEMA 1981a.

57. US FEMA 1981b.

58. Green and Parker 1994: 9. See also Quarantelli 1986.

59. Rogers 1980.

60. US FEMA 1981a: n.p.

61. Harker and Wilmore 1979: Sec. 7:4.

62. Ibid.: Appendix C.

63. Iklé and Kincaid 1956: 44–45.

64. Strope, Nehnevajsa, and Dresch 1974: 16.

65. Calvan 1983: 28–29. This is depicted in Peter Watkins' epic film *The Journey* (1983–85).

66. Calvan 1983: 36.

67. Farace 1972: 25.

68. Harker and Coleman 1975: 52.

69. Laurino, Trinkl, and Dresch 1980: 9.

70. Ibid.: 115. See also Laurino, Trinkl, Miller, and Harker 1977: vii.

71. Edwards 1996: 120.

72. Kraake, Helling, and Huber 1993: 136–37.

73. Edwards 1996: 340–41.

74. NARA RG 396 Entry 1029 650 42/05/05, Box 7, Operation Alert 1959: Extracts from OCDM Region IV Report of the Regional Phase, July 8–9–10, 1959, Joseph Borus, "Manpower Task Force Report": 4.

Afterword: Dismantling Civil Defense

1. Ken Farrell, interview with author, 2000. See also Farrell, Coyne, and Jewsbury 1986.

2. Paul Joseph Watson and Alex Jones. Prison Planet Web site, www.prisonplanet.com/articles/july2005/090705bombingexercises.htm, accessed 25 May 2006.

3. McEwan 2005b: A-31.

4. US DHS 2005.

5. Amacher 2003: 34–37, 40–43.

6. US FEMA 2005.

7. American Red Cross Web site, www.redcross.org. Accessed 17 December 2005.

8. Rush University Medical Center, Chicago 2005, in collaboration with the Uniformed Services University of the Health Sciences, offers several for-credit programs, including emergency mental health after a suicide bombing, psychiatric sequelae in a survivor of 9/11, and disaster planning for inhalational anthrax, pulmonary toxicants, SARS, and smallpox.

9. Gellman and Schmidt 2002: A1. The 1950s' plans are supplemented by President Reagan's National Security Decision Directive 188, "Government Coordination for National Security Emergency Preparedness," 16 September 1985, in Simpson 1995: 457, 591–94.

10. Associated Press Report 2002.

11. NATO AC/98-D/80 Annex, NATO Civil Defence Committee, "Informing the Public," 3 July 1959: 11.

12. Starbucks Coffee Company 2004. This was not renewed in 2005: it would have seemed tactless in the aftermath of Hurricane Katrina's devastation of the Gulf Coast.

13. Carey and O'Connor 2004: A9. During the height of the anthrax scare in 2001, as spores were sent through the post to seemingly random recipients as well as politicians, 25 percent of Americans polled claimed to maintain emergency supplies of food, water, or clothing. Hilts 2001: B7.

14. Smith 2005: B2.

15. McEwan 2005a.

16. "Three-Day Bioterrorism," 2002: A11; Hu 2002: A23; and S. Kershaw 2003: A19.

17. E. Ross 2005.

18. In 2005, Britain published "Preparing for Emergencies: What You Need to Know" and distributed it to all households, occasioning much derision. See also Bruce, Donovan, and Hornof 2004.

19. Wells 1948. Wells states in his preface to *The World Set Free* that the novel was written in 1913 and published early in 1914. He credits Soddy 1909 for scientific insight.

20. Peterson 1983; Royal Society of Canada 1985; Peattie 1984: 32–36; Ehrlich 1984: 1–15; and Forrow and Sidel 1998: 456–61. Edward Teller 1987 was a stubborn voice against this.

21. See Robinson 1959; Auerbach and Warren 1969: 126–47; US National Academy of Sciences 1975; Weart 1988: 203; and NARA RG 396 1009, Box 1, Letter from Philip Wylie, 15 February 1955.

22. "Ready or Not?: System Failure" 2005.

23. Withington 2003: 15–16.

24. Sanger 2001: A1, B6.

25. NARA RG 397 Entry #55 650 42/29/07–02, Box 8, "Questions and Answers on Crisis Relocation Planning," 9 August 1978.

26. A. C. Cowan 2006; DePalma 2006; "More Domestic Spying" 2006.

WORKS CITED

Archives

Bristol City Libraries (BCL), Bristol
British Library (BL) Department of Manuscripts, London
Diefenbunker Archive (DA), Canada's Cold War Museum, Carp Ontario
Dwight D. Eisenhower Presidential Library (DDEPL), Abilene, Kans.
East Sussex Records Office, Lewes
Harold Washington Library (HWLC), Chicago
John F. Kennedy Library (JFKL), Boston
National Archives (NARA), College Park, Md.
National Archives of Canada (NAC), Ottawa
National Archives of Ireland (NAI), Dublin
National Archives of the United Kingdom/Public Records Office (PRO), London
National Library of Medicine (NLM), Bethesda, Md.
National Security Archive, Washington, http://www.gwu.edu/~nsarchiv
North Atlantic Treaty Organization (NATO), Brussels
Northwestern University Special Collections, Evanston, Ill.
Scout Association Archive, London
Stanford University Libraries, Stanford, Calif.
Swarthmore College (SPC), Swarthmore, Pa.

Artistic Works and Non-Print Media

The Atomic Bomb: Its Effects and How to Meet Them. 1952. Directed by David H. Villiers. Produced by Ronald H. Riley. Verity Films. Filmstrip.
Communications for Civil Defense. 1950s. Bell Telephones of Canada. Filmstrip.
The Day After. 1983. Directed by Nicholas Meyer. ABC-TV. Videocassette.
The Day that Made a Difference. 1964. US OCD. Filmstrip.
Diefenbunker footage. 1994. Videocassette.
Duck and Cover. 1952. US FCDA and Safety Commission of the National Education Association. Produced in cooperation with the Public Schools of Astoria and New York, N.Y. Archer Productions Inc. Filmstrip.

A Hole in the Ground. 1963. Royal Observer Corps. Filmstrip.

The Journey. 1983–85. Directed by Peter Watkins. Produced by Swedish Peace and Arbitration Society (Stockholm) and Canadian National Film Board (Ottawa). Filmstrip.

Memorandum to Industry. 1966. US OCD. Filmstrip.

Nuclear Roof. ca. 1961. Produced by the Canadian Army and Foundation Group of Companies. Filmstrip.

On the Beach. 1959. Produced and directed by Stanley Kramer. United Artists. Filmstrip.

Operation Lifesaver. 1956. Directed by Isobel Kehoe. National Film Board. Filmstrip.

"Ready or Not?: System Failure." 2005. ABC-TV *Primetime,* 15 September. Executive Producer Lisa Soloway. Videocassette.

Rehearsal for Disaster. ca. 1956–57. US FCDA. Filmstrip.

Six Feet Under, "The Plan." 2002. Written by Kate Robin. Directed by Rose Troche. HBO. Season 2, episode 16. Videocassette.

Tony n' Tina's Wedding. 1988. Artificial Intelligence. Produced by Joseph and Dan Corcoran. Directed by Larry Pelligrini. Edison Hotel, New York. Performance.

W5: Open Target. 1988. Produced by CTV. Videocassette.

The War Game. 1966. BBC. Written and produced by Peter Watkins. Filmstrip.

War of the Worlds. 1938. Adapted by Howard Koch from the novel by H. G. Wells. Filmstrip.

Interviews and Correspondence

Biggs, Bob, Corporal (ret.). Interview with author, 24 August 2004.

Farrell, Ken. Interview with author, 18 August 2000.

Fox, Louise. Interview with author, 26 July 2004.

Hurt, Donald. Interview with Melissa Hurt, 21 April 2003.

———. Correspondence with author, 23 April 2003.

Pollock, Della. Lecture delivered at Northwestern University, 20 October 2000.

Smith, Anne-Marie. Correspondence with author, 5 July 2005.

Published Sources

Abbott, H. Porter. 2002. *The Cambridge Introduction to Narrative.* Cambridge: Cambridge University Press.

Abrams, Herbert L. 1984. "Medical Resources after Nuclear War." *Bulletin of the Atomic Scientists* 40, no. 10: 23–26.

"Acting and Reacting 6. — The Living Image." 1951. *Casualties Union Journal* 2, no. 5 (May): 6.

Adelman, Irma. 1972. "Economic System Simulations." In *Simulation in Social and Administrative Science Overviews and Case-Examples,* edited by Harold Guetzkow, Philip Kotter, and Randall L. Schultz, 210–25. Englewood Cliffs: Prentice-Hall.

A.J.M. 1960. "The 500 Who Didn't Hide." *Liberation:* 3–5.

Alberta Civil Defence. 1955. *Operation "Lifesaver."* Edmonton.

———. 1950s. *Wardens' Manual.* Edmonton.

Allen, T. B. 1987. *War Games: The Secret World of the Creators, Players, and Policy Makers Rehearsing World War III Today.* New York: McGraw-Hill.

Allnutt, Bruce C. 1971. *A Study of Consensus on Social and Psychological Factors Related to Recovery From Nuclear Attack.* McLean, Va.: Human Sciences Research Inc.

Altman, James W. 1960. "Laboratory Research on the Habitability of Public Fallout Shelters." In *Symposium on Human Problems in the Utilization of Fallout Shelters, 11 and 12 February 1960*, edited by George W. Baker and John H. Rohrer, 157–66. Washington: National Research Council.

Altman, James W., Robert W. Smith, Rheda L. Meyers, Frank S. McKenna, and Sara Bryson. 1960. *Psychological and Social Adjustment in a Simulated Shelter*. Pittsburgh: American Institute for Research.

Amacher, Peter. 2003. "You're on Your Own—Again." *Bulletin of the Atomic Scientists* 59, no. 3: 34–37, 40–43.

American Association of School Administrators. National Commission on Safety Education. National Education Association. 1966. *A Realistic Approach to Civil Defense: a Handbook for School Administrators*. Washington.

American Council on Education. Committee on Civil Defense and Higher Education. 1954. *Civil Defense and Higher Education*. Washington: American Council on Education.

American Psychiatric Association. 1952. *Diagnostic and Statistical Manual: Mental Disorders*. Washington: American Psychiatric Association.

———. 1954. *Psychological First Aid in Community Disasters*. Washington: American Psychiatric Association.

———. 1956. *Disaster Fatigue: The Cause and Treatment of Psychological Disorders in Civil Disaster*. Washington: American Psychiatric Association.

———. 1968. *DSM-II: Diagnostic and Statistical Manual of Mental Disorders*. Washington: American Psychiatric Association.

———. 1980. *DSM-III: Diagnostic and Statistical Manual of Mental Disorders*. Washington: American Psychiatric Association.

Anderson, Martha Willis. 1964. *Levels of Activity*. Pittsburgh: Office of Civil Defense.

Anstruther Defence Establishment Preservation Trust. 1994. "Scotland's Secret Bunker: A Guide & History 1951–1993." Press release.

Aristotle. 1966. *Metaphysics*. Translated by Richard Hope. Ann Arbor: University of Michigan Press.

"The Army Joins C.D. Atom Exercise." 1951. *Alert: the Official Organ of the National Federation of Civil Defence Associations* 18 (April): 4.

Associated Press Report. 2002. "Congress Mulls Doomsday Plan." 31 May. CBS News. http://www.cbsnews.com/stories/2002/05/30/politics/main510562.shtml. Accessed 19 August 2005.

Associated Universities, Inc. 1952. *Report of the Project East River. Prepared under Signal Corps Contract No. DA-19-025-SC-96*. New York: Associated Universities.

Atkinson, Tom. 1968. "Public Responses during an International Crisis." In *Annual Progress Report Civil Defense Research Project March 1967–March 1968*, 290–311. Oak Ridge, Tenn.: Oak Ridge National Laboratory.

"Atomic Defence Training." 1949. *Casualties Union Journal* 15 (November): 12–13.

Auerbach, Stanley I., and Shields Warren. 1969. "Medical and Ecological Effects of Nuclear Weapons." In *Survival and the Bomb: Methods of Civil Defense*, edited by Eugene P. Wigner, 126–47. Bloomington: Indiana University Press.

Auerswald, Philip E., Lewis M. Branscomb, Todd M. La Porte, and Erwann O. Michel-Kerjan, eds. 2006. *Seeds of Disaster, Roots of Response: How Private Action Can Reduce Public Vulnerability*. Cambridge: Cambridge University Press.

Austin, J. L. 1962. *How to Do Things with Words*. 2d ed. Cambridge, Mass.: Harvard University Press.

Bacon, Wallace A. 1966. *The Art of Interpretation*. New York: Holt, Rinehart and Winston.

Baker, George W., and Dwight W. Chapman, eds. 1962. *Man and Society in Disaster*. New York: Basic Books.

Baker, John Overend. 1951. *Civil Defence and You*. London: Jordan and Sons.

Baraibar, Aitor. 1999. "Stelarc's Post-Evolutionary Performance Art: Exposing Collisions between the Body and Technology." *Women and Performance* 11, no. 1: 157–68.

Barba, Eugenio. 2000. "The Deep Order Called Turbulence: The Three Faces of Dramaturgy." *TDR: The Drama Review* 44, no. 4 (winter): 55–66.

Baudrillard, Jean. 2002. *The Spirit of Terrorism*. London: Verso.

Beck, Elsie Jane. 1975. "She Also Told It to the Marines," *Foresight* 2, no. 4 (July–August): 22–23.

Bennett, Scott H. 2003. *Radical Pacifism: The War Resisters League and Gandhian Nonviolence in America, 1915–1963*. Syracuse: Syracuse University Press.

Bentz, Richard, et al. 1956. *Some Civil Defense Problems in the Nation's Capital Following Widespread Thermonuclear Attack*. Chevy Chase, Md.: Operations Research Office, Johns Hopkins University.

Berenbaum, M. C. 1960. "The Civil Defence Fraud." *New Statesman* 60, no. 1538 (3 September): 292.

Beres, Louis René. 1983. "Subways to Armageddon." *Society* 20, no. 6: 7–10.

Berger, Peter. 1975. "Sociological Perspectives—Society as Drama." In *Life as Theater: A Dramaturgical Sourcebook*, edited by Denis Brissett and Charles Edgley, 13–22. New York: Aldine de Gruyter.

Biderman, Albert D. 1959. *The Relevance of Studies of Internment for the Problem of Shelter Habitability*. Vol. 2. Washington: National Research Council.

Billheimer, John W., Robert Bullemer, Arthur Simpson, and Robert Wood. 1976. *Impacts of the Crisis Relocation Strategy on Transportation Systems. Vol. II: Planning Guidelines. Vol. III: Prototype Plans. Final Report*. Washington: Defense Civil Preparedness Agency.

Blair, Bruce G., John E. Pike, and Stephen I. Schwartz. 1998. "Targeting and Controlling the Bomb." In *Atomic Audit: the Costs and Consequences of U.S. Nuclear Weapons since 1940*, edited by Stephen I. Schwartz, 197–268. Washington: Brookings Institution Press.

Blau, Herb. 1990. *The Audience*. Baltimore: Johns Hopkins University Press.

Bloomfield, Lincoln P. 1982. *The Foreign Policy Process: A Modern Primer*. Englewood Cliffs, N.J.: Prentice-Hall.

Bloomfield, Lincoln P., and Cornelius J. Gearin. 1973. "Games Foreign Policy Experts Play: The Political Exercise Comes of Age." *Orbis* 16, no. 4 (winter): 1008–31.

Boleslavsky, Richard. 1933. *Acting: The First Six Lessons*. New York: Theatre Arts Books.

Bolsover, Phil. 1982. *Civil Defence: The Cruellest Confidence Trick*. 2d ed. London: CND.

Boyer, Paul. 1985. *By the Bomb's Early Light: American Thought and Culture at the Dawn of the Atomic Age*. New York: Pantheon.

———. 1998. *Fallout: A Historian Reflects on America's Half-Century Encounter with Nuclear Weapons*. Columbus: Ohio State University Press.

Boyer, Robert D. 1979. *Realism in European Theatre and Drama, 1870–1920: A Bibliography*. Westport, Conn.: Greenwood.

Boy Scout Association. 1941. *Collection of Drug Plants by the Boy Scouts*. London: Boy Scout Association.

Boy Scouts of America. 1951a. *Family "Be Prepared" Plan*. New York: Boy Scouts of America.

———. 1951b. *Pattern for Survival: A Guide for Unit Leaders*. New York: Boy Scouts of America.

———. 1951–64. *Annual Reports to Congress*. Washington: United States Government Printing Office.

———. 1972. *Emergency Preparedness*. New Brunswick, N.J.: Boy Scouts of America.

Boyne, Roy. 2001. *Subject, Society and Culture*. London: Sage.

Brantl, Virginia M. 1958. "Operation Rebound." *American Journal of Nursing* 58, no. 11: 1550–51.

Brecht, Bertolt. 1964. *Brecht on Theatre*, edited and translated by John Willett. New York: Hill and Wang.

Brewer, Garry D., and Martin Shubik. 1979. *The War Game: A Critique of Military Problem Solving*. Cambridge, Mass.: Harvard University Press.

Briggs, Raymond. 1982. *When the Wind Blows*. London: Hamish Hamilton.

Brooks, Keith, Eugene Bahn, and L. LaMont Okey. 1967. *The Communicative Act of Oral Interpretation*. Boston: Allyn and Bacon.

Brown, Joanne. 1988. " 'A Is for Atom, B Is for Bomb': Civil Defense in American Public Education, 1948–1963." *Journal of American History* 75, no. 1: 68–90.

Brown, William M. 1963. *Strategic and Tactical Aspects of Civil Defense with Special Emphasis on Crisis Situations*. Harmon-on-Hudson, N.Y.: Hudson Institute.

———. 1971. *Recovery From a Nuclear Attack: A Study Based Upon a Hypothetical 1973 War Scenario*. Topanga, Calif.: self-published.

Bruce, James A., Kenneth F. Donovan, and Monica J. Hornof. 2004. *Public Safety and Emergency Preparedness Canada*. Ottawa: Science Applications International Corporation (SAIC Canada).

Burns, Robert. 1896. *The Poetry of Robert Burns*. Vol. 1, edited by William Ernest Henley and Thomas F. Henderson. Edinburgh: T. C. and E. C. Jack.

Butler, Robert. 2003. *The Art of Darkness: Staging the Phillip Pullman Trilogy*. London: Oberon Books.

Callon, Michel, and Bruno Latour. 1981. "Unscrewing the Big Leviathan." In *Advances in Social Theory and Methodology: Toward an Integration of Micro- and Macro-Strategies*, edited by K. Knorr-Cetina and A. V. Cicourel, 277–303. Boston: Routledge and Kegan Paul.

Calvan, Tracy. 1983. *Crisis Relocation Plans: The Realities of Planning for Nuclear Attack in New York State*. Albany: New York Assembly Standing Committee on Governmental Operations Subcommittee on Military and Civil Defense.

Cameron, Dale C. 1950. "Psychiatric Implications of Civil Defense." *American Journal of Psychiatry* 106: 587–93.

Campbell, Duncan. 1982. *War Plan UK: The Truth about Civil Defence in Britain*. London: Burnett.

Campbell, Norman. 1961. "Carp 'War Shelter' for Federal Govt." *Citizen* (Ottawa), 11 April.

Canada Central Mortgage and Housing Corporation. 1960. *Your Basement Fallout Shelter. Blueprint for Survival No. 1*. Ottawa.

Canada Department of Agriculture. 1961. *Fallout on the Farm. Blueprint for Survival No. 3.* Ottawa.

Canada Department of National Health and Welfare. 1965. *Casualty Simulation.* Ottawa.

Canada Department of National Health and Welfare, Civil Defence Canada. 1951. *Personal Protection under Atomic Attack. Civil Defence Manual No. 4.* Ottawa.

———. 1952. *The Warden Service.* Ottawa.

Canada Department of National Health and Welfare, Information Services Division. 1958. *National Civil Defence Day Friday September 19th 1958. Promotional Guide.* Ottawa.

Canada Department of Public Works. 1974. *Public Protection: Concept and Policy.* Ottawa.

Canada Department of Public Works, Development Engineering Branch. 1964. *Fallout Protection Survey. A Study of Procedures and Techniques Prepared for Federal Emergency Measures Organization.* Ottawa.

Canada Director of EMO for Halifax. Welfare Advisory Committee. 1964. *Welfare Plan for Local Disaster.* Rev. ed. Halifax.

Canada EMO. 1961. *Eleven Steps to Survival. Blueprint for Survival No. 4.* Ottawa.

———. 1962. *Simpler Shelters.* Ottawa.

———. 1968a. *Fallout Protection Survey of Canada. Alberta Region Survey Results. Analysis Study No. 1.* Ottawa.

———. 1968b. *Project Phoenix: Final Report.* Ottawa.

Canada EMO and DND. 1970. *Fallout Protection Surveys.* Ottawa.

Canada EPC. 1979. *A Guide to Civil Emergency Planning for Municipalities.* Ottawa.

———. 1983. *Study on the Psychological Effects of Disasters on Operational Personnel.* Ottawa.

———. 1987. *Vital Points Manual.* Ottawa.

———. 2000. *Plan for Tomorrow . . . TODAY! The Story of Emergency Preparedness Canada 1948–1998.* Ottawa.

Cantril, Hadley. 1940. *The Invasion from Mars: A Study in the Psychology of Panic.* Princeton: Princeton University Press.

Carey, Benedict, and Anahad O'Connor. 2004. "As Public Adjusts to Theatre, Alerts Cause Less Unease." *New York Times,* 3 August, A9.

Carey, Michael J. 1982. "The Schools and Civil Defense: The Fifties Revisited." *Teachers College Record* 84, no. 1: 115–27.

Carnicke, Sharon M. 1998. *Stanislavsky in Focus.* Amsterdam: Harwood.

Carr, C. 2002. "Hunger Artist: The Twelve Days of Marina Abramovic." *Village Voice* 47, no. 49 (4–10 December): 57.

Cartegena Declaration on Refugees. 1984. Adopted at the "Coloquio Sobre La Proteccion Internacional de los Refugiados en Américan Central, México y Panamá," Cartegena, Colombia.

Casualties Union. 1957a. *Atlas of Injury.* London: Casualties Union.

———. 1957b. *Casualties Union Founded 1942. Brief History.* London: Casualties Union.

———. 1957c. *Report of the General Committee for the Period 1st November, 1955–31st March, 1957.* London: Casualties Union.

———. 1962. *The Top Level First Aider: What the Casualty Expects.* London: Casualties Union.

———. 1963. *Twenty-one Years in Your Hands.* London: Casualties Union.

"Casualties Union Library." 1955. *Casualties Union Journal* 3, no. 10 (winter): 198.

Chaput, Marcel, and T. K. Groves. 1956. *Data for Planning Reception and Protection in Southern*

Ontario in a Nuclear War. Ottawa: Department of National Defence, Defence Research Board Operational Research Group. No. 189.

Chenault, William W., and Cecil H. Davis. 1975a. *Prototype Reception/Care Plan to Meet the Welfare, Shelter, and Related Needs of Populations Affected by Crisis Relocation. Reception/Care Plan for Fremont County.* McLean, Va.: Defense Civil Preparedness Agency and Human Sciences Research.

———. 1975b. *Reception/Care Planning for Crisis Relocation.* McLean, Va.: Human Sciences Research, Inc.

Chester, V., G. A. Cristy, and C. M. Haaland. 1975. *Strategic Considerations in Planning a Counterevacuation.* Oak Ridge, Tenn.: Oak Ridge National Laboratory, Health Physics Division, Emergency Technology Section.

Chicago Civil Defense Corps. 1951. *Chicago Alert: a City Plans its Civil Defense against Atomic Attack.* Chicago.

———. 1955. *Annual Report of the Chicago Civil Defense Corps for Year Ending December 31st, 1954.* Chicago.

Christiansen, Nancy, and Walter H. Wickham. 1961. "Air-Raid Game." *Jack and Jill,* 34–35.

Churcher, John, and Elean V. M. Lieven. 1983. "Images of Nuclear War and the Public in British Civil Defense Planning Documents." *Journal of Social Issues* 39, no. 1: 117–32.

"Civil Defence, 1953." 1953. *Casualties Union Journal* 3, no. 1 (September): 5–6.

Clanahan, Russell B. 1974. "Disaster's Mental Casualties. *Foresight* (March/April): 12–15.

[Clark, Paul]. 1958. *Report on a Study of Non-Military Defense.* Santa Monica, Calif.: RAND.

Clarke, Lee. 1999. *Mission Improbable: Using Fantasy Documents to Tame Disaster.* Chicago: University of Chicago Press.

Clarke, Magnus. 1982. *The Nuclear Destruction of Britain.* London: Croom Helm.

Clarke, Robin. 1986. *London under Attack: The Report of the Greater London Area War Risk Study Commission.* Oxford: Basil Blackwell.

Claxton, Eric C. 1943. *Practical Rescue Training: A Handbook for Wardens and other Civil Defence Personnel.* London: Pitman.

———. 1950. "Commentary." *Casualties Union Journal* 2, no. 2 (October): 26–27.

———. 1955. "Protection of Casualties." *Casualties Union Journal* 3, no. 8 (summer): 143.

———. 1990. *More Ways than One of Fighting a War: The Story of a Battle School for Civil Defence and the Creation of Casualties Union.* Lewes, Sussex: Book Guild Ltd.

———. 1992. *The Struggle for Peace: The Story of Casualties Union in the Years Following the Second World War.* Lewes, Sussex: Book Guild.

Columbia Broadcasting System Inc. 1951. *Homemaker's Manual of Atomic Defense.* New York: Columbia Broadcasting System Inc.

Committee on Behavioral Research. 1962. *Emergency Planning and Behavioral Research.* Washington: National Research Council.

Conway, Edward A. 1954. "Let's Get Out of Here!: What the 'New Look' in Civil Defense can Mean for You." *America (National Catholic Weekly Review)* 91, no. 3: 65.

Costley, J. A. 1983. *Civil Defence in the Health Service.* Sheffield: Trent Regional Health Authority.

Cowan, A. C. 2006. "Silence is Broken in Librarians' Record Case." *New York Times,* 31 May, A20.

Cowan, Judy. 1994. *The Kelvedon Hatch Secret Bunker*. Brentwood, Essex: Kelvedon Hatch Museum.

Crease, Robert P. 1993. *The Play of Nature: Experimentation as Performance*. Bloomington: University of Indiana Press.

Crossley, George. 1982. *Civil Defence in Britain. Peace Studies Papers. No. 7*. London: University of Bradford School of Peace Studies and Houseman.

———. 1985. *The Civil Defence Debate in Britain 1957–83: An Account and Critical Analysis of the Major Issues in the Debate about Civil Defence against Nuclear Attack*. Bradford, Yorkshire: University of Bradford.

Danzig, Elliott R., and Arthur I. Siegel. 1955. *Emergent Leadership in a Civil Defense Evacuation Exercise*. Philadelphia: Federal Civil Defense Administration.

Danzig, Elliott R., Paul W. Thayer, and Lila R. Galante. 1958. *The Effects of a Threatening Rumor on a Disaster-Stricken Community*. Disaster Study No. 10. Vol. 517. Washington: National Research Council.

Davis, Tracy C. 2003. "Theatricality and Civil Society." In *Theatricality*, edited by Tracy C. Davis and Thomas Postlewait, 127–55. Cambridge: Cambridge University Press.

Day, Elizabeth. 2004. "Queen Was to Flee to Canada in Event of Nuclear Attack." *Ottawa Citizen*, 28 March, A8.

de Kadt, Emanuel J. 1964. *British Defense Policy and Nuclear War*. London: Frank Cass.

"The Demonstrators' Statement." 1955. *WRL News* 73, 3.

Dent, Michelle. 2004. "Staging Disaster: Reporting Live (Sort of) From Seattle." *TDR: The Drama Review* 48, no. 4: 109–34.

Denzin, Norman K. 2003. *Performance Ethnography: Critical Pedagogy and the Politics of Culture*. Thousand Oaks, Calif.: Sage.

DePalma, Anthony. 2006. "Terror Arrests Reveal Reach of Canada's Surveillance Powers." *New York Times*, 8 June, A12.

Diacon, Diane. 1984. *Residential Housing and Nuclear Attack*. London: Croom Helm.

Diamond, Elin. 1996. "Introduction." In *Performance and Cultural Politics*, edited by Elin Diamond, 1–12. London: Routledge.

Diderot, Denis. 1830. *The Paradox of Acting*. Translated by Walter Herries Pollock. Reprint, New York: Hill and Wang, 1957.

Dierst, Glenn V. 1962. "Alert Warning and Communication System for Industry." *Industrial Security* 6, no. 3 (July): 31–33, 123.

Disaster Research Group. Division of Anthropology and Psychology. 1962. *Emergency Planning and Behavioral Research*. Washington: National Research Council.

District of Columbia Office of Civil Defense. 1960s. *Instructions to Shelter Occupants for Emergency Use of Shelters*.

Dolan, Jill. 2001. "Performance, Utopia, and the 'Utopian Performative.'" *Theatre Journal* 53, no. 3: 455–79.

Dreyfuss, Leonard. 1951. Address in *Institute on Mental Hygiene Aspects of Civil Defense: Proceedings*, 14–16. Trenton: New Jersey Department of Defense, Division of Civil Defense.

"Drive for Mass Shelters." 1962. *Life* 52, no. 2 (12 January): 34–43.

Dudley, Michael Quinn. 2001. "Sprawl as Strategy: City Planners Face the Bomb." *Journal of Planning Education and Research* 21, no. 1: 52–63.

Dudziak, Mary L., ed. 2003. *September 11 in History: A Watershed Moment?* Durham, N.C.: Duke University Press.

Dunnigan, James F. 1997. "Wargames at War." www.hyw.com/Books/WargamesHandbook/9-wargam.htm. Accessed 2 December 2005.

Dyer, George Bell, and Charlotte Leavitt Dyer. 1962. *Exercises on an Assumption of Violence: A Sensible and Active American Family Approach to the Peculiar Problems of Our Times.* New Hope, Pa.: Dyer Institute of Interdisciplinary Studies.

Eastman, Samuel Ewe. 1965. *The Effects of Nuclear Weapons on a Single City.* Arlington, Va.: Institute for Defense Analyses, Economic and Political Studies Division.

Eden, Lynn. 2004. *Whole World on Fire: Organizations, Knowledge, and Nuclear Weapons Devastation.* Ithaca: Cornell University Press.

Edwards, Paul N. 1996. *The Closed World: Computers and the Politics of Discourse in Cold War America.* Cambridge, Mass.: MIT University Press.

Ehrlich, Anne. 1984. "Nuclear Winter." *Bulletin of the Atomic Scientists* 40, no. 10: 1–15.

El-Ayouty, Yassin, ed. 2004. *Perspectives on 9/11.* Westport, Conn.: Praeger.

El Paso County Crisis Relocation Plan (Prototype). 1976. Vol. IV Annex B: *Law and Order Services for Risk Area: El Paso County and Colorado Springs.* Santa Barbara: Mission Research Corporation.

Erickson, Harold M., et al. 1953. *Mental Health Implications in Civilian Emergencies.* Washington: HEW, Public Health Service, National Institutes of Health, National Institute of Mental Health.

Erikson, J. 1976. "Loss of Communality at Buffalo Creek." *American Journal of Psychiatry* 133: 302–5.

Etter, H. S., J. I. Pond, D. P. Schultze, and W. E. Strope. 1962. *The Family Occupancy Test, 4–6 November 1960.* San Francisco: Naval Radiological Defense Laboratory.

Etter, H. S., R. A. Goldbeck, R. H. Heiskell, J. H. Sheard, and W. E. Strope. 1960. *Preliminary Report on the Shelter Occupancy Test of 3–17 December 1959.* San Francisco: Naval Radiological Defense Laboratory.

Fairchild, J. W., and Juan O. Gonzalez. Office of Civil Defense. 1963. *Simulated Occupancy Test: Francis Family Shelter, Tucson, Arizona July 5, 1963–July 15 1963.* Gainesville: Engineering and Industrial Experiment Station, College of Engineering, University of Florida.

"Fallout Shelters." 1961. *Life* 51, no. 11 (15 September): 95–108.

Farace, Richard V. 1972. *An Analysis of a Community Shelter Plan Information Campaign.* East Lansing: Michigan State University Press.

Farrell, Ken G., L. J. Coyne, and J. E. Jewsbury. 1986. *Home Fallout Protection.* Ottawa: Public Works Canada.

Fisher, Jennifer. 1997. "Interperformance: The Live Tableaux of Suzanne Lacy, Janine Antoni, and Marina Abramovic." *Art Journal* 56 (winter): 28–33.

Fitzpatrick, Margaret Mary. 1950. *The Role of Women in Wartime Britain, 1939–1945: Industry, Armed Forces, Civil Defense, Community Facilities, Voluntary Organizations.* Washington: U.S. Department of Labor Women's Bureau.

Flanigan, Frank M. Office of Civil Defense. 1964. *Simulated Occupancy Test—Family Shelter—Bozeman, Montana . . . February 1–March 7 1964.* Gainesville: Florida Engineering and Industrial Experiment Station, College of Engineering, University of Florida.

Fogleman, Charles W., and Vernon J. Parenton. 1959. "Disaster and Aftermath: Selected Aspects of Individual and Group Behavior in Critical Situations." *Social Forces* 38, no. 2 (December): 129–35.

Foreman, Kathleen, and Clem Martini. 1995. *Something Like a Drug: An Unauthorized Oral History of Theatresports*. Red Deer, Alberta: Red Deer College Press.

Form, William H., and Charles P. Loomis, et al. 1956. "The Persistence and Emergence of Social and Cultural Systems in Disasters." *American Sociological Review* 21, no. 2: 180–85.

Forman, Robert E. 1963. "Resignation as a Collective Behavior Response." *American Journal of Sociology* 169, no. 3 (November): 285–90.

Forrow, Lachlan, and Victor W. Sidel. 1998. "Medicine and Nuclear War: From Hiroshima to Mutual Assured Destruction to Abolition 2000." *Journal of the American Medical Association* 280, no. 5 (5 August): 456–61.

Freedman, Lawrence. 2000. *Kennedy's Wars: Berlin, Cuba, Laos, and Vietnam*. Oxford: Oxford University Press.

Freytag, Gustav. 1968. *Technique of the Drama: An Exposition of Dramatic Composition and Art*. Translated by Elias J. MacEwan. Reprint, New York: Benjamin Blom. (Orig. pub. 1863.)

Fritz, Charles E. 1961. "Disaster." In *Contemporary Social Problems: An Introduction to the Sociology of Deviant Behavior and Social Disorganization*, edited by Robert K. Merton and Robert A. Nisbet, 651–94. New York: Harcourt, Brace, and World.

Fritz, Charles E., and Harry B. Williams. 1957. "The Human Being in Disasters: A Research Perspective." *Annals of the American Academy of Political and Social Science* 309: 42–51.

Fritz, Charles E., Harry B. Williams, and J. H. Matthewson. 1957. *Convergence Behavior in Disasters*. Washington: National Research Council.

Fromm, Erich, Herman Kahn, and Michael Maccoby. 1962. "The Question of Civil Defense — A Debate." *Commentary* 33, no. 1 (January): 1–23.

Fuoss, Kirk W. 1995. "'Community' Contested, Imagined, and Performed: Cultural Performance, Contestation, and Community in an Organized-Labor Social Drama." *Text and Performance Quarterly* 15, no. 2 (April): 79–98.

Garrett, Ralph L. 1976a. *Civil Defense and the Public: An Overview of Public Attitude Studies*. Washington: Defense Civil Preparedness Agency.

———. 1976b. "Social and Psychological Response to the Shelter Environment." In Swedish Civil Defence Administration, *Survival in Shelters*, 135–41. Swedish Civil Defence Administration: Stockholm.

Garrison, Dee. 1994. "The Civil Defense Protest Movement in New York City, 1955–1961." In *Not June Cleaver: Women and Gender in Postwar America, 1945–1960*, edited by Joanne Meyerowitz, 201–26. Philadelphia: Temple University Press.

———. 2006. *Bracing for Armageddon: Why Civil Defense Never Worked*. New York: Oxford University Press.

Gebauer, Gunter, and Christoph Wulf. 1995. *Mimesis: Culture, Art, Society*. Translated by Don Reneau. Berkeley: University of California Press.

Geerhart, Bill. 2001. "Watch out Below." *Bulletin of the Atomic Scientists* 57, no. 1: 6–7.

Gellman, Barton, and Susan Schmidt. 2002. "Shadow Government Is at Work in Secret." *Washington Post*, 1 March, A1.

Gent, J. C., Surgeon Capt. 1959. "Civil Defence Exercise." *Journal of the Royal Naval Medical Service* 45, no. 3: 199–25.

George, Alice L. 2003. *Awaiting Armageddon: How Americans Faced the Cuban Missile Crisis.* Chapel Hill: University of North Carolina Press.

Georgia Department of Public Defense, Civil Defense Division, and State Department of Education. 1952. *Civil Defense Manual for Georgia Schools.* Atlanta.

Ghamari-Tabrizi, Sharon. 2005. *The Worlds of Herman Kahn: The Intuitive Science of Thermonuclear War.* Cambridge, Mass.: Harvard University Press.

Glass, Albert J. 1957. "Psychological Consideration in Atomic Warfare." Working paper, Headquarters, Army Medical Service School, Brooke Army Medical Center, Fort Sam Houston, Texas, Symposium on the Management of Mass Casualties, March 1957: 266–68.

Glasstone, Samuel, ed. 1957. *The Effects of Nuclear Weapons.* Washington: U.S. Atomic Energy Commission.

Goffman, Erving. 1959. *Presentation of Self in Everyday Life.* Garden City, N.Y.: Doubleday.

———. 1974. *Frame Analysis: An Essay on the Organization of Experience.* Cambridge, Mass.: Harvard University Press.

Gordon, Mel. 1988. *The Grand Guignol: Theatre of Fear and Terror.* New York: Da Capo Press.

Graham-White, Anthony. 1976. "'Ritual' in Contemporary Theatre and Criticism." *Educational Theatre Journal* 28: 318–24.

Graubard, Morlie H., and Carl H. Builder. 1980. *Rand's Strategic Assessment Center: An Overview of the Concept.* Santa Monica, Calif.: RAND.

Greater London Council. 1966. *Greater London Civil Defence Newsletter,* no. 1 (August).

———. 1985. Public Relations Branch. *Blackout to Whitewash: Civil Defence Since 1937.* London: Greater London Council Public Relations Branch.

Grebler, Leo. 1956. "Continuity in the Re-building of Bombed Cities in Western Europe." *American Journal of Sociology* 61, no. 5 (March): 463–69.

Green, C. H., and D. J. Parker. 1994. "Evacuation: Enhancing Response." In *Problems Associated with Large Scale Evacuations.* Easingwold Papers No. 5. Easingwold, York: HO Emergency Planning College, 1–26.

Greenberg, Bradley S., Duane Pettersen, and John Kochevar. 1966a. *The Development of Values and Beliefs in Young Americans toward Fallout Shelters and Civil Defense (Pilot Study Report No. 1).* Washington: Office of Civil Defense.

———. 1966b. *The Development of Values and Beliefs in Young Americans toward Fallout Shelters and Civil Defense Pilot Study No. 2.* Washington: Office of Civil Defense.

Greenberg, Bradley S., Joseph R. Dominick, and Edward Razinsky. 1968. *A Pilot Study of Young Americans' Beliefs and Knowledge About Civil Defense. Report #1.* Washington: Office of Civil Defense.

Greenblat, Cathy Stein. 1981. "Gaming-Simulation and Social Science: Rewards to the Designer." In *Principles and Practices of Gaming-Simulation.* Rev. ed., edited by Cathy Stein Greenblat and Richard D. Duke, 41–46. Beverly Hills: Sage.

Greene, Owen, et al. 1982. *London After the Bomb: What a Nuclear Attack Really Means.* Oxford: Oxford University Press.

Grinspoon, Lester. 1963. "Fallout Shelters and Mental Health." *Medical Times* 91, no. 6: 517–20.

Groom, Walter R. 1953. "Full Benefit from the Use of Trained Casualties." *Casualties Union Journal* 3, no. 7 (spring): 131–32.

Gross, E., and O. E. Collins. n.d. *Attitudes of Men at AC&W Sites in Japan.* Randolph AFB, Tex.: Crew Research Laboratory, Research Report No. 174.

Grossman, Andrew D. 2001. *Neither Dead Nor Red: Civilian Defense and American Political Development During the Early Cold War*. New York: Routledge.

Guetzkow, Harold. 1967. "Some Correspondences between Simulations and 'Realities' in International Relations." In *New Approaches to International Relations*, edited by Morton A. Kaplan, 202–69. New York: St. Martin's Press.

Guide for Crisis Relocation Contingency Planning. A Prototype Risk Area Plan. Working Draft. 1976. Washington: Defense Civil Preparedness Agency, October.

Haaland, Carsten M. 1968. "Civil Defense Systems Analysis." In *Annual Progress Report Civil Defense Research Project March 1967–March 1968*, November, 36–56. Oak Ridge, Tenn.: Oak Ridge National Laboratory.

Haaland, Carsten M., Conrad V. Chester, and Eugene P. Wigner. 1976. *Survival of the Relocated Population of the U.S. after a Nuclear Attack*. Oak Ridge, Tenn.: Atomic Energy Commission and Federal Emergency Management Agency.

Hack, Vincent I., Lieut. Col. 1959. "Simulation of Military Casualties." *Journal of the American Medical Association* 171, no. 2: 193–95.

Hammes, John Anthony, R. Travis Osborn, et al. 1963. *Shelter Occupancy Studies at the University of Georgia. A Summary of the Final Report*. Springfield, Va.: Clearinghouse for Federal Scientific and Technical Information.

Hanifan, Donald T., and Dunlap and Associates Inc. Western Division. 1963. *Physiological and Psychological Effects of Overloading Fallout Shelters*. Santa Monica, Calif.: Office of Civil Defense.

Hare, A. Paul, and Herbert H. Blumberg. 1988. *Dramaturgical Analysis of Social Interaction*. Westport, Conn.: Praeger.

Harker, Robert A. 1970. *Transattack Environment Scenarios*. Palo Alto, Calif.: URS Research Company.

Harker, Robert A., and Allen E. Wilmore. 1979. *Crisis Relocation Management Concepts Derived From Analyses of Host Area Requirements*. Washington: Defense Civil Preparedness Agency.

Harker, Robert A., and Charlie C. Coleman. Defense Civil Preparedness Agency. 1975. *Application of Simulation Training Exercises to Crisis Relocation Planning Final Report*. Palo Alto: Center for Planning and Research.

Harvey, Ernest C., and Robert W. Hubenette. 1974. *Alternative Hosting and Protective Measures*. Stanford: Stanford Research Institute. (Orig. pub. 1968.)

Hausrath, Alfred H. 1971. *Venture Simulation in War, Business, and Politics*. New York: McGraw-Hill.

Haydon, Peter T. 1993. *The 1962 Cuban Missile Crisis: Canadian Involvement Reconsidered*. Toronto: Canadian Institute of Strategic Studies.

"Hay's Wharf 1950 (Eighth Annual Meeting and Open Competition)." 1951. *Casualties Union Journal* 2, no. 3/4 (March): 61–62.

Heartney, Eleanor. 2002. "Import/Export: The Body East." *Art in America* (April): 44–49.

Heer, David M. 1965. *After Nuclear Attack*. New York: Praeger.

Heiskell, R. H. 1963. *Environmental Studies of a 100-Man Underground Shelter*. San Francisco: Naval Radiological Defense Laboratory.

Henderson, Clark, and Walmer E. Strope. 1978. *Crisis Relocation of the Population at Risk in the New York Metropolitan Area*. Menlo Park, Calif.: Stanford Research International, September.

Henrikson, Margot. 1997. *Dr. Strangelove's America: Society and Culture in the Atomic Age*. Berkeley: University of California Press.

Hersey, John. 1946. *Hiroshima*. Harmondsworth: Penguin.

Herts and Essex Nuclear Free Zone Councils' Joint Committee. 1991. *Still Planning for War? Planning Assumptions Study Final Report*. Vol. 3. Herts and Essex Nuclear Free Zone Councils' Joint Committee.

Hilts, Philip J. 2001. "Americans Skeptical about Bioterrorism Risk." *New York Times*, 9 November, B7.

Hirschfelder, J. O., et al. 1950. *The Effects of Atomic Weapons*. Washington: United States Government Printing Office.

Hoffman, John M. 1959. "Sensible Survival Measures for the Doctor's Family." *Northwest Medicine* 58, no. 8: 1151, 1153.

Holmström, Mårten. 1976. "Experiment with Five Persons in a Closed Air Raid Shelter." In *Survival in Shelters*, by Swedish Civil Defence Administration, 123–41. Stockholm: Swedish Civil Defence Administration.

Hopley, Russell J. 1948. *Civil Defense for National Security*. Washington: United States Government Printing Office, October.

Howard, Katherine Graham. 1977. *With My Shoes Off*. New York: Vantage.

Hu, Winnie. 2002. "A Mock Nuclear Emergency, Within Limits." *New York Times*, 25 September, A23.

Iklé, Fred C., and Harry V. Kincaid. 1956. *Social Aspects of Wartime Evacuation of American Cities with Particular Emphasis on Long-Term Housing and Reemployment*. Washington: National Research Council.

Indiana Department of Public Instruction. 1960. *Civil Defense Education in Our Indiana Schools*. Indianapolis.

Industrial College of the Armed Forces. 1954. *Mobilization of the National Economy in the Face of Atomic Attack: Oral Presentations*. Washington.

"In the News with Civil Defence: Exercise 'Shuttlecock.' " 1958. *Casualty Simulation: the Journal of the Casualties Union* 5, no. 2: 21–22.

"In the News with Civil Defence: N.H.S.R. Exercise 'Gory.' " 1960. *Casualty Simulation* 5, no. 10: 165–66.

Isaacs, Stella (Dowager Marchioness of Reading). 1954. *It's the Job That Counts, 1939–1953: A Selection from the Speeches and Writings of the Dowager Marchioness of Reading, Chairman of Women's Voluntary Service for Civil Defence*. London: privately published.

Izzo, Gary. 1997. *The Art of Play: The New Genre of Interactive Theatre*. Portsmouth, N.H.: Heinemann.

Jackson, Pauline M., and Robert A. Harker. 1969. *Analogy between New Orleans Transattack Environment Scenarios and Hurricane Camille*. Washington: Office of Civil Defense.

Jackson, Shannon. 2004. *Professing Performance: Theatre in the Academy from Philology to Performativity*. Cambridge: Cambridge University Press.

Janis, Irving Lester. 1949. *Psychological Aspects of Vulnerability of Atomic Bomb Attacks*. Santa Monica, Calif.: RAND.

———. 1951. *Air War and Emotional Stress: Psychological Studies of Bombing and Civilian Defense*. The RAND Series. New York: McGraw-Hill.

————. 1962. "Psychological Effects of Warning." In *Man and Society in Disaster*, edited by George W. Baker and Dwight W. Chapman, 55–63. New York: Basic Books.

JHK and Associates. 1973. *Report: Contingency Planning for Crisis Relocation*. Alexandria, Va.: Defense Civil Preparedness Agency.

————. 1977. *Crisis Relocation Transportation Requirements. Defense Civil Preparedness Agency. A Feasibility Study of Crisis Relocation Planning for California*. Washington: Defense Civil Preparedness Agency.

Jones, Amelia. 2005. "Stelarc's Technological 'Transcendence'/Stelarc's Web Body: The Insistent Return of the Flesh." In *Stelarc: The Monograph*, edited by Marquard Smith, 87–124. Cambridge, Mass.: MIT Press.

Juchem, Marguerite R., and Colorado Department of Education. *Organizing Colorado Schools for Civil Defense*. Denver, 1953.

Kahn, Herman. 1962. "A Rational Basis for Decision Making on Civil Defense Policy." Taken from testimony before Subcommittee on Government Operations, House of Representatives, U.S. Congress, 1961. Testimony 7 and 9 August 1961." In *Behavioral Science and Civil Defense*, edited by George W. Baker and Leonard S. Cottrell Jr., 21–52. Washington: National Research Council.

————. 1984. *Thinking the Unthinkable in the 1980s*. New York: Simon and Schuster.

Kaplan, Fred. 1984. *The Wizards of Armageddon*. New York: Simon and Schuster.

Katz, Elihu. 1960. *Joy in Mudville: Public Reaction to the Surprise Sounding of Chicago's Air Raid Sirens*. Chicago: National Opinion Research Center, University of Chicago.

Keiser, Lester. 1968. *The Traumatic Neurosis*. Philadelphia: J. B. Lippincott.

Kennedy, Dennis. 2001. "Sports and Shows: Spectators in Contemporary Culture." *Theatre Research International* 26, no. 3: 277–84.

Kennedy, John F. 1962. "Broadcast on the Berlin Crisis. 25 July 1961." In *Public Papers of the Presidents of the United States. John F. Kennedy, 1961*. Washington: United States Government Printing Office.

Kennedy, Robert. 1969. *Thirteen Days: A Memoir of the Cuban Missile Crisis*. New York: Norton.

Kentucky Department of Military Affairs Division of Civil Defense. 1964. *A Civil Defense Plan for Kentucky Schools*. Frankfort, Ky.

Kershaw, Baz. 1992. *The Politics of Performance: Radical Theatre as Cultural Intervention*. London: Routledge.

Kershaw, Sarah. 2003. "Terror Scenes Follow Script of Never Again." *New York Times*, 13 May, A19.

Kincade, William Hadley. 1980. "U.S. Civil Defense Decision-Making: The Ford and Carter Administrations." 2 vols. PhD diss., American University.

Kirby, Michael. 1965. *Happenings*. New York: E.P. Dutton.

Klein, Jennie. 2002. "Biospheria." *New Art Examiner* 29, no. 5 (May–June): 74–81.

Klonglan, Gerald E., George M. Beal, and Joe M. Bohlen. 1964. *Family Adoption of Public Fallout Shelters. A Study of Des Moines, Iowa*. Iowa Agricultural and Home Economics Experiment Station Project No. 1529. Sociological Studies in Civil Defense. Rural Sociology Report. No. 30. Ames: Iowa State University.

Konijn, Elly A. 2000. *Acting Emotions: Shaping Emotions on Stage*. Translated by Barbara Leach with David Chambers. Amsterdam: Amsterdam University Press.

Kraake, Swantje, Klaus Helling, and Reiner K. Huber. 1993. "On a Research Game for Crisis

Management." In *International Stability in a Multipolar World: Issues and Models for Analysis*, edited by Reiner K. Huber and Rudolf Avenhaus, 133–44. Baden-Baden: Nomos Verlagsgesellschaft.

Krajnc, Anita. 2000. "The Art of Green Learning: From Protest Songs to Media Mind Bombs." *International Politics* 37, no. 1: 19–40.

Krugler, David. 2006. *This Is Only a Test: How Washington, D.C. Prepared for Nuclear War*. Houndsmills, U.K.: Palgrave-Macmillan.

Lamers, William M. 1959. *Disaster Protection Handbook for School Administrators*. Washington: American Association of School Administrators.

Lane, Christopher. 2003. "The Poverty of Context: Historicism and Nonmimetic Fiction." *PMLA* 118, no. 3: 450–69.

Laurence, William L. 1950. *The Hell Bomb*. New York: Knopf.

Laurie, Peter. 1979. *Beneath the City Streets: A Private Inquiry into Government Preparations for National Emergency*. London: Granada.

Laurino, Richard, Frank Trinkl, Carl F. Miller, and Robert A. Harker. 1977. *Economic and Industrial Aspects of Crisis Relocation: An Overview*. Washington: Defense Civil Preparedness Agency.

Laurino, Richard, Frank Trinkl, and Francis Dresch. 1980. *Key Economic Problems and Guidelines for Crisis Relocation*. Palo Alto: Center for Planning and Research.

Law, John. 1999. "After ANT Complexity, Naming and Topology." In *Actor Network Theory and After*, edited by John Law and John Hassard, 1–14. Oxford: Blackwell.

Lawson, John Howard. 1960. *Theory and Technique of Playwriting*. 1936. Reprint, New York: J.P. Putnam's Sons.

Lay, James S., Jr. 1960. Memorandum for the National Security Council, 14 July. Reproduced from National Archives Records Administration by National Security Archive, http://www.gwu.edu/~nsarchiv/NSAEBB/NSAEBB43/doc4.pdf. Accessed 3 December 2005.

Leavitt, Jane T. 1974. *Local Vital Facilities Lists: Identification of Industries and Facilities Essential to the Life Support of the Prototype San Antonio, Texas Crisis Relocation Area*. Alexandria, Va.: Institute for Defense Analyses, Program Analysis Division.

Lee, David B. 1990. "War Gaming: Thinking for the Future." *Airpower Journal* (summer): 40–51.

Lerner, Melvin. 1965. "The Effect of Preparatory Action on Beliefs Concerning Nuclear War." *Journal of Social Psychology* 65: 225–31.

"Lethargy Troubled 3 Women Shut in Fall-Out Refuge." 1965. *Times* (London), 23 March, 16.

Levine, Gene N., and John Modell. 1964. *The Threat of War and American Public Opinion*. New York: Department of Defense.

Light, Jennifer S. 2003. *From Warfare to Welfare: Defense Intellectuals and Urban Problems in Cold War America*. Baltimore: Johns Hopkins University Press.

Little, Richard G., Paul B. Pattak, and Wayne A. Schroeder. 1998. *Use of Underground Facilities to Protect Critical Infrastructures: Summary of a Workshop*. Washington: National Academy Press.

Livingston, Lawrence Jr., Bertrand Klass, and John Rohrer. 1954. *Operations Walkout, Rideout, and Scat: Studies of Civil Defense Dispersal Test Exercises in Spokane, Bremerton, and Mobile*. Washington: National Research Council.

London Boroughs Association. 1989. *Civil Defence*. London: London Nuclear Information Unit.

Los Alamos Scientific Laboratory, DOD, and Atomic Energy Commission. 1950. *The Effects of Atomic Weapons*. Washington: United States Government Printing Office.

Louisiana Civil Defense Agency, Department of Education. 1953. *Louisiana Civil Defense Guide for Schools*. Baton Rouge.

Lowry, Ira S., and U.S. Atomic Energy Commission. 1966. *The Postattack Population of the United States*. Project Agreement No. 3. Santa Monica, Calif.: RAND.

Mack, Raymond W., and George Walter Baker. 1961. *The Occasion Instant: The Structure of Social Responses to Unanticipated Air Raid Warnings*. Washington: National Research Council.

"Make Up Your Mind!" 1951. *Casualties Union Journal* 2, no. 7 (October): 134.

Malina, Judith. 1972. *The Enormous Despair*. New York: Random House.

———. 1984. *The Diaries of Judith Malina 1947–1957*. New York: Grove.

Maloney, Sean. 1997. "Dr. Strangelove Visits Canada: Projects Rustic, Ease, and Bridge, 1958–1963." *Canadian Military History* 6, no. 1 (spring): 42–56.

Mandel, Robert. 1985. "Professional-Level War Gaming: An Assessment." In *Theories, Models, and Simulations in International Relations. Essays in Honor of Harold Guetzkow*, edited by Michael Don Ward, 482–500. Boulder: Westview.

Margolin, Deb. 2000. "Mining My Own Business: Paths between Text and Self." In *Method Acting Reconsidered: Theory, Practice, Future*, edited by David Krasner, 127–34. New York: St. Martin's Press.

Maryland Department of Education. 1964. *Civil Defense Manual for the Schools of Maryland*. Pikesville: Maryland Civil Defense Agency.

Marzani, Carl, Field Marshal Montgomery, Fred Warner Neal, and Leo Szilard. 1962. *Shelter Hoax and Foreign Policy*. New York: Marzani and Munsell, Inc.

Mast, Robert H. 1966. *Impact of the Cuban Missile Crisis: Patterns of Response*. Washington: Office of Civil Defense.

May, Ernest R., and Philip D. Zelikow. 1997. *The Kennedy Tapes: Inside the White House during the Cuban Missile Crisis*. Cambridge, Mass.: Belknap Press.

McAuley, Gay. 1999. *Space in Performance: Making Meaning in the Theatre*. Ann Arbor: University of Michigan Press.

McCamley, N. J. 1998. *Secret Underground Cities*. Barnsley: Leo Cooper.

———. 2002. *Cold War Secret Nuclear Bunkers*. London: Leo Cooper.

McConachie, Bruce. 2001. "Doing Things with Image Schemas: The Cognitive Turn in Theatre Studies and the Problem of Experience for Historians." *Theatre Journal* 53, no. 4 (December): 569–94.

McDermott, Edward A. 1962. "Public Support of Civil Emergency Planning." In *Behavioral Science and Civil Defense*, edited by George W. Baker and Leonard S. Cottrell Jr., 3–6. Washington: National Research Council.

McEnaney, Laura. 2000. *Civil Defense Begins at Home: Militarization Meets Everyday Life in the Fifties*. Princeton: Princeton University Press.

McEwan, Ian. 2005a. *Saturday*. London: Jonathan Cape.

———. 2005b. "The Surprise We Expected." *New York Times*, 8 July, A–31.

McGrath, L. 1997. "Creating the Casualty: Role Simulation in Accident and Emergency Training." *Accident and Emergency Nursing* 5, no. 9: 99–101.

McIlroy, Andrew. 1997–1998. "No Interest, No Time, No Money: Civil Defense in Cleveland in the Cold War." *Ohio History* 106: 59–86.

McKenzie, Jon. 2001. *Perform or Else: From Discipline to Performance.* London: Routledge.

Mechling, Elizabeth Walker, and Jay Mechling. 1991. "The Campaign for Civil Defense and the Struggle to Naturalize the Bomb." *Western Journal of Speech Communication* 55, no. 2: 105–33.

" 'Medusa' Men Toiled in Sleet Storm." 1951. *Western Daily Press and Bristol Mirror*, 12 February, 4.

Messinger, Sheldon L., Harold Sampson, and Robert D. Towne. 1975. "Life as Theatre: Some Notes on the Dramaturgic Approach to Social Reality." In *Life as Theater: A Dramaturgical Sourcebook*, edited by Denis Brissett and Charles Edgley, 32–42. New York: Aldine de Gruyter.

Michigan Office of Civil Defense and Michigan Department of Public Instruction. 1955. *Civil Defense and Safety Manual: A Program for Michigan Schools.* Lansing.

Michigan's Upper Peninsula Women's Civil Defense Conference [report]. 1953. Marquette, Michigan, September 23.

Miller, Delbert C. 1960. "Some Implications for Shelter Living Based on a Study of Isolated Radar Bases." In *Symposium on Human Problems in the Utilization of Fallout Shelters 11 and 12 February 1960*, edited by George W. Baker and John H. Rohrer, 51–57. Washington: National Research Council.

Miller, Roy I., and Richard D. Duke. 1981. "Gaming: A Methodological Experiment." In *Principles and Practices of Gaming-Simulation*, edited by Cathy Stein Greenblat and Richard D. Duke, 213–23. Rev. ed. Beverly Hills: Sage.

Minnich, Michael. 1960. "Testing the Plan: Emergency Plan and Organization." *Industrial Security* 4, no. 3: 70–74.

"More Domestic Spying: Now We Learn that the NSA Sought Records of Every Phone Call in the Country. What Else Don't We Know?" 2006. Editorial, *Wall Street Journal*, 12 May, A20.

"The Moscow-Peking Conflict: Differing National Interests Come to the Fore." 1963. *The Militant*, 21 October, 4.

Murray, Janet H. 1997. *Hamlet on the Holodeck: The Future of Narrative in Cyberspace.* New York: Free Press.

Nathan, James A. 1992. "The Heyday of the New Strategy: The Cuban Missile Crisis and the Confirmation of Coercive Diplomacy." In *The Cuban Missile Crisis Revisited*, edited by James A. Nathan, 1–39. New York: St. Martin's Press.

National Education Association, National Commission on Safety Education. 1966. *Current Status of Civil Defense in Schools with Guidelines for Action.* Washington: United States Government Printing Office.

National Military Establishment, Office of the Secretary of Defense. 1948. *A Study of Civil Defense.* Washington.

National Opinion Research Center. 1954. *Human Reactions in Disaster Situations.* Chicago: University of Chicago.

National Recreation Association. 1951. *Emergency Recreation Services in Civil Defense.* New York.

Nehnevajsa, Jiri. 1975. *Crisis Relocation: Perspectives of Americans.* Pittsburgh: University of Pittsburgh.

————. 1976. *Volunteering for Civil Defense: Insights from a 1972 Survey*. Pittsburgh: University of Pittsburgh.

Nehnevajsa, Jiri, Dorothy V. Brodie, Donna J. Krochmal, and Richard H. Pomery. 1964. *Civil Defense and Society*. Washington: Office of Civil Defense.

"The Newbridge Experiment." 1981. *Protect and Survive Monthly* 6: 18–19.

New England Telephone and Telegraph Company. 1964. "'Take Shelter' the Announcer Said then the Door was Shut." *Telephone Topics*.

Nicholson, Helen M. 1951. "All the World's a Stage." *Casualties Union Journal* 2, no. 3/4 (March): 68–70.

————. 1955. "Call a Spade a Spade! and Don't Call It a Wheelbarrow." *Casualties Union Journal* 3, no. 8 (summer): 152–53.

NORAD Headquarters. 1978. *NORAD Regulation 55–86: Battle Damage Scripting Procedures for Exercises*.

North Carolina Department of Public Instruction. 1953. *The Schools and Civil Defense*. Raleigh.

Northcutt, Susan Stoudinger. 1999. "Women and the Bomb: Domestication of the Atom Bomb in the United States." *International Social Science Review* 74, no. 3/4: 129–39.

Oakes, Guy. 1993. "The Cold War Conception of Nuclear Reality: Mobilizing the American Imagination for Nuclear War in the 1950's." *International Journal of Politics, Culture, and Society* 6, no. 3: 343–63.

————. 1994. *The Imaginary War: Civil Defense and American Cold War Culture*. New York: Oxford University Press.

————. 1995. "The Cold War System of Emotion Management: Mobilizing the Home Front for World War III." In *The Age of Propaganda*, edited by Robert Jackall, 275–96. New York: New York University Press.

"One Week After, Two Weeks After . . ." 1984. *Bulletin of the International Civil Defence Organisation* (Geneva) 343 (January): 4–5.

Openshaw, Stan, Philip Steadman, and Owen Greene. 1983. *Doomsday: Britain after Nuclear Attack*. Oxford: Basil Blackwell.

Opinion Research Corporation. 1961. *A Report on Two Pilot Studies on Public Attitudes toward Fallout Shelters*. Princeton: Department of Defense, Office of Civil Defense.

Oregon Civil Defense Agency. 1952. *Civil Defense Manual, Oregon Schools*. Salem.

————. 1958. *Civil Defense in Oregon Schools: A Planning and Instruction Guide*.

Organization of African Unity. 1974. Convention Governing the Specific Aspects of Refugee Problems in Africa. Addis Ababa.

Ozorak, Paul. 1998. *Bunkers Bunkers Everywhere*. Ottawa.

"Pageant of Civil Defence: Sombre Theme of an Ancient Carnival." 1950. *Times* (London), 10 November, 3.

Parrino, Paul S. 1964. "Civil Defense Emergency Hospital—Plans and Training for Maximum Utility." *Journal of the Indiana State Medical Association* 57, no. 7: 780–82.

Peace Data Association. 1982. *Civil Defence Is No Defence. Region 2 Direct Action Handbook (and Supplement)*. Leeds: Peace Data Association.

Pearson, Mike, and Michael Shanks. 2001. *Theatre/Archaeology*. London: Routledge.

Peattie, Lisa. 1984. "Normalizing the Unthinkable." *Bulletin of the Atomic Scientists* 40, no. 3: 32–36.

Pedlow, Gregory W., ed. 1997. *NATO Strategy Documents 1949–1969*. Brussels: NATO.

Perla, Peter. 1990. *The Art of Wargaming: A Guide for Professionals and Hobbyists*. Annapolis: United States Naval Institute Press.

Peterson, Jeannie. 1983. *The Aftermath: The Human and Ecological Consequences of Nuclear War*. New York: Pantheon.

Peterson, Val. 1953. "Panic: The Ultimate Weapon?" *Colliers*, 21 August.

Pfister, Manfred. 1991. *The Theory and Analysis of Drama*. Translated by John Halliday. Cambridge: Cambridge University Press.

Phelan, Peggy. 1993. *Acting Out: The Politics of Performance*. London: Routledge.

Pike, John E., Bruce G. Blair, and Stephen I. Schwartz. 1998. "Defending Against the Bomb." In *Atomic Audit: The Costs and Consequences of U.S. Nuclear Weapons since 1940*, edited by Stephen I. Schwartz, 269–326. Washington: Brookings Institute.

Plato. 1921. *Parmenides*. In *Plato in Twelve Volumes*, vol. 4. Translated by Harold N. Fowler. Cambridge, Mass.: Harvard University Press.

Poole, Robert, S. V. Lloyd, and M. D. Hally. 1989a. *Nuclear Disaster: War and Civil Defence in North West England*. Abridged version. Bury: North West Planning Assumptions Study.

———. 1989b. *Nuclear Disaster: War and Civil Defence in North West England*. 9 vols. Bury: North West Planning Assumptions Study.

Poulter, C. W., and C. D. O. Willesden, compilers. 1957. *Painting the Picture: Civil Defence*. London: Civil Defence Corps Middlesex Division.

Pritchard, John W., Detroit Public Schools, and Wayne University Joint Committee on Civil Defense. 1956. *Civil Defense in the Schools*. Vol. 2. 2d ed. Detroit: Board of Education of the City of Detroit.

Procyshyn, Alexei. n.d. "The Metaphysics of Experience and the Autonomy of the Work of Art." The Centre for the Study of Theory and Criticism. University of Western Ontario. http://www.uwo.ca/theory/skandalon/skandalon/pdf_files/sk_art_1_1h.htm. Accessed 5 December 2005.

Quarantelli, E. L. 1986. *Sociopsychological Aspects of Evacuating or Sheltering Health Care Facilities in the Event of a Nuclear Power Plant Accident*. Preliminary Paper #115. Newark, Del.: Disaster Research Center, University of Delaware.

Quarantelli, E. L., and Russell R. Dynes. 1977. "Response to Social Crisis and Disaster." *Annual Review of Sociology* 3: 23–49.

Ransohoff, Jerry N. 1959. " 'OPAL 58' Surprise 'Paper Evacuation' Moves 13 Hospitals to Non-target Area." *Hospitals* 33, no. 9: 51–53, 108.

Ranum, Marcus J. 2004. *The Myth of Homeland Security*. Indianapolis: Wiley.

Raser, John R. 1969. *Simulation and Society: An Exploration of Scientific Gaming*. Boston: Allyn and Bacon.

Rayner, Jeanette F. 1960. *An Analysis of Several Surveys Relative to Problems of Shelter Habitability*. Vol. 1. Washington: National Research Council.

Realist [pseud.]. 1949. "Acting and Reacting. 3.—Pain, Fear and Re-Assurance." *Casualties Union Journal* 15 (November): 6.

Rees, David. 1984. "Soviet Preparedness." *Conflict Studies* 163: 1–32.

"Research News." 1949. *Casualties Union Journal* 15 (November): 12–15.

"Response and Responsibility in Acting." 1946. *Casualties Union Journal* 3 (summer): 87–88.

Richardson, Brian. 1996. "Introduction: The Struggle for the Real: Interpretive Conflict, Dramatic Method, and the Paradox of Realism." In *Realism and the American Tradition*, edited by William W. Demastes, 1–17. Tuscaloosa: University of Alabama Press.

Ricoeur, Paul. 1984. *Time and Narrative.* Vol. 1. Translated by Kathleen McLaughlin and David Pellauer. Chicago: University of Chicago Press.

Ridenour, Louis N. 1962. "Pilot Lights of the Apocalypse." In *Great Science Fiction by Scientists*, edited by Groff Conklin, 280–88. New York: Collier. (Orig. pub. in *Fortune* 33 [(January 1946]: 116ff.)

"The Rights of Non-Conformity." 1955. *Commonweal* (15 July): 363–64.

Roach, Joseph. 1993. *The Player's Passion: Studies in the Science of Acting*. Ann Arbor: University of Michigan Press. (Orig. pub. 1985.)

Robinson, Donald. 1959. *The Fact of Disaster*. Garden City, N.Y.: Doubleday.

Rockett, Frederick C. 1964. *Source Book on Non-Military Defense. Volume IV. Civilian Behavior Under Nuclear Stress*. Harmon-on-Hudson, N.Y.: Hudson Institute.

Rogers, George Oliver. 1980. *Presidentially Directed Relocation: Compliance Attitudes*. Washington: Defense Civil Preparedness Agency.

Rogers, George Oliver, and Jiri Nehnevajsa. 1984. *Behavior and Attitudes under Crisis Conditions: Selected Issues and Findings*. Washington: United States Government Printing Office.

Rose, Kenneth D. 2001. *One National Underground: The Fallout Shelter in American Culture*. New York: New York University Press.

Ross, Bernard H. 1971. "American Government in Crisis." PhD diss., New York University.

Ross, Emma. 2005. "WHO Urges Rehearsal of Flu Plans." *Boston Globe*, 8 November. http://www.boston.com/news/world/europe/articles/2005/11/08/. Accessed 22 November 2005.

Royal Society of Canada. 1985. *Nuclear Winter and Associated Effects: A Canadian Appraisal of the Environmental Impact of Nuclear War*. Ottawa.

Rush University Medical Center. 2005. *Terrorism and Disaster: What Clinicians Need to Know*. Chicago.

Sagan, Scott D. 1993. *The Limits of Safety: Organizations, Accidents, and Nuclear Weapons*. Princeton: Princeton University Press.

Saigh, Philip A., and J. Douglas Bremner, eds. 1999. *Posttraumatic Stress Disorder: A Comprehensive Text*. Needham Heights, Mass: Allyn and Bacon.

Salinger, Pierre. 1966. *With Kennedy*. Garden City, N.Y.: Doubleday.

Salopek, Marijan. 1989. "Western Canadians and Civil Defence: The Korean War Years, 1950–1953." *Prairie Forum* 14, no. 1: 75–88.

Sanger, David E. 2001. "Bush Seeks New Volunteer Force for Civil Defense." *New York Times*, 9 November, A1, B6.

Sauter, Willmar. 2000. *The Theatrical Event: Dynamics of Performance and Perception*. Iowa City: University of Iowa Press.

Schechner, Richard. 1982. "Collective Reflexivity: Restoration of Behavior." In *A Crack in the Mirror: Reflexive Perspectives in Anthropology*, edited by Jay Ruby, 39–81. Philadelphia: University of Pennsylvania Press.

———. 1986. *The Anthropology of Performance*. New York: Performing Arts Journal.

———. 1993. *The Future of Ritual: Writings on Culture and Performance*. London: Routledge.

———. 1998. "The Street Is the Stage." In *Radical Street Performance: An International Anthology*, edited by Jan Cohen-Cruz, 196–207. London: Routledge.

————. 2002. *Performance Studies: An Introduction*. London: Routledge.

Schnun, Paula P. 1991. "PTSD and Combat-Related Psychiatric Symptoms in Older Veterans." *PTSD Quarterly* 2, no. 1 (winter): 1–8.

Scott, William A. 1955. *Public Reaction to a Surprise Civil Defense Alert in Oakland, California, Federal Civil Defense Administration*. Ann Arbor, Mich.: Federal Civil Defense Administration.

Scudamore, J. M., G. M. Trevelyan, M. V. Tas, E. M. Varley, and G. A. W. Hickman. 2002. "Carcass Disposal: Lessons from Great Britain Following the Foot and Mouth Disease Outbreaks of 2001." *Revue Scientifique et Technique de L'Office International Des Epizooties* (Scientific and Technical Review) 21, no. 3: 775–87.

Seliger, Jerome S., and Joan Kelley Simoneau. 1986. *Emergency Preparedness: Disaster Planning for Health Facilities*. Rockville, Md.: Aspen Publishers.

Sherry, Michael S. 1995. *In the Shadow of War: The United States since the 1930s*. New Haven: Yale University Press.

Shoef, Corina. 2004. "In Search of the Theatre's Social 'Eventness.'" In *Theatrical Events: Borders, Dynamics, Frames*, edited by Vicky Ann Cremona, Peter Eversmann, Hans van Maanen, Wilmar Sauter, and John Tulloch, 357–71. Amsterdam: Rodopi.

Shute, Nevil [pseud.]. 1957. *On the Beach*. New York: W. Morrow.

Simpson, Christopher. 1995. *National Security Directives of the Reagan and Bush Administrations: The Declassified History of U.S. Political and Military Policy, 1981–1991*. Boulder: Westview.

Simulatics Corporation. 1966. *Crisis Level and Civil Defense Attitudes*. Cambridge, Mass.: Office of Civil Defense.

Sismondo, Sergio. 2004. *An Introduction to Science and Technology Studies*. Oxford: Blackwell.

Smith, Leef. 2005. "Pentagon Conducts Emergency Drills." *Washington Post*, 9 June, B2.

Smith, Wilbur, and Associates. 1954. *An Evacuation Study of the Milwaukee Metropolitan Area for the Federal Civil Defense Administration. Supplement and Chapter Dealing with the Traffic Control and Supervision Prepared by the Traffic Institute, Northwestern University Evanston, Illinois*. New Haven, Conn.

"So Who's Worried." 1961. *Telegram* (Toronto), 8 October, 7.

Soddy, Frederick. 1909. *Interpretation of Radium*. London: John Murray.

South Yorkshire Fire and Civil Defence Authority. 1988a. Press Release, 14 December.

————. 1988b. *South Yorkshire Civil Defence Plans*. 9 vols. Barnsley: South Yorkshire Fire and Civil Defence Authority.

Stanford Research Institute and Lehigh University Institute of Research. 1953. *Impact of Air Attack in World War II: Selected Data for Civil Defense Planning. Division I: Physical Damage to Structures, Facilities, and Persons. Volume 1: Summary of Civil Defense Experience*. Bethlehem, Pa.: Federal Civil Defense Administration.

Starbucks Coffee Company. 2004. "Be Prepared: It's an Easy Way to Ease Your Mind."

States, Bert O. 1996. "Performance as Metaphor." *Theatre Journal* 48, no. 1: 1–26.

Steed, Judy. 1985. "Getting Ready for Doomsday." *Globe and Mail* (Toronto), 20 July.

Stone, Jeremy J. 1963. "The Question of Crisis Evacuation." In *Arms Control and Civil Defense*, Annex I. Harmon-on-Hudson, N.Y.: Hudson Institute.

Stouffer, Samuel A., et al. 1949. *The American Soldier: Combat and Its Aftermath*. Princeton, N.J.: Princeton University Press.

Strope, Walmer E., Clark D. Henderson, and Charles T. Rainey. Center for Planning and Research. 1976. *The Feasibility of Crisis Relocation in the Northeast Corridor*. Arlington, Va.: Defense Civil Preparedness Agency.

———. 1977. *Draft Guidance for Crisis Relocation Planning in Highly Urbanized Areas*. Washington: Defense Civil Preparedness Agency.

Strope, Walmer E., Jiri Nehnevajsa, and Francis W. Dresch. 1974. *An Alternative Population Assignment Strategy for Crisis Relocation*. Washington: Defense Civil Preparedness Agency.

Strope, Walmer E., J. I. Pond, and D. P. Schultze. 1960. *Preliminary Report on the Shelter Occupancy Test of 25–29 July 1960*. San Francisco: Naval Radiological Defense Laboratory.

"Study Circles Reach Five Hundred." 1964. *Casualties Union Journal* 6, no. 3 (summer): 47.

Sullivan, Roger J., Kurt Guthe, William H. Thoms, and Frank L. Adelman. 1979. *Survival during the First Year After a Nuclear Attack*. Arlington: Federal Emergency Management Agency.

Taylor, Diana. 2003. *The Archive and the Repertoire: Performing Cultural Memory in the Americas*. Durham, N.C.: Duke University Press.

Teller, Edward. 1987. *Better a Shield than a Sword: Perspectives on Defense and Technology*. New York: Free Press.

Thiong'o, Ngũgĩ wa. 1997. "Enactments of Power: The Politics of Performance Space." *TDR: The Drama Review* 41, no. 3: 11–30.

"This is the Diefenbunker!" 1961. *Telegram* (Toronto), 11 September.

Thomas, Andy, ed. 1977. *The County Warbook*. Manchester: Mole Express.

Thompson, E. P. 1980. *Protest and Survive*. London: CND.

Thompson, James. 1985. *Psychological Aspects of Nuclear War*. Chichester: British Psychological Society and John Wiley and Sons.

Thompson, John B. 1995. *The Media and Modernity: A Social Theory of the Media*. Stanford: Stanford University Press.

"Three-Day Bioterrorism Drill Begins in an Oklahoma Town." 2002. *New York Times*, 13 April, A11.

Tierney, John. 2003. "Ridge Gets the Joke, but Hasn't Lost His Focus." *New York Times*, 17 March, A19.

Towle, Donald D. 1950. "When an A-Bomb Explodes." *The Review of the Order of St. John* 23, no. 5 (June): 7.

Tracey, Michael. 1982. "Censored: The War Game Story." In *Nukespeak: The Media and the Bomb*, edited by Aubrey Crispen, 38–54. London: Comedia.

Trachtenberg, Marc. 1990. "New Light on the Cuban Missile Crisis." *Diplomatic History* 14, no. 2 (spring): 241–47.

———. 1999. *A Constructed Peace: The Making of the European Settlement, 1945–1963*. Princeton: Princeton University Press.

Turner, Victor. 1981. *From Ritual to Theatre: The Human Seriousness of Play*. New York: Performing Arts Journal.

Tuthill, Curtis E., and H. Rowland Ludden. 1961. *Attitude Factors in the Acceptance of a Prototype Dual-Purpose Underground Classroom Fallout Shelter the Rockinghorse Elementary School, Montgomery Co., MD*. Washington: Office of Civil Defense.

Tyhurst, J. S. 1957. "Psychological and Social Aspects of Civilian Disaster." *Canadian Medical Association Journal* 76: 385–93.

Tyrrell, Ivan. 1982. *The Survival Option: A Guide to Living Through Nuclear War*. London: Jonathan Cape.

Ubersfeld, Anne. 1999. *Reading Theatre*. Translated by Frank Collins. Foreword by Paul Perron and Patrick Debbèche. Toronto: University of Toronto Press.

United Kingdom. 1949a. *Statutory Instruments 1949 No. 2145. The Civil Defence (Burial) Regulations*. Vol. I. London: His Majesty's Stationery Office.

———. 1949b. *Statutory Instruments 1949 No. 2147. The Civil Defence (Evacuation and Care of the Homeless) Regulations*. Vol. I. London: His Majesty's Stationery Office.

———. 1951. *Statutory Instruments 1951 No. 1223. The Civil Defence (Emergency Feeding) Regulations*. Vol. I. London: His Majesty's Stationery Office.

———. 1952. *Statutory Instruments 1952 No. 2138. The Civil Defence (Billeting) Regulations*. London: Her Majesty's Stationery Office.

United Kingdom Civil Defence Department. 1950. *Atomic Warfare*. London: Her Majesty's Stationery Office.

———. 2005. *Preparing for Emergencies: What You Need to Know*. London: His Majesty's Stationery Office.

United Kingdom Departments of State and Official Bodies and HO. 1963. *Civil Defence Handbook no. 10. Advising the Householder on Protection against Nuclear Attack*. London.

United Kingdom Health Protection Agency. 2001. *Foot and Mouth Disease: Disposal of Carcasses. Second Report on Results of Monitoring Public Health*. http://www.hpa.org.uk/infections/topics_az/footmouth/SecondFMDMonitoring_finalversion.pdf. Accessed 5 December 2005.

United Kingdom HO. 1965. *York Experiment Test of Government Advice on Fall-out Shelters*. London.

———. 1976. *Protect and Survive*. London.

United Kingdom HO. Emergency Planning College. 1994. *Problems Associated With Large Scale Evacuations. Easingwold Papers No. 5*. Easingwold, York: Emergency Planning College.

United Kingdom HO and Scottish Home and Health Department. 1983. *Civil Defence. The Basic Facts*, London.

United Nations General Assembly. 1951. Convention Relating to the Status of Refugees. 28 July.

United States. 1952. *Statutes at Large. Containing the Laws and Concurrent Resolutions Enacted During the 81st Congress of the U.S.A. 1950–51*. Vol. 64, Part 1: 1245–57. Washington: United States Government Printing Office.

United States Congress (89th Congress 1st Session). 1965. *Congressional Testimony and Actions on Civil Defense: Excerpts January–June 1965*. MP-30-A. Washington: Office of Civil Defense.

United States DCPA. 1973. *Operations for Population Relocation During Crisis Periods. Volume IV —Host Jurisdiction Checklist*. Washington.

———. 1974. *Fact Sheet on Crisis Relocation Planning*. Battle Creek, Mich.: Staff College.

United States Department of Agriculture Economic Research Service. 1964. *Homemaker's Estimates of How Long Food on Hand Could Be Made to Last a Civil Defense Study*. Washington: USDA Economic Research Service.

United States Department of Commerce, Bureau of Public Roads. 1956. *A Preliminary Report on Highway Needs for Civil Defense*. Washington.

United States DHS. 2005. "Ready.gov." http://www.ready.gov/business/index.html. Accessed 5 December 2005.

United States DOD. 1966. *Background of Civil Defense and Current Damage Limiting Studies*. Washington.

———. 1975a. *High Risk Areas for Civil Preparedness Nuclear Defense Planning Purposes.* Washington.

———. 1975b. *Mandate for Readiness. Defense Civil Preparedness Agency Annual Report 1974.* Washington.

———. 1977. *Preparing Crisis Relocation Planning Emergency Public Information.* Working Draft. Washington.

United States DOD, OCD. 1960. *School Shelter: An Approach to Fallout Protection.* Washington.

———. 1961a. *Fallout Protection: What to Know and Do about Nuclear Attack.* Washington.

———. 1961b. *The Family Fallout Shelter.* Washington. (Orig. pub. 1959.)

———. 1963a. *Annual Report of the Office of Civil Defense for the Fiscal Year 1963,* Washington.

———. 1963b. *National School Fallout Shelter Design Competition Awards.* Washington.

———. 1968a. *Annual Report of the Office of Civil Defense for the Fiscal Year 1968.* Washington.

———. 1968b. *In Time of Emergency: A Citizen's Handbook on Nuclear Attack [and] Natural Disasters.* Washington.

———. 1971. *New Dimensions. Ninth Annual Report of the Office of Civil Defense Fiscal Year Ended June 30, 1970.* Washington.

———. 1972. Publications Catalog. Washington.

———. 1974. Publications Catalog. Washington.

———. 1976. Publications Catalog. Washington.

United States DOD, OCDM. 1961. *Conelrad.* Washington: United States Government Printing Office.

United States Executive Office of the President. OCDM. 1958. *The National Plan for Civil and Defense Mobilization.* Washington.

United States FCDA. 1952a. *Annual Report for 1951.* Washington.

———. 1952b. *Bert the Turtle Says Duck and Cover.* Washington.

———. 1952c. *Civil Defense in Schools. Technical Manual.* Washington: United States Government Printing Office.

———. 1953. *Annual Report for 1952.* Washington.

———. 1954a. *Annual Report for 1953.* Washington.

———. 1954b. *A Report on the Washington Conference of National Women's Advisory Committee.* Washington.

———. 1955a. *Facts about Fallout.* Washington.

———. 1955b. *Home Protection Exercises.* 3d ed. Washington: United States Government Printing Office, July.

———. 1956a. *Annual Report for 1955.* Washington.

———. 1956b. *The Church and Civil Defense.* Washington: United States Government Printing Office.

———. 1956c. *Fifth Survey of the U.S. Public's Information and Knowledge Concerning Civil Defense. A Report of a National Study in June 1956.* 2 Vol. Ann Arbor.

———. 1956d. *Mortuary Services in Civil Defense.* Washington: United States Government Printing Office.

———. 1956e. *Rural Family Defense.* Washington.

———. 1957a. *Battleground U.S.A.: An Operation's Plan for the Civil Defense of a Metropolitan Target Area.* Washington: United States Government Printing Office.

————. 1957b. *Facts about Fallout Protection*. Washington.

————. 1957c. "Survival in Public Shelters: A Paper on a Technical Study of Hypothetical Nuclear Attack on the Metropolitan Area of St. Louis." Washington.

United States FCDA and Department of Commerce Bureau of Public Roads. 1956. *A Preliminary Report on Highway Needs for Civil Defense*. Washington.

United States FCDA, National Academy of Sciences, and National Research Council Department of Anthropology and Psychology. 1958. *Behavior in an Emergency Shelter: A Field Study of 800 Persons Stranded in a Highway Restaurant During a Heavy Snowstorm*. Washington: Disaster Research Group.

United States FEMA. 1979. *A Report to the President on Comprehensive Emergency Management*. Washington.

————. 1980. *High-Risk Areas*.

————. 1981a. CRP *Table-Top Exercise Fast-Forward*.

————. 1981b. *Special Problems of Blacks and Other Minorities in Large Scale Population Relocation*. Washington: National Capitol Systems.

————. 1981c. *US Crisis Relocation Planning*. Washington.

————. 1983a. *Crisis Relocation. Tabletop. Exercise #26*.

————. 1983b. *Crisis Relocation. Tabletop. Exercise #55*.

————. 1983c. *Crisis Relocation. Tabletop. Exercise #57*.

————. 1983d. *Morgan County Crisis Relocation. Tabletop. Exercise #51*.

————. 1983e. *Soviet Civil Defense*. Washington.

————. 1985. FEMA Publications Catalog.

————. 2005. "FEMA for Kids." www.fema.gov/kids. Accessed 5 December 2005.

United States National Academy of Sciences. 1975. *Worldwide Effects of Nuclear War*. Washington: United States Government Printing Office.

United States OCDM. 1960. *Index to Publications*. Washington.

————. 1961. *Information Bulletin*. Washington.

United States OCDM and Executive Office of the President. 1960. *Annual Report of the Office of Civil and Defense Mobilization for Fiscal Year 1959*. Washington.

United States President, Executive Order. 1952. "Preparation by Federal Agencies of Civil Defense Emergency Plans, Executive Order 10346." *Federal Register* 17, no. 78 (19 April): 3477. Microfiche.

————. 1953. "Safeguarding Official Information in the Interests of the Defense of the United States, Executive Order 10501." *Federal Register* 18, no. 220 (10 November): 7049, 7051–7054. Microfiche.

————. 1962. "Prescribing Responsibilities of the Office of Emergency Planning in the Executive Office of the President, Executive Order 11051." *Federal Register* 27, no. 191 (2 October): 9683–89. Microfiche.

United States President, National Security Decision Directive 188. 1985. "Government Coordination for National Security Emergency Preparedness." 16 September.

United States President's Science Advisory Committee. 1976. *Security Resources Panel. Deterrence and Survival in the Nuclear Age (The "Gaither Report" of 1957)*. Washington: United States Government Printing Office.

United States Public Law 920. 1951. *Federal Civil Defense Act of 1950*. 81st Cong., 2d sess., 11, 12, Jan.

University of Maryland, College Park. Bureau of Business and Economic Research. 1955. "Balti-more and the H-Bomb." *Studies in Business and Economics* 9, no. 2.

University of Michigan Survey Research Center. 1950. *Public Thinking about Atomic Warfare and Civil Defense. Five Americans State their Conceptions of Atomic Warfare and the Problem of Civil Defense. Illustrative Interviews*. Ann Arbor.

Vale, Lawrence J. 1987. *The Limits of Civil Defence in the USA, Switzerland, Britain and the Soviet Union: The Evolution of Policies since 1945*. New York: St. Martin's Press.

Valley Forge Foundation and FCDA. 1951. *The Alert America Convoys*. Washington.

Vanderbilt, Tom. 2002. *Survival City: Adventures among the Ruins of Atomic America*. Princeton, N.J.: Princeton Architectural Press.

Vernon, Jack A. 1959. *Project Hideaway: A Pilot Feasibility Study of Fallout Shelters for Families*. Princeton, N.J.: Princeton University.

Walker, James E. C., John W. Raker, and William F. Voboril. 1964. "Operation Disaster—Boston." *New England Journal of Medicine* 271, no. 12: 605–10.

Wallis, George Washington. 1963. "Some Social Dimensions of Attitudes toward Civil Defense." PhD diss., Florida State University.

Walter, Nicholas. 1963. *The RSGs 1919–1963*. London: B. Potter.

Walton, Bruce. 1994. "We Couldn't Run, So We Hoped We Could Hide." *Smithsonian* 25, no. 1 (1 April): 46–58.

Ward, Frazer. 2001. "Gray Zone: Watching Shoot." *October* 95 (winter): 114–30.

Washington (State) Department of Civil Defense. 1952. *Washington State Women in Civil Defense 1952*. Olympia.

Waskow, Arthur I., and Stanley L. Newman. 1962. *The Shelter-Centered Society*. New York: Ballantine Books.

Weart, Spencer R. 1988. *Nuclear Fear: A History of Images*. Cambridge, Mass.: Harvard University Press.

Welbrock-Smith, J. 1960. "Have You Been Neglected?" *Casualty Simulation* 5, no. 10 (autumn): 169.

Wells, H. G. 1913. *Little Wars*. London: Frank Palmer.

———. 1948. *The First Men in the Moon, The World Set Free, and Short Stories*. London: Odhams Press.

Welsh, James M. 1983. "The Modern Apocalypse: *The War Game*." *Journal of Popular Film and Television* 11, no. 1: 25–41.

Westcott, James. 2003. "Marina Abramovic's *The House with the Ocean View*." *TDR: The Drama Review* 47, no. 3 (fall): 129–36.

Westlake, E. J. 2002. "'The Bomb that Blew Up Seattle': Jason Sprinkle and the Performance of Municipal Identity." *TDR: The Drama Review* 46, no. 1 (spring): 29–38.

Westwood, L. 1998. "More Than Tea and Sympathy." *History Today* 48, no. 6: 3–5.

White, Eston T., and Val E. Hendrix. 1982. *Defense Requirements and Resource Allocation*. Washington: National Defense University.

Wilkie, Fiona. 2002. "Kinds of Place at Bore Place: Site-Specific Performance and the Rules of Spatial Behaviour." *New Theatre Quarterly* 18, no. 3 (August): 243–60.

Williams, Harry B., and George W. Baker. 1959. *Summary Report. Operation 4:30: A Survey of the Responses to the Washington, D.C., False Air Raid Warning*. Washington: National Research Council.

Wilson, Andrew. 1968. *The Bomb and the Computer*. London: Barrie and Rocklif.

Winkler, Allan M. 1984. "A 40-Year History of Civil Defense." *Bulletin of the Atomic Scientists* 40, no. 6 (June/July): 16–22.

Winter, Sidney G. 1967. *The Federal Role in Postattack Economic Organization*. Santa Monica, Calif.: RAND.

Withey, Stephen B. 1954. *4th Survey of Public Knowledge and Attitudes Concerning Civil Defense—a Report of National Study in March 1954*. Ann Arbor: University of Michigan.

Withington, Thomas. 2003. "Civil Defense: March, Citizens, March." *Bulletin of the Atomic Scientists* 59, no. 6 (November/December): 15–16.

Wittner, Lawrence S. 1997. *Resisting the Bomb: A History of the World Nuclear Disarmament Movement, 1954–1970. Volume 2: The Struggle against the Bomb*. Stanford: Stanford University Press.

Wolfenbarger, Bob. 1963. "Doomsday Comes and Goes in Test to Survive A-War." *Western Electric GHQ*, 31 December, 5.

Wolford, Lisa. 1996. *Grotowski's Objective Drama Research*. Jackson: University of Mississippi Press.

Women's Voluntary Service for Civil Defence. 1957. *One in Five*. London: Women's Voluntary Service for Civil Defence.

———. 1963. *Report on 25 Years Work. WVS Civil Defence, 1938–1963*. Southampton: Her Majesty's Stationery Office.

Yegorov, P. T., I. A. Shlyakhov, and N. I. Alabin. 1970. *Civil Defense: A Soviet View*. Washington: United States Government Printing Office.

Zuckerman, Edward. 1984. *The Day After World War III*. New York: Viking.

INDEX

Calgary, 159–60, 162, 309

Cambodia, 251

Campaign for Nuclear Disarmament, 32, 54–55, 164. *See also* Peace and anti-nuclear movements

Canadian civil defense. *See* Civil defense exercises in Canada; Civil defense in Canada

Carter, Jimmy, 21

Castro, Fidel, 385 n. 107

Casualties Union, 52, 95–96, 99, 199–204; acting and, 199–204, 206–7, 210–11, 218, 377 n. 25; faking (make-up) and, 199–210, 204–5, 209–10, 212, 215, 218, 379 n. 61; first aid training and, 200, 202, 204; Leatherhead Rescue School and, 199–200, 204, 217; nuclear injuries and, 204–7, 214–15; psychiatric injuries and, 211, 215–17; rescue training and, 199–200, 206; spread of techniques and, 204, 207, 217; staging and, 200–204, 218

Censorship and propaganda, 232, 239, 383 n. 72. *See also* Public awareness literature

CENTO, 251

Charlottetown, 97–98, 102, 162, 306

Chekhov, Anton, 260; *The Cherry Orchard*, 71

Chemical warfare. *See* Atomic, biological, and chemical warfare

Chénier, Marie-Joseph, *Charles IX*, 89

Chicago, 32, 33, 35, 46, 148, 187, 305, 320

Children, 45, 53–54, 109, 114, 123, 140, 141, 143, 145, 159, 165, 267–74, 325, 332; Boys' and Girls' Clubs, 28; Campfire Girls, 41; 4-H Clubs, 28, 41; Future Farmers of America, 28, 41. *See also* Education; Scouting movement

China, 248, 289

Church. *See* Religion

Churchill, Winston, 51–52, 261

Cincinnati, 379 n. 61

Citizen Corps (U.S.), 335

Civil Contingency Reaction Force (U.K.), 335

Civil Defense Corps (U.K.): in exercises, 66, 84, 95–96, 164–65, 207, 211, 276; partici-

pation in, 18–19, 25–26, 35–38, 128, 204; recruitment and, 25, 109; training of, 31, 38, 271

Civil defense exercises conducted by NATO: "CIVLOG [19]64," 184; "CIVLOG [19]65," 248–60, 262, 265, 278, 288; "CIVLOG [19]65," 69; "Fallex [19]62," 49, 52, 65, 230, 248, 274, 288; "Fallex [19]63," 52; "Fallex [19]64," 248; "Fallex [19]66," 306

Civil defense exercises in Canada: "Alert," 33; "Alert III," 65; "Co-Operation I," 65; "Co-Operation II," 266–68, 284; "Co-Operation III," 268–69; "Co-Operation" series, 288; "Fifth Key," 81–83; "Lifesaver," 159–60, 162; "Rainex 2," 310; "Second Phase," 283; "Tocsin [19]60," 65, 97–99, 195, 306; "Tocsin [19]63," 80, 248, 310; "Tocsin [19]66," 301–10; "Tocsin B 1961," 65, 76–77, 162, 185, 193, 296; "Wintex 73," 300; "Wintex/Prime Rate 75," 300

Civil defense exercises in United Kingdom: "Battledore," 208; "Beagle II," 283; "Bluebell," 164–66; "Britannia," 270, 320, 365 n. 86; "Bull Ring," 208; "Clearsite," 68, 164; "Damage Control," 365 n. 93; "Dustbath," 191, 194; "Dutch Treat," 65; "Exodus I," 52, 164; "Exodus II," 164; "Fall," 211–13, 214; "Foil," 365 n. 86; "Gory," 209; "Hard Rock," 54–55; "High Heels," 232; "Janus [19]63," 274; "Janus [19]64," 274–75; "Life Line II," 213; "Maybee," 164; "Medical Britannia," 365 n. 86; "Medusa," 94–96, 206; "Mercian Trump," 292; "Mercian Trump II," 292–93; "Minerva [19]65," 275–76; "Minerva [19]68," 276; "Minor Key," 310; "Nifty Nugget," 319; "Parapluie," 52; "Phoenix Five," 265, 365 n. 93; "Pikadon," 378 n. 43; "Review," 163–64; "Scrum Half," 265; "Second Lap," 365 n. 93; "Short Commons," 273; "Shuttlecock," 208; "Torquemada," 365 n. 93; "Triad," 211; "Warpost," 76; "Zedroad," 69, 164, 165; "Zeta," 67–68, 164

Economy, 21, 22, 81, 82, 154, 192, 230–31,
236, 248, 284, 327–29; in computing
calculations and gaming, 312–29, 245;
debt and, 328; economic controls, 230,
231–34, 237, 268, 316–18, 328; emergency
agencies and, 232; employment stabilization and, 263; Federal Reserve Bank and,
316–17; inflation and, 318–19; insurance
and, 317–18; rationing and, 231, 233, 238,
243, 274, 318; stockpiles and, 226, 233,
240; taxation and, 318–19; trade and,
22; wage, rent, price, and credit controls
and, 230, 237, 238–39. *See also* Industry;
International trade; Manpower
Edmonton, 160, 162, 186, 306, 309
Education, 106–8, 115, 167, 284, 334; curricula, 110–16, 237; universities, 113, 332
Eisenhower, Dwight D., 27, 55, 77, 109–
10, 115, 122, 153, 180, 196, 231, 266, 278;
Atoms for Peace and, 111; National Shelter Policy and, 130–31; participation in
exercises of, 185
Electro-magnetic pulse, 57, 81, 176–77
Emergency and rest centers (public), 65–66,
97, 163, 324. *See also* Crisis Relocation
Planning; Relocation sites
Emergency Broadcast System (U.S.), 183. *See
also* CONELRAD
Emergency legislation, 22, 232–34, 238, 243
Emergency powers, 232. *See also* Emergency
legislation
Energy, fuel, and petroleum, 17, 22, 49, 81,
91, 228, 232, 234, 243, 244, 247, 250, 251,
259, 273, 275–76, 280, 283, 309, 335
Espionage and sabotage, 21, 61, 97, 187, 227
Essential records (duplicate records), 23, 49,
113, 224–25, 233, 239, 243
Evacuation and population dispersal, 14,
44–45, 49, 50–51, 68, 75, 80, 83, 113,
159–80, 269–71, 275, 276, 326, 336, 379
n. 61; British evacuation in World War II,
159, 162, 163; logistics of, 158, 160–62,
166, 272, 320–26; manpower and, 234;
prelocation and, 226, 241, 380 n. 12;

spontaneous dispersal, 162–63, 225, 262;
strategic, 171–72, 321; tactical, 159–72,
272–73, 321, 332. *See also* Stay-put policy
Event structure, 22, 68–70, 75–84, 183, 193–
94; attack, 17; post-attack, 63–64, 92,
208, 213, 234–35, 329; pre-attack, 226,
248; restoration phase, 249
Executive Branch. *See* White House
Executive Reserve (U.S.), 232, 239
Exercises. *See* Civil defense exercises conducted by NATO; Civil defense exercises
in Canada; Civil defense exercises in
United Kingdom; Civil defense exercises
in United States; Command post exercises; Field exercises; Public (community)
shelter tests; Tabletop exercises; War
games and exercises

"Fallex" exercises: "Fallex [19]62," 49, 52, 65,
230, 248, 274, 288; "Fallex [19]63," 52;
"Fallex [19]64," 248; "Fallex [19]66," 306
Fallout, 14–18, 55, 84, 121, 171, 192, 194, 207;
advice to public about, 28; gamed in ex-
ercises, 66, 67, 178–80, 187–89, 191, 208,
248, 251, 267, 275, 276, 310, 317, 323, 334–
35; ignored in exercises, 163, 378 n. 39. *See
also* Radiological defense
False alarms, 33–35, 120
Families, provision for civil defense workers,
241. *See also* Children; Women
FEMA (Federal Emergency Management
Agency), 20, 69, 125, 332, 335–36
Field exercises, 66, 69, 95–96, 277–78, 285
Finland, 251, 263
Food: in civil disasters, 132–33; in Cuban
Missile Crisis, 240, 242; in exercises, 72,
136, 141, 147, 190, 194, 233, 234, 251–52,
267, 268, 273–79, 283, 308, 309, 318, 324,
379 n. 61; as exercise and planning pri-
ority, 22, 196, 225, 230, 248; home stocks
of, 43–44, 112, 153; mass feeding, 112, 113,
226, 228, 271–73
France, 249, 251, 252, 259, 265
Freytag, Gustav, 78–79

Role play. *See* Actors and acting

Royal Observer Corps (U.K.), 38

Rural regions: civil defense planning and, 44; disposal of dead in, 280, 285; in exercises, 146–49, 267; fallout shelters and, 152, 186, 240; post-attack recovery and, 84, 154, 335; shelter tests and, 146–49

Sabotage. *See* Espionage and sabotage

Salinger, Pierre, 227, 236, 237

San Antonio, 120

Schechner, Richard, 86–87; on dark play, 98; on direct theater, 156, 207, 259; on play acts, 254–56; on restored behavior, 98

Schlesinger, Arthur M., 29

Scotland, 65, 67, 162, 204, 265, 270, 271, 273, 291–92, 392 n. 6

Scouting movement, 25–28, 31, 40, 159, 204, 224, 237, 270, 272

Seattle, 50

September 11 attacks, 3, 311, 331–37, 377 n. 25

Shakespeare, William: *Hamlet*, 71, 78, 250; *Henry V*, 89; *Julius Caesar*, 78; *Othello*, 75

Sharmat, Mary, 53–54

Sheffield, 37, 67, 76, 164, 272–73

Shelter, 14–15, 18, 83–84, 89–90, 108, 110, 114, 121–22, 127–57, 240. *See also* Home shelters; Public (community) shelters; Relocation sites; Shielding

Shielding, 14–15, 189, 240, 323, 326–27, 331. *See also* Fallout; Shelter

Shute, Nevil, *On the Beach*, 55–56, 57

Site-specific performance, 127, 157. *See also* Relocation sites

South Africa, 204, 228

Southampton, 270

Soviet Union. *See* U.S.S.R.

"Spade Fork" exercises, 224, 230, 231–36, 237, 238, 244–46, 247, 260, 278

Spain, 251

Spectatorship, 52, 55, 93, 94, 99, 155, 165, 166, 195–97, 207, 208, 218–19, 246, 255, 256

Spokane, 166–67

Stanislavsky, Konstantin, 307

Stay-put policy, 83, 98, 163, 265, 269, 270,

271. *See also* Evacuation and population dispersal

Stelarc (performance artist), 155

St. John Ambulance Service, 204, 206

St. John, New Brunswick, 162

St. John's, Newfoundland, 372 n. 1

St. Louis, 130

Sunningdale civil defense training center (U.K.), 62, 271, 274, 275

Supreme Court: in Canada, 299; in United States, 228, 241, 243

Survivalists, 176–77

Suspension of disbelief, 2, 61, 74, 85, 86, 126, 157, 195, 224, 260, 278, 305–7, 319, 330. *See also* Plays; Realism; Spectatorship

Sweden, 227, 251

Switzerland, 227, 251, 259

Syndicates, 66–69, 75–76, 94, 266–79, 283, 285, 379 n. 61

Systems analysis, 59–60, 68–69, 313–20, 397 n. 45

Tabletop exercises, 324–27, 332; Dial-a-Scenario, 327; Fast Forward, 324; Morgan City, Missouri, 324

Targets, vital points, and risk areas: anticipated pattern and extent of, 3, 15, 17, 18, 21, 23, 108, 113, 161–62, 171, 240, 299, 320–25, 328, 397 n. 41, 397 n. 46; in exercises, 97, 159, 186, 189, 234, 250, 266–67, 271; in fiction, 11

Taylor, Diana, 288, 314; on scenarios, 277–78, 311

Teller, Edward, 30

Thatcher, Margaret, 10, 19

Theater. *See* Rehearsals

Thiong'o, Ngũgĩ wa, 256

"Tocsin" exercises: "Tocsin [19]60," 65, 97–99, 195, 306; "Tocsin [19]63," 80, 248, 310; "Tocsin [19]66," 301–10; "Tocsin B 1961," 65, 76–77, 162, 185, 193, 296

Tony n' Tina's Wedding (Corcoran and Corcoran), 258

Toronto, 161–63, 180, 320

Trade unions, 45

Tracy C. Davis is the Barber Professor of Performing Arts and Professor of Theatre and English at Northwestern University. She is the author of *The Economics of the British Stage, 1800–1914* and *George Bernard Shaw and the Socialist Theatre* and is president of the American Society for Theatre Research.

Library of Congress Cataloging-in-Publication Data
Davis, Tracy C.
Stages of emergency: Cold War nuclear civil defense / Tracy C. Davis.
p. cm.
Includes bibliographical references and index.
ISBN 978-0-8223-3959-5 (cloth : alk. paper) — ISBN 978-0-8223-3970-0 (pbk. : alk. paper)
1. Civil defense—United States—History—20th century. 2. Civil defense—Canada—History—20th century. 3. Civil defense—Great Britain—History—20th century. 4. Nuclear warfare. I. Title.
UA927.D39 2007
363.350973'09045—dc22   2006033808